Contending Theories of International Relations

Contending Theories of International Relations

A Comprehensive Survey

Fourth Edition

James E. Dougherty

St. Joseph's University

Robert L. Pfaltzgraff, Jr.

The Fletcher School of Law and Diplomacy, Tufts University

LONGMAN

An imprint of Addison Wesley Longman, Inc.

New York • Reading, Massachusetts • Menlo Park, California • Harlow, England
Don Mills, Ontario • Sydney • Mexico City • Madrid • Amsterdam

Contending Theories of International Relations: A Comprehensive Survey, Fourth Edition

Acquisitions Editor: Margaret Loftus
Supervising Production Editor: Lois Lombardo
Project Coordination and Text Design: York Production Services
Cover Design: Paul Lacy
Manufacturing Manager: Hilda Koparanian
Electronic Page Makeup: ComCom
Printer and Binder: RR Donnelley & Sons Company
Cover Printer: Phoenix Color Corp.

Library of Congress Cataloging-in-Publication Data

Dougherty, James E.
    Contending theories of international relations: a comprehensive survey / James E. Dougherty,
Robert L. Pfaltzgraff, Jr.—4th ed.
        p.   cm.
    Includes bibliographical references and index.
    ISBN 0-673-99756-1
    1. International relations.   I. Pfaltzgraff, Robert L.
    II. Title.
    JX1395.D67   1996
    3278.01—dc20   96-14654
                                                 CIP

ISBN 0-673-99756-1

12345678910—DOC—99989796

Contents

Preface

With this new edition, *Contending Theories of International Relations* moves toward the end of its third decade of university and college use. Although major changes have been made to take account of the new literature of recent years, we have endeavored to preserve the basic elements of the approach that guided us in the preparation of the first three editions:

1. An *interdisciplinary method* that draws insights from traditional, behavioral–scientific, and postbehavioral fields, as well as normative theory, and that includes the various great debates of international relations
2. An *effort to integrate* newer with older theories, as well as insights from different perspectives into international phenomena
3. An *impartial presentation* of contending theories and theorists, along with the views of their critics where appropriate
4. The *ample citation of scholarly sources* on which our discussions and analyses are based

This fourth edition has been substantially revised to reflect not only the paradigmatic debate sparked by the transformed global system and the end of the Cold War, but also the large number of newer writings on neorealist and structural-realist theories, democratic peace theory, and other neoliberal theory; the emerging discussion about why the Cold War ended as it did; the long peace, or why the Cold War did not result in war between the United States and the Soviet Union; implications of the end of the Cold War for international-relations theory; structural and institutionalist theories; theories about the causes of anarchy and the conditions for cooperation and political integration; the debate about structure–agent relationships within and among the levels of analysis; post–Cold War deterrence; postmodernist–postbehavioralist theory; the causes of war; game theory and bargaining theory; geography and war; constructivist–reflectivist theories; and recent developments in theories of decision making, crisis, and crisis management. Wherever possible, we have endeavored to show relationships among the various theories of international relations. We have also addressed issues related to the nature of theory itself. These issues include the ongoing consideration of how theory is developed, the epistemological basis for knowledge, and the issue of rationality in the decisions of individuals and the foreign policies of governments. Encompassed in this discussion is the debate about the extent to which all theory in the social sciences, and international relations in particular, is normative. Such topics are considered in this edition, building on earlier editions of *Contending Theories of International Relations.*

Because of space constraints, we have reduced or eliminated surveys of certain theories that appeared in the earlier editions to make room for the substantial new material that has appeared in the burgeoning literature of international-relations theory in the 1990s. The field of international theory is always changing in its substantive and methodological dimensions. Yet we remain convinced that in international relations, as in the social sciences generally, theory can be understood best when it is linked to and builds on the enduring insights of the past. At the same time, as we move toward and beyond the end of the twentieth century, changes in the international system seem to be outpacing the ability of our theories either to explain change or to explain the phenomena that are the necessary object of theoretical development and analysis. Therefore, we need to ask what endures from the past to form a basis on which to develop post–Cold War international-relations theory into the next century. We confront a debate about the extent to which, in a fragmenting structure that includes failed states, the anarchy that is said to exist at the international level differs appreciably from that at other levels of analysis, and yet, at the same time, there exists at least a certain minimum fragile order. The theoretical discussion of such issues is addressed in the chapters that follow.

It is our purpose to assist undergraduate and graduate students, as well as the general reader, in their quest for a greater understanding of the rapidly evolving field of theory. Because a single text can do no more than describe alternative approaches and point to stimulating avenues for further exploration and study, we provide extensive bibliographical notes for the interested readers. For the fourth edition, large numbers of new source references have been added to those retained from the previous edition. It is to be hoped that undergraduate students preparing term papers, as well as graduate students and others working on more advanced research topics, will benefit from this bibliographical information.

The authors embarked on this project more than 25 years ago. While codirecting the graduate seminar in international-relations theories at the University of Pennsylvania, we became aware that students felt overwhelmed by the great variety of theories that were beginning to abound in the field. It was our purpose to come to their assistance—not by propagating a single favorite theory, but by surveying the full panoply of the literature available, and trying to assess the various theories as objectively as we could, setting forth the theoretical points of intersection or overlap, of convergence or divergence. We know full well that this field is so vast and complex that the achievement of a single, unified, parsimonious yet powerful explanation of international phenomena may always prove to be elusive. Yet today more than ever, theory is a fascinating and important area for study, reflection, and research. The expanding literature of international-relations theory, together with the rapidity and extent of change in the global system, increases the need for a comprehensive survey of the many older and newer theories.

In earlier editions we noted many persons who profoundly deserved thanks for their contributions to our intellectual development and to this work. That debt remains, for this present edition, like contemporary theory itself, built on all that has gone before. We wish especially to acknowledge our gratitude to colleagues at St. Joseph's University (especially Professors David H. Burton, Elwyn F. Chase, Jr., and Frank X. Gerrity), the Fletcher School of Law and Diplomacy, Tufts University, and the Institute for Foreign Policy Analysis. Over the course of decades, our colleagues have contributed much to our understanding of international relations. We express thanks to the many students who have posed, and continue to ask, challenging questions about theories of international relations. Both of us have benefited immeasurably from discussions with policymakers in the United States and abroad, whose perspectives furnish an indispensable basis for assessing the relationship between theory and practice in the world as it exists, in contrast to the world as we might wish it to be.

We would be remiss not to single out those who rendered valuable comments for this edition and, in particular, the reviewers commissioned by HarperCollins, who provided useful critiques that were used to the fullest extent possible in the preparation of this edition: Paul F. Diehl, University of Illinois; Kurt Taylor Gaubatz, Stanford University; Ted Hopf, University of Michigan; William E. Kelly, Auburn University; Roberta McCalla, University of Wisconsin-Madison. We are also grateful to Professor Richard H. Shultz, Jr., of the Fletcher School of Law and Diplomacy, Tufts University, for materials related to the discussion of low-intensity conflict in Chapter 8. We express our thanks to colleagues at the Institute for Foreign Policy Analysis, especially Dr. Jacquelyn K. Davis and Dr. Charles M. Perry, Executive Vice President and Director of Studies, respectively, for valuable insights into the linkage between theory and policy.

Marjorie Duggan, of the Institute for Foreign Policy Analysis, furnished indispensable help in preparing the manuscript for publication, keeping track of numerous revisions and renumbering of footnotes, as well as typing all the completed drafts. We also acknowledge the assistance of Roberta Breen and Howard Madnick, both of the Fletcher School of Law and Diplomacy, and Lawrence Rothenberg, of the Institute for Foreign Policy Analysis, in tracking down sources. To all who assisted in the production of this edition, we express our gratitude. May this edition contribute to an understanding of theories of international relations for an emerging generation of scholars, students, and policymakers in the increasingly complex and heterogeneous world of the late twentieth century and into the next millennium.

James E. Dougherty
Robert L. Pfaltzgraff, Jr.

Chapter
1

Theoretical Approaches to International Relations

*T*he pace of global change has quickened dramatically since 1989, when the dismantling of the Berlin Wall, together with profound political transformation in Central-Eastern Europe, signaled the collapse of the Soviet empire and of the Soviet Union itself. For four decades prior to 1989, the overarching concern of Western governments, and many theorists of international relations, had been to deter nuclear war and any conventional conflict that could escalate to the nuclear level. After 1989, the substantial reduction of military forces in Europe, the dissolution of the Warsaw Pact, the re-unification of Germany, and the devolution of Gorbachev's Soviet Union to Yeltsin's Commonwealth of Independent States ushered in an abrupt discontinuity in what had been a familiar world scene—frightening at times, but an environment to which we had become accustomed, and one which had seemed immune to drastic alteration.

Throughout the Cold War period, the international system retained a seemingly recognizable shape, despite swings between deep freezes and warming détentes. Analysts developed coherent theories and engaged in sometimes esoteric debates about realism versus idealism, mutual deterrence and balanced arms control, stability and instability, national interests and international security; about the theory and practice of crisis management, regional integration, and the viability of alliances under strain; and so forth. Most, but not all, analysts in the field shared a common conceptual paradigm and professional vocabulary that enabled them to carry on a meaningful discussion or argument about such things as power, strategy, and foreign-policy decision making under conditions of bipolarity or multipolarity. There were many disagreements, but they fitted into the comprehensive framework based on the international system of a bipolar world.

In the aftermath of the Cold War, we are in the midst of a fundamental paradigm shift in our thinking about the future of world politics. The importance of paradigmatic change lies in the fact that the paradigm provides the essential basis for theory. The paradigm furnishes a comprehensive framework for the identifica-

1

tion of the variables about which the theory is to be developed. As the first stage in theory building, the paradigm (framework for theoretical analysis) describes the phenomena to be investigated. In international relations, these phenomena refer to the numbers and types of actors. The paradigm is essentially a means of selecting what will be the object of theory. It will help direct attention to the kinds of relationships to be investigated among the units that compose the paradigm. To what extent, it is asked, is the international system based on state actors or units other than states? What are the defining characteristics of such entities? What was termed a *traditional paradigm* was said to be "state centric." To speak of paradigmatic shift is to emphasize the transformation of a paradigm consisting of states to one that has a multiplicity of differing types of actors. Subsequent chapters of this text highlight the ongoing discussion and debate about the changing paradigm and its significance for the future of international-relations theory.

To indicate the order of magnitude of the shift required, it would be an exaggeration to compare it with the transition from the Ptolemaic view of the astronomical universe to the modern scientific view that emerged with Galileo's telescopic observation of the relationship between the earth and the sun in the early seventeenth century. Such a comparison, however, has the merit of showing how difficult it can be for elites and institutions to move from well-trodden terrain into the unknown. Galileo and other leading contributors to the new scientific vision of that era met with not only scientific, but also religious and philosophical opposition, yet they were all convinced that the old earth-centered paradigm was wrong. Hence, the aforementioned analogy is not entirely apt. The Ptolemaic theory, though satisfying to all but a few thinkers for many centuries, never conformed to cosmic reality. In contrast, the dominant paradigm of the Cold War period shared by most analysts and policymakers bore at least some resemblance to what was widely perceived to be international political reality from the late 1940s to the late 1980s. Nonconformist critics had a point when they asserted that the Soviet communist system could not last forever. Nonetheless, not even these critics predicted the surprising events of 1989 and after—itself an issue for consideration in our theories of international relations, addressed in subsequent chapters.

The comparison is faulty in at least one other important respect. It took the great astronomers and mathematical scientists of Europe—Copernicus, Brahe, Kepler, Galileo, and Newton—a century and a half to complete their paradigm shift. International theorists are under pressure to produce a new grand conceptual vision in a much shorter time frame—preferably less than a decade—and to do so in a global setting that, unlike the planets in the solar system, is undergoing dramatic and rapid change. Policymakers and diplomats are compelled to deal with emerging problems on an ad hoc basis, relying on practical or intuitive political wisdom (as they have usually done in the past), or responding, as democratic leaders must, by trying to balance a variety of conflicting demands. "The search for a new geopolitical cartography to replace the somewhat oversimplified Cold War notion of a world divided between democracy and totalitarianism," suggests John Lewis Gaddis, might begin with a look at "the forces of integration and fragmentation in the contemporary international environment."[1] Integration may not be always good, nor fragmentation always bad. Nations must now strive to balance one set of forces against another. (For example, neither a strong imperialist Russia nor a chaotically weak one is desirable.)

The end of the Cold War spawned several shorthand descriptions of the transformed global setting. A former deputy director of the U.S. State Department's policy planning staff, Francis Fukuyama, in a widely cited and controversial book, proclaimed the triumph of democracy as "the end of history."[2] During the Persian Gulf crisis of 1990–1991, President Bush spoke of "a new world order" of cooperation among nations and peaceful settlement of disputes—an era in which the United Nations might be able to live up to the original expectations of its founders. At the same time, Bush was criticized for acting out a balance-of-power policy á la Nixon and Kissinger while employing the rhetoric of Presidents Woodrow Wilson and Jimmy Carter, with emphasis on democracy, human rights, and international law.[3]

Indeed, the early 1990s were years of almost euphoric hope in a universal march toward popular democracy and market economies. From all quarters, analysts were noting the obvious fact that there was only one superpower left, without being quite sure what that meant. For well over a decade, writers had been pointing to a decline in the utility of military power (largely because the possessors of nuclear weapons had found them to be militarily unusable), noting that concerns about economic security were overtaking those of military security. The chorus of voices among politicians and media pundits demanding a "peace dividend"— defense cuts and a shift of resources to domestic programs—grew louder. Talk about threats of war and the need for nuclear deterrence became far less fashionable than it had been in the late 1970s and early 1980s. Illustrative of this perspective, John Mueller argued that among modernized nations, war has become so catastrophic and repulsive as to be "subrationally unthinkable—rejected not because it's a bad idea but because it remains subconscious and never comes off as a coherent possibility."[4] Michael Howard asserted optimistically that, although wars are still likely to occur in less developed societies, it is "quite possible that war . . . between highly developed societies may not recur, and that a stable framework for international order will become firmly established."[5]

Decades of frustratingly slow arms-control negotiations had finally produced reductions in the stockpile of nuclear weapons and in conventional forces deployed in Central Europe, which had seemed, and actually promised to be, unattainable during the Cold War. Nevertheless, even after the Cold War, the two principal erstwhile rivals continued to maintain sufficient capabilities to pose a potential threat to each other's existence. Moreover, governments expressed increasing concern about the dangers of the proliferation of weapons of mass destruction, including nuclear, biological, and chemical capabilities, to additional independent centers of control in more volatile regions of the world, where conflicts might break out and escalate. Another cause for concern was the possibility that terrorist groups might gain access to stolen nuclear materials, available on the black market.

"War," wrote Zbigniew Brzezinski, in a vein echoing John Mueller, "has become a luxury that only poor nations can afford."[6] Afford it they did, either as independent not-so-poor, oil-producing states (Iraq vs. Kuwait); national groups of different religious traditions fighting for territory in fragmented multinational states (Eastern Orthodox Serbs, Roman Catholic Croats, and Muslim Bosnians in the former Yugoslavia); and various civil wars of a nationalist, religious, secessionist, or tribal character (Iraqi government vs. Kurds and marshland Shiite Arabs; Buddhist Sinhalese vs. Hindu Tamils in Sri Lanka; conflicts in the former Soviet republics of Georgia, Azerbaijan, and Tadjikistan; and Hutus versus Tutsis in Rwanda—to mention only a few). By the mid-1990s, the United Nations Security Council had so much on its diplomatic plate—more than two dozen peacekeeping and peace-enforcing operations, actual or proposed—that it was running substantial deficits because poor members were unable to pay, and rich members (including the United States) were falling into arrears in meeting their financial obligations. The United Nations and its member nations had to set priorities. In the postindustrial, information-age democracies, the political focus became less international and more domestic, except for the fact that the preoccupation of voters with jobs, inflation, and the qualify of life (in the home and in the environment)— coupled with the concern of economists and bankers over interest rates, international competitiveness, currency fluctuations, trade gaps, corporate restructuring, deficits, and debts—forced their governments to give high-priority attention to trends shaping the global economy. There has been much speculation concerning the possibility that armed conflict among the great powers was being replaced by the prospect of trade wars among the world's principal economic centers—North America, the European Community/Union, and Japan (or the Pacific Rim)— conflicts replete with their own jargon relative to gaps and imbalances, unfair trade practices, and retaliatory moves to force foreign markets to open.

Samuel P. Huntington was not quite satisfied with any of the foregoing nascent paradigms. He was particularly critical of what he called "endism"—end of the Cold War, end of history, end of war among the industrially advanced nations.[7] Later, in an article that provoked considerable debate, Huntington wrote,

> It is my hypothesis that the fundamental source of conflict in this new world will not be primarily ideological or primarily economic. The great divisions among humankind and the dominating source of conflict will be cultural. Nation-states will remain the most powerful actors in world affairs, but the principal conflicts of global politics will occur between nations and groups of civilizations. The clash of civilizations will dominate global politics.[8]

His list includes seven or eight civilizations—Western, Confucian, Japanese, Islamic, Hindu, Slavic–Orthodox, Latin American, and perhaps African—each with its own distinctive religion; modes of thought and expression; traditions regarding the state, marriage, and the family; law and authority; perspectives on liberty and equality; emphases on tradition and change; and so on. Civilizational differences, Huntington held, are real and basic enough to produce prolonged, violent conflict. Communications technology, global trade and investment, migration, and other factors have made once homogeneous civilizations more permeable to each other, but each has a distinctive approach to the vital issues of our time— human rights, the natural environment, national security, economic development, and the kinds of ethnic, linguistic, territorial, regional, and other conflicts that have intensified since the end of the ideological Cold War. Not only Islam, but also

Christianity, Judaism, Buddhism, and Hinduism are all manifesting a fundamentalist reaction against secular, materialist Western culture.[9] If Huntington's analysis is correct, it might imply for the future a shift from the nation-state to larger cultural entities as basic units for the study of international relations—or at least for some aspects of it. (A half century ago, the historian Arnold Toynbee had urged a "civilizational approach.") Huntington's prognosis, of course, may not be on the mark. He drew fire from several critics.[10] Fouad Ajami, for example, noted that Huntington, while conceding that states will remain the most powerful international actors, points to a coming war of civilizations. According to Ajami, Huntington viewed civilizations as watertight compartments, underestimating the degree to which all non-Western civilizations have been remade by the West's secularism and modernity, and apparently forgot that "civilizations do not control states; states control civilizations."[11] If Huntington is correct (and his views are treated more fully in our discussion of environmental theories), this might imply for the future a shift from the nation-state to larger cultural entities as the basic units for the study of international relations.

The prudent scholar may deem it unwise to fasten too early and too exclusively on any one of the theoretical paradigms now being offered from several quarters. Previous editions of this text reflected a conviction that no single approach can explain adequately, with comprehensiveness and subtlety, the full range of phenomena that make up the ever-evolving *complexe internationale*. As we show subsequently, the post–Cold War literature abounds in diverse views on why the international structure has changed. No one can predict with certainty whether the emerging system will be more stable and safer or more unstable and dangerous than before.[12] International-relations theory is now in a highly tentative phase, which makes it all the more challenging and interesting. If we think that ideas have consequences in history, then we must admit that some of the ideas now burgeoning on the academic scene might have some impact on the shape of the world beyond the year 2000, especially in view of the fact that the revolution in telecommunications now facilitates an unprecedented global circulation of ideas. International theory changes constantly, along with the total environment and the human response to it. In ancient times, the pace of change was slow and hardly noticeable; in our age, it appears to increase at an exponential rate, partly because of the information explosion. Today's theoretical explanations may have to be refined and corrected tomorrow as new data are discovered, more accurate classifications and measurements made, and more insightful analyses performed here and abroad.

Imre Lakatos, a Hungarian mathematician, has suggested the criteria for determining whether the replacement of an older theory by a newer one represents scientific progress. His formula is somewhat inelegant but clear, and it has been quoted by scientific theorists of international relations:

A scientific theory T is *falsified* if and only if another theory T' has been proposed with the following characteristics: (1) T' has excess empirical content over T: that is, it predicts *novel* facts, that is, facts improbable in the light of, or even forbidden, by T; (2) T' explains the previous success of T, that is, all the unrefuted content of T is included (within the limits of observable error) in the content of T'; and (3) some of the excess content of T' is corroborated.[13]

In all scientific fields, new theory builds on old. A certain degree of conceptual continuity is essential for rational discourse. As John Lewis Gaddis has observed, "visions of any future have to proceed from the awareness of some kind of past; otherwise . . . there can be no language for expressing them."[14] No matter which paradigm, if any, may ultimately hold sway, it will not be able to ignore the concepts of power and influence, in one form or another—political, military, economic, ideological, religious and cultural, related to control of communications, or whatever else may shape the forces of historical development. We cannot prescind from any of those significant dimensions that affect the tone and tint of international politics and the dialectical process of contradictory demands in which modern governments must fashion their foreign policies.

In this introductory chapter, we show how the field of international relations has developed historically and how its scope has been defined since World War II. We discuss the nature and function of theory, as well as various types of theory, and we indicate some of the different approaches that may be adopted. We offer a few thoughts on the relation between theory and practice. That discussion is followed by a look at the level-of-analysis problem: Who are the international actors to be studied? We then briefly review the not entirely arcane debate between traditionalists and behavioralists and conclude by noting some of the difficulties of trying to formulate a cumulative theory in this field.

EARLY APPROACHES TO INTERNATIONAL-RELATIONS THEORY

Efforts at theorizing about the nature of interstate relations are quite old. We can find seminal ideas in ancient China—in the writings of Mo-Ti, Mencius, Confucius, and Lord Shang—and in India—in the Code of Manu, dealing with honorable conduct in warfare and the inviolability of diplomats, and in the works of Kautilya, who had a complex theory of the balance of power among princely states. (References are made to Chinese and Indian thought in Chapter 5.)

More pertinent to international theory in the West is the heritage of thought from classical Greece and Rome. The reflections of Plato and Aristotle on the subject were rather sketchy, but their philosophies (which might be characterized roughly as idealist or utopian and realist or empirical, respectively) were comprehensive enough to include war and the necessity for military defense of the city-state on which they focused their attention. The ancient Greek historian Thucydides expanded his view to encompass the Greek city-state system and analyzed problems of diplomacy, imperialism, the making of alliances, war and peace, the motives that drive political action (fear, honor, and interest), and the dialectic clash of power versus moral values. Any student of international relations can still read with profit Thucydides's great history, *The Peloponnesian War*.[15] Following the failure of the Greek city-states to form an effective federal structure and their consequent decline, Alexander the Great, the Cynics, and the Stoics bequeathed to the West the idealist concept of *cosmopolitanism*—citizenship in a world state.

During its days as a vigorous young republic, Rome and its jurists developed the *ius gentium* (law of nations), a body of legal principles and practices common to the various Mediterranean peoples with whom Rome was in contact, and which would later be looked on as a customary basis for a law between nations.[16] In the later days of the Roman Empire, there were no real international relations characteristic of a state system, but Roman legal ideas on the just war survived to be developed by patristic writers and theologians in Christian medieval Europe (see Chapter 5). Niccolò Machiavelli marked a radical departure from the long tradition of ethical political theory by reflecting the new secular imperatives and Byzantine diplomacy of the Italian city-state system in Renaissance times. Machiavelli's *The Prince,* a harbinger of modern realist analysis of power realities in the state system, ushered in what purported to be a value-free approach to the science of statecraft.[17]

Two centuries before Machiavelli, Dante Alighieri (1265–1321) was convinced that the proper work of humankind was the development of intellect and culture, for which work a peaceful world was essential. His *De Monarchia (On World Government)* was the first powerful appeal in Western political literature for international organization under a world ruler capable of monopolizing military power and enforcing peace among princes without disturbing the internal autonomy of political communities.[18] (The question as to whether Dante's formula is a contradiction in terms may recur frequently to the student, upon reading subsequent chapters, especially those dealing with power, the international system, and the causes of war.)

The French were prolific producers of plans for international organization and the promotion of peace. Pierre Dubois (1250–1322) called for a regional union of Christian princes to establish peace in Europe by displacing their aggressive urges in an effort to recover the Holy Land from Turkish infidels. The Pope (then a client of France at Avignon) would summon a council, which would create an arbitration court with an effective system of sanctions to settle intra-European disputes peacefully.[19] Emeric Crucé (1590–1648), convinced that most people yearn to live in peace, stressed the cooperative over the conflictual aspects of international relations; exalted the role of the merchant in trade over that of the warrior in war (who becomes less useful and more dangerous in times of peace); opposed imperialism and colonialism on the practical grounds that the political and economic costs exceed the gains; and suggested that a neutral city be made an international center for peacemaking diplomacy. Crucé favored a freezing of the territorial status quo in Europe and, like Dutch scholar Desiderio Erasmus, looked toward the complete eradication of war, in this respect parting company with Hugo Grotius, who defended war as an instrument of justice, provided that its conduct be limited by the law of nations (see Chapter 5). The Duc de Sully (1560–1641), a chief minister of Henry IV, envisaged an equilibrium of strength among the Europeans (to be achieved partly through a reduction of territory ruled by the Hapsburg monarchy), and propounded a grand design for a confederation of the Christian states of Western Europe, with a council permanently headquartered at a central location for the peaceful settlement of disputes. Any redistribution of territory was to take into account the wishes of national populations. Abbé de Saint-Pierre (1659–1743) also proposed organizing the Christian states of Europe into a federal union, which he hoped would ally defensively with a counterpart grouping that it would try to form in Asia. (Crucé, by the way, in sharp contrast to Dubois and Sully, both of whom saw the Turks as a convenient outlet for the fighting energies of Christian Europe, would have accorded the Ottoman Sultan a place of honor in the peace organization.)[20]

In general, the French writers—whether they adopted the regional or the more universal approach—relied heavily on diplomacy, arbitration, and adjudication in their plans for perpetual peace. Those of the Enlightenment period showed a marked preference for commerce and trade over war for the achievement of foreign-policy goals, as well as a particular abhorrence for war waged in the name of religion. Some stressed the need for severe sanctions against disturbers of the peace; others did not. They did not all agree on the importance of maintaining the territorial status quo. Most of them assigned a role to France as the natural leader of Europe, because they believed (as good Cartesians) that France was unique among nations in being ruled by reason rather than by passions. The major exception was Jean-Jacques Rousseau (1712–1778), who began by editing Saint-Pierre's project for perpetual peace and ended by criticizing it and altering it substantially. Although regarded as a romantic because of his idyllic interpretation of innocent, benevolent human nature in the state of nature, Rousseau was quite the cynical realist in his theory of human behavior, the state, and interstate relations. Parting company with what he called the "absurdly reasonable" Saint-Pierre, Rousseau insisted that human beings are seldom led by reason and its logical calculations but often by passions. Human nature is basically peaceful; it becomes warlike only when it enters society; war is a product of civilization; it is the institution of private property that has alienated humans from their original freedom and happiness, corrupting them by creating inequality, a class system, a law based on force, and a self-serving ruling elite capable of tyrannizing and impoverishing their subjects while making war to aggrandize their power. In this regard, Rousseau may be regarded as a forerunner of Karl Marx. Whereas citizens within the state are controlled by law, princes continue to exist in a state of nature, ruled only by the law of the strongest.

Rousseau's compatriot, Jean Bodin (1530–1596), had much earlier formulated the doctrine of sovereignty, which made the monarch supreme *internally* within the realm, but equal *externally* vis-à-vis other sovereign rulers. Bodin, however, was enough of a traditionalist to hold that the sovereign's power is not unlimited, for the prince is bound by the law of God, the natural law of reason, and the law of nations (*ius gentium,* based on immemorial custom, e.g., the principle that treaties are to be kept—*pacta sunt servanda*). Rousseau did not set much store by such limits. He relied on the balance of power to preserve order of a sort within the anarchic state system, but not peace, for the maintenance of the balance sometimes prescribed war as a method. Rousseau, convinced that princes would not consent to restrictions on their power and freedom of action, and that their ministers like to utilize the occasion of war to advance their own private interests, was extremely skeptical concerning the prospects for Saint-Pierre's federation, given his belief that human rationality is only potential, while people are actually so alienated by corrupt civilization that they cannot see what is in their own best interest.[21]

Among the English, William Penn (1644–1718), a Quaker, and Jeremy Bentham (1748–1832), a Utilitarian philosopher, formulated plans for universal and perpetual peace, as did the German idealist philosopher, Immanuel Kant (1724–1804). Penn, anxious to replace what he called the "Logic of Fish," whereby states feed upon each other, proposed that the European princes remove themselves from the state of nature and subject themselves to an effective system of international law and order. He wanted the princes to preserve domestic sovereignty but to renounce it in their relations with each other by establishing a legislative assembly in which the voting power of each member would be proportionate to the personal income of the ruler and the value of the territory ruled.[22] Bentham sought to pacify and maximize the happiness of European nations through disarmament, the emancipation of distant colonies, and an international court or congress. The latter was to rely on open diplomacy, the power of public opinion, and a free press to support its reasonable, practical decisions.[23] Kant, convinced that history was moving in a progressive direction, and that even wars would eventually contribute toward an end of international anarchy, argued that states with republican constitutions would gradually expand the zone of peace, renouncing war and arms races among themselves and building a federation of free states under law, based not on force but on principles of right.[24] (The recent debate over the Kantian thesis concerning democracy and peace is examined in Chapter 8.)

Political philosophers of the seventeenth and eighteenth centuries—Thomas Hobbes (1588–1679), Baruch Spinoza (1632–1677), and John Locke (1632–1704) among them—agreed fully with the peace writers that sovereign monarchs exist, with regard to each other, in a state of nature and recurring wars, but they were much less sanguine on the prospects for international government. From the sixteenth century onward, such thinkers as Francesco Guicciardini (1483–1540), François Fénelon (1650–1715), David Hume (1711–1766), and Friedrich von Gentz (1764–1832) looked upon the balance of power as the most prudent policy to be pursued by monarchs interested in maintaining the independence of their own realms and overall stability, but not necessarily peace, in Europe.[25] The founding theorists of modern international law—Francisco de Vitoria (1480–1549), Alberico Gentili (1552–1608), Francisco de Suárez (1548–1617), Hugo Grotius (1583–1645), Christian von Wolff (1679–1754), Emmerich de Vattel (1714–1767), and others—all viewed war as a sort of substitute judicial proceeding not only permitted but sometimes even required under the law of nations as a means of restoring justice and punishing wrongdoing states for violating well-established rights. Even so when the right to go to war (*ius ad bellum*) was justly invoked, the war had to be conducted in a just, proportionate, limited manner (*ius in bello*) according to widely recognized rules.[26] These and other early theorists are cited in succeeding chapters; many of the issues they raised have never been settled with finality.

Despite the classical writings just summarized, some may consider it surprising that Martin Wight, with the period prior to the first World War I in mind, noted that if by *international theory*, we mean a "tradition of speculation about relations between states, a tradition imagined as the twin of speculation about the State to which the name 'political theory' is appropriated, such a tradition does not exist."[27] Wight suggested that one explanation for this absence is that since the time of Hugo Grotius, the Dutch jurist and statesman, and Samuel Pufendorf (1632–1694), the German jurist and historian, nearly all speculation about the international community had fallen under the heading of international law. Wight noted that most writing on interstate relations before this century was contained in the political literature of the aforementioned peace writers, buried in the works of historians, cloistered in the peripheral reflections of philosophers, or harbored in speeches, dispatches, and memoirs of state leaders and diplomats. Wight concluded that in the classical political tradition, "international theory, or what there is of it, is scattered, unsystematic, and mostly inaccessible to the layman," as well as being "largely repellent and intractable in form."[28] The only theory that infused the thinking of the period—and it was a theory somewhat dearer to practicing diplomats than to academicians—was that of the balance of power. Indeed, it was a collection of what seemed to be commonsense axioms rather than a rigorous theory.

Whether international theory should be separated from traditional theory has been the object of debate. How different are international phenomena from other classes of objects with which political theory deals? This issue recurs in various forms in our discussion of theories of international relations. Chris Brown sees the theory of relations among states as an integral part of a much older, more venerable Western theory of speculation about the political order. That theory was not merely empirical, but normative as well, dealing with the moral dimension of politics, the *ought* as well as the *is*. "At its most basic," writes Brown, normative theory "addresses the ethical nature of the relations between communities/states, whether in the context of the old agenda, which focused on violence and war, or the new(er) agenda, which mixes these traditional concerns with the modern demand for international distributive justice."[29] The normative dimension has received even greater attention among international theorists since the end of the Cold War—especially with regard to such issues as the need to strengthen international peacekeeping institutions, humanitarian intervention in ethnic conflicts, and the formulation of more cooperative international policies and programs related to trade, technology transfer, economic development, hunger and malnutrition, environmental preservation, human rights, health, and other problems pertinent to the quality of life.

The period of European history from the end of the Thirty Years War in 1648 to the outbreak of World War I in 1914 constituted what has often been seen as the golden age of diplomacy, the balance of power, alliances, and international law in a state system characterized also by numerous wars. Nearly all political thought focused on the sovereign nation-state—the origins, functions, and limitations of governmental powers, the rights of individuals within the state, the requirements of order, and the imperatives of national self-determination and independence. The economic order was presumed simplistically to be separate from domestic politics and divorced from the international politics of diplomacy. Governments were expected to promote and protect trade, but not to regulate it. Various branches of socialist thinking sought to strike out in new directions, but socialists, despite their professed internationalism, did not really produce a coherent international theory. They advanced a theory of imperialism borrowed largely from John A. Hobson (1858–1940), the British economist, and thus derivative from an economic theory indigenous to the capitalist states.[30] (See Chapter 6.) Until 1914, international theorists almost uniformly assumed that the structure of international society was unalterable, and that the division of the world into sovereign states was necessary and natural.[31] The study of international relations consisted almost entirely of diplomatic history and international law, rather than of investigation into the processes of the international system.

MODERN APPROACHES TO INTERNATIONAL-RELATIONS THEORY

Some impetus to the serious study of international relations in this country came when the United States emerged as a world power, but ambiguities in American foreign policy, combined with the trend toward isolationism during the 1920s and 1930s, hindered the development of international-relations as an intellectual discipline. Although there have been many intellectual contributions to the development of international relations theory, the leading role of the United States assured that, as a result, much of the theory of international relations that emerged in the twentieth century, and especially after World War II, would be written in the United States or would have the United States as a central element. Nevertheless, American contributions to international-relations theory have been heavily influenced not only by their roots in Western political theory, but also by the numbers of immigrant scholars, especially in the realist school. Theorists such as Hans J. Morgenthau, Nicholas J. Spykman, Arnold Wolfers, Robert Strausz-Hupé, and Henry Kissinger brought with them an intellectual tradition that enriched American scholarship, as well as theory and policy.

From its inception as a field or discipline after World War I until the present, international-relations theory has been derived from an Anglo-American tradition that extends from the writings of E. H. Carr and Alfred Zimmern to Martin Wight and Hedley Bull, and, most recently, the work of Barry Buzan and Chris Brown, to mention only some of the major and seminal British contributions.[32] In the United States, following World War I, intellectual idealists who shared Woodrow Wilson's vision of the League of Nations contrasted sharply with those political leaders who, feeling pressures for a so-called return to normalcy, blocked the United States' entry into the world organization. Americans demanded a moral and peaceful international order, but they were unwilling to pay the price. This dichotomy between noble impulses and tendencies toward isolationism was clearly reflected in the Kellogg–Briand Treaty of 1928, which outlawed war by moralistic declaration but provided no adequate means of enforcement.[33]

For a decade or more after the Treaty of Versailles, the two most popular approaches to teaching world affairs in American universities included courses in current events and courses in international law and organization. Current-events courses were designed more to promote international understanding than to apply social science or other methodologies to theoretical development.[34] Courses in international law emphasized discrepancies between the formal obligations of states (especially League of Nations members) and their actual conduct in an era of struggle among powers anxious to preserve the international status quo and those determined to overturn it.[35]

Whereas some British and American scholars in the period between the two world wars focused on the study of international law and organization, others looked for more dynamic, comprehensive evaluations of forces and events in inter-state relations. Leading diplomatic historians searched for the alleged causes or origins of the Great War of 1914–1918.[36] Other historians explored the phenomenon of nationalism, long regarded (up to today) as the most potent political force in the modern world, despite the advent of universalist ideologies.[37] Specialized writings appeared in several areas—problems of security, war, and disarmament;[38] imperialism;[39] diplomacy and negotiation;[40] the balance of power;[41] the geographical aspects of world power (which built on the work of Alfred Thayer Mahan and Sir Halford Mackinder, treated in Chapter 4);[42] the history of international-relations theory;[43] and economic factors in international relations.[44] For example, Sir Norman Angell, one of the most prolific British writers of his time and the recipient of the 1933 Nobel Peace Prize, suggested that war between highly industrialized states was a futile exercise because free trade had given rise to unprecedented interdependence, which in turn made international cooperation essential to their individual and collective well-being. (See Chapter 5.)

E. H. Carr and the Crisis of World Politics

By the 1930s, within international-relations literature, there was a growing recognition of the gap between the utopians and the realists (discussed in greater detail in Chapter 2). The academic climate after World War I made it conducive for utopians to concern themselves with the means of preventing another war. Consequently, this task spurred the serious study of international relations. No scholars in that period more trenchantly analyzed the philosophical differences between utopians and realists than did Edward Hallett Carr, in his celebrated work,[45] which, although published in 1939, did not have its impact in America until after World War II. Carr used the term *utopians* for idealists who placed emphasis on international law and organization, as well as on the influence of morality and public opinion in the affairs of nations. He probably did not intend the more pejorative connotation that attached to the term *utopians* after World War II as naïve opponents of power politics expounded by realists. Indeed, since the end of the Cold War, as we show in Chapter 2, where Carr's work is treated more fully, the idealist concept of the harmony of national interests in peace has received new attention in a more recent neoliberal–neorealist debate.

As World War II approached, the gap between utopian optimism and the events of the day widened. The failures of the League of Nations in the 1930s cast doubt on the harmony of interest in peace, which appeared to accord with the interests of satisfied, status-quo powers with democratic governments, but not with the perceived needs of revisionist, totalitarian, or authoritarian states seeking boundary changes, enhanced status, greater power, and, especially in the case of Nazi Germany, revenge for the humiliation of the post–World War I settlement imposed by the Versailles treaty. Contrary to the utopian assumption, national self-determination did not always produce representative governments. Instead, the overthrow of the old monarchical order gave rise in many places, including Russia, to a more pervasive and oppressive totalitarian state.

The world consisted not principally of peace-loving states based on the realization of an international harmony of interest in peace. Instead, increasingly some of the major actors embraced ideologies such as fascism and communism—joined, for example, in the infamous Molotov–Ribbentrop Pact of August 1939 between the Soviet Union and Nazi Germany, which set the stage for Adolph Hitler's invasion of Poland, the outbreak of World War II, the partition of Poland, and the absorption of the Baltic states into the Soviet Union, all in contravention of the standards of international conduct set forth in utopian theory. Those states that most strongly embodied and were the intellectual centers of utopian theory themselves fell far short of its precepts. The United States had rejected Wilson's call for internationalism and had refused to join the League of Nations, reverting instead to isolationism. In Britain the carnage of World War I that had resulted in the loss of much of a generation of manhood spawned a pacifism whose effect was to restrict greatly any ability to bring necessary force to bear within or outside the League of Nations against expansionist states such as Nazi Germany and Fascist Italy, as well as imperial Japan, until the onset of World War II. Such was the international setting that marked the decline of the utopian phase and provided fertile intellectual ground for the reassertion and reformulation of a realist theory of international relations after World War II.

Post–World War II Realism

Not surprisingly, World War II and its immediate aftermath shifted Western thinking on international relations further away from the idealism of the early League of Nations period toward an older and resurgent realism, from law and organization to the elements of power. Even idealistically inclined analysts—and there were many who had supported the war effort for reasons of the highest moral idealism—became skeptical of utopian programs and called instead for a merger of international law and organization with effective power to ensure international peace, the security of nations, and the equitable settlement of disputes.

Throughout the post–World War II period, both the onset of the Cold War and the emergence of the United States as a power with global interests and commitments generated within American universities a heightened interest in the study of international relations. War veterans in college showed a keen concern over foreign affairs. Under the impact of critical international developments associated with the Cold War, the United States government greatly expanded its operations in the areas of national military security, alliances and other international organizations, and economic-development assistance to foreign countries. All of these operations, of course, increased the need for trained personnel. For the first time, many American industries became aware of international trade and investment possibilities. Scientists, alarmed at the implications of the new nuclear technology that they had just produced, entered politics as crusading novices, warning of dangers confronting humanity. Civic-minded persons zealously organized councils and associations to educate and exhort in order to make citizens more aware of international problems.

Academic scholars in Britain and the United States, the two countries in which the universities had shown the most progress in the interwar curricular development of international relations, produced analyses designed to be suitable to the postwar reality. Several works published in the late 1940s emphasized the power approach to the study of international relations. One of the more frequently quoted English authors was Martin Wight, already noted in this chapter, who wrote that

> what distinguishes modern history from medieval history is the predominance of the idea of power over the idea of right; the very term "power" to describe a state in its international aspect is significant; and the view of the man in the street, who is perhaps inclined to take it for granted that foreign politics are inevitably power politics, is not without a shrewd insight.[46]

The textbooks in international relations published during the first two decades after World War II generally recognized power as a central concept in the field.[47] The text that had the greatest impact on the university teaching of international relations, that of Hans J. Morgenthau, explained nation-state behavior on the basis of national interest (defined in terms of power) as the normal objective pursued by governments when possible. The other important textbooks of that period devoted on the average at least three chapters to the nature of power and the elements or factors of national power. Most contemporary political scientists and students of international relations continue to regard power not as a wanton destructive thing, but as a combination of persuasive influence and coercive force capable of being used for positive as well as negative purposes, as a variable of major importance.[48]

THE DEVELOPMENT OF INTERNATIONAL-RELATIONS THEORY

The earlier textbooks contained some theoretical observations on such topics as nationalism, imperialism, colonialism, the emergence of the Third World, ideology and propaganda, and the impact of economic and technological factors on international relations. Some contained chapters on alliances, regional or functional integration, disarmament or arms control, and such specific techniques of foreign policy as intervention, nonalignment, and isolation. Seldom was there an effort to draw precise linkages among the theories, or to find out whether partial theories could be fitted together into a larger, coherent whole.[49] This is not to suggest that the authors necessarily lacked their own informing theory. However, they did not present generalized theory in a systematic manner. Indeed, several of them were probably suspicious of single, overarching theories.

Throughout the period since the late 1940s, there has been a steady development of methodologies and techniques for research, analysis, and teaching in international relations, which have contributed to the growth of theory.[50] The effort toward comprehensive theory-building began with the great debate between realists and utopians. Subsequently, the 1960s witnessed a considerable expansion of interest in theoretical analysis,[51] and in its validation by means of such methodologies as content analysis and bivariate and multivariate correlations. Insights from the biological, psychological, anthropological, sociological, economic, and other behavioral sciences were borrowed in the effort to explain international politics. There was an emphasis on abstract model building, as well as on a variety of new approaches to the understanding of (a) ecological factors and the individual relationships between humans and their milieu, (b) regional integration, (c) interaction in the international system, (d) the causes of war, (e) the conditions for deterrence, (f) arms races and arms control, (g) decision making, (h) games theory, and (i) related subjects in foreign policy and international relations, all of which are treated in subsequent chapters.

Theory and Its Types

The student should not be frightened by the word *theory*. Theory is nothing but systematic reflection on phenomena, designed to explain them and to show how they are related to each other in a meaningful, intelligent pattern, instead of being merely random items in an incoherent universe. Every discipline requires theory to guide research, to provide a basis for explanation, and if possible, to lead to a predictive capability. Biological, chemical, and other scientists seeking cures for diseases can hardly proceed in a purely hit-and-miss fashion without any theory to give them a sense of purpose and direction. Social scientists who would recommend to policymakers how to reduce the incidence of domestic crime or decrease the likelihood of war in an international crisis need theory in order to penetrate to the underlying causes of the problems they wish to solve.

In every field, there are different kinds of theory—almost as many, perhaps, as there are different questions to be answered. Not all theorists show interest in all the questions or all the theories. Even in such an exact science as astronomy, there continue to be fundamental disagreements over basic questions regarding the origin of the solar system, the nature of black holes, and whether the universe is expanding or contracting. As in all scientific fields, in international relations there are comprehensive or grand theories on the one hand, and partial or middle-range theories on the other. Most of the better-known writers usually devote their attention to one favorite approach in either category, or else assume a dominant grand theory while pursuing their own work on a narrower front.

Grand theory purports to explain in a generalized way a wide range of phenomena. Examples include the realist or power theories of Hans J. Morgenthau and Henry A. Kissinger; the neorealist theories of Kenneth Waltz and Gottfried-Karl Kindermann; the systems theories of Morton Kaplan and Richard Rosecrance; the neo-Marxist theories of the capitalist world economy of Immanuel Wallerstein and Christopher Chase-Dunn; and the *dependencia* theories of J. Samuel and Arturo Valenzuela and others.

Examples of partial, middle-range theories designed to explain a limited range of phenomena with as few variables as necessary include those pertaining to (a) the influence of the geographical environment (Alfred Thayer Mahan, Halford

Mackinder, Nicholas Spykman, Harold and Margaret Sprout); (b) communications patterns and community building (Karl Deutsch); (c) functionalism and sector integration (David Mitrany, Ernst Haas, Leon Lindberg, and Joseph S. Nye); (d) deterrence (Bernard Brodie, Herman Kahn, Glenn Snyder and Paul Diesing, and Robert Jervis); (e) international development and conflict (Nazli Choucri and Robert North); (g) alliance behavior (William Riker and Stephen Walt); (h) bargaining behavior (Thomas Schelling and Anatol Rapaport); and (i) decision making (Richard Snyder, Graham Allison, and Glenn Paige).

Even the effort to classify theories as grand or middle range can provoke debate. They are not completely disjunctive categories; some theories might fall in between, and others might not fit well into either. The decision-making theory of Richard Snyder and his colleagues, for example, is not so much an explanatory theory with predictive power as it is a precise taxonomy or classificatory scheme, a conceptual framework that provides a researcher doing a single or comparative case study in decision making with an orderly framework for collecting and analyzing data. Other theories of decision making—such as the "cybernetic" (John Steinbruner), "satisficing behavior" (Herbert Simon), "bureaucratic" (Morton Halperin), and "rational actor" or "organizational process" (Graham Allison) theories—come closer to being explanatory. All of the aforementioned theories, plus others, are treated in subsequent chapters. The purpose of mentioning them here is to indicate that there are not only many different theories, but also various types of approaches to theorizing about international relations. Authorities in the field are not at all agreed on which would be better—to build grand theory first and let the formulation of middle-range theories flow from it, or to test out and solidify a number of middle-range theories before proceeding to a higher, more abstract level. Stanley Hoffmann, for example, prefers to start with grand theory, whereas J. David Singer would lean toward laying the foundation with middle-range, empirically based theories. The situation has changed little since Glenn Snyder and Paul Diesing wrote,

> In our teaching and research, we are like travelers in a houseboat, shuttling back and forth between separate "islands" of theory, whose relatedness consists only in their being commonly in the great "ocean" of "international behavior." Some theorists take up permanent residence on one island or other, others continue to shuttle, but few attempt to build bridges, perhaps because the islands seem too far apart.[52]

At the risk of oversimplifying, we can say that those who adopt a careful, counting approach prefer the more modest hypotheses that become embodied in middle-range or even small-scale theories, whereas those of a more philosophizing bent favor the larger, more sweeping vision. Modern academicians who are often unjustly accused of knowing and writing more and more about less and less significant things often exhibit impatience or contempt toward the products of generalizing minds. Kenneth Boulding, on the other hand, shunned scholarly research on a narrow scale and urged those who would understand the international system to abandon the microscope and the infinitesimally trivial and take up the telescope to encompass the whole universe as it evolves through space and time.[53] Only then, he wrote, can we begin to see how the international human society on this tiny planet fits into the increasingly complex, interactive scheme of the larger universe. Because inevitable change is the fundamental law, he argued, we must throw off the apparently unchanging concepts of power politics inherited from Thucydides, Machiavelli, and Hobbes, and recognize that threat and conflict will sooner or later give way to mutually beneficial cooperation and integration. Boulding struck a novel and refreshing note that probably sounds more comforting to the philosopher than to the responsible policymaker, who thinks not in terms of aeons or centuries but of next year, next week, or tomorrow. The main point at the moment is that much depends on one's general philosophical outlook, including one's view of history and human nature, as well as whether human nature remains pretty much the same or undergoes genuine progressive development from egoism to altruism during the course of history. Obviously, society changes outwardly as a result of accumulated knowledge and the impact of education, science, technology, production, economics, religion, and culture. However, whether human beings experience equally profound internal change in their psychological and moral qualities is a different question.

THE DEFINITION AND SCOPE OF INTERNATIONAL RELATIONS

Definition is only the beginning, not the end, of systematic inquiry. Modern science began, as Alfred North Whitehead noted in a 1925 lecture, when emphasis was shifted from the Aristotelian method of classification to the Pythagorean–Platonist method of measurement, yet he hastened to add that classification is necessary for orderly, logical thought.[54] Every disciplinary field should be able to define itself clearly, just as every scientific thinker should undertake a research project with a precise notion of the phenomenon to be investigated. When the subject of international relations was just emerging as a field of study, academicians on both sides of the Atlantic had difficulty coming to grips with its nature and scope. In 1935, Sir Alfred Zimmern suggested that "the study of international relations extends from the natural sciences at one end to moral philosophy . . . at the other." He defined the field not as a single subject or discipline but as a "bundle of subjects . . . viewed from a common angle."[55] Many teachers since his time have wryly noted with Zimmern that students who major in international relations wish that they knew more about history, politics, economics, geography, demography, diplomacy, international law, ethics, religion, and nearly every branch of contemporary science and technology. Certainly those who achieve enduring distinction within the field seem to be those prepared by a liberal educational background for a life of active inquiry, based on an insatiable interest in the international dimension.

Nicholas J. Spykman, among the first to propose a rigorous definition, used the term *interstate relations*, which, however, he did not expect would gain wide acceptance: "International relations are relations between individuals belonging to different states, . . . international behavior is the social behavior of individuals or groups aimed at . . . or influenced by the existence or behavior of individuals or groups belonging to a different state."[56] Loosely defined, the term *international relations* could encompass many different activities—international communications, business transactions, athletic contests, tourism, scientific conferences, educational exchange programs, and religious missionary activities. International-relations scholars have never agreed on where the boundaries of their field lie.

Frederick S. Dunn once warned that the word *scope* is dangerously ambiguous because it implies the existence of clearly discernible boundary lines as readily identifiable as a surveyor's mark.

> A field of knowledge does not possess a fixed extension in space but is a constantly changing focus of data and methods that happen at the moment to be useful in answering an identifiable set of questions. It presents at any given time different aspects to different observers, depending on their point of view and purpose. The boundaries that supposedly divide one field of knowledge from another are not fixed walls between separate cells of truth but are convenient devices for arranging known facts and methods in manageable segments for instruction and practice. But the foci of interest are constantly shifting and these divisions tend to change with them.[57]

He went on to suggest, quite sensibly, that the "subject-matter of international relations consists of whatever knowledge, from any sources, may be of assistance in meeting new international problems or understanding old ones."[58]

For more than a decade after World War II, scholars debated whether international relations could be called a discipline with a methodology and substantive content of its own, or whether it was so encyclopedic as to belong to several disciplines. Quincy Wright regarded it as "an emerging discipline," one in the process of formation, and argued that it meets the definitional criteria of its critics as well as do most academic disciplines, in the development of which history has played as much a part as logic has played.[59] Morton A. Kaplan—insisting that international relations lacks the character of a discipline because there is "no common disciplinary core to be enriched as there had been in the companion subject-matter of political science," no set of unique skills and techniques, and no developed body of theoretical propositions—preferred to recognize international politics merely as a subdiscipline of political science.[60]

Frederick S. Dunn wrote that international relations may "be looked upon as the actual relations that take place across national boundaries, or as the body of knowledge which we have of those relations at any given time."[61] This is a fairly standard approach, but is it adequate? It is comprehensive, and it does not limit the subject to official relations between states and governments. However, is this delineation too broad, and would it be better to include transnational relations on the basis of their political significance, for example, by focusing on the influences that they exert on the world's political units? As students of politics, we are concerned with relationships between or among all of the actors—state and nonstate, international and transnational—to the extent that they contribute to an understanding of political phenomena. We define international politics as the effort of one state, or other international actor, to influence in some way another state, or other international actor. An influence relationship may encompass the actual or threatened use of military force, or it may be based entirely or partly on other inducements, such as political or economic ones. International politics, moreover, like all politics, represents the reconciliation of varying perspectives, goals, and interests. Thus, international politics includes many but not necessarily all transactions or interactions that take place across national frontiers.

Stanley Hoffmann found that "debates which try to determine the scope of a social science are rather pointless" because there are no immutable essences in social relationships. In his view, all definitions are bound to involve ambiguities and difficulties, especially in the case of a field marked by constant flux. Preferring a formula that leads to perceptive investigations and does not violate common sense, Hoffmann suggests an operational definition of the field to encompass "the factors and the activities which affect the external policies and the power of the basic units into which the world is divided."[62] He warns, however, against trying to gather everything within the fold, noting that "a flea market is not a discipline."

The prudent international theorist will avoid the Scylla and Charybdis of either including trivia or excluding significant phenomena. A field that is too broad or cluttered cannot be comprehended by the human mind and may seem to outsiders in other academic disciplines to be intellectually arrogant, if not downright imperialistic. On the other hand, if something can be shown to be relevant to a full understanding of an issue that belongs to international relations, it should not be kept outside the walls on the grounds that it is part of a different academic preserve. Much depends, of course, on the nature of the problem under investigation and on the degree to which material from another field can be incorporated and handled competently. As for the scope of our field, more is said in a subsequent section, when we take up the level-of-analysis problem and the units or actors on which we should focus our attention.

Should international theory emphasize the contemporary scene? There is an inescapable attractiveness about the present, bounded by what has recently happened and what is imminently about to happen. Fascination with the contemporary is heightened by the attention it receives in the news media, by the preoccupation of policymakers, and by the fact that research funding is more readily available for such policy-oriented topics of current interest and concern as Islamic fundamentalism, trade wars, international terrorism, drug traffic, intergovernmental cooperation on environmental issues, and so on. Nevertheless, most experienced scholars in international relations realize that a knowledge of history is essential because it broadens immensely the database from which extrapolations into the future are to be made, and it also refines our ability to formulate hypotheses that approximate social reality.

Morton Kaplan opens his principal work on the international system with a tribute to history: "There is one respect in which a science of international politics must always be indebted to history. History is the great laboratory within which international action occurs."[63] Kaplan calls for investigations into the ancient Greek city-state system, the Italian state system of the Renaissance period, and the balance-of-power system that dominated Europe during the eighteenth and nineteenth centuries, so that typical system behaviors in different eras might be compared.[64] In his view, international theorists should be interested in all systems—past, present, future, and hypothetical.[65] (Kaplan's theory is examined in Chapter 3.)

If we limit our attention exclusively to the existing nation-state system and ignore the vast record of the past out of which present reality evolved, we seriously restrict our ability to imagine possible futures. The history of international relations is not an international theory, but as a primary source of empirical data, it is part of the essential raw material with which the theoretician works.[66] One can hardly grasp, for example, integration theory (cf. Chapter 10) without some knowledge of the European Community/Union's development and of the factors that prevented other regions from achieving comparable success.

The Nature and Function of Theory

A theory—any theory, in any field—is a general explanation of certain selected phenomena, set forth in a manner satisfactory to someone acquainted with the characteristics of the reality being studied. It need not be acceptable to all experts; indeed, it may satisfy the expounder and horrify all others. Powerful theories are those that exercise great influence on the thinking of large numbers, perhaps the overwhelming majority, of knowledgeable persons for a long time before being replaced by new theories. (Among the enduring theories are those of the economists that address the division of labor and the principle of comparative advantage; those of social theorists pertaining to the ethnocentrism of groups—the preference for traditional and familiar over new and alien ways—and the relationship between external conflict and internal cohesiveness; those of physicists focussed on conservation of energy and the relativity of the time–space continuum; and those of international theorists in the realist school pertaining to the nearly universal tendency of states to seek their interests, as defined in terms of power.) In the social sciences, however, not even the most powerful theories command unquestioning assent within a disciplinary field. As we survey throughout this text a variety of theories, it becomes clear that no single generalization, principle, or hypothesis has yet been demonstrated with sufficient force to serve as the foundation for a universally accepted comprehensive theory of international relations.

As Martin Hollis and Steve Smith point out, two basic intellectual approaches have shaped the development of the social sciences, including the study of international-relations and the development of international-relations theory.[67] The first has its origin in natural science, which seeks explanations for the phenomena with which it deals. The second can be traced to the study of history and to a quest for an understanding of the meaning of phenomena. The first tradition is termed *scientific* because it relies on scientific method as the essential basis for explanation; the second has been termed *hermeneutic* because it is essentially interpretive. Explanatory theory is based on a quest for unifying themes, for an understanding of the causes of human behavior, for the discovery of laws that govern how people and collectivities—including nations, coalitions, and alliances—act under specified circumstances. In contrast, understanding connotes experience and interpretation—how those who have been a part of a major event, such as the Cuban Missile Crisis or the end of the Cold War—have viewed the situation. The search for causal explanation has been likened to the outside observer who views the phenomena being studied with the goal of developing theory based on what is observed. Contrasted is the approach that focuses on getting the inside story, including who said what to whom, what were the thoughts of two great leaders, and what were the dynamics of their relationship. Taken together, Hollis and Smith suggest, these two intellectual traditions—based respectively on causal explanation and interpretive understanding—have shaped the evolution of the study of international relations and theorizing about the phenomena with which it is concerned. Both have a role to play in the theoretical development of the social sciences. Exactly what their respective contributions have been, or could be, remains an object of debate, as we note in subsequent chapters.

In literature on the philosophy of science, the term *theory* has assumed a specific meaning. A theory is defined as a symbolic construction, a series of interrelated hypotheses, together with definitions, laws, theorems, and axioms. A theory sets forth a systematic view of phenomena by presenting a series of propositions or hypotheses that specify relations among variables in order to present explanations and make predictions about the phenomena. In the physical sciences, a theory may be viewed as a system consisting of the following elements: (1) a set of axioms, the truth of which is assumed and can be tested only by testing their logical consequences—an axiom cannot be deduced from other statements contained in the system; (2) statements, or theorems, that are deduced from the axioms, or from other theorems and definitions; and (3) definitions of descriptive terms contained in the axioms.[68] A theory is a group of laws that are deductively connected. Some of the laws are premises from which other laws are deduced. Those laws deduced from the axioms are the theorems of the theory. Whether a law is an axiom or a theorem depends on its position in a theory.

A theory does not necessarily depend on empirical referents for validity; it need only state logically deduced relationships among the phenomena with which the theory is concerned.[69] According to Abraham Kaplan, the ability to apply the theory successfully is not a necessary condition for its success because the failure of the application may be traceable to many factors external to the theory itself.[70] Nonetheless, the development of empirical referents makes possible the testing of a theory. Carl Hempel has offered the following analogy:

> A scientific theory might therefore be likened to a complex spatial network: Its terms are represented by the knots, while the threads connecting the latter correspond, in part, to the definitions and, in part, to the fundamental and derivative hypotheses contained in the theory. The whole system floats, as it were, above the plane of observation and is anchored to it by rules of interpretation. These might be viewed as strings which are not part of the network but link certain parts of the latter with specific laces in the plane of observation. By virtue of those interpretive connectors, the network can function as a scientific theory. From certain observational data, we may ascend, via an interpretive string, to some point in the theoretical network, thence proceed, via definitions and hypotheses, to other points from which another interpretive string permits a descent to the place of observation.[71]

In the field of international relations, as in all the social sciences, theory is somewhat more diffuse and less precise than one finds in the physical sciences (for reasons that are explained later) and may assume several different forms. Theory has been equated with a philosophy, an ideology, a set of interrelated concepts, a set of interrelated hypotheses with a requisite amount of supporting evidence, and a set of axioms and concepts from which hypotheses may be derived. Theory may be deductive or inductive, a distinction that is elaborated subsequently. It may be a description and analysis of the political behavior of rational actors, based on a single dominant motive such as power. Rather than describing how rational actors do in fact behave, it may be normative, indicating how they ought to behave—a subject on which more is said subsequently.

Relation Between Theory and Practice

Despite their complementarity, basic differences exist between academic social-science theory and political-diplomatic practice. There are also differences, perhaps less basic, between general theoretical approaches to international relations and the policy sciences that deal with the foreign-policy problems of particular states, just as there are differences between the policy sciences and the actual conduct of diplomacy. Each of the several levels of knowledge and action has a legitimacy of its own that ought not to be disparaged by one who happens to be operating at another level. In all cases, it is useful to keep in mind the distinction between the scholar, who seeks to achieve a theoretical understanding of phenomena and to formulate generalizations about political behavior based on a high level of probability, and the decision maker, who has to choose a specific course of action in a concrete set of circumstances, in which probability analysis may not be an adequate basis on which to make important policy choices.

Long ago, Aristotle differentiated between knowing and doing, between the speculative intellect and the practical intellect.[72] David Hume drew a sharp contrast among three classes of knowledge: (1) *deductive reasoning*, which relates to the logical and necessary truths of mathematics and metaphysics; (2) *empirical knowledge*, which pertains to apparently causal relationships that are not really rationally necessary; and (3) *value judgments*, which derive from an accumulation of historical facts as they have affected human emotion and intuition. For Hume, politics and morals must always be inextricably bound with value judgments and hence can be neither deductive nor empirical.[73] To state the problem of theory and practice in Humean terms, we might assert that whereas the pure theorist is usually concerned principally with deductive thought processes to reach generalized formulations, the policymaker has a principal interest in the empirical and inductive knowledge derived from personal experience rather than from any systematic research effort. The policymaker is concerned also with the subtle details of the political values, forces, and preferences operating in a particular situation in all its existential reality rather than with a universal abstraction or probability. Whereas the social theorist wishes to concentrate primarily on elements common to many situations, the decision maker invariably wants complete detailed information about those elements that are unique to the case at hand.

However, lest anyone receive the wrong impression, we stress that the differing emphases of theorist and practitioner do not alter the desirability that each should try to appreciate the modes of knowledge peculiar to the other. Neither can afford to dismiss generalized or particularized knowledge. Leaders in the late twentieth century must weigh and mix different theories in their ongoing efforts to understand developments, choose appropriate policies, and predict outcomes. They will be likely, however, to continue to prefer their own intuitional theories—the cumulative effect of their own education and political experience, whether in elected, appointed, or usurped offices, in executive, legislative, or diplomatic positions. These intuitional theories may serve as more reliable guideposts to policy choices than may abstract theoretical constructs developed in academic circles and often couched in terminology unfamiliar to policymakers. Academic theoreticians aim at understanding; practical politicians must choose courses of action. The former try to prescind from day-to-day events; the latter cannot.

Finally, we must remember that political leaders are usually preoccupied with shaping the foreign policies of their own countries vis-à-vis major allies and adversaries. Their span of attention in the international realm is limited by the greater amount of time and effort they must devote to domestic matters. They can seldom afford the luxury of thinking about the entire international system. The international theorist may be deeply interested in the foreign policies of a number of states, depending on the precise phenomenon being investigated, but realizes that international relations are more than merely the sum of the foreign policies of nations. Even though there is a strong linkage between international and domestic politics and economics,[74] there is an inwardness to the making of foreign policy that requires a nationally specific perspective. The academic scholar who deals with international theory views the subject from a larger perspective and focuses on the net results of interactive processes that national policymakers may try to understand and influence, but not always completely or successfully. Let us quickly add that a great deal of our substantive knowledge about international relations has always come and will continue to come from studies of national and comparative foreign policies.[75] The two approaches intersect in many places but are not identical.

Deductive and Inductive Theorizing

Two eminent theorists in the field—Quincy Wright and James N. Rosenau—offered, at an interval of two decades, some useful advice to would-be theorists of international relations. According to Wright, "a general theory of international relations means a comprehensive, coherent and self-correcting body of knowledge contributing to the understanding, the prediction, the evaluation and the control of the relations among states and of the conditions of the world."[76] Wright's mandate is quite ambitious: He has a grand theory in mind, one that covers all aspects of the field. It should be expressed in generalized propositions that are as clear, as accurate, and as few as possible. It should not be cluttered up with a lot of exceptions. In short, the theory should be *parsimonious*—that is, it should state an important truth as accurately, elegantly, and briefly as possible. Scientists have always been disposed to equate scientific truth with aesthetic beauty, and the latter with intellectual simplicity. Every part of the theory should be logically consistent with every other part. The theory should be formulated in a manner conducive to continual updating and improvement in the light of new evidence. Thus, it should be capable of constant verification and refinement. It should contribute to an objective understanding of international reality, rather than one distorted by national perspective. Theory, said Wright, should enable us to predict at least some things and should help us to arrive at value judgments—even if the process of moral assessment may not be entirely consistent with the value-free tradition of Western science.[77] Wright himself agrees, and we agree with him, that a theory fulfilling all these ideal requirements would be extremely difficult, and perhaps impossible, to achieve.

James Rosenau agrees with Stanley Hoffmann that being able to define *theory* precisely furnishes no guarantee that one will be able to theorize imaginatively or creatively. Rosenau would distinguish more sharply than Wright between empirical and normative (or ethical) theory. He considers both types important but fears that both can be distorted if what is and what ought to be are mixed too closely together.* The theorist, Rosenau insists, must assume that in human affairs there is an underlying order, that things do not happen randomly, but that their causes can be explained rationally (even when what we call "irrational behavior" is involved). He urges the theorist to seek not the unique but the general, and to sacrifice detailed descriptions of the single case in favor of the broader, more abstract patterns that encompass many instances. The theorist should be ready to tolerate ambiguity and to be contented with probabilities rather than certainties and absolutes. One must give the mind free rein to play with unusual, even absurd, ideas that may produce insights into previously unthought-of explanations. International phenomena should be looked on as puzzles or mysteries awaiting solution by the inquisitive mind. Finally, the theorist must always be ready to be proven wrong.[78] (Many are, sooner or later.)

The summaries just given make it clear that Wright had general deductive theory in mind, while Rosenau's advice seems pointed somewhat more toward empirical, inductive, and middle-range theories. These are the two basic approaches to theorizing in the Western intellectual tradition. The deductive method can be traced to Plato, who used it to construct his ideal republic. One begins with an abstract concept, model, or major premise—flowing from a set of definitions and assumptions drawn more from wisdom than from systematically collected evidence—and then proceeds by plausible, logical steps to deduce (draw out) subordinate propositions and necessary conclusions. Deduction is a *formal* process of deriving hypotheses from axioms, assumptions, and concepts logically integrated. The hypotheses so derived, in a scientific conception, should be tested with data that are not impressionistic, but rather are systematically and carefully selected.

Take, for example, the view expounded by Morgenthau and Waltz that all political communities are concerned in one way or another with *power*—acquiring, consolidating, or expanding power, projecting an image of power to preserve

---

*The subject of disarmament provides an example of what Rosenau means. Those who assign the highest priority and urgency to disarmament on the international agenda may underestimate the political, psychological, technical, and strategic problems involved. Those who have specialized in studying the empirical–historical–technical data on disarmament may have reached such pessimistic conclusions as to overestimate the difficulties of ever reaching arms limitation agreements.

it, balancing power for security, or accommodating to the power of another political community. This is an example of a deductive theory. Theorists of power have not pulled it out of thin air. Far from disdaining empirical data, they have developed their ideas on the basis of an extensive reading and interpretation of historical evidence. It is a mistake, therefore, to equate deductive theory with nonempirical theory, even when combined with a certain philosophy regarding human nature. The deductive differs from the inductive method in the way that historical factual evidence is collected, converted into usable data, analyzed, and interpreted for purposes of theory. The deductive thinker may arrive at a concept, model, or major premise in an impressionistic, intuitive, or insightful manner rather than according to strict methodological criteria for selecting cases, rigorous coding rules for classifying events, or mathematically precise ways of determining correlations.

The inductive approach entails a different route toward generalizing from experience. Instead of leaping to a conclusion by way of an inner mental light, as it were, the inductive empiricist is more careful about observing, categorizing, measuring, and analyzing facts. This method is traceable to Aristotle, who wrote his *Politics* after examining the constitutions of some 150 Greek city-states. The inductive thinker may consider the deductive method excellent in mathematics, logic, and metaphysics but prefers to investigate physical and social phenomena by observing a number of instances in the same class, and by describing in detail both the research procedures followed and the substantive results, so that others (who may be skeptical) can replicate (repeat) the work if they wish to do so. The inductive method produces no certainties, only probabilities, and in the social sciences (as contrasted with physics or chemistry), these probabilities are usually not of a very high order. For that matter, certainties are not produced by the deductive method, or by the methods used by chemists, physicists, or biologists. Newton was the greatest physicist of his age, but Einstein demonstrated that his work was partial and flawed, just as eventually even Einstein's work may be superseded by a new theory. In international-politics research, it is rare to obtain statistical correlations at high levels of significance—such as, "point 05," meaning that there would be only five chances in a hundred that the results were due to coincidence.

Deduction and induction should not be regarded as either competitive or mutually exclusive approaches. Some scholars will prefer one over the other and will make better progress with one than the other. Theory building requires a fruitful combination of the two, plus something more, discussed here soon. The argument that in the nuclear age, a bipolar international system is more stable than a multipolar one, and vice versa, is not amenable to empirical proof, so it usually proceeds by logical deduction from assumed premises regarding the amount of uncertainty in the system, the number of actors to whom the states must allocate their attention, and the destructive power of nuclear weapons. (See the references to Singer, Waltz, and Bueno de Mesquita in Chapter 8.) On the other hand, the middle-range theoretical proposition that governments find it relatively easy to pursue policies of regional economic integration in periods of prosperous growth and tend to retrench toward national particularism at times of recession can be arrived at by deduction and can then be tested by reference to the evaluation of the European Economic Community/Union (see Chapter 10).

Kenneth N. Waltz distinguishes theories from empirical data, statistical correlations, hypotheses, and inductively reached laws or generalizations. Statistical correlations, even when significant, are not facts, and they can never establish causal connections. We can arrive at laws and empirical generalizations through inductive methods, and these may identify invariable or probable associations but cannot explain them. The ancient Babylonians were familiar with the laws of tidal movements, which they could observe, measure, and predict, but they could not explain those laws. Explanation is the function of theory, which cannot be reached by deduction alone, for deduction merely proceeds logically from initial premises and thus can provide no powerful new explanations. Theories have to be invented by a creative intellectual process that takes a number of disparate laws and generalizations, simplifies them by isolating a few key factors, abstracting them from what is not relevant, aggregating them in a previously unknown way, and synthesizing them in a new, ideal, quasi-perfect explanatory system. Such a process can hardly be taught. A textbook can do no more than show how others have theorized. Students can judge for themselves whether a particular theory is insightful, satisfying, and promising. It is hoped that a survey of theories will inspire those who study them to embark on their own road to theorizing.

The Level-of-Analysis Problem: The Actors and Their Relationship to Each Other

In all the social sciences—politics, economics, and sociology, for example—one cannot help wondering where to begin, where to focus attention, where to try to get a handle on the subject, and how to distinguish between the sources of explanation and the objects of analysis. In all these fields, the micro and macro perspectives have their ardent partisans. Determining the proper fulcrum point is particularly difficult in international relations because of the comprehensiveness of the field. On which of many possible levels of analysis should we focus our attention? Which are the proper units of study—or actors? From the micro to the macro level, one can draw up a lengthy inventory of logical candidates, from empires (either long extinct or recently dissolved) down to the International Olympic Committee (IOC), Amnesty International, and McDonald's fast-food chain. In Waltz's international theory, the focus of levels of analysis has been individuals, states, and the global system.[79] According to Barry Buzan, the levels of analysis have emphasized essentially three ideas: (1) *interactive capacity,* the types and intensities of interaction of which any one unit is capable with respect to others in the system; (2) *structure,* how the units are arranged with respect to each other and how they are differentiated from each other; and (3) *process,* the extent to which the units interact with each other in recurrent patterns. The levels of analysis provide a conceptual basis for asking such questions as, "What is the effect of systemic structure (e.g., bipolarity) on the behavior of states or other units?" By the same token, how the interactive capacity of the units shapes the structure is of importance.[80]

Individuals   Although most international theorists would probably reject the notion that individuals are international actors (nearly all legal authorities have sinilarly denied them any status as subjects of international law), a classical liberal would argue that the individual should be the foundation for any social theory because only individuals are real, while society is an abstraction. Although few theorists would agree with the classical liberal position, and most would probably tend to think that social forces produce the heroic figure more often than the other way around, it cannot be denied that scholars in the fields of history, politics, and international relations do pay attention to leaders who have played a prominent role on the world stage. Moreover, those who survey, for example, the attitudes of voters on international issues are, for all practical purposes, placing the individual at the center of their investigations. It bears repeating, however, that most theorists do not do this, but rather subsume individuals into a nation-state or other organizational context, such as those decision-making units (treated in Chapter 11) that play key roles in formulating foreign policies on behalf of states.

Subnational Groups   These may take many forms: political parties, the communications media, and organized interest groups of a nongovernmental nature that seek to influence foreign policies by lobbying or shaping public opinion. These actors fall primarily within the scope of foreign-policy studies, both national and comparative. International theorists, however, while not placing them at the center of their attention, are obliged to recognize their relevance because of the undoubtedly significant linkage between domestic and international politics. Numerous important examples will come to mind if one thinks about the implications of (a) the Iran–arms–hostages–Contras affair that preoccupied U.S. policymakers in the 1980s, (b) the relation between media coverage and international terrorism, (c) the rise of xenophobic protest movements against immigrants in Europe, and (d) the impact, in parliamentary systems of government, that ethnic minorities can have on the foreign policies of their countries, as for example when Greek constituents prompted the U.S. Congress to cut off aid to Turkey for having invaded Cyprus in 1974 or when Dutch and other European church groups rallied more than a million opponents to the deployment of NATO intermediate-range missiles in 1980.

Nation-States   Realist theorists subscribe to what is called the "state-centric" view of international relations, focusing on the action of states and governments. They recognize other realities mentioned in this inventory, and they take those realities into account as appropriate, but they insist that all others, whether less or more extensive, are subordinate to nation-states, which are the principal actors at the international level. In recent centuries, the world was divided into imperialist powers and colonial territories or protectorates. The number of states claiming to be legally sovereign and politically independent has increased steadily in this century: Whereas there were only about 60 in the 1930s, there were more than 180 as we moved toward the year 2000. Throughout the various eras of history, the patterns of political organization have always reflected some relationship with political, military, economic, technological, cultural, and other forms of power (including religious and psychological). Realists do not assert that currently existing nation-state structures will endure forever, but they have no doubt that those structures are now firmly entrenched and are likely to constitute the basic units of international political reality for a long time to come.[81] Nonstate actors derive their significance from states, or from the degree to which they either can influence the policies and behavior of states or can be used by states as policy instruments.

Transnational Groups and Organizations Not Made Up of States This category includes all entities—political, religious, economic–commercial, and so on—that operate transnationally (across one or more international boundaries) but do not have governments or their formal representatives as members, what are termed *nongovernmental organizations* (NGOs). For centuries, the Catholic church was recognized as an indisputable example. In more recent times, this broad category has included communist parties, national liberation guerrilla movements, international terrorist groups (such as Hezbollah), international arms dealers, and many international nongovernmental organizations.[82] In recent years, there has been a growing awareness of Islamic fundamentalism (with its center in Shiite Iran) as a force of considerable transnational potential, regardless of the term's vagueness and the fact that, historically, Islam has not been characterized by either a priesthood or a hierarchical organization.

Among the transnational phenomena that have attracted academic attention since the mid-1970s is the multinational corporation (MNC)—a term that has been subjected to a variety of subtle definitional refinements by other scholars.[83] MNCs, in contrast to nation-states, regard boundaries and territory as irrelevant. Despite the amount of concern expressed over their potential for politically intervening in host countries (especially in the Third World), they are primarily interested in profits rather than politics, except insofar as the latter affects the former. Apart from the deductive literature on dependency and interdependence (treated in Chapter 6) and the limited number of case studies of specific MNCs in specific countries, there has not yet been an impressive amount of scientific research on the role of MNCs in the international political system, on their political power in comparison with that of host states, and on the degree to which they are controllable or uncontrollable by home countries, host countries, or international organizations. Much of the debate has been normative, turning on whether MNCs have been beneficial or harmful to less developed countries (or less advantaged social classes) in the Third World, a subject that is treated in greater detail in Chapter 6. There can be no doubt, however, that General Motors, Westinghouse, Royal Dutch Shell, British Petroleum, SONY, Volkswagen, and International Telephone and Telegraph are important transnational firms and international actors.

International Groups and Organizations with States or Their Representatives as Members These include both limited-membership groups such as the Organization of Petroleum Exporting Countries (OPEC), the European Community/Union, the Arab League, and the Association of South East Asian Nations (ASEAN); such principal international actors in this century as the League of Nations, the United Nations, and the World Court; and such specialized agencies as the United Nations Educational, Scientific and Cultural Organization (UNESCO); the World Health Organization (WHO), the Food and Agriculture Organization (FAO), the International Bank for Reconstruction and Development (IBRD), the International Monetary Fund (IMF), the International Civil Aviation Organization (ICAO), the International Telecommunications Union (ITU), the International Fund for Agricultural Development (IFAD), the World Trade Organization (WTO) created in December 1994 by the Uruguay round of the General Agreement on Tariffs and Trade (GATT), and other intergovernmental bodies that report to the UN Economic and Social Council. During the Cold War, the two major regional security groups—the North Atlantic Treaty Organization (NATO) and the now defunct Warsaw Treaty Organization (WTO)—rivaled the United Nations in importance. A study by the Union of International Associations estimated that the number of national representatives of more than 110 countries in more than 2,100 international organizations exceeded 54,000.[84] Most of these carry on routine administrative activities that do not attract the interest of the international theorist. On those occasions, however, when the ICAO debates what to do about the hijacking of aircraft by terrorists, or when the adequacy of the International Atomic Energy Agency (IAEA) safeguards system becomes an issue in regard to compliance with the provisions of the Nuclear Non-Proliferation Treaty, the specialized agencies are removed from obscurity into the spotlight of international politics and become for a time at least bit players if not full-fledged actors.

The International System   At the most comprehensive and abstract level, we come to the international or global system, which is given detailed treatment in Chapter 3. At this level of analysis, the emphasis is on the whole rather than on its component parts, or what is termed a *holistic/systemic focus.* The behavioral patterns of the parts are presumed to be shaped by the structures that constitute the system. In this macrocosmic, global scheme, specific nation-states and other international actors are not absent, but they are present in blurred rather than sharp outline. J. David Singer has noted that the nation-state level produces richer descriptions and causal explanations (e.g., of how and why specific wars begin), whereas the systemic model is more conducive to broader generalizations about how all states normally behave within the structure that is said to constitute the international system. To focus on the state as the unit actor is to engage in what is termed *reductionist* or *atomistic analysis of the parts* rather than analysis of the whole. Singer sees Morgenthau's thesis that states seek their national interest defined in terms of power as a systemic theory, a general rule to which one might be able to find some exceptions that do not vitiate the rule.[85]

Generally speaking, those who favor an international-systems-level approach are convinced that the international system exerts a more profound effect on the component parts than the other way around. A holistic/systemic approach assumes not only that the whole is greater than the sum of its parts, but also that the structure of the system molds the behavior of the units. This, of course, is a modern version of the ancient philosophical problem known as the "one and the many," one of those profound and recurring problems that seem always to defy solution but that make the intellectual life fascinating. In earlier historical periods, it was possible to recognize partial international systems (e.g., the Greek and Italian city-state systems). There was a Mediterranean state system of sorts before Rome became an empire, but an empire precludes the kind of international relations that mark a system of more or less equal, independent states. The Romans may have been aware of the Chinese empire, but they can scarcely be said to have carried on international relations with China. The system of feudalism that prevailed in medieval Europe was such a complex set of hierarchical and autonomous relationships—papacy and empire, kingdoms, principalities, duchies, lords and vassals, free cities, leagues, guilds, and corporations—that our modern concept of state could not apply. (*Il stato* came in with Machiavelli.)

As we show subsequently (Chapters 3, 6, and 8), the modern nation-state system and what is called the "world capitalist system" began a process of gradual development some five centuries ago. Europe became an international state system during the period following the Thirty Years War (1618–1648). Two centuries ago, the United States entered the system, as did the Latin American republics (at least formally) a few decades later. The Ottoman Empire and Japan were the first non-Western states to enter the state system. The period from the end of the First World War to the start of the Second World War witnessed fundamental fragmenting changes in that system; World War II completed the transition to a new system with bipolar and multipolar characteristics (1945–1991). The global system during that period exerted an increasing impact on its component state members, just as changes within the component state members themselves shaped the international systemic structure. The source of such changes and their consequences—within and among the levels of analyses—represents a crucially important focal point for international-relations theory building.

Realists and neorealists continue to concentrate on the nation-state as a central unit. The nation-state is assumed to be a rational actor pursuing its national interest (viewed in terms of power) within an anarchical society, an international system of self-help in which security, defined as survival, remains the primary concern. Pluralists who study MNCs, international organizations, terrorist groups, and the burgeoning importance of economic interdependence insist that the realists are too narrow and single-minded in their approach, if not absolutist and simplistic. Foreign-policy decisions that affect the international system are not really taken by nation-states, which are abstractions reified by the realists. Instead, decisions are taken by groups or individuals who can act with the authority of the state.[86] Moreover, the pluralists contend, many significant decisions are taken outside the framework of nation-states—by international organizations, by international regimes, or by MNCs (which, invested with formidable economic resources, may pursue policies different from those of governments).[87] Marxists and some international-systems analysts are convinced that global structures and processes (whether capitalist or other) predominate over those of states and that the global system should be the principal object of serious investigation.[88]

The international-systems level provides a neat, manageable yet comprehensive model that assigns homogeneous goals to all national actors, but it also gives rise to simplistic images of look-alike nation-states, while underestimating their differences and exaggerating the degree to which the total system determines member–actor behavior. Focusing on the nation-state, by way of contrast, enables us to see the unique characteristics and situational circumstances of the actors, but it also involves the risk of excessive differentiation, which may obscure the general patterns for which the theorist is searching.

Politics, Economics, and Interdependence   Since World War II, the study of international relations in American universities has usually been organized within departments of political science, or else those departments have played a pivotal role in interdisciplinary programs. Political scientists traditionally have focused their attention on the policies and actions of governments, but in recent decades they have become interested in a broader range of phenomena that influence and are influenced by politics and diplomacy. In the international field, no less than in the domestic one, the tendency has been to expand the concept of the political to include trends in economics, science, and technology, and even in education, culture, and religion. Today, international relations encompass the operations of MNCs, trade balances, fluctuations in the value of currencies, satellite communications, the superconductivity revolution, the information highway, environmental pollution, Islamic fundamentalism, and the Olympic games, insofar as they have political aspects.

No sensible observer would deny that the world has become progressively integrated in this century, as a result of economic and technological developments that link together in unprecedented fashion all parts of the global system. It has not become politically or culturally integrated, however. Indeed, many nations, regions, and subnational groups have sought to resist or limit integrative processes (discussed in Chapter 10) by asserting their own identity and independence, by violent action if necessary, against larger unifying or centralizing forces.[89] Wherever we look, we can see the centrifugal forces of fragmentation competing with the centripetal forces of integration.

Powerful new transnational forces have emerged on the international scene since the early 1970s, which make even more complex the development of global consensus leading to an effective political authority. One of the most frequently cited modern definitions of *politics*—that of David Easton, who described politics as the process whereby societal values are authoritatively allocated[90]—is illustrative. To the extent that such a definition presupposes the organization of a society under effective authority able to take decisions on values and priorities by way of the budget process, and able to enforce its laws by holding in the background the threat of sanctions, the model of the national political system cannot be extended to the international realm because there is no effective authority in existence at this level. Easton himself admitted that "decisions and actions performed by international systems rely for their acceptance on accord with the perceived self-interest of the participating members," among whom "the impact of a sense of legitimacy is still extremely low."[91]

Raymond Aron, Stanley Hoffmann, Roger D. Masters, Kenneth N. Waltz, and several other theorists in the realist school have frequently warned against losing sight of the crucial difference between national societies in which values, law, and power are often quite highly centralized, and the international system in which they are so decentralized that each state, taking into account its own interest, can decide which norms it will observe and which ones it will ignore.[92] At the same time, the present international system contains numerous examples of political units characterized by civil war and anarchy. As a whole, the anarchical international system of the 1990s was far more peaceful than Bosnia.

Since the early 1980s, several international theorists have sought to bridge the wide gap, as it were, between national and international systems, between the political and economic orders, and between the realists and pluralists–globalists by spotlighting the concepts of interdependence and international regimes. Both concepts are discussed more fully in the chapters on realism and on systems. Here it is sufficient to note that *interdependence* carries the connotation that nation-states are becoming increasingly sensitive and vulnerable to economic–technological changes in other nation-states and in the global system as a whole, and that they are slowly adjusting their policies accordingly.[93] *International regimes,* discussed more fully in Chapter 3, are those sets of governing arrangements—procedures, norms, rules, and, in some cases, special functional institutions—designed to regulate and control certain kinds of transnational activity, where such regulation and control would seem to be a matter of common interest (or at least coincident interest) among several or many states.[94] Examples would be the international regimes designed to manage currency exchange rates (in the IMF), to remove impediments to international trade (in the periodically revised GATT), and to prevent the proliferation of nuclear weapons through the Nuclear Non-Proliferation Treaty, the safeguards system of the IAEA, and various agreements among nuclear-supplier countries to regulate their exports.

The state-centric system as known in the past is now being transformed into what Seyom Brown calls

> a global polyarchy in which national states, subnational groups, and transnational interests and communities are vying for the support and loyalty of individuals and [in which] conflicts are prosecuted and resolved on the basis of ad hoc power plays and bargaining among shifting combinations of these groups. . . . The institutions with the greatest coercive capabilities—national governments—. . . are losing a good deal of their legitimate authority.[95]

In this polyarchic system, states find themselves under contradictory pressures from above and below. Outer and downward forces emanate from international organizations (regional and global), a growing awareness of interdependence, and calls for integration and cooperation to deal with vital issues of peacekeeping, security, proliferation of mass-destruction weapons, trade and investment, human rights, migration, economic development, democratization and environment, along with the revolution in information technology. Various forces are making for polarization, secession, and fragmentation from within existing states. Benjamin R. Barber painted a bleak emerging picture of the "Lebanonization" of several states wracked by cultural, ethnic, linguistic, and religious conflict, in which groups that once managed to live together now manifest new tribalist attitudes. Forces from outside and inside are amplified by scientific–technical progress that gives instantaneous global coverage by the electronic media.[96] Nevertheless, despite the strains under which they must operate, Fouad Ajami and Michael Mann suggest states have proven intelligent and resourceful enough to survive as principal actors in the international system.[97]

The Controversy Between Traditionalists and Behavioralists

The 1960s witnessed a great debate between traditional advocates of a classical approach to international relations and those who preferred the methods of the newer behavioral sciences, which placed emphasis on quantification as a basis for precision in the development of what was hoped would be a cumulative theory linking various islands of theory in a grand or general theory of international relations based on interlinked propositions. The acerbity of that debate has now worn off, and the controversy seems less relevant in the contemporary field of international-relations theory. At the time, however, it reflected a fundamental dichotomy in the American discipline of political science. A summary of the principal arguments on each side can still contribute to an understanding of how international-relations theory evolved in the second half of the twentieth century. The two perspectives were less polarized in the 1990s than they once were, but by no means could they be said to have merged synthetically.

At the core of this debate was the question of *epistemology,* how we acquire knowledge.[98] Behavioralism rested on what is termed a *positivistic epistemology,* according to which knowledge arises from our sensory experience, from what we observe about the world around us. Such an approach contrasts with *metaphysics,* which traces knowledge to sources that lie beyond observation, or empiricism, and encompass human reasoning, contemplation, intuition, and introspection. In the field of international relations, as we have already seen in this chapter, we deal largely in concepts such as the international system, the state, the regional subsystem, or alliances. Because concepts are by their very nature abstractions, their components cannot be observed. Behavioral science has only limited relevance to the development of international-relations theory if the phenomena with which we deal cannot be subjected to empirical analysis.

Hedley Bull called "classical" that "approach to theorizing that derives from philosophy, history, and law, and that is characterized above all by explicit reliance upon the exercise of judgment and by the assumption that if we confine ourselves to strict standards of verification and proof there is very little of significance that can be said about international relations."[99] Traditionalists are usually skeptical of the effort to predict or to apply probability analysis to human affairs. They will occasionally use quantitative data to illustrate a point they are trying to make in an otherwise discursive presentation, but they are critical of the proclivity of some contemporary analysts to quantify in order to demonstrate by tortuous statistical analysis a proposition that ought to be obvious to a person of common sense. Traditionalists are typically but not rigidly interested in the single and unique event, case, situation, or problem, which they seek to understand in the subtlety of detail, including its relationships with other relevant phenomena. Often the traditionalist will study several cases of a similar nature, drawing appropriate comparisons and contrasts along the way, but there is a danger that the very selection of a limited number of cases might bias the results. (Scientists, too, of course, may rely on a small number of case studies to develop, illustrate, or test a general model.) Traditionalists would insist that they are at least as meticulous in gathering, sifting, weighing, and interpreting evidence as any other social scientists. They would highlight the fact that they make use of judgment, intuition, and insight as essential in arriving at their conclusions, after having reviewed and digested all the data that they deem relevant and reliable.

The behavioral-quantifying approach places considerable emphasis on what it regards as scientifically precise methods. Different social scientists stress different methods or combinations of methods—attitude surveys, content analysis, simulation and gaming, statistical correlations, model building, and the use of computer-driven quantitative analysis as a basis for achieving precision in measurement and analysis.[100] Nevertheless, the scientific approach should not be fully equated with quantitative methodology, although the latter is much more likely to be employed, and certain to be used on a grander scale, in the scientific than in the traditional approach. Charles Kegley and Eugene Wittkopf have noted that some behavioralists themselves wondered whether they "had become preoccupied with method to the exclusion of real-world problems [and] had focused on testing interesting [hypotheses] but ones that were largely trivial and meaningless to the policymakers responsible for protecting their nations and making the world a better place in which to live."[101]

The traditionalist often criticizes the behavioralist for (a) allegedly being too confident of the ability to generalize, to convert problematic statements into causal propositions, and to use these propositions to predict behavior in an area in which things are not predictable; (b) attributing to abstract models a congruence with reality that the models do not have; (c) avoiding the substantive issues of international politics because, in the zeal for scientific method, the behavioralist may never have really mastered those issues in all their complexity; and (d) succumbing to a fetish for measurement that ignores crucially important qualitative differences among the phenomena being measured.[102]

Behavioralists assert that when they test for statistical correlation between two factors, they are determining whether the relationship between the two might be merely coincidental, and when they engage in multivariate analysis, they are trying to find out which of several factors constitutes the most reliable predictor of a particular outcome.[103] The scientific analyst regards the traditionalist's distrust of precise method, quantification, and verification through statistical testing as irresponsible and arrogant.[104] Traditionalists have responded by asserting that in their own way, they perform a careful content analysis of the primary and secondary sources (documentary and otherwise) that they adduce as evidence—speeches, press statements, government reports, diplomatic messages, personal memoirs, newspaper accounts and commentaries, interviews, scholarly studies, and so on—and intuitively select what they deem important and relevant without the need for a systematic counting of words and phrases. The traditionalist remains convinced that the essence of politics is the qualitative difference—that subtle shade or nuance of meaning that can be communicated in the choice of a single word or phrase but that does not lend itself to quantification.

Into a Post-positivist Era: Postmodernism

Several factors have converged to create the basis for yet a third debate about the nature of, and prospects for, international-relations theory.[105] The end of the Cold War, together with disillusionment and dissatisfaction with quantitative–empiricist–positivist–cumulative theory promised by the behavioral revolution (second debate), helps shape the intellectual setting for this latest debate. However, there are other crucially important dimensions as well. These dimensions include a questioning of the paradigms that have dominated the development of international-relations theory, notably the realist–neorealist, the pluralist, and the globalist models discussed in this and other chapters. The dimension of the third debate, which criticizes the behavioral revolution on methodological grounds, is termed *postempiricist*. Its proponents point to the impossibility, as they see it, of constructing a value-free, objective, or completely unbiased social science, including such a theory, or theories, of international relations. The postempiricist is concerned not as much with paradigmatic issues as with the need to question the epistemological and methodological basis for the development of empiricist knowledge about international relations that was central to the behavioral revolution.

Somewhat broader in focus, postmodernism questions not only the basis for the development of knowledge, but also the nature, meaning, and value of modernity itself, based as it is on the eighteenth-century Enlightenment. Modernization, flowing from the Enlightenment principles, has represented progress leading perhaps ultimately to perfection, as suggested, for example, in utopian theory, addressed in later chapters. The postmodernist rejects the inevitability, as well as the idea, of progress, or the notion that history is moving with meaning toward any specific goal, including the perfection inherent in the Enlightenment thought that forms the intellectual core of modernity. Instead, progress, if it comes at all, will be the product of discontinuity. Therefore, to the postmodernist, unacceptable restrictions to intellectual inquiry result when the methodological rigidity of the natural sciences is applied to the social sciences; further, the paradigms on which theoretical development has been premised are similarly constraining. Instead, postpositivism, with postempiricist and postmodernist emphasis, celebrates diversity, both methodologically and conceptually. For the postmodernist, modernity was neither inevitable nor necessary, but simply the product of a particular period of European history. In turn, this era has shaped the conception of reality on which our social-science theories have been based.

To the postmodernist, existing paradigms represent a particular view of the world and, as such, preclude, or greatly restrict, the possibility of alternative ways of constructing reality. Upon such paradigms, we base the facts that shape our theoretical understanding of the world. Thus, theory is the product of our perception of reality, based on cognition. The theories on which we rely shape the way in which we see the world and influence the data that we develop or obtain in the process of conducting our research. How we view the world is also influenced by language, how we communicate what we construct as reality. A paradigm that produces a realist (or other) theory has important implications for policy and other action, based on the assumptions contained in the theory about such phenomena as power. According to the postmodernist, reality—including modernism itself—is socially constructed and created by humans within a specific context and time. Other structures than those that presently exist could have been developed. How and why those socially constructed structures came about is related to the question of who makes such choices. A major focus of postmodernist thought is the identity of those who make the choices on which reality is socially constructed. This focus leads to issues of authority structure and its ideological basis, as well as the implications of gender for social structures. What is regarded as important, as well as what is considered insignificant, is determined by the identity of those making the choices that produce the socially constructed reality of the day. An emerging literature of feminist international-relations theory, within this postmodernist context, points to the male-identity dominance in shaping the reality on which theory is based.[106] According to this approach, the politics of identity—whether it is based on such factors as masculinity, femininity, ethnicity, race, religion, age, generation, or ideology—need to be addressed as part of a postmodernist critique of modernity as it has been shaped by the Enlightenment.

Postmodernism represents a deconstruction of existing theory, without putting any clearly developed alternative in its place. It is considered to be critical theory that does not provide necessary criteria or priorities for constructing an alternative paradigm or even an adequate basis for developing alternative theory. In celebrating diversity, postmodernism, according to Yosef Lapid, carried to its logical conclusion, represents a form of epistemological anarchy that would give equal emphasis to nearly any approach. In this case, he asserts, the result may be theoretical proliferation without theoretical growth.[107] Taking a different perspective, Richard K. Ashley and R. B. J. Walker contend that the complexity of the global setting, with its proliferating problems and challenges to existing structures, theory, and knowledge, creates the need for new thinking that questions "all presumptively sovereign centers of interpretation and judgment" and therefore welcomes the dissidence of postmodernism.[108] Such international ferment is regarded as the essential prerequisite to the development of alternative theories of international relations. Postmodernism itself, however, as John A. Vasquez asserts, contains a logical contradiction in its assumption that reality is a social construction in which there are no permanent truths. In this case, postmodernism itself must also be nothing more than a social construction that has no immanent truth. If postmodernism is correct that there is no enduring explanation of history or international behavior over vast time periods, then the postmodernist effort to set forth such an explanation is fundamentally flawed.[109]

Let us now illustrate many of the issues we have just discussed by examining one of the classic theories of international relations, Balance of Power.

TRADITIONAL THEORY: BALANCE OF POWER

The oldest, most persistent, and most controversial of all theories of international politics—the balance of power—was recognized at least implicitly in ancient India and in ancient Greece, although it was never formally articulated. David Hume noted that although the term *balance of power* was associated with the state system of Europe, "the maxim of preserving the balance of power is founded so much on common sense and obvious reasoning that it is impossible it could altogether have escaped antiquity," concluding that it had been practiced from ancient times to the eighteenth century.[110]

Insofar as it could be called a formal theory of international politics, the modern concept of balance of power was associated with the Newtonian conception of a universe in equilibrium. (Frequently, a social-science theory has been adapted from a physical-science theory, or at least influenced by the development of one.) Actually, the notion of equilibrium is basic to many sciences. Chemists speak of a solution in stable equilibrium. Economists perceive a balance of countervailing forces, such as supply and demand. Biologists warn against human activities that disturb the balance of nature between organisms and environment. Political writers often analyze the interaction of interest groups or of governmental branches within national society in terms of checks and balances.[111] Naturally, theorists of international social reality employ balance as a central organizing concept for the power relations of nation-states, and then assume that the latter are driven, almost by a law of their own nature, to seek their security by some form of power balancing.

Balance of Power: Problems of Definition

The term *balance of power* has been roundly criticized for causing considerable semantic and definitional confusion. Ernst B. Haas found at least eight distinct meanings for the term: (1) any distribution of power, (2) equilibrium or balancing process, (3) hegemony or the search for hegemony, (4) stability and peace in a concert of power, (5) instability and war, (6) power politics in general, (7) a universal law of history, and (8) a system and guide to policymakers.[112] "The trouble with the balance of power," wrote Inis L. Claude, Jr., "is not that it has no meaning, but that it has too many meanings." The term has been used to connote equilibrium and disequilibrium, or any distribution of power whether balanced or unbalanced, or as both policy and system (either automatic and self-regulating or wholly dependent on manipulation by shrewd political leaders). Claude concluded that the concept of the balance of power is extremely difficult to analyze because those who write about it not only fail to provide precise clues as to its meaning but often "slide blissfully from one usage of the term to another and back again, frequently without posting any warning that plural meanings exist."[113]

It is true that the concept of balance of power is riddled with ambiguity. Many political leaders have sought a unilateral superiority rather than an objective bilateral balance with their principal rival. Nevertheless, it is theoretically possible to conceive of the *balance of power* as a situation or condition, as a universal tendency or law of state behavior, as a guide for stateleadership, and as a mode of system-maintenance that is characteristic of certain types of international systems. As long as we think in terms of equilibrium rather than of superiority, these four usages need not be inconsistent with each other.

Conceived as a situation or a condition, *balance of power* implies an objective arrangement in which there is relatively widespread satisfaction with the distribution of power. The universal tendency or law describes a probability and enables one to predict that members of a system threatened by the emergence of a disturber of the balance—that is, a power seemingly bent on establishing an international hegemony—will form a countervailing coalition. Balance of power as a policy guide prescribes to stateleaders who would act rationally that they should maintain eternal vigilance and be prepared to organize a countervailing coalition against the disrupter of equilibrium. Balance of power as a system refers to a multinational society in which all essential actors preserve their identity, integrity, and independence through the balancing process.[114]

Balance of Power: Purposes and Functions

Various purposes and functions were attributed to the balance of power in classical theory, as expounded by Bolingbroke, Gentz, Metternich, and Castlereagh. It was supposed to (1) prevent the establishment of a universal hegemony, (2) preserve the constituent elements of the system and the system itself, (3) ensure stability and mutual security in the international system, and (4) strengthen and prolong the peace by deterring war—that is, by confronting an aggressor with the likelihood that a policy of expansion would meet with the formation of a counter-coalition. The traditional methods and techniques of maintaining or restoring the balance were (1) the policy of divide and rule (working to diminish the weight of the heavier side by aligning, if necessary, with the weaker side), (2) territorial compensations after a war, (3) creation of buffer states, (4) the formation of alliances, (5) spheres of influence, (6) intervention, (7) diplomatic bargaining, (8) legal and peaceful settlement of disputes, (9) reduction of armaments, (10) armaments competitions or races, and (11) war itself, if necessary, to maintain or restore the balance.

A review of the list of objectives and methods will show that there were internal inconsistencies in the theory and in the practice. These were probably unavoidable, given the historic oscillation between stable and unstable equilibria within the nation-state system. If the balance of power had worked perfectly as all political leaders expected, and if the existing distribution of power had posed no threat to their national security, then the balance of power as situation, law, policy, and system would almost certainly have contributed to the prolongation of peace. However, the dynamics of the international political system were conducive neither to serene stability nor to prudent rational decision making at all times. Moreover, stateleaders pursuing only what they considered their own legitimate national interest—a term closely associated with the balance-of-power system—may have appeared in the eyes of other leaders of state as conspiring to overturn the international system and gain predominance. Conversely, a government embarked on a hegemonial path might not provoke the formation of a countercoalition until it was too late to prevent a large-scale war declared to restore the balance. In theory, the balance helped preserve the peace and identity of member states, but in practice, balance-of-power policy sometimes led to war and to the partitioning of less essential actors (such as Poland in the 1790s). However, keeping the peace and preserving all the lesser members intact were subordinate goals to the more fundamental aims of preserving the multistate system by observing the maxim expressed by Friedrich Gentz: "If the states system of Europe is to exist and be maintained by common exertions no one of its members must ever become so powerful as to be able to coerce all the rest put together."[115]

Another key concept in the classical theory must be mentioned. Under normal circumstances, with several nations seeking to maximize their power position through the various methods and techniques of balance-of-power politics, no one nation gains hegemony, and a precarious equilibrium is maintained. Even so, for various reasons, the balance might be on the verge of breaking down. At this point, an impartial and vigilant holder of the balance emerges, which is strong enough to restore the balance swiftly once it is disturbed. Historically, England played this role in the European state system. In a famous memorandum published on January 1, 1907, Sir Eyre Crowe wrote that it had "become almost a historical truism to identify England's secular policy with the maintenance of this balance by throwing her weight now in this scale and now in that, but ever on the side opposed to the political dictatorship of the strongest single state or group at a given time."[116] Winston Churchill reiterated this as a fundamental tenet of British foreign policy in 1936.[117] Although the theory of the balance of power, as a policy guide to state-leaders, has shaped British policy, it has been set within a far broader international context, at least in realist theory, in which the balance of power is a central element. According to Henry Kissinger, whose own statecraft was based on balance-of-power principles, the balance of power serves to restrict the ability of states to dominate each other and to limit the scope of conflicts. Its goal is not so much peace as it is moderation on the part of states, leading to stability. Kissinger views the balance of power not as an automatic mechanism but instead one of two possible outcomes of a situation in which states are obliged to deal with each other. One state can become so powerful that it dominates the others, or else the "pretensions of the most aggressive member of the international community are kept in check by a combination of the others; in other words, by the operation of a balance of power, chosen by prudent leaders."[118]

Critiques of Balance of Power

For many generations, the balance of power has encountered criticism for reasons other than the semantic vagueness mentioned earlier. Nicholas J. Spykman held that the theory inadequately explained the practice:

> The truth of the matter is that states are interested only in a balance (imbalance) which is in their favor. Not an equilibrium, but a generous margin is their objective.

There is no real security in being just as strong as a potential enemy; there is security only in being a little stronger. There is no possibility of action if one's strength is fully checked; there is a chance for a positive foreign policy only if there is a margin of force which can be freely used.[119]

Although the balance of power has its place in realist theory, Hans J. Morgenthau found the balance of power deficient on several grounds. The multistate system precluding a single state from achieving universal dominion has been preserved only at the price of frequent and costly wars. He held that the balance of power was (1) *uncertain* because no completely reliable means of measuring, evaluating, and comparing power exist; (2) *unreal* because stateleaders try to compensate for its uncertainty by aiming for superiority; and (3) *inadequate* for explaining national restraint during most of the years from 1648 to 1914 because it does not give sufficient credit to the restraining influence of the basic intellectual unity and moral consensus then prevailing in Europe.[120]

Ernst B. Haas has observed that using the balance of power as a policy guide assumes a high degree of flexibility in national decision making. The vigilant political leader must engage in a constant power calculus and be ready to enter into a countervailing coalition, regardless of ideological differences, economic interests, and domestic political attitudes. Haas had questioned the degree to which policymakers, especially in democratic countries, can enjoy the kind of flexibility that the balance-of-power theory would seem to demand.[121] It should be pointed out, however, that the Anglo-American democracies managed sufficiently to overcome their aversion to communism in World War II to enable them to align with the Soviet Union against Nazi Germany. In the second generation of the Cold War, the United States adopted a balance-of-power approach, especially during Henry Kissinger's tenure as U.S. National Security Advisor and Secretary of State, vis-à-vis the People's Republic of China and the Soviet Union, and evolved a better relationship with both China and the Soviet Union than either Beijing or Moscow could have had with each other. In other words, the United States attempted to exploit the Sino–Soviet rift to develop a de facto alignment with China, the weaker of the two sides, against the Soviet Union as a means of restraining Moscow's global strategies and ambitions.

Kenneth N. Waltz defended the balance-of-power theory against those critics who, in his view, have misunderstood certain crucial points. Every theory, he argued, must begin with some assumptions. He assumed that states are unitary actors that seek, at a minimum, to preserve themselves and, at a maximum, to dominate others if possible. They strive to achieve their objectives through internal efforts (e.g., increasing capabilities) and external efforts (e.g., strengthening their own alliance and weakening that of the adversary). He then adds the condition that states are operating in a self-help system with no superior referee. Those who do not help themselves as well as others do so will become disadvantaged. Assumptions, Waltz points out, are neither true nor false, but they are essential for the construction of a theory. In Waltz's theory of structural realism, the balance of power is rooted inescapably and necessarily in the international system of states. Thus, he parts company with other theorists of the balance of power—Hume,

Churchill, Organski, Morgenthau, Haas, Kissinger, and others—who have held that the balance-of-power policy is something to be followed voluntarily by wise and prudent political leaders. For Waltz, the tendency toward equilibrium is automatic, regardless of whether "some or all states consciously aim to establish and maintain a balance, or whether some or all states aim for universal domination." If the results to be produced (i.e., balance) depend on some or all states consciously working for it, then international politics can be explained by theories of national bureaucratic policymaking, and an international balance-of-power theory would have nothing to explain. Waltz wanted a theory applicable to the international system irrespective of the behavior of particular states.[122]

Balance of Power: Contemporary Models

Several modern, nontraditional, and scientific theoreticians have found the balance-of-power theory to be worthy of attention. Morton A. Kaplan makes it one of his six heuristic models of international systems. He devotes more space to the balance-of-power system with its essential rules than to any of the other systems.[123] (For a discussion of Kaplan's system models, see Chapter 3.) Arthur Lee Burns, after studying the problem of the system in stable balance, concludes that "the most stable arrangement would seem to be a world of five or some greater odd number of Powers, independent and of approximately equal strength," because these powers would not be readily divisible into two equal sides.[124] For simplicity in calculating relationships, and for the certainty and stability that such simplicity would yield, Burns held that, optimally, the most stable system would be a world of "five roughly equal blocs, each including a family of exchangeable client nations."[125]

More recently, R. Harrison Wagner has argued that any number of actors from two through five can produce a stable system, but that the most stable system is one with three actors.[126] Several analysts in the field of nuclear deterrence and arms-control theory have updated and cast into highly sophisticated forms the categories of balance-of-power thinking.[127] Also, although many intellectuals and academicians regard the balance-of-power theory as a crude, unsophisticated, naïvely simplistic, or obsolete theory of international politics, large numbers of stateleaders, politicians, diplomats, pundits, journalists, and people-in-the-street still regard it as an adequate explanation of what actually happens in the international system and the basis on which foreign policy ought to be formulated and conducted. The theory retained a charm and a validity for analysts of strategic-arms limitations and others during the Cold War concerned with the relationship of the United States, the Soviet Union, China, Western Europe, Japan, and other potential power centers in the global system. In the aftermath of the Cold War, the United States has focused strategic attention on regions of major interest, including Southwest Asia and Northeast Asia. A major object of U.S. security strategy has been to assure a form of equilibrium and, principally, to prevent Iraq or Iran from dominating the Persian Gulf or to restrain, if necessary, North Korea in the Korean peninsula and China vis-à-vis Taiwan. Thus the post–Cold War world provides an ample context for the conceptual discussion of the balance of power.

Can There Be a Scientific International Theory?

Having discussed the traditionalist–behavioralist controversy as one of the major debates of international-relations theory, as well as the postmodernist critique of positivism, we return to the question of the extent to which there can, or cannot, be scientific international-relations theory. The meaning of *scientific* is relative. The term *science* connotes nothing more than a body of knowledge and a way of discovering new knowledge. Whatever satisfies intelligent human beings in any age as the optimum means of enlarging their intellectual frontiers will pass muster as being scientific.

Genuine scientific progress is usually made when one starts out by accepting that body of knowledge of the field already generally accepted by scholars, but not necessarily uncritically. Individuals may wish to reorganize somewhat the existing body of knowledge to enhance their own working comprehension of it. Nonetheless, the individual must take something as given—something already based on empirical observation, experience, and human reflection. If learning is social, the individual cannot begin every day to create the universe de novo.

Once the investigator has mastered the existing knowledge, and organized it for his or her purposes, the investigator pleads a meaningful ignorance: "Here is what I know; what do I not know that is worth knowing?" This is a very important question. Once an area has been selected for investigation, the question should be posed as clearly as possible, and it is here that quantification can prove useful,[128] provided that mathematical methods are combined with carefully constructed theories, hypotheses, or research questions. Achieving a satisfactory merger of appropriate tools of analysis with solid typologies is one of the most difficult aspects of formulating a worthwhile and testable hypothesis in the realm of political reality, where the names we call things and the words we use are of crucial importance. Surveying the field of international relations, or any sector of it, we see many disparate elements and keep sifting them through various permutations in our minds, wondering whether there may be any significant relationships between A and B or between B and C. By a process that we are compelled to call "intuition" until we learn much more about it than we now know, we perceive a possible correlation, hitherto unsuspected or not firmly known, between two or more elements. At this point, we have the ingredients of a hypothesis that can be expressed in measurable referents and that, if validated, would be both explanatory and predictive. (In the strictest scientific sense, what we cannot predict we cannot fully explain,[129] but that is an extremely demanding criterion of explanation in the social sciences.)

From here on, the scientific method becomes more familiar. The hypothesis must be tested. This testing demands the construction of an experiment or the gathering of data in other ways. In either case, every effort must be made to eliminate the influence of the unknown, and to make certain that the evidence sought pertains to the hypothesis and to nothing else. The results of the data-gathering effort are carefully observed, recorded, and analyzed, after which the hypothesis is discarded, modified, reformulated, or confirmed. Findings are published, and others are invited to replicate this knowledge-discovering adventure, and to confirm or deny the findings. This, very roughly, is what we usually mean by the scientific method. At every step of the way, there is emphasis on precision of thought and language and on a distinction between what is assumed and what is empirically testable.

Application of scientific method during the past 250 years has produced impressive results in the physical sciences in the form of generalized laws. In physics, astrophysics, chemistry, biology, and certain areas of psychology, a high degree of predictability has been achieved. Even the exact sciences, however, with all their powerful methodologies, reach limits to what can be known at any given moment. According to Werner Heisenberg's principle of indeterminacy, for example, it is not possible to determine simultaneously both the position and the movement of a particle of matter.[130] In all the sciences, physical and social, we find that our efforts to measure a phenomenon may dislocate or change the thing we are trying to measure.

The Search for Recurring Patterns

Anyone claiming to be a scientific theorist, whether traditional or future-oriented behavioral, is bound to search for regularities. Nonetheless, we should remember that there are peculiar difficulties confronting all social scientists, and if we keep these in mind, we are more likely to make intellectual progress than if we ignore or forget them. The social scientist studying human affairs encounters problems concerning the relation of the observer to the observed to a greater degree than the scientist studying atoms, molecules, or stars. The physical scientist requires certain instruments and techniques that are fairly standardized and that work in the same way for all observers. Physical scientists, no matter how excited they might be about their work, usually avoid the kind of emotional involvement with the observed phenomenon that might influence their perception and their judgment. In the investigation of human society, objective observation is much more likely to be infused with subjective purpose. A physicist or a chemist who happens to be an ardent pacifist in personal outlook is not prone to be swayed by this conviction in the analytic approach to the more fissionable atoms, as compared with other atoms. However, social scientists who have strong preconceptions about such subjects as war, terrorism, national values, world population and hunger, disarmament, international organization, or the conflict between democracies and dictatorships are much more likely to run into difficulty in their efforts to achieve the complete detachment that the scientific method presupposes. (There is no need for social scientists to apologize for this human involvement.) Although the method is supposed to be value-free, the phenomenon being examined is often overladen with value implications that influence the intellectual and psychological set of the observer–analyst. Social scientists hardly agree on which of these two attitudes produces the greater perceptual distortion in the study, let us say, of the problems of war and peace: a purely neutral or nonethical desire to understand human aggressiveness for the purpose of explaining it and predicting its manifestations, or a moral commitment to study war, with a view toward abolishing it in order to make the world a better place. Undoubtedly, theory building will continue to be characterized by the interpenetration of these two distinct purposes, both within individual minds and within the field as a whole.[131]

The peculiarities of the observer–observed relationship in the social sciences give rise to additional difficulties. Some of these are well known and frequently cited, such as the inability to conduct controlled experiments in order to isolate the factors being studied. Even the most ruthless totalitarian regime, whatever the efficiency of the technical means of social control at its disposal, would be extremely hard pressed to conduct a strictly controlled scientific experiment with a single nation, not to mention two or more. The point is that in attempting to study any large social aggregates scientifically, the conditions of control for the sake of exactitude must be established primarily through the clarification of one's own thought processes, rather than in the confusing and uncontrollable social universe.

Other problems are less readily recognized. Given the comprehensibility of the field, the sheer mass of pertinent data seems to exceed the bounds of human mastery. Many data are inaccessible and remain so either for a very long time (in governmental archives) or forever (in the minds of individuals who forget or die before they transmit to scholars all that they know about what really happened). The scholar and theorist, therefore, often arrives at generalized conclusions from sketchy evidence that might be unreliable on grounds quite apart from its incompleteness. At the same time, the information revolution is enhancing our ability to gain access to data. On-line sources such as the Internet provide direct access to vast information sources in many parts of the world without the user having to leave home or office, library or laboratory.

There is also the problem of language, in which all theory must be couched. Even the exact sciences have not been immune from difficulties in relating language to observation, or verbal symbols to experience. It is inaccurate to say that the exact sciences require quantitative symbols, whereas the social sciences rely on qualitative symbols: Every physical science and every social science require some empirical foundation, and the method is not empirical unless it entails the essential functions of naming and counting. In all the sciences, counting is a very simple thing. An important separator between the physical sciences and the social sciences is the realm of qualitative language, or the naming process. No one debates the meaning of such terms as *liquid, vapor, magnetic, electrically charged, sodium chloride,* or *nuclear fission.* However, in analyzing the social universe, we constantly face terms such as *democratic, aggressive, revolutionary, illegal, discriminatory, violent,* and the concept of the state itself. We have already noted the multiple means attached to the term *balance of power.* Not one of these terms is invested with complete semantic clarity. Thus, although all social scientists can count, and a great many understand the process of statistically correlating dependent and independent variables, or of performing factor analysis, there is reason to believe that the basis of agreement on what is being counted or measured in the field of international relations is very narrow and precarious indeed.

CONCLUSION

Our purpose in this chapter has been to show generally how the study of international relations has evolved, in order to set the stage for examining the major theories, past and present, in detail.

In Quincy Wright's major work, *A Study of International Relations,* after admitting that international relations is still "an emerging discipline manifesting little unity from the point of view of method and logic,"[132] he suggested that the field might best be understood if approached through four basic intellectual perspectives. In his opinion, all social reality can be conveniently divided into four categories: (1) the *actual* (what was or what is, known through the method of description); (2) the *possible* (what can be, known through the method of theoretical speculation); (3) the *probable* (what will be, known through the method of prediction); (4) the *desirable* (what ought to be, known through the method of ethical, valuational, or normative reflection). These four categories, says Wright, correspond to history, art, science, and philosophy.[133] The authors find this categorization to be useful in thinking about the various meanings of international-relations theory.

To sum up, the essential function of international theory is to enable us to improve our knowledge concerning international reality, whether for the sake of pure understanding or for the more active purpose of changing that reality. Theory helps us to order our existing knowledge and to discover new knowledge more efficiently. It provides a framework of thought in which we define research priorities and select the most appropriate available tools for the gathering and analysis of data about phenomena. Theory directs our attention to significant similarities and differences and suggests relationships not previously perceived. At its best, theory serves as a proof that the powers of the human mind have been applied to a problem at hand with foresight, imagination, and profundity, and this proof inspires others to further efforts for purposes either of agreeing or disagreeing.

There is no one model for theory. Social theorizing occurs at many levels and through many disciplinary perspectives, with several experiments at interdisciplinary approaches under way. International theory, which goes beyond foreign-policy theory, contains components that are intended to be descriptive, speculative, explanatory, predictive, and normative. A single scholar may emphasize any one of these, but the more highly developed the field of international theory as a whole becomes, the more likely will it involve a synthesis of what is, what might be, what probably will be, and what ought to be. Good theory may be inductive or deductive; micro or macro; highly specific, midrange, or grand, in the sense of being as comprehensive as the state of our knowledge at any given time permits and of explaining as wide a number of phenomena with as few variables as necessary. All of these approaches may be valid and useful when handled with intelligence and methodological care and when applied to the appropriate level, or levels, of analysis in the study of international relations.

NOTES

1. John Lewis Gaddis, "Toward the Post–Cold War World," *Foreign Affairs,* 70 (Spring 1991), 102–103.
2. Francis Fukuyama, "The End of History?" *The National Interest* (Summer 1989), 3–5, 8–15, 18. Fukuyama, following in the philosophical footsteps of Hegel, as interpreted by the Russian émigré to Paris Alexandre Koujève, predicted that henceforth the movement of the civilized world would be ineluctably toward a universal state of liberal democracy and bourgeois consumerism.

3. Joseph S. Nye, Jr., "What New World Order?" *Foreign Affairs,* 71 (Spring 1992), 84. See also Stanley Hoffmann, "Delusions of World Order," in Steven L. Spiegel and David J. Pervin, eds., *At Issue: Politics in the World Arena,* 7th ed. (New York: St. Martin's Press, 1994).

4. John Mueller, *Retreat from Doomsday: The Obsolescence of Major War* (New York: Basic Books, 1989). In a review of that book, Carl Kaysen has concluded that, although technological and economic changes since the nineteenth century have made war among industrial powers so much more humanly costly, physically destructive, economically unprofitable, and opposed to the political goals of democratic publics, nevertheless, a certain culture lag affects governmental and political elites. In Kaysen's view, even though conscious attitudes toward war have changed, war has not yet quite become "subrationally unthinkable." "Is War Obsolete?" *International Security,* 14 (Spring 1990), 42–64; quotation on p. 43.

5. Michael Howard, *The Lessons of History* (New Haven, CT: Yale University Press, 1991), p. 176.

6. Zbigniew Brzezinski, "Selective Global Commitment," *Foreign Affairs,* 70 (Fall 1991), 5. His advice to makers of foreign policy, not incompatible with that of John Lewis Gaddis, was to pursue a course of "functionally pragmatic transnationalism". Ibid.

7. Samuel P. Huntington, "No Exit: The Errors of Endism," *The National Interest* (Fall 1989).

8. Samuel P. Huntington, "The Clash of Civilizations," *Foreign Affairs,* 72 (Summer 1993), 22–49, quoted at p. 22.

9. Ibid., 25–29. (Huntington is discussed further in Chapter 2.)

10. See the symposium "On 'The Clash of Civilizations.'" (Fouad Ajami, Robert L. Bartley, Liu Binyan, Jeane J. Kirkpatrick, Kishore Mahbubani, Gerard Piel, and Albert L. Weeks), *Foreign Affairs,* 72 (September/October 1993), 2–26; Arnold Toynbee, *War and Civilization* (NY: Oxford University Press, 1950). Also, M. F. Ashley Montagu, ed. *Toynbee and History: Critical Essays and Reviews* (Boston: Porter Sargent Publisher, 1956).

11. Fouad Ajami, "The Summoning," *Foreign Affairs,* 72 (September/October, 1993), 2–9, quoted at p. 9. Samuel P. Huntington reiterated his position that there is no better framework than the civilizational for understanding the post–Cold War world. "If Not Civilizations, What?" *Foreign Affairs,* 72 (November/December 1993), 186–194.

12. See John Mearsheimer, "Why We Will Soon Miss the Cold War," *Atlantic Monthly,* 266 (1990), 35–50; Charles W. Kegley, Jr. and Gregory A. Raymond, "Must We Fear a Post–Cold War Multipolar System?" *Journal of Conflict Resolution,* 36 (September 1992), 573–585; Christopher Layne, "The Unipolar Illusion: Why New Great Powers Will Rise," *International Security,* 17 (Spring 1993), 5–51.

13. Imre Lakatos, *The Methodology of Scientific Research Programs,* Vol. I (London: Cambridge University Press, 1978), p. 32 (Emphasis in original).

14. John Lewis Gaddis, "International Relations Theory and the End of the Cold War," *International Security,* 17 (Winter 1992/1993), 6.

15. Thucydides, *The History of the Peloponnesian War,* trans. Rex Warner (Harmondsworth, England: Penguin Books, 1954). See also William T. Bluhm, *Theories of the Political System: Classics of Political Thought and Modern Political Analysis* (Englewood Cliffs, NJ: Prentice-Hall, 1965), chap. 2; John H. Finley, Jr., *Thucydides* (Cambridge, MA: Harvard University Press, 1942); Peter J. Fliess, *Thucydides and the Politics of Bipolarity* (Baton Rouge: Louisiana State University Press, 1966); Robert Gilpin, Kenneth Waltz, and Robert Keohane have claimed Thucydides as a forerunner of neorealism. For a critical view, see "Thucydides and Neorealism," *International Studies Quarterly,* 33 (March 1989), 3–27.

16. Sir Henry Sumner Maine, *Ancient Law* (first published 1861; Tucson, AZ: University of Arizona Press, 1986), pp. 37–52; R. and A.J. Carlyle, *A History of Medieval Political Theory in the West*, 6 vols., (London: William Blackwood & Sons, 1903–1936), I, pp. 23 ff.; H. F. Jolowicz, *Historical Introduction to the Study of Roman Law* (Cambridge, England: Cambridge University Press, 1932), pp. 46–48; A. P. D'Entreves, *Natural Law* (London: Hutchinson's University Library, 1955), pp. 19, 24–30.

17. Niccolò Machiavelli, *The Prince and the Discourses* (New York: Random House Modern Library, 1940); James Burnham, *The Machiavellians* (New York: Macmillan, 1956); Friedrich Meinecke, *Machiavellism: The Doctrine of Raison d'Être and Its Place in Modern History*, trans. Douglas Scott (New Haven, CT: Yale University Press, 1957).

18. Dante Alighieri, *On World Government*, trans. Herbert W. Schneider, 2nd ed. rev. (New York: Liberal Arts Press, 1957); Etienne Gilson, *Dante and Philosophy*, trans. David Moore (New York: Harper & Row Torchbooks, 1963), part III.

19. Dubois's *De Recuperatione Terrae Sanctae* is discussed in Frank M. Russell, *Theories of International Relations* (New York: Appleton, 1936), pp. 105–110.

20. For excellent summaries of Crucé's *Le Nouveau Cyneé*, Sully's *Grand Dessein*, and Abbé de Saint-Pierre's *Project for Making Peace Perpetual in Europe*, see Frank M. Russell, op. cit. pp. 163–174, 188–191. Crucé and Saint-Pierre are also treated in Torbjörn L. Knutsen, *A History of International Relations Theory* (Manchester, England: Manchester University Press, 1992), pp. 81–82 and 120–121.

21. Knutsen, op. cit. pp. 58–64, 113–127; Russell, op. cit. 185–186, 191–194.

22. Russell, op. cit. pp. 175–178.

23. Ibid., pp. 194–197.

24. Ibid., pp. 197–201; Knutsen, op. cit., pp. 111–113, 125–127.

25. Evan Luard, ed., *Basic Texts in International Relations* (New York: St. Martin's Press, 1992), pp. 377–399.

26. Russell, op. cit., pp. 137–160; Luard, op. cit., pp. 147–152; Knutsen, op. cit., pp. 84–87.

27. Martin Wight, "Why Is There No International Theory?" *International Relations*, II (April 1960), 35–48, 62.

28. Ibid., pp. 37–38.

29. Chris Brown, *International Relations Theory; New Normative Approaches* (New York: Columbia University Press, 1992), pp. 3–8; the passage quoted is on p. 3. For other sources that support Brown's thesis, see F. H. Hinsley, *Power and the Pursuit of Peace: Theory and Practice in the History of Relations Between States* (Cambridge, England: Cambridge University Press, 1967); John A. Vasquez, ed., *Classics of International Relations* (Englewood Cliffs, NJ: Prentice-Hall, 1986); and the works cited previously by Russell, by Knutsen, and by Luard.

30. See Chapter 6, the section on the Marxist–Leninist theories of imperialism.

31. Martin Wight, op. cit., p. 40.

32. See, for example, Steve Smith, ed., *International Relations: British and American Perspectives* (Oxford, England: Basil Blackwell Ltd., 1985); Barry Buzan, "From International System to International Society: Structural Realism and Regime Theory Meet the English School," *International Organization*, 47(3) (Summer 1993), 327–352; Norman D. Palmer, "The Study of International Relations in the United States: Perspectives of Half a Century," *International Studies Quarterly*, 24(3) (September 1980), 343–364; Ekkehart Krippendorf, "The Dominance of American Approaches in International Relations," *Millenium: Journal of International Studies*, 16(2) (Summer 1987), 207–214; Christopher Hill and Pamela Beshoff, eds., *Two Worlds of International Relations: Academics, Practitioners and the Trade in Ideas* (London and New

York: Routledge, 1994); Brian C. Schmidt, "The Historiography of Academic International Relations," *Review of International Studies*, 20 (4) (October 1994), 349–368; and Hayo Krombach, "International Relations as an Academic Discipline," *Millennium*, 21 (92), 243–262.

33. Grayson Kirk, *The Study of International Relations in American Colleges and Universities* (New York: Council on Foreign Relations, 1947), p. 4; Foster Rhea Dulles, *America's Rise to World Power, 1898–1954* (New York: Harper & Row, 1963), pp. 158–161. For an excellent treatment of the dichotomy, see Robert E. Osgood, *Ideals and Self-Interest in America's Foreign Relations* (Chicago: University of Chicago Press, 1953).

34. Kenneth W. Thompson, "The Study of International Politics: A Survey of Trends and Developments," *Review of Politics*, XIV (October 1952), 433–443. See also Norman D. Palmer, "The Study of International Relations in the United States: Perspectives of Half a Century," *International Studies Quarterly*, 24(3) (September 1980), 343–364; William C. Olson and A. J. R. Groom, *International Relations Then and Now: Origins and Trends in Interpretation* (New York: Harper and Collins, 1991).

35. James L. Brierly, *The Law of Nations*, 2nd ed. (New York: Oxford University Press, 1936); Clyde Eagleton, *International Government* (New York: Ronald Press, 1932); Charles G. Fenwick, *International Law*, 2nd ed. (New York: Appleton, 1934); Norman L. Hill, *International Administration* (New York: McGraw-Hill, 1931); Hersch Lauterpacht, *The Function of Law in the International Community* (New York: Oxford University Press, 1933); J. B. Moore, *A Digest of International Law* (Washington, DC: Government Printing Office, 1906); Lassa F. L. Oppenheim, *International Law: A Treatise*, 4th ed. (London: Longmans, 1928); Pitman B. Potter, *An Introduction to the Study of International Organization*, 3rd ed. (New York: Appleton, 1928).

36. Sidney B. Fay, *The Origins of the World War*, 2nd ed. (New York: Macmillan, 1930); G. P. Gooch, *History of Modern Europe, 1878–1919* (New York: Holt, Rinehart and Winston, 1923); R. B. Mowat, *European Diplomacy, 1815–1914* (London: Longmans, 1922); Bernadotte E. Schmitt, *The Coming of the War, 1914* (New York: Scribner's, 1930); Raymond J. Sontag, *European Diplomatic History, 1871–1932* (New York: Appleton, 1933); G. P. Gooch and Harold W. Temperly, *British Documents on the Origins of the War, 1889–1914* (London: His Majesty's Stationery Office, 1928). For a historiographical appraisal of the work of American historians, see Warren I. Cohen, *The American Revisionists: The Lessons of Intervention in World War I* (Chicago: University of Chicago Press, 1967).

37. Carlton J. H. Hayes, *Essays on Nationalism* (New York: Macmillan, 1926); Hans Kohn, *A History of Nationalism in the East* (London: George Routledge, 1932), *Nationalism in the Soviet Union* (London: George Routledge, 1933), and *The Idea of Nationalism* (New York: Macmillan, 1944).

38. Philip J. Noel-Baker, *Disarmament* (New York: Harcourt Brace, 1926); James T. Shotwell, *War as an Instrument of National Policy* (New York: Harcourt Brace, 1929); J. W. Wheeler Bennett, *Disarmament and Security Since Locarno, 1925–1931* (New York: Macmillan, 1932).

39. Parker T. Moon, *Imperialism and World Politics* (New York: Macmillan, 1926); Herbert I. Priestley, *France Overseas: A Study of Modern Imperialism* (New York: Appleton, 1938).

40. Harold Nicolson, *Peacemaking, 1919* (Boston: Houghton Mifflin, 1933), and *Diplomacy* (London: Oxford University Press, 1939).

41. Carl J. Friedrich, *Foreign Policy in the Making: The Search for a New Balance of Power* (New York: Norton, 1938); Alfred Vagts, "The United States and the Balance of Power," *Journal of Politics*, III (November 1941), 401–449.

42. James Fairgrieve, *Geography and World Power* (New York: Dutton, 1921); Nicholas J. Spykman, "Geography and Foreign Policy, I," *American Political Science Review,* XXXII (February 1938), 213–236, and the following two books: *America's Strategy in World Politics* (New York: Harcourt Brace, 1942) and *The Geography of Peace* (New York: Harcourt Brace, 1944). Spykman also wrote two articles with Abbie A. Rollins, "Geographic Objectives in Foreign Policy I," *American Political Science Review,* XXXII (June 1939), 391–410, and "Geographic Objectives in Foreign Policy II," ibid. (August 1939), 591–614. The theories of Mahan and Mackinder are treated in Chapter 4 in this text.

43. Frank M. Russell, *Theories of International Relations* (New York: Appleton, 1936).

44. Sir Norman Angell, *The Great Illusion* (New York: G. P. Putnam's Sons, 1933). See also J. D. B. Miller and Norman Angell, *Futility of War: Peace and the Public Mind* (London: Macmillan, 1986), especially chaps. 2 and 3.

45. E. H. Carr, *The Twenty-Years' Crisis, 1919–1939: An Introduction to the Study of International Relations* (London: Macmillan, 1939; New York: Harper & Row [Torchbooks], 1964).

46. Martin Wight, *Power Politics, Looking Forward,* Pamphlet No. 8 (London: Royal Institute of International Affairs, 1946), p. 11.

47. Hans J. Morgenthau, Politics Among Nations (New York: Knopf; several editions, 1948–1978; brief edition revised by Kenneth Thompson New York: McGraw-Hill, 1993); Frederick L. Schuman, *International Politics: An Introduction to the Western State System,* 4th and 5th eds. (New York: McGraw-Hill, 1948, 1953); Robert Strausz-Hupé and Stefan T. Possony, *International Relations* (New York: McGraw-Hill, 1950, 1954); Norman D. Palmer and Howard C. Perkins, *International Relations* (Boston: Houghton Mifflin, 1953, 1957, 1969); Norman J. Padelford and George A. Lincoln, *The Dynamics of International Politics* (New York: Macmillan, 1962); Ernst B. Haas and Allen S. Whiting, *Dynamics of International Relations* (New York: McGraw-Hill, 1956); Harold and Margaret Sprout, *Foundations of National Power* (Princeton, NJ: Van Nostrand, 1945, 1951) and *Foundations of International Politics* (Princeton, NJ: Van Nostrand, 1962); Quincy Wright, *The Study of International Relations* (New York: Appleton-Century-Crofts, 1955), pp. 23–24; Charles P. Schleicher, *Introduction to International Relations* (Englewood Cliffs, NJ: Prentice-Hall, 1954) and *International Relations: Cooperation and Conflict* (Englewood Cliffs, NJ: Prentice-Hall, 1962); Frederick H. Hartmann, *The Relations of Nations* (New York: Macmillan, 1957, 1962); A. F. K. Organski, *World Politics* (New York: Knopf, 1958); Lennox A. Mills and Charles H. McLaughlin, *World Politics in Transition* (New York: Holt, Rinehart and Winston, 1956); Fred Greene, *Dynamics of International Relations* (New York: Holt, Rinehart and Winston, 1964); W. W. Kulski, *International Politics in a Revolutionary Age* (Philadelphia: Lippincott, 1964, 1967). The reader's attention is called to the following reviews of the earlier international-relations texts: Richard C. Snyder, "Toward Greater Order in the Study of International Politics," *World Politics,* VII (April 1955), 462–478; Fred A. Sondermann, "The Study of International Relations: 1956 Version," *World Politics,* X (July 1958), 639–647; Kenneth E. Boulding, "The Content of International Studies in College: A Review," *The Journal of Conflict Resolution,* VIII (March 1964), 65–71; and Dina A. Zinnes, "An Introduction to the Behavioral Approach: A Review," *The Journal of Conflict Resolution,* XII (June 1968), 258–267. For a content analysis of some later textbooks and other teaching materials, see James N. Rosenau et al., "Of Syllabi, Texts, Students and Scholarship in International Relations: Some Data and Interpretations on the State of a Burgeoning Field," *World Politics,* XXIX (January 1977), 263–340.

48. Georg Schwarzenberger, *Power Politics: A Study of World Society* (New York: Praeger, 1951), pp. 13–14. (The third edition of this work appeared in 1964.) For recent discussions of efforts to clarify the notion of power, see David V. J. Bell, *Power, Influence and Authority* (New York: Oxford University Press, 1975); Jack H. Nagel, *The Descriptive Analysis of Power* (New Haven, CT: Yale University Press, 1975); and David A. Baldwin, "Power Analysis and World Politics," *World Politics,* XXXI (January 1979), 161–194.

49. Horace V. Harrison, writing in 1964, criticized not only the textbooks but nearly all writing in international theory as being partial, implicit rather than explicit, too narrowly focused, designed to serve particular professional interests, and incapable of providing a guide either to research or to action. He added, however, that some progress toward more general theories had begun since the later 1950s. See his introduction to the book he edited, *The Role of Theory in International Relations* (Princeton, NJ: Van Nostrand, 1964), pp. 8–9.

50. William T. R. Fox and Annette Baker Fox, "The Teaching of International Relations in the United States," *World Politics,* XIII (July 1961), 339–359. See also Quincy Wright, op. cit., chaps. 3 and 4; Grayson Kirk, op. cit.; Waldemar Gurian, "On the Study of International Relations," *Review of Politics,* VIII (July 1946), 275–282; Frederick L. Schuman, *The Study of International Relations in the United States, Contemporary Political Science: A Survey of Methods, Research and Training* (Paris: United Nations Educational, Scientific, and Cultural Organization, 1950); Frederick S. Dunn, "The Present Course of International Relations Research," *World Politics,* II (October 1949), 142–146; Kenneth W. Thompson, op. cit.; L. Gray Cowen, "Theory and Practice in the Teaching of International Relations in the United States," in Geoffrey L. Goodwin, ed., *The University Teaching of International Relations* (Oxford, England: Basil Blackwell, 1951); John Gange, *University Research on International Relations* (Washington, DC: American Council on Education, 1958); Richard N. Swift, *World Affairs and the College Curriculum* (Washington, DC: American Council on Education, 1959); Edward W. Weidner, *The World Role of Universities,* Carnegie Series in American Education (New York: McGraw-Hill, 1962), especially the chapters dealing with student-abroad programs, exchange programs, and international programs of university assistance.

51. The appearance of several anthologies in international theory in the early 1960s attested to a burgeoning interest in the field. See William T. R. Fox, ed., *Theoretical Aspects of International Relations* (Notre Dame, IN: University of Notre Dame Press, 1959); Charles A. McClelland, William C. Olson, and Fred A. Sondermann, eds., *The Theory and Practice of International Relations* (Englewood Cliffs, NJ: Prentice-Hall, 1960); Ivo D. Duchacek, ed., with the collaboration of Kenneth W. Thompson, *Conflict and Cooperation Among Nations* (New York: Holt, Rinehart and Winston, 1960); Klaus Knorr and Sidney Verba, eds., "The International System: Theoretical Essays," *World Politics,* XIV (October 1961); James N. Rosenau, ed., *International Politics and Foreign Policy: A Reader in Research and Theory* (New York: Free Press, 1961); Horace V. Harrison, ed., op. cit.

52. Glenn H. Snyder and Paul Diesing, *Conflict Among Nations: Bargaining, Decision-making, and System Structure in International Crises* (Princeton, NJ: Princeton University Press, 1977), pp. 21–22.

53. Kenneth E. Boulding, *Ecodynamics: A New Theory of Societal Dynamics* (Beverly Hills, CA: Sage Publications, 1978), p. 9.

54. Alfred North Whitehead, *Science and the Modern World* (New York: Macmillan, 1925), pp. 41–44.

55. Alfred Zimmern, "Introductory Report to the Discussions in 1935," in Alfred Zimmern, ed., *University Teaching of International Relations, Report of the Eleventh Session of the International Studies Conference* (Paris: International Institute of Intellectual Cooperation, League of Nations, 1939), pp. 7–9. Later, C. A. W. Manning prepared a pamphlet for UNESCO on the university teaching of international relations, in which he took a similar position. There is an international-relations complex that has to be viewed from a universalistic angle, and none of the established disciplines as traditionally taught can be relied on to supply this necessary perspective. See P. D. Marchant, "Theory and Practice in the Study of International Relations," *International Relations*, I (April 1955), 95–102.

56. Nicholas J. Spykman, *Methods of Approach to the Study of International Relations, Proceedings of the Fifth Conference of Teachers of International Law and Related Subjects* (Washington, DC: Carnegie Endowment for International Peace, 1933), p. 60.

57. Frederick S. Dunn, "The Scope of International Relations," *World Politics*, I (October 1948), 1–42.

58. Ibid., p. 144.

59. Quincy Wright, *The Study of International Relations* (New York: Appleton-Century-Crofts, 1955), pp. 23–24.

60. Morton A. Kaplan, "Is International Relations a Discipline?" *The Journal of Politics*, XXIII (August 1961), p. 463.

61. Frederick S. Dunn, op. cit., p. 143.

62. Stanley Hoffmann, ed., *Contemporary Theory in International Relations* (Englewood Cliffs, NJ: Prentice-Hall, 1960), pp. 4–6. Raymond Aron has similarly noted that, although the definitional difficulty is real, it should not be exaggerated because every scientific discipline lacks precise outer limits. More important than knowing where phenomena become or cease to be data of international relations, says Aron, is the field's principal focus of interest. For him, this focus is on interstate relations. *Peace and War: A Theory of International Relations*, trans. Richard Howard and Annette Baker Fox (New York: Praeger, 1968), pp. 5–8.

63. Morton A. Kaplan, *System and Process in International Politics* (New York: Krieger, 1976), p. 3. In an article written as a rejoinder to Bull's criticism of the scientific writers, Kaplan accused the traditionalists of using history ineptly, of falling into the trap of overparticularization and unrelated generalization, and of being unaware that many writers in the modern scientific school regard history as a laboratory for the acquisition of empirical data. See his "The New Great Debate: Traditionalism vs. Science in International Relations," *World Politics*, XIX (October 1966), 15–16.

64. Morton A. Kaplan, "Problems of Theory Building and Theory Confirmation in International Politics," in Knorr and Verba, eds., op. cit., p. 23; Morton A. Kaplan, *New Approaches to International Relations* (New York: St. Martin's, 1968), pp. 399–404. See also George Modelski, "Comparative International Systems," *World Politics*, XIV (July 1962), 662–674, in which he reviews Adda B. Bozeman, *Politics and Culture in International History* (Princeton, NJ: Princeton University Press, 1960). See also Hoffmann, op. cit., pp. 174–180; James D. Fearon, "Counterfactuals and Hypothesis Testing in Political Science," *World Politics*, 43(2) (January 1991), 169–195.

65. Morton A. Kaplan, *System and Process in International Politics*, chap. 2.

66. "The substance of theory is history, composed of unique events and occurrences. An episode in history and politics is in one sense never repeated. It happens as it does only once. In this sense, history is beyond the reach of theory. Underlying all theory, however, is the assumption that these same unique events are also more concrete instances

of more general propositions. The wholly unique, having nothing in common with anything else, is indescribable." Kenneth W. Thompson, "Toward a Theory of International Politics," *American Political Science Review,* XLIX (September 1955), 734.

67. Martin Hollis and Steve Smith, *Explaining and Understanding International Relations* (Oxford, Englnd: Clarendon Press, 1990), pp. 1–7; 45–91; 196–216.

68. See Fred N. Kerlinger, *Foundations of Behavioral Research* (New York: Holt, Rinehart and Winston, 1966), p. 11, and Robert Brown, *Explanation in Social Science* (Chicago: Aldine, 1963), p. 174.

69. Gustav Bergman, *The Philosophy of Science* (Madison: University of Wisconsin Press, 1958), pp. 31–32.

70. Abraham Kaplan, *The Conduct of Inquiry* (San Francisco: Chandler, 1964), p. 319.

71. Carl G. Hempel, *Fundamentals of Concept Formation in Empirical Science* (Chicago: University of Chicago Press, 1952), p. 36.

72. *The Ethics of Aristotle,* trans. D. P. Chase (New York: Dutton, 1950), Book VI, p. 147. Hans J. Morgenthau, echoing Aristotle, stressed the difference between what is worth knowing intellectually and what is useful for practice. "Reflections on the State of Political Science," *Review of Politics,* XVII (October 1955), 440.

73. David Hume, "A Treatise of Human Nature: Part III. Of Probability and Knowledge," in *The Essential David Hume,* Introduction by Robert P. Wolff (New York: New American Library, 1969), pp. 53–99. See Sheldon S. Wolin, "Hume and Conservatism," *American Political Science Review,* XLVII (December 1954), 999–1016. Michael Polanyi, too, has treated the difference between the theory of affairs and the practice of affairs. *Personal Knowledge* (Chicago: University of Chicago Press, 1958), pp. 4–9ff.

74. For analyses of linkages between domestic political structures and processes on the one hand and foreign policy on the other, see James Rosenau, *Linkage Politics* (New York: Free Press, 1969); Henry A. Kissinger, "Domestic Structure and Foreign Policy," in *American Foreign Policy: Three Essays* (New York: Norton, 1969); Wolfram Hanreider, "Compatibility and Consensus: A Proposal for the Conceptual Linkage of External and Internal Dimensions of Foreign Policy," in Hanreider, ed., *Comparative Foreign Policy: Theoretical Essays* (New York: McKay, 1971); and Jonathan Wilkenfeld, ed., *Conflict Behavior and Linkage Politics* (New York: McKay, 1973).

75. Fred A. Sondermann, "The Linkage Between Foreign Policy and International Politics," in James N. Rosenau, ed., op. cit., pp. 8–17.

76. Quincy Wright, "Development of a General Theory of International Relations," in Horace V. Harrison, ed., op. cit., p. 20.

77. Ibid., pp. 21–23.

78. James N. Rosenau, *The Scientific Study of Foreign Policy,* rev. ed. (London: Frances Pinter, 1980), pp. 19–31.

79. Kenneth N. Waltz, *Theory of International Politics,* chap. 1, "Laws and Theories." (Reading, MA: Addison Wesley, 1979).

80. Barry Buzan, "The Level of Analysis Problem in International Relations Reconsidered," in Ken Booth and Steve Smith, eds., *International Relations Theory Today* (University Park: Pennsylvania State University Press, 1995), pp. 204–205.

81. See J. David Singer, "The Level-of-Analysis Problem in International Relations," in Knorr and Verba, eds., op. cit., pp. 77–92. Reprinted in James N. Rosenau, ed., *International Politics and Foreign Policy: A Reader in Research and Theory,* rev. ed. (New York: Free Press, 1969), pp. 20–29. K. J. Holsti concedes that the classical paradigm, postulating sovereign states as principal actors in an anarchic global system, has been much pilloried in recent decades, but he insists that it remains the dominant paradigm

and still commands the allegiance of most international theorists. *The Dividing Discipline: Harmony and Diversity in International Theory* (Boston, MA: Allen & Unwin, 1985), p. 11.

82. The subject of other-than-state actors is fully explored in Richard W. Mansbach, Yale H. Ferguson, and Donald E. Lampert, *The Web of World Politics: Non-State Actors in the Global System* (Englewood Cliffs, NJ: Prentice-Hall, 1976).

83. Samuel P. Huntington, "Transnational Organizations in World Politics," *World Politics,* XXV (April 1973) 333–368; Joseph S. Nye, Jr., "Multinational Corporations in World Politics," *Foreign Affairs,* 53 (October 1974) 153–175; Robert Gilpin, *U.S. Power and the Multinational Corporation* (New York: Basic Books, 1975); David E. Apter and Louis Wold Goodman, eds., *The Multinational Corporation and Social Change* (New York: Praeger, 1976); Raymond Vernon, *Storm over the Multinationals: The Real Issues* (Cambridge, MA: Harvard University Press, 1977); George Modelski, ed., *Transnational Corporations and World Order* (San Francisco: Freeman, 1979); Charles W. Kegley, Jr., and Eugene R. Wittkopf, eds., "The Rise of Multinational Corporations: Blessing or Curse?" in chap. 5 of their *World Politics: Trend and Transformation* (New York: St. Martin's, 1981); Joan Edelman Spero, *The Politics of International Economic Relations,* 3rd ed. (New York: St. Martin's, 1985), chaps. 4 and 8; and Robert T. Kudrle, "The Several Faces of the Multinational Corporation," in Jeffrey A. Frieden and David A. Lake, eds., *International Political Economy* (New York: St. Martin's, 1987).

84. Kegley and Wittkopf, eds., op. cit., p. 106.

85. J. David Singer, in Rosenau, ed., op. cit., p. 23.

86. The pluralists' critique of the realists is well described in Paul R. Viotti and Mark V. Kauppi, *International Relations Theory: Realism, Pluralism, Globalism* (New York: Macmillan, 1987), pp. 7–8, 192–193.

87. Ibid., p. 204; Kegley and Wittkopf, eds., op. cit., p. 139.

88. Viotti and Kauppi, op. cit., p. 9.

89. Cf. Joseph S. Nye, ed., *International Regionalism: Readings* (Boston: Little, Brown, 1968); Walker Connor, "Nation-Building or Nation-Destroying?" *World Politics,* XXIV (April 1972) 320–355.

90. David Easton, *The Political System* (New York: Knopf, 1959), pp. 129–131.

91. David Easton, *A Systems Analysis of Political Life* (New York: John Wiley and Sons, 1965), p. 284. Nevertheless, Easton holds that in some small degree at least, it is proper to consider decisions taken through appropriate international structures and procedures as authoritative; p. 284 and pp. 484–488. Even in some rare cases, however, of United Nations Security Council resolutions that are considered by international law authorities to be legally binding, states remain politically free to decide for themselves whether to comply, because no effective enforcement mechanism exists.

92. Raymond Aron, "What Is a Theory of International Relations?" *Journal of International Affairs,* XXI(2) (1967), 190; Stanley Hoffmann, *The State of War* (New York: Praeger, 1965), chap. 2; Roger D. Masters, "World Politics as a Primitive Political System," *World Politics,* XVI (July 1964); Kenneth N. Waltz, *Theory of International Politics,* p. 113.

93. Robert O. Keohane and Joseph S. Nye, *Power and Interdependence: World Politics in Transition,* second edition (Glenview, IL: Scott, Foresman and Company, 1989) chap. 1.

94. Ibid., pp. 5, 19–22; Ernst B. Haas, "On Systems and International Regimes," *World Politics,* XXVII (January 1975) and "Why Collaborate? Issue-Linkage and International Regimes," *World Politics,* XXXII (April 1980); Stephen D. Krasner, "Transforming International Regimes: What the Third World Wants and Why," *International Studies Quarterly,* 25 (March 1981); and the special issue of *International*

Organization, XXXVI (Spring 1982) devoted to international regimes and edited by Stephen D. Krasner.

95. Seyom Brown, *New Forces, Old Forces and the Future of World Politics* (New York: HarperCollins, 1995), p. 253.
96. Benjamin R. Barber, "Jihad v. McWorld," *The Atlantic* (March 1992). As early as 1972, Walker Connor had examined the phenomenon of state fragmentation. "Nation-Building or Nation-Destroying," *World Politics,* XXIV (April 1972).
97. Fouad Ajami (see Notes 10 and 11); Michael Mann, "Nation-States in Europe and Other Continents: Diversifying, Developing, Not Dying," *Daedalus,* 122(3) (1993), 115–140.
98. For a discussion of the critiques of behavioralism, see Donald J. Puchala, "Woe to the Orphans of the Scientific Revolution," in Robert L. Rothstein, ed., *The Evolution of Theory in International Relations* (Columbia: University of South Carolina Press, 1991), pp. 39–61.
99. Hedley Bull, "International Theory: The Case for a Classical Approach," *World Politics,* XVIII (April 1966), 361. Bull's essay is reprinted in the volume by Knorr and Rosenau, eds., op. cit.; cf. p. 20.
100. Klaus Knorr and James N. Rosenau, op. cit., p. 14.
101. Charles W. Kegley, Jr., and Eugene R. Wittkopf, *World Politics: Trend and Transformation,* 4th ed. (New York: St. Martin's Press, 1993), p. 27.
102. All of these and other criticisms are presented by Hedley Bull, op. cit.
103. J. David Singer, "The Incompleat Theorist: Insight Without Evidence," in Knorr and Rosenau, eds., op. cit., pp. 72–73.
104. Klaus Knorr and James N. Rosenau, op. cit., p. 16.
105. Its already extensive literature includes J. Baudrillard, *Seduction* (New York: St. Martin's Press, 1990); J. Der Derian and M. J. Shapiro, eds., *International/Intertextual Relations: Postmodern Readings of World Politics* (Lexington, MA: Lexington Books, 1989); M. Foucault, *The Archaeology of Knowledge* (New York: Pantheon, 1972); Jim George, *Discourses of Global Politics: A Critical (Re)Introduction to International Relations* (Bouldler, CO: Lynne Rienner Publishers, 1994), especially pp. 139–233; Jurgen Habermas, *The Philosophical Discourse of* Modernity, Twelve Lectures, trans. Frederick G. Lawrence (Cambridge, MA: MIT Press, 1995); M. Hollis and S. Smith, *Explaining and Understanding International Relations* (Oxford, England: Oxford University Press, 1990); Yosif Lapid, "The Third Debate: On the Prospects of Theory in a Post-Positivist Era," *International Studies Quarterly,* 33 (1989), 235–254; J. F. Lyotard, *The Postmodern Condition* (Minneapolis: University of Minnesota Press, 1984); P. M. Rosenau, *Postmodernism and the Social Sciences* (Princeton, NJ: Princeton University Press, 1992).
106. This feminist literature includes M. L. Adams, "There's No Place Like Home: On the Place of Identity in Feminist Politics," *Feminist Review,* (31) (1989), 22–33; F. Anthias and N. Yuval-David with H. Cain, eds., *Racialized Boundaries, Race, Nations, Gender, Colour, and the Anti-Racist Struggle* (London: Routledge, 1993); M. Cooke and A. Wollacott, eds., *Gendering War Talk* (Princeton, NJ: Princeton University Press, 1993); A. Curthoys, "Feminism, Citizenship and National Identity," *Feminist Review,* (44) (1993), 19–38; C. Enloe, *Bananas, Beaches and Bases: Making Feminist Sense of International Politics* (London: Pandora, 1989); P. Holden and A. Ardener, eds., *Images of Women in Peace and War* (London: Macmillan, 1987); M. Hutchinson, *The Anatomy of Sex and Power* (New York: William Morrow and Company, 1990); S. Jeffords, *The Remasculinization of America: Gender and the Vietnam War* (Bloomington: Indiana University Press, 1989); C. Mackinnon, *Towards a Feminist Theory of the State* (Cambridge, MA: Harvard University Press, 1989); N. Funk and M. Mueller,

eds., *Gender Politics and Post-Communism* (London: Routledge, 1993); V. Moghadam, *Identity Politics: Cultural Reassertion and Feminisms in International Perspectives* (Boulder, CO: Westview Press, 1993); V. S. Peterson, ed., *Gendered States: Feminist (Re)Visions of International Relations Theory* (Boulder, CO: Lynne Rienner, 1992); V. S. Peterson and A. S. Runyan, *Global Gender Issues* (Boulder, CO: Westview Press, 1993); Christine Sylvester, *Feminist Theory and International Relations in a Post-Modernist Era* (Cambridge, England: Cambridge University Press, 1994); and J. A. Tickner, *Gender in International Relations: Feminist Perspectives on a Changing Global Security* (New York: Columbia University Press, 1992).

107. Yosef Lapid, "Prospects of International Theory in a Post-Positivist Era," *International Studies Quarterly,* 33 (1989), 249.

108. Richard K. Ashley and R. B. J. Walker, "Reading Dissidence/Writing the Discipline: Crisis and the Question of Sovereignty in International Studies," *International Studies Quarterly,* 34 (1990), 368.

109. John A. Vasquez, "The Post-Posivitivist Debate: Reconstructing Scientific Enquiry and International Relations Theory After Enlightenment's Fall," in Ken Booth and Steve Smith, eds., *International Relations Theory Today* (University Park: Pennsylvania State University Press, 1995), p. 225.

110. David Hume, *Essays and Treatises on Several Subjects* (Edinburgh: Bell and Bradfute, and W. Blackwood, 1925), Vol. I, pp. 331–339. Reprinted in Arend Lijphart, ed., *World Politics* (Boston: Allyn & Bacon, 1966), pp. 228–234.

111. All these examples are cited in Hans J. Morgenthau, *Politics Among Nations,* op. cit., pp. 161–166.

112. Ernst B. Haas, "The Balance of Power: Prescription, Concept or Propaganda?" *World Politics,* V (July 1953), 442–477.

113. Inis L. Claude, Jr., *Power and International Relations* (New York: Random House, 1962), pp. 13, 22.

114. This paragraph and the one following constitute a synthesis from several different sources. For fuller treatment of the balance of power, see Inis L. Claude, Jr., op. cit.; Edward V. Gulick, *Europe's Classical Balance of Power* (Ithaca, NY: Cornell University Press, 1955); Sidney B. Fay, "Balance of Power," in *Encyclopedia of the Social Sciences,* Vol. II (New York: Macmillan, 1930); Alfred Vagts, "The Balance of Power: Growth of an Idea," *World Politics,* I (October 1948), 82–101; and Paul Seabury, ed., *Balance of Power* (San Francisco: Chandler, 1965).

115. Quoted in Edward V. Gulick, op. cit., p. 34.

116. "Memorandum on the Present State of British Relations with France and Germany," in G. P. Gooch and Harold V. Temperly, eds., op. cit., III, 402.

117. Winston S. Churchill, *The Gathering Storm* (Boston: Houghton Mifflin, 1948), pp. 207–210.

118. Henry Kissinger, *Diplomacy* (New York: Simon and Schuster, 1994), p. 20.

119. Nicholas J. Spykman, *American Strategy and World Politics* (New York: Harcourt Brace, 1942), pp. 21–22.

120. Hans J. Morgenthau, op. cit., chap. 14.

121. Ernst B. Haas, "The Balance of Power as a Guide to Policy-Making," *Journal of Politics,* XV (August 1953), 370–398.

122. Kenneth N. Waltz, *Theory of International Politics,* op. cit., pp. 117–123.

123. Morton A. Kaplan, *System and Process,* op. cit., pp. 22–36. Particularly important to his theory is the list of six essential rules of the balance-of-power system on p. 23.

124. Arthur Lee Burns, "From Balance to Deterrence: A Theoretical Analysis," *World Politics,* IX (July 1957), 505. Whereas Burns prefers five as the optimal number required for security, Kaplan says that five is the minimal number required for secu-

rity, but that security increases with the number of states up to some as-yet-undetermined upper limit. "Traditionalism vs. Science" in *International Relations,* op. cit., p. 10.

125. Arthur Lee Burns, op. cit., p. 508.

126. R. Harrison Wagner, "The Theory of Games and the Balance of Power," *World Politics,* 38 (July 1986), 575.

127. See Glenn H. Snyder, "Balance of Power in the Missile Age," *Journal of International Affairs,* XIV (1) (1960); John H. Herz, *Balance Systems and Balance Policies in a Nuclear and Bipolar Age,* op. cit., and the books and articles cited subsequently in the extended discussion on deterrence and arms control in Chapter 9 of this text.

128. For examples of quantitative studies in international relations, see Claudio Cioffi-Revilla, *The Scientific Measurement of International Conflict: Handbook of Datasets on Crises and Wars, 1495–1988 A.D.* (Boulder, CO: Lynne Reimer Publishers, 1990); Daniel Frei and Dieter Ruloff, *Handbook of Foreign Policy Analysis* (London: Martinus Nijhoff, 1989); Francis W. Hoole and Dina A. Zinnes, eds., *Quantitative International Politics* (New York: Praeger Publishers, 1976); P. Terrence Hopmann, Dina A. Zinnes, and J. David Singer, eds., *Cumulation in International Relations Research* (Denver, CO: University of Denver/Graduate School of International Studies, 1981); Morton A. Kaplan, ed., *New Approaches to International Relations* (New York: St. Martin's Press, 1968); Urs Luterbacher and Michael D. Ward, eds., *Dynamic Models of International Conflict* (Boulder, CO: Lynne Rienner Publishers, 1985); Richard L. Merritt and Stin Rokkan, eds., *Comparing Nations: The Use of Quantitative Data in Cross-National Research* (New Haven, CT: Yale University Press, 1966); John E. Mueller, ed., *Approaches to Measurement in International Relations: A Non-Evangelical Survey* (New York: Appleton, 1969); Emerson, M.S. Niou, Peter C. Ordeshook, and Gregory F. Rose, *The Balance of Power: Stability in International Systems* (New York: Cambridge University Press, 1989); Charles W. Kegley, Jr., and Gregory A. Raymond, *When Trust Breaks Down: Alliance Norms and World Politics* (Columbia, SC: University of South Carolina Press, 1990); James N. Rosenau, ed., *International Politics and Foreign Policy* (New York: Free Press, 1969); James N. Rosenau, ed., *In Search of Global Patterns* (New York: Free Press, 1976); Rudolph J. Rummel et al., *Dimensions of Nations* (Evanston, IL: Northwestern University Press, 1967); Rudolph J. Rummel, *Understanding Conflict and War* (Five volumes) (London: Sage Publications, 1981); Bruce M. Russett, *International Regions in the International System* (Chicago, IL: Rand McNally, 1967); Bruce M. Russett, ed., *Peace, War, and Numbers* (London: Sage Publications, 1972/1977/1978); J. David Singer, *Quantitative International Politics: Insights and Evidence* (New York: Free Press, 1968); J. David Singer, ed., *The Correlates of War,* 5, 1 and 2 (London: Collier Macmillan Publishers, 1979); J. David Singer and Paul F. Kiehl, *Measuring the Correlates of War* (Ann Arbor, MI: University of Michigan Press, 1990); J. David Singer and Michael D. Walker, eds., *To Auger Well: Early Warning Indicators in World Politics* (London: Sage Publications, 1979); J. David Singer and Richard Stoll, *Quantitative Indicators in World Politics: Timely Assurance and Early Warning* (New York: Praeger Publishers, 1984); Frank W. Wayman and Paul F. Diehl, eds., *Reconstructing Realpolitik* (Ann Arbor, MI: University of Michigan Press, 1994).

129. Carl G. Hempel and Paul Oppenheim, "Studies in the Logic of Explanation," *Philosophy of Science,* XV (1948), 135–175.

130. Werner Heisenberg, *Physics and Philosophy* (New York: Harper & Row, 1958), pp. 179, 183, 186. It should be pointed out that the principle of indeterminacy is often referred to less accurately by social scientists as "the uncertainty principle."

131. See Quincy Wright, *A Study of International Relations,* chap. 7; "Educational and Research Objectives," *Western Political Quarterly,* XI (September 1958), 598–606. Another penetrating discourse on the role of normative theory in contrast to a purely value-free approach to international relations is to be found in Charles A. McClelland, "The Function of Theory in International Relations," *Journal of Conflict Resolution,* IV (September 1960), 311–314.

132. Quincy Wright, *A Study of International Relations,* op. cit., p. 26.

133. Ibid., p. 11, and chaps. 8–11.

Chapter
2

From Realist to Neorealist Theory

THEORETICAL FOUNDATIONS

Realist theory, the foundations of which can be traced from the ancient world to the twentieth century, held a dominant position in the study of international relations in the years extending from the end of World War II into the early 1980s. Central to realist theory are several assumptions that shaped the paradigm which formed the basis for much of the theoretical development of that period: (1) that the international system is based on nation-states as the key actors; (2) that international politics is essentially conflictual, a struggle for power in an anarchic setting in which nation-states inevitably rely on their own capabilities to ensure their survival; (3) that states exist in a condition of legal sovereignty in which nevertheless there are gradations of capabilities, with greater and lesser states as actors; (4) that states are unitary actors and that domestic politics can be separated from foreign policy; (5) that states are rational actors characterized by a decision-making process leading to choices based on maximizing the national interest; and (6) that power is the most important concept in explaining, as well as predicting, state behavior.

Although there are areas of disagreement among realist theorists, as discussed in this chapter, there is overall consensus that realism has been preoccupied with two essential questions: (1) What accounts for state behavior in general and in particular for the survival of states? and (2) What produces and accounts for the dynamics of the international system?[1] In realist theory, answers to such questions are sought at the state level and at the system level. More recently, the study of international relations, and its theoretical agenda, have been shaped by neorealism which, since the early 1980s, together with structural realism, has come to occupy a position of central importance as a reformulation of classical realist theory.

Both realism and neorealism have been the object of great debate. Realist theory, as noted in Chapter 1 and discussed in this chapter, represented both a critique of, and an alternative to, what was termed *utopian theory*. The late twentieth-century counterpart to the utopian–realist controversy came in the form of a debate with a neoliberal school of theory, also discussed in this chapter. Realist thought is based on an international system, the defining characteristic of which is anarchy, by which is meant the absence of legal authority. The essence of sovereignty is the legal equality of states. Because states exist in a condition of sovereignty, there is no higher legal authority than the state. Nevertheless, states are not equal in capabilities. Some have vast means at their disposal. Others have meager power. Whatever hierarchy exists in the international system is the result of differentiation among states in their capabilities. Although states form alliances or coalitions, they are ultimately compelled to rely on their own means to ensure their survival. In this sense, the international system leads states to engage in self-help.

The ultimate means by which states achieve security, based on self-help, is found in armaments. If each state arms against one or more other states, the result is what has been called a "security dilemma."[2] The basic issue is this: At what point does the effort of one state to ensure its security come to be perceived by another state as a threat to that state's security? Because all states exist in a self-help system, levels of trust are low. One state cannot be certain that another state's efforts to arm for its own defense are not also intended to provide an offensive capacity. Therefore, a margin of safety will be sought in the form of yet greater armaments. Such suspicion on both sides is said to lead to an arms race. This is the security dilemma that characterizes an international system, the structure of which is anarchic, or based on power but lacking authority. (On arms races, see Chapter 8.)

Before addressing the principal assumptions and characteristics of realist theory, and drawing contrasts with utopian theory, it is appropriate to suggest that realism and utopianism, as David Baldwin asserts, are "loaded terms."[3] They connote, in some minds, the study of the world in hard-headed and realistic terms, versus an approach characterized by wishful thinking and soft-headed (utopian) analysis. Such terminology, including the use of the term *liberal,* or *neoliberal,* is unfortunate, for it inaccurately attaches to theories labels that may obfuscate as much as they illuminate. Utopian thought describes a world that its proponents would like to create. Realist thought attempts to describe a world that is said to exist. Although realist theory attaches central importance to power, utopian theory acknowledges power, which it seeks to subordinate to international institutions that possess authority. Both theories set forth prescriptions for bringing about change, although they differ in fundamental respects, not about the existence of power as a key variable, but about the extent of its importance and the prospects for, as well as the means by which, change can be brought about. We turn first to a brief discussion of utopian theory and what has been termed the utopian–realist debate.

The Utopian-Realist Debate

To a large extent, what was called "the utopian–realist controversy"—one of the great debates of international-relations theory—was focused on the extent to which political behavior and the anarchical circumstances of international politics could be transformed to a condition of world order, based on cooperative normative standards and global interdependence. This debate is described in great detail by E. H. Carr, in the context of diplomacy between the two World Wars.[4] Carr saw the utopians, for the most part, as intellectual descendants of eighteenth-century

Enlightenment optimism, nineteenth-century liberalism, and twentieth-century Wilsonian idealism.[5] Emphasizing how international relationships ought to be conducted, the utopians disdained balance-of-power politics, national armaments, the use of force in international affairs, and the secret treaties of alliance that preceded World War I. Instead, they stressed international legal rights and obligations, a natural harmony of interest in peace—reminiscent of Adam Smith's invisible hand[6]—as a regulator for the preservation of international peace, a heavy reliance on reason in human affairs, and confidence in the peace-building function of world public opinion.

Utopianism in international-relations theory is based on the assumption, drawn from the eighteenth-century Enlightenment, that environing circumstances shape human conduct and that such factors can be altered as a basis for changing human behavior. In sharp contrast to realist theory, utopianism holds that humankind is perfectible, or at least is capable of significant improvement. At the international level, the political environment can be transformed by the development of new institutions such as the League of Nations and the United Nations. By the establishment of norms of conduct, political behavior can be altered. Once such standards are set forth, it will be possible to create educated electorates and leadership capable of accepting those standards. It is assumed that enlightened public opinion can be expected to make rational decisions. Central to utopian theory, moreover, was the assumption of a harmony of interest in peace at the level of the collectivity, or nation-state, based on the interest of the individual in a peaceful world. The highest interest of the individual coincides with that of the larger community. If states have not embraced peace, it is because the leadership has not been responsive to the will of the people. An international system based on representative governments (a world made safe for democracy, in the words of Woodrow Wilson) would necessarily be a peaceful world. It is for this reason that a principal tenet of utopian theory was national self-determination. If people are free to select the form of government under which they live, they will choose representative forms of rule. The result will be to create the necessary framework for the realization of the harmony of interest in a peaceful world. As we show later, especially in Chapter 8, the relationship between democracy and peace has been an enduring part of international-relations theory.

Utopianism arose at an initial stage in the development of twentieth-century international-relations theory, although theories of international relations are deeply rooted in Western thought, as we have noted in our brief survey in Chapter 1.[7] In E. H. Carr's words, "International relations took its rise from a great and disastrous war; and the overwhelming purpose which dominated and inspired the pioneers of the new science was to obviate a recurrence of this disease of the international body politic."[8] It was the destructiveness of World War I that had led to the quest for international norms and institutions in the form of the League of Nations Covenant and the collective security framework established by its founders. In Carr's perspective, the wish is said to be the father of thought, in the sense that an abiding desire to abolish war or to reduce its destructiveness shaped the approach to international-relations theory. Carr asserts that purpose, or teleology, precedes and conditions thought. At the beginning of the establishment of a new field of inquiry, the element of wish is overwhelmingly strong, and the inclination to analyze facts and means is weak or nonexistent.[9] The utopian perspective guided the development of international-relations theory in the decades between the two world wars, especially in the Anglo-American setting. The dominant approach was to embrace what was international and to condemn what was national, and to evaluate events of the day by reference to the extent to which they conformed to the standards established by international legal norms and the League of Nations. There arose a substantial literature, highly normative in content, the purpose of which was, as stated in the foreword to one such volume by G. Lowes Dickinson, "to disseminate knowledge of the facts of international relations, and to inculcate the international rather than the nationalistic way of regarding them . . . for the world cannot be saved by governments and governing classes. It can be saved only by the creation, among the peoples of the world, of such a public opinion as cannot be duped by misrepresentation nor misled by passion."[10] (In addition to Dickinson, the list of contributors to this utopian literature included Nicholas Murray Butler, James T. Shotwell, Alfred Zimmern, Norman Angell, and Gilbert Murray.)

Realists, in contrast to utopians, stressed power and interest rather than ideals in international relations. Realism is basically conservative, empirical, prudent, suspicious of idealistic principles, and respectful of the lessons of history. It is more likely to produce a pessimistic than an optimistic view of international politics. Realists regard power as the fundamental concept in the social sciences (such as energy is in physics), although they admit that power relationships are often cloaked in moral and legal terms. Moreover, they criticize the utopian for preferring visionary goals to scientific analysis. Thus, although the utopian hoped for change that might permit disarmament, the realist emphasized national security and the need for military force and balance of power to support diplomacy, based on the assumption that national security represents the greatest and most immediate need of the state. To the realist, appeals to reason and to public opinion, as well as reliance on international organizations, namely the League of Nations, had proved woefully weak supports for keeping the peace in the 1930s; for example, they did not save Manchuria and Ethiopia from aggression, just as in subsequent decades, they did not prevent the Cold War or the regional and ethnic conflicts that have come after the Cold War.

Analyzing international relations between the two World Wars, Carr contended that "the inner meaning of the modern international crisis is the collapse of the whole structure of utopianism based on the concept of the harmony of interests."[11] In his view, the utopian theory of that era merely justified the interests of the dominant English-speaking status-quo powers, of the satisfied versus the unsatisfied, of the haves versus the have-nots. In particular, the harmony of interest in peace, a central tenet of utopian theory, applied more to those states, such as Great Britain and the United States, satisfied with the outcome of World War I, than to revisionist, dissatisfied states, such as Germany, Italy, and Japan.

Nevertheless, Carr, a pragmatist, took utopians and realists to task. He suggested that whereas the utopians ignore the lessons of history, the realists often read history too pessimistically. Whereas the idealist exaggerates freedom of choice, the realist exaggerates fixed causality and slips into determinism. While the idealist may confuse national self-interest with universal moral principles, the realist runs the risk of cynicism and fails to provide any ground for purposive and meaningful action[12]—that is, the realist denies that human thought modifies human action. To the utopian, purpose precedes observation; the vision of a Plato comes before the analysis of an Aristotle. The vision may even seem totally unrealistic. Carr cites the alchemists who tried to turn lead into gold, noting that when their visionary project failed, they began examining facts more carefully, thus giving birth to modern science.[13] He concludes that sound political theories contain elements of utopianism and realism, of power as well as of moral values.[14]

The Neorealist–Neoliberal Debate

E. H. Carr

The utopian–realist debate about which E. H. Carr and others wrote has been replaced by an intellectual successor generation on both sides of the divide, in the form of a neoliberal–neorealist debate. Its defining characteristics bear some resemblance to the earlier controversy, although there are important differences as well. The neorealist–neoliberal debate contains as a key element discord not about the existence of anarchy, which both sides acknowledge to exist, but rather its meaning and implications, as well as the extent to which development of institutions such as the United Nations, the North Atlantic Treaty Organization, or the European Community/Union can transcend the basic structural characteristics of the anarchic international system. Neoliberal institutionalist theory, as it has been termed, contains the basic realist assumptions that states are the principal actors; that states act in accordance with their conception of national interest; that power remains an important variable; and that the structure of world politics is anarchic. According to Robert Keohane, neorealists and neoliberal institutionalists, if they are to understand international relations, need to find whatever common ground exists between them on the role of institutions. Keohane, himself in the liberal institutionalist camp, acknowledges that "the fact that international institutions are used by states to pursue their interests does not demonstrate how significant they will be when interests change."[15] He goes on to assert that "realists and institutionalists agree that without a basis either of hegemonic dominance or common interests, international institutions cannot long survive." Furthermore, neorealist and neoliberal institutionalists agree that possibilities exist for international cooperation, but they diverge on the likelihood of its success.

Keohane

    Stated in contemporary terms, the end of the Cold War has transformed the structure of international politics. In Europe, the system of the Cold War, to the extent that it was bipolar, has been replaced by political fragmentation, including the breakup or weakening of alliance structures, as well as the disintegration of states and the resurgence of intrastate ethnic conflict. The contemporary global setting contains elements of cooperation and conflict, together with patterns of behavior that draw states into collaborative arrangements, as well as conflictual situations. The test for neoliberalist institutionalists will be the extent to which organizations such as the European Community/Union, the Western European Union, the Organization for Security and Cooperation (OSC) in Europe, and NATO will be able to diminish or eliminate post–Cold War conflicts. From the neorealist perspective, such clashes, reflecting the dramatically changed structure of the international system, cannot be effectively managed within international institutions, unless those institutions somehow reflect the structure of the international system within which they exist. According to the neorealist logic, in John Mearsheimer's words, "NATO was basically a manifestation of the bipolar distribution of power in Europe during the Cold War, and it was that balance of power, not NATO *per se*, that provided the key to maintaining stability on the continent."[16] According to the neorealist, international institutions provide no substitute for reliance on the capabilities of the state. Nevertheless, the neorealist–neoliberal debate has moved away from the sharp delineation that existed during the utopian–realist era to an effort toward synthesis. Such an evolution, discussed in a later section of this chapter, provides a potential basis for further progress in international-relations theory.

Before discussing in somewhat greater detail neorealist theory, it is necessary to set forth classical realist theory in its essential elements. To do so, it is important briefly to examine its intellectual origins.

Antecedents of Realist Theory

Realist theory has intellectual roots that can be traced to the ancient world. In his celebrated history of the Peloponnesian War, Thucydides (400 B.C.) wrote, "What made war inevitable was the growth of Athenian power and the fear which this caused in Sparta."[17] His conception of the importance of power, together with the propensity of states to form competing alliances, is said to place Thucydides well within the realist school. The statement from Thucydides's writings that "the strong do what they have the power to do and the weak accept what they have to accept"[18] typifies much of twentieth-century realist thought. Just as Thucydides had developed an understanding of state behavior in the ancient world from his observation of relations between Athens and Sparta, Niccolò Machiavelli (1469–1557) analyzed interstate relations in the Italian system of the sixteenth century. In his writings in general, and *The Prince* in particular, Machiavelli is clearly linked to realist theory by (a) his emphasis on the ruler's need to adopt moral standards different from those of the individual in order to ensure the state's survival, (b) his concern with power, (c) his assumption that politics is characterized by a clash of interests, and (d) his pessimistic view of human nature.[19]

Thomas Hobbes (1588–1679), like Machiavelli, viewed power as crucial in human behavior: Man has a "perpetual and restless desire of power after power that ceaseth only in death."[20] Hobbes believed that "covenants, without the sword, are but words and of no strength to secure a man at all."[21] Without a strong sovereign, chaos and violence follow: "If there be no power erected, or not great enough for our own security, man will and may lawfully rely on his own strength and art for caution against all other men."[22]

Like other modern realists, Hobbes concerned himself with the underlying forces of politics and with the nature of power in political relationships. Although Hobbes believed that a strong sovereign was mandatory for maintaining order within the political system, he saw little prospect for fundamentally changing human behavior or the anarchic setting. In his emphasis on strong political institutions for managing power and preventing conflict, Hobbes paradoxically was closer to proponents of world government or, to be more precise, world empire than to realists who stress a balance of power among major political groups. Hobbes regarded the latter condition as analogous to an anarchical state of nature, but he doubted the possibility of establishing a world empire. His response to the condition of anarchy described by realists was the creation of a hierarchical order in which ultimate power would be vested in the sovereign.

Georg Hegel (1770–1831), more than any other political philosopher, elevated the position of the state. Although realist writers are usually by no means Hegelian, Hegel's belief that the state's highest duty lies in its own preservation is found in realist theory. Hegel reasoned that "since states are related to one another as autonomous entities and so as particular wills on which the validity of treaties depends, and since the particular will of the whole is in content a will for its own welfare it follows that welfare is the highest aim governing the relation of one state to another."[23] Moreover, Hegel held that the state has an "individual totality" that develops according to its own laws. The state has objective reality; that is, it exists apart from its citizens. Hegel held that the state has moral standards different from and superior to those of the individual. Without imputing superior status to state moral standards, realist theory contains the proposition that behavior on behalf of the state may require conduct that would not be acceptable within a civilized society.

Among the antecedents of realist theory is the work of Max Weber (1864–1920), whose writings dealt extensively not only with the nature of politics and the state, but also with power as central to politics. Although the richness of Weber's political thought cannot be encompassed in a short analysis, suffice it to suggest that, with respect to realist theory, many of the formulations contained in his work shaped subsequent generations of writing and scholarship. For Weber, as for later realists, the principal characteristic of politics is a struggle for power. The power element of political life is especially evident at the international level because "every political structure naturally prefers to have weak rather than strong neighbors. Furthermore, as every big political community is a potential aspirant to prestige, it is also a potential threat to all its neighbors; hence, the big political community, simply because it is big and strong, is latently and constantly endangered."[24] Among the dimensions of politics as a struggle for power, moreover, is that of economics. In Weber's thought, economic policy stands in a subordinate relationship to politics, inasmuch as the "power political interests of nations" encompass an economic struggle for existence.

Among the concerns of realists with which Weber before them was preoccupied is the ethical problem of intentions versus consequences, or what is also termed the absolute ethic of conviction and the ethic of responsibility. To adhere to an absolute ethic is to take actions in keeping with that ethic without regard for their consequences. However, according to Weber, leaders in an imperfect world confront the need to behave by a political ethic, in which the achievement of good ends may make necessary the utilization of less than morally acceptable means. For Weber the ethic of conviction cannot be separated from an understanding of the consequences of such action, which in turn gives concrete meaning to an ethic of responsibility. In contemporary realist thought, the meaning of the ethic of responsibility comes forth in the notion that each political action must be judged on specific merits, rather than in accordance with some abstract, universal standard.

The Weberian ethic of conviction and the ethic of consequences assumed in much of realist theory the formulation, as Hans Morgenthau suggests, that abstract moral principles cannot be universally applied to specific political actions. The political leader operates in an anarchic society lacking authoritative political institutions, legal systems, and commonly accepted standards of conduct. Acting on behalf of state interests, the political leader necessarily embodies a standard of conduct substantially different from that of the individual within a civilized political unit. Here we confront the realist assumption that, while the international system is anarchical, within the nation-state, law and order generally prevail—the unitary state in an anarchic society. The leader of state, by oath of office, is sworn to safeguard the state from external threat, to provide for its common defense, and ultimately to ensure its survival in a world of anarchy. Because there is no legally or politically superior authority, the power of the state becomes the ultimate guarantee of security. The protection of the state from its enemies in an international system containing revolutionary and expansionist states inevitably leads the political leader to adopt or to condone policies that would be deemed unacceptable among individuals or groups within a civilized state. For these reasons, the realist holds that politics is not a function of ethical philosophy. Instead, political theory, including realist theory, is derived from political practice and historical experience.

In contrast, utopian thought was based on the idea that politics can be made to conform to an ethical standard. Norms of behavior, such as those specified in international law and organization, can be established and made the basis for international behavior. This utopian assumption is challenged in realist theory, which posits instead that there are severe limitations in the extent to which political reform, institutional development, or education can alter political behavior, based as it allegedly is not only on the anarchical structure of the international system but also on a human nature that itself is flawed, power-seeking, and otherwise imperfect. Hence, realist theory emphasizes the balance of power as a regulatory mechanism to prevent any one state or other political group from achieving hegemony.

Although the term *structure* refers to the units of the international system and their relationship to each other, including the distribution of power, and holds that systemic structural characteristics decisively shape behavioral patterns, other variables also have important implications for state actors. Classical realist writers pointed to the importance of geographical location. Geography is said to shape the options available to states. Even in the nuclear age, when any state can be targeted by highly accurate missiles armed with atomic warheads launched with intercontinental range, geography nevertheless renders certain states more vulnerable than others to foreign conquest. Reflecting this dimension of realist theory, Henry Kissinger maintains that "both the American and the European approaches to foreign policy were the products of their own unique circumstances. Americans inhabited a nearly empty continent shielded from predatory powers by two vast oceans and with weak countries as neighbors. . . . The anguishing dilemmas of security that tormented European nations did not touch America for nearly 150 years."[25] The extent to which the location of a state exposes it to, or affords it protection from, hostile neighbors is said to influence its foreign policy.

Power and International Behavior

According to realist theory, states operate in an anarchic system in which their policies are based on national interest backed by power. Because the structure of the system includes the distribution of power, it follows that power is a key concept in realist–neorealist theory. Furthermore, if we cannot develop techniques for measuring power, our ability to understand relationships among units in the structure will be severely limited. Therefore, realist–neorealist theory has included both the conceptualization and measurement of power. Although power is the key variable shaping international behavior, according to realist–neorealist theory, power nevertheless represents one of the most important, yet troublesome, concepts in international-relations theory. Because of its crucial importance in realist–neorealist theory, the need to define, as well as to refine, the meaning of power is abundantly apparent. According to Robert Gilpin, the "number and variety of definitions (of power) should be an embarrassment to political scientists."[26] In its basic meaning, power connotes the ability of one actor to influence another actor to do, or not to do, something desired by that actor. The actor exerting such influence does so by means of the capabilities that it has available. According to David Baldwin, "The most common conception of power in social science treats power as a type of causal relationship in which the power wielder affects the behavior, attitudes, beliefs, or propensity to act of another actor."[27] As if to confirm Robert Gilpin's characterization of power, we confront within and beyond realist–neorealist theory numerous definitions of power. Kenneth Waltz, as Baldwin points out, rejects a causal conception of power, preferring instead to suggest "the old and simple notion that an agent is powerful to the extent that he affects others more than they affect him."[28] Waltz goes on to maintain that it is possible to rank the capabilities of states by reference to "how they score on *all* of the following items: size of population and territory, resource endowment, economic capability, military strength, political stability and competence."[29]

The diversity of definitions of power, characteristic of its pervasive presence in realist–neorealist writings, can be illustrated by reference to other literature, in this case that of the realist era of the middle years of the twentieth century. According to Nicholas J. Spykman, "All civilized life rests in the last instance on power." Power is the ability to move the individual or the human collectivity in some desired fashion, through "persuasion, purchase, barter, and coercion."[30] Robert Strausz-Hupé maintained that international politics is "dominated by the quest for power," and that "at any given period of known history, there were several states locked in deadly conflict, all desiring the augmentation or preservation of their power."[31] Arnold Wolfers argued that power is "the ability to move others or to get them to do what one wants them to do and not to do what one does not want them to do." Moreover, he deemed it important "to distinguish between power and influence, the first to mean the ability to move others by the threat or infliction of deprivations, the latter to mean the ability to do so through promises or grants of benefits."[32] John Burton, himself clearly not an exponent of the realist school of theory or of realpolitik, suggests that "there is probably no greater common factor in all thinking on international relations than the assumption that States depend for their existence upon power, and achieve their objectives by power, thus making the management of power the main problem to be solved."[33] According to Robert Gilpin, power encompasses the military, economic, and technological capabilities of states, while prestige consists of the "perceptions of other states with respect to a state's capacities and its ability and willingness to express its power."[34]

The power of a state is said to consist of capabilities, some of which are economic in nature—such as levels of industrialization and productivity, gross national-al product, national income, and income on a per capita basis. In an analysis of the economic dimensions of international politics and the political aspects of international economics, assessing power in its intertwined economic and political contexts, Charles P. Kindleberger defines power as "strength capable of being used efficiently," that is, "strength *plus* the capacity to use it effectively"[35] in support of some objective. Thus, like several other writers, Kindleberger distinguishes between means and ends, or the use of means for the attainment of ends. Thus, strength is a means that exists even in the absence of its use for some goal, whereas power is the use of strength for a particular purpose. According to Kindleberger, "Prestige is the respect which is paid to power. Influence is the capacity to affect the decisions of others. Force is the use of physical means to affect those decisions. Dominance is defined as the condition under which A affects a significant number of B's decisions without B affecting those of A."[36] Power thus conceptualized is related to adaptability and flexibility in a nation's economy. Such is the meaning of efficiency in the use of power. Thus, power is dynamic and changing, rather than static in nature. Those states or other entities best able to adjust to change are likely to possess power, and to make most effective use of it in support of posited goals.

According to Klaus Knorr, power, influence, and interdependence are inextricably related. Two states can be in conflict over some issues while cooperating on others. "When they cooperate, they benefit from the creation of new values, material or nonmaterial. When they are in conflict, they attempt to gain values at each other's expense. In either case, they are interdependent."[37] Power becomes important in conflictual situations, whereas influence is central both in circumstances of conflict and in cooperative relationships. Power may be used coercively or noncoercively. "When power is used coercively, an actor (B) is influenced if it adapts its behavior in compliance with, or in anticipation of, another actor's (A) demands, wishes, or proposals." Knorr suggests that the term *power* is employed by some writers to identify all influence, whether coercive or noncoercive. He prefers to invoke the term *power* to designate "only the exercise of coercive influence."[38] Developing a model for the analysis of the utility of military power by one actor (A) against another actor (B), Knorr identifies four basic factors: (1) B's estimate of the costs of complying with A's threat, (2) B's estimate of the costs of defying A's threat, (3) B's bargaining skill relative to A's, and (4) B's propensity to act rationally and to assume risks.[39] Knorr holds that many variables "intervene in determining whether or not a military threat will be effective, and to what extent."[40]

In the context of power, interdependence is said to connote the ability of one state to influence another in some way. If the interdependence is mutual, each could damage both the other and itself by severing the relationship that exists between them. Such a conception of interdependence has shaped the deterrence relationship of the nuclear age. The survival of each nuclear power is dependent on the decision of one or more of the others not to destroy it with atomic weapons. In this sense, there is a form of interdependence. The costs and the benefits of exercising power by each party in an interdependent relationship increase as the level of interdependence grows. According to David Baldwin, dependency relationships represent a form of influence in which one actor's ability, for example, to cut off the supply of a critical resource, such as oil, to another actor may furnish the basis for influence of the disadvantaged party in other areas as well.[41] Clearly related is the issue of cost in analyzing the relationship between power and dependency. The level of dependency is determined either by the opportunity costs of forgoing the object at issue—for example, oil—or by the extent to which the dependent state can substitute another supplier or another source of energy for oil.[42] Similarly, James A. Caporaso maintains that the nature of dependence would include (1) the magnitude of the dependent state's interest in a desire for a good, (2) the extent of the control of the good in question by the party exerting influence, and (3) the ability of the dependent state to find an alternative source for the commodity for which there exists a particular level of dependence.[43]

Viewing power as a multidimensional influence relationship, K. J. Holsti suggests that power consists of (1) the acts by which one actor influences another actor, (2) the capabilities utilized for this purpose, and (3) the response elicited. Holsti conceptualizes power as a means to an end, even though some political leaders may seek influence as an end in itself, just as some people may value money not only for what it can buy but also for its own sake. In short, Holsti defines power as the "general capacity of a state to control the behavior of others."[44] Stated differently, answers are sought to the following questions: In light of our goals, what kind of behavior do we seek to obtain from another actor, and how can such an actor be induced to do what we want? What capabilities are available for use in support of our goal? What is likely to be the response to our effort to influence the behavior of the other actor?[45] In such an analysis of power, the idea of causation is implicit, to return to the aforementioned conception of power set forth by David Baldwin. Possessing power is said to be conducive to its threatened or actual use to produce a desired result. Those who object to causally based theories of political behavior logically fault power theory that is based on causation.[46] In such a critique, we are brought back to one of the enduring questions of power and political behavior: To what extent can the intentions of states as political actors be inferred from the capabilities in their possession? Is there a causal relationship in which the possession of capabilities shapes the intentions of their possessors and their propensity to use power? Or, can a powerful state refrain from using its power?

It is generally agreed that power is situationally specific. Although power is far less fungible than money, the unit of account by which economic power is measured, some aspects of power are more fungible than others and might be so rank ordered. If power must be related to the situation in which it is used, or available for use, Baldwin maintains, categorizing states as great powers or small powers is inadequate if not misleading because such terms relate to a generalized, rather than to a specific, situational context, or to a particular issue area.[47] The need exists, it is suggested, for students of international politics to examine the multiple distributional patterns of power in a large number of issue areas, while recognizing the limitations of power analysis resulting from the absence of a common denominator of political value for comparing different forms and uses of power.

Jack H. Nagle has suggested that the "measurement and observation of preferences will be a fundamental difficulty in the study of power, severely restricting outcomes over which power can be measured."[48] Nagle argues for power analysis based on data that relate preferences causally to explanations of outcomes. He contends that this problem extends to motivation theory in psychology, as well as to game theory and to decision theory. According to Herbert Simon and Roderick Bell, the essential prerequisite for the measurement of power is a theoretical framework or theory of power.[49] The use of cardinal numbers to measure power implies that the observed or measured units have the same properties as, or are isomorphic to, the cardinal numbers. Thus, the problem of power measurement relates more to the deficiencies inherent in existing theory than in the measurement techniques themselves. In yet another approach to power measurement, Jacek Kugler and William Domke have constructed a framework based on the resources available to a government and its ability to extract, mobilize, and utilize them in support of a specific goal. National strength is defined as the sum of a state's internal capabilities (societal base) and external resources (in the form of help from allies or assistance of other lands from abroad). States that are directly threatened are likely to be more able than other states to mobilize resources. States under stress of war are capable of mobilizing vast resources. According to this analysis, differences in the form of government—pluralistic or totalitarian— do not decisively shape the level of resource mobilization. These authors also found that, while richer nations can mobilize greater amounts of societal resources, poorer states are more effective in raising their levels of extraction because of greater political slack in less developed countries that can be mobilized during times of stress.[50]

Efforts have been made to measure power, and especially influence, by reference to communications—who communicates with whom, who consults with whom. (Such measures have also been used in the study of political integration, discussed in Chapter 10.) It is hypothesized that the more a person, group, or nation is the recipient rather than the originator of communications, the greater the influence of that entity over others. Steven Brams has hypothesized that two nations have an influence relationship with each other that is symmetrical if the transactions between them are approximately equal.[51] If one nation receives the preponderant number of transactions, it exercises asymmetrical influence over the other.[52] Such a proposition can be, and has been, tested with the use of international visit data, but without conclusive results.

In recent work designed to synthesize and analyze efforts to measure power, Michael P. Sullivan acknowledges that a major difficulty arises from the need to specify the type of international behavior to be explained by reference to power as the key explanatory variable. In the absence of such specificity, he claims, we may erroneously conclude that different types of international behavior can be explained by the same measurement of power.[53] Furthermore, Sullivan maintains, power as an attribute, or capability, must be distinguished from power as influence. Although states with the greatest power are likely to be the most influential, there are exceptions to this generalization—we may need an alternative explanation to that of power as the key variable. In his discussion of power, Sullivan notes a large number of measurable elements: population, territory, resources, levels of education and skills, gross national product, the scientific–technological base, exports and imports, foreign investment, military expenditures, size of armed forces, agricultural production, and food supply. Beyond such measurements at the national level, it is possible to specify systems-level power measures. They would include alliance and nongovernmental organization membership, as well as the distribution of capabilities throughout the system as a basis for giving operational meaning to bipolarity and multipolarity. Our ability to categorize the polarity of international systems depends on the extent to which it is possible to develop adequate techniques for measuring power and alignment.

Because power provides the core concept in realist theory for understanding state behavior, the need for greater definitional clarity is abundantly apparent. Although power has been defined as the aggregate of the capabilities available to the state, the power of one state also is said to be relative to the aggregate capabilities of the state with which it has a conflictual relationship. It has been suggested, as noted previously, that power is situational, or dependent on the issue, object, or goal for which it is employed. Economic power, however vast, cannot halt armored divisions, just as military power itself would not be sufficient to ensure global trade dominance. To specify and compare attributes, or capabilities, represents power in its static dimension. What is most important is the outcome of the interactive process, whether it be who wins wars or who wins trade negotiations. This is power in its dynamic setting. Finally, the literature on power, as we have seen, includes influence, the extent to which capabilities translate into the ability to shape the behavior of others to produce a desired outcome. Realist theory left such definitional and measurement problems to be addressed by the neorealist successor generation and others concerned with understanding the role of power in historic, contemporary, and future global settings.

Realist International-Relations Theory: The Midtwentieth Century

The major assumptions of realist theory, deeply rooted in history and political thought, gained intellectual ascendancy in writings that included the work of the Protestant theologian Reinhold Niebuhr; the diplomat–policy-planner–historian George F. Kennan; the geographer–political scientist Nicholas J. Spykman; policy-maker–historian–strategic analyst Henry Kissinger; the political scientist and student of geopolitics Robert Strausz-Hupé; and the seminal writings of Hans J. Morgenthau. Morgenthau casts a long, deep intellectual shadow over the neorealist as well as the classical realist landscape. Although space does not permit a detailed examination of the writings of these and other major contributors, we turn to a brief description and assessment of Hans Morgenthau as theorist and George F. Kennan and Henry Kissinger, respectively, as theorists–policymakers.

Hans J. Morgenthau   No twentieth-century writer has had a greater impact on the development of realist theory than Hans J. Morgenthau (1904–1980). The realist concepts related to rationally determined national interest, power, balance of power, and the management of power in an anarchic world were nowhere more fully developed than in Morgenthau's work. It is to Morgenthau that critics of realist theory usually turn and to whom those who seek to adapt realist theory to a neorealist reconceptualization refer as a necessary beginning point.

Essential to Morgenthau's realist theory are six basic principles. First, he suggested that political relationships are governed by objective rules deeply rooted in human nature. Because these rules are "impervious to our preferences, they can be challenged only at the risk of failure."[54] If these rules themselves cannot be changed, Morgenthau held that society can be improved by first understanding the laws that govern society and then by basing public policy on that knowledge. In theorizing about international politics, moreover, it is necessary to employ historical data for examining political acts and their consequences. In evaluating and assimilating these vast amounts of historical data, Morgenthau asserts, the student of politics should attempt to view the issue from "the position of a statesman who must meet a certain problem of foreign policy under certain circumstances," and ask "what the rational alternatives are from which a statesman may choose who must meet this problem under these circumstances (presuming always that he acts in a rational manner), and which of these rational alternatives this particular statesman, acting under these circumstances, is likely to choose. It is the testing of this rational hypothesis against the actual facts and their consequences that gives meaning to the facts of international politics."[55]

Second, Morgenthau posited that political leaders "think and act in terms of interest defined as power" and that historical evidence proves this assumption.[56] This concept, central to Morgenthau's realist theory, gives continuity and unity to the seemingly diverse foreign policies of the widely separated nation-states. Moreover, the concept "interest defined as power" makes it possible to evaluate actions of political leaders at different points in history. In his view, international politics is a process in which national interests are accommodated or resolved on the basis of diplomacy or war.

> The concept of the national interest presupposes neither a naturally harmonious, peaceful world nor the inevitability of war as a consequence of the pursuit by all nations of their national interests. Quite to the contrary, it assumes continuous conflict and threat of war to be minimized through the continuous adjustment of conflicting interest by diplomatic action.[57]

Third, Morgenthau acknowledged that the meaning of interest defined as power is not easily determined. However, in a world in which sovereign nations compete for power, survival constitutes the minimum goal of foreign policy and the core national interest. All nations are compelled to protect "their physical, political, and cultural identity against encroachments by other nations." Thus, national interest is identified with national survival. "Taken in isolation, the determination of its content in a concrete situation is relatively simple, for it encompasses the integrity of the nation's territory, of its political institutions, and of its culture."[58] As long as the world is divided into nations in an anarchic global setting, Morgenthau asserted, the "national interest is indeed the last word in world politics." Interest, then, is the essence of politics, which is defined as a struggle for power.

Once its survival is assured, the nation-state may pursue lesser interests. Morgenthau assumed that nations ignore the national interest only at the risk of destruction. To illustrate the meaning of national interest and the need to distinguish between the most vital and the lesser national interests, Morgenthau sets forth several historical examples.[59] If Great Britain, in 1939 to 1940, had based its policy toward Finland on legalistic–moralistic considerations, backed with large-scale military aid against Soviet aggression, then Britain's position might have been weakened sufficiently to ensure its destruction by Nazi Germany. Britain would have neither restored Finland's independence nor safeguarded its own most vital national interest, that of physical survival. Only when the national interest most closely related to national survival has been safeguarded can nations pursue lesser interests.

Fourth, Morgenthau stated that "universal moral principles cannot be applied to the actions of states in their abstract, universal formulation, but that they must be filtered through the concrete circumstances of time and place."[60] In pursuit of the national interest, nation-states are governed by a morality that differs from the morality of individuals in their personal relationships. In the actions of leaders of state as stateleaders, the political consequences of a particular policy become the criteria for judging it. To confuse individual morality with state morality is to court national disaster. Because the primary official responsibility of stateleaders is the survival of the nation-state, their obligations to the citizenry require a different mode of moral judgment from that of the individual. This is not to suggest that Morgenthau ignored ethical or moral considerations. He could envisage no conception of national interest that would condone policies of mass extermination, torture, and the indiscriminate slaughter of civilian populations in war. He saw ethics as providing a system of restraints on political conduct, while nevertheless, as Greg Russell suggests, urging the realist to "view the moral significance of political action as a product of the ineluctable tension between the moral command and the requirements of political success."[61]

Fifth, Morgenthau asserted that political realism does not identify the "moral aspirations of a particular nation with the moral laws that govern the universe."[62] In fact, if international politics is placed within a framework of defining interests in terms of power, "we are able to judge other nations as we judge our own."[63] This aspect of Morgenthau's realism bears resemblance to the thought of Reinhold Niebuhr, a leading twentieth-century Protestant theologian who wrote extensively on international relations and foreign policy.

Sixth, and finally, Morgenthau stressed the autonomy of the political sphere. Political actions must be judged by political criteria. "The economist asks: 'How does this policy affect the welfare of society, or a segment of it'? The lawyer asks:

'Is this policy in accord with the rules of law'? The realist asks: 'How does this policy affect the power of the nation?'"[64]

In power struggles, nations follow policies designed to preserve the status quo, to achieve imperialistic expansion, or to gain prestige. In Morgenthau's view, domestic and international politics can be reduced to one of three basic types: "A political policy seeks either to keep power, to increase power, or to demonstrate power."[65]

Although the purpose of a status-quo policy is to preserve the existing distribution of power, the nation adopting such a policy does not necessarily act to prevent all international change. Instead, status-quo nations seek to thwart change that may produce fundamental shifts in the international distribution of power. Morgenthau cites the Monroe Doctrine as an example of a status-quo policy that fulfills his two criteria. First, it was designed to maintain the prevailing power balance in the Western hemisphere. Second, it expressed the unwillingness of the United States to prevent all change. Instead, the United States would act only against change that threatened the existing distribution of power. Likewise, treaties concluded at the end of wars invariably codify the then-prevailing status quo.

Imperialism is the second major alternative available to nations. This is a policy designed to achieve a "reversal of existing power relations between nations."[66] The goals of imperialist powers include local preponderance, continental empire, or world domain. Nations may adopt imperialistic policies as a result of victory, defeat, or the weakness of other states. A state for which its leaders expect victory may alter its objectives from the restoration of the status quo to a permanent change in the distribution of power. Moreover, a defeated nation may adopt an imperialistic policy to "turn the scales on the victor, to overthrow the status quo created by victory, and to change places in the hierarchy of power."[67] Finally, the existence of weak states may prove irresistible to a strong state.

To attain imperialistic objectives, states may resort to military force or to cultural and economic means. Military conquest is the oldest and most obvious form of imperialism. Economic imperialism is not as effective a technique as military conquest, but if one imperialistic state cannot gain control over another by armed force, it may attempt to do so by economic means. Cultural imperialism represents an attempt to influence the human mind "as an instrument for changing the power relations between two nations."[68] (For an examination of theories of imperialism, see Chapter 6.)

According to Morgenthau, states may pursue a policy of prestige. This may be "one of the instrumentalities through which the proponents of status quo and of imperialism achieve their ends."[69] The objective is to "impress other nations with the power one's own nation actually possesses, or with the power it believes, or wants other nations to believe, it possesses."[70] Morgenthau suggested two specific techniques of this policy: diplomacy and display of force. A policy of prestige succeeds when a nation gains such a reputation for power that the actual use of power becomes unnecessary—the political shadow allegedly cast in the form of influence by the attributes or capabilities that constitute power noted earlier in this chapter.

Morgenthau was concerned not only about the quest for power, but also with the conditions for international peace. His concept of international order is closely related to his concept of national interest. The pursuit of national interests that are not essential to national survival contributes to international conflict. In the twentieth century, especially, nations have substituted global objectives for more limited goals that, in Morgenthau's view, constitute the essence of national interest. Modern nationalism, combined with the messianic ideologies of the twentieth century, has obscured the national interest. In the guise of extending communism or making the world safe for democracy, nations intervene in the affairs of regions not vital to their security. For example, Morgenthau opposed U.S. military intervention in Vietnam because Southeast Asia allegedly lay beyond the most vital interests of the United States, and because the United States would have found it impossible, except perhaps with a vast expenditure of resources, to maintain a balance of power in Southeast Asia. In contrast, he expressed great concern about Soviet influence in Cuba because of its geographic location in close proximity to the United States. Thus Morgenthau applied his theoretical analysis to major issues of U.S. Cold War national interest and security, writing extensively on topics of importance.

Even in an international system without the ideologically motivated foreign policies that he saw during the Cold War, Morgenthau held that competition between opposing nation-states is likely. Like many other realists, Morgenthau viewed the balance of power as the most effective technique for managing power in an anarchic international system based on competitive relationships among states. He defined balance of power as (1) a policy aimed at a certain state of affairs, (2) an actual state of affairs, (3) an approximately equal distribution of power, and (4) any distribution of power. However, it is not the balance of power itself, but the international consensus on which it is built that preserves international peace. "Before the balance of power could impose its restraints upon the power aspirations of nations through the mechanical interplay of opposing forces, the competing nations had first to restrain themselves by accepting the system of the balance of power as the common framework of their endeavors." Such a consensus "kept in check the limitless desire for power, potentially inherent, as we know, in all imperialisms, and prevented it from becoming a political actuality."[71]

The international consensus that sustained the balance of power before the twentieth century had ceased to exist. Structural changes in the international system at least drastically limited, if not rendered ineffective, the classical balance of power. In Morgenthau's view, the balance of world power during the Cold War rested with two nations, the United States and the Soviet Union, rather than with several great powers, as it had in earlier eras. He contended that allies of one superpower could shift their alignment to the other superpower, but they could not alter significantly the distribution of power because of their weakness relative to either the United States or the Soviet Union, nor was any third power of sufficient strength as to be capable of intervening on either side and greatly changing the power distribution.

Like the balance of power, diplomacy plays a crucial role in the preservation of peace. According to Morgenthau, the diplomat's role had been diminished by the development of advanced communications, by public disparagement of diplomacy and diplomats, and by the tendency of heads of government to conduct their own negotiations in summit conferences. The rise in importance of international assemblies, the substitution of open diplomacy for secrecy, and the inexperience on the part of the superpowers contributed to the decline of diplomacy during much of the twentieth century. Morgenthau clearly preferred a diplomacy similar to that of the international system before the twentieth century. His views on traditional diplomacy as a means for adjusting national interests resembled those of Sir Harold Nicolson, a leading twentieth-century British diplomat and theoretician of diplomatic practice.[72]

If it is to be revived as an effective technique for managing power, Morgenthau asserted, diplomacy must meet four conditions: (1) It must be divested of its crusading spirit, (2) foreign-policy objectives must be defined in terms of national interest and must be supported with adequate power, (3) nations must view foreign policy from the point of view of other nations, and (4) nations must be willing to compromise on issues that are not vital to them. If diplomacy could be restored to a position of importance, Morgenthau believed, it might not only contribute to peace through accommodation, but also to creating an international consensus on which more adequate world political institutions could be built.

George F. Kennan   Because of the importance of understanding why and how the Cold War ended when it did, it is appropriate to assess the realist writings of George F. Kennan (1904–). As a key architect of containment strategy, Kennan occupies a position of major importance both in the history of the Cold War and in the formulation of early U.S. policy. Writing in 1947, Kennan maintained that "the main element of any U.S. policy toward the Soviet Union must be that of a long-term, patient but firm and vigilant containment of Russian expansive tendencies."[73] Kennan called for a "policy of firm containment, designed to confront the Russians with unalterable counterforce at every point where they show signs of encroaching upon the interest of a peaceful and stable world." Outlining in some detail the principles of such a strategy, Kennan concluded that "the United States has in its power to increase enormously the strains under which Soviet policy must operate, to force upon the Kremlin a far greater degree of moderation and circumspection than it has had to observe in recent years, and in this way to promote tendencies which must eventually find their outlet in either the breakup or the gradual mellowing of Soviet power."[74] Thus Kennan, in retrospect, foresaw with considerable clarity the possibility that, over time, the Soviet Union would face internal contradictions that would lead to its collapse. Such a prognosis is worth recalling in light of the events that unfolded with such rapidity in the years leading into the 1990s that resulted in the disintegration of the Soviet Union and the end of the Cold War. (See pp. 235–236 infra.)

Like other realist theorists of his generation, Kennan based his analysis on an understanding of geography and political relationships. He assumed that military strength on a scale capable of reaching the United States could be mobilized only in a few parts of the world, namely, in "those regions where a major industrial power, enjoying adequate access to raw materials, is combined with large reserves of educated and technically skilled manpower." These geographically important regions include Europe and Asia.[75] In particular, Kennan viewed the relationship between Germany and Russia to be crucial to European and transatlantic security. When they had the means to do so, both had sought to expand into East Central Europe. The key to security in and beyond Europe lay in the ability to develop a relationship that contained Russian and Soviet power and established for Germany and its neighbors an acceptable state of affairs. Given the importance of the German–Russian relationship and Kennan's belief in the pursuit of limited foreign-policy objectives, as discussed here subsequently, Kennan, both in his earlier and later writings, saw no great urgency about the problems of other regions of the world.[76] Kennan objected to efforts to extend the containment doctrine beyond Europe. He objected to the universalization of containment to situations and times different from those during which he formulated it, just as he opposed in his writings other efforts to develop and apply abstract principles to all foreign-policy problems.[77] The United States, he maintained, was largely unable to effect fundamental change in Third World regions because of the "enormity of the problems in relation to available resources" and because of the "necessity of concentrating such resources elsewhere."[78]

In his writings into the 1990s, Kennan reaffirmed his commitment to a United States foreign policy based on strictly limited capabilities and goals. "In an age of nuclear striking power, national security can never be more than relative; and to the extent that it can be assured at all, it must find its sanction in the intentions of rival powers as well as in their capabilities."[79] His conception of United States national interest in the late twentieth century was narrowly defined—perhaps, according to one reviewer, verging on isolationism.[80] His global conception of the role of the United States was based on the reduction of external commitments to an indispensable minimum: "the preservation of the political independence and military security of Western Europe and Japan."[81]

Although George F. Kennan has written extensively about Russia and the Soviet Union, his contributions to realist theory have had the United States as their focus. Kennan divided United States foreign policy into two periods: the first from the American Revolution to the middle nineteenth century, and the second from that time to the midtwentieth century.

In the first period, for which Kennan clearly shows preference, the United States evolved basic goals that found expression in such documents as the Declaration of Independence and the U.S. Constitution. American leaders of state developed a foreign policy designed to achieve their objectives. In defining and shaping the limits of foreign policy, American leaders concluded that

> the first and obvious answer was that one ought to protect the physical intactness of our national life from any external or political intrusions—in other words, that we ought to look to the national security. Secondly, one could see to it that insofar as the activities of our citizens in pursuit of their private interests spilled beyond our borders and into the outside world, the best possible arrangements were made to promote and protect them.[82]

According to Kennan, American goals were fixed, limited, and devoid of pretensions of international benevolence or assumptions of moral superiority or inferiority on the part of one nation or another. Erroneously, in Kennan's estimation, Americans projected to the international arena assumptions based on their own national experience. Because they believed that the political and legal framework of the United States had contributed decisively to domestic tranquillity, American leaders focused on creating a comparable international order in an effort to minimize the likelihood of conflict.

> I see the most serious fault of our past policy formation to lie in something that I might call the legalistic–moralistic approach to international problems. This approach runs like a red skein through our foreign policy of the past fifty years [1900–1950]. It has in it something of the old emphasis on arbitration treaties, something of the Hague Conferences, and schemes for universal disarmament, something of the more ambitious American concepts of international law, something of the Kellogg Pact, something of the idea of a universal "Article 51," something of the belief in World Law and World Government. . . . It is the belief that it should be possible to suppress the chaotic and dangerous aspirations of governments by the acceptance of some system of legal rules and restraints.[83]

Moreover, Kennan asserted that American political leaders in this first period frankly and confidently dealt with power realities.[84] Recognizing the importance of power factors in international politics, the United States strived to restrain the European powers in their territorial ambitions in the Western hemisphere. The United States encouraged movements toward political independence and gave guarantees to new countries that had severed their links with European powers. "All of this involved power considerations. Yet none of it was considered evil or Machiavellian, or cynical. It was simply regarded as a response to the obvious and logical requirements of our situation."[85]

In contrast, Kennan assessed U.S. policy in a later period, when America allegedly lost sight of the power factor and substituted legalistic–moralistic assumptions and objectives for earlier foreign-policy goals. If Americans forgot the power factor in the nineteenth century, this was only natural and inevitable. Geographically separated from Europe, shielded by the British navy from continental European powers, and preoccupied with domestic development, Americans especially in the second half of the nineteenth century cultivated a spirit of romanticism:

> We were satisfied, by this time, with our own borders, and we found it pleasant to picture the outside world as one in which other peoples were similarly satisfied with theirs, or ought to be. With everyone thus satisfied, the main problem of world peace, as it appeared to us, was plainly the arrangement of a suitable framework of contractual engagements in which this happy status quo, the final fruit of human progress, could be sealed and perpetuated. If such a framework could be provided, then, it seemed, the ugly conflicts of international politics would cease to threaten world peace.[86]

In addition to criticizing the American assumption of an international harmony of interests, Kennan asserted that Americans had lost sight of the fact that the rules governing the behavior of individuals are likely to differ drastically from those that exist in relations between states. Governmental behavior at the international level cannot be subjected to the same moral standards that are applied to human behavior:

Moral principles have their place in the heart of the individual in the shaping of his own conduct, whether as a citizen or as a government official. But when the individual's behavior passes through the machinery of political organization and merges with that of millions of other individuals to find its expression in the actions of government, then it undergoes a general transformation, and the same moral concepts are no longer relevant to it. A government is an agent, not a principal; and no more than any other agent may it attempt to be the conscience of its principal.[87]

Nevertheless, even though the use of force in international affairs cannot be completely ruled out, this "does not constitute a reason for being indifferent to the ways in which force is applied—to the moral implications of weapons and their use."[88] Finally, Kennan objected to a concept of international affairs that would lead one nation to consider its own purposes moral and those of its opponent immoral. "A war fought in the name of high moral principle finds no end short of some form of total domination."[89] Thus, the introduction of moralistic principles would encourage nations to pursue unlimited national objectives, to choose total war, and to impose laws of unconditional surrender on defeated opponents. In sum, the pursuit of moralistic principles is incompatible with the pursuit of essentially limited foreign-policy objectives.

Henry A. Kissinger   Another scholar who has drawn from history—in this case, diplomatic history—is Henry A. Kissinger (1923–). As a realist, Kissinger is notable for having contributed both to its literature and to the practice of statecraft as National Security Advisor to Presidents Nixon and Ford and as Secretary of State. Kissinger's theory of international relations is derived from his analysis of early nineteenth-century Europe. In *A World Restored,* based on his doctoral dissertation, Kissinger wrote,

> The success of physical science depends on the selection of the crucial experiment; that of political science in the field of international affairs, on the selection of the crucial period. I have chosen for my topic the period between 1812 and 1822, partly, I am frank to say, because its problems seem to me analogous to those of our day. But I do not insist on this analogy.[90]

Kissinger's fascination with this period lies in the insights that might be provided into the exercise of power by stateleaders such as Castlereagh and Metternich for the development of an international structure that contributed to peace in the century between the Congress of Vienna and the outbreak of World War I. Kissinger studied the nature and quality of political leadership, the impact of domestic political structures on foreign policy, and the relationship between diplomacy and military policy in stable and revolutionary international systems. His objective, as a key architect of U.S. foreign policy in the Nixon–Ford Administrations (1969–1977), was to help bring into existence a *pentapolar* (five-poled) international system based on the economic capabilities of the United States, Japan, and a unifying European Community, together with the political–military capabilities of China and the Soviet Union. Such a system contained asymmetrical power centers in which the United States, because of its vast political–military *and* economic resources, had a unique role to play. What was called the "Nixon Doctrine" had as a central tenet the emergence of a new international system of greater complexity than the older Cold War bipolar structure. Despite its unsurpassed resources, American global power was eroding as a result of the trauma of the Vietnam War, the emergence of the Soviet Union as a nuclear superpower, and the vibrant economies of Europe and Japan. At the same time, the Sino–Soviet conflict created for the United States new opportunities for a triangular diplomacy, in which the United States might develop with Moscow and Beijing, respectively, a better relationship than either could enjoy with the other.[91] As Kissinger (and President Nixon) saw it, the major challenge was to create, as at the time of the Congress of Vienna, an international system based on sufficient major power consensus that each of its principal members had a stake in ensuring the preservation of such a global structure.

Like Morgenthau, Kissinger views with disfavor the injection of ideology into the international system. Ideology not only contributes to the development of unlimited national objectives, but it also eventually creates states that have the goal of overthrowing the existing international system. In the absence of agreement among powers about the framework for the system—or its legitimacy—the conduct of diplomacy becomes difficult, even impossible. Hence, we understand the emphasis in the Nixon–Ford–Kissinger foreign policy on creating a stable structure for the international system: "All nations, adversaries and friends alike, must have a stake in preserving the international system. They must feel that their principles are being respected and their national interests secured. They must, in short, see positive incentive for keeping the peace, not just the dangers of breaking it."[92]

Such a conception for the late twentieth century drew heavily on the theoretical framework developed by Kissinger in *A World Restored.* His quest for a stable international system as a policymaker, moreover, was based on a belief in the need for a "certain equilibrium between potential adversaries"—namely, the United States and the Soviet Union. In his memoir, Kissinger wrote, "If history teaches anything it is that there can be no peace without equilibrium and no justice without restraint."[93] However, the global system of the late twentieth century differed substantially from that of the early nineteenth century described by Kissinger in *A World Restored.*

> The classical concept of balance of power included continual maneuvering for marginal advantages over others. In the nuclear era, this is not realistic because when both sides possess such enormous power, small additional increments cannot be translated into tangible advantage or even usable political strength. And it is dangerous because attempts to seek tactical gains might lead to confrontation which would be catastrophic.[94]

Realist writers, Kissinger concluded, have often sought to separate domestic politics from foreign policy. The conduct of an effective diplomacy is said to be difficult, if not impossible, if it must be subject, in both its conception and its execution, to the continuous scrutiny of public opinion in a democracy such as the United States. Flexibility, characteristic of Kissinger's style of diplomacy, can be achieved in secrecy more easily than in a policy process open to the glare of publicity.

Nevertheless, in Kissinger's theory of international relations, the domestic political structure of states is a key element. His stable and revolutionary system models of international politics, noted earlier, are linked to the domestic political structures of the states in either system. Stable international systems are characterized by actors with domestic political structures based on compatible notions about the means and goals of foreign policies. By definition, governments with stable domestic political structures do not resort to revolutionary or adventuristic foreign policies to restore or preserve domestic cohesion. In contrast, revolutionary systems contain actors with domestic political structures that contrast sharply with each other. Kissinger contends that

> when domestic structures—and the concept of legitimacy on which they are based— differ widely, statesmen can still meet, but their ability to persuade has been reduced for they no longer speak the same language. But when one or more states claims universal applicability for their particular structure, schisms grow deep indeed.[95]

Thus, Kissinger, in effect, links his conception of domestic political structure not only to his models of stable and revolutionary systems, but also to the notion of legitimacy set forth in *A World Restored*. Presumably, domestic political structures that are compatible are conducive to the development of consensus, or legitimacy, at the international level. Those eras of stability among states coincide with the presence, at the national level, of compatible political structures based on a modicum of stability.

NEOREALISM

The realist tradition has furnished an abundant basis for the formation of what is termed a *neorealist approach* to international-relations theory. Neorealism purports to refine and reinvigorate classical realism by developing propositions based on the disaggregation of independent and dependent variables, and by integrating what is termed *classical realist theory* into a contemporary framework based on comparative analysis. A neorealist theory would inject greater rigor into the realist tradition by defining key concepts more clearly and consistently, and developing a series of propositions that could be subjected to empirical testing and investigation. Neorealism has embraced work that is termed *structural realism,* identified with the writings of Kenneth Waltz,[96] as well as a series of efforts explicitly to build on classical realism, and in particular the writings of Hans Morgenthau. For neorealism, power remains a key variable, although it exists less as an end in itself than as a necessary and inevitable component of a political relationship. Among those efforts is the work of Gottfried-Karl Kindermann.[97] According to Kindermann, "just as the instrument of power and of sanctions does not exhaust the nature of law, the nature of politics is also not exhausted by primarily referring to power as its most important tool."[98]

Indeed, the neorealist approach represents an effort not only to draw from classical realism those elements of a theory adequate to the world of the late twentieth century, but also to link conceptually other theoretical efforts. Thus the structural realism of Kenneth Waltz draws heavily on systems constructs, and the neorealism of Kindermann's Munich School of Neorealism has as its basis what is termed a *constellation analysis,* an integrated multimethod system of inquiry. Constellation analysis represents an effort, characteristic of neorealist theory as further examined subsequently herein, to move from the single-factor approach of classical realism (Morgenthau's "concept of interest defined as power") in order to encompass phenomena at each of the levels of analysis extending from the impact of domestic factors on foreign policy to the implications of international systemic structure for interactive patterns. Constellation analysis includes six categories for inquiry and analysis: (1) system and decision, including linkages between domestic and foreign policy and decision making; (2) perception and reality, including the subjective images of decision makers; (3) interest and power, including how decision makers define the role of power in achieving foreign-policy goals, based on conceptions of national interest; (4) norm and advantage, encompassing how legal, moral, or ideological postulates shape the conduct of units of the international system, as well as systemic structures themselves; (5) structures and interdependence, including the effects of structures on levels of interdependence and overall interactive patterns; and (6) cooperation and conflict, or how all of the aforementioned categories shape the strategies of actors toward other actors and lead to patterns of cooperation, conflict, or neutrality. Constellation analysis is intended as a neorealist theory to explain the behavior of individual actors (e.g., states) within an international constellation. Constellation analysis is also designed to analyze multidimensional patterns of interaction within a polycentric setting consisting of two or more monocentric action systems (e.g., states).

While retaining the concept of power as an indispensable variable in explaining political change and dynamics, neorealism, as developed by the Munich school, posits politics, not power, as its key concept, both in domestic politics and at the international level. This form of neorealism has as a basic premise the existence of an international system consisting of interactive elements that are to be studied by reference to concepts derived from classical realist theory, but also based on variables drawn from cross-cultural comparative analysis. To quote again from Kindermann's description: "Neorealism, in other words, proceeds from the assumption that a much higher degree of concrete and quasi-institutionalized cross-disciplinary cooperation is required before essential progress can be made in our ability to analyze and, if possible, to predict political action processes of systems as complex as, for instance, the nation-state and its structurally essential subsystems."[99]

Neorealism has as its focus the international system as the structure that shapes the political relationships that take place among its members. For structural realism, international politics is more than the summation of the foreign policies of states and the external balance of other actors in the system. Thus, Kenneth Waltz argues for a neorealist approach based on patterned relationships among actors in a system that is anarchical. In this respect, drawing on the paradigm of international politics of classical realism, structural realism contains an emphasis on those features of the structure that mold the way in which the components relate to one another.

According to Waltz, the term *structure* connotes the way in which the parts are arranged. In domestic politics, there is said to be a hierarchical relationship, in which units stand in formal differentiation from one another by reference to their degree of authority or the function that they perform. By contrast, the international system lacks comparable governmental institutions. Actors stand in a horizontal relationship with each other, with each state the formal equal (sovereignty) of the other. Waltz defines structure by the principle (hierarchical or anarchic) by which it is organized. Furthermore, Waltz defines structure by the specification of functions of the units. The more hierarchical the system, the greater the differentiation of functions; the more anarchical, the greater the similarity in function among the units.[100] Finally, structure is defined by the distribution of capabilities among the units, including, for example, the extent to which it consists of actors that are similar to or widely different from each other as to the means in their possession. In keeping with classical realism, Waltz treats states as "unitary actors who, at a minimum, seek their own preservation and, at a maximum, strive for universal domination." Therefore, in the realist tradition, he points to the necessary emergence of a balance of power.

The focus of structural realism is the arrangement of the parts of the international system with respect to each other. According to Waltz, "The concept of structure is based on the fact that units differently juxtaposed and combined behave differently and in interacting produce different outcomes."[101] Basic to an anarchic system, by virtue of its structure, is the need for member units to rely on whatever means or arrangements they can generate in order to ensure survival and enhance security. In such a system, based as it is on the principle of self-help, states pursue one or both of two basic courses of action, in keeping with Waltz's approach to structure as a variable conditioning, or circumscribing, political behavior. They engage in internal efforts to increase their political, military, and economic capabilities and to develop effective strategies. They also undertake external attempts to align, or realign, with other actors.

The structure of the system, notably the number of actors and their respective capabilities, shapes the patterns of interaction that will take place, including the number of states aligned with each other in opposing groupings as part of a balance of power. In the anarchical structure, all units confront the minimal need or functional requirement for security, although there are wide variations among them in their respective capabilities for this purpose. Indeed, differences among states in the means possessed for security represent the principal distinguishing characteristic separating one from the other.

In Waltz's perspective, international systems are transfigured by changes in the distribution of capabilities among their units. As structures change, so do interactive patterns among the members, as well as the outcomes that such interactions can be expected to produce. Although capabilities constitute attributes of the units, their distribution among the various units forms a defining characteristic of the structure of the system, and in this case, of structural realism. In sum, central to structural realism, and especially to the approach developed by Waltz, is the proposition that only a structural transformation can alter the anarchical nature of the international system.

If structure defines the arrangement of the parts of the international system in the structural realism of Waltz, what accounts for change in the structure? According to Waltz, structures emerge from the coexistence of the primary political units of a given era. They may be city-states, nations, or empires. His approach to structural realism does not address the question of how and why such political units come into existence at a particular time in history. His concern is not with the units or with the combinations of units at the national or subnational levels. Stated differently, Waltz's structural realism does not approach international-relations theory from a reductionist theoretical perspective. In contrast to structural realism, a reductionist theory would explain international phenomena principally by reference to the actions of the separate states and their internal characteristics. Structural realism in itself, Waltz admits, does not furnish a comprehensive theory of international relations; this would require, for example, a theory of domestic politics because the units shape the system's structure, just as the structure affects the units. Changes in systems, including their transformation, originate not in their structure, but in their parts. Unit-level forces are said to shape the possibilities for systemic change.[102]

Other contemporary neorealist analysis has as its focus change at the international level, based on a reinterpretation of classical realist theory. According to Robert Gilpin, states engage in cost–benefit calculations about alternative courses of action available to them.[103] To the extent that the anticipated benefits exceed the costs, states are likely to attempt to make changes in the system. In this respect, Gilpin attempts to refine the rationality assumption that is contained in classical realist theory. In Gilpin's formulation, a state will attempt to change the international system by means of territorial, political, or economic expansion until the marginal costs of additional change become equal to or exceed the marginal benefits. An international system is in a condition of equilibrium to the extent that its major actors are satisfied with the territorial, political, and economic status quo. It is acknowledged that every state or group in the system could benefit from some form of change; therefore, the costs of changing form the principal barriers to disruptive or destabilizing action. The distribution of power represents the principal means for controlling the behavior of states. Dominant states maintain a network of relationships within the system for this purpose.

In deciding on foreign policies that would produce change in the international system, Gilpin suggests, states usually make trade-offs among various objectives. They do not attempt to achieve one goal at the sacrifice of all others, but instead engage in a *satisficing* (sic) approach, designed to attain various combinations of desired results.[104] Historically, states have had as their goal the conquest of territory that, before the Industrial Revolution and the advent of advanced technology, represented the principal means for enhancing security or wealth. Furthermore, states strive to increase their influence over other states by means of threats, coercion, alliances, and spheres of influence. Finally, an increasingly important goal of states lies in the extension of influence in the global economy. In keeping with the satisficing principle, subgoals are by no means mutually exclusive. Among the objectives of states, Gilpin asserts, those considered to be most important are defined as vital interests on whose behalf the state is willing to go to war.

International systems are said to undergo essentially three types of change. First and of fundamental importance is an alteration in the nature of the actors or the types of entities—empires, states, or other units—that compose a particular international system, which Gilpin terms *systems change*. Examples include the rise and decline of the Greek city-state system, the medieval European state system, and the emergence of the nuclear state system leading to the present era. What, it is asked, are the particular sociopolitical, economic, and technological factors that give rise to the organizational framework with which groups or individuals advance their interests? A system changes as the cost–benefit ratio of membership in the existing system is altered.

A second dimension of change has as its focus not the system itself but instead the components within which change takes place. All international systems are characterized by the rise and fall of powerful states that shape patterns of international interactions and establish the rules by which the system operates. Thus, the distribution of power within the system is altered. Here, the emphasis is placed not on the rise and fall of international systems but instead on the growth and decline of their constituent elements—that is, the greater or lesser powers and, in particular, the replacement of one dominant entity by another such actor. Whereas classical realist theory was derived largely from the European state system, a comparative study of international systems including earlier, non-Western systems would yield an understanding of how and why systemic change takes place. Finally, the third element of this neorealist theory of change has as its focus the nature of its members' political, economic, or sociocultural interactions. In sum, the study of change embraces the system itself, its constituent elements, and the interactive process among them.

The propensity of states, or other actors, to seek to extend their territorial control, political influence, and economic domination is said to be a function of their power. Such a process, according to Gilpin, continues until the marginal costs of further change equal or exceed the marginal benefits. As the size of the state and the extent of its control grow, there eventually comes a point at which the cost expansion relative to the derived benefits limits the capacity for control and for further expansion. A system in which the cost of expansion equals or exceeds the perceived benefits is said to be in equilibrium. By the same token, an equilibrium, once reached, is itself subject to change because there is a tendency for the economic costs of maintaining the status quo to increase faster than the economic capacity to support it. Therefore, disequilibrium represents a gap between the units of the international system and the capacity of the dominant states to maintain the existing system.

Such is the condition that results in the decline of a principal actor, a phenomenon that can be observed historically in the Roman, Byzantine, Chinese, and British empires in successive ages. In place of the one dominant actor, there eventually arises a new equilibrium reflecting the altered distribution of power. As its relative power grows, a rising state attempts to extend its control of territory and to increase its influence, usually at the expense of the dominant, but declining, power. The power in decline has essentially several options: to attempt to increase capabilities to match the rising unit; to reduce commitments and thus to acquiesce, gracefully, in altered circumstances; to enter into alliances or other arrangements with other powers; or to make concessions to the rising power. However, Gilpin suggests, the primary means by which the issue of disequilibrium has been resolved throughout history has been by war, the result of which has usually been a redistribution of power between the victorious and the vanquished. Thus, international politics consists of forces leading to conflict or accommodation in a succession of international systems marked by change. "Ultimately," Gilpin concludes,

> international politics still can be characterized as it was by Thucydides: the interplay of impersonal forces and great leaders. . . . World politics is still characterized by the struggle of political entities for power, prestige, and wealth in a coalition of global anarchy. Nuclear weapons have not made the resort to force irrelevant; economic interdependence does not guarantee that cooperation will triumph over conflict; a global community of common values and outlook has yet to displace international anarchy.[105]

The neorealist theory developed by Kenneth Waltz sparked an unfolding debate that has dominated the international-relations theoretical landscape since the early 1980s. Much of the discussion has focused on the boundary between the system and the unit levels. Central to Waltz's theory is his assertion that international relations can be divided into system and unit levels of analysis, with what he terms *structure* representing the system level of analysis. The focus of Waltz's theoretical effort, as already noted, lies at the system level. Therefore, he gives relatively little attention to unit factors because they lie outside his definition of structure. According to critics, as a result of his emphasis on system structures, Waltz has neglected the role of the units, as well as the impact of the structure of the units themselves on the behavioral patterns of their members. If structure at the international systemic level shapes actor behavior at the state unit level, why, it is asked, does not structure influence how the members of the unit themselves behave?

This question includes the assumption, also set forth by Waltz's neoliberal institutionalist critics, that a theory of international politics must include the domestic politics of the units, to the extent that they shape foreign policy. According to such a conclusion, Waltz can be faulted either for drawing too narrowly the conceptual boundary between the system and its units or for having too narrowly defined the term *structure* and assuming that the system level contains only structure. According to neoliberal institutionalists, for example, international organizations are systemic-level phenomena that may shape system structure. The extent to which they do so represents at the very least a question to be addressed in the development of theory. According to Barry Buzan, who, together with Charles Jones and Richard Little, have been in the forefront of the effort both to refine neorealism and to synthesize neorealist and neoliberal institutionalist theory, Waltz's focus on power and its distribution at the structure level "heavily discounts the authority and organizational dimensions of international parties."[106] Instead, it is suggested that, in addition to power, there is general agreement that "rules, regimes, and international institutions need to be brought into the definition of international political structure."[107]

Such a critique of Waltz leads logically to the proposition that system structure contains a series of variables, including, but not confined to, power and its distribution in the form of capabilities among the units of the system. Buzan, Jones, and Little introduce what they term *deep structure,* by which they mean that political structure encompasses anarchy (no central government) as well as hierarchy (central government over the units). Buzan, Jones, and Little's deep structure encompasses organizational principles based on hierarchy and anarchy. If the units of the system are similar, their relationship to each other is based logically on sovereignty, with each defining itself as having ultimate authority and independence. If the units are different in terms of the governmental functions that they perform, or seek to undertake, this means that they do not have, or claim to have, complete sovereignty. To the extent that units are sovereign over a limited sphere, they exist in a hierarchical setting, or at least in a structure in which organizations such as the European Community/Union and the United Nations "undertake some governmental, or at least government-like, functions."[108]

Furthermore, Buzan, Jones, and Little suggest that deep structure includes not only power and institutions, but also rules and norms. System structure contains what is termed the *international political system,* as well as the international societal system, with its emphasis on cultural, legal, and normative behavioral dimensions. Although the sovereign state represents the dominant unit in the modern international system, the state is not the exclusive basis for government. To the extent that other factors shape the structure, Waltz's conception of system structure, however useful as a point of departure, must be broadened within and beyond the political sector. According to Buzan, Jones, and Little, those additional sectors, beyond the political, that would be necessary to understand international-system structure would include the economic and societal as well as the strategic (by which they mean the exercise of control by coercion).

Having opened Waltz's conception of system structure in this fashion, Buzan, Jones, and Little assert that the structural and unit levels of analysis are linked and that, therefore, a theory of structural realism must develop such linkages. Whereas Waltz largely excludes the unit level, Buzan, Jones, and Little maintain that a theory of international relations requires as great rigor at the unit level as at the system-structure level. Neorealist, or structural realist, theory can be adapted to accommodate such a broadening of its scope. Waltz had suggested that the unit level provides two sources of explaining international behavior: the attributes of the units and the interactions among them. Whereas Waltz confines such explanations to the unit level, Buzan, Jones, and Little attempt to link the unit and the system-structure levels. They assert that "explanation of behavior in terms of possession of a capability by a unit is quite different from explanation in terms of the distribution of a capability within the system."[109] Stated differently, they maintain that how states choose to use their capabilities is not the same as how actors are ranked in the system structure, according to their respective capabilities. At the unit level, there are action–reaction patterns that form a process. How power is employed, as well as the outcome of the interactive process, should be distinguished from power as a capability, or from power in its static, bean-counting, dimension, to recall the discussion of power earlier in this chapter. Leaving largely intact Waltz's boundary between the system structure and unit levels, Buzan, Jones, and Little seek to clarify the conceptual boundary between the two levels and to develop a clearer understanding between power at the unit and the system-structure levels.

Buzan, Jones, and Little also suggest that there are unit capabilities, the nature of which affects system structure. Specifically, these include technology and shared norms and organizations. Technology provides an important means by which units interact, just as norms and organizations shape the systemic setting within which interaction takes place. Technology produces interactive patterns and opportunities illustrated by the difference between those available in the era of horse-drawn carriage and the sailing ship, contrasted with the jumbo jet and global telecommunications and information networks. To the extent that shared norms exist, institutions can be built that may in turn strengthen and broaden patterns of interaction. According to Buzan, Jones, and Little, the systemic dimension of interaction, in contrast with the unit or structure, is largely missing from classical realism and from Waltz's neorealism and necessarily forms a component of a broadened neorealist–structural-realist theory.

This effort to rethink and expand neorealist theory includes a focus on the relationship between system transformation and system continuity. If world history unfolds within an anarchic setting and if world history nevertheless exhibits dramatic systemic change, it follows that neorealist theory—and anarchy in particular—"needs to be treated as a differentiated structural property which can undergo transformation."[110] According to Buzan, Jones, and Little, it is necessary to move beyond Waltz's identification of structure as the defining characteristic of the international system. Instead, the states as units of the international system themselves are shaped by their respective structures. Those decision makers, or agents of the state, face not only the constraints imposed by the structure of the international system, but also the constraints imposed by the structure of the state itself. From distinctive domestic settings, Buzan, Jones, and Little suggest, greatly differing types of states may emerge. Contrary to Waltz's assertion, the anarchic structure of the international system does not produce homogeneous units. The heterogeneity of the international system at any time in history can be explained partially by the fact that domestic structures affect the units that form the international system. The types of interaction among units and their foreign policies in general are shaped by domestic constraints.

The structural realism developed by Buzan, Jones, and Little rejects the realist–neorealist assumption that anarchy characterizes only the international system and that in contrast, the units are hierarchical in their domestic structures. Instead, according to these structural realists, units have differing structures, extending from empires to republics and including states as well as nonstate actors. Furthermore, in their international actions, the units exhibit cooperative as well as competitive behavior. They develop alliances, coalitions, regimes, norms, and institutions for international cooperation. Such features, common to the international system, are said to be explainable by reference to the structure of the international system.

Although the anarchic society produces states that are sovereign, this sovereignty does not mean that anarchy is incompatible with cooperation and interdependence. Thus, Buzan, Jones, and Little attempt to broaden neorealist theory to encompass competition *and* cooperation. They believe that structural-realist theory, with its emphasis on system structure as well as on unit structure and the relationship between domestic and international systemic constraints, provides a basis for developing a comprehensive theory of international relations. The domestic structure of states, together with the international systemic level of interactive capabilities such as technology, shapes the interactive capacity of the system, with consequences for its structure. Change and continuity are affected by interactive elements between the international system and its units. The neorealist theory of Waltz, as broadened by Buzan, Jones, and Little, nevertheless retains structural analysis as its core theoretical concept, together with an international system based on anarchy but still including patterns of cooperation.

Thus, the neorealist reformulation of realist theory includes an effort to bridge domestic and international politics and specifically to relate domestic structures to international structures. Although survival represents the ultimate goal of the state, according to realist theory, how the state achieves this objective depends on the ability of its leaders, in the words of Michael Mastanduno, David A. Lake, and G. John Ikenberry, to "meet and overcome challenges from, and maintain the support of, societal groups and conditions."[111] The leaders of states seek control over resources to advance their international and domestic agendas and to preserve their leadership legitimacy. States attempt to accumulate economic wealth and technological strength, for both the international and the domestic benefits that may result. States engage in international strategies termed *external extraction* and *external validation.*[112] *External extraction* refers to the accumulation of resources from beyond the state borders, such as access to global markets or resources, that can be useful in achieving domestic objectives. *External validation* is defined as the attempts made by leaders to make use of their authoritative status within the international community to enhance their domestic status. For example, the ability of the leadership of a new state to gain international recognition is often seen as an essential basis for strengthening domestic legitimacy. Because the state is central to neorealist theory, what is needed is a broadening of neorealist theory to encompass a recognition of the fact that states participate simultaneously in international and domestic arenas. Neorealist theory, it is suggested, needs to take into account the proposition that states pursue goals in one arena that affect their pursuit in another arena. States may respond to international events through domestic actions and may attempt to solve domestic problems through actions at the international level. The combinations of strategies at each of these levels, together with the relationship between such strategies and international–domestic structures, represent an important emerging dimension of neorealist theory.

The effort to refine neorealist theory encompasses the reformulation of power, as well as the development of a greater understanding of the conditions under which cooperation rather than competition will be chosen as the preferred option. Addressing such issues, Charles L. Glaser sets forth what is termed *contingent realism,* in which he proceeds from realist–structural assumptions but reaches different conclusions from those reached by realists and structural realists.[113] Under a broad range of contingencies, states, in a self-help system, decide to cooperate as a means of resolving the security dilemma. According to Glaser, a state will weigh the advantages and risks of an arms race against the benefits and costs of entering an arms-control agreement. To the extent that arms competition is perceived as diminishing rather than contributing to security, adversaries are likely to prefer cooperative arrangements, such as arms-control agreements. In this sense, such states engage in self-help but in a cooperative rather than a competitive form. This theoretical analysis is carried one step further to include a rethinking of power, the focus of which is shifted to military capabilities with an emphasis on considerations of offense and defense. Glaser suggests that a state seeking security in an anarchic setting, deciding whether to pursue competitive or cooperative strategies, confronts two fundamental questions: (1) Which will provide the necessary military forces to deter an adversary or to provide defense in the event of deterrence failure? (2) What levels and types of capabilities will provide for one state's security without threatening the other side's ability to deter and defend? Contingent-realist theory emphasizes what is termed the *offense–defense balance*, defined as the ratio of the cost of offensive forces to the cost of defensive capabilities. According to contingent-realist theory, the greater the emphasis on defense, the less the need for arms control. Because large increases or asymmetries in offensive forces are needed to gain significant military advantage, arms control will be necessary as a means of restraining arms races. In addressing such issues, contingent realism opens neorealist–structural-realist theory to inputs from theories of cooperative behavior, theories of arms control, and game theory. To the extent that such theories are integrated, we have enlarged the basis for a comprehensive theory of international relations.

REALISM–NEOREALISM: LIMITATIONS AND CONTRIBUTIONS

The neorealist–structural-realist reformulations of classical realist theory in themselves represent an ongoing critique of what may be termed a realist tradition in international-relations theory. To trace the evolution of realist theory from its classical to contemporary versions is to set forth critiques in the form of refinements. Neorealist and structural-realist theory sought both to deepen and to broaden classical realist theory. Specifically, this meant the development of greater rigor in the effort theoretically to define and to link system structure to actor behavior. It also encompassed efforts to assess the meaning of domestic structures for the foreign policies of states in a self-help international system. Last but not least, without abandoning power as a centrally important variable in an anarchic society, an effort has been made not only to define and measure power, but also to delineate its limitations.

Recent critiques of realism, moreover, have focused on its relevance for explaining the end of the Cold War and the post–Cold War world. It is said that realist theory, as the dominant paradigm of the Cold War era, based on a struggle for power between the United States and the Soviet Union, does not adequately account for the collapse of the Soviet Union and the withdrawal of Soviet military forces from Central Europe without a shot having been fired. Juxtaposed, however, is a realist explanation of the collapse of the Soviet Union, based on the proposition that the Cold War was the result of the rise of Soviet power, which posed a perceived threat to the United States and its allies. As long as the Soviet leadership believed that the Soviet Union could maintain the power to compete, the competition continued. Once the Soviet leadership, after Mikhail Gorbachev came to power, concluded that it no longer had the capabilities needed for competition with the West, the Cold War came to an end. During the Cold War, the Soviet Union was a state attempting to challenge the hegemonic position of the United States. It failed to do this because of the distribution of power, which by the end of the Cold War had shifted in favor of the United States.[114] In short, the essential premise set forth in the containment strategy, outlined by George F. Kennan, was fulfilled.

Because of its rich heritage and multiple intellectual sources, realist theory is said to rest on what has been termed a *fractured foundation,* the effect of which is to undermine realism's structural integrity. According to Thomas R. Cusack and Richard J. Stoll, and as set forth in this chapter, there are major inconsistencies and disagreements among realists about (1) the system level, (2) the actors within the system, and (3) certain technical relations. Cusack and Stoll, themselves part of the contemporary effort to provide a critique and revision of realist theory, make use of computer simulation to examine models of international systems, or what they term *realpolitik systems.*[115]

At the international-system level, there is a diversity of views among realists, according to Cusack and Stoll, about the extent to which moderation and restraint, for example in pursuit of national interest, are essential requirements for, or the inevitable consequences of, a system based on principles of realist theory. They suggest, furthermore, that there is debate or confusion among realists about how important the distribution of power is, as well as what form it should take, together with the significance of uneven patterns of growth among the actors of the system. At the actor level, there are said to be disputed assumptions about the fundamental characteristics of the actors that constitute the system. Some realists view the state as a rational actor and military entity, from which domestic factors are largely excluded. Others have questioned the assumption of the state as a rational actor, the decisions and policies of which are purposeful.

The differences in technical relations, noted previously, to which Cusack and Stoll refer, include the extent to which war manifests itself in behavioral patterns among states and its role in the survival of the international system and its units. Realists do not have a commonly accepted theoretical understanding of the conditions under which states resort to armed combat, contrasted with attempts to find solutions other than war to resolve major differences. Last but not least, neorealist theory, notably in the formulation developed by Waltz, does not account for structural change. As John Lewis Gaddis suggests, if it is true that systemic structures affect the distribution of capabilities among units, and if shifts in this distribution can produce changes in such structures, is it not the case that those shifts are the result of changes in the capabilities of states within the system?[116] Actions within the units, to the extent that they shape the capabilities of states as units, then have important implications for international systemic structure.

Because classical realist and neorealist–structural-realist theory is said often to provide an explanation of state behavior in an anarchic system, it is appropriate to test its essential propositions in the context of the international system. In other words, if we examine in historical detail the period between the formation of the modern state system, following the Treaty of Westphalia in 1648, and the twentieth century, do we find that the essential premises advanced by realist theory are substantiated? Without having amassed historical evidence for or against realist theory, Paul Schroeder concludes that in most cases, states did not respond to "crucial threats to their security" by resorting to self-help, defined as the use of their own power, alone or in combination with that of other states in the form of a balance of power.[117] Instead, other strategies were more likely to be employed, including simply ignoring the threat, hiding from the threat by declaring neutrality or by adopting a strictly defensive position, or withdrawing into isolation. Other efforts included attempts to surmount international anarchy by creating institutional arrangements based on international consensus. Yet another approach came in the form of *bandwagoning,* joining the stronger side in order to receive advantage in the form of protection, even at the cost of sacrificing some independence.

Such behavior, according to Schroeder, has been more common than resorting to self-help in the form of balancing, especially in the case of smaller states. For example, during the Napoleonic wars, states large and small at some point either hid or engaged in bandwagoning rather than fighting or balancing France. In the years leading to World War II, states such as the Netherlands, Denmark, and Norway refused either to arm or to join an alliance to oppose Nazi Germany. Instead, they remained strictly neutral. Great Britain and France sought not to balance, but instead to appease, Germany by abandoning Czechoslovakia, which otherwise might have contributed to a balance of power against Germany. Schroeder concludes that the major problem with neorealism is its effort to prescribe and predict a "determinate order for history without having adequately checked this against the historical evidence." The result is said to be a theory that obstructs new insights and hypotheses, while overlooking "large bodies of inconvenient facts."[118]

For several reasons, the national-interest concept has been the object of criticism. According to one critique, "That national interest is a necessary criterion of policy is obvious and unilluminating. No statesman, no publicist, no scholar would seriously argue that foreign policy ought to be conducted in opposition to, or in disregard of, the national interest."[119] Moreover, it is difficult to give operational meaning to the concept of national interest. Stateleaders are constrained, or given freedom, by many forces in interpreting the national interest. They are often the captive of their predecessors' policies. They interpret national interest as a result of their cultural training, values, and the data made available to them as decision makers. According to Michael Joseph Smith, realists, having adopted Max Weber's ethic of responsibility, discussed earlier in this chapter, have not presented a competent set of criteria for judging responsibility. Although, and perhaps because, they minimize the relevance of ethics to international relations, they appear not to recognize that "their judgment of morality and their definition of the national interest rested on their own hierarchy of values."[120]

Among the focal points of neorealist analysis is an effort to reformulate and refine the national-interest concept to encompass a perceived calculus of benefits and losses, in accordance with alternative posited goals for the state. Specifically, the regime concept (described in Chapter 10) includes an attempt to adapt national interest to a theoretical framework related to state motivation in the formation of what are defined as international regimes for collaboration or cooperation.

Realist writers, it has been noted, have been criticized for their efforts to draw from the Eurocentric system of the past a series of political concepts for the analysis of a vastly different contemporary global international system. The pursuit of limited national objectives, the separation of foreign policy from domestic politics, the conduct of secret diplomacy, the use of balance of power as a technique for the management of power, and the pleas for nations to place reduced emphasis on ideology as a conditioner of international conduct have little relevance to the international system today. By urging that nations return to the practices of an earlier period, some realist writers overestimate the extent to which such change in the present international system is possible. If nations obey laws of nature, which the realist purports to have discovered, why is it necessary to urge them, as realists do, to return to practices supposedly based on such laws?[121] Although history provides many examples of international behavior that substantiate classical realist theory, historical data offer deviant cases. In calling on stateleaders to alter their behavior, the realist becomes normative in theoretical orientation and fails to provide an adequate explanation as to why political leaders sometimes do not adhere to realist tenets in foreign policy.

In emphasizing power as the principal motivation for political behavior, realist theory has not produced an acceptable definition of power. Similarly, the term *balance of power* has numerous meanings, as discussed in Chapter 1. There are formidable problems of measuring power, as noted earlier in this chapter. There is no common unit into which power is converted for measurement in realist writings. Moreover, power is necessarily related to the objective for which it is to be used. The amount and type of power vary with national goals. In addition, realists have been criticized for allegedly having placed too much emphasis on power, to the relative exclusion of other important variables. In Stanley Hoffmann's view, "It is impossible to subsume under one word variables as different as: power as a condition of policy and power as a criterion of policy; power as a potential and power in use; power as a sum of resources and power as a set of processes."[122]

Neorealism and, specifically, structural realism, have encountered several criticisms, including an alleged disregard for history as a process that is continually undergoing redefinition, in which individuals contribute to the molding of each successive era. In this respect, the neorealist is considered to have departed from classical realism, which held that the stateleader was shaped by but also had an important influence on history. Far from being the captives of a particular system, the individual person holds the potential to be the master of structures, not simply the object. Moreover, neorealism is faulted for having presumably reduced politics to those dimensions that are conducive to interpretation by reference to rational behavior under various structural constraints. Because of its focus on structure, neorealism is said to have ignored the social basis and social limits of power. It is said that power cannot be reduced to capabilities; instead, power consists also of psychological factors such as public morale and political leadership, as well as situational factors and the extent to which power is exercised within a consensual, as contrasted with a conflictual, framework. The state-as-actor world of neorealism is faulted for having imputed to the state the role of unitary actor, the behavior of which is shaped by the structure of the international system. Neorealism, it is suggested, was statist before it was structuralist.[123] In response, neorealists deny that realism is, in fact, structural determinism. Although structural elements exert a powerful constraining influence on political behavior, the neorealist does not consider all of human political conduct to be determined by the structure within which the polity is organized, nor does the neorealist accept the criticism that the state-as-actor world represents a negation of the role of those individuals or groups of persons who act as the actual decision makers.[124]

Despite its critics, realism ranks as the most important attempt thus far to isolate and focus on a key variable in political behavior—namely, power—and to develop a theory of international relations. If only as a result of having stated its premises in such bold fashion, realism has painted a sharply contoured global theoretical landscape that can be (as it has been) modified by another generation of theory builders. In Robert O. Keohane's words, "Realism provides a good starting point for the analysis of cooperation and discord, since its tautological structure and its pessimistic assumptions about individual and state behavior serve as barriers against wishful thinking."[125] According to R. B. J. Walker, political realism should be viewed "less as a coherent theoretical position in its own right than as the site of a great many contested claims and metaphysical disputes."[126] For example, realism, Walker points out, and as this chapter illustrates, contains structural and historicist traditions. To a far greater extent than their predecessors, realist students of international relations attempted to construct theory from historical data. In addition to their efforts to determine how national actors in fact behaved, realists developed a body of normative theory, with prescriptions particularly for policymakers. The problems to which realist thought has addressed itself—the interaction and behavior of human beings as decision makers, the nature of power, the goals of foreign policy, the techniques for measuring and managing power, the impact of environmental factors on political behavior, the purposes and practices that ought to guide political leaders, and the impact of structures of alternative international systems—are central both to the study of international politics and to the practice of statecraft. Because realist theory, both in its classical and contemporary forms, addresses issues that are crucially important to international relations, its impact has been pervasive and enduring.

NOTES

1. Thomas R. Cusack and Richard J. Stoll, *Exploring Realpolitik: Probing International Relations Theory with Computer Simulation* (Boulder, CO: Lynne Rienner Publishers, 1990), p. 53.
2. John H. Herz, "Idealist Internationalism and the Security Dilemma," *World Politics*, 5(2) (January 1950), 157–180. See also Paul R. Viotti and Mark V. Kauppi, *International Relations Theory: Realism, Pluralism, Globalism* (New York: Macmillan Publishing Company, 1987), p. 49.

3. David A. Baldwin, "Neoliberalism, Neorealism, and World Politics," in David A. Baldwin, ed., *Neorealism and Neoliberalism: The Contemporary Debate* (New York: Columbia University Press, 1993), pp. 9–10. See also Ronan P. Palan and Brook M. Blair, "On the Idealist Origins of the Realist Theory of International Relations," *Review of International Studies,* 19 (4) (October 1993), 385–400.

4. E. H. Carr, *The Twenty-Years' Crisis, 1919–1939: An Introduction to the Study of International Relations* (London: Macmillan, 1939; New York: Harper & Row [Torchbooks], 1964).

5. Arnold Wolfers, "Statesmanship and Moral Choice," *World Politics,* I (January 1949), 175–195, and "Political Theory and International Relations," in Arnold Wolfers and Lawrence Martin, eds., *The Anglo-American Tradition in Foreign Affairs* (New Haven, CT: Yale University Press, 1956); Kenneth W. Thompson, "The Limits of Principle in International Politics: Necessity and the New Balance of Power," *Journal of Politics,* XX (August 1958), 437–467. George F. Kennan has commented as follows on the American legalistic–moralistic approach to international problems: "Our national genius, our sense of decency, our feeling for compromise and law, our frankness and honesty—had not these qualities succeeded in producing on this continent a society unparalleled for its lack of strain and violence? There was no reason why the outside world, with our assistance, should not similarly compose itself to a life without violence." From *Realities of American Foreign Policy,* excerpted in David L. Larson, ed., *The Puritan Ethic in United States Foreign Policy* (Princeton, NJ: Van Nostrand, 1966), p. 34.

6. Adam Smith and other eighteenth-century economists, following in the individualistic steps of John Locke, taught that people in a competitive system, when they seek their own private gain, are led by an "invisible hand" to promote the interest of the whole society.

7. For an extensive examination of its origins, see Torbjörn L. Knutsen, *A History of International Relations Theory: An Introduction* (Manchester, England: Manchester University Press, 1992), especially pp. 11–24.

8. E. H. Carr, *The Twenty Years' Crisis, 1919–1939: An Introduction to the Study of International Relations* (London: Macmillan and Company Ltd., 1962), p. 9.

9. Ibid., p. 5.

10. G. Lowes Dickinson, *Causes of International War* (London: Swarthmore Press Ltd., 1920). Other works illustrative of the literature of utopian international theory include Norman Angell, *The Great Illusion* (see Chapter 1, Note 44); Nicholas Murray Butler, *Between Two Worlds: Interpretations of the Age in Which We Live* (New York: Charles Scribner's Sons, 1934); Nicholas Murray Butler, *A World in Ferment: Interpretations of the War for a New World* (New York: Charles Scribner's Sons, 1917); G. Lowes Dickinson, *The International Anarchy, 1904–1914* (New York and London: Century Company, 1926); Harold Josephson, *James T. Shotwell and the Rise of Internationalism in America* (Cranbury, NJ: Associated University Presses, 1975); Gilbert Murray, *The Ordeal of This Generation* (New York and London: Harper & Row, 1929); James T. Shotwell, *The Autobiography of James T. Shotwell* (New York: Bobbs-Merrill Company, 1961); James T. Shotwell, *The History of History* (New York: Columbia University Press, 1939); Alfred Zimmern, *America & Europe and Other Essays* (Freeport, NY: Books for Libraries Press, 1929, reprinted 1969); Alfred Zimmern, *The League of Nations and the Rule of Law, 1918–1935* (New York: Russell & Russell, 1939, reissued 1969). See Alfred Zimmern, "The Problem of Collective Security" in *Neutrality and Collective Security,* Harris Foundation Lectures, 1936 (Chicago: University of Chicago, 1936), pp. 3–89.

11. E. H. Carr, op. cit. p. 62; see especially chaps. 1–6.
12. Ibid., p. 92.
13. Ibid., pp. 5–6.
14. Ibid., pp. 10, 20–21, 93–94.
15. Robert O. Keohane, "Institutional Theory and the Realist Challenge After the Cold War," in David A. Baldwin, ed., *Neorealism and Neoliberalism: The Contemporary Debate* (New York: Columbia University Press, 1993), pp. 294–295. See also Robert Powell, "Anarchy in International Relations Theory: The Neorealist–Neoliberal Debate," *International Organization,* 48(2), (Spring 1994), 313–344; Charles W. Kegley, Jr., ed., *Controversies in International Relations Theory: Realism and the Neoliberal Challenges* (New York: St. Martin's Press, 1995); Ethan B. Kapstein, "Is Realism Dead? The Domestic Sources of International Politics," *International Organization,* 49 (4) (Autumn 1995), 751–774.
16. John J. Mearsheimer, "The False Promise of International Institutions," *International Security,* 19(3), (Winter 1994–1995), 14. See also John J. Mearsheimer, "Back to the Forties: Instability in Europe After the Cold War," *International Security,* 15(1), (Summer 1990), 5–56; Joseph M. Grieco, "Anarchy and the Limits of Cooperation: A Realist Critique of the Newest Liberal Institutionalism," in David A. Baldwin, ed., *Neorealism and Neoliberalism: The Contemporary Debate* (New York: Columbia University Press, 1993), pp. 116–140. See also Robert O. Keohane and Lisa L. Martin, "The Promise of Institutionalist Theory," *International Security,* 20(1) (Summer 1995), 39–62; John Gerard Ruggie, "The False Premise of Realism," *International Security,* 20(1) (Summer 1995), 62–71. Charles A. Kupchan and Clifford A. Kupchan, "The Promise of Collective Security," *International Security,* 20 (1) (Summer 1995), 52–61. For a collection of recent articles from *International Security* related to neorealist theory, see Michael E. Brown, Sean M. Lynn-Jones, and Steven E. Miller, eds., *The Perils of Anarchy: Contemporary Realism and International Security: An International Security Reader* (Cambridge MA: MIT Press, 1995).
17. Thucydides, *History of the Peloponnesian War,* M. I. Finley, ed.; Rex Warner, trans. (Harmondsworth, England: Penguin, 1972), p. 49. For a critical view of realist–neorealist uses of the work of Thucydides, see Daniel Garst, "Thucydides and Neorealism," *International Studies Quarterly,* 33 (1989), 3–27. See also Steven Forde, "International Realism and the Science of Politics: Thucydides, Machiavelli, and Neorealism," *International Studies Quarterly,* 39 (2) (June 1995), 141–160.
18. Thucydides, *History of the Peloponnesian War* (Harmondsworth, England: Penguin, 1980), p. 402.
19. Niccolò Machiavelli, *The Prince* (Harmondsworth, England: Penguin, 1961), chaps. 10–14.
20. Thomas Hobbes, *Leviathan,* edited and with an introduction by Michael Oakeshott (Oxford, England: Basil Blackwell, 1946), p. 64.
21. Ibid., p. 109.
22. Ibid.
23. George W. F. Hegel, *Philosophy of Right* (Oxford, England: Clarendon, 1942), p. 264; Friederich Meinecke, *Machiavellism: The Doctrine of Raison d'Etat and Its Place in Modern History* (New York: Praeger, 1965), p. 360.
24. Max Weber, *Economy and Society,* Guenther Roth and Claus Wittich, eds. (2 vols.) (Berkeley and Los Angeles: University of California Press, 1978), p. 911.
25. Henry Kissinger, *Diplomacy* (New York: Simon and Schuster, 1994), p. 20.
26. Robert Gilpin, *U.S. Power and the Multinational Corporation: The Political Economy of Foreign Direct Investment* (New York: Basic Books, 1975), p. 24.

27. David A. Baldwin, "Neoliberalism, Neorealism, and World Politics," in David A. Baldwin, ed., *Neorealism and Neoliberalism: The Contemporary Debate* (New York: Columbia University Press, 1993), p. 16.

28. Kenneth Waltz, *Theory of International Politics* (Reading, MA: Addison-Wesley, 1979), p. 192.

29. Kenneth Waltz, *Theory of International Politics,* p 131.

30. Nicholas J. Spykman, *America's Strategy in World Politics* (New York: Harcourt Brace, 1942), p. 11.

31. Robert Strausz-Hupé and Stefan T. Possony, *International Relations* (New York: McGraw-Hill, 1954), pp. 5–6.

32. Arnold Wolfers, *Discord and Collaboration* (Baltimore: Johns Hopkins Press, 1962), p. 103.

33. John. W. Burton, *International Relations: A General Theory* (New York: Cambridge University Press, 1967), p. 46.

34. Robert Gilpin, *War and Change in World Politics* (New York: Cambridge University Press, 1981), p. 33.

35. Charles P. Kindleberger, *Power and Money: The Politics of International Economics and the Economics of International Politics* (New York: Basic Books, 1970), pp. 56, 65.

36. Ibid., p. 56.

37. Klaus Knorr, *The Power of Nations: The Political Economy of International Relations* (New York: Basic Books, 1975), p. 3. See also by the same author, *Power and Wealth: Military Power and Potential* (Lexington, MA: D. C. Heath, 1970); *On the Uses of Military Power in the Nuclear Age* (Princeton, NJ: Princeton University Press, 1966).

38. Klaus Knorr, *The Power of Nations: The Political Economy of International Relations,* op. cit., p. 4.

39. Ibid.

40. Ibid., p. 10.

41. David A. Baldwin, "Power Analysis and World Politics: New Trends Versus Old Tendencies," *World Politics,* XXXI(2) (January 1979), 177. See also Oran R. Young, "Interdependencies in World Politics," *International Journal* (Autumn 1969), 726–750.

42. David Baldwin, "Interdependence and Power: A Conceptual Analysis," *International Organization,* 34(4) (Autumn 1980), 499.

43. James A. Caporaso, "Dependence, Dependency, and Power in the Global System," *International Organization,* 32 (Winter 1978), 32.

44. K. J. Holsti, *International Politics: A Framework for Analysis* (Englewood Cliffs, NJ: Prentice-Hall, 1967), p. 193.

45. Ibid., pp. 194–195.

46. See, for example, Jack H. Nagle, *The Descriptive Analysis of Power* (New Haven, CT, and London: Yale University Press, 1975), p. 11; Robert A. Dahl, "Cause and Effect in the Study of Politics," in Daniel Lerner, "Power," in *International Encyclopedia of the Social Sciences* (New York: Free Press, 1968).

47. David A. Baldwin, "Power Analysis and World Politics: New Trends Versus Old Tendencies," *World Politics,* XXXI(2) (January 1979), 161–194.

48. Jack H. Nagle, *The Descriptive Analysis of Power,* op. cit., p. 122.

49. Herbert Simon, "Notes on the Observation and Measurement of Power," and Roderick Bell, "Political Power: The Problem of Measurement," in Roderick Bell, David V. Edwards, and R. Harrison Wagner, eds., *Political Power: A Reader in Theory and Research* (New York: Free Press, 1969), pp. 26–27, 73–78.

50. Jacek Kugler and William Domke, "Comparing the Strength of Nations," *Comparative Political Studies,* 19(1) (April 1986), 39–69.

51. Steven Brams, *Superpower Games: Applying Game-Theory to the Superpower Conflict* (New Haven, CT: Yale University Press, 1985). See also Klaus Knorr, *The Power of Nations: The Political Economy of International Relations,* p. 11. See also by the same author, *Power and Wealth: Military Power and Potential,* op. cit.; *On the Uses of Military Power in the Nuclear Age,* op. cit. Wayne H. Ferris, *The Power Capabilities of Nation-States: International Conflict and War* (Lexington, MA: D. C. Heath, 1973).

52. Steven Brams, op. cit., p. 267.

53. Michael P. Sullivan, *Power in Contemporary International Politics* (Columbia, SC: University of South Carolina Press, 1990), p. 103.

54. Hans J. Morgenthau, *Politics Among Nations,* 5th ed., rev. (New York: Knopf, 1978), p. 4. For a retrospective assessment of Morgenthau's political philosophy, see Kenneth Thompson and Robert J. Myers, eds., *Truth and Tragedy: A Tribute to Hans J. Morgenthau,* augmented edition (New Brunswick and London: Transaction Books, 1984). See also Jaap W. Nobel, "Morgenthau's Struggle with Power: The Theory of Power Politics and the Cold War," *Review of International Studies,* 21 (1) (January 1995), 61–86.

55. Ibid., p. 5.

56. Ibid.

57. Hans J. Morgenthau, "Another 'Great Debate': The National Interest of the United States," *American Political Science Review,* LXVI (December 1952), 961.

58. Ibid. See also Hans J. Morgenthau, *In Defense of the National Interest* (New York: Knopf, 1951); Charles A. Beard, *The Idea of the National Interest* (New York: Macmillan, 1934). The idea of the national interest as a basis for decision making is examined in Chapter 11.

59. Hans J. Morgenthau, *Politics Among Nations,* pp. 11–14.

60. Ibid., p. 10.

61. Greg Russell, *Hans J. Morgenthau and the Ethics of American Statecraft* (Baton Rouge, LA, and London: Louisiana State University Press, 1990), p. 161.

62. Hans J. Morgenthau, *Politics Among Nations*, p. 11.

63. Ibid.

64. Ibid., p. 12.

65. Ibid., p. 36.

66. Ibid., p. 43.

67. Ibid., p. 58.

68. Ibid., p. 64.

69. Ibid., p. 77.

70. Ibid., p. 78.

71. Ibid., pp. 226–227.

72. See, for example, Harold Nicolson, *Diplomacy,* 3rd ed. (New York: Harcourt, Brace and Company, 1963); *Evolution of Diplomatic Method* (New York: Macmillan, 1962); *The Congress of Vienna* (London: Constable, 1946); Morgenthau, *Politics Among Nations,* pp. 540–548.

73. "The Sources of Soviet Conduct," written by George F. Kennan under the pseudonym "X," was originally published in *Foreign Affairs* in 1947, and reprinted in *Foreign Affairs,* 65(4) (Spring 1987), 852–869. See also George F. Kennan, "Containment Then and Now," *Foreign Affairs,* 65(4) (Spring 1987), 885–891.

74. Ibid.

75. George F. Kennan, *Realities of American Foreign Policy* (Princeton, NJ: Princeton University Press, 1954), pp. 63–64.

76. George F. Kennan, *Russia, the Atom and the West* (London: Oxford University Press, 1958) pp. 676–671.

77. George F. Kennan, *Memoirs, 1925–1950* (Boston: Little, Brown, 1967), p. 367. For more recent reflections on his earlier life and times, see George F. Kennan, *Sketches from a Life* (New York: Pantheon Books, 1989); George F. Kennan, *At a Century's Ending: Reflections 1982–1995* (New York: W.W. Norton & Company, 1996).

78. Ibid., p. 230.

79. George F. Kennan, "Morality and Foreign Policy," *Foreign Affairs* (Winter 1985/1986), 206.

80. See Richard Rovere, "Containers," *The New Yorker* (August 8, 1977), 70–73.

81. George F. Kennan, *The Cloud of Danger: Current Realities of American Foreign Policy,* (Boston, MA: Little, Brown, 1977) p. 229.

82. George F. Kennan, *Realities of American Foreign Policy* (Princeton, NJ: Princeton University Press, 1954), p. 11.

83. George F. Kennan, *American Diplomacy, 1990–1950* (New York: Mentor Books, 1957), pp. 93–94. See also Charles Burton Marshall, op. cit., p. 56: "Our national experience has been such as to root in our minds an excess of confidence in the political efficacy of documents—in the capability of statesmen to resolve the future by agreement on the written word."

84. George F. Kennan, *Realities of American Foreign Policy,* p. 13.

85. Ibid., p. 14.

86. Ibid., p. 16.

87. Ibid., p. 48.

88. George F. Kennan, "World Problems in Christian Perspective," *Theology Today,* XVI (July 1959), 155–172.

89. George F. Kennan, *American Diplomacy,* p. 87.

90. Henry A. Kissinger, *A World Restored—Europe After Napoleon: The Politics of Conservatism in a Revolutionary Age* (New York: Grosset and Dunlap, 1964).

91. For a detailed description of the Nixon Doctrine, see Henry Kissinger, *Diplomacy* (New York: Simon & Schuster, 1994), especially pp. 703–732.

92. Henry A. Kissinger, *White House Years* (Boston: Little, Brown and Company, 1979), p. 55.

93. Ibid., p. 232.

94. Henry A. Kissinger, "The Nature of the National Dialogue," Address to the Pacem in Terris III Conference, Washington, October 8, 1973. Reprinted in Henry A. Kissinger, *American Foreign Policy,* 3rd ed. (New York: Norton, 1977), p. 126.

95. Henry A. Kissinger, "Domestic Structure and Foreign Policy," in *American Foreign Policy,* op. cit., p. 12.

96. Kenneth M.Waltz, *Theory of International Politics* (Reading, MA: Addison-Wesley Publishing Company, 1979).

97. Gottfried-Karl Kindermann, *The Munich School of Neorealism in International Politics,* unpublished manuscript, University of Munich, 1985.

98. Ibid., pp. 10–11.

99. Ibid., p. 12. See also, Reinhard Meier-Walser, "Neorealismus ist mehr als Waltz—Der Synoptische Realismus der Münchener Schule," *Zeitschrift für Internationale Beziehungen,* 1(1) (June 1994), pp. 115–126; Gottfried-Karl Kindermann et al., *Grundelemente der Weltpolitik* (Munich: Piper Publishing House, 1991).

100. Kenneth Waltz, *Theory of International Politics,* op. cit., pp. 93–101.

101. Ibid., p. 81. For additional analysis of the concept of anarchy and system structure, see Barry Buzan, "Peace, Power, and Security: Contending Concepts in the Study of International Relations," *Journal of Peace Research,* 21(2) (1984), 109–125; Joseph M. Grieco, "Anarchy and the Limits of Cooperation: A Realist Critique of the Newest Liberal Institutionalism," *International Organization,* 42(3) (Summer 1988), 485—507.

102. Kenneth Waltz, *Theory of International Politics*, op. cit., pp. 60–67.

103. Robert Gilpin, *War and Change in World Politics* (New York: Cambridge University Press, 1981), pp. 9–11.

104. Gilpin, *War and Change in World Politics*, p. 20. Gilpin borrows the term "satisficing" from Herbert Simon, who contrasts "the goal of *maximizing* with the goal of *satisficing*, of finding a course of action that is 'good enough'." Herbert Simon, "A Behavioral Model of Rational Choice," in Herbert Simon, ed., *Models of Man: Social and Rational* (NY: John Wiley and Sons, 1957), especially p. 204–205, 247, 250, 252–253, 261 and 271.

105. Ibid., p. 230.

106. Barry Buzan, Charles Jones, and Richard Little, *The Logic of Anarchy: Neorealism to Structural Realism* (New York: Columbia University Press, 1993), p. 36.

107. Ibid., p. 37.

108. Ibid., p. 38.

109. Ibid., p. 52.

110. Ibid., p. 82.

111. Michael Mastanduno, David A. Lake, and G. John Ikenberry, "Toward a Realist Theory of State Actors," *International Studies Quarterly*, 33 (1989), 463–464.

112. Ibid., p. 464.

113. Charles L. Glaser, "Realists as Optimists: Cooperation as Self-help," *International Security*, 19(3), (Winter 1994/1995), 50–90.

114. For an extended statement of this position, see William C. Wohlforth, "Realism and the End of the Cold War," *International Security*, 19(3) (Winter 1994/1995), 91–129.

115. Thomas R. Cusack and Richard J. Stoll, *Exploring Realpolitik: Probing International Relations Theory with Computer Simulation* (Boulder, CO, and London: Lynne Rienner Publishers, 1990), especially pp. 21–40.

116. John Lewis Gaddis, "International Relations Theory and the End of the Cold War," *International Security*, 17(3) (Winter 1992/1993), 34.

117. Paul Schroeder, "Historical Reality vs. Neorealist Theory," *International Security*, 19(1) (Summer 1994), 116–117.

118. Ibid., pp. 147–148.

119. Thomas I. Cook and Malcolm Moos, "The American Idea of International Interest," *American Political Science Review*, XLVII (March 1953), 28.

120. Michael Joseph Smith, *Realist Thought from Weber to Kissinger* (Baton Rouge, LA, and London: Louisiana State University Press, 1986), p. 235.

121. Cecil V. Crabb, *American Foreign Policy in the Nuclear Age* (New York: Harper & Row, 1965), pp. 458–459.

122. Stanley Hoffmann, *Contemporary Theory in International Relations* (Englewood Cliffs, NJL Prentice-Hall, 1960). op. cit., p. 32. For a more recent critique of realist theory, see Stanley Hoffmann, *Janus and Minerva: Essays in the Theory and Practice of International Politics* (Boulder, CO, and London: Westview Press, 1987), especially pp. 70–85.

123. Richard K. Ashley, "Poverty of Neorealism," in Robert O. Keohane, ed., *Neorealism and Its Critics* (New York: Columbia University Press, 1986).

124. Robert G. Gilpin, "The Richness of the Tradition of Political Realism," in Robert O. Keohane, ed., op. cit., pp. 316–321.

125. Robert O. Keohane, *After Hegemony: Cooperation and Discord in the World Political Economy* (Princeton, NJ: Princeton University Press, 1984), p. 245.

126. R. B. J. Walker, "Realism, Change, and International Political Theory," *International Studies Quarterly*, 31 (March 1987), 67.

Chapter
3

Systemic Theories of Politics and International Relations

DEFINITION, NATURE, AND APPROACHES TO SYSTEMS THEORY

The term *system* is widely used in social-science literature and in particular in political science and international-relations writings and discourse. Neorealist–structural-realist theory, as we have seen in Chapter 2, attaches primary importance to the structural characteristics of the international system (numbers and types of actors and distribution of capabilities among them) in establishing the behavioral patterns of the units composing the system. The term *system* has been used in other theoretical contexts as well. In this chapter we first discuss the meaning of *system* and describe its usage. We then build on the neorealist–structural-realist theory of the previous chapter, with emphasis on the extensive writings on *polarity*, how alternative international systemic structures are said to affect the interactive patterns within such structures.

Theorizing based on systems brings together two fundamental approaches to international-relations theory. The first is focused on actors and the interaction that takes place between them, whether they are individuals, groups of people such as nations, or bureaucratic units. This approach has been termed *reductionist* because its focus is the development of explanations or theory at the level of the individual participants or units. The second approach places emphasis on the structures that provide the framework within which such interaction occurs. Structure is said to have a decisive impact on the interaction of actors. According to structural theory, the actions of individuals or groups, when aggregated, produce patterns of behavior that may be fundamentally different from the behavior patterns of the individual. In this sense, the behavioral characteristics and the impact of behavioral patterns, or interactions, of the aggregate are greater than, and differentiated from, those of its individual parts.[1] As Robert W. Cox suggests, the actor–interaction approach seeks explanations for the motivations, as well as for the consequences of such interactions.[2] The structural approach attempts to explain how the structures within which actors exist affect the interactions

100

between the actors, and how and why changes in the structure take place. As we have noted elsewhere, the structural approach has been termed *holistic* or *systemic* because it is based on the development of explanations at a more macro level of analysis.[3]

According to John Gerard Ruggie, the study of change is necessarily and by definition the study of structure.[4] Examples of change include the collapse of the Roman Empire, the rise of the modern state system, and the demise of the Soviet Union. It is structure that establishes interactive patterns, which change as structure changes. To add one more term to this discussion, we introduce *structuralism*, which assumes the existence of structures that are permanent and immutable. Thus, the structure that shapes international interactive patterns is immanent, although its characteristic features, including the numbers of actors and the distribution of capabilities among them, may undergo change from time to time. Structures provide the framework within which actors, or agents as the term is often used, respond and relate to one another. Within such structures, systems are groups of actors, or agents, that are interacting with each other. How the actors relate to each other and the relationship between the structure and the actors–agents (the structure–agency relationship) forms a critically important part of the quest for an understanding of change at the systemic, holistic level. According to Richard Little, an important key to understanding how large-scale historical change comes about appears to lie in the relationship between structure and agency.[5] Taking our discussion one step farther, systems, together with agents and structures, form the three concepts composing what is termed a *structurationist ontology*.

Alexander Wendt and Raymond Duvall describe the relationship between structures and agents as one of "codetermined irreducibility." The systems of interaction among agents are made possible by the structure in which they exist. These authors define *social systems* as the "regularized practices of agents that make possible the social structures that make those practices, and the agents who engage in those practices, themselves possible."[6] Interactions among agents shape the structure, which, in turn, has an impact on the interactions. Social structures arise out of interactive patterns, just as social structures have implications for the interactive patterns themselves.

The term *system* has been used in several ways in writings about international relations. This includes systems analysis, which describes a variety of techniques, such as cost-effectiveness studies, which are designed to allow rational-choice decisions regarding the allocation of resources. In the literature of political science, however, "systems analysis" has often been used interchangeably with "systems theory," insofar as it is employed to describe conceptual frameworks and methodologies for understanding the operation of political systems. As Robert J. Lieber has suggested, "Systems analysis is really a set of techniques for systematic analysis that facilitates the organizing of data, but which possesses no ideal theoretical goals. By contrast, systems theory subsumes an integrated set of concepts, hypotheses, and propositions, which (theoretically) are widely applicable across the spectrum of human knowledge."[7] We define *systems theory* as a series of statements about relationships among independent and dependent variables, in which changes in one or more variables are accompanied, or followed, by changes in other variables or combinations of variables. As Anatol Rapoport has suggested, "A whole which functions as a whole by virtue of the interdependence of its parts is called a system, and the method which aims at discovering how this is brought about in the widest variety of systems has been called general systems theory."[8] John Burton has written that the concept of system connotes "relationships between units. The units of a system are of the same 'set,' by which is meant that they have features in common that enable a particular relationship."[9] The human nervous system, a car motor, the Hilton Hotel chain, an Apollo spacecraft, the Federal Reserve system, a fish tank in a marine-ecology experimental project, and the "balance of power"—all of these are systems.

A system can be described in its successive states. It may be loosely or tightly organized, stable or unstable. A stable system requires an input of considerable power to upset it; an unstable system is more precarious, and its balance is more easily disturbed. Every system seeks to establish, maintain, and return after disturbance to some sort of equilibrium. The equilibrium itself may be stable or unstable. A stable equilibrium is capable of absorbing new components and processing a variety of inputs while continuing to function normally, adjusting to changes, and correcting its behavior by making appropriate reactions to *negative feedback* (i.e., information that it is deviating from course).

Smaller systems (or subsystems) may exist within larger systems. According to John Burton, "Whereas the subsystem is a system in itself that can be isolated (though in isolation its functional relevance will not always be apparent) a system level refers to a complex of relationships comprising all units at that level. Systems have different features at different levels."[10] Every system has boundaries that distinguish it from its operating environment. Every system is, in some sense, a communications net that permits the flow of information leading to a self-adjusting process. Every system has inputs and outputs; an output of a system may reenter that system as an input, through what is termed *feedback.*

Closely related to systems theory is the term *interdependence,* used to characterize relationships in a global international system. Interdependence is said to be the result of interaction among components of a system. The greater the level of interdependence among states, for example, the greater is likely to be the loss of control that they experience over all or part of their decision-making independence. At an abstract level, Wolf-Dieter Eberwein suggests that interdependence is a "property resulting from the specification of the relationships existing between the actors in the global environment on the one hand, and the dynamics these relationships entail on the other hand."[11] According to Robert O. Keohane and Joseph S. Nye, interdependence always carries with it costs, "since interdependence restricts autonomy, but it is impossible to specify *a priori* whether the benefits of a relationship will exceed the costs. This will depend on the values of the actors as well as on the nature of the relationship."[12] The same authors conceptualize interdependence as having two dimensions: sensitivity and vulnerability. "Sensitivity involves degrees of responsiveness within a policy framework—how quickly do changes in one country bring costly changes in another, and how great are the costly effects?"[13] They suggest that "vulnerability can be defined as an actor's liability to suffer costs imposed by external events even after policies have been altered."[14] Interdependence, with its sensitivity and vulnerability dimensions, can be social, political, economic, military, or ideological in nature, as Keohane and Nye demonstrate in their analysis. It follows that interdependence is not symmetrical. As R. Harrison Wagner suggests, an interdependent relationship between parties that are not equal is likely to be characterized either by "dependence," defined as need, or by "asymmetry," which refers to a situation in which "one party needs the benefits derived from a relationship more than the other."[15] In turn, interdependence as a concept is closely related to power and dependency theory, discussed respectively in Chapters 2 and 6.

Also widely used in international-relations studies, and especially in systems theory, as we have seen, is the term *interaction*. The greater the level of interdependence, the greater the amount of interaction. Systems are hypothesized patterns of interaction. As the level of interdependence and the amount of interaction grow, the complexity of the system increases. In turn, interdependence and interaction, like systems theory itself, are closely linked to integration theory, which is discussed in Chapter 10. Interaction consists not only of demands and responses— the actions—of nation-states, international organizations, and other nonstate actors, but also of transactions across national boundaries, including trade, tourism, investment, technology transfer, and, more broadly, the flow of ideas.

Examining the international system of the late twentieth century, Andrew M. Scott characterized interaction in the following way:

> Hundreds of actors are pouring actions into the international arena at the same time, and those actions are being variously deflected and aggregated and combined with one another. . . . In an undirected aggregative process, the behavior of individual actors is purposive, but the process as a whole knows no purpose and is under no overall direction. . . . A process that is only partly under control does not become quiescent because the control element has ceased to be adequate, but rather, continues to function and produces results only some of which are intended.[16]

In short, problems (inputs), in the international system are multiplying faster than solutions can be found, thus leading to systems overload. Patterns of interdependence and interaction grow more complex as a result of the pervasive impact of technology on the international system. Under such conditions, it is hypothesized, the *structural requisites*—that is, those needs that must be satisfied for a system to function effectively—become more numerous.[17]

Interdependence and interaction provide focal points for many writers in explaining systems transformation. The emergence in the late twentieth century of a global international system for the first time in history, in place of the Eurocentric system that endured from the Treaty of Westphalia in 1648 until the twentieth century, is related to the global diffusion of technology that has created extensive and unprecedented levels and types of interaction. Edward L. Morse refers to the twofold effects of modernization as "the emergence of certain forms of interdependence among a large set of states and the transnational nature of the international system."[18] Here, interdependence is defined as "the outcome of specified actions of two or more parties (in our case, of governments) when the outcomes of these actions are mutually contingent." Morse sets forth a series of propositions about interdependence within the international system. For example, the greater the degree of interdependence, the greater the likelihood of crisis. "Interdependence does not only breed crises and various forms of linkage, it also increases the potential for any single party to manipulate a crisis for its own domestic or foreign political ends."[19]

Other writers have sought to define interdependence and to ascertain the extent to which levels of interdependence are rising or declining. According to Hayward Alker, a "synthetic, multifaceted definition of interdependence is possible." Interdependence is a "social relationship among two or more cross-state actors observable in terms of actual or anticipated interactions among them."[20] Richard Rosecrance and Arthur Stein view interdependence, in the most general sense, as consisting of "a relationship of interests such that if one nation's position changes, other states will be affected by that change," or, in an economic sense, "interdependencies are present when there is an increased national 'sensitivity' to external economic developments."[21] They take issue with the conclusion of Karl Deutsch and his associates (see Chapter 10) that levels of transactions, especially trade, in the international stage, relative to those within states, were declining in much of the twentieth century. In their view, the growth in the service sector, most pronounced in highly industrialized states, had been underestimated in gross national product (GNP) calculations for earlier periods, especially the previous century. The authors noted the existence of a paradox in the contemporary international system: "The vertical integration of nationalist processes has moved to a new peak. The horizontal interaction of transnational processes is higher than at any point since World War I."[22]

Although in recent decades, systems theory has had a major influence on the study of politics, the idea of systems was not unknown to earlier political writers. For example, Thomas Hobbes, in Chapter 22 of his *Leviathan,* writes of systems.[23] Modern students of politics have adapted the concept of systems from the physical sciences and the social sciences, on which systems theory has had a major impact. For example, one of the most important exponents of systems theory, Ludwig von Bertalanffy, suggested that the ever-increasing specialization within modern science begets fragmentation among disciplines: "The physicist, the biologist, the psychologist and the social scientist are, so to speak, encapsulated in a private universe, and it is difficult to get a word from one cocoon to the other."[24] The growth of disciplines and greater academic specialization threaten to fragment the scientific community into isolated enclaves unable to communicate with each other. Systems theory represents a response to this problem. Another theorist of systems, Anatol Rapoport, suggested that systems theory has the potential of reestablishing approaches that emphasize the functional relationship between parts and whole without sacrificing scientific rigor. He maintained that the analogies established or conjectured in systems theory are not mere metaphors. According to Rapoport, these analogies are rooted in actual correspondences between systems or theories of systems.[25] Bertalanffy discerned similar viewpoints and conceptions in various fields. Disciplines such as physics and chemistry study phenomena in dynamic interaction. In biology, there are problems of an organismic nature. In such seemingly diverse disciplines, it is essential, according to Bertalanffy, to "study not only isolated parts and processes, but the essential problems that are the organizing relations that result from dynamic interaction and make the behavior of parts different when studied in isolation or within the whole."[26]

In short, Bertalanffy, like Rapoport, suggested the presence of structural similarities—*isomorphism*[27]—in the principles that govern the behavior of intrinsically dissimilar entities. This is because they are in certain respects *systems*—that is, "complexes of elements standing in interaction." Because of such structural similarities, systems theory is said to offer a "useful tool *providing* on the one hand, models that can be used in, and transferred to, different fields, and *safeguarding*, on the other hand, from vague analogies which have often marred the progress in these fields."[28] According to Peter Nettl, systems theory "is an attempt to explore structural isomorphisms and homeomorphisms between systems."[29]

James Rosenau and Systems, Cascading Interdependence, and Postinternational Politics

In the late twentieth century, the international system is said to have entered an era of what James M. Rosenau calls "cascading interdependence," based on rapidly changing patterns of interaction among such phenomena as "resource scarcities, subgroupism, the effectiveness of governments, transnational issues, and the aptitudes of publics."[30] It is characterized by the expanding interdependence and fragmentation of a decentralizing world that Rosenau calls "postinternational politics."[31] The postinternational politics to which Rosenau refers may evolve in either chaotic or coherent patterns.

Questions about the nature and evolution of postinternational politics must be answered ultimately by the empirical examination of issues. Thus, postinternational politics differs fundamentally from postmodernism, the proponents of which reject an epistemology based on empirism as the necessary basis for theoretical development, as noted in Chapter 1. Taken together, the rise to political consciousness and assertiveness of previously quiescent groups and their coalescence; the extensive impact of technology in such forms as the information and communications revolution; the widening availability, or diffusion, of technologies for war or peace; the widening and deepening of economic and other forms of transactions resulting both in conflictual and cooperative solutions point to what Rosenau calls "interlocking tensions that, being interlocked, derive strength and direction from each other and cascade throughout the global system."[32]

The rise of subgroups in a fragmenting world means that the loyalties of individuals have been transferred from a larger to a smaller entity, with a consequent weakening of the authority of the established nation-state. The "crisis of authority" to which Rosenau refers diminishes the utility of conceiving of the state as an appropriate focal point for theory building. It is both inadequate and misleading to refer to a "state system." Instead, the effect of cascading interdependence is to distribute power in erratic fashion among state entities and numerous subsystems at many levels.[33]

Such is the meaning of cascading interdependence that individuals and groups occupy various roles in differing systems, including systems of which they may previously have been members, as well as those in which they are currently participating as official policymakers or in a private capacity. The resultant patterns of interaction create what Rosenau calls "role conflicts," reflected in the "values, capabilities and histories that differentiate the various systems in which the policymaking position is situated."[34] Roles are viewed as containing expectations held by the participants both of themselves and of others with whom they are dealing. The fact that role occupants as policymakers envisage a variety of results from the interactive process in which they are engaged on a policy issue lends importance to scenarios as relevant focal points. To quote Rosenau,

> They [role scenarios] are . . . the basis on which publics participate in global life, with choices among various scenarios underlying the degree to which they are active and the direction which their collective actions take. Stated more emphatically, role scenarios are among the basic understandings and values that are transmitted through political socialization and that sustain collectivities across generations. . . . Put in still another way, the task of leadership is that of selling action scripts, of getting publics to regard one set of scripts as more viable and valid than any other they may find compelling.[35]

In Rosenau's formulation, it is the existence of shared action scripts about how collectivities, or systems, resolve their problems that holds them together. It is the emergence of a cascade of disparate interacting action scripts based on changing role scenarios that lies at the center of the crisis of authority depicted by Rosenau. If the cohesiveness of groups and systems is measured by the extent to which the role scenarios of its members are compatible or congruent, it is the cascading of subgroups across the world that characterizes and contributes to disaggregation. As Rosenau states it,

> The more crises of authority cascade subgroupism across the global landscape, the more extensive is the disaggregation of wholes into parts that, in turn, either get aggregated or incorporated into new wholes. That is, cascading interdependence can readily be viewed as continuous processes of systemic formation and reformation.[36]

Thus, Rosenau posits the existence of open systems subject to inputs based on recurrent phenomena, the cumulative effect of which is to yield patterns of disorder. Cascading interdependence is a function of interaction dynamics producing not necessarily just cooperation but also the conflict that is inherent in systemic breakdown. Hence, the concept of cascading interdependence is said to furnish a basis for analyzing authority relationships, the dynamics of sociopolitical aggregation, and the adaptive mechanisms of systems in which the threatened or actual use of force or the prospect for cooperative behavior represents points along a continuum.

Building on this analysis, Rosenau asserts that the prevailing global system, or global order, is characterized principally by the extent to which its units are connected to each other.[37] The defining characteristic of the present era is the degree to which such units are linked in real time. Within this overall context, global order is sustained at three basic levels of interactive patterns. First, there is what is termed the *ideational* or *intersubjective level,* based on what people perceive to be the ordering of the world. This level would include academic and media commentators, the speeches of political leaders, and theorists such as those represented in this volume. The second basic level of activity sustaining global order, according to Rosenau, exists at the *behavioral level,* what people actually do on a regular basis to maintain existing global arrangements, based on their ideational understandings or perceptions. This may include negotiations, instances of resorting to war, threats to enemies, and promises to allies. The third level of patterns sustaining global order, in Rosenau's model, is the *institutional level,* which consists of the institutions and regimes within or through which states and other actors act in keeping with their ideational and behavioral expressions. The extent to which global affairs at any time in history are orderly depends on activity within all three of these levels, which, within and among themselves, are viewed by Rosenau as an interactive set of dynamics producing change in the global system.

The order that characterizes the international system does not presume either the existence or the absence of government. Governance can be present without government, just as government can exist without governance. The examples of governments incapable of governing are numerous. According to Rosenau, governance without government means simply that systems, as such, are defined by their capacity to perform necessary functions, as we have noted in other discussions of systems in this chapter. The functions to which Rosenau refers include coping with external challenges, preventing conflicts among its constituent units from tearing the system apart, obtaining necessary resources, and developing policies based on goals. Although governments exist to perform such functions, such institutions appear to be inadequate in an era of rapid change. Under such circumstances, these functions are performed to the extent that they are based on shared goals that form the essential basis for, and defining characteristic of, governance. *Governance,* as a broader term than *government,* is necessarily dependent on either intersubjective consensus or shared goals. Although governance can exist without government, government can hardly be effective without the consensus on which its authority is based. To the extent that they embody governance, the regulatory mechanisms of systems do not necessarily depend on the existence of governments endowed with formal authority and police powers.

Kenneth Boulding and Systems Complexity

Systems are characterized by greater or lesser levels of complexity, and these varying levels of complexity have been of interest in the social sciences. From his work in economics and general systems theory, Kenneth Boulding attempted to classify systems according to levels of increasing complexity: mechanical, homeostatic, biological, equivalent to higher animals, and human.[38] The process of gathering, selecting, and using information essential to preservation is far more complex in the human system than in a simple mechanical system. A thermostat, for example, reacts only to changes in temperature and ignores other data. The simpler the system, the fewer the data essential for survival. In contrast to simple systems, humans have a capacity for self-knowledge, which makes possible the selection of information based on a particular cognitive structure, or mental representation, as a basis for decision making, discussed in Chapter 12. The mental representation called an "image" can furnish the framework for the restructuring of the stimulus information into something fundamentally different from the information itself. The resulting human behavior is a response not to a specific stimulus, but to a knowledge structure effecting a comprehensive view of the environment. Difficulties in the prediction of system behavior arise to account for the image's intervention between stimulus and response. To a far greater extent than simple systems, complex systems have a potential for collapse because the image has screened out information essential for survival.

Social and political systems are structured from the images of participant human actors. Boulding gives the term *folk knowledge* to the collective images of the members of political systems. The decisions of political leaders conform to the dictates of folk knowledge, screening out conflicting information. The information-gathering apparatus of both national and international systems usually serves to confirm both the images of the leading decision makers and the folk knowledge of the systems. Boulding was convinced that the elimination of the influence of folk knowledge on decision making would have as great an effect on international behavior as the removal of medieval notions about cosmology had on developing modern science. Boulding considered the idea of image crucial in understanding systems and in studying such political phenomena as conflict and decision making. Thus, systems theory contributes to conceptualization at a level "between the highly generalized constructions of pure mathematics and the specific theories of the specialized disciplines."[39]

Talcott Parsons

In sociology, Talcott Parsons was the foremost twentieth-century student of systems theory. Parsons postulated the existence of an actor oriented toward attaining anticipated goals by means of a normatively regulated expenditure of energy.[40] Because the relationships between actors and their situation have a recurrent character or system, all action occurs in systems. Although Parsons recognized that there can be action between an individual and an object, he was more concerned with action in a societal context, with what he calls an "action system." Parsons's action system places people both in the role of subjects and in the role of objects. Subject (alter) and object (ego) interact in a system. If actors gain satisfaction, they develop a vested interest in the preservation and functioning of the system. Mutual acceptance of the system by the actors creates an equilibrating mechanism in the system.

At any given time, a person is a member of several action systems, such as family, employer, and nation-state. Three subsystems compose the Parsonian system: (1) the personality system, (2) the social system, and (3) the cultural system. These subsystems are interconnected within the action system, so that each affects the other. In summary, Parsons conceived of society as an interlocking network of action systems. A change in one subsystem affects the other subsystems and the whole action system.

It is possible, Parsons suggested, to distinguish and study the actions that persons (actors) perform as members of a specific system of action. Action is based on the choices among alternative courses that actors believe to be open to them. In Parsons's view, action is "a set of oriented processes," in which there are two major *vectors,* the motivational orientations and the value orientations. Supposedly, the course of action that actors adopt is based on a previous learning experience, as well as on their expectations about the behavior of the persons with whom they are interacting. According to Parsons, interaction makes the development of culture possible at the human level, and it provides culture with a significant determinant of patterns of action in a social system.[41]

Parsons proposed a set of five dichotomous pattern variables as constituting the basic dilemmas that actors face in all social action. These variables describe the alternatives available to actors confronted with problematic situations. The pattern variables are grouped as follows: (1) universalism–particularism; (2) ascription–achievement; (3) self-orientation–collectivity-orientation; (4) affectivity–affective-neutrality; and (5) specificity–diffuseness. The universalism–particularism dichotomy distinguishes between judging objects in a general frame of reference and judging them in a particular scheme. Whereas the impartial dispensation of justice under law is universalistic, kinship behavior is particularistic. The ascription–achievement dichotomy refers to values governing human advancement in social and political systems—whether, for example, birth and wealth count for more than intellectual ability and education. The self-orientation–collectivity-orientation dichotomy categorizes action as being taken on behalf of the unit initiating the action or as being initiated on behalf of other units. Businesses, for example, tend to be self-oriented, whereas governments are collectivity oriented. The affectivity–affective-neutrality variable indicates an individual's sensitivity or insensitivity to emotional stimuli. The specificity–diffuseness variable distinguishes between those relationships that are diffuse and all-encompassing, such as a marriage, and those that are specific and highly structured, such as an interaction between a sales clerk and a customer. Although diffuseness characterizes traditional societies, specificity of function is a mark of modernized societies.

Parsons's pattern variables provide a framework for describing recurring and contrasting patterns in the norms of social systems. Many authors deem the Parsonian pattern variables as useful in examining social and political systems. For example, Parsons suggested that a bureaucracy is built on universalistic and achievement norms, and that the contractual relationships among business corporations are based on norms of specificity. Such variables may be used, for example, in a discussion either of international relations or of political parties at the national or local level.

In his theory, Parsons attached great importance to equilibrium as a means of measuring fluctuations in the ability of a social system to cope with problems that affect its structure.[42] Systems theory assumes the interdependence of parts in determinate relationships, which impose order on the components of the system. Although equating order with equilibrium, Parsons asserted that equilibrium is not necessarily synonymous with "static self-maintenance or a stable equilibrium. It may be an ordered process of change—a process following a determinate pattern rather than random variability relative to the starting point. This is called a moving equilibrium and is well exemplified in growth."[43] Social systems are characterized by a multiple-equilibrium process because social systems have many subsystems, each of which must remain in equilibrium if the larger system is to maintain equilibrium.

Parsons was concerned with how social systems endure stress, how they enhance their position, and how they disintegrate. If societal equilibrium and ultimately the social system itself are to be maintained, four functional conditions are prerequisite: (1) *pattern maintenance*—the ability of a system to ensure the reproduction of its own basic patterns, values, and norms; (2) *adaptation* to the environment and to changes in the environment; (3) *goal attainment*—the capacity of the system to achieve whatever goals the system has accepted or set for itself; and (4) *integration* of the different functions and subsystems into a cohesive, coordinated whole. In Parsons's social system, families and households are the subsystems that serve the function of pattern maintenance. Adaptation occurs in the economy and in areas of scientific and technological change. The polity—the government in particular—performs the function of goal attainment. The integrative function is fulfilled by the cultural subsystems, which include mass communications, religion, and education. Parsons's functional prerequisites have been adapted, in varying forms, to the study of politics, which is itself one of his subsystems, and they have influenced the international-systems writers discussed in this chapter.[44] Although Parsons briefly addressed the concept of international systems, he saw in the international system patterns of interaction similar to those within the action system at the domestic level. The major problem for the international system, as well as for the domestic system, is that of maintaining equilibrium, which is important if a system is to manage its inner tensions.[45]

According to Parsons, the formulation of common values that cut across national boundaries is essential to international order. Although the international system is deficient in such values, the importance attached to economic development and national independence over the past two generations represents their emergence, at least in rudimentary form, as consensus-building forces at the global level. Parsons saw the need for procedural consensus–agreement among participants in international politics about the institutions and procedures for the settlement of problems and differences. He also called for the differentiation of interests among peoples in a pluralistic fashion so that they will cut across the historic lines of partisan differentiation. In domestic political and social systems, people achieve greater unity as a result of their cross-cutting cleavages—such as, some Protestants being Democrats and others being Republicans. Such pluralistic differentiation at the international level would enhance the prospects for international stability.[46]

David Easton and Others

Several political scientists have developed, adapted, and employed systems theory. These scholars have concerned themselves with the political system, which has been defined by Gabriel Almond as "that system of interactions to be found in all independent societies which performs the functions of integration and adaptation (both internally and vis-à-vis other societies) by means of the employment, or the threat of employment, of more or less legitimate physical compulsion."[47] Karl Deutsch, who also adhered to the functional prerequisites of Parsons, held that a system is characterized by transactions and communications. He was concerned with the extent to which political systems are equipped with adequate facilities for collecting external and internal information as well as for transmitting this information to the points of decision making. Those political systems that survive stress can receive, screen, transmit, and evaluate information.[48] According to David Easton, systems theory is based on the idea of political life as a boundary-maintaining set of interactions embedded in and surrounded by other social systems that constantly influence it.[49] Further, political interactions can be distinguished from other kinds of interactions by the fact that they are oriented principally toward the "authoritative allocation of values for a society."[50]

Such scholars share an interest in functions performed by the political system—an interest in the means by which the system converts inputs into outputs. Easton in particular has been identified with what is termed input–output analysis. The principal inputs into the political system are demands and supports, whereas the major outputs are the decisions allocating system benefits. Almond addressed the question of how political systems engage in (a) political socialization, (b) interest articulation and aggregation, and (c) political communication. Such factors represent means for making demands on the political system; therefore, they are input functions. Almond was concerned particularly with political output functions involving rule making, rule application, and rule adjudication. His output functions, in the case of the American political system, correspond to the legislative, executive, and judicial branches, respectively.

The system represents an effort to cut across the boundaries separating seemingly discrete disciplines. Easton, for example, maintains that at the international and national levels, it is possible to find sets of relationships through which values are authoritatively allocated. Unlike certain other systems, however, the international system lacks universal or even strongly held feelings of legitimacy; nevertheless, its members make demands with the expectation that these will be converted into outputs. According to Easton, writing in 1965, authorities in this case are much "less centralized than in most modern systems, less continuous in their operation and more contingent on events, as in the case of primitive systems. But, nonetheless, historically the great powers and, more recently, various kinds of international organizations, such as the League of Nations and the United Nations, have been successful, intermittently, in resolving differences that were not privately negotiated and in having them accepted as authoritative."[51] Employing his systems model, Easton suggested the possibility of studying and categorizing political systems, at both the national and international levels, according to their capacity for authoritatively allocating values.

Structural–Functional Analysis

Systems theory encompasses a basic concern with structural–functional analysis that attempts to examine the performance of certain kinds of functions within such seemingly different entities as a biological organism and a political system. Structural–functional analysis builds on the early twentieth-century work of anthropologists Bronislaw Malinowski (1884–1942) and A. R. Radcliffe-Brown (1881–1955). Subsequently, Robert K. Merton developed a framework for structural–functional analysis in the field of sociology.[52] Proponents of structural–functional analysis assume that it is possible, first, to specify a pattern of behavior that satisfies a functional requirement of the system and, second, to identify functional equivalents in several different structural units. Structural–functional analysis contains as concepts structural and functional requisites. A *structural requisite* is a pattern or observable uniformity of action necessary for the continued existence of the system.[53] A *functional requisite* is a generalized condition, given the level of generalization of the definition and the unit's general setting.[54] Moreover, an effort is made to distinguish between functions (or what Levy calls "eufunctions") and dysfunctions. According to Merton, "eufunctions are those observed consequences which make for the adaptation or adjustment of the system."[55] Thus, structural–functional analysis may enable the researcher to avoid the pitfall of associating particular functions with particular structures and, for this reason, may prove useful in comparative research and analysis. According to John Weltman, the utilization of systems theory in the study of international relations represents a "mode of analysis growing out of, and conditioned by, two pervasive currents of thought—functional sociology and general systems theory." He suggests that functional sociology and general systems theory, taken together, are mutually reinforcing. "The functional sociologists are more concerned with activity than with the entity within which this activity occurs, to which it is related, and in terms of which it is assessed." In contrast, for systems theory, he proposes, "The nature of the entity within which activity occurs is paramount, often to the exclusion of direct concern with the concrete activity itself."[56]

Both the Parsonian functional prerequisites and the functions set forth by theorists such as Almond and Easton can be located and described within a given political system. Such functions relate to the system's goals, to the system's maintaining an equilibrium, and to the system's ability to interact with and adapt to changes within the environment. Structural–functional analysis provides, at a minimum, a classificatory scheme for examining political phenomena.[57]

Systems concepts have been applied to studies in international integration, foreign-policy decision making, and conflict. Systems theory has been used at several analytical levels of immediate interest to the student of international politics:

- The development of models of international systems in which patterns of interaction are specified
- The study of the processes by which decision makers in one national unit, interacting with each other and responding to inputs from the domestic and international environment, formulate foreign policy—although, as Raymond Tanter has suggested, "international systems approaches may imply interaction models, whereas foreign policy approaches may suggest decision-making models"[58]

- The study of interaction between a national political system and its domestic subsystems—such as public opinion, interest groups, and culture—in order to analyze patterns of interaction
- The study of external *linkage groups*—that is, other political systems, actors, or structures in the international system with which the national system under examination has direct relations
- The examination of the interaction between external linkage groups[59] and those internal groups most responsive to external events, such as foreign-affairs elites, the military, and business people engaged in world trade

These analytic foci are by no means mutually exclusive: Understanding decision-making processes and systems at the national level is essential to understanding interaction among the national units of the international system. As we have noted in Chapter 2, the structural realist is concerned with the international systemic level of analysis as the source of crucially important behavioral patterns. To focus on national decision making is to study what may be termed a subsystem of the international system. In this chapter, we are concerned in particular with those theorists whose focus includes the international system and its regional subsystems. In subsequent chapters, including decision-making and integration theory, we examine other applications of systems theory.

THE NATURE OF SYSTEMS AT THE INTERNATIONAL LEVEL

In the study of international relations, Morton A. Kaplan suggests the existence of a system of action that he defines as "a set of variables so related, in contradistinction to its environment, that describable behavioral regularities characterize the internal relationships of the variables to each other and the external relationships of the set of individual variables to combinations of external variables."[60] Systems theory is said to provide a basis for the examination of linkages, which are recurrent sequences of behavior that originate in one system and are reacted to in another. If such sequences of interactions can be isolated and examined, it may be possible to gain theoretical insights into the nature of the interdependence of national and international systems.

George Modelski defines an international system as a social system having structural and functional requirements. International systems consist of a set of objects, together with the relationships among these objects and among their attributes. International systems contain patterns of action and interaction among collectivities and among individuals acting on their behalf.[61] Richard N. Rosecrance concludes that a system comprises disturbance inputs, a regulator that undergoes changes as a result of the disturbing influence, and environmental constraints that translate the state of the disturbance and the state of the regulator into stable or unstable outcomes.[62]

The systems approach has had many adherents because supposedly it furnishes a framework for organizing data, integrating variables, and introducing materials from other disciplines. Kaplan has suggested that systems theory permits the integration of variables from different disciplines.[63] Rosecrance believes that systems theory helps link "general organizing concepts" with "detailed empirical investigation." In his work, the concept of system provides a framework for studying the history of a particular period and enhances the prospects for developing a "theoretical approach which aims at a degree of comprehensiveness."[64] Dissatisfied with past approaches to the study of international relations, Charles A. McClelland pointed to systems theory as a response to the need "to gather the specialized parts of knowledge into a coherent whole."[65] Other writers have suggested that, by virtue of the inherent complexity of global politics, there exists no entity known as an international system. Instead, there are "multiple issue-based systems." International politics is hypothesized as consisting of "many distinctive and overlapping systems that differ from each other in terms of their structural properties and in terms of the purposes of the individuals and groups that constitute them. If we allow that these multiple systems can overlap and/or become linked, then it becomes apparent that there is more than a single relevant global system as well as many that are less than global in domain."[66]

It is useful to draw a distinction between the international system as a *system* of states and as a *society* of states. It is possible, as in the case of the history of relations among the basic political units of the world, to have an international system without the existence of an international society. Whenever there is interaction—in the form, for example, of diplomatic communications, the exchange of ambassadors, and the conclusion of agreements—there is said to be an international system. In Hedley Bull's view, however, an international society decides when a group of states "conceive themselves to be bound by a common set of rules in their relations with one another, and share in the working of common institutions . . . such as the forms of procedures of international law, the machinery of diplomacy and general international organization, and the customs and conventions of war."[67] In this respect, he suggested that structures shape the norms of behavior that govern society. An international society is characterized by shared normative standards or rules of conduct in the form, for example, of international law. At the same time, an international society has as its prerequisite an international system. Among the international societies of the past, Hedley Bull included the classical Greek city-state system, the Hellenistic states in the era from the collapse of Alexander's empire and the Roman conquest, China in the Period of Warring States, the state system of ancient India, and the modern state system, from its Eurocentric origins to its present global structure.[68]

Just as there are similarities in their definitions of systems, those writers discussed in this chapter whose work has dealt primarily with the international level have common elements in their respective international-systems frameworks. First, each has an interest in those factors that contribute to stability or instability in the international system. Second, there is a common concern with the adaptive controls by which the system remains in equilibrium, or a steady state. Such preoccupation in the study of political and social systems is analogous to the interest of biologists in homeostasis in living organisms. Third, there is a shared interest in assessing the impact on the system of the existence of units with a greater or lesser ability to mobilize resources and to utilize advanced technology. Fourth, there is a consensus among writers that domestic forces within the national political units exert a major effect on the international system. Fifth, they are concerned, as part of their interest in the nature of stability, with the capacity of the international system to contain and deal effectively with disturbances within it. This leads to a shared interest in the role of national and supranational actors as regulators in an international system that is characterized by dynamic change.

There is an emphasis on the role of elites, resources, regulators, and environment as factors that enhance or detract from system stability. Moreover, the flow of information is crucial to the functioning and preservation of the system. In fact, systems theory owes much to principles of cybernetics developed by Norbert Wiener and applied by scholars such as Karl W. Deutsch to the study of politics (see Chapter 10). Interaction among the units of a system occurs as a result of a communications process. In short, central to systems theory are several categories of questions, concepts, and data:

- The internal organization and interaction patterns of complexes of elements hypothesized or observed to exist as a system
- The relationship and boundaries between a system and its environment and, in particular, the nature and impact of inputs from and outputs to the environment
- The functions performed by systems, the structures for the performance of such functions, and their effect on the stability of the system
- The homeostatic mechanisms available to the system for the maintenance of steady state or equilibrium
- The classification of systems as open or closed, or as organismic or nonorganismic systems
- The structuring of hierarchical levels of systems, the location of subsystems within systems, and the patterns of interaction both among subsystems and between subsystems and the system itself

This last category may be restated as the problem of level of analysis, including international subsystems, or subordinate state systems, to which students of international relations have addressed themselves at considerable length over the past two generations.[69] (Reference has previously been made to the level-of-analysis problem, especially in Chapter 1.) Several scholars have attempted to specify patterns of interaction within models and within actual political units in the North Atlantic area, the Middle East, and Asia. Regions have been treated as subsystems of the international system. Research on international subsystems has had several focal points: (1) an attempt to specify as precisely as possible patterns of interaction among units in one international subsystem, (2) an effort to compare two or more international subsystems, and (3) studies of relationships between a subsystem and the international system.[70]

Richard N. Rosecrance

Although students of international relations have traditionally turned to historical materials for the construction and validation of theories, their work has been faulted often for its lack of comparability or for its failure to develop adequate criteria for the selection of data. Proponents of systemic theories of politics, such as Rosecrance and Kaplan, have turned to history in an effort to construct models of international systems. Rosecrance analyzed nine historical systems between 1740 and 1960, each of which was demarcated by significant changes in diplomatic techniques and objectives.[71] Rosecrance discerns the existence of recurring phenomena in the nine international-systems periods, from which he developed two models. Concerned with the conditions for international stability, he selected as his basic elements disturbance input, the regulator mechanism that reacts to the disturbance, the environmental constraints that influence the range of possible outcomes, and finally the outcomes themselves. Disturbance input included such forces as ideologies, domestic insecurity, disparities between nations in resources, and conflicting national interests. The regulator mechanism consisted of capabilities such as those deriving from the Concert of Europe, the United Nations, or an informal consensus that, it is often pointed out by historians, the major European nations shared in the eighteenth century. The third element, the presence of environmental constraints, limits the range of possible outcomes. Systems were judged to be equilibrial or disequilibrial, depending on whether the regulator or the disturbance was stronger. From these elements, Rosecrance developed and examined four basic determinants for each of his nine systems: elite direction (attitudes), degree of elite control, resources available to the controlling elites, and the capacity of the system to contain disturbances. Given his choice of determinants, it is evident that Rosecrance attached considerable importance to the domestic sources of international behavior.

Among his domestic determinants, Rosecrance emphasized the elites of national units. First, was the elite satisfied with its position domestically, or did it feel threatened by events in the international system? Second, the control or security of the elite within the society that it commanded was a determinant in each of the international systems: Did the elites perceive a weakening in their internal position? Third, emphasis was placed on the availability of disposable resources to the elite and its ability to mobilize those resources. Finally, Rosecrance viewed the system's capacity to mitigate and contain disturbances as a determinant of equilibrium.[72]

Morton A. Kaplan

The work of Morton A. Kaplan, which attempted to specify rules and patterns of interaction within models of alternative international systems, represented a seminal contribution to international-systems model building in the early 1960s. According to Kaplan, the classic statement of systems theory is to be found in the work of W. Ross Ashby on the human brain.[73] Although Ashby is concerned with the human brain and Kaplan with international politics, both were preoccupied in their respective fields (a) with a system as a set of interrelated variables, distinguishable from its environment; and (b) with the manner in which the set of variables maintains itself under the impact of disturbances from the environment.

Accordingly, Kaplan constructed six models of hypothetical international systems that provide a theoretical framework within which to generate and test hypotheses.[74] Within each model, he developed five sets of variables: essential rules, transformation rules, actor classificatory variables, capability variables, and information variables. The so-called *essential rules* are essential because they describe the behavior necessary to maintain equilibrium in the system.[75] The *transformation rules* specify the changes that take place as inputs other than the inputs necessary for equilibrium to enter the system. The *actor classificatory variables* set forth the structural characteristics of actors. *Capability variables* indicate armament levels, technologies, and other elements of power available to actors. *Information variables* refer to the levels of communication within the system. The rules refer to the kinds of actors; their capabilities, motivations, and goal orientations; their styles of political behavior; and the structural characteristics of each of Kaplan's six systems—the balance of power, loose bipolar, tight bipolar, universal–international, hierarchical, and unit veto. These six systems can be ranked along a scale of integrative activity, with the unit-veto system as the least integrated and the hierarchical system as the most integrated.

In Kaplan's models, changes in the system are the result of changes in the value of the parameters or constants. He acknowledged that few, if any, existing international systems conform fully with any of his models of hypothetical systems. Nevertheless, he is prepared, so long as the theory set forth in the model explains behavior when "suitable adjustments are made for the parameters of the system," to continue to employ that model. The system has changed when a different theory, or systems model, is needed to account for its behavior. Thus, the utility of Kaplan's models lies in the extent to which they provide a basis for comparing behavior within any given existing international system with one or another of the six models. Moreover, by specifying rules for system change, via a step-level function (that is, a system response to a disturbance input of such a nature as to transform the system itself), Kaplan claimed to have built into his models a means of understanding how international systems are transformed.

Kaplan's models represent a spectrum ranging from more loosely to more tightly organized international-system models. Moreover, in his scheme, national actors are classified according to structural categories—directive or nondirective systems, which in turn may be system dominant or subsystem dominant. In this work, Kaplan was concerned with (1) the organizational focus of decisions, including the nature of actors' objectives and the instruments available to attain them; (2) the distribution of rewards, including the extent to which they are allocated by the system or by the subsystem; (3) the alignment preferences of actors; (4) the scope and direction of political activity; and (5) the flexibility or adaptability of units in their behavior.

Propositions drawn from models of international systems were examined in historical case studies. In one such endeavor, Kaplan's models were tested for formal logical consistency with the use of mathematical tools and the computer.[76] The models were then applied to historical periods, such as the Chinese warlord system of the early twentieth century and the Italian city-state system of the fourteenth and fifteenth centuries. The author of a study of the Chinese warlord system found that this was "basically a 'balance of power' system operating under many unfavorable parameters." Moreover, this was a "balance of power system in which the actors either deliberately or unwittingly violated many of the essential behavioral rules that are necessary for the stability of such a system."[77] Among the conclusions of a study of the Italian city-state system were that, by and large, essential rules contained in the balance-of-power model were not violated, essential and even nonessential actors were preserved, the territorial capabilities of actors did not change greatly, equilibrium became both less static and less stable, and inevitably, the system disintegrated.[78]

Utilizing an approach similar to events data, but drawing on diplomatic history rather than current events, Patrick J. McGowan and Robert M. Rood examined the rate of alliance formation in the period between 1814 and 1914, in order to test hypotheses drawn from Kaplan's balance-of-power model. Specifically, they hypothesized that "in a balance of power international system, a decline in the systemic rate of alliance formation precedes system changing events, such as general war."[79] They tested hypotheses concerning the formation of alliances as a stochastic process. "That is, in a balance of power system alliances occur from time to time, and these events over time are subject to probability laws because the past behavior of the alliance process has no influence on future behavior."[80] There was a tendency, in the nineteenth-century European balance-of-power system, for alliances to be formed "quickly upon one another or with a lag of about three and one-half years." They note that "a clear cut decline in systems flexibility occurred after 1909, and that this period immediately preceded an event (World War I) that destroyed the European balance of power, perhaps forever."[81] They conclude that the data analyzed strongly supported Kaplan's balance-of-power model. The subject of how alliances relate to the amount of war in the international system is taken up in the following section and in Chapter 8.

Thus Kaplan's models, although less complex than the international system of the real world, were designed to facilitate comparisons with the real world, to contribute to a meaningful ordering of data, and to build theory at the macrolevel. Only two of them—the balance of power and the loose bipolar systems—can be clearly discerned in history. However, the case can be made that a third model (the unit-veto system) is partially validated in the contemporary role of the nuclear powers, while a fourth model (the universal–international system) exists in normative theory and in the aspirations of those scholars and practitioners, past and present, who seek to create such a global system.

THEORIES OF POLARITY AND INTERNATIONAL STABILITY

The relationship between the structure of the international system, based on the distribution of power throughout the international system, and the incidence of war has been the object of theorizing both in traditional and contemporary writings. *Polarity* refers to the number of actors and the distribution of capabilities among them and thus connotes the structure of the system. We have noted the debate about the importance of international-system structure itself that is found, for example, in neorealist–structural-realist theory. The discussion has also encompassed debate about the relationship between the distribution of power and stability. Specifically, are international systems containing two poles (bipolarity) more or less prone to war than international systems containing larger numbers of actors with power more widely distributed (multipolarity)?[82] Although Kaplan, in his models, focused on essential rules for the operation of several international systems, other scholars, including Karl W. Deutsch, J. David Singer, Kenneth N. Waltz, and Richard N. Rosecrance, theorized about the implications of multipolarity and bipolarity for the frequency and intensity of war. Deutsch and Singer contended that "as the system moves away from bipolarity toward multipolarity, the frequency and intensity of war should be expected to diminish."[83] They assumed that coalitions of blocs of nations reduce the freedom of alliance members to interact with outside countries. The greater the number of actors who are not alliance members, the greater the number of possible partners for interaction in the international system. Although alliance membership minimizes both the range and the intensity of conflict among those countries that are alliance members, the range and intensity of conflicts with actors outside the alliance are said to be increased.

Although interaction among nations is as likely to be competitive as it is to be cooperative, the more limited the possibility for interaction, the greater the potential for instability. Deutsch and Singer assumed that the international system is but a special case of the pluralism model—namely, that "one of the greatest threats to the stability of any impersonal social system is the shortage of alternative partners."[84] Interaction with a great number of nations produces cross-cutting loyalties that reduce hostility between any single dyad of nations.

Another hypothesis in support of a correlation between the number of actors and war is based on the "degree of attention that any nation in the system may allocate to all of the other nations or to possible coalitions of nations."[85] The greater the number of dyadic relationships, the less the amount of attention that an actor can give to any one dyadic relationship. If some minimal percentage of a nation's external attention is needed for "behavior tending toward armed conflict, and the increase in the number of independent actors diminishes the share that any nation can allocate to any other single actor, such an increase is likely to have a stabilizing effect upon the system."[86] Multipolarity is said to reduce the prospects for an arms race because a country is likely to respond only to that part of the increase in armaments spending of a rival power that appears to be directed toward it, rather than toward the other powerful countries.

The polarity literature is often unclear about whether the number of poles, or power centers, or the distribution of capabilities among them represents the determinant of the level and types of conflict. Furthermore, how powerful does a state have to be in order to qualify for polar status? What is the gap that must exist between those states, on the one hand, that are the key, polar actors in the system and, on the other, those states that are not polar actors? Neorealist–structural-realist theory, as we have noted elsewhere, holds that it is the distribution of capabilities that explains interactive patterns, including the prospects for peace or war.

Neorealist–structural-realist theorists count the number of especially powerful states relative to the remaining states in order to determine whether the system is unipolar, bipolar, or multipolar. Polarity is also measured by the extent to which states form alliances or coalitions. Neorealist–structural-realist theorists also point to the importance of the distribution of capabilities among polar states. However, they do not focus on disparities in capabilities between or among the polar states.

According to Edward D. Mansfield, placing sole or primary reliance on the number of poles as a basis for measuring the distribution of power assumes that the poles do not differ substantially among themselves in their power, or that they are structurally equivalent, equal, or symmetrical.[87] The fact that polar powers—such as the United States and the Soviet Union during the Cold War—were not equally powerful is in itself of theoretical importance. He suggests that there are important differences between the number of poles and the concentration of power among their respective members and the consequent theoretical implications for war, peace, and stability in the system. If, for example, there is a bipolar structure containing two equal or equivalent states, each of which is more powerful than any remaining state in the system, the system will remain stable so long as one or the other bipolar power does not create inequality by increasing its own capabilities or forming alliances with lesser states. According to balance-of-power theorists, Mansfield points out, war becomes more likely when power inequalities exist among the major, polar actors. Accordingly, both the number of poles and the level of power concentration among the polar states form an important determinant of whether war will break out.

SYSTEM STRUCTURE AND STABILITY

Although there is, as we have seen, little agreement among writers on the subject of polarity, some contend that a multipolar world is likely to be less stable than a bipolar system. With fewer important actors and greater certainty in military and political relationships, the prospects for misunderstandings and conflict are said to be less under conditions of bipolarity than in a multipolar world. Stanley Hoffmann, for example, suggested that the existence of the five uneven power centers, which were hypothesized to exist in the early 1970s, was not only undesirable, but also dangerous because the balance of uncertainty is increased and might lead to an arms race.[88] Another writer, Ronald Yalem, saw an emerging tripolar world (United States, Soviet Union, and China), in which two powers would tend to coalesce against the third. Because of the tripling of the number of bilateral interactions in comparison with the more simple interaction pattern in a bipolar world, and the additional patterns of potential conflict, there was said to be a greater possibility for conflict in a tripolar world. Stability in such a system depends on the ability of each state to prevent the emergence of a bipolar alignment against itself. Each must resist the temptation to form bipolar alignments against the third major power. Yalem writes, "Without any 'balancer of power' to affect the inherent tendency of two of the principals to combine against the third, or a strong supranational actor to regulate tripolarity, the system is likely to be susceptible to continual instability."[89]

Empirical studies by J. David Singer and Melvin Small yielded conclusions not fully in support of the hypothesis about bipolarity–multipolarity and the outbreak of war. Analyzing historical data for the period from 1815 to 1945 for possible correlations between alliance aggregation and the onset of war, Singer and Small tested the following hypotheses: (1) the greater the number of alliance commitments in the system, the more war the system will experience; and (2) the closer the system is to bipolarity, the more war it will experience.[90]

For the entire period under examination, the hypothesis about alliance aggregation and the outbreak of war was not confirmed. In the nineteenth century, alliance aggregation and occurrence of war correlated inversely, whereas in the twentieth century, the variables covaried. In addition, the authors discovered that regardless of "whether we measure amount of war by numbers of wars, the nation-months involved, or battle deaths incurred, alliance aggregation and bipolarity predict strongly away from war in the nineteenth century and even more strongly toward it in the twentieth."[91] In short, for the period 1815 to 1899, the evidence presented by Singer and Small failed to support the theory about bipolarity and conflict presented earlier by Deutsch and Singer.

Although such a study using aggregate data can show the existence of correlations, it cannot, as Singer and Small acknowledge, establish a causal relationship. Conceivably, a third variable may be the causal factor affecting the other two variables. Such a third variable might be the perceptions of national decision makers or the existence of nuclear weapons, which vastly increased for the United States and the Soviet Union the risk–gain calculus during the Cold War. For example, leaders may "step up their alliance-building activities as they [perceive] the probability of war to be rising,"[92] or they may seek to defuse political escalation to war, as the United States and the Soviet Union did at the time of the Cuban Missile Crisis in 1962.

Another study tested hypotheses about the balance of power for a much shorter period—1870 to 1881. Drawing on international-events data, specifically a coded compilation of significant diplomatic events drawn from diplomatic histories, Brian Healy and Arthur Stein found that the alliances of the period—the Three Emperors' League of 1873 and the Dual Alliance of 1879—did not lead to an increase in cooperation among allies and an increase in conflict between allies and other states. In the case of the Three Emperors' League, Germany was the object of sharply increased hostility by an ally, Russia, and even by Austria. The authors concluded that there was a decrease in cooperation between members of the Three Emperors' League and outside states, although this decrease was less than what occurred within the league itself. Similarly, the period following the formation of the Dual Alliance of 1879 between Germany and Austria was marked by a deterioration in relations between the two signatories, together with an improvement in relations with Russia, against which the Dual Alliance was directed.

These findings point to a modification of the Singer–Small hypothesis, as well as the proposition advanced by Arthur Lee Burns and others, in which the alignment of two or more states with each other heightens the opposition of others and enhances the risk of war. Moreover, the formation of the Three Emperors' League was followed by a decline in interactions among allies, from which Healy and Stein concluded that interactions between members of the league and outside states probably increased. However, the findings of this study supported the proposition that there was a tendency toward equilibrium in this international system based on a multipolar balance of power, with the inference that "unbalanced relationships are more likely to be unstable than are balanced relationships," and "the tension caused by the unbalanced relationship induces a change in interaction behavior."[93]

In our discussion of neorealist–structural-realist theory (Chapter 2), we noted efforts to broaden such theoretical focus to encompass propositions and findings from the systemic and the unit actor levels. The focus of such efforts is the impact of the structure of the system on the prospects for war or peace. The next step beyond theorizing such as that represented in this section is to engage in empirical tests in an effort to determine the effects of international-system structures on peaceful or warlike behavior on the part of the various state actors. Bruce Bueno de Mesquita and David Lalman, in such a study, examined whether, between 1816 and 1965, wars in Europe were a function of the number of poles (bipolar or multipolar), the tightness of such poles, and the distribution of power among the actors in the system.[94] Confining their analysis to major actors in the system, they measured the tightness or looseness of polarity by clustering European states according to their alliance commitments and the similarity of their foreign policies. They found low correlations among the three variables. In other words, whether a state went to war was not directly related to bipolarity or multipolarity, measured by the tightness of alliances or the distribution of power among the actors of the system. Nevertheless, they concluded that low correlations do not necessarily mean that these variables, taken separately, are not important in understanding the relationship between an international-system structure and conflict.

At the unit-actor level, de Mesquita and Lalman addressed the question of the extent to which decision makers take into account systemic-level considerations in shaping their respective policies. In other words, what do they do if confronted with the choice between a policy leading to greater stability or peace at the level of the international system and a policy that enhances the security of the individual state. Here, these authors construct a model that contains the assumption that decision makers subjectively assessed the anticipated gains and losses from either challenging or not challenging a potential adversary in a crisis situation. The probability that the challenger will use force increases in proportion to the expected gains from such action. Finally, their model contains the assumption that decision makers, in deciding whether to challenge a potential adversary based on the perceived gains at the actor-unit level, also take into account such international-system-level variables as polarity, the nature of alliances, and the distribution of power among major actors. Although conceding that decision makers may have factored into their calculations the international-system-level effects, de Mesquita and Lalman found no evidence that they act as if they were constrained by the system structural attributes examined.

The end of the Cold War is widely acknowledged to represent a profound structural change in the international system. Specifically in Europe, the bipolar structure that sharply divided the continent, based on the alliance relationships set forth in NATO and the Warsaw Pact, has disintegrated. The result, according to John Mearsheimer, is that the likelihood of major crises in Europe will increase.[95] His assessment, based on structural analysis, derives from the familiar structuralist assumption that the number of actors and the distribution of capabilities among them shape the intensity and frequency of armed conflict. Mearsheimer contends that the absence of war in Europe since the end of World War II and until the Balkan wars of the 1990s was the result of the bipolar power distribution, the approximate equality of military capabilities between the two sides, and the existence of a large nuclear arsenal under the control, respectively, of the United States and the Soviet Union. The collapse of the Soviet Union, the unification of Germany, and the decline of the United States as an actor in Europe reflects an emerging multipolar structure that, like other multipolar systems, will be prone to instability.

According to Mearsheimer, the long peace that was the defining characteristic of Cold War, based on military equivalence underwritten by nuclear deterrence, contrasts sharply with eras of war and violence in Europe before 1945. The many armed conflicts of this earlier period arose essentially from the imbalances of power among the major states of the multipolar system. Although the particular wars that broke out had specific and unique causes and origins, it was the power imbalance that permitted such factors to lead to the outbreak of hostilities. This destabilizing feature of earlier eras is contrasted, in Mearsheimer's work, with the bipolarity based on rough military parity and nuclear deterrence that, in contrast, was highly stable. Domestic factors, including nationalism, contributed to the wars of the past, just as domestic structures of the Cold War era contributed to peace. Nevertheless, according to Mearsheimer, the "keys to war and peace lie more in the structure of the international system than in the nature of the individual states."[96] Therefore, Mearsheimer argues for the "limited and carefully managed" proliferation of nuclear weapons in Europe to compensate for the withdrawal of Soviet and U.S. nuclear capabilities from the region. Specifically, the balance that he favors in a multipolar post–Cold War Europe encompasses proliferation to include, but ideally not extend beyond, Germany as a means of achieving balance between Germany and Russia.

The issue of polarity and its implications for stability have been addressed by other contributors to this literature. As John Gaddis points out, systems theory provides criteria that furnish a basis for differentiating between stable and unstable political configurations, although, it should be added, the application of such criteria, as this section of this chapter illustrates, does not lead to agreed conceptions of which types of systems are stable or unstable. Gaddis himself, building on the work of Deutsch and Snyder, suggests that *stable systems* are defined as capable of retaining their essential characteristics, preventing any one state from dominating the system, ensuring the survival of its members, and preventing the outbreak of major war.[97] Stable systems are said to be self-regulating to the extent that they have the means to counteract pressures that might jeopardize their survival. System survival depends to a great extent on the existence of agreed procedures among the principal members for resolving disputes.

The Cold War system, Gaddis suggests, largely met such criteria. Power, especially in its military dimension, was highly polarized between the United States and the Soviet Union. The resulting bipolar structure was relatively simple. Unlike the more intimate Eurocentric multipolar systems of the nineteenth century that required the political–diplomatic skills of stateleaders such as Metternich or Bismarck to keep them intact, the bipolar structure lent itself to the development and preservation of alliances that themselves contributed to predictability about the behavior of members and thus enhanced stability.

As the diversity of perspectives represented in this section suggests, there is little agreement among scholars about the relationship between multipolarity–bipolarity and international stability. In marked contrast to Deutsch and Singer, Kenneth Waltz and others, including Mearsheimer, argue that a bipolar international system, with its inherent disparity between the superpowers and the lesser states, and with both superpowers in possession of vast nuclear weapons arsenals, appears to be more stabilizing than a multipolar system. Having the capacity to inflict and control violence, the superpowers are "able both to moderate other's use of violence and to absorb possibly destabilizing changes that emanate from uses of violence that they do not or cannot control."[98] In such a system, both superpowers, following their instinct for self-preservation, continually seek to maintain a balance of power based on a wide range of capabilities, including military and technological strength. Military power is most effective when it deters an attack. Hence, Waltz sees utility in the maintenance of strength by each of two competing superpowers in a bipolar system because states "supreme in their power have to use force less often."[99] According to Waltz, "Bipolarity is expressed as the reciprocal control of the two strongest states by each other out of their mutual antagonism. . . . each is very sensitive to the gains of the other."[100] Waltz's theory is supported by Alvin M. Saperstein,[101] who discusses the stability implications of a transition from a bipolar to a tripolar world. Describing an international system in which each of the tripolar actors has a competitive relationship with the others, he concludes that stability decreases as system complexity increases. The greater the number of actors (three vs. two) constituting the system, the more complex and less stable it becomes. Furthermore, with additional actors, the level of uncertainty rises about the responses of the various parties in crisis situations. Complexity, instability, and uncertainty—all of which are enhanced in tripolar, compared with bipolar, systems—provide the ingredients of war. This work, based on a nonlinear mathematical model of international competition, accords with Waltz's contention that a bipolar world is more stable than a multipolar system.

In another refinement of tripolar dynamics, Randall L. Schweller[102] attempts to describe the interactive patterns among the three leading states in such systems. The distribution of capabilities among such states, as well as their foreign-policy orientation (*revisionist states*, which seek to increase their resources, or *status-quo states*, which seek to keep their resources), shapes behavior in what he calls "complex unit structure interactions," thus representing a critique of Waltz's theory, regarded as "all structure and no units." The principal criterion for a state to constitute one of the three poles is that it must possess more than half the resources (military potential) of the most powerful state in the system. By systems stability, Waltz he means that no actor in the system is eliminated. According to Schweller, the most unstable of tripolar systems is one in which the distribution of resources is equal because two of the poles (A and B), if they are revisionist, may combine their resources in an effort to destroy the third polar member (C). If only one pole is revisionist, the prospects for stability are enhanced. A tripolar system, in which all three members (A, B, and C) are of equal strength and revisionist, represents an especially destabilizing situation. If two revisionist states (B and C) align against the third revisionist state (A), the latter has no additional state or states to which to turn to create a counterbalance and therefore risks elimination. By contrast, a tripolar structure in which all three members are status quo states represents the most stable system.

Variants on this model include a tripolar system in which one party (A) is slightly stronger than the other two (B and C), while the latter two (B and C), if they combine their resources, would be greater than the first power (A). If the slightly stronger state (A) is also a revisionist power, its attractiveness as an alliance or alignment partner to either of the other two states (B and C) is very low. The latter two states (B and C) have a major incentive to align with each other in order to restrain the stronger, revisionist power (A). However, if the slightly stronger state (A) is a status-quo power, it may provide an attractive coalition partner against either of the other two states (B and C), and specifically against the one that is revisionist. If both states (B and C) are revisionist, the slightly stronger state (A) will have an interest in prolonging their rivalry by playing the role of balancer, although such a course may be risky to the extent that it leads the two rivals to set aside their differences, if only temporarily, in order to eliminate the balancer. Somewhat paradoxically, Schweller concludes that a tripolar system is most likely to be stable under conditions in which there is inequality in resources among the three members. He regards this as a balance-of-power situation in which, even if each of the three poles is revisionist, two of them join together for the purpose of blocking the hegemonic aspirations of the third state. However, he also suggests that if any coalition consisting inevitably of stronger and weaker members went to war and defeated the third pole, the result would be a situation in which the remaining weaker member would be at the mercy of the stronger member. Under such circumstances, realizing the ultimate unstable outcome, no coalition would be formed. Each of the three poles attempts to maximize its advantage without resorting to war that would, by eliminating one of the actors, result in instability. The only exception to this proposition, according to Schweller, is a case in which two of the three poles are status-quo states, which may be motivated to go to war to destroy a revisionist state that they regard as a threat to their security.

As an example of behavior in a tripolar system within the definition of poles, World War II pitted the United States and the Soviet Union against Germany. Thus, two of the three poles (the Soviet Union and Germany) were revisionist. As a status-quo power, the United States had the support of Britain, also a status-quo state. Japan, while not a polar state, was like Britain a second-ranking great power but, unlike Britain, it was a revisionist state. The principal structural characteristic of the system—tripolarity—shaped the alignment patterns.

As a predictor of stability in the international system, polarity has been challenged by analyses of historical periods of European diplomacy and wars. Ted Hopf[103] suggests that the key to explaining international politics in sixteenth-century Europe lies in variables other than polarity. These include the existing state of the technical offensive–defensive military balance, the ease with which military capabilities were acquired, and the nature of strategic systems. Although attention has been focused extensively on twentieth-century international systems, previous eras offer insight into polarity issues. Between 1495 and 1521, the European system was multipolar, followed by a bipolar period (Hapsburg and Ottoman Empires) from 1521 to 1529. Hopf claims that the multipolar Europe of the first period, consisting of Austria, England, France, Spain, the Ottoman Empire, and Venice, was characterized by 26 separate wars. During the subsequent bipolar period, there were 25 discrete wars. The average duration of wars did not differ appreciably from one period to the next. Although it is not possible, from this analysis, to suggest a direct relationship between the other variables studied and stability, differences in polarity did not affect the number, frequency, or intensity of wars. Furthermore, the relative stability of the Cold War era, defined by the absence of war between the United States and the Soviet Union, was attributable not to the bipolar structure, it is suggested, but instead to the ability of each side to destroy the other and therefore to deter military action. Thus, the offense–defense balance, shaped by the ultimate destructiveness of nuclear weapons, rather than polarity, accounted for the long period of Cold War stability.

Offering an alternative system, Richard N. Rosecrance is critical of both the Deutsch–Singer and the Waltz models, respectively, of multipolarity and bipolarity, and argues instead for bimultipolarity. Criticizing Waltz's formulation of bipolarity, Rosecrance contends that a bipolar world in which the two superpowers are intensely and vitally interested in the outcome of all major international issues is essentially a zero-sum game. Hence, the motivation for expansion and the potential for conflict between the bloc leaders are said to be greater in a bipolar system than in a multipolar world.[104]

Although the intensity of conflict may be lower in a multipolar world than in a bipolar system, Rosecrance suggests that the frequency of conflict will be greater in a multipolar world because of a greater diversity of interests and demands. "If a multipolar order limits the consequences of conflict elsewhere in the system, it can scarcely diminish their number. If a bipolar system involves a serious conflict between the two poles, it at least reduces or eliminates conflict elsewhere in the system."[105] Another criticism is that, while reducing the significance of any change in the power balance, multipolarity increases the uncertainty as to what the consequences will be. Thus, it makes policymaking complex and the achievement of stable results difficult.

The alternative system proposed by Rosecrance combines the positive features of bipolarity and multipolarity without their attendant liabilities. In bimultipolarity, "the two major states would act as regulators for conflict in the external areas; but multipolar states would act as mediators and buffers for conflict between the bipolar powers. In neither case would conflict be eliminated, but it might be held in check."[106] The bipolar nations, and in particular the superpowers, would seek to restrain each other from attaining predominance, while acting together from a mutual interest in minimizing conflict or challenge in the multipolar region of the globe. The multipolar states, although having rivalries stemming from a diversity of national perspectives and interests, would have a common interest in resisting the ambitions of the bipolar powers. Therefore, the probability of war would be lower in a bimultipolar system than in either a strictly bipolar or a strictly multipolar system. Rosecrance concluded that the increase of multipolarity would enhance the prospects for détente between the superpowers, and thus for collaboration between them on the resolution of problems of a multipolar nature.

As an alternative to each of the foregoing models, Oran R. Young suggests the need for a model that emphasizes "the growing interpenetration of the global or systemwide axes of international politics on the one hand and several newly emerging but widely divergent regional areas or subsystems on the other hand."[107] Critical of the bipolar and multipolar models for their focus on essentially structural problems, to the neglect of the dynamics of international systems, Young develops a "discontinuities model" that encompasses the concurrent influence of global and regional power processes in patterns that are strongly marked by elements of both congruence and discontinuity.[108] Young used the concepts of congruence and discontinuity to refer to the degree to which "patterns of political interests and relationships of power are similar or dissimilar as between the global area and various regional areas and as between the different regional areas themselves."[109] Young's conception of discontinuities is similar to the model of a world of multiple issue-systems, noted earlier.[110] The crisscrossing, overlap, and linkage phenomena entail acute boundary identification problems: Where does system X end and system Y begin?

No final answer can be given to such questions because system boundaries, like systems themselves, are imposed by analysts for particular research purposes and are constantly changing. Some actors—including military or economic superpowers—and certain issues—such as nationalism and economic development—are relevant throughout the international system, although the regional subsystems of the international system have unique features and patterns of interaction. Young proposes a model in which the existence of such discontinuities is emphasized. Young's discontinuities model is designed to generate useful insights about (a) the variety and complexity of interpenetration among subsystems, (b) the trade-offs and the possibilities for manipulation across subsystems, (c) the problems of incompatibility of the actors with systemwide interests, and (d) the relationships between various subsystems and the global patterns of international politics.

This survey of theories about the relationship between polarity and stability clearly reveals the wide areas of disagreement. As Charles W. Kegley, Jr. and Gregory A. Raymond suggest, the deductive models on which such theorizing is based must be supplemented by insights derived from inductive empirical analyses,[111] including historical data. Deductive reasoning that proceeds from differing sets of assumptions will produce logically consistent relationships between phenomena such as polarity and stability, as we have seen in the extensive literature on this topic.

The term *stability*, as we have noted, connotes the absence of major war between the major states in the system. It is appropriate to ask, as Kegley and Raymond do, whether stability means more than simply the absence of major war and encompasses the absence of major threats to global peace. To the extent that, as in the Cold War era, there were endemic threats to the peace, the world of that era was peaceful but not stable. Therefore, the key to stability would lie in the reduction or removal of threats to peace. The fact that the Cold War superpowers went to the brink of war, without ever actually crossing that threshold, may be more attributable to the restraining influence of nuclear weapons than to the bipolar structure of the system. Unless the relationship, respectively, between nuclear weapons and superpower stability, and between bipolarity and superpower stability, can somehow be disentangled, according to Kegley and Raymond, we cannot assess the relative importance of either of these variables (nuclear weapons or bipolarity) in determining the requirements for stability. If nuclear weapons are the independent variable to carry forward such deductive logic, it follows that a multipolar system in which its major actors each possessed nuclear weapons would be stable.

REGIONAL SUBSYSTEMS IN THE INTERNATIONAL SYSTEM

As part of the systems perspective in international-relations theory, the interest of scholars in delineating subsystems has increased substantially in the past generation. It has been noted elsewhere in this chapter and in Chapter 10 that systems theory and integration theory have been closely associated in the literature of international-relations theory. Because much of the theorizing about integration has focused on the regional level, it follows that integration studies and the regional subsystem have also been linked in the writings of scholars, especially since the early 1960s. As Michael Banks noted in 1969, "A number of attempts have been made to approach regional subsystems from the traditionally ideographic standpoint of area studies, but in a way which employs at least some of the more cogent of the systems' insights into the patterns of world politics."[112] According to Louis Cantori and Steven Spiegel, the regional subsystem consists of "one state, or of two or more proximate and interacting states which have some common ethnic, linguistic, cultural, social, and historical bonds, and whose sense of identity is sometimes increased by the actions and attitudes of states external to the system."[113] The systems are delineated by four pattern variables:

1. The nature and level of cohesion, or the "degree of similarity or complementarity in the properties of the political entities being considered and the degree of interaction between these units"
2. The nature of communications within the region
3. The level of power in the subsystem, with power defined as the "present and potential ability and the willingness of one nation to alter the internal decision-making processes of other countries in accordance with its own policies"
4. The structure of relations within the region[114]

In order to take account of overlap between subsystems and boundary diffuseness in regional membership, it is necessary, as the authors suggest, to divide each subsystem into first, a *core sector*, a principal focus of international politics within a given region; second, a *peripheral sector*, including states that play a role in the political affairs of the region but are separated from the core as a result of social, political, economic, organizational, or other factors; and third, an *intrusive system* that takes account of external powers, the participation of which in the subsystem is important.

Another scholar, William R. Thompson, has reviewed and synthesized the literature of international subsystems. According to Thompson, the attributes set forth in this literature include proximity of actors to each other; patterns of relations or interactions exhibiting regularity; *intrarelatedness*, with a change in one part of the subsystem affecting other parts; internal and external recognition as distinctive units of power that are relatively inferior to those of the dominant system; the effects of change in the dominant system being greater on the subsystem than vice versa; a certain (unspecified) degree of shared linguistic, cultural, historical, social, or ethnic bonds; a relatively high level of integration, including perhaps explicit institutional relations; intrasystem actions that are predominant over external influences; distinctive military forces; a form of regional equilibrium; and a common level of development.[115] Thus, one can say that the level of consensus on the attributes of a subsystem is low.

Thompson concludes, "Strictly speaking, regional subsystems need not be geographical regions per se. Rather, the subsystems consist of the interactions of national elites, not the physical entities of political units, of which interactions are observed to have more or less regional boundaries. In this sense, it should only be necessary to employ the minimal regional criterion—namely, general proximity."[116] From his analysis, the author infers that the "necessary and sufficient conditions for a regional subsystem include: regularity and intensity of interactions so that a change in one part affects other parts; general proximity of actors; internal and external recognition of the subsystem as distinctive; and provision of at least two, and probably more, actors in the subsystem."[117]

Using such criteria, it is possible to identify many subsystems, although their boundaries may differ for different purposes. From an institutional perspective, we may identify the European Union as a subsystem. From a geographic and cultural perspective, we may view Western Europe as yet another subsystem. The existence of a state such as the United Kingdom, France, or Germany within each of these subsystems provides a series of inputs from the international environment into its foreign policy. Elsewhere in the world, we could develop a series of regional subsystems that help to shape the foreign policies of the states that are core or peripheral members, or that are located outside the subsystem.

World-System Analysis

Central to the analysis of systems is the study of their structures and processes. World-system analysis represents an attempt to assess the relationships of structure and process within contemporary and historical contexts. Of fundamental importance is the assumption that the origins of the modern world system can be traced to as long ago as the late fifteenth century. For several centuries, therefore, the present world system, together with its various subsystems, has been evolving from lesser to greater levels of complexity, based on increasing forms of interaction. It is possible to observe and to analyze a series of structures and processes in the world system that display elements of continuity over a period of at least 500 years. Indeed, the world system of the late twentieth century, however distinctive it may appear from that of earlier eras, nevertheless is based on modifications of the same structures and processes found in previous centuries. In this sense, world-system analysis represents an intellectual reaction to what have been deemed to be excessively abstract, ahistorical social-science models. History is deemed to be a vital ingredient, not merely as a basis for descriptive narrative—not the principal goal of the proponents of world-system analysis—but instead as the crucially important means of discerning and comparing repetitive phenomena and, in particular, cyclical phases, which are described in greater detail later in this chapter.

World-system analysis forms an effort, in keeping with much of the study of international phenomena, to cut across traditional disciplinary boundaries. It is based on the assumption that the world system contains a series of interdependent political–military, economic, and cultural subsystems, and that it is difficult, if not self-defeating, to examine, for example, patterns of political and economic interaction in isolation from each other. World-system analysis shares with structural realism the fundamental assumption that, as William R. Thompson puts it, "behavior within the system can best be explained in terms of world system structure and its critical processes."[118] However, for world-system analysis, structures exist at many levels. Thus, to quote Thompson again, "The operating assumption is that analysts must at some point decipher the pervasive structural context within which all behavior is conducted, regardless of the level of interaction."[119] Such processes and structures should be studied in integrated fashion, by which is meant within a context that not only cuts across academic disciplinary boundaries, but also brings into focus what is termed *world-system time*.

In world-system analysis, it is posited that rhythms and cycles in the processes of the system can be identified and examined. The world system of the past half-millennium contains a series of such phenomena. Of importance are not years and decades themselves, but instead the longer-term fluctuations that may be seen in the system. A large number of cycles are identified by various contributors to the world-system analysis literature. According to Immanuel Wallerstein, the world system has been characterized historically by the development of a division of labor between the core area and its periphery, and by the rise and fall of hegemonic powers and the gradual territorial expansion of such states and their eventual decline, together with successive periods of growth and stagnation in the world economy.[120] In economic terms, at any given time, the core area encompasses those states having the most efficient agricultural–industrial production, together with the highest level of capital accumulation. With such a frame of reference, Wallerstein discerns a first stage (1450–1600) in the development of the modern world economy, during which time the core area shifted from the Mediterranean to northwest Europe. This was a period, of course, in which the economy was primarily agrarian. This was followed by an era of systemwide stagnation in a second stage, beginning in about 1600 and extending as long as 150 years. Only in a third stage, beginning in 1750 and extending into the twentieth century, did the industrial dimension become predominant, followed in turn by global economic expansion and consolidation.

Of central importance in Wallerstein's analysis for students of international politics is the relationship that is drawn between the core–periphery division of labor in economic terms and the concentration or diffusion of power with respect to more or less dominant states. There have been only brief periods of hegemonic power associated with the world system of the past 500 years. These included the Netherlands (1625–1672/75), Great Britain (1763–1815ca, 1850–1873), and the United States (1945–1965/1967). According to Wallerstein, such eras are characterized by the concentration within the hegemonic state of agriculture and industry, as well as financial resources. The shortness of such periods is attributed to the high cost of preserving hegemony and the eventual spread of economic capabilities to rival core states. With the cyclical decline of hegemonic control, there follows a period of power diffusion and competition among rival core powers.

Since the mid-1970s, George Modelski has developed a form of world-system analysis based on what he calls "long cycles of world leadership."[121] Such phenomena represent a pattern of regularity in balance in the world system. According to Modelski, the basic unit of the modern world system (since 1500) is a world region. Before the modern period, such regions existed in relative isolation from each other. It was only with the Age of Exploration that such interaction intensified. The greater the extent and scope of interregional interaction, the more complex is the world system—a characteristic of the modern world contrasted with that of the premodern period.

In an examination of interactive patterns that bears some resemblance to traditional geopolitical analysis (see Chapter 2), Modelski views the development of the contemporary world system as the direct result of sea power. By means of increasing mobility over the oceans, a complex international system was forged, in place of the premodern system in existence for more than a millennium before 1500 and based on a single path of interaction—namely, the so-called "silk road," linking China with Europe through Central Asia and the Middle East. Based on sea power, a succession of leading states came into existence. They included the Iberian order, in turn under Portuguese and Spanish hegemony, followed by a period of Dutch supremacy, which was superseded by the maritime dominance of Great Britain and ultimately by the United States. Rejecting the realist thesis of endemic and pervasive anarchy, Modelski instead suggests that periods of global leadership under leading maritime states have been accompanied by international stability. It is in the interval between the decline of one hegemonic maritime state and the rise of another that international conflict increases. Leading world states have shown a remarkable capability to forge mechanisms such as alliances and coalitions for collaborative behavior within various forms of a balance of power.

The long cycle to which Modelski refers contains a pattern that begins in the aftermath of a major war. For example, the Italian wars at the end of the sixteenth century, together with the conflicts between France and Spain, were followed by the rise of Iberian dominance in place of the Italian states of the previous era. Succeeding cycles, featuring the rise and decline of leading states, were punctuated by the wars that, in their time, were systemwide or global in nature, culminating of course in World War II. At the height of its capabilities, a leading world state possesses power in excess of 50 percent of that generally available in the system as a whole.

Of central importance as theoretical antecedents for Modelski are the balance of power, sea power, and transnationalism. Within the balance of power, leading states pursued strategies designed to preserve, or restore, stability—for example, by aiding a weaker state threatened by the power of a stronger one. The literature of sea power, and in particular that of Alfred Thayer Mahan, represents an important contribution to the study of interactive patterns of direct importance to world-system analysis. Finally, transnationalism, in the totality of the forces conducive to interdependence, represents a focal point for world-system analysis because, in Modelski's words, "it sets up a useful tension between the nation-state, a creation of the modern world, and the forces supplementing it or possibly transcending it in a post-modern system."[122] Modelski regards the long-cycle theory of world-system analysis as having potentially important predictive power, even though skepticism and caution are justified. If, for example, system time can be clearly delineated from one cycle to the next, it might be possible not only to discern recurring patterns of cyclical behavior but also to assess the position of various states in the present cycle. To the extent that such an assessment is deemed possible, the world system of the decades that lie ahead is said to be characterized by a tendency toward increased fragmentation, along with greater competition among major powers in a system of heightened complexity. (See "long cycle" theories in Chapter 8.)

In the world-system concept, it is the level of concentration of power—political, military, and economic—that shapes the structure of the system. In this respect, world-system analysis resembles other theories in which structural elements provide defining characteristics of the relationships among entities within the system. It follows that rules for the operation of the system are formulated during periods of high power concentration under the leadership of a dominant state. The rhythm of the system is that of alterations in the concentration of capabilities followed by major wars. In the wake of a fragmentation of power comes a period of warfare, succeeded in turn by a reconcentration of capabilities in the hands of a newly emergent leading state. According to Kenneth Organski, for example, the international system is divided into two tiers of major powers—a dominant state and the lesser of great powers. Taken together, such states are divided between those that are satisfied with the status quo and those that seek to change the existing distribution of capabilities. The erosion of the position of the dominant power, part of the cyclical evolution of world-system analysis, leads dissatisfied actors to threaten or actually to resort to using force in order to effect changes in their favor.

CRITIQUES OF SYSTEMS THEORY

Although systems theory has been one of the major approaches to the study of politics, it has also been the object of criticism. Harold and Margaret Sprout acknowledged that "most systems theorists would stop far short of claiming that social and biological structures and functions are isomorphic in any but a purely metaphysical sense." Nevertheless, the Sprouts questioned "whether one derives clearer and richer insights into the operations of political organizations by endowing them even metaphorically with pseudobiological structures and pseudopsychological functions."[123] Another critic, Stanley Hoffmann, contended that by combining the ideal of a deductive science with the desire to achieve predictability, systems theorists produce a tautology.

> If one builds a model of the behavior of certain groups (for instance, nations) based on a set of hypotheses about the variables which are supposed to determine the behavior of the groups, if, further, some of these hypotheses are highly questionable, and if, finally, the model rests on the assumption that these groups are interchangeable, then the "predictions" about the groups' behavior will be a mere restatement in the future tense of the original hypotheses, and thus comprise a totally arbitrary set of propositions about the groups concerned. Such is the danger of "formal models of imaginary worlds, not generalizations about the real world." It is the triumph of form over substance.[124]

Implicit in Hoffmann's critique is the contention that systems theorists use inappropriate techniques borrowed from other disciplines, such as sociology, economics, cybernetics, biology, and astronomy. At the same time, Hoffmann faults models that contain essential rules or patterns of interaction, such as those of Kaplan, for being deficient in empirical referents.

> The construction of purely abstract hypotheses based on a small number of axioms, from which a number of propositions are deduced, either is a strange form of parlor game, too remote from reality to be "testable," or else rests on postulates about the behavior of the included variables, which are either too arbitrary or too general: the choice is between perversion and platitude.[125]

Hoffmann contends that systems theory, because it aims at a high level of generalization and uses tools from other disciplines, does not "capture the stuff of politics." The emphasis that many systems models place on communications theory reduces individuals and societies to communications systems, to the relative neglect of the substance of the messages that these networks carry. Stated differently, measuring the quantity of transactions or interactions, without reference to the qualitative dimension, is inadequate. What the transactions or interactions contain is likely to be as important as, and probably more important than, their number.

Other writers are critical of systems theory. Jerone Stephens calls for research on the requisites that international systems must fulfill and the ranges within which they can be fulfilled without transforming the system. He maintained that international-relations scholars must avoid a further proliferation of works that merely advocate systems theory in favor of empirical studies of international systems, a criterion characteristic of the debate about the emphasis to be placed, respectively, on theory or empiricism, and on deductive or inductive analysis. Stephens writes, "We have had enough heuristic formulations already to last most students of politics a lifetime, and it is now time to ask for results of this heuristic deluge, and if none are forthcoming, to move on to other ways of studying politics."[126]

Similarly, George Modelski suggested that systems theory has been "devoid of significant insights" in the study of international relations. "System is a concept of high generality and what is true of all systems, while relevant to world politics, is usually not specific enough to add greatly to our appreciation of that narrowly circumscribed field. What is more, for some practitioners of what has come to be known as systems theory, the mere utterance and frequent repetition of the magic term system has become a ritual act of special potency, expected to confer upon the utterer instant admission not only to the circle of the initiated, but also to a sesame of political wisdom." Modelski concluded "that the usefulness of a specific systems approach to international relations may now be approaching its end, despite the fact that the influence expected by it will undoubtedly prove to have been a lasting one."[127] In the same vein, Steven J. Brams suggested, "Verbal formulations abound of the functions systems perform, but notably lacking in most of these systems paradigms is what empirical referents the concepts employed have that would allow propositions linking them to be tested empirically."[128] In the years since such critiques were formulated, there is much evidence to suggest that systems theory, however useful as a construct, has not provided a basis for the development of cumulative theory.

Systemic studies have been faulted for having failed allegedly either to specify or to clarify adequately their epistemological bases. Without such preliminary investigation, writers on systems theory have turned at an early stage of their work to substantive statements about power and stability without having set forth definitions or clearly specified variables. According to Oran Young, such a tendency to dispense with preliminaries "leads to obscurity with regard to conceptual choices" and to ambiguities and confusion within the works of single writers.[129] For example, there is confusion about the distinction between concrete and analytical constructs, the relevance of concepts such as environment, and the use of organismic analogies. There has been disagreement among students of systems theory about deductive and inductive studies, quantitative techniques for the manipulation of data, and the relative merits of comparative analyses and historical studies.[130]

According to John Weltman, "systems theory has not been applied in any uniform fashion." In this perspective, "The context of the applied (systems) theory ranges from stylistic allusion to a full display of its complex conceptual paraphernalia."[131] Thus the problems of definition, scope, and method that divide proponents of systems theory resemble those that beset the study of international relations and political science at a more general level. As a result, the contribution of systems theory to the methodological and conceptual development of international-relations theory is uncertain but will continue to attract interest until more adequate and promising approaches are found for the development of macrolevel theory. Nevertheless, systems theory has provided a conceptual framework within which to identify key variables and to ask crucially important questions about relationships among structure, agent, and system. Systems theory affords a basis for examining the sources of behavior within and among the various levels of analysis that compose the totality of international-relations theory. A large number of the theories, treated in this and previous chapters and in subsequent chapters, have been shaped by systemic approaches to theorizing.

NOTES

1. Richard Little, "Structuralism and Neo-Realism," in Margot Light and A. J. R. Groom, eds., *International Relations: A Handbook of Current Theory* (London: Frances Pinter, 1985), p. 76. See also William C. Olson and A. J. R. Groom, *International Rela-*

tions Then and Now: Origins and Trends in Interpretation (London: HarperCollins Academics, 1991), pp. 222–225.

2. Robert W. Cox, "Production, the State, and Changes in World Order," in Ernst-Otto Czempiel and James N. Rosenau, eds., *Global Changes and Theoretical Challenges: Approaches to World Politics for the 1990s* (Lexington, MA, and Toronto: Lexington Books, 1989), pp. 37–38.

3. See Richard Little, "The Systems Approach," in Steve Smith, ed., *International Relations: British and American Perspectives* (Oxford, England: Basil Blackwell, in association with the British International Studies Association, 1985), p. 74.

4. John Gerard Ruggie, "International Structure and International Transformation: Space, Time, and Method," in Ernst-Otto Czempiel and James N. Rosenau, eds., *Global Changes and Theoretical Challenges: Approaches to World Politics for the 1990s* (Lexington, MA, and Toronto: Lexington Books, 1989), p. 21. See also Stephen Haggard, "Structuralism and Its Critics: Recent Progress in International Relations Theory," in Emanuel Adler and Beverly Crawford, eds., *Progress in Postwar International Relations* (New York: Columbia University Press, 1991), pp. 403–437.

5. For a discussion of this issue, see Richard Little, "International Relations and Large-Scale Historical Change," in A. J. R. Groom and Margot Light eds., *Contemporary International Relations: A Guide to Theory* (London: Pinter Publishers, 1994), pp. 9–10.

6. Alexander Wendt and Raymond Duvall, "Institutions and International Order," in Ernst-Otto Czempiel and James N. Rosenau, eds., *Global Changes and Theoretical Challenges: Approaches to World Politics for the 1990s* (Lexington, MA: Lexington Books, 1989), pp. 58–59.

7. Robert J. Lieber, *Theory and World Politics* (Cambridge, MA: Winthrop, 1972), p. 123. See also Oran R. Young, *Systems of Political Science* (Englewood Cliffs, NJ: Prentice-Hall, 1968), p. 19; Michael Banks, "Systems Analysis and the Study of Regions," *International Studies Quarterly*, 13(4) (December 1969), 345–350.

8. Anatol Rapoport, "Foreword," in Walter Buckley, ed., *Modern Systems Research for the Behavioral Sciences* (Chicago: Aldine, 1968), p. xvii. (Italics added in text.) See also James E. Dougherty, "The Study of the Global System," in James N. Rosenau, Kenneth W. Thompson, and Gavin Boyd, eds., *World Politics: An Introduction* (New York: Free Press, 1976), pp. 597–623.

9. John W. Burton, *Systems, States, Diplomacy and Rules* (Cambridge, England: Cambridge University Press, 1968), p. 6.

10. Ibid., p. 14.

11. Wolf-Dieter Eberwein, "In Favor of Method, or How to Deal with International Interdependence," in Ernst-Otto Czempiel and James N. Rosenau, eds., *Global Changes and Theoretical Challenges: Approaches to World Politics for the 1990s* (Lexington, MA: Lexington Books, 1989), pp. 92–93.

12. Robert O. Keohane and Joseph S. Nye, *Power and Interdependence: World Politics in Transition,* Second Edition (Glenview, IL: Scott, Foresman and Company, 1989), pp. 9–10.

13. Ibid., p. 12.

14. Ibid., p. 13.

15. R. Harrison Wagner, "Economic Interdependence, Bargaining Power, and Political Influence," *International Organization*, 42(3) (Summer 1988), 461. For an extended treatment of the economic dimensions of interdependence, see John Gerard Ruggie, ed., *The Antinomies of Interdependence: National Welfare and the International Division of Labor* (New York: Columbia University Press, 1983).

16. Andrew M. Scott, "The Logic of International Interaction," *International Studies Quarterly,* 21(3) (September 1977). 438.

17. According to Scott, they consist of environmental and resource requisites, system flow requisites (materials, people, energy, technology, information), trained personnel and their services, and control and guidance requisites; ibid., 445.

18. Edward L. Morse, *Modernization and the Transformation of International Relations* (New York: Free Press, 1976), p. 14.

19. Ibid., p. 130.

20. Hayward R. Alker, Jr., "A Methodology for Design Research on Interdependence Alternatives," *International Organization,* 31(1) (Winter 1977), 31.

21. Richard Rosecrance and Arthur Stein, "Interdependence: Myth or Reality?" *World Politics,* XXVI(1) (October 1973), 2.

22. Ibid., p. 21.

23. Hobbes defines systems as follows: "By systems I understand any numbers of men joined in one interest or one business of which some are regular and some irregular." Thomas Hobbes, *Leviathan,* Introduction by Michael Oakeshott (Oxford, England: Basil Blackwell, 1946), p. 146.

24. Ludwig von Bertalanffy, "General Systems Theory," in *General Systems,* I (1956), pp. 1–10; reprinted in J. David Singer, ed., *Human Behavior and International Politics: Contributions from the Social-Psychological Sciences* (Chicago: Rand McNally, 1965), p. 21. See also Roy R. Grinker, ed., *Toward a Unified Theory of Human Behavior* (New York: Basic Books, 1956).

25. Anatol Rapoport, op. cit., p. xxi.

26. Bertalanffy, op. cit., p. 21. He has suggested that a system implies any arrangement or combination of parts or elements in a whole, which may apply to a cell, a human being, or a society. See also "General Systems Theory: A New Approach to a Unified Theory of Science," *Human Biology,* XXIII (1951), 302–304.

27. Isomorphism may be defined as "a one-to-one correspondence between objects in different systems which preserves the relationship between the objects." A. Hall and R. Fagen, "Definition of a System," *General Systems,* I (1956), 18.

28. Ibid., p. 22. (Italics in original.)

29. Peter Nettl, "The Concept of Systems in Political Science," *Political Studies,* 14 (September 1966), 305–338.

30. James N. Rosenau, "A Pre-Theory Revisited: World Politics in an Era of Cascading Interdependence," *International Studies Quarterly,* 28(3) (September 1984), 255.

31. James N. Rosenau, "Global Changes and Theoretical Challenges: Toward Postinternational Politics for the 1990s," in Ernst-Otto Czempiel and James N. Rosenau, eds., *Global Changes and Theoretical Challenges: Approaches to World Politics for the 1990s* (Lexington, MA, and Toronto: Lexington Books, 1989), p. 19.

32. Ibid., p. 262.

33. Ibid., p. 264.

34. Ibid., p. 268.

35. Ibid., p. 272.

36. Ibid., p. 281.

37. James N. Rosenau, "Governance, Order, and Change in World Politics," in James N. Rosenau and Ernst-Otto Czempiel (eds.), *Governance Without Government: Order and Change in World Politics* (New York: Cambridge University Press, 1992), pp. 1–29.

38. Kenneth E. Boulding, *The Image: Knowledge in Life and Society* (Ann Arbor: University of Michigan Press, 1956), p. 8; "Political Implications of General Systems

Research," *General Systems Yearbook*, VI (1961), 17. For a treatment of image theory and international conflict, see chap. 7, pp. 290–298.

39. Kenneth E. Boulding, *Beyond Economics* (Ann Arbor: University of Michigan Press, 1968), p. 83.

40. Talcott Parsons and Edward A. Shils, eds., *Toward a General Theory of Action* (New York: Harper & Row Torchbooks), p. 53.

41. Parsons defines a social system as a "system of interaction of a plurality of actors, in which the action is oriented by rules which are complexes of complementary expectations concerning roles and sanctions. *As a system*, it has determinate internal organization and determinate patterns of structural change. It has, furthermore, as a system, a variety of mechanisms of adaptation to changes in the external environment. These mechanisms function to create one of the important properties of a system, namely, a tendency to maintain boundaries. A total social system which, for practical purposes, may be treated as self-sufficient—which, in other words, contains within approximately the boundaries defined by membership all the functional mechanisms required for its maintenance as a system—is here called a *society*." (Italics in original.) Parsons and Shils, ibid., pp. 195–196.

42. Talcott Parsons, "An Outline of the Social System," in Talcott Parsons, Edward A. Shils, Kaspar Naegele, and Jesse R. Pitts, eds., *Theories of Society* (New York: Free Press, 1961), p. 37.

43. Talcott Parsons and Edward A. Shils, "Toward a General Theory of Action," in Parsons et al., eds., op. cit., p. 107. Parsons defines *process* as "any mode in which a given state of a system or a part of a system changes into another state," *An Outline of the Social System*, op. cit., p. 201.

44. According to Parsons, the traditional focus of political science has been on such concrete phenomena as government and constitutions rather than on conceptual schemes such as systems. Classical political theory has consisted primarily of the normative and philosophical problems of government instead of empirical analysis of its processes and determinants. Parsons acknowledges that government, which is "one of the most strategically important processes and foci of differentiated structures within social systems," forms therefore one of the most crucial disciplines of the social sciences. However, Parsons calls for a shift in focus of the study of political science from the concrete phenomena of government to a more sharply theoretical and empirical emphasis; ibid., p. 29.

45. Talcott Parsons, "Order and Community in the International Social System," in James N. Rosenau, ed., *International Politics and Foreign Policy* (New York: Free Press 1961), pp. 120–121. For the implications of Parsons's work for sociological theories of conflict, see Chapter 8, Note 1.

46. Talcott Parsons, *Sociological Theory and Modern Society* (New York: Free Press, 1967), pp. 467–488.

47. Gabriel Almond, "Introduction," in Gabriel Almond and James S. Coleman, eds., *The Politics of the Developing Areas* (Princeton, NJ: Princeton University Press, 1960), p. 7. See also Gabriel A. Almond and G. Bingham Powell, Jr., *Comparative Politics: A Developmental Approach* (Boston: Little, Brown, 1966), especially chap. 2.

48. Karl W. Deutsch, *The Nerves of Government* (New York: Free Press, 1964), pp. 250–254.

49. David Easton, *A Framework for Political Analysis* (Englewood Cliffs, NJ: Prentice-Hall, 1965), p. 25.

50. Ibid., p. 50.

51. David Easton, *A Systems Analysis of Political Life* (New York: Wiley, 1965), pp. 284–285, 484–488. See also N. B. Nicholson and P. A. Reynolds, "General Systems,

the International System and the Eastonian Analysis," *Political Studies,* XV(1) (1967), 12–31.

52. See Robert K. Merton, *Social Theory and Social Structure* (New York: Free Press, 1957).

53. Ibid.

54. Marion J. Levy, Jr., "Functional Analysis," *International Encyclopedia of Social Sciences,* VI (New York: Macmillan and Free Press, 1968), 23.

55. Robert K. Merton, op. cit., p. 51. In addition, Merton distinguishes between manifest and latent functions. *Manifest functions* are those with patterns that produce consequences that are both intended and recognized by the participants. *Latent functions* consist of patterns with results that are unintended and unrecognized by participants.

56. John J. Weltman, *Systems Theory in International Relations: A Study in Metaphoric Hypertrophy* (Lexington, MA: Lexington Books, 1973), p. 14.

57. See A. James Gregor, "Political Science and the Uses of Functional Analysis," *American Political Science Review,* LXII (June 1968), 434–435. Even though the point is not central to international theory, the student should be aware of the important distinction drawn in recent years by scholars of comparative politics between static or equilibrium models of the system with dynamic or developmental models. See Gabriel A. Almond, "A Developmental Approach to Political Systems," *World Politics,* XVII (January 1965), 182–214.

58. Raymond Tanter, "International Systems and Foreign Policy Approaches: Implications for Conflict Modeling and Management," in Raymond Tanter and Richard A. Ullman, eds. *Theory and Policy in International Relations* (Princeton, NJ: Princeton University Press, 1972), p. 8.

59. James Rosenau has defined *linkage* as "any recurrent sequence of behavior that originates in one system and is reacted to in another." "Toward the Study of National–International Linkages," in James N. Rosenau, ed., *Linkage Politics* (New York: Free Press, 1969), p. 45.

60. Morton A. Kaplan, *System and Process in International Politics* (New York: Wiley, 1962), p. 4.

61. George Modelski, "Agraria and Industria: Two Models of the International System," in Klaus Knorr and Sidney Verba, eds., *The International System: Theoretical Essays* (Princeton, NJ: Princeton University Press, 1961), pp. 121–122.

62. Richard N. Rosecrance, *Action and Reaction in World Politics* (Boston: Little, Brown, 1963), pp. 220–221.

63. Morton A. Kaplan, op. cit., p. xii.

64. Richard Rosecrance, op. cit., p. 267.

65. Charles A. McClelland, "Systems History in International Relations: Some Perspectives for Empirical Research and Theory," *General Systems, Yearbook of the Society for General Systems Research,* III (1958), 221–247.

66. Donald E. Lampert, Lawrence S. Falkowski, and Richard W. Mansbach, "Is There an International System?" *International Studies Quarterly,* 22(1) (March 1978), 146.

67. Hedley Bull, *The Anarchical Society: A Study of Order in World Politics* (New York: Columbia University Press, 1977), p. 13.

68. Ibid., pp. 15–16.

69. See J. David Singer, "The Level-of-Analysis Problem in International Relations," in Klaus Knorr and Sidney Verba, eds., op. cit., pp. 77–92. See also *International Studies Quarterly* (Special Issue on International Subsystems), XIII (December 1969).

70. For studies on international subsystems, see Michael Brecher, *The States of Asia: A Political Analysis* (New York: Oxford University Press, 1963), pp. 88–111; Leon N.

Linkberg, "The European Community as a Political System," *Journal of Common Market Studies,* V (June 1967), 348–386; Karl Kaiser, "The U.S. and EEC in the Atlantic System: The Problem of Theory," ibid., pp. 388–425; Stanley Hoffmann, "Discord in Community: The North Atlantic Area as a Partial International System," in Francis O. Wilcox and H. Field Haviland, Jr., eds., *The Atlantic Community: Progress and Prospects* (New York: Praeger, 1963), pp. 3–31; see *International Studies Quarterly* (Special Issue on International Subsystems), XIII (December 1969).

71. Richard Rosecrance lists past international systems as follows: (1) eighteenth century, 1740–1789; (2) Revolutionary Imperium, 1789–1814; (3) Concert of Europe, 1814–1822; (4) truncated concert; 1822–1848; (5) shattered concert, 1848–1871; (6) Bismarckian concert, 1871–1890; (7) imperialist nationalism, 1890–1918; (8) totalitarian militarism, 1918–1945; (9) postwar, 1945–1960.

72. Richard Rosecrance, op. cit., pp. 280–296.

73. W. Ross Ashby, *Design for a Brain* (New York: Wiley 1952). Kaplan makes this assertion in "Systems Theory," in James C. Charlesworth, ed., *Contemporary Political Analysis* (New York: Free Press, 1967), p. 150.

74. According to Kaplan, "The conception that underlies System and Process is fairly simple. If the number, type, and behavior of nations differ over time, and if their military capabilities, their economic assets, and their information also vary over time, then there is some likely interconnection between these elements such that different structural and behavioral systems can be discerned to operate at different periods of history. This conception may turn out to be incorrect, but it does not seem an unreasonable basis for an investigation of the subject matter. To conduct such an investigation requires systematic hypotheses concerning the nature of the connections of the variables. Only after these are made can past history be examined in a way that illuminates the hypotheses. Otherwise the investigator has no criteria on the basis of which he can pick and choose from among the infinite reservoir of facts available to him. These initial hypotheses indicate the areas of facts which have the greatest importance for this type of investigation; presumably if the hypotheses are wrong, this will become reasonably evident in the course of attempting to use them." Morton A. Kaplan, "The New Great Debate: Traditionalism vs. Science in International Relations," *World Politics,* XX (October 1967), 8.

75. According to Kaplan, "The models are not equilibrium models in the Parsonian sense. Thus they are not static but respond to change, when it is within specified limits, by maintaining or restoring system equilibrium. Equilibrium does not have an explanatory function within such systems. Rather it is the equilibrium that is to be explained; and the model itself constitutes the explanation by indicating the mechanisms that restore or maintain equilibrium." Morton A. Kaplan, "The Systems Approach to International Politics," in Morton A. Kaplan, ed., *New Approaches to International Relations* (New York: St. Martin's, 1968), p. 388.

76. See Donald L. Reinken, "Computer Explorations of the Balance of Power: A Progress Report," in Morton A. Kaplan, ed., *New Approaches to International Relations,* op. cit., pp. 459–481.

77. Hsi-Sheng Chi, "The Chinese Warlord System as an International System," in Morton A. Kaplan, ed., ibid., p. 449.

78. Winfried Franke, "The Italian City-State System as an International System," in Morton A. Kaplan, ed., ibid., p. 449.

79. Patrick J. McGowan and Robert M. Rood, "Alliance Behavior in Balance of Power Systems: Applying a Poisson Model to Nineteenth Century Europe," *American Political Science Review,* LXIX(3) (September 1975), 862. The authors note that Poisson

sampling, as utilized in their study, "consists of observing the process over a predetermined amount of time, length, or other dimensions, and counting the number of events which occur." Quoted from Howard Raiffa and Robert Schlaifer, *Applied Statistical Decision Theory* (Cambridge, MA: MIT Press, 1961), p. 283.

80. Ibid., p. 861.
81. Ibid., p. 869.
82. For an extended analysis of this debate, see Bruce Bueno de Mesquita and David Lalman, "Empirical Support for Systemic and Dyadic Explanations of International Conflict," *World Politics*, XLI(1) (October 1988), 1–20.
83. Karl W. Deutsch and J. David Singer, "Multipolar Power Systems and International Stability," *World Politics*, XVI (April 1964), 390. For an earlier theoretical analysis of multipolarity and international stability, see Arthur Lee Burns, "From Balance to Deterrence: A Theoretical Analysis," *World Politics*, IX (July 1957), 494–529. Burns examines several propositions, including the following: The closer the alliance between any two or more powers, the greater the increase of opposition or pressure (other things being equal) between any one of the two and any third power or group powers: other things being equal, considerations of long-run security determine an optimum degree of short-run security; any system embodying the balance of power has some intrinsic tendency to increase that number; a deterrent state or system will emerge from a power-balancing system whenever the development of military technology makes (1) the physical destruction of all of an opponent's forces impossible and (2) the physical destruction of the economy very easy.
84. Karl Deutsch and J. David Singer, op. cit., p. 394.
85. Ibid., p. 392.
86. Ibid., p. 400.
87. Edward D. Mansfield, "Concentration, Polarity, and the Distribution of Power," *International Studies Quarterly*, 37 (1993), 105–128.
88. Stanley Hoffmann, "Weighing the Balance of Power," *Foreign Affairs*, 50 (July 1972), 618–643.
89. Ronald Yalem, "Tripolarity and the International System," *ORBIS* (Winter 1972), 1055.
90. International wars (in which at least one participant on each side is an independent and sovereign member of the international system) with total battle-connected deaths of more than 1000 were included in the data. To operationalize the dependent variable, the duration and magnitude of each war were measured by the "nation-months-of-war measure" (p. 259); the sum of the months which all nations individually experienced as participants in the war. Furthermore, a distinction was made between major and minor powers, and their wars and nation-months were calculated separately. To operationalize and quantify the independent variable, namely, "the extent to which alliance commitments reduced the interaction opportunities," (p. 261) two dimensions were considered: (1) the nature of the obligation (whether it was a defense pact, neutrality pact, or entente); and (2) the nature of the signatories' power status (whether it was between two major, two minor, or one major and one minor power). After the alliances were discovered and classified, the data on each type of alliance for each year were converted into a percentage figure as follows: (1) percentage of all in any alliance; (2) percentage of all in defense pact; (3) percentage of majors in any alliance; (4) percentage of majors in defense pact; and (5) percentage of majors in any alliance with minor. J. David Singer and Melvin Small, "Alliance Aggregation and the Onset of War," in J. David Singer, ed., *Quantitative International Politics* (New York: Free Press, 1968), pp. 246–286. See also Alan Ned Sabrosky, ed., *Polarity and War:*

The Changing Structure of International Conflict (Boulder, CO, and London: West-view Press, 1985).

91. J. David Singer and Melvin Small, ibid., p. 283.
92. Ibid., p. 284.
93. Brian Healy and Arthur Stein, "The Balance of Power in International History: Theory and Reality," *The Journal of Conflict Resolution*, XVII(1) (March 1973), 57.
94. Bruce Bueno de Mesquita and David Lalman, "Empirical Support for Systemic and Dyadic Explanations of International Conflict," *World Politics*, XLI(1) (October 1988), 1–20.
95. John J. Mearsheimer, "Back to the Future: Instability in Europe after the Cold War," *International Security*, 15(1) (Summer 1990), 5–7. For an alternative perspective on the post–Cold War international system structure, see Charles Krauthammer, "The Unipolar Moment," special edition, *America and the World, Foreign Affairs*, 70(1) (1991), 23–33.
96. John J. Mearsheimer, "Back to the Future: Instability in Europe after the Cold War," ibid., 5–7.
97. John Lewis Gaddis, *The Long Peace: Inquiries into the History of the Cold War* (New York: Oxford University Press, 1987), p. 218.
98. Kenneth N. Waltz, "International Structure, National Force, and the Balance of World Power," *Journal of International Affairs*, XXI(2) (1967), 220.
99. Ibid., p. 223.
100. Ibid., p. 230.
101. Alvin M. Saperstein, "The 'Long Peace'—Result of a Bipolar Competitive World?" *Journal of Conflict Resolution*, 35(1) (March 1991), 68–79.
102. Randall L. Schweller, "Tripolarity and the Second World War," *International Studies Quarterly*, 37 (1993), 73–103.
103. Ted Hopf, "Polarity, the Offense–Defense Balance, and War," *American Political Science Review*, 85(2) (June 1991), 474–493.
104. Richard N. Rosecrance, "Bipolarity, Multipolarity, and the Future," *Journal of Conflict Resolution*, X (September 1966), 318.
105. Ibid., p. 319.
106. Ibid., p. 322. Another study with a focus on the relationship between polarity and armed conflict concludes in similar vein: Based on the research contained in this volume, it may well be that the best prospects for stability in the emerging international order reside in a continuation of power bipolarity, and cluster multipolarity, not unlike Rosecrance's bimultipolarity, the political expression of which was the Nixon Doctrine itself. Alan Ned Sabrosky, "Beyond Bipolarity: The Potential for War," in Alan Ned Sabrosky, ed., *Polarity and War: The Changing Structure of International Conflict* (Boulder, CO, and London: Westview Press, 1985), p. 217.
107. Oran R. Young, "Political Discontinuities in the International System," *World Politics*, XX (April 1968), 369.
108. Ibid., p. 370.
109. Ibid.
110. Donald E. Lampert, Lawrence S. Falkowski, and Richard W. Mansbach, "Is There an International System?" *International Studies Quarterly*, 22(1) (March 1978), 150.
111. Charles W. Kegley, Jr. and Gregory A. Raymond, "Must We Fear a Post–Cold War Multipolar System?" *Journal of Conflict Resolution*, 36(3) (September 1992), 574–575.
112. Michael Banks, "Systems Analysis and the Study of Regions," *International Studies Quarterly*, 13(4) (December 1969), 357. Other early efforts to study regional subsystems include Mario Barrera and Ernst B. Haas, "The Operationalization of Some Variables Related to Regional Integration," *International Organization*, 23(1) (Winter 1969),

150–160; Joseph S. Nye, Jr., ed., *International Regionalism Readings* (Boston: Little, Brown, 1968); Stanley Hoffmann, "Discord in Community: The North Atlantic Area as a Partial International System," *International Organization,* 17(3) (Summer 1963), 521–549; Michael Brecher, "International Relations and Asian Studies: The Subordinate State System of Southern Asia," *World Politics,* 15(2) (January 1963), 213–235; Larry W. Bowman, "The Subordinate State System of Southern Africa," *International Studies Quarterly,* 12(3) (September 1968), 231–261; Michael Brecher, "The Middle East Subordinate System and Its Impact on Israel's Foreign Policy," *International Studies Quarterly,* 13(2) (June 1969), 117–139; see *International Studies Quarterly,* (Special Issue on International Subsystems), 13(4) (December 1969), prepared by Peter Berton, especially articles by John H. Sigler, "News Flow in the North African International Subsystem"; Thomas W. Robinson, "Systems Theory and the Communist System"; Donald C. Hellmann, "The Emergence of an East Asian International Subsystem"; Leonard Binder, "The Middle East as a Subordinate International System," *World Politics,* X (1958), 408–429. See also Michael Banks, "Systems Analysis and the Study of Regions," *International Studies Quarterly,* 13 (1969), 335–360; Karl Kaiser, "The Interaction of Regional Subsystems: Some Preliminary Notes on Recurrent Patterns and the Role of Superpowers," *World Politics,* XXI (1968), 84–107; and Kathryn D. Baols, "The Concept Subordinate International System: A Critique," in Richard A. Falk and Saul H. Mendlovitz, eds., *Regional Politics and World Order* (San Francisco: Freeman, 1973).

113. Louis J. Cantori and Steven L. Spiegel, *The International Politics of Regions: A Comparative Approach* (Englewood Cliffs, NJ: Prentice-Hall, 1970), p. 607.

114. Ibid., pp. 7–20.

115. William R. Thompson, "The Regional Subsystem: A Conceptual Explication and a Propositional Inventory," *International Studies Quarterly,* 17(1) (March 1973), 93. This article contains an extensive list of propositions about regional subsystem behavior drawn from the literature of the past generation.

116. Ibid., p. 96.

117. Ibid., p. 101.

118. William R. Thompson, "Introduction: World System Analysis With and Without the Hyphen," in William R. Thompson, ed., *Contending Approaches to World System Analysis* (Beverly Hills, CA: Sage Publications, 1983), p. 9.

119. Ibid.

120. Immanuel Wallerstein, *The Modern World-System: Capitalist Agriculture and the Origins of the European World Economy in the Sixteenth Century* (New York: Academic Press, 1974); *The Modern World-System II: Mercantilism and the Consolidation of the European World-Economy, 1600–1750* (New York: Academic Press, 1980).

121. George Modelski, "Long Cycles of World Leadership," in William R. Thompson, ed., op. cit., p. 115.

122. Ibid., p. 131.

123. Harold and Margaret Sprout, *The Ecological Perspective on Human Affairs with Special Reference to International Politics* (Princeton, NJ: Princeton University Press, 1965), p. 208; Harold and Margaret Sprout, *An Ecological Paradigm for the Study of International Politics,* Research Monograph No. 30, Center of International Studies (Princeton, NJ: Princeton University Press, 1968), pp. 2–10.

124. Stanley Hoffmann, "Theory as a Set of Questions," in Stanley Hoffmann, ed., *Contemporary Theory in International Relations,* (Englewood Cliffs, NJ: Prentice-Hall, 1960), p. 44. The quotation in this excerpt is from Ralph Dahrendorf, "Out of Utopia: Toward a Reorientation of Sociological Analysis," *American Journal of Sociology,* LXIX (September 1958), 120.

125. Stanley Hoffmann, "International Relations: The Long Road to Theory," in James N. Rosenau, ed., *International Politics and Foreign Policy* (New York: Free Press, 1961), p. 426.

126. Jerone Stephens, "An Appraisal of Some System Approaches in the Study of International Systems," *International Studies Quarterly,* 16(3) (September 1972); 348.

127. George Modelski, "The Promise of Geocentric Politics," *World Politics,* 22(4) (July 1970), 631; *Principles of World Politics* (New York: Free Press, 1972), p. 8.

128. Steven J. Brams, "The Search for Structural Order in the International System: Some Models and Preliminary Results," *International Studies Quarterly,* 13(3) (September 1969), 278.

129. Oran B. Young, *A Systemic Approach to International Politics,* Research Monograph No. 33, Center of International Studies (Princeton, NJ: Princeton University Press, 1968), p. 1.

130. Ibid., pp. 2–3.

131. John J. Weltman, *Systems Theory in International Relations: A Study in Metaphoric Hypertrophy,* op. cit., p. 311.

Chapter
4

Environmental Theories

THE ROLE OF ENVIRONMENT IN INTERNATIONAL RELATIONS

The role of environing factors, including the physical milieu (geography) and the social milieu (culture), as conditioners of political behavior, has attracted major theoretical interest for many generations. Especially until the end of World War II, the study of international relations drew heavily on geography as an explanation for state behavior. States were said to be advantaged, or handicapped, by geographic location and circumstances. With the dawn of the nuclear age and the development of postindustrial societies, environing factors, notably the role of geography, diminished in salience. Nuclear systems capable of intercontinental range greatly diminished whatever security had been derived from geographic location. By the same token, postindustrial societies depend more on access to information-based technologies and intellectual capabilities than on physical control of territory containing national resources. Japan, although devoid of national resources such as coal and iron, nevertheless became the world's second largest economy based on cutting-edge technologies. Despite its remoteness from Europe and Asia, the United States and European–Asian states became equally vulnerable to a nuclear strike delivered by intercontinental ballistic missiles (ICBMs) capable of reaching their targets within minutes. In the generation after World War II, as noted in other chapters, theories of international relations drew heavily on concepts derived from academic disciplines other than geography. Nevertheless, throughout this period environing factors were never totally ignored. Environing factors encompass what Harold and Margaret Sprout, whose writings spanned the decades preceding and following World War II, termed *human* as well as *nonhuman, intangible* as well as *tangible* factors, the physical environment (geography) and the social environment (culture).[1] Taken together, the physical and social environment compose what has been termed the *milieu*. Since the 1970s, however, the environing and geographic dimension has received renewed attention. The focus is less on the geopolitical concerns of the earlier period than on the relationship between geography and conflict, as discussed in this chapter. At the same time, since the 1960s, there has been extensive interest in the analysis of the implications of resource scarcity and depletion for international relations, including conflict.[2]

Before turning to the most recent work on environing factors, we survey earlier theories. Interest in the impact of geographical and broader environmental factors on politics extends back to the ancient world. Aristotle, for example, believed that people and their environment are inseparable, and that they are affected both by geographical circumstances and by political institutions. Location near the sea stimulated the commercial activity on which the city-state was based; temperate climate favorably affected the development of national character, human energy, and intellect.[3] Writing in the late sixteenth century, Jean Bodin, too, maintained that climatic circumstances influence national characteristics, as well as the foreign policies of states. According to Bodin, the extremes of northern and temperate climates offer conditions most favorable to building a political system based on law and justice. Northern and mountainous regions were said to be conducive to greater political discipline than were southern climes, which fail to spark initiative.[4] Montesquieu, one of the great eighteenth-century French philosophers, pointed to various climatic factors that he felt influenced the political divisions of Western Europe, in contrast to the great plains of Asia and Eastern Europe, and contributed to a spirit of political independence. According to Montesquieu, islands could preserve their freedom more easily than continental countries because they are isolated from foreign influences.[5] Here, Montesquieu had in mind Britain, which had evolved unique political institutions that he greatly admired, and which had withstood invasion from continental Europe since 1066.

In American history, Frederick Jackson Turner hypothesized that the existence of the frontier, pushed westward by succeeding generations of settlers until the end of the nineteenth century, shaped the American character and intellect—"that practical, inventive turn of mind, quick to find expedients; that masterful grasp of material things, lacking in the artistic but powerful to affect great ends; that restless, nervous energy; the dominant individualism, working for good and evil, and withal that buoyancy and exuberance which comes with freedom—these are the traits of the frontier, or traits called out elsewhere because of the existence of the frontier."[6] The rise of social-Darwinian analysis in the late nineteenth century also provided an important intellectual stimulus to environmentally oriented studies of international affairs, insofar as it transferred to the social order a scientific perspective in which the evolutionary development of a species was a function of its ability to adjust to its physical habitat. The concept of the survival of the fittest was adapted from living organisms to the state, as exemplified in the geopolitical writings of Friedrich Ratzel, discussed later in this chapter.

Environmental factors encompass resources and population, as well as the impact of population on resources, including the availability of food supplies. The notion that there are severe limits to growth is central to the thought of Thomas Robert Malthus and to many of the writings on imperialism. Beginning in 1798, with his *Essay on the Principle of Population as it Affects the Future Improvement of Society,* Malthus hypothesized that population growth will always outpace the increase in food supplies. If unchecked, population will rise in geometric progression, although the means of subsistence will be augmented only in arithmetic progression. As a result, poverty will be the inevitable fate of mankind, unless population growth is checked by war, famine, and disease. J. A. Hobson and Vladimir

Lenin, in their respective analyses of imperialism, saw a quest for access to markets and raw materials, leading capitalist states to become imperialistic. For Lenin, the ultimate effect of capitalism, as noted in Chapter 6, would be a struggle among capitalist states for the world's remaining markets and raw materials.

In a more contemporary study, Nazli Choucri and Robert C. North hypothesized that there is an inextricable relationship between population growth and resource demand, and that the more advanced the level of technology, the greater will be the need for resources. A population increase of 1 percent is said to make necessary a 4 percent increase in national income merely to maintain living standards at their existing level.[7] As technology advances, together with population growth, societies seek greater access to resources. As societies attempt to extend their interests outward in light of resource needs, the likelihood of conflict is enhanced. Here, Choucri and North draw linkages among resource factors, domestic growth, and foreign policy. Their hypotheses are examined in greater detail in Chapter 8, along with the writings of Quincy Wright, who emphasized the relationship between conflict and cultural, political, institutional, and technological change.

Peace is said to be dependent on an equilibrium among many forces and to be jeopardized by a transformation in factors such as demography. Rapid increases in population in the past century have produced cultural interpenetration and have greatly increased communication. As a result, what Quincy Wright termed *technological distance* has narrowed, while the opportunities for friction and for conflict among people have increased.[8] Wright postulated that the growth in size of states had made it more necessary and more likely that conflict would be resolved without violence, but it had also made more severe those conflicts that could not be settled by peaceful means.[9]

Thus, at the end of the twentieth century, population, as well as resource and technology factors—the so-called global issues of the present era—have contributed to a literature focused on the implications of population growth for resource scarcity, the implications of resource scarcity for potential conflict, the relationship between resources and geography, and the impact of technology on resources and geography.[10] Technology has made possible the exploitation of resources in inhospitable and once inaccessible environments, such as the seabed, and in the years to come in outer space. At the same time, technology has created the great need for resources that has contributed to their depletion and has raised the specter of resource scarcity unless alternative sources or substitutes are found.

The political significance of one or another geographical location has been influenced decisively by technology and by resource issues. The geopolitical significance of the Strait of Hormuz, commanding the entrance to the Gulf, lies in the location of vast oil reserves in such neighboring states as Saudi Arabia, Kuwait, Iraq, and Iran. In historical context, major emphasis was placed on the importance of the seas. In the writings of Alfred Thayer Mahan, the geopolitical significance of the seas stemmed from the mobility they conferred, by virtue of the ability of the sailing vessel and later the steamship to move military resources most effectively from one point to another. Subsequent changes in technology had the effect of enhancing the importance of other geographical elements, although the vast bulk of world trade still moves by sea.

The end of the Cold War stimulated renewed thinking about environmental factors. The growth in numbers and influence of intergovernmental organizations, as well as players other than the sovereign states as important actors, contributed to a need to reconsider the implications of environing factors for political relationships. Such entities, as well as other transnational forces, such as the information revolution, challenge the sovereignty of the geographically based nation-state. Forces leading to the breakup of existing states, including the Soviet Union and Yugoslavia, have transformed the global map. The bipolar world of the Cold War has been replaced by new spatial patterns analyzed with reference to environmental considerations.

For example, Robert Kaplan has pointed to a post–Cold War world characterized principally by pockets or islands of affluence, notably North America, Western Europe, and parts of the Pacific rim.[11] These advanced societies are linked in an unprecedented global network of trade, investment, technology transfer, instantaneous communications, and mobility of persons and ideas. They stand in sharp contrast to surrounding regions, the defining features of which include political fragmentation, ungovernability, major population increases, declining living standards, spreading disease, ethnic and sectarian conflict, resource depletion, and the rise of radical, fundamentalist ideologists. Much of Africa, portions of South America, and parts of Central Asia and South Asia fall within this category. Kaplan sketches a world in which states disintegrate under a tidal wave of refugees from environmental and social disaster. Wars break out over scarce resources, including water, while the distinction between war and crime becomes increasingly blurred. Private armies fight each other, as well as state security forces. To describe what he terms the bifurcated world of the post–Cold War era, Kaplan uses the analogy of "a stretch limo in the potholed streets of New York City, where homeless beggars live. Inside the limo are the air-conditioned post-industrial regions of North America, Europe, the emerging Pacific Rim, and a few other isolated places, with their trade symmetry and computer-information highways. Outside is the rest of mankind, going in a completely different direction."[12]

Much of the essence of international relations is the study of states and other interacting units within a spatial setting. Conflicts take place across or within the geographical boundaries of states. Wars have been waged over control of territory and resources. Therefore, *political geography,* the relationship between geography and politics, has been of enduring importance from a theoretical, as well as a policy, perspective. As George J. Demko and William B. Wood point out, political geography has as its principal focus the study of how societies make decisions affecting relationships between people and their environment, as well as spatial patterns of human settlement.[13] Encompassed in this definition are individuals and groups of people, as well as social institutions and governments. Environmental factors include national and human-created systems—national resources and urban areas, the latter based on decisions taken by individuals or groups of individuals to settle in specific geographic locations. *Political geography* then represents the study of how and why people adapt to and modify their environments.

Such decisions span a spectrum that encompasses natural ecosystems, the market for various goods and services, relations between states dependent on the same national resources, and the quest of different groups of people for control of territory that they covet.

Closely related is the term *geopolitics,* which moves the study of the relationship between geography and politics to include the study of power in its geopolitical dimension. *Geopolitics* refers to the impact of geography (spatial features) on political power. As Saul B. Cohen has suggested, "The essence of geopolitical analysis is the relation of international political power to the geographical setting. Geopolitical views vary with the changing geographical setting and with man's interpretation of the nature of this change."[14] According to Raymond Aron, the term *geopolitical* encompasses a "geographical schematization of diplomatic-strategic relations with a geographic-economic analysis of resources, with an interpretation of diplomatic attitudes as a result of the way of life and of the environment (sedentary, nomadic, agricultural, seafaring)."[15] Ewan Anderson suggests that geography, as part of geopolitics, consists of very small areas that form what he terms the *epicenters of geopolitical upheaval,* with consequences that can extend far beyond their point of origin.[16] As examples, he cites the Strait of Hormuz at the entrance to the Persian Gulf, the Spratley Islands in the South China Sea, the Strait of Malacca that connects the Indian Ocean and the South China Sea, and, during the Cold War, the divided city of Berlin. Such geopolitically important areas, so-called flashpoints, are considered later in this chapter. In Colin Gray's perspective, "Physical geography alone, while providing important constraints and opportunities, is given specific strategic meaning only with reference to time, technology, relative national effort, and choices effected among strategies and tactics."[17] Several of the theories discussed in other chapters attach varying degrees of importance to the environment, including but not confined to geography.

The most recent thinking about spatial relationships encompasses what Demko and Wood term a *geopolinomic world*[18] and what Edward N. Luttwak terms *geoeconomics.*[19] In place of maps based on national boundaries, it is telecommunication channels that assume primary significance. Decisions about where to locate a production facility are made not with regard for frontiers between states but instead on the basis of such factors as the availability of needed labor and hospitality to investment. The geopolinomic map of the world is drawn by international financial networks, investment patterns, the movement of people and ideas, and the flow of vast amounts of information. Among the results is a world of region states, noted later in this chapter. In a geopolinomic world, the internationalization of capital and the accelerating flow of information weaken the political foundations of the geographically defined state. Such entities, based in fixed territorial dimensions, are destabilized or even dissolved by the forces associated with information technologies. In a geoeconomic world, power is measured by the ability, with high levels of research and development, to conquer the markets of the future by achieving decisive technological superiority. Access to emerging markets becomes more important than actual physical control of territory.

The revolution in technology that shapes postindustrial societies has produced yet another spatial relationship, termed *cyberspace.* This concept is not defined in traditional territorial geographical terms but instead is directly related to the information highway. Whereas human interaction before and during the industrial age took place along defined sea lines of communication and transportation routes determined by rail lines and highways, the information highway exists as a multimedia, multichannel, internetted global communications capability. Cyberspace provides the means to bypass and circumvent traditional state sovereignty and transcend geographically bound entities. In cyberspace, we gain access to unprecedented amounts of information in the immediate time frame. Whether in war or in business, the key to success lies in commanding access to information. Just as control of particular geographic territories was deemed essential to industrial-age warfare, in the postindustrial era, the crucial ingredient in planning and executing a military operation lies in having access to large amounts of information, together with the ability to process such data and to incorporate it into our thought processes.

ENVIRONING FACTORS: EARLIER TWENTIETH-CENTURY APPROACHES

Whether implicitly or explicitly, environing factors are deeply rooted in much of international-relations theory. Illustrative of the place of such factors are utopian and realist theory and their most recent manifestations in the form of neoliberal and neorealist–structural-realist theory discussed in Chapter 2. Utopian and realist theory and their more contemporary intellectual counterparts discuss the human actor in relation to the environment. Nonetheless, they broaden the notion of environment to include the products of human culture, as well as the physical features of the earth. Drawing on the writings of theorists of the Enlightenment, utopian theorists claimed that international behavior could be changed by transforming the institutional setting. Schemes for international organization and world government, as well as for establishing norms for international conduct, were designed to alter human behavior by changing the international political environment. In contrast, as the analysis undertaken in Chapter 2 reveals, realists in international relations often held that the geographical location of states will condition, if not determine, political behavior. Among the most influential realist theorists who also wrote extensively on the impact of geography on international politics were Nicholas J. Spykman and Robert Strausz-Hupé. If the political behavior of national units is in large part the product of environmental circumstances, including geography, in which nations find themselves, the perennial task of the political leader is to work within the parameters established by the environment. Moreover, writers who have used the constructs of systems theory, discussed in Chapter 3, have emphasized the environment. Systems may be open or closed. The open systems, both biological and social, by definition, are susceptible to, and dependent for their survival on, inputs from, and outputs into, their environment. In so-called closed or self-contained systems, inputs from an external environment have been eliminated, although environmental factors have often been incorporated into closed systems.

One of the major earlier twentieth-century historians of global civilization in historic context, Arnold Toynbee, held that civilizations are born in environments that pose difficult challenges.[20] The challenged civilization develops an élan vital, which carries it through equilibrium toward another challenge, thereby inspiring another response. The challenge–response cycle is potentially infinite, although it is retrospective, thus not allowing us to predict the potential response to a challenge. He examined five types of challenging stimuli. Two were physical: (1) *hard country*—that is, a country possessing a harsh climate, terrain, and soil—and (2) *new ground*—the exploration, opening up, and development of a wilderness into productive land. The three nonphysical stimuli include (1) those challenges emanating from another state, (2) continuous external pressure against a state, and (3) a stimulus of penalization—that is, if a state loses the use of a particular component, it is likely to respond by increasing correspondingly the efficiency of another component. Toynbee added that overly severe physical challenge can arrest the development of civilization. The Polynesian, Eskimo, Arabian nomad, Spartan, and Osmanli civilizations were retarded as a result of physical challenges they could not meet.

The breakdown of civilizations results from the degeneration of the creative minority into a "dominant minority which attempts to retain by force a position that it has ceased to merit." This in turn provokes a "secession of a proletariat which no longer admires and imitates its rulers and revolts against its servitude."[21] Thus, the society loses its social cohesiveness. Vertical schisms between geographically segregated communities and horizontal schisms between classes or groups that are geographically contiguous but socially segregated characterize the disintegration of a civilization. The horizontal schism may occur when a dominant minority retains its ruling position by force but loses its right to that role as a result of its loss of complexity. Toynbee's schema is related to modern, more complex theories of social revolution, treated in Chapter 8.

GEOGRAPHICAL FACTORS OF NATIONAL POWER

With the advent of industrial-age communication–transportation technologies, increased attention was given to geography, focusing on population–resource distribution, the strategic location of states, and the forward projection of national power. Because geopolitics has as its focal point national power and the control of territory, it followed that those political entities most able to project their capabilities over greater distances would constitute the dominant industrial-age powers. According to numerous writers—including, for example, Kenneth Boulding and subsequently Patrick O'Sullivan—there is an inverse relationship between power and distance from its core area.[22] In O'Sullivan's words, "Most of the conflicts [since the mid-1950s] have arisen in the crush zone between the great powers. The force fields of the hegemonies may be thought of as extending out from their cores, overwhelming smaller nations with their power, surrounding the spheres of influence of lesser powers and lapping against each other at the edges."[23] To be sure, the impact of technology has been of such importance, as noted elsewhere in this chapter, that the political significance of geography has been altered, although not eliminated. To the extent that weapons of mass destruction can be launched from any point on earth, from under the oceans, or from outer space, to strike a target anywhere on earth, the distinction between greater power at its core compared with the periphery has lost its previous significance.[24] However, the capabilities available to political entities are numerous, with some more easily moveable than others. In an era before the airplane and the missile, when military capabilities were most easily moved by sea, the political unit most able to master sea power became the dominant state. At an abstract level, the relationship between geography and power—geopolitics—resides in the ability, at any time, of one state or another to move power in order to influence or control desired territory deemed to be of strategic importance. In the geopolinomic or geoeconomic world, the relationship between geography and power is found in the ability to move goods, services, and information most efficiently and rapidly from one point to another.

For the most part, those writers concerned with the environment have tended to stress the importance of such factors as determinants, or at least conditioners, of political behavior. Environment not only limits human conduct, but also provides opportunities. Of particular importance are climatic and geographical factors. Uneven distribution of resources, as well as differences in geographical and climatic endowments, shape the potential power of a state. The size of the country influences the availability of indigenous natural resources, and the climate affects the mobilization of human resources necessary for exploiting those natural resources. Variations in those factors may have crucially important implications for the structure of political systems, even influencing their capacity for survival under stress.

If political behavior is affected by environment, individuals have some capacity for choice, even within the constraints furnished by environing circumstances. Of particular importance to writers such as Alfred Thayer Mahan (1840–1914), an American naval officer and historian; Sir Halford Mackinder (1861–1947), a British geographer; and Giulio Douhet, an Italian advocate of air power; as well as Harold and Margaret Sprout, is the impact of technological change on our environment. Technology, it is suggested, does not render environmental factors unimportant or obsolete. Rather, it replaces one set of environmental factors with still another set. Mahan saw naval capabilities as the key to national power; Mackinder considered the technology of land transportation as crucial; Douhet focused on the technology of air power as it was altering the conduct of warfare earlier in the twentieth century by extending our capacity for projecting power far beyond historical confines. The advent of the technologies of the late twentieth century for the extension of control both on the earth's surface and in inner and outer space has enhanced the interest of scholars and policymakers in geopolitical and geopolinomic relationships. Thus, for example, in this age of ICBMs, analysts engaging in the constant calculus of deterrence consider such geographic factors as a country's size and population distribution, together with weapon deployments on land or sea, as relevant to targeting strategies. In the age of the information highway, the ability to receive, transport, and process vast amounts of data—to achieve information dominance—is said to represent the key to power.

Although we possess some limited capacity to change our environment, we remain circumscribed in our behavior by environmental factors. Central to geopolitical theories has been the question of the extent to which environmental factors can be modified to suit human needs. This question is not new. It long separated Anglo-American and French theorizing about geopolitical relationships. A French school of geographical possibilist thought, represented by Lucien Febvre and Vidal de la Blache, rejected the determinism of Anglo-American and German environmental theories. Drawing on the intellectual heritage of the Enlightenment, French students of geography suggested that the natural environment could be modified. In fact, human free will was said ultimately to determine the options available. Environment, and geography in particular, is but one of many forces governing the development of human activity.[25] Twentieth-century geopolitical writers fall somewhere between a strictly determinist and a possibilist interpretation. If environment does not determine the boundaries of human conduct, it nevertheless provides an important, if not crucial, conditioning influence. As Ladis K. D. Kristof has suggested, "The modern geopolitician does not look at the world map in order to find out what nature compels us to do but what nature advises us to do, given our preferences."[26]

We turn now to the writings of representative geopolitical theorists from the United States and Europe. Among the Americans, we focus on Mahan and the Sprouts, as well as subsequent, more recent writings on political geography, with an emphasis on the relationship between territorial boundaries and conflict and the efforts to define and describe the post–Cold War geopolitical and geopolinomic environment. Mahan concentrated on the impact of naval power on national political potential. The Sprouts probed the implications of a broad range of environmental factors for political behavior. In addition to Mahan and the Sprouts, a list of the most eminent American students of geopolitical relationships includes such diverse earlier twentieth-century writers as Isaiah Bowman, James Fairgreave, C. W. Hayes, Richard Hartshorne, Stephen B. Jones, George F. Kennan, Owen Lattimore, Homer Lea, General William ("Billy") Mitchell, Ellen Churchill Semple, Alexander P. de Seversky, Nicholas J. Spykman, Robert Strausz-Hupé, Frederick Jackson Turner, Hans A. Weigert, Karl A. Wittfogel, Derwent Whittlesey, and Quincy Wright.

MAHAN, THE SEAS, AND NATIONAL POWER

Alfred Thayer Mahan wrote during the period of the last great wave of European imperial expansion and the rise of the United States to the status of a world power. His ideas greatly influenced Theodore Roosevelt who, first as Assistant Secretary of the Navy and later as President, contributed decisively to the rise of the United States as a leading naval power. Mahan's analysis of maritime history, particularly the growth of British global influence, led him to conclude that control of the seas, and especially of strategically important narrow waterways, was crucial to great power status.[27] Mahan based his theory on the observation that the rise of the British Empire and the development of Britain as a naval power had occurred simultaneously. The world's principal sea routes had become the empire's internal communications links. Except for the Panama Canal, Britain controlled all of the world's major waterways and narrow seas or *choke points*—those bodies of water to which access, or passage through, could be controlled relatively easily from either shore: Dover, Gibraltar, Malta, Alexandria, the Cape of Good Hope, the Strait of Malacca at Singapore, the Suez Canal, and the entrance to the St. Lawrence River.

The ocean commerce of Northern Europe passed either through the narrow Strait of Dover, under British guns, or around the northern tip of Scotland, where the British navy maintained constant vigil. Britain and the United States enjoyed greater access to the oceans than did Germany and Russia. Movement by sea was easier than over land, and the land masses were surrounded by oceans. States with ready access to the oceans had greater potential for major power status than states that were land-locked. Islands had an advantage over states sharing land boundaries with other states. Maritime states formed alliances more for purposes of commerce than of aggression.

In Mahan's analysis, sea power was crucial to national strength and prosperity. The capacity of a state to achieve such status was dependent on its geographic position, land configuration, extent of territory, population, national character, and form of government. For example, nations such as Britain or Japan, isolated by water, must maintain large naval forces if they are to be great powers, because for nations with long coastlines, the sea is a frontier and their position relative to other states is a function of their capacity to operate beyond that frontier. Geographical position contributed to Britain's power—with sufficient proximity to continental Europe to strike potential enemies and adequate distance from continental Europe to be reasonably safe from invasion. By focusing sea power in the Northeastern Atlantic and the English Channel, Britain could control the world commerce of European powers because there were no rivals to British sea power until the rise after 1890 of German, Japanese, and U.S. naval forces.

Such an option was not open to France, whose power had to be divided to protect its eastern frontier and its Mediterranean and Atlantic coastlines. In Mahan's analysis, the length of the coastline and the quality of the harbors were important factors, although an abundance of territory may constitute a source of weakness if the land does not have adequate levels of population and natural resources. Mahan held that the size and character of population and an aptitude for commercial pursuits, particularly those of international trade, indicated a capacity in a nation to become a major power. A nation with a large portion of its population skilled in maritime pursuits, especially shipbuilding and trade, had the potential to become a great maritime state. In sum, Mahan correlated national power and mobility over the seas, because at the time he wrote, transportation over land was primitive in contrast to the relative facility of movement over the frictionless oceans.

Building on the Work of Mahan

Other writers have viewed seapower as an essential part of power projection. Since the sixteenth century, navies have been critically important both in preserving the home base of the naval power from attack and in safeguarding friendly communications and commercial routes, while denying enemies access to the seas. Building on Mahan's work, George Modelski and William R. Thompson, tracing the relationship between sea power and global politics, concluded that sea power has represented the sine qua non for global operations.[28] Leading naval powers not only protect sea lines of communication, but also play a critical part in preserving the status quo established as a result of previous major wars. Major navies represent a necessary, but not sufficient, condition for global power status. They confer intercontinental mobility, giving their possessors the means, as the United States demonstrated in the Cuban Missile Crisis of 1962, to block the forces of a challenger. Although land forces were indispensable to the ultimate defeat and occupation of an opponent, as in World War II, it was naval power that linked the various theaters of operation by conferring indispensable mobility on the leading possessors of such capabilities.

Modelski and Thompson go so far as to suggest that sea power has been an essential part of world politics since 1500, directly related to the long-cycle approach. It was at the beginning of the sixteenth century that the global system was transformed into an oceanic system, as a result of naval technologies linking previously isolated continents and opening the world for European imperial expansion and colonization. Successively, Portugal in the sixteenth century, the Netherlands in the seventeenth century, the United Kingdom in the eighteenth and nineteenth centuries, and the United States in the twentieth century, became major powers based on their ability to master the naval innovations of the era and to contribute decisively to maintaining international order. Each long cycle lasted approximately 100 years and was identified with a state having vast maritime capabilities. As noted in Chapter 3, the long cycle, represented by the work of Modelski and Thompson, as well as other contributors, holds that over time, the world system displays regularities that are both repetitive and evolutionary. This includes global powers and global wars. Such conflicts have had a crucially important naval dimension because maritime power is indispensable to intercontinental interaction. The technological innovation that has marked evolution toward greater complexity during each succeeding long cycle has been associated with sea power.

Mackinder and the Heartland

Like Mahan, Sir Halford Mackinder saw an intimate relationship between geography and technology. If the technology of the earlier era had enhanced the mobility of sea power over land power, the technology of the early twentieth century gave to land power the dominant position. The railroad, and subsequently the internal combustion engine and the construction of a modern highway and road network, made possible rapid transportation within much of the land mass of Eurasia. Until then, the inner regions of Eurasia had been landlocked. Mackinder noted that Eurasia's river systems drain into none of the major seas of the world. The Arctic freezes much of the northern Eurasian coast. Nonetheless, with the advent of the railroad, the Middle East was becoming as accessible to Germany by land in the early twentieth century as it had been to Britain by sea in previous centuries. Although Britain, as a small island, was what Mackinder termed the *legatee* of a depreciating estate, the major Eurasian powers sat astride the greatest combination of human and natural resources. Mackinder saw the struggle between land power and sea power as a unifying theme of history. The first cycle in the evolution of sea power was completed in the closing of the Mediterranean Sea by the Macedonians. In the next cycle in the evolution of sea power, Mackinder noted that Rome, a land power, had defeated maritime Carthage, and once again the Mediterranean had become a closed sea.[29] In both these cycles in the ancient era—the Macedonian–Greek and the Roman–Carthaginian—a land power had successfully challenged a sea power. In modern times, Britain found it difficult, if not impossible, to withstand pressures from land powers. Technology, once favorable to sea power, was said to be tipping the advantage in the early twentieth century to land power.

First, in a famous paper read before the Royal Geographic Society of London in 1904, and later, just after World War I, in his book *Democratic Ideals and Reality,* Mackinder suggested that the pivot area of international politics was that vast expanse of territory stretching from the East European and Siberian plains:

> As we consider this rapid review of the broader currents of history, does not a certain persistence of geographical relationship become evident? Is not the pivot region of the world's politics that vast area of Euro-Asia which is inaccessible to ships, but in antiquity lay open to the horse-riding nomads, and is today about to be covered with a network of railroads?[30]

This area, which coincided with the czarist Russian Empire, "occupies the central strategical position" and possesses "incalculably great" resources. (This pivot area Mackinder called the "Heartland.") The region, he suggested, was surrounded by the "inner crescent," which includes such countries on the periphery of Eurasia as Germany, Turkey, India, and China. This region in turn is surrounded by the "outer crescent," which includes such countries as Britain, South Africa, and Japan.

Mackinder formulated the famous dictum:

Who rules East Europe commands the Heartland
  Who rules the Heartland commands the World Island Eurasia
  Who rules the World Island commands the World.[31]

Mackinder feared the rise of Germany and later the Soviet Union as mighty land states capable of becoming great naval powers. While emphasizing the growing importance of land power, Mackinder did not deprecate the role of sea power. Sea power was as vital to world power as it had ever been. In the twentieth century, however, broader land bases were necessary for sea power than had been needed in the nineteenth century. Mackinder's world island had the potential to become the greatest sea power, even though its heartland would remain invulnerable to attack by sea power. In the twentieth century, the state controlling the heartland and hence the world island would become a leading sea power in the same way as Macedonia and Rome, although primarily land powers, had eventually gained control of the seas. In fact, Mackinder correctly foresaw international politics in the first half of the twentieth century as being principally a struggle between Germany and Russia for control of the heartland and adjacent areas on the Eurasian land mass. What he did not foresee, of course, was the collapse of the

Soviet Union, based on its inability to link politically that vast region between Central-Eastern Europe, including part of Germany, in a political framework capable of exerting compelling pressure from the Eurasian heartland into and beyond the rimlands. The organizational and ideological failures of communism proved to have a greater impact on world power than the heartland resource base about which Mackinder had written. Such a conception has influenced the thought of other writers, including many of the realist school considered in Chapter 2, who have posited that the state capable of dominating Eurasia would have within its grasp the means to control remaining portions of the world.

Without necessarily referring to Mackinder or stating their assumptions as explicitly, American policymakers have had as a principal objective to prevent the domination of the Eurasian land mass by a hostile power—hence, the American interest in alliances with Western Europe and Japan and in security commitments elsewhere on the rimlands of Eurasia, including the Middle East. From this conception derived American diplomacy, especially evident in the Nixon–Kissinger foreign policy of the 1970s and in subsequent administrations during the Cold War, to strengthen links between the United States and the People's Republic of China, and thus to help prevent a reconciliation between the two largest land powers of Eurasia—China and the Soviet Union.

During World War II, Mackinder revised his theory to include in an Atlantic community a counterpoise to the aggregation of power in Eurasia. Although he accurately foresaw that the Soviet Union would emerge from World War II as the "greatest land power on the globe" and "in the strategically strongest defensive position," the nations of the North Atlantic basin would form a counterpoise, which in fact occurred with the formation of the Atlantic Alliance in 1949 as East–West tensions deepened in the early post–World War II period.[32] According to Mackinder, together, Britain, France, and the United States could provide power adequate to prevent a resurgence of German aggression and to balance the Soviet Union. Other writers, such as Nicholas J. Spykman and Stephen B. Jones, suggested that the rimland of Eurasia might prove strategically more important than the heartland if new centers of industrial power and communications were created along the circumference of the Eurasian land mass. The rimland hypothesis was a central theoretical foundation of the policy for containment of the Soviet Union, beginning with the Truman Doctrine and the Marshall Plan in 1947, during the Cold War, and extending into the 1990s.[33]

The advent of the airplane, and subsequently the means to penetrate outer space, provided a whole new dimension to geopolitics. Once again, technology had the effect of altering the significance of specific geopolitical relations. Just as Mahan and Mackinder had based their geopolitical theories on an analysis of the implications, respectively, of technologies facilitating movement over the seas and the land, Giulio Douhet, writing in the 1920s, saw the airplane as conferring unprecedented possibilities for the conduct of warfare against targets previously invulnerable to attack and destruction. As long as human activities were restricted to the earth's surface, they were subject to constraints imposed by the terrain. Although the seas are uniform in character, human mobility via the oceans is limited by virtue of the coastlines that surround them. No such impediments to mobility exist in the air. Writing with great foresight in 1921, Douhet concluded,

> The airplane has complete freedom of action and direction; it can fly to and from any point of the compass in the shortest time—a straight line—by any route deemed expedient. . . . By virtue of this new weapon, the repercussions of war are no longer limited by the farthest artillery range of surface guns, but can be directly felt for hundreds and hundreds of miles over all the lands and seas of nations at war. . . . There will be no distinction any longer between soldiers and civilians.[34]

It followed that the wars of the future would differ radically from those of the past, and that control of the air would confer on states unprecedented mobility of power and the capacity to inflict devastation on an adversary's military forces and industry.

Writing during World War II, and building on the writings of Douhet and the ideas of U.S. General Billy Mitchell, Alexander de Seversky emphasized the implications of advances in technology for rapid increases in the range of aircraft. This would render unnecessary the aircraft carrier, he predicted, because planes could operate from land bases to attack targets in the enemy's homeland. Thus, the unprecedented mobility conferred by technology for human-operated flight, noted by Douhet, was given even greater emphasis by Alexander de Seversky. Air power made possible not only greater mobility, but also freed people to an unprecedented extent from dependence on an extensive ground organization, including bases for refueling, as the range of aircraft, and thus their operating radius, grew.[35] Control of air space became as complex a problem as control of the land and the sea.

From Heartland to Core–Periphery

Mackinder's "heartland–rimland" relationship differs fundamentally from the geopolitical concept of core (center)–periphery based on dependency theory. Nevertheless, both share the idea that much of Europe lies within the heartland or the core (center) area. According to the core–periphery spatial structure, the postcolonial world contains a core of affluent states, surrounded by a large number of poor former colonies that, despite their nominal independence, remain heavily dependent on the core for their economic existence. According to Immanuel Wallerstein, whose world-systems work is discussed in Chapter 3, the geographical expansion of the European economy, beginning about 1450, had created a global economy by the first decade of the twentieth century. The core–periphery as a spatial setting is based on the explicit assumption that the periphery did not join the world economy as a full and equal partner. The core and the periphery are characterized by productive processes based on comparative advantage. The core area contains units with relatively high wages, advanced technology, and a diversified economy capable of producing many different kinds of goods and services. This contrasts with the periphery, the defining characteristics of which are low wages, a relative absence of advanced technology, and a production base lacking great breadth. Viewed in contemporary context, according to Taylor, there are three core areas encompassing Western Europe, North America, and Japan. Such spatial relationships are familiar in the present global setting. They represent an effort to categorize states and regions as geographic entities by reference to their economic attributes and, in doing so, to consider the implications of such characteristics for conflict. For example, do the fault lines for future conflict lie between or within core–periphery areas? To what extent does the spatial structure described by writers such as Taylor and Wallerstein shape the emerging conflict map?

GEOPOLITICS: THE POLITICAL SIGNIFICANCE OF SPATIAL FACTORS

Friedrich Ratzel (1844–1904), a German geographer, coined the term *Anthropogeographie,* which meant a synthesis of geography, anthropology, and politics. Thus, the new discipline of political geography was born in Germany in the nineteenth century. This new discipline was directed to the study of people, the state, and the world as organic units. The state was seen as a living organism that occupies space and that grows, contracts, and eventually dies, although Ratzel himself stopped short of imputing to the state an objective reality, asserting instead that states "are not organisms properly speaking but only aggregate-organisms," the unity of which is forged by "moral and spiritual forces."[36]

As already noted in this chapter, political geographers addressed themselves to the question of people's relationship to nature. They were concerned with the implications of climate, topography, and natural resources for civilization. In fact, Ratzel attributed the development of superior civilizations, which he identified principally with Europe, to favorable climatic conditions. He contended that humankind was engaged in an unending struggle for living space, an idea that later was integrated in the form of the term *lebensraum* into the thought of Haushofer and Hitler as a geopolitical rationalization for the military aggression of the Third Reich in World War II. A state's land area indicates its power position. States strive to extend their territorial frontiers. The urge for territorial expansion is greatest among strong states. Boundaries therefore are constantly shifting. They form the zones of conflict between states, as dynamic frontiers. In twentieth-century German geopolitical writings and in Spykman's work,[37] boundaries (dynamic frontiers) are viewed as demarcations of zones in which expansion has temporarily ceased.

Rudolf Kjellen (1864–1922), a Swedish geographer, first used the term *geopolitics* to describe the geopolitical bases of national power. Adhering to an organic theory of the state, he held that states, like animals in a Darwinian theory, engage in a relentless struggle for survival. States have boundaries, a capital, and lines of communication, as well as a consciousness and a culture. Although Kjellen wrote metaphysically and imputed to the state the quality of a living organism, he nevertheless concluded that "the life of a state is, ultimately, in the hands of the individual."[38] He considered the emergence of a few great powers as a result of efforts of strong states to expand.

In the interwar period, the followers of Kjellen and Ratzel used geopolitics to develop a framework for German national expansion. Karl Haushofer (1869–1946) founded the German Academy at the University of Munich in 1925, together with the journal *Zeitschrift für Geopolitik.* Both received active support from the Third Reich.[39] Haushofer's influence was considerable in military circles and became the basis for many of Hitler's conceptions of Nazi expansion.

For Haushofer, geopolitics represented the relationship of political phenomena to geography. Geopolitics enabled German leaders to establish national objectives and policies. The purpose of geopolitics, in Haushofer's conception, was to place the systematic study of geography at the disposal of a militarized Germany by relating national power to geographic factors, collecting relevant geographical information, and presenting a propaganda rationale for Nazi expansion and aggression. Thus, for Haushofer and his followers, geopolitics and power politics became synonymous. The geopolitical concepts developed by Haushofer (including lebensraum and dynamic frontiers), to the extent that they shaped Hitler's view of the world, contributed to the outbreak of World War II. In this respect, they stand in sharp contrast to other types of geopolitical analysis, based on a scientific knowledge of geography and its relationship to technology, resources, and population.

THE SPROUTS AND HUMAN–MILIEU RELATIONSHIPS

Harold Sprout (1901–1980) and Margaret Sprout (1903–) made a major contribution to the development of hypotheses for examining environing relationships. The Sprouts emphasized the importance of geography in examining political behavior,[40] contending that most, if not all, human activity is affected by the uneven distribution of human and nonhuman resources.[41] The Sprouts rejected unidimensional, geopolitical theories in favor of an ecological perspective because it appeared to provide a more integrated, holistic view of the international environment, which took account of its physical and nonphysical features. The environment (milieu) was viewed as a multidimensional system, in which the perceptions held by political leaders of environmental conditions (the psychomilieu), as well as the conditions themselves, were the objects of study and analysis. Such research emphasized the *interrelationship* of geography, demography, technology, and resources, and it focused on the importance of perceptual variables, as well as quantitative factors such as population and territorial size.

The milieu is said to affect human activities in only two respects. First, through the psychomilieu, it can influence human decisions only if human beings perceive factors related to the milieu. Second, through the *operational milieu,* such factors can limit individual performance or the outcome of decisions, based on perceptions of the environment.[42] Thus, decisions may be taken on the basis of erroneous perceptions of the environment, with potentially disastrous consequences. The task confronting the decision maker, therefore—to link the Sprouts' analysis to decision-making theories considered in Chapter 11—is to narrow the gap between the perceived and the real environment.

The Sprouts regarded geography as "concerned with the arrangement of things on the face of the earth, and with the association of things that give character to particular places." They believed that geography affected all human and nonhuman, tangible and intangible phenomena that "exhibit areal dimensions and variations upon or in relation to the earth's surface."[43] Every political community has a geographical base. Each political community is set on a territory that is a unique combination of location, size, shape, climate, and natural resources. Thus, transactions among nations must entail significant, even crucial, geographical considerations. The Sprouts noted that international statecraft exhibits in all periods "more or less discernible patterns of coercion and submission, influence and deference; patterns reflected in political terms with strong geographic connotations."[44]

Cognitive Behavioralism and the Operational Milieu

Important to the Sprouts is the concept of cognitive behavioralism. This concept assumes that a person consciously responds to the milieu through perception "and in no other way."[45] Erroneous ideas about the milieu may be just as influential as accurate ideas in forming moods, preferences, decisions, and actions. The Sprouts proceed to distinguish between the environment as the observer perceives it and the environment as it actually exists. The so-called *psychomilieu* may be compared to Plato's shadows in the cave—"images or ideas which the individual derives from interaction between what he selectively receives from his milieu, by means of his sensory apparatus, and his scheme of values, conscious memories, and subconsciously stored experience."[46] Failure to perceive the limiting condition may result in severe consequences. Inflated illusions about and misinterpretations of geographic circumstances may have similar unfortunate effects.[47] Popular attitudes, as well as the decisions of stateleaders, are based on geographical conceptions that "depend in no small degree upon the kinds of maps to which they are accustomed," as is noted in greater detail in a later section of this chapter. Therefore, an analysis of political behavior must take account of assumptions that political leaders make about their milieu.

The decisional entity, acting within the operational milieu and having a psychomilieu,[48] is an environed organism (an individual or a population) rather than an abstraction (the state). It is this decisional entity that is a principal concern of the social scientist and a particular interest of the student of international relations and of decision making, as noted in Chapter 11. Thus, the Sprouts object to terminology such as the "state's motivation" and the "state's needs." They do not apply *psychoecological* (relating to the psychological relation between organism and environment) concepts to social organization for much the same reason that they reject giving human attributes to the national or international system. They attribute these concepts only to human beings. They believe that political discussion on such an abstract level muddies rather than clarifies an understanding of the workings of international politics.[49]

Although political decisions are based on the stateleader's perceptions of the milieu, the results of these decisions are limited by the objective nature of the operational milieu—that is to say, by "the situation as it actually exists and affects the achievements and capabilities of the entity in question (whether a single individual, group, or community as a whole)."[50] In short, the operational milieu exists, even though it may not be fully discernible by the political actor. So far as decision making is concerned, the Sprouts do not see the milieu as inevitably conditioning, drawing, or compelling the policymaker and dictating her or his choices.

Thus, the ecological perspective provides a framework for the consideration of three types of phenomena: (1) the perceived psychomilieu; (2) the actions of individuals or groups; and (3) the outcomes of their actions in the operational milieu.[51] The three fundamental concepts of importance to the Sprouts include environment, environed entities, and entity–environmental relationships.[52]

The Sprouts emphasize that technology and social change play a large role in environmental relationships. Although technology has obviously not altered the physical layout of lands and seas, it has added new dimensions to the international milieu. Geography, environed organisms, the psychomilieu, technology, the operational milieu, and beliefs all affect each other. "Substantial changes either in the environment or in the genetic makeups of the organisms involved are likely to start chain reactions that ramify throughout the entire 'web-of-life' within the biotic community."[53] The interrelatedness of the ecological paradigm has grown increasingly with the mounting complexity of modern society resulting from expanding populations and advanced technology. It is increasingly difficult to "isolate and classify human political events as merely domestic matters or foreign affairs, or as political, sociological, or economic." In fact, the complexity of interrelatedness "within and between national communities, and the increasing irrelevance of the time honored distinction between domestic and international questions, constitute major datum points in the ecological perspective on international politics."[54] The focal point for empirical analysis since the mid-1980s has increasingly been the linkage between domestic politics and foreign policy. Such relationships have only increased in magnitude and complexity since the Sprouts' work.

In their study of environmental relationships, the Sprouts drew four major conclusions. First, the ecological perspective and frame of reference provide a fruitful approach to the analysis of foreign policy and the estimation of a state's capabilities. Second, it is helpful to distinguish analytically between the relation of environmental factors to policy decisions and their relation to the operational results of decisions. In the Sprouts' judgment, much of the confusion clouding the discussion of environmental factors in international politics stems from the failure to make this distinction explicit. Third, the ecological approach is a useful complement to the study of both the foreign policy and the international capabilities of states. The Sprouts' paradigm entails the examination of such limiting conditions as the level of available technology, the cognition of essential factors, and the ratio of available resources to commitments.[55] Finally, they see the ecological approach as broadening the study of international politics by integrating into it relevant theories and data from geography, psychology, sociology, and other systems of learning.

Cognitive Evolution and Constructivist–Reflectivist Approaches

The social milieu that was central to the Sprouts' work has been the object of more recent work. The principal focus of what are termed constructivist–reflectivist approaches is the assumption that our understanding of the world, as well as the intellectual tools used for viewing that world, are not objectively derived, but instead are the result of socially constructed concepts. In a way, the proponents of this approach suggest that "the world is in the eye of the beholder" and then proceed to ask where those interpretations of the world come from and how they influence the behavior of individual and state actors.

According to Alexander Wendt, constructivism is a structural theory based on the assumption that states are the principal units of analysis, but that the key structures are socially constructed. What came to be defined as state or national interests was the result of the social identities of the actors. Such interests and identities are in more or less constant flux in what are termed *intersubjective systemic structures*, consisting of what Wendt terms *shared understandings, expectations, and social knowledge*.[56] Similarly, Nicholas Greenwood Onuf maintains that social reality is what people construct or constitute as social reality.[57] Those activities that are deemed to be the most important to the interests of the members of a social unit such as a state are by definition political in nature. When such activities extend beyond the immediate locale or boundaries of the unit, they become international relations. According to Onuf, the terms *construct* and *constitute* are synonymous in the theoretical sense that people and society construct, or constitute, each other. Thus, there is an interactive process in which people constituting a group or a unit continuously construct in their individual and collective mind the reality that forms the basis for and is shaped by the decisions made.

The reflectivist component of this approach arises from the assumption that institutions emerge as a result of a deliberative process that, in turn, shapes the social milieu. The initiatives that develop are reflective of values, norms, and practices that, according to Robert Keohane, differ from one culture to another, and that may undergo change from one era to another.[58] Changing attitudes toward slavery and racial and other forms of discrimination are illustrative of the reflectivist phenomena to which proponents of this approach point. How such changes come about and how they are embedded or reflected in institutional change, both at the national and international levels, is the essence of constructivist–reflectivist theory.

To the constructivist–reflectivist, regimes and other institutions are more than the aggregate of rules and norms. Arising out of shared need, knowledge, and interest, as suggested in the constructivist–reflectivist literature, existing institutional arrangements themselves may contribute to a learning process that enhances the prospects for convergent state policies.[59] Stated differently, regimes, as well as institutions having greater authority and structure than regimes, may enhance cognitive evolution.

According to Emanuel Adler, there is a dynamic relationship between historical and structural forces that helps explain the nature of change.[60] At any moment in history, states and those actors composing states are affected by their respective interpretations of the world that are the result of socially constructed concepts. Just as science progresses by means of paradigmatic development—one construct being replaced by another as knowledge evolves—social processes are embedded in regimes and institutions that produce among relevant actors what is termed *intersubjective consensus.* In a fashion analogous to scientific revolution, there may be dramatic or evolutionary changes in shared beliefs about political practice, acceptable social behavior, and values based on what Adler terms *cognitive evolution.* Because our ideas, beliefs, and behavior are learned from other people, the source of collective learning lies in the ability of groups to transmit to each other the products of their respective cognitive experiences. There is a dynamic process in which cognitive evolution is aggregated at the national level and more broadly within the international system. Learning, in this sense, is defined as the ability of policymakers to adopt new interpretations of reality—to create a novel intersubjective consensus—that are introduced into the political system first at the national level and subsequently at the international level. It follows that, as the Sprouts maintained, the environment does not instruct policymakers or determine their options any more than scientific knowledge itself is the basis for international behavior. Instead, Adler suggests, common political action results from the extent to which a particular set of premises is shared within and among institutions, nation states, and other groups. Contrasted with static theories of international relations, cognitive evolution represents a process of innovation and political selection that has the effect of channeling action in novel directions.

Cognitive evolution has essentially three dimensions: (1) *innovation,* the creation of new values and expectations that are accepted by a group; (2) *selection,* the extent to which values and expectations become embedded in the minds of the group; and (3) *diffusion,* the degree to which new values and expectations spread from one group or state to another. In the process that constitutes cognitive evolution, epistemic communities, defined as elites with a shared understanding of a particular subject, who develop a strategy for achieving their goals, play a major innovative role.[61] In the selection process just described, states are of major importance, whereas in the diffusion phase, cognitive evolution is advanced at the international level by regimes and other institutional structures reflective of an evolving intersubjective consensus that shapes the global social milieu.

SPATIAL RELATIONSHIPS AND CONFLICT: RECENT WORK

Scholars have focused on other relationships between environment and political behavior as well. Writing in the mid-1970s, George Liska examined the nature of equilibrium in the international system, with specific reference to conflict and geopolitical factors. He concluded that conflict between continental and maritime states has been a recurrent phenomenon in international relations, especially in the European system:

> The qualitative disparity between principally land-based and sea-oriented states proved commonly incapable of assimilation by competitive or other interactions. The schism was conspicuously manifest whenever a strong land power staged, and the dominant maritime power resisted to the point of vetoing, a drive for seaborne outreach that would expand the scope of the balance of power and adapt its functioning to overseas extensions of the system's continental core.[62]

In an effort to determine the impact of insular status on nations, two other authors—Robert Holt and John Turner—compared the policies of Britain, Sri Lanka, and Japan.[63] Their analysis revealed that insular polities have a "more active involvement" with other countries than noninsular polities. Insular polities are more limited than noninsular states in the range of foreign policies available to them. These authors found similarities in the foreign policies of Britain and Japan. Both countries attempted to occupy sections of the Eurasian mainland, especially those areas from which invasions might be mounted against them. Both tried to maintain a balance of power among mainland nations by supporting the weaker coalition. Both sought alliances with powers outside the region to strengthen their position with respect to more proximate continental national units.

In assessing the effect of noncontiguity on the integration of political units, Richard Merritt's study of territorially discontiguous polities indicated that centrifugal forces increased with distance.[64] Not surprisingly, especially before the present information age, there was greater communication with neighboring than with physically distant peoples. The noncontiguous polity depends on the external environment to preserve communication links among its physically separated parts. Daily dependence on communications makes noncontiguous polities sensitive to shifts in the international environment that affect communications. Such polities have been concerned with the application of international law to internal waters, territorial waters, high seas, air rights, and land access, to cite only the modern history of problems experienced by such states as Malaysia, Pakistan (1947–1974), the United Arab Republic (Egypt–Syria, 1958–1962), and the now-defunct West Indies Federation.

There is an extensive and recent literature on the relationship between resource scarcity and conflict. Within the next half century, it is suggested, increases in world population will accelerate the depletion of renewable resources such as water, agricultural land, forests, and fisheries, together with nonrenewable resources, including fossil fuels and other minerals such as bauxite and iron ore. According to Thomas F. Homer-Dixon, reductions that are occurring in the amount or the quality of resources are reducing the overall total available, while increases in population divide what remains into smaller portions.[65] Population growth and resource depletion converge to produce conflicts in many parts of the developing world. The sources of environmental scarcity are said to lie in environmental change such as drought or soil erosion; population growth, which places greater pressure on existing resources; and the unequal distribution of resources, which limits access. Basing his findings on conclusions from numerous case studies of conflicts in which resource issues were present, Homer-Dixon suggests that states have fought more over nonrenewable than renewable resources. Oil and minerals, as nonrenewable resources, are more directly linked to national power than are forests or fish, renewable ones. The renewable resource most likely to contribute to interstate resource wars is water.

Homer-Dixon finds that environmental scarcity leads to economic deprivation, which contributes to civil strife and increases economic and political pressures on governments, possibly resulting in a weakening of state legitimacy. Increased gaps between population groups within a state as a result of resource scarcity produce grievances and rivalries, leading to conflict. As a result of resource scarcity, population groups may find it necessary to migrate in search of land and other resources. According to Homer-Dixon, such groups often spark ethnic conflicts in areas to which they move. Economic pressures on such groups, resulting from resource scarcity, can contribute to conflicts, including insurgency against state authority. Homer-Dixon sees major empirical support for the proposition that environmental scarcity will rise sharply in the decades ahead. Increases in population, greater resource consumption, and inequalities in access to resources will have an unprecedented impact on many regions. The potential for violent conflicts arising out of resource issues will grow dramatically.

Since the early 1960s, as noted at the beginning of this chapter, the emphasis placed on geography and conflict has had essentially two focal points for empirically based research, as Paul F. Diehl points out: (1) geography as a variable that is especially important in facilitating conflict; and (2) the role of geography in itself as a source of conflict.[66] The first focal point includes work that addresses such questions as how geography affects the likelihood that states will go to war with each other. The second focal point centers on the study of conflict in which control of a particular territorial area has been the source of conflict.

Geography, and specifically the location of political entities in close proximity to each other, is said to create opportunities for conflict to the extent that states sharing borders with each other are more likely to engage in conflict than are states that are noncontiguous. Such work takes as its point of departure findings contained in Lewis F. Richardson's *Statistics of Deadly Quarrels*.[67] Richardson found a strong, positive correlation between the number of frontiers a state had and the extent of its participation in wars with other states. The greater the number of borders, the greater the likelihood that a nation would be a party to international conflict. Richardson found that contiguity was a common factor in the armed conflicts that he studied, and the shared frontiers increase the number and types of interactions that states have with each other.

Richardson's work provided the basis for a large number of other empirical studies in which hypotheses about the relationship between geographic contiguity and war were tested. For example, building on Richardson's writings, Harvey Starr and Benjamin A. Most extended the concept of geographic contiguity to include not only the borders of the homeland (metropole) to each other, but also their overseas territorial extensions of states that had far-flung empires.[68] Illustrative of this definition, Great Britain as an imperial power with territories in nearly every part of the world shared colonial frontiers with as many as 68 other nations between 1946 and 1965, the period chosen by Starr and Most for their study. Such a condition led Great Britain into conflicts in many parts of the world, from Southeast Asia (Malaya) to East Africa (Kenya), from Palestine in the Middle East to Belize in South America. Thus, the notion of contiguous land borders of the metropole does not exhaust the types of borders that must be considered in assessing the relationship between frontiers and wars. Frontiers encompass not only contiguous land borders, but also borders across water. For example, island states that claim jurisdiction over surrounding waters may place themselves in conflict with neighboring states, as in the case of Greece and Turkey over the Aegean. Starr and

Most found that certain states, such as France and Great Britain, engaged in fewer armed conflicts, as their colonial possessions gained independence in the period between 1945 and 1965. Modifying Richardson's general finding that more borders lead to more war, Starr and Most concluded that the growth in numbers of homeland borders has tended to produce less war, while larger numbers of colonial borders were accompanied by more war.[69] According to Starr and Most, moreover, contiguous states are more likely to be perceived as threatening than those that are most distant. States that have many borders face a security dilemma to that extent that they must cope with more than one potential aggressor that is located in close proximity.

Two other major contributors to this literature, Paul F. Diehl and Gary Goertz, suggest that, throughout history, conflict has been more often based on concrete territorial issues than on abstract political goals.[70] Basing their work on 775 territorial changes during the period between 1816 and 1980, they find that almost all major wars began with at least one of the parties contiguous to the dispute site. War is more likely when the locus of the dispute is proximate to one or both of the protagonists. Stated differently, states are more likely to defend territorial assets closer to home than to acquire new and more distant areas by military means. Contiguity and willingness to resort to violence in defense of such territory are closely related. Thus Diehl and Goertz find that it is geographic proximity to an area in dispute, rather than shared borders with a state, that is a predictor of war. Nonetheless, they agree with Starr and Most that the opportunity for conflict is enhanced by geographic proximity.

Another discussion of literature on the relationship between geography and conflict is what is termed the *spatial correlation of events*. The term *spatial* refers to geographical areas defined by their sociopolitical characteristics. Examples of spatial units include urban areas, industrialized regions, and core–periphery concepts, as components of a political system. John O'Loughlin finds that, while immediate neighbors may be of greatest concern to a state, conflict may spread from its point of origin to involve other states within geographic regions.[71] According to O'Loughlin, the border–war relationship must be broadened to include spatial effects that extend to states that are in close proximity to conflict, but which are not the immediate parties in the conflict. Such states may perceive themselves to be increasingly vulnerable to the effects of war or heightened tensions between neighboring states, as in the case of the rapid expansion of the geographic zone of conflict in the weeks leading to the outbreak of World War I.

As in epidemiology, in which the increase in a particular disease in one country is directly related to its incidence in a neighboring state, so conflict may spread. There tends to be a clustering of conflict in particular regions, or what has been termed *shatterbelts*, geographic regions from which conflict escalates to engage outside powers. Such regions are said to include Europe, the Middle East, East Asia, Southeast Asia, Sub-Saharan Africa, and South Asia. A large number of the wars of the twentieth century originated in such regions. According to Philip L. Kelly, a *shatterbelt* is defined as a geographic region over which major powers engage in competition because they have strong perceived national interests.[72] Therefore, the potential for major conflict escalation is present. The outbreak of crisis in such regions, in light of major power interests, holds important potential for such intervention, providing the spatial dimension within a specific geographical setting for conflict. There are regional groupings of states having common borders, according to Andrew M. Kirby and Michael D. Ward, which tend to engage in armed conflict.[73] Such states are situated in regions constituting shatterbelts.

Closely related as a focal point of analysis is the role of geography in the diffusion of conflict beyond its immediate point of origin. This includes the extent to which states sharing borders with other states experiencing internal conflict are likely to undergo similar uprisings. According to Most and Starr, the occurrence of war in one state increases the likelihood that there will be war in one or more other states—perhaps in domino-like fashion.[74] They use the example of France's withdrawal from Indochina, the Middle East, and Africa as French colonial possessions, which erupted in wars leading to independence. To elaborate this concept, the French retreat from its overseas territories coincided generally with comparable moves by other European imperial powers, including Belgium, Great Britain, and the Netherlands, followed by Portugal. Pressures for independence, backed in many cases by violence, occurred in a spatially defined regional context—Southeast Asia, South Asia, the Middle East, North Africa, and Sub-Saharan Africa. The outbreak of conflict in support of independence in one colonial territory provided impetus for comparable activity in adjacent territories. Thus, conflict tended to diffuse across space from one state to another in the period studied by Most and Starr.

THE CLASH OF CIVILIZATIONS?

The end of the Cold War led to other efforts to rethink the geopolitical divisions, or fault lines, that form the basis for future conflict. In place of U.S.–Soviet rivalry and the dividing lines that differentiated the Western world from the Soviet bloc and from the Third World of less developed states, Samuel P. Huntington suggests that culture and civilization will define the future conflicts.[75] Wars will take place between Western and non-Western civilizations. The geopolitical significance of states will be determined by their location on or near the cultural divide separating civilizations. According to Huntington, the world of the future will be shaped by interaction among several major civilizations, including Western, Confucian, Japanese, Islamic, Hindu, Slavic–Orthodox, Latin American, and possibly African civilizations. Huntington points to several factors that are contributing to the clash of civilizations. They include deeply rooted religious differences; increasing intercivilization interaction, producing paradoxically growing awareness of differentiation; the weakening of the nation-state as a source of group identity, with religion often moving in to fill the resulting gap; the dewesternization and indigenization of elites in non-Western societies; the relative immutability of cultural characteristics; and the growth of economic regionalism, the effect of which is to reinforce civilization-consciousness.

To identify the geographic points for crisis and conflict, it is essential to understand where the fault lines lie between civilizations. According to Huntington, the critical dividing boundary in Europe runs along the frontier between Finland and Russia and between the Baltic states and Russia. It separates Catholic western Ukraine from Orthodox eastern Ukraine, and it divides Transylvania from the remainder of Romania. In the Balkans, the historic frontier between the Hapsburg and Ottoman empires, along the line between Croatia and Slovenia, represents another zone of conflict, as we have seen all too vividly in the Balkan wars of the 1990s. Huntington buttresses his thesis by reference to the bloody clashes between Muslims and Hindus, between Pakistan and India. Those states containing populations of different civilizations are likely to face disintegrative pressures, as we have already seen in the breakups of the Soviet Union and of Yugoslavia. Thus, Huntington views civilization as the determining factor shaping the social and psychomilieus, to use the Sprouts' terminology and, as a result, the geopolitical configuration within which future conflicts will erupt.

REDEFINING THE MEANING OF BORDERS

The advent of postindustrial society, based on unprecedented flows of information, alters the significance of boundaries within a broader context of spatial relationships. According to Friedrich Kratochwil, the concept of territorial sovereignty as the organizing principle of international politics contends with transnational exchanges that cut across the boundaries of existing states.[76] Kratochwil discusses the function of boundaries in territorial and nonterritorial social organizations. In the state system, boundaries defined zones of exclusive jurisdiction. The interdependence of states is measurable by the extent to which territorial boundaries are crossed by various types of interaction, including economic networks. Territorial frontiers are supplemented or superseded by boundaries based, for example, in markets for goods and services. Kratochwil suggests three types of exchanges that are affected by boundaries. First, these exchanges include the relationship between the unit and its environment. Second, they encompass exchanges between the unit and other units. Third, they involve exchanges that take place between the core of the unit and its periphery. Taken together, such exchanges constitute a system that can be studied by reference to the nature and types of exchanges within and among the three categories of transactions.

Closely related is the spatial relationship set forth by Kenichi Ohmae, who concludes that the emerging geopolitical map features economic borders that are not the lines of division between civilizations or states, but instead the contours of information flows.[77] As a result, we are in the midst, he suggests, of the development of region states that transcend existing national borders. He cites as examples the economic relationship that links Hong Kong and Southern China; the region between San Diego and Tijuana; and the triangle encompassing Singapore, neighboring sections of Malaysia, and parts of Indonesia.[78] The ability to shift capital instantaneously from one part of the world to another produces in this sense a borderless world within the context of geopolinomics and geoeconomics, noted earlier in this chapter. Capital flows need not be tied to the physical movement of goods, with traditional trade representing only a small and decreasing amount of economic activity across borders. The defining characteristic of region states is their possession of capabilities for full participation in the global economy. This participation includes receptivity to foreign investment and foreign products, and extensive economic links, based on access to vast and increasing amounts of information.

CRITIQUES OF ENVIRONMENTAL THEORIES

Critics of environmental theories, including the Sprouts, take issue with writers who engage in environmentalistic rhetoric and assume that attitudes or decisions are determined, influenced, or in some other way causally affected by environmental factors.[79] Although the Sprouts reject environment as a determinant of politics, they conceive as crucial (a) the actor's perception of environmental factors and (b) limitations to human activity posed by the environment.[80]

According to Strausz-Hupé, geographic conditions have been modified by humans throughout history: "Geographic conditions determine largely where history is made, but it is always man who makes it."[81] Although deriving his own work from the geopolitical concepts in Mackinder's writings, Spykman criticized Mackinder for overestimating the potentialities of the heartland and underestimating those of the inner crescent. "If there is to be a slogan for the power politics of the Old World, it must be 'Who controls the Rimland rules Eurasia; who rules Eurasia controls the destinies of the world.'"[82] Spykman also noted that a combination of sea powers had never been aligned against a grouping of land powers. "The historical alignment has always been in terms of some members of the Rimland with Great Britain and Russia together against a dominating Rimland power."[83] In his analysis of the German geopolitical school, Strausz-Hupé asserted that "there is, in short, no historical evidence in support of the causal nexus alleged by the advocates of *lebensraum* . . . to exist between population pressure and national growth in space."[84] Historically, national expansion has resulted from conditions other than population pressure. For example, Japanese expansionism in Asia antedated the upsurge in Japan's population. Nor does large space necessarily equate with national power, as the collapse of the Soviet Union, once the world's largest land state territorially, amply confirms, although "whenever large space was thoroughly organized by a state, small nations . . . were not able to withstand its expansive force."[85] According to Derwent Whittlesey, Haushofer's conception of geopolitics was illogical, in that it based the need for lebensraum on Germany's high birth rates. Because the birth rates of the Slavic territories to the east were even higher, their need for territory should have been greater than that of Germany.[86]

Finally, it is often asserted that technological change has rendered both Mackinder's heartland concept and Haushofer's geopolitical theory obsolete. In the discussion following Mackinder's presentation of his paper, "The Geographical Pivot of History," to the Royal Geographic Society, Leopold Amery asserted, "Both the sea and the railway are going in the future . . . to be supplemented by the air as a means of locomotion, and when we come to that, a great deal of this geographical distribution must lose its importance, and the successful powers will be those who have the greatest industrial basis."[87] According to Strausz-Hupé, "If it [the

Heartland] ever was a valid concept (for which there is no convincing evidence), there is no guarantee that modern technology will not invalidate it. It may, indeed, have done so already."[88] The Sprouts criticize the theories of both Mahan and Mackinder as being outmoded as a result of innovations in military technology and "paramilitary and nonmilitary forms of political interaction."[89] Kristof faults geopolitical writers for having "marshaled facts and laws of the physical world to justify political demands and support political opinions. One of the best examples of the hopelessly contradictory arguments to which this may lead is a concept akin in spirit to that of the 'natural boundary,' namely, the concept of the 'harmonic state.'"[90]

Although the psychomilieu—the world as it is perceived—is central to the work of writers such as the Sprouts, other writers have focused specifically on the effects of alternative types of maps—the visual presentation of spatial and geographical relationships—as they relate to the formation of images about the world. Since World War II, special emphasis has been placed on the distortion introduced into political analysis by earlier reliance on Mercator equator-based projections. Such maps failed to present the idea of the earth as a sphere and therefore as having geographical unity and continuity. The Mercator projection provided an erroneous conception of distances—for example, the proximity of the United States to Russia across the Arctic. Viewing the world as a sphere makes evident that, for example, Buenos Aires is farther from the United States than is every European capital, including Moscow.

The advent of air power, and its indispensable contribution to the Allied victory in World War II, contributed decisively to the alteration in traditional Mercator-type conceptions of geography, for the shortest distance by air between two points lay in a line that followed the contour of the earth. In its place came asymmetrical projections based mostly on spherical pole-centered maps. Numerous writers during World War II pointed to the need for such alternative maps. The need for such maps became apparent also because, as Richard E. Harrison and Hans W. Weigert, writing in the 1940s, pointed out:

> We continued using it (the Mercator projection) when land power and land-based air power became pivotal in the greatest of all world conflicts. In a world war that is mainly being fought in the northern hemisphere this proved to be an almost fatal misjudgment; for the Mercator projection whose center of accuracy is along the equator cannot possibly show the relationship between the power spheres of the contending great Powers.[91]

If maps shape a person's perceptions of the world, they also reflect the shared constructs of geographic and spatial relationships that are prevalent. Maps are drawn and redrawn to take account of those geographical factors deemed to be important at a given time. As Alan Henrikson has written, "One can regard such things as maps as pure subjective ideographs, or as constructs with only a mathematical relation to objective reality, or even as mere reflections of the material processes of history, in which case they would have no independent determining power. . . . The global maps that helped to guide and explain the war effort (World War II)—and were thus an essential part of the war's intellectual history—were traces on the human mind, etched there not only by man's experience but by man's imagination."[92] This idea is reflected in the works of Richard Edes Harrison and Robert Strausz-Hupé, who went so far as to suggest that the "psychological isolationism" of the United States resulted from the deficiencies of maps, notably the utilization of two-dimensional (Mercator) projections instead of those representing the earth as a globe.[93] According to W. H. Parker, Mackinder viewed the map of the world not as "the physical or political map found in an atlas, but a mental map in which the various horizontal distinctions and movements of global phenomena are vertically integrated in dynamic interaction."[94]

Technological changes may have altered the significance of the theorizing of certain of the writers examined in this chapter, although advanced technology has rendered environmental relationships ever more important. As many writers have suggested, modern science and technology have transformed the environment in intended, but also in unintended ways.[95] Science and technology have brought uninvited guests in such forms as air pollution, traffic congestion, and resource scarcity. In the twentieth century, the pace of scientific–technological innovation has quickened beyond any historical precedent, and people in all parts of the globe have been drawn into the orbit of modern technology. Whether changes wrought by technology are affecting the environment in ways beyond the means of coping with them remains an unanswered question. What is certain is that inextricable relationships or linkages exist among technology, geography, and international politics.

CONCLUSION

Thus, at the end of the twentieth century, the focus on the milieu in the literature of international relations represents a convergence of several principal interests of scholars and policymakers. These include resource scarcity and conflict, population growth, the relationship of geography to political power, the emergence of post–Cold War geopolitical relationships, and the increased importance of geopolinomic and geoeconomic concepts. In short, a new set of geopolitical or geostrategic relationships has come into existence, largely as a result of the pervasive impact of technology on international relations generally and, specifically, on the foreign policies of states. Because the perception of the milieu, and the impact of the milieu itself, is central to decision making and to political behavior generally, those concerned with the development of theories of political behavior at the international level have taken renewed interest in environmental relationships. Political systems have been hypothesized to be open systems—susceptible to inputs from, and making outputs to, their environments. Last but not least, the issues of pollution and ecology and of population growth and food supply have led to efforts both to forecast trends and to develop models often neo-Malthusian in nature. The milieu then provides a unique focal point not only for older and contemporary theorizing, but also for analytical and normative theory in international relations in the years ahead, for in the final analysis, all foreign policies and other patterns of international interaction are set within a political, social, cultural, and geographic environment.

NOTES

1. Harold and Margaret Sprout, *The Ecological Perspective on Human Affairs with Special Reference to International Politics* (Princeton, NJ: Princeton University Press, 1965), p. 27. The Sprouts set forth the following definitions: *Environment* may be defined as a generic concept under which are subsumed all external forces and factors to which an organism or aggregate of organisms is actually or potentially responsive; or it may be limited to the material and spatial aspects of the surrounding world, to the exclusion of the melee of human social relations.
2. For a survey of such writings, see Paul F. Diehl, "Geography and War: A Review and Assessment of the Empirical Literature," *International Interactions,* 17(1) (1991), 11–27.
3. Aristotle, *The Politics of Aristotle,* trans. Ernest Barker (Oxford, England: Clarendon, 1961), pp. 289–311.
4. Jean Bodin, *Six Books of the Commonwealth,* trans. F. J. Tooley (New York: Macmillan, 1955), pp. 145–157.
5. Baron de Montesquieu, *The Spirit of Laws* (Worcester, MA: Isaiah Thomas, 1802), Vol. I, pp. 154–159, 259–274.
6. Frederick Jackson Turner, "The Significance of the Frontier in American History," in Donald Sheehan, ed., *The Making of American History,* Book II (New York: Dryden, 1950), p. 200.
7. Nazli Choucri, "Population Resources and Technology: Political Implications of the Environmental Crisis," in David A. Kay and Eugene B. Skolnikoff, eds., *World-Eco-Crisis: International Organizations in Response* (Madison: University of Wisconsin Press, 1972), p. 24. See also Nazli Choucri and Robert C. North, "Population and (In)security: National Perspectives and Global Imperatives," in David Dewitt, David Haglund, and John Kirton, eds., *Building a New Global Order: Emerging Trends in International Security* (New York: Oxford University Press, 1993), pp. 229–256.
8. Quincy Wright, *A Study of War* (Chicago and London: University of Chicago Press, 1965), p. 1144.
9. Ibid., p. 1285.
10. See, for example, Susan L. Cutter, "Exploiting, Conserving, and Preserving Natural Resources"; Roger E. Kasperson, "Global Environmental Hazards: Political Issues in Societal Responses"; Phyllis Mofson, "Global Ecopolitics"; George J. Demko, "Population, Politics, and Geography: A Global Perspective"; and William B. Wood, "Crossing the Line: Geopolitics of International Migration" in George J. Demko and William B. Wood, eds., *Reordering the World: Geopolitical Perspectives on the Twenty-first Century* (Boulder, CO: Westview Press, 1994), pp. 123–205.
11. Robert D. Kaplan, "The Coming Anarchy," *The Atlantic Monthly* (February 1994), 44–76.
12. Robert D. Kaplan, ibid., 60.
13. George J. Demko and William B. Wood, "Introduction: International Relations Through the Prism of Geography," in George J. Demko and William B. Wood, eds., *Reordering the World: Geopolitical Perspectives on the Twenty-first Century* (Boul-

der, CO: Westview Press, 1994), p. 8. See also Martin Ira Glassner, *Political Geography* (New York: John Wiley and Sons, 1993), especially pp. 3–9; J. R. V. Prescott, *Political Geography* (London: Methuen and Company Limited, 1972), pp. 1–26; J. C. Archer and F.M. Shelley, "Theory and Methodology in Political Geography," and S. D. Brunn and K. A. Mingst, "Geopolitics," in Michael Pacione, ed., *Progress in Political Geography* (London: Croom Helm, 1985), pp. 11–76; Harm J. De Blij, *Systemic Political Geography* (New York: John Wiley and Sons, 1973), especially pp. 1–14.

14. Saul B. Cohen, *Geography and Politics in a World Divided*, 2nd ed. (New York: Oxford University Press, 1973), p. 29.

15. Raymond Aron, *Peace and War* (Garden City, NY: Doubleday, 1966), p. 191.

16. Ewan W. Anderson, *An Atlas of World Political Flashpoints: A Sourcebook of Geopolitical Crisis* (London: Pinter Reference, 1993), p. xiii.

17. Colin S. Gray, *The Geopolitics of Super Power* (Lexington: University Press of Kentucky, 1988), p. 45.

18. George J. Demko and William B. Wood, "Introduction: International Relations Through the Prisms of Geography," in George J. Demko and William B. Wood, eds., *Reordering the World: Geopolitical Perspectives on the Twenty-first Century*, pp. 10–11.

19. Edward N. Luttwak, *Endangered American Dream* (New York: Simon and Schuster, 1993), pp. 307–325.

20. For an examination of Toynbee's challenge–response hypothesis, see Arnold Toynbee, *A Study of History*, abridgement of Vols. I-IV by D. C. Somervell (London: Oxford University Press, 1956), pp. 60–139. Andrew M. Scott has proposed the challenge–response concept as a central approach to the study of international affairs, closely related to the balance-of-power idea. "Challenge and Response: A Tool for the Analysis of International Affairs," *Review of Politics,* XVIII (1956), 207–226.

21. Toynbee, op. cit., p. 246. Toynbee defines *breakdown* as the termination of growth.

22. Kenneth D. Boulding, *Conflict and Defense* (New York: Harper & Row, 1963); Patrick O'Sullivan, *Geopolitics* (New York: St. Martin's Press, 1986).

23. O'Sullivan, ibid., p. 69.

24. See, for example, Albert Wohlstetter, "Illusions of Distance," *Foreign Affairs,* 46(2) (1968), 242–255.

25. See Harold and Margaret Sprout, *The Ecological Perspective on Human Affairs,* op. cit., pp. 83–98; Lucien Febvre, *A Geographical Introduction to History* (New York: Knopf, 1925), pp. 358–368; P. W. J. Vidal de la Blache, *Principles of Human Geography,* Emmanuel de Martonne, ed. (New York: Holt, Rinehart and Winston, 1926); O. H. K. Spate, "How Determined Is Possibilism?" *Geographical Studies,* IV (1957), 3–8; George Tatham, "Environmentalism and Possibilism," in Griffith Taylor, ed., *Geography in the Twentieth Century* (New York: Philosophical Library, 1951), pp. 128ff, 151ff. See also Manus I. Midlarsky, "Environmental Influences on Democracy," *Journal of Conflict Resolution,* 39(2) (June 1995), 224–262.

26. Ladis K. D. Kristof, "The Origins and Evolution of Geopolitics," *Journal of Conflict Resolution,* IV (March 1960), 19. See also R. J. Johnston, *Geography and State: An Essay in Political Geography* (New York: St. Martin's Press, 1982), especially pp. 1–28, 120–187; J. R. V. Prescott, *Political Geography* (New York: St. Martin's Press, 1972), especially pp. 1–75; Kliot, Nurit, and Waterman, eds., *Pluralism and Political Geography: People, Territory and State* (New York: St. Martin's Press, 1983), especially pp. 9–36.

27. Alfred Thayer Mahan, *The Influence of Seapower upon History, 1660–1783* (Boston: Little, Brown, 1897), especially pp. 281–329. See also Margaret Tuttle Sprout,

"Mahan: Evangelist of Sea Power," in Edward Mead Earle, ed., *Makers of Modern Strategy: Military Thought from Machiavelli to Hitler* (Princeton, NJ: Princeton University Press, 1943), pp. 415–445; Harold and Margaret Sprout, *The Rise of American Naval Power* (Princeton, NJ: Princeton University Press, 1942); William Reitzel, "Mahan on Use of the Sea," and James A. Field, Jr., "The Origins of Maritime Strategy and the Development of Seapower," in B. Mitchell Simpson III, ed., *War, Strategy and Maritime Power* (New Brunswick, NJ: Rutgers University Press, 1977), pp. 77–107.

28. George Modelski and William R. Thompson, *Seapower in Global Politics, 1494–1993* (Seattle: University of Washington Press, 1988). See especially pp. 3–26.

29. Halford Mackinder, *Democratic Ideals and Reality* (New York: Norton, 1962), pp. 35–39.

30. Halford Mackinder, "The Geographical Pivot of History," *Geographical Journal,* XXIII (April 1904), 434. For an extended discussion and critique of Mackinder's thought and writings on geography and geopolitics, within the broader context of his life and times, see W. H. Parker, *Mackinder: Geography as an Aid to Statecraft* (Oxford, England: Clarendon Press, 1982), especially chaps. 5–8.

31. Halford Mackinder, op. cit., p. 150. See also Hans W. Weigert, "Mackinder's Heartland," *The American Scholar,* XV (Winter 1945), 43–45.

32. Halford J. Mackinder, "The Round World and the Winning of the Peace," *Foreign Affairs,* XXI (July 1943), 601.

33. See Stephen B. Jones, "Global Strategic Views," *Geographic Review,* XLV (October 1955), 492–508; Nicholas J. Spykman, *The Geography of the Peace* (New York: Harcourt Brace and Company, 1944), p. 43; and George F. Kennan, "The Sources of Soviet Conduct," *Foreign Affairs,* XXV (July 1947), 566–582. Spykman, in discussing the value of the Heartland's "interior lines" with respect to the periphery or rimland, suggested that the relations between center and circumference are of one sort if the maritime powers are trying to apply their leverage around the rimland from afar; but these relations are changed if local centers of power and communications are developed around the rimland; op. cit., p. 40.

34. Giulio Douhet, *The Command of the Air,* trans. Dino Ferrari (New York: Coward-McCann, 1942), pp. 10–11.

35. Alexander P. de Seversky, *Victory Through Air Power* (New York: Simon & Schuster, 1942).

36. Friedrich Ratzel, *Anthropogeographie,* 2nd ed. (Stuttgart, Germany: J. Engelhorn, 1899), Part I, p. 2. See Kristof, op. cit., p. 22.

37. See, in particular, Nicholas J. Spykman and Abbie A. Rollins, "Geographic Objectives in Foreign Policy I," *American Political Science Review,* XXXIII (June 1939), 391–393.

38. Rudolf Kjellen, *Der Staat als Lebensform,* trans. M. Langfelt (Leipzig: S. Hirzel Verlag, 1917), pp. 218–220. See Kristof, op. cit., p. 22.

39. For a discussion of the development of the German Academy, see Donald H. Norton, "Karl Haushofer and the German Academy, 1925–1945," *Central European History,* I (March 1958), 82. According to its rules and regulations, the objectives of the academy were "to nourish all spiritual expressions of Germandom and to bring together and strengthen the unofficial cultural relations of Germany with areas abroad and of the Germans abroad with the homeland, in the service of the all-German folk-consciousness."

40. Harold and Margaret Sprout, *The Ecological Perspective on Human Affairs,* op. cit., p. 9.

41. Harold and Margaret Sprout, *An Ecological Paradigm for the Study of International Politics*, Monograph No. 30 (Princeton, NJ: Center for International Studies, 1968), p. 21.

42. Ibid., p. 11.

43. Ibid., p. 13. The definition is quoted by the Sprouts from Preston F. James et al., *American Geography: Inventory and Prospect* (Syracuse, NY: Syracuse University Press, 1954), p. 4.

44. Harold and Margaret Sprout, *The Ecological Perspective on Human Affairs,* op. cit., p. 15.

45. Ibid., p. 140.

46. Ibid., p. 28.

47. See Harold and Margaret Sprout, *An Ecological Paradigm for the Study of International Politics,* op. cit., pp. 39–41. For the implications of perception in foreign-policy decision making, see Chapter 11.

48. Ibid., p. 11.

49. Ibid., p. 42.

50. Ibid., p. 34.

51. Harold and Margaret Sprout, *The Ecological Perspective on Human Affairs,* op. cit., p. 8.

52. Harold and Margaret Sprout, *An Ecological Paradigm for the Study of International Politics,* op. cit., p. 62.

53. Ibid., p. 20.

54. Ibid., p. 56.

55. Ibid., p. 64.

56. Alexander Wendt, "Collective Identity Formation and the International State," *American Political Science Review,* 88(2) (June 1994), 384–396. For other constructivist literature, see, for example, Edward Rhodes, "Constructing Peace and War: An Analysis of the Power of Ideas to Shape American Military Power," *Millennium: Journal of International Studies,* 24(1), (Spring 1995), 53–85; and Jonathan Mercer, "Anarchy and Identity," *International Organization,* 49(2), (Spring 1995), 229–252.

57. Nicholas Greenwood Onuf, *World of Our Making: Rules and Rule in Social Theory and International Relations* (Columbia, SC: University of South Carolina Press, 1989), especially pp. 35–65.

58. Robert O. Keohane, "International Institutions: Two Approaches," *International Studies Quarterly,* 32 (1988), 379–395.

59. Peter M. Haas, "Do Regimes Matter? Epistemic Countries and Mediterranean Pollution Control," *International Organization,* 43(3) (Summer 1989), 378.

60. Emanuel Adler, "Cognitive Evolution: A Dynamic Approach for the Study of International Relations and Their Progress," in Emanuel Adler and Beverly Crawford, eds., *Progress in Postwar International Relations* (New York: Columbia University Press, 1991), pp. 43–88.

61. See, for example, Emanuel Adler and Peter M. Haas, "Conclusion: Epistemic Communities, World Order, and the Creation of a Reflective Research Program," *International Organization,* 46(1) (Winter 1992), 367–390; Peter M. Haas, "Do Regimes Matter? Epistemic Communities and Mediterranean Pollution Control," *International Organization,* 43(3) (Summer 1989), 377–403.

62. George Liska, *Quest for Equilibrium: America and the Balance of Power on Land and Sea* (Baltimore and London: Johns Hopkins Press, 1977), p. 4.

63. Robert T. Holt and John E. Turner, "Insular Polities," in James N. Rosenau, ed., *Linkage Politics* (New York: Free Press, 1969), pp. 199–236.

64. Richard L. Merritt, "Noncontiguity and Political Integration," in James Rosenau, ed., ibid., pp. 237–272.

65. Thomas F. Homer-Dixon, "Environmental Scarcities and Violent Conflict: Evidence from Cases," *International Security,* 9(1) (Summer 1994), 5–40. See also Thomas Homer-Dixon, Jeffrey Boutwell, and George Rathjens, "Environmental Scarcity and Violent Conflict," *Scientific American,* (February 1993); Thomas Homer-Dixon, "Environmental Scarcity and Global Security," *Headline Series* (New York: Foreign Policy Association, 1993).

66. Paul F. Diehl, "Geography and War: A Review and Assessment of the Empirical Literature," *International Interactions,* 17(1) (1991), 16–23.

67. Lewis F. Richardson, *Statistics of Deadly Quarrels* (Chicago: Quadrangle Books, 1960).

68. Harvey Starr and Benjamin A. Most, "The Substance and Study of Borders in International Relations Research," *International Studies Quarterly,* 20(4) (December 1976), 581–621.

69. Harvey Starr and Benjamin A. Most, "A Return Journey: Richardson, 'Frontiers' and Wars in the 1946–1965 Era," *Journal of Conflict Resolution,* 22(3) (September 1978), 441–467.

70. Paul F. Diehl and Gary Goertz, "Territorial Changes and Militarized Conflict," *Journal of Conflict Resolution,* 32(1) (March 1988), 103–122; Gary Goertz and Paul F. Diehl, *Territorial Changes and International Conflict* (London and New York: Routledge, 1992), especially pp. 105–127. See also Paul F. Diehl, "Contiguity and Military Escalation in Major Power Rivalries, 1816–1980," *The Journal of Politics,* 47 (1985), 1203–1211; David Garnham, "Dyadic International War 1816–1965: The Role of Power Parity and Geographic Proximity," *Western Political Quarterly,* 27 (1976), 231–242; J. R. V. Prescott, *The Geography of Frontiers and Boundaries* (Chicago: Aldine Publishing Co., 1965), especially pp. 90–152.

71. John O'Loughlin, "Spatial Models of International Conflicts: Extending Current Theories of War Behavior," *Annals of the Association of American Geographers,* 76(1) (1986), 63–79.

72. Philip L. Kelly, "Escalation of Regional Conflict: Testing the Shatterbelt Concept," *Political Geography Quarterly,* 5(2) (April 1986), 161–180.

73. Andrew M. Kirby and Michael D. Ward, "The Spatial Analysis of Peace and War," *Comparative Political Studies,* 20(3) (October 1987), 303–304.

74. Benjamin A. Most and Harvey Starr, "Diffusion, Reinforcement, Geopolitics, and the Spread of War," *The American Political Science Review,* 74 (December 1980), 932–945.

75. Samuel P. Huntington, "The Clash of Civilizations?" *Foreign Affairs,* 72(3) (Summer 1993), 22–48. See also "Comments: Responses to Samuel P. Huntington's 'The Clash of Civilizations?'" *Foreign Affairs,* 72(4) (September–October 1993), 1–26; Samuel P. Huntington, "If Not Civilizations, What? Paradigms of the Post–Cold War World," *Foreign Affairs,* 73(5) (November/December 1993), 187–194.

76. Friedrich Kratochwil, "Of Systems, Boundaries, and Territoriality: An Inquiry into the Formation of the State System," *World Politics,* 39 (October 1986), 27–52; Friedrich Kratochwil, Paul Rohrlich, and Harpreet Mahajan, *Peace and Disputed Sovereignty* (Lanham, MD: University Press of America, 1985), especially pp. 3–47.

77. Kenichi Ohmae, *The End of the Nation State: The Rise of Regional Economics* (New York: Free Press, 1995), especially pp. 79–100.

78. Kenichi Ohmae, "New World Order: The Rise of the Region State," *The Wall Street Journal* (August 16, 1994), p. A12.

79. Harold and Margaret Sprout, *Foundations of International Politics* (Princeton, NJ: Van Nostrand, 1962), p. 54. Examples of such rhetoric include "The mountains of Japan have pushed the Japanese out upon the seas making them the greatest seafaring people of Asia." "England, *driven* to the sea by her sparse resources to seek a livelihood and to find homes for her burgeoning population, and sitting athwart the main sea routes of Western Europe, seemed *destined by geography* to command the seas." (Italics in original.)

80. Harold and Margaret Sprout, *The Ecological Perspective on Human Affairs*, op. cit., p. 11.

81. Robert Strausz-Hupé, *Geopolitics*, op. cit., p. 173.

82. Nicholas Spykman, *The Geography of the Peace*, op. cit., p. 43.

83. Ibid., p. 181.

84. Robert Strausz-Hupé, op. cit., pp. 164–165.

85. Ibid., p. 181.

86. Derwent Whittlesey, "Haushofer: The Geopolitician," in Edward Mead Earle, ed., op. cit., p. 400.

87. *Geographical Journal*, XXIII (April 1904), 441.

88. Robert Strausz-Hupé, op. cit., pp. 189–190. A half-century after Leopold Amery made his comment about the airplane, long-range bombers carrying nuclear bombs had become prime symbols of international power, and analysts were still arguing, not quite conclusively, as to whether the advent of air power and nuclear energy had rendered the Heartland concept obsolete. See W. Gordon East, "How Strong Is the Heartland?" *Foreign Affairs*, XXIX (October 1950), 78–93; and Charles Kruszewski, "The Pivot of History," *Foreign Affairs*, XXXII (April 1954), 338–401.

89. Harold and Margaret Sprout, *Foundations of International Politics*, op. cit., pp. 338–339.

90. Ladis Kristof, op. cit., p. 29.

91. Richard E. Harrison and Hans W. Weigert, "World View and Strategy," in Hans W. Weigert and Vilhjalmut Stefansson, eds., *Compass of the World: A Symposium on Political Geography* (New York: Macmillan, 1947), p. 76.

92. Alan K. Henrikson, "The Map as an Idea: The Role of Cartographic Imagery During the Second World War," *The American Cartographer*, 2(1) (1975), 46–47.

93. Richard Edes Harrison and Robert Strausz-Hupé, "Maps, Strategy and World Politics," in Harold and Margaret Sprout, eds., *Foundations of National Power* (Princeton, NJ: Princeton University Press, 1945), pp. 64–68.

94. W. H. Parker, op. cit., p. 133. The phenomena to which Mackinder referred are *lithosphere* (land); *hydrosphere* (water); *atmosphere* (air); *photosphere* (light); *biosphere* (life); and *psychosphere* (mind) (pp. 133–134).

95. See, for example, Robert Strausz-Hupé, "Social Values and Politics: The Uninvited Guests," *Review of Politics*, XXX (January 1968), 59–78. Another writer, George F. Kennan, who, like Strausz-Hupé, was examined in Chapter 2 on Realism, has suggested the need for an international organization for the collection, storage, and retrieval and dissemination of information and the coordination of research and operational activities on environmental problems at the international level. See George F. Kennan, "To Prevent a World Wasteland," *Foreign Affairs*, XLVIII (April 1970), 404.

Chapter
5

The Older Theories of Conflict and War

PREREQUISITES OF
A GENERAL THEORY OF CONFLICT AND WAR

All theorists of international relations recognize the problem of war as a central one. The stability of the international system is usually defined in terms of its proximity to or remoteness from the occurrence or likelihood of large-scale war. Scholarly works probing the causes of war continue to be published.[1] Prior to World War I, writes Michael Howard, historians were interested in the causes of specific wars but devoted little attention to the quest for the causes of war in general. War as a recurring phenomenon was taken for granted. In Howard's view, the causes of war have not changed fundamentally throughout the centuries. Just as Thucydides had written that the causes of the Peloponnesian War were "the growth of Athenian power and the fear this caused in Sparta," some of the principal causes of World War I were the growth of Germany's power and the fear this aroused in Britain. War, according to Howard, does not happen by accident nor does it arise out of subconscious, emotional forces, but rather from a "superabundance of analytic rationality."[2] The fears of those who make the decision for war may be rational or irrational, or both in combination. If fear is a basic cause of war, then we are forced to conclude that war is the product of irrational as well as rational factors, and that an understanding of its causes—as well as of ways to prevent, control, limit, regulate, and terminate it—would seem to require a comprehensive approach to the problem. Whether war as an institutionalized form of state behavior can ever be totally abolished from the international system is a larger question that cannot be answered until we understand the causes of war.

Among the recent efforts to understand at a general level the origins of war, Donald Kagan, surveying conflicts from the Peloponnesian War (431–404 B.C.) to the Cuban Missile Crisis of 1962, reaches several conclusions. He sees war not as an aberration, but instead as a recurring phenomenon. It is a uniquely modern Western characteristic, not substantiated by historic experience, to believe that humans can so transform themselves as to make war obsolete or impossible. According to Kagan, basing his conclusions on comparative historical analysis, war is the result of competition for power. In a world of sovereign states, such competition is a normal condition that sometimes leads to war. He also finds that states seek power not only for greater security or economic gain, but also for "greater prestige, respect, deference, in short, honor." Kagan also concludes that "fear, often unclear and intangible, not always of immediate threats but also of more distant ones, against which reassurance may not be possible, accounts for the persistence of war as a part of the human condition not likely to change."[3]

Unfortunately, we still do not know what are the causes of war, or if we do know them, we are far from being in agreement about them. No single general theory of conflict and war exists that is acceptable to social scientists in their respective disciplines, or to authorities in other fields from which social scientists borrow insights. If a comprehensive theory is ever to be developed, it will probably require inputs from biology, psychology and social psychology, anthropology, history, political science, economics, geography, theories of communications, organization, games, decision making, military strategy, functional integration, and systems, as well as philosophy, theology, and religion. Such a vast synthesis of human knowledge may be impossible to achieve. Merely to contemplate the need for it, however, serves to warn us against what Alfred North Whitehead called "the fallacy of the single factor." We cannot identify any single cause of conflict or war; the causes are not only multiple but they have kept multiplying throughout history.

The term *conflict* usually refers to a condition in which one identifiable group of human beings (whether tribal, ethnic, linguistic, cultural, religious, socioeconomic, political, or other) is engaged in conscious opposition to one or more other identifiable human groups because these groups are pursuing what are or appear to be incompatible goals. Lewis A. Coser defines conflict as a "struggle over values and claims to scarce status, power, and resources in which the aims of the opponents are to neutralize, injure, or eliminate their rivals."[4] Conflict is an interaction involving humans; it does not include the struggle of individuals against their physical environment. Conflict implies more than mere competition. People may compete with each other for something that is in shortage without being fully aware of their competitors' existence, or without seeking to prevent the competitors from achieving their objectives. Competition shades off into conflict when the parties try to enhance their own position by reducing that of others, try to thwart others from gaining their own ends, and try to put their competitors out of business or even to destroy them. Conflict may be violent or nonviolent (i.e., in terms of physical force), dominant or recessive, controllable or uncontrollable, and resolvable or insoluble under various sets of circumstances. Conflict is distinct from tensions, insofar as tensions usually imply latent hostility, fear, suspicion, the perceived divergence of interests, and perhaps the desire to dominate or gain revenge; however, tensions do not necessarily extend beyond attitudes and perceptions to encompass actual overt opposition and mutual efforts to thwart one another. They often precede and always accompany the outbreak of conflict, but they are not the same as conflict, and they are not always incompatible with cooperation. The causes of tension, however, are probably closely related to the causes of conflict. Moreover, if tensions become powerful enough, they themselves may become contributory or preliminary causes of the occurrence of conflict, insofar as they affect the decision-making process.

What Coser has provided is a sociological definition. He is interested in conflict between groups. Other analysts insist that the term *conflict* must embrace not only intergroup but also interpersonal and intrapersonal phenomena. Society would not have to be concerned about conflict within the individual if it were not for the plausible assumption that there is a significant relationship between conflicts within the inner structure of the individual and conflicts in the external social order. No theory of conflict can ignore this relationship. The internal and the external can never be completely separated. Neither can the one ever be reduced completely to the other and derived solely from it. Psychological states alone cannot explain social behavior, and social conditions alone cannot explain individual behavior.

Conflict is a universally and permanently recurring phenomenon within and between societies. It is not necessarily continuous or uniformly intense. Many societies experience periods of relative peace, both internal and external. Quite probably, however, a certain amount of low-level, muted, almost invisible conflict goes on constantly in all societies, even those apparently most peaceful. (Individual criminal behavior can certainly be considered a form of violent conflict.) Conflict, as we stated previously, need not issue in violent behavior—it may be carried on by subtle political, economic, psychological, and social means. Politics itself is a process for resolving conflict. Whether large-scale, organized international warfare can ever be eliminated from human affairs—as were the institutions of slavery and human sacrifice, also considered natural at one time—remains a subject for debate.

Perhaps the most that can be realistically hoped for at present is that the most destructive forms of organized international violence (such as nuclear war and conventional wars that might escalate to the level of nuclear war) can be deterred indefinitely as a result of intelligent policies of mutual restraint on the part of governments until effective methods of international peace enforcement emerge, assuming that they eventually will. However, it is too much to expect that all social conflict can ever be abolished, or even that political violence at all levels can be permanently ruled out. H. L. Nieburg has argued that violence is a natural form of political behavior; that the threat of inflicting pain by resorting to violence will always be a useful means of political bargaining within domestic and international society; and that the threat of resorting to force demonstrates the seriousness with which the dissatisfied party sets forth its demands against the satisfied, the establishment, the defender of the status quo in order to confront the latter starkly with the alternatives of making adjustments or risking dangerous escalation of violence.[5] Many social scientists, including several identified with the peace movement, recognize that total elimination of conflict from the human situation is not only impossible but also undesirable, because conflict in some forms is a condition of social change and progress.[6]

MICRO- AND MACROTHEORIES OF CONFLICT

Most social sciences can be roughly divided into two groups, depending on whether they adopt the micro or the macro—or holistic or reductionist—approach to the study of the human universe. Do we seek the origins of conflict in the nature of human beings or in their structures and institutions? Generally speaking, psychologists, and social psychologists, biologists, games theorists, and decision-making theorists take as their point of departure the behavior of individuals, and from this, they draw inferences to the behavior of the species. Moreover, sociologists, anthropologists, geographers, organization and communication theorists, political scientists, international-relations analysts, and systems theorists typically examine conflict at the level of groups, collectivities, social institutions, social classes, large political movements, religious or ethnic entities, nation-states, coalitions, and cultural systems. Some scholars—economists, for example—might divide their efforts between the macro- and the microdimensions. One historian might prefer to study the clash of nation-states, while another might prefer to concentrate on the unique factors in the personality, background, and decisional behavior of an individual stateleader that prompted the stateleader to opt for war or peace in a specific set of circumstances. (Microcosmic theories are treated in Chapter 7; macrocosmic, in Chapter 8.)

Historically, the intellectual chasm between the macro- and the microperspectives of human conflict was nowhere better illustrated than in the earlier polarity of psychology and sociology. The former field analyzed conflict from a knowledge of the individual, the latter from a knowledge of collective behavior. Psychologists have tended to approach human problems as arising from the inner psychic structure of the individual, whence they assumed that complexes, tensions, and other disorders were projected into the external social situation. Conversely, sociologists have been disposed to conduct their analysis of all human problems at the level of social structures and institutions, and to trace the effects of disorders at that level back to the psychic life of individuals. The sharpness of the cleavage as it was perceived around the turn of the century is reflected in Emile Durkheim's statement that "every time that a social phenomenon is directly explained as a psychic phenomenon, one may be sure that the explanation is false."[7] The long-standing antipathy of Freudian analysis toward the Marxian dialectic (so severe that for several decades Freudian psychology was completely taboo in the Soviet Union) provides a well-known if somewhat extreme example of the divergent perspectives of the two fields.[8]

In the twentieth century, especially in recent decades, the distance between the two fields has narrowed. Psychologists have recognized the importance of institutions, groups, and the total cultural environment in shaping the individual's psychic life. For their part, sociologists have paid increasing attention to the role of psychic factors in social processes. Social psychologists, in particular, have sought to bridge the gap between the two parent disciplines. While it would be going too far to conclude that the gap has yet been fully bridged, increasing numbers of social scientists are becoming convinced that it is impossible to construct an adequate theory of conflict without fusing the macro- and the microdimensions into a coherent whole.[9] In recent years, as Michael Haas has noted, social scientists, armed with statistical methods and aided by computers, have begun for the first time to study international conflict systematically and to accumulate a definitive body of scientific knowledge about the subject. Nonetheless, theory on international conflict, he concludes, remains at a primitive level partly because "most empirical researchers have been bulldozing exhibitionistically without attempting to put the subject in order analytically."[10]

INDIVIDUALS AND INTERNATIONAL CONFLICT

Social psychologists are more hesitant today than were their predecessors two or three decades ago to extrapolate the explanations of complex social behavior, particularly at the level of international relations, from their knowledge of individual psychic behavior. In the past, some psychologists who were concerned with the problem of conflict assumed too readily that the explanation of group aggression is a mere corollary of the explanation of individual aggression. They took the Platonic notion that the state is the individual "writ large" and converted this into a pseudoscientific analogy under which society came to be uncritically regarded as the psychological organism writ large. Social psychologists are now much less confident in this respect. Stephen Withey and Daniel Katz have warned against the attempt to "explain the functioning of social systems by a simple reduction of a macroscopic process."[11] Herbert C. Kelman has also pointed out that many earlier writings on war and peace by psychologists and psychiatrists were not germane to the interactions of nation-states. Kelman held that the earlier writers tended to overemphasize individual aggressive impulses. These writers took it for granted that the behavior of states is merely the aggregate of individual behaviors, ignoring the fact that individuals differ widely in their roles, interests, and ability to influence final decisions. The behavior of such a large collectivity as a nation, according to Kelman, cannot be considered a direct reflection of the motives and personal feelings of either its citizens or its leaders.

Only by analyzing international relations, not by automatically applying psychological findings about the individual, can we identify those points at which such application is relevant. Kelman defined war as a societal and intersocietal action conducted within a national and international political context. Of crucial importance in the study of international relations is the process by which nations develop their national policies and decide on war. In part, such an explanation includes the motivations and perceptions of individuals as policymakers and relevant publics playing various roles as part of a larger society. However, Kelman cautioned that psychological analysis is useful to the study of aggressive behavior in an international context only if we know where and how such individuals fit into the larger political and social framework of the nation and the international system, as well as the constraints under which they operate.[12]

Most specialists in the fields of political science and international relations would heartily endorse Kelman's conclusion. Psychological factors alone might go a long way toward explaining instances of anomic violence (i.e., apparently spontaneous and irrational outbursts by either a crowd or an individual), but even in these cases, social scientists are now more wary of the fallacy of the single factor. At more complex levels of politicized conflict, where violence reflects to a much greater extent some degree of planning, organization, management, and even institutionalization, the need for circumspection in explaining phenomena by reference to purely psychological factors becomes commensurately greater.

CONFLICT AND SOCIAL INTEGRATION

Social scientists are divided on the question of whether social conflict should be regarded as something rational, constructive, and socially functional or something irrational, pathological, and socially dysfunctional. Most Western psychologists and social psychologists seem to regard all violent forms of individual, group, and politicized aggression as irrational departures from normal, desirable behavior. By way of contrast, most sociologists and anthropologists in Europe and America (with the notable exception of the Parsonian school, which, like a majority of psychologists, stresses the importance of compromise and adjustment) have been willing to attribute a constructive purpose to conflict, insofar as it helps to establish group boundaries, strengthens group consciousness and sense of self-identity, and contributes toward social integration, community building, and socioeconomic change in a progressive direction.[13] Karl Marx, of course, who was more sociologist than economist, placed the greatest emphasis on class conflict and the final conflict between the proletariat and the bourgeoisie as the forceps that is supposed to give birth to a just social order. Many social scientists tend to divide on the issue, some regarding violent conflict as irrational, while others judge it good or bad, depending on the context in which it arises; the political, economic, or social values at stake; the costs incurred in comparison with anticipated gains; and the net outcome for the group, the nation, or the international system.

VARIETIES OF CONFLICT

Several salient questions occur at the outset of our inquiry. Should we study the phenomenon of conflict in terms of conscious motivations? Do people really fight about what they say they are fighting about? Instead, must we go beyond stated reasons, regard them with suspicion as mere self-rationalizations, and try to penetrate to the real—that is, unconscious, murky, and sordid impulses that drive people to aggressive behavior? Is this a false dichotomy? If we look carefully, we see that microscientists are more inclined to probe beneath the surface into the unconscious, the innate, the instinctive (to use an obsolete term), whereas macroscientists are somewhat more willing to lend credence to conscious motivations, for these motivations pertain to thought, language, and communications patterns, which, in contrast to internal psychic forces, are products of society. Given that the human being is a symbolic animal, words are crucial links between the unconscious and the conscious, between micro and macro.

International war is one form of social conflict—undoubtedly the most important single form in terms of its potential consequences for the individual and nations. However, there are many other forms of social conflict: civil war, revolution, coup, guerrilla insurgency, political assassination, sabotage, terrorism, seizure of hostages, prison riots, strikes and strike-breaking, sit-ins, threats, displays of force, economic sanctions and reprisals, psychological warfare, propaganda, tavern brawls, labor–management disputes, flare-ups at collegiate or professional sports events, divorce contests and legal wrangling over the custody of children, intrafamily fights, and felonious crimes.

A crucial question that arises frequently in the social sciences, regardless of the phenomenon under investigation, is whether we are dealing with the one or the many. Can we understand war as a separate conflict phenomenon in isolation, or must we study it as one highly organized manifestation, at a specific social-structural level, of a general phenomenon? Social scientists are far from agreement as to whether human conflict can be satisfactorily explained as a continuum in which violent outbursts differ only by such accidents as the nature of the parties, the size, the duration, the intensity, the nature of the issues and the objectives sought, the processes and modes of conflict, and the weapons employed, but not in their underlying causes; or whether human conflict is an indefinite series of discrete phenomena, each of which, despite a superficial external resemblance to the others, requires its own unique theoretical explanation.

THEORIES OF WAR AND ITS CAUSES IN ANTIQUITY

Most of the older theories of war and its causes we would now call "prescientific," even though some of them were based on empirical evidence, drawn from history and human experience. Several of the earlier theories contain perceptive insights that continue to merit our attention as part of our cultural heritage. They enable us to see how the problem of war was looked upon in other historical epochs, and why it was not always regarded as the greatest of evils; they reflect conscious motivations for and rationalizations of war, which at the level of human decision making can be causal; they provide philosophical, religious, political, and psychological arguments for and against war, both in general and in specific circumstances.

China   In virtually all the ancient religious–ethical civilizations, the problem of war was approached not only as one of political–military strategy, but also as one of spiritual and moral dimensions. Ancient China produced a broad range of theories from pacifism, or peace, to bellicism, or war. Mo-Ti preached a doctrine of universal love, with which the waging of war was deemed utterly incompatible; he called war large-scale murder and attacked it on grounds that it profits nobody (as Norman Angell subsequently asserted in the early twentieth century). Confucius and his disciple Mencius taught that states, in dealing with one another, should observe good faith and moderation; they should also avoid imperialism, intervention in the affairs of other states, and aggressive wars of conquest. Like many modern idealists, they believed that diplomats should rely on the reasonableness and justice of their positions, rather than on the threat of force, to win their case. However, the Confucians were not pacifists; they did not counsel nonresistance to attack. Confucius, although he looked on war as an evil, insisted that when it comes, it must be waged vigorously. As a prerequisite of success, the army must have a clear idea of why it is fighting and a strong conviction that its cause is just. Mencius played down the value of alliances and warned rulers not to depend on them; the real strength of a state lies less in strong forts than in the morale of its people and the moral stamina of its defenders. (In the twentieth century, Mao Zhedong stressed that in war, the power of humans counts for more than the power of weapons.) To the right of the Confucians were the legalists, including the real or legendary Lord Shang, the Machiavelli of ancient China, who advised rulers to make the peasants work long and hard and to fill peasants' lives with drudgery, so that when war comes, they will greet it as a welcome relief.[14]

India   Whereas China extolled the scholar, Indian Hindu (but not Buddhist) culture assigned a higher place to the warrior class. War was accepted as part of the eternal scheme of things and was more highly institutionalized in India than in China. Rule calculated to mitigate the severity of war had the sanction of Indian religious authorities. Unfair, unchivalrous, and inhumane practices in war were condemned; not even in war was there an unqualified right to kill; certainly a king must not kill those enemies who throw down their arms and beg for mercy. Nonetheless, even those Hindu and Buddhist teachers who protested against war took it for granted that war was a naturally recurring phenomenon. The ancient Buddhist doctrine of *ahimsa* ("harmlessness toward all living things"), famous as one of the sources from which Gandhi derived his doctrine of nonviolence, was not understood to forbid the waging of war; actually, it promoted vegetarianism long before it contributed to pacifism.[15]

Greece   The Greeks in general had a similarly fatal attitude toward war. The philosopher Heraclitus postulated endless strife as one of the endless underlying processes of reality, along with the attracting force of love; the two alternate with each other in gaining the ascendancy and then being driven out but never eliminated. In his view, if war should perish, the universe would be destroyed, for strife is justice, through which all things come into being and pass away.[16] The Greeks did not produce much in the way of pacifist thought. The Athenians especially always seemed ready to fight for their freedom and independence, and sometimes for imperialistic ends.

Even in his most utopian work, *The Republic,* Plato was unable to dispense with the role of military guardians. He suggested that there would be no need for a warrior group to defend the state if people could be contented with a simple, frugal existence—having neither the desire to plunder foreigners, nor wealth to tempt them to aggression. However, people want "courtesans and cakes," imposing public temples and theaters, fine fabrics, elegant dwellings, and exotic spices—all the fruits and comforts of civilization. War, said Plato, results from the unwillingness of human beings to live within the limits of necessity.[17] Aristotle accepted war as a legitimate instrument for settling interstate disputes, but he never praised it. Rather, he insisted that, just as humans must engage in economic activity in order to enjoy the life of leisure and culture, so they must occasionally carry on war in order to have peace. He strongly criticized Sparta for gearing its educational and legal system to war as the ultimate end of politics.[18]

Pericles, a peerless propagandist, used his famous Funeral Oration to glorify not war but the heroism of those Athenians who died defending the open, democratic society against the closed society of the garrison state of Sparta. The historian

Thucydides lamented the destructiveness of war, accepted it grudgingly as a matter of defense rather than conquest or annihilation, and perhaps came as close as any Greek writer to a skeptical view of the utility of war when he pragmatically warned stateleaders to take time over their decision to opt for war. He recorded (or composed) the words of one diplomatic envoy urging a king to ponder the unpredictability of war before making the fatal commitment. "The longer a war lasts," he wrote, "the more things tend to depend on accidents. . . . (and) we have to abide their outcome in the dark."[19]

Because the Greeks prized limit or measure as the key to human perfection, as well as moderation in all things, and because they regarded themselves as superior to all non-Greeks (*barbaroi*), they sought to assuage the damaging effects of war among their own city-states, which shared cultural values. Thus, the treaty of the Amphictyonic League of Delphi prohibited war among members except for good cause, and it forbade taking Greeks as slaves, killing civilians, and burning member cities or cutting off their water supply.[20]

The Greeks never worked out carefully the idea of the just war. This task was taken up by the Romans who, in the early Roman republic, were much more unabashedly moral and legalistic than the Greeks had been in their approach to war. The Romans were meticulous in observing the rules of war—rules of their own devising under the *ius fetiale,* that part of the sacred law that regulated the solemn swearing of treaties, the settlement of disputes between states, and the declaration of war. It was the function of the *fetial judges,* a religiopolitical college of priest officials, to determine whether a neighboring community had so wronged Rome as to justify a resort to military force.

The Romans apparently felt obliged to convince themselves, before embarking on war, that their cause was just and pious (*justum et pium*). The most commonly recognized causes were (1) the violation of Rome's territorial dominions; (2) violation of ambassadors' diplomatic immunity by inflicting physical harm; (3) violation of a treaty obligation; (4) rendering aid to an enemy of Rome; (5) desecration of sacred places; and (6) refusing to surrender those who had committed serious offenses against Rome.[21]

Romans were inclined to look on a military defeat as a sign that the gods did not find their cause just; this was a powerful incentive to bravery on the battlefield. The Romans usually demanded satisfaction from the offending party within a specified period. If this was not forthcoming, a herald would read the formal declaration and hurl a spear into the soil of the enemy state, indicating the precise moment when war broke out. War and peace were simultaneously incompatible. Two states were either at war or at peace with each other. There was no room for that ambiguity or uncertainty often found in Oriental history and during the U.S.–Soviet Cold War, when limited conflict and uneasy cooperation were commingled. The Romans, even more than the Greeks, believed at least in theory that no greater force should be used in war than required by "legitimate military necessity," and that deliberate efforts should be made to regularize belligerent proceedings.[22] Practice, however, sometimes overcame theory, as it often does in the passions of war. Rome treated Spain with harsh brutality, callously enslaved more intelligent Greeks and other civilized peoples, and finally succumbed to Cato's oft-repeated admonition, "Carthage must be destroyed" (*Carthago delenda est*).[23]

Islam   The prophet Muhammad preached the holy war (*jihad*) as a sacred duty and a guarantee of salvation, and for several centuries, Muslim theorists assumed that the world was divided into the *dar al-Islam* (the peaceful abode of the true believers and those who submitted to their tolerant rule) and the *dar al-harb* (the territory of war). Inasmuch as Islam was a universalist system of belief, the two territories were always theoretically at war with each other because war was the ultimate device for incorporating recalcitrant peoples into the peaceful territory of Islam. The jihad, therefore, was more a crusade than the *bellum justum* ("just war"), familiar to medieval Christian writers. The concept of the jihad as a permanent state of war against the non-Muslim world had become almost obsolete in modern times, at least prior to the emergence of Muammar Qhaddhafi in Libya, Ayatollah Khomeini in Iran, and various radical fundamentalist groups (e.g., the Muslim Brotherhood) and militant terrorists (e.g., Jihad), who call for a holy war against enemies of Islam. Several modern writers have stressed that the term *jihad* refers less to military conflict than to the spiritual struggle for perfection within the heart of individuals.[24] Mahatma Gandhi declared that he was able to perceive the origins of the doctrine of nonviolence and love for all living things not only in the sacred Hindu and Buddhist writings and the Bible, but also in the Koran.[25]

Judaism   The predominant historical attitudes toward war that are found in Western culture are a product of several different sources, including the Judeo-Christian religious tradition, Greek philosophy, Roman legalism, European feudalism, Enlightenment pacifism, and modern scientism, humanitarianism, and other ideologies. The ancient Jewish scriptures reflect the paradox of human yearning for a peaceful existence amidst the constant recurrence of war. Surrounded by hostile peoples, the Israelites relied heavily on a combination of religious prophetism and military organization for nation building, defense, and territorial expansion. In the earlier history of the Jews, Yahweh often appeared as a warrior-god. Joshua, Gideon, Saul, and David fought wars for Yahweh's honor and glory, to demonstrate Yahweh's power, as well as Yahweh's special relationship to the chosen people. Once the promised land had been won from the Canaanites, and kings took over from judges, the wars of Israel and Judah became less ferocious, and themes of love, justice, and peace became more prominent in the Jewish scriptures.[26]

War and Christianity   The early Christians were divided in their attitude toward the use of military force by the state. During the first three centuries of the early Catholic Church's history, when Christianity was regarded an alien and subversive creed within the Roman Empire, there was a strong tendency toward pacifism, especially among the intellectuals, many of whom believed that the Christian both as private person and as a citizen should respond to injury by turning the other cheek, regardless of the consequences for the state. Pacifism, however, did not become the orthodox Christian doctrine. The dominant view among the leaders of the church was that political authority was divinely instituted for the benefit of the individual, and that when force was used justly, it was a good, not an evil. People are enjoined to turn the other cheek when their own rights are violated, because they seek a salvation beyond history, but the state, which must safeguard the temporal social good here and now, may have to resort to force at times. Saint Ambrose and Saint Augustine, writing after Christians in the West had begun to assume responsibility for the social order, baptized the ancient Roman doctrine of the just war as a "sad necessity in the eyes of men of principle."[27]

Scholastic philosophers in the Middle Ages considerably refined the just-war doctrine. The decision to initiate violent hostilities could not be taken by a private individual, but only by public authority. Rulers were enjoined against resorting to war unless they were morally certain that their cause was just (*jus ad bellum*)—that is, that their juridical rights had been violated by a neighboring ruler. Even then, they were exhorted to exhaust all peaceful means of settling the dispute before initiating the use of force, and these means usually included arbitration. Furthermore, there had to be a reasonable prospect that the resort to force would be more productive of good than of evil and would restore the order of justice. The war had to be waged throughout with a right moral intention, and it had to be conducted by means that were not intrinsically immoral (*jus in bello*), for what begins as a just war could become unjust in its prosecution. These were the common teachings of such medieval writers as Antoninus of Florence and St. Thomas Aquinas. Emphasis was placed on what would later be called the "principles of proportionality and discrimination." Under the first, the suffering and destruction caused by the war should not be disproportionate to the cause justifying the resort to war; under the second, innocent populations were considered immune as targets of military action.[28]

Throughout the Middle Ages, the Catholic Church attempted to impose ethical controls on the conduct of war by specifying times when fighting could not be carried on, sites where battle was prohibited, types of weapons that could not legitimately be employed, and classes of persons that were either exempted from the obligation of military service or protected against military action. This effort to soften the cruelty of warfare was by no means new in Western culture. The ancient Greeks and Romans had been familiar with such agreed rules of war as those forbidding wanton destruction of populations, the burning of cities, and the severance of water supplies. Many circumstances of medieval European culture, including the common values of Christendom, the nature of feudalism, prevailing economic conditions, the Teutonic tradition of the chivalric warrior, and the crude state of the military sciences, actually reinforced the moral efforts of the Catholic Church to mitigate the harshness of warfare during the medieval period.[29]

In the period of transition from medieval to modern Europe, three outstanding exceptions to the dominant theory and practice of morally limited warfare can be identified. These were invariably expressions of ideological conflict that ran counter to the distinctive tendencies of medieval culture: (1) the Crusades of the twelfth and thirteenth centuries, fought against an alien and "infidel" civilization;

(2) the wars of the fourteenth and fifteenth centuries, especially between the French and English, in which the forces of national feeling made themselves felt for the first time on a large scale; and (3) the religious wars that followed the Reformation. In all of these cases, war ceased to be a rational instrument of monarchical policy for the defense of juridical rights. The concept of war as a small-scale affair of skirmish and maneuver lost its primacy when large numbers of nonprofessional (i.e., nonchivalric) warriors, both volunteers and mercenaries, became enmeshed with cultural, national, or religious antipathies. When a cherished set of values or a way of life was thought to hinge on the outcome of an encounter, war became an all-consuming psychological and moral experience. Hence, the battles of Antioch, Crécy, Poitiers, Agincourt, and Magdeburg were bitter and bloody in the extreme. In the Thirty Years War between Catholics and Protestants (1618–1648), the population of Germany was reduced from 21 million to 13 million.[30]

THE PHILOSOPHICAL THEORIES
OF THE NATION-STATE PERIOD

During the classical period of the balance of power that was ushered in by the Treaty of Westphalia in 1648, the concept of limited war regained currency in Europe. At the beginning of the modern nation-state period in the sixteenth and seventeenth centuries, the traditional Western doctrine of the just war was reaffirmed by scholastic theologians and philosophers, such as Victoria and Suarez, as well as by the earliest systematic expounders of international law—Grotius, Ayala, Vattel, Gentilis, and others. For these writers—as we saw in Chapter 1—the just war emerged as a substitute juridical proceeding—a sort of lawsuit in defense of the legal rights of the state, prosecuted by force in the absence of an effective international judicial superior capable of vindicating the order of justice. Virtually all the classical European writers on international war insisted on the necessity of sparing the lives of the innocent in war. The slaying of the guiltless could never be directly intended; at best, it was condoned as an indirect effect as incidental to the legitimate operations of a just war.[31]

In the latter half of the seventeenth century, after the violence of the religious wars had subsided, the pendulum swung back again toward more moderate forms of warfare. From then through most of the eighteenth century, the Age of Reason, wars were less ideological and more instrumental in the traditional sense. Armies were larger, but also better organized, supplied, disciplined, and trained, officered largely by aristocrats who tried, not very successfully, to imbue lower-class ranks with the ideals of the old chivalric code. John U. Nef suggests a number of factors that influenced the trend toward greater restraint: a growing distaste for violence; a raising of the comfort level among the European bourgeoisie; the refinement of manners, customs, and laws by an aristocracy that now admired gentility, agility, and subtlety more than prowess in battle; the pursuit of commerce; and the growth of the fine arts, combined with zealous efforts to apply reason to social affairs. All these factors, Nef concludes, helped to weaken the will for organized fighting.[32]

Down to the time of the French Revolution, the states of Europe were not willing to pursue objectives that required inflicting a great deal of destruction on the enemy. This period witnessed the emergence of economic motivations for conflict, but, although it is true that colonial and commercial rivalries were added to dynastic feuds as causes of international disputes, the rise of the bourgeoisie helped buttress pacifist rather than militarist sentiments, for the bourgeoisie desired more than anything else an orderly international community in which conditions of trade would be predictable. The very fact that the leading commercial nations of Western Europe were also developing naval power helped to soften the effects of warfare in the eighteenth century, insofar as naval forces could carry on hostile engagements without directly involving land populations. Such land warfare as did take place was usually characterized by adroit maneuver, surprise, march and countermarch, and rapier thrusts at the enemy's supply lines, as exemplified in the campaigns of Turenne, Saxe, and Marlborough. War, in the century of drawing-room culture, was not entirely unrelated to the game of chess or the minuet. The prevailing sense of restraint probably led to a slowdown in the rate of innovation in military technology. Encounters between armies in the field were often looked on as mere adjuncts to the diplomatic process, designed to strengthen or weaken the bargaining positions of envoys during prolonged negotiations.

MODERN PACIFIST THEORIES

Meanwhile, the post-Renaissance and Enlightenment periods had witnessed the rise in Europe of a school of pacifist thought that rejected the medieval moral–legal doctrine of war. The pacifist writers—Erasmus, More, Crucé, Fenelon, Penn, Voltaire, Rousseau, Kant, and Bentham—took their stand either on Stoic and early Christian radical positions or on the newer European ideals of cosmopolitanism, humanitarianism, and bourgeois internationalism. Practically all of them exhibited a pronounced skepticism in their attitudes toward war and the military profession. It was particularly fashionable to compare unfavorably the destructive life of the soldier with the useful life of the merchant. The abolition of force from international politics came to be looked on as the noblest objective of stateleaders. The quest for human happiness unmarred by any trace of the tragic became for European intellectuals the great goal of life.[33]

The philosophers were not agreed among themselves as to whether happiness was to be achieved through the application of scientific and technical reason or through people's return to nature and rediscovery of their original simplicity. Nonetheless, rationalists and romantics alike were convinced that society was about to break the shackles of traditional authority and superstition; dispel the historical curses of ignorance, disease, and war; and embark—in the vision of Condorcet—on the absolutely indefinite perfectibility of humanity, which knows no limit other than the duration of the globe on which nature has placed us.[34] "The people, being more enlightened," wrote Condorcet, "will learn by degrees to regard war as the most dreadful of all calamities, the most terrible of all crimes."[35] The era was marked by a bitter cynicism concerning the concept of the just war, which was regarded as mere propaganda calculated to cloak the aggressive urges of ambitious monarchs. No one at the time denounced the stupidity and incongruities of war with more scathing sarcasm than Voltaire, who poked fun at the two kings, each of whom had *Te Deums* sung in his own camp after the battle.[36] There was an anticipation, reflected in the writings of Montesquieu, that the transition from monarchical to republican institutions would be accompanied by a shift from the spirit of war and aggrandizement to that of peace and moderation. (See Chapter 8, the section on "Democracies, War, and Peace.") The period abounded in projects for abolishing war and establishing perpetual peace.[37]

The hopes of the Enlightenment writers proved ill-founded at the end of the eighteenth century. Liberal nationalist ideology was born in France during the Revolution and its Napoleonic aftermath, eventually sparking nationalist reactions elsewhere in Europe. The French introduced the *levée en masse,* the citizen conscript army—the nation at arms, backed by all the organizable resources of a newly industrializing society. Thus, France became the prototype of economic regimentation, large-scale factory production for war, and the mobilization of popular opinion in support of national expansionist policies. The charismatic little Corsican was virtually the first to wage total war in modern times. For a while, his powerful army was unconquerable. Military casualties reached unprecedented proportions.[38]

Napoleon, however, had left the European balance of power in a shambles. The conservative reaction of 1815 and thereafter, masterminded by Metternich and Talleyrand and based on the principle of a return to monarchical legitimacy, restored the classical idea of the balance of power—a Newtonian notion of an international universe in equilibrium—to a central place in the thinking of European leaders of state.[39] This restoration helped to limit war and, with the exception of the Franco–Prussian War, minimize the harsh effects of a developing military technology for a hundred years. Standing armies were reduced in size everywhere outside of Russia and Prussia. In Western Europe, the conviction grew that science, industry, communications technology, the growth of liberal parliamentary institutions, education, and international trade were all combining to make war obsolete and perhaps impossible. The era of the Concert of Powers, of which the Pax Britannica was an important feature, was marked by astute diplomacy and short wars rather than by lengthy, destructive engagements between military forces. Bismarck, the most canny manipulator of war, as an adjunct of his diplomacy toward Denmark, Austria, and France, in his efforts to unify Germany under Prussia's leadership, preferred to wield an iron fist in a velvet glove.[40] Throughout the nineteenth century, Europe experienced no conflict as bloody as the American Civil War, which was in several respects a prototype of modern total war in which powerful political and ideological motivations pitted the industrial technology of emerging capitalist liberalism against the traditional values of an agrarian, slave-holding aristocracy.[41]

Appearances in Europe, however, were somewhat deceptive. Despite the return to limited war, fought for limited political objectives (e.g., the unification of Germany), the latter decades of the nineteenth century witnessed the spread of universal conscription in Europe, the mass production of new automatic weapons, armaments races, the creation of alliances, increasing colonial and commercial rivalries among the powers, and the growth of a popular press that could be converted into a powerful instrument for stirring belligerent sentiments. The rise of modern war industry had an ambiguous significance. On the one hand, it served to make war more frightful and more unprofitable, and hence less readily undertaken. On the other hand, it served to make it much more likely that war, when it did come, would be total in nature, absorbing all available energies. The closely packed battle, in which mass is multiplied by velocity, became a dominant feature in modern European military thought.[42] Emphasis was placed on means of rapid mobilization—the telegraph for ordering up reserves, the railroad for transporting troops and equipment to the front, and steamships for getting them to the colonial territories of Asia and Africa. The speed of mobilization was so critical that the decision to mobilize became tantamount to a declaration of war by 1914.[43]

Jonathan Dymond's Uncompromising Pacifism

Throughout the nineteenth century, the pacifist movement slowly extended its influence in England and the United States. Jonathan Dymond, an English Quaker, argued that war, like the slave trade, would begin to disappear when people would refuse to acquiesce in it any longer and begin to question its necessity. Dymond denied that the patriotic warrior celebrated in song and story for having laid down his life for his country deserves such praise. The officer, he said, enters the army in order to obtain an income, the private because he prefers a life of idleness to one of industry. Both fight because it is their business, or because their reputation is at stake, or because they are compelled to do so. Dymond anticipated the contentions of the socialists and the later exponents of the devil theory of war by insinuating that the industrialists who profit from war combine forces with the professional military for the purpose of promoting war. He declared that the Christian scriptures require the individual to refrain from violence under all circumstances. All distinctions between just and unjust war, between defensive and aggressive war he dismissed as being in vain. War must be either absolutely forbidden or else permitted to run its unlimited course.[44] Dymond is one of the early voices of that modern movement of uncompromising pacifism that seeks not only to give religious advice to the conscience of the individual, but also to exert an influence on the policy of states—or at least those states in which the climate of opinion is sufficiently liberal to permit the propagation of the pacifist doctrine.

The aversion of modern intellectual pacifists to war cannot be explained purely in terms of religious and humanitarian factors. Since the nineteenth century, economic considerations, either liberal or socialist in their foundation, have entered into the thinking of most pacifists on the subject of war and peace. From Richard Cobden's era in the midnineteenth century down to very recent times, many liberal pacifists have been convinced that there exists an intrinsic and mutually causal relationship between free trade and peace, and that the abolition of trade barriers is the only means of effecting permanent peace. The heirs of this intellectual tradition in the contemporary era are the neoliberals (discussed in Chapter 2) and the interdependence theorists (discussed in Chapter 6).

Sir Norman Angell and War as an Anachronism

The liberal view that war represents the greatest threat to the economic health of modern industrial civilization reached its culmination in the writings of Norman Angell, an English publicist who achieved prominence in the 1920s and 1930s and whose work formed part of the utopian phase of international relations described previously. Shortly before World War I, Angell argued that warfare in the industrial age had become an unprofitable anachronism. The economic futility of military power, he declared, had been amply demonstrated by recent history, which showed that even when victory in war seems at first glance to bring with it substantial economic gains, such appearances are misleading and illusory. Nearly everyone thought that the Germans had reaped an advantage from the huge indemnity that France was forced to pay after being defeated in the Franco-Prussian War of 1870 to 1871, but, Angell argued, the indemnity actually induced an inflation that hurt the German economy. No nation, he went on to say, can genuinely improve its economic position either through war or through those imperialistic operations that involve costly preparations for military defense. Angell was convinced that the factors that really do constitute prosperity have not the remotest connection with military or naval power, all our political jargon notwithstanding.[45]

In the final analysis, Angell was a rationalist who believed that war could be eliminated through the growth and progressive application of human reason to international affairs. The modern technical state could no longer expect to profit from waging war but could only anticipate the disintegration of its own society. Once people become convinced that war has lost its meaning except as a form of mutual suicide, thought Angell, disarmament and peace would be possible. He was confident that peace was primarily a matter of educating the publics of democratic societies, and he chose to couch his homilies in terms of the economic self-interest of an interdependent European community, rather than in terms of traditional religious morality. In any case, he had no doubt that once human beings fully realized the irrelevance of military force for the attainment, promotion, and preservation of prosperity or socioeconomic well-being, then political wars would cease as religious wars did in the West a long time ago. It is worth noting the parallel between the thought of Norman Angell with that of Herbert Spencer in the nineteenth century and of George Liska in the middle of the twentieth, all of whom held that industrial nations are bound to eschew war.[46] Moreover, most contemporary strategic theorists (to be surveyed in Chapter 9), who come from a great diversity of perspectives, have concluded that nuclear war makes no sense, that no gain could be worth its cost, that it is unwinnable, and that nuclear weapons can have no use except a deterrent one. Deterrence theorists, it might be said, think that Angell's theory could not be demonstrably validated until after the advent of nuclear weapons on a large scale, producing a balance of terror.

BELLICIST THEORIES

Modern Western theories of conflict and war, including those of utopian pacifism, cannot be understood without some reference to the appearance, following the French Revolution, of a militarist school of thought within the West. "Bellicism," as this school might be called, developed at least partly in conscious reaction to idealistic pacifism. Perhaps it would be more accurate to say that the two tendencies in Western thought fed on each other as polar opposites. Western culture has never lacked thinkers who stressed conflict and tension over cooperation and harmony in social reality.

Most Western theorists of military strategy from the period of the French Revolution until the early 1960s (when the emphasis shifted from conventional strategy to the study of guerrilla warfare and counterinsurgency) showed a distinct preference for direct over indirect strategies, for the bludgeoning attack of the massed army over the graceful rapier thrust, for the frontal assault and the quick decision over the more patient strategy of maneuver, encirclement, attrition, and negotiation. The concept of total war has often been traced to the writings of Karl von Clausewitz, who at times expressed quite vividly the idea of war as an act of force pushed to its utmost bounds, as he did in the following passage:

> Now philanthropic souls might easily imagine that there was an artistic way of disarming or overthrowing our adversary without too much bloodshed and that this was what the art of war should seek to achieve. However agreeable this may sound, it is a false idea which must be demolished. He who uses this force ruthlessly, shrinking from no amount of bloodshed, must gain an advantage if his adversary does not do the same. Thereby he forces his adversary's hand, and thus each pushes the other to extremities to which the only limitation is the strength of resistance on the other side. Never in the philosophy of war can we introduce a modifying principle without committing an absurdity. So we repeat our statement: War is an act of force, and to the application of that force there is no limit.[47]

Yet, according to an eminent twentieth-century strategist of limited war and opponent of total-war thinking, Sir Basil H. Liddell Hart, Clausewitz has often been misinterpreted. As a student of Immanuel Kant, Clausewitz appreciated the difference between the ideal and the real, between the tendency of thought for the sake of clarity to carry an idea to an extreme, abstract form and the significant modifications that practical reality imposes on the abstraction. Clausewitz spoke of absolute war as a logical extreme to which military combat can be carried within the mind—a context in which each side strives for perfection of effort to break the other's will to resist—but he also recognized that there is no such thing in the real world, where war should be and is an instrument of state policy, "a continuation of politics by other means." Thus, war is always subordinate to and limited by politics. Human beings always fall short of absolute efforts; they can never devote all of their resources to war because there is a continuing demand that many other needs be met. The aims for which a war is undertaken and the means used to wage it are to be controlled by a political intelligence. Echoing the ancient Chinese strategist Sun Tzu, the Prussian theorist suggested that the decisive battle need not always be fought. Especially when the two warring sides are relatively equal in capabilities, they may wish to avoid a mutually destructive war of attrition, more costly than any political objective to be gained would be worth. Clausewitz was willing to contemplate limited war not for any moral or humanitarian reasons in the sense of the medieval just-war doctrine, but rather for reasons concerning the interests of the state.[48]

Other philosophers of the nineteenth century—Hegel, Nietzsche, Treitschke, Fichte, and Bernhardi—seemed at times to exalt power and war as ends in themselves. Hegel, for whom reality was the dialectical clash of ideas, was a communitarian who thought that the individual is shaped by national culture, and regarded the autonomous, sovereign nation-state as the concretization of the absolute in history, the march of God in the world. On the subject of war, he has perhaps been misunderstood. He did not glorify war and its brutality, but because he valued the nation so highly, he accepted war as a phenomenon that could contribute to national unity. Hegel left himself open either to misunderstanding or to justifiable criticism when he said that through war, the ethical health of nations is maintained, just as the motion of the winds keeps the sea from the foulness which a constant calm would produce.[49] Such views led Martin Wight, mistakenly, according to Chris Brown, to identify the Nazis and communists as Hegel's offspring.[50]

The harshest nineteenth-century critic of the values that underlay not only the Western Christian civilization of his day but even those of pure original Christianity was Friedrich Nietzsche. Emphasizing as he did the will-to-power as the basic determinant of human behavior, Nietzsche looked on the Christian ethos, marked by self-denial, resignation, humility, respect for weakness, and the renunciation of power, as the foe of the truly creative impulses in a personal religion of failure that inhibits the full development of the superman. Even more than for Hegel, war for Nietzsche plays an indispensable role in the renewal of civilizations. In the following passage, published in 1878, the German philosopher, who was determined to destroy all old categories of thought, seemed to adumbrate in a very stark way the theory of the moral equivalent of war that William James would express more optimistically in 1912:

> For the present, we know of no other means whereby the rough energy of the camp, the deep impersonal hatred, the cold-bloodedness of murder with a good conscience, the general order of the system in the destruction of the enemy, the proud indifference to great losses, to one's own existence and that of one's friends, the hollow earthlike convulsion of the soul, can be as forcibly and certainly communicated to enervated nations as is done by every great war. Culture can by no means dispense with passions, vices and malignities. When the Romans, after having become Imperial, had grown rather tired of war, they attempted to gain new strength by gladiatorial combats and Christian persecutions. The English of today, who appear on the whole to have also renounced war, adopt other means in order to generate anew those vanishing forces; namely, the dangerous exploring expeditions, sea voyages, and mountaineerings, nominally undertaken for scientific purposes, but in reality to bring home surplus strength from adventures and dangers of all kinds. Many other such substitutes for war will be discovered, but perhaps precisely thereby it will become more and more obvious that such a highly cultivated and therefore necessarily enfeebled humanity as that of modern Europe not only needs wars, but the greatest and most terrible wars—consequently occasional relapse into barbarism—lest, by the means of culture, it should lose its culture and its very existence.[51]

Lesser minds than Nietzsche's followed in his tracks. Johann Gottlieb Fichte, an ardent advocate of Machiavelli's ideas of raison d'état, warned that a neighboring power may be an ally against a common foe but will seek to gain at the friend's expense as soon as the common threat has disappeared; this is not a matter of choice, but a dictate of political wisdom. Thus, it is not enough to defend the national territory; the ruler must be constantly watching the entire situation and never fail to oppose any detrimental developments or to exploit possibilities of gain. Whoever fails to increase power is sure to decrease as others pursue their advantages.[52] The German historian Heinrich von Treitschke, who spoke for the Prussian military caste, also drew his inspiration from Machiavelli. Convinced that the independent sovereign nation-state is the highest political achievement of which the individual is capable, he rejected as intolerable the concept of a genuine universal political community. War is frequently the only means available to the state to protect its independence, and thus the ability and readiness to wage war must be preserved in a carefully honed condition. The state ought to be oversensitive in matters of national honor, so that the instinct of political self-preservation can be developed to the highest possible degree. Whenever the flag is insulted, there must be an immediate demand for full satisfaction, and if this is not forthcoming, "war must follow, however small the occasion may seem."[53] There is nothing reprehensible in this, for in Treitschke's eyes, war itself is majestic and sublime.[54]

The ideas voiced by Clausewitz, Hegel, Nietzsche, and Treitschke were echoed by several philosophers of military history in Europe and in the United States. General Friedrich von Bernhardi, strongly influenced by the Darwinian concept of survival of the fittest (which he understood only superficially), correlated war with human progress, holding that "those intellectual and moral factors which insure superiority in war are also those which render possible a general progressive development among nations."[55] The geopolitical writings of Kjellen and Ratzel, as well as the twentieth-century German students of geopolitics represented by Haushofer, were indebted intellectually to Darwinian concepts. (See Chapter 4, in which the geopolitical theories are examined.)

Alfred Thayer Mahan also saw history as a Darwinian struggle in which fitness is measured in terms of military strength. The habits of military discipline, he thought, are necessary underpinnings of an orderly civilian structure. He viewed the nations of the world as economic corporations locked in a fierce survival competition for resources and markets. Unlike the Marxists, however, he attributed this not merely to the impulses of capitalism, but rather to human nature and the fact that the supply of economic goods is finite. Contradictions of national self-interest, along with wide and irreducible discrepancies of power, opportunity, and determination, produce the conditions of permanent conflict and render it unrealistic to expect violence to be eliminated from international affairs. Mahan deemed futile all efforts to substitute law for force, since all law depends on force for its efficacy. Finally, Mahan defended the institution of war against the accusation that it was immoral and un-Christian. He argued that war is the means whereby nation-states carry out the mandates of their citizens' consciences. A state should go to war only when it is convinced of rightfulness, but once it has committed its conscience, there is no choice but war (not even arbitration), for the material evils of war are less than the moral evil of compliance with wrong.[56] (Mahan's views on the geopolitics of maritime power are treated in Chapter 4.)

BELLICISTS AND ANTIDEMOCRATIC THEORISTS

As the nineteenth century gave way to the twentieth, the intellectual polarization of Western pacifists and bellicists became complete. The bellicists and their doctrines may be classified as follows.

1. *Realistic positivism,* was represented by such turn-of-the-century Italian writers as Vilfredo Pareto (1848–1923) and Gaetano Mosca (1858–1941). Pareto, an economist and sociologist, and Mosca, a political scientist, both expounded the concepts of rule by the elite, the importance of coercive instruments in the maintenance of social unity and order, and the inevitable recurrence of revolution. Mosca was not as antihumanitarian and antidemocratic as Pareto, but he shared Pareto's prejudice against pacifism, fearing that if war should be eliminated, nations would grow soft and disintegrate.[57]

2. *Social Darwinists* and nationalists with proclivities toward social Darwinism included such proponents as the sociologists William Graham Sumner and Ernst Haeckel and the jurist Oliver Wendell Holmes.[58]

3. Certain *pessimistic philosophers of history* included Oswald Spengler (1880–1936) and Bendetto Croce (1866–1952). Spengler, a German historian, was particularly fascinated by the will-to-power, the virility of barbarians, the subjugation of weaker peoples, and the law of the jungle, while he suffered from a special dread of a worldwide revolution of the nonwhite people against the whites.[59] Croce, an Italian philosopher and political leader, although a critic of the excesses of militarism, regarded war as a necessary tragedy of the human condition, indispensable to human progress, and regarded the dream of perpetual peace as fatuous.

4. The forerunners and cryptorepresentatives of *racist theory* and/or *fascism,* as well as the actual archetypes of those ideologies, included writers such as Houston Stewart Chamberlain, Arthur de Gobineau, Giovanni Gentile, Alfredo Rocco, Georges Sorel, Gabriel d'Annunzio, and Benito Mussolini.[60]

It would be unfair to insinuate that all the foregoing schools of thought should be linked with the fascists, or even that all fascists were or are racists, but all exalted, in varying degrees, the role of force and virile action in social processes. The aforementioned individuals are more appropriately treated in works on political theory or intellectual (and anti-intellectual) history, but serious students of international relations cannot afford to ignore the impact these writers had on the thinking of their time, nor should students overlook the influential role of conscious ideas and persisting attitudes in decision making and social conflict.

ANARCHISM AND THE MARXIST SOCIALISTS

Finally, there were the anarchists and the Marxist socialists. These two movements of an extremist nature, antithetical in many respects, produced contrary offshoots, some theoretical and some practical. Both movements helped dialectically to strengthen the theory of pacifism and the practice of politicized violence as an instrument either of abolishing the state or of promoting class revolution as a prelude to establishing a cooperative or a socialist order. The Marxist–Leninist theory of imperialism and war is examined in the next chapter. Here, a brief word about anarchism is in order, because it is often misunderstood by the public at large and because it constitutes a more significant tendency of the contemporary mind, especially the minds of Western youth and anti-Western liberationists, than is generally recognized.

Anarchism is the doctrine that opposes established political authority in all its forms. Anarchists view life as a moral drama in which the individual is arrayed against the state and all the oppressive instruments of coercion that they associate with government—bureaucracies, courts, police, and the military, as well as the institutions of private property and religion. They seek liberation from these and all forms of external constraint on human freedom. Firmly convinced of humanity's innate goodness and reasonableness, a benign anarchist who follows Kropotkin believes that the basic law of society is not conflict but mutual aid and cooperation. The anarchist, according to Irving Louis Horowitz, in addition to being antipolitical is also antitechnological and antieconomic.[61] Thus anarchists are essentially foes of capitalist and socialist alike: If the former keeps government merely to protect their bourgeois interests and manage their affairs, the latter would replace capitalist tyranny with socialist tyranny—the dictatorship of the proletariat.

Some branches of anarchism—notably collectivist, communist, syndicalist, and conspiratorial—openly espoused the use of violence both in theory and as a tactical necessity. Sergei Nechaev (1847–1882), a disciple of the Russian revolutionary agitator Mikhail Bakunin (1814–1876), adopted a creed of "propaganda by deed" and "universal pan destruction." He advocated the nihilistic tactic of assassination for its effects of psychological terror and the demolition of existing institutions.[62] Enrico Malatesta (1850–1932), an Italian journalist, regarded well-planned violence as an apt means of educating the working classes as to the meaning of the revolutionary struggle.[63] Similarly, the French journalist Georges Sorel (1847–1922) perceived value in proletarian acts of violence that serve to delineate the separation of classes. Such violence, he maintained, helps to develop the consciousness of the working class and keeps the middle class in a chronic state of fear, always ready to capitulate to the demands made on it, rather than run the risk of defending its position by resorting to force.[64]

Not all anarchists have been advocates of violence. Individualist anarchists in America, such as Henry David Thoreau (1817–1862) and Benjamin R. Tucker (1854–1939), eschewed violence as unrespectable. They preferred to emphasize nonviolent civil disobedience. The two most influential pacifist anarchists of modern times—Mahatma Gandhi (1869–1948) and Leo Tolstoy (1828–1910)—

radically opposed a pure religious ethic to a person's willingness to submit to the state, which they excoriated for brutalizing the masses and converting military heroism into a virtue. Deeming it imperative that the law of force be superseded by the law of love, yet finding this impossible within the framework of the existing nation-state system, they insisted that the latter must give way to a universal society.[65]

Anarchism has sometimes been quite trenchant in its moral criticism of existing institutions, but it has not made a significant contribution toward a scientific understanding of the sources of human conflict. Where one finds in anarchist writings a keen insight into group sociology (e.g., in Sorel's awareness of the group-integrating function of externally directed violence), this usually reflects borrowing from more dispassionate social scientists (e.g., Sorel was strongly influenced by Durkheim). In recent decades, the chief appeal of anarchist theories in the United States, which have a long history in this country, has been to intellectuals, artists, black militants, students, youth, and others identified with the counterculture, and, especially in the late 1960s, the protest against the Vietnam War. The terrorist seeks to transform society by delivering random, indiscriminate blows regardless of the guilt or innocence of those targeted, thus producing widespread insecurity and senseless shocks that shake society to its foundations. Propaganda by deed remains the preferred strategy of nihilists who, like Verloc in Joseph Conrad's novel, *The Secret Agent,* ask what response can be made "to an act of destructive ferocity so absurd as to be incomprehensible, inexplicable, almost unthinkable—in fact, mad? Madness alone is truly terrifying, inasmuch as you cannot placate it either by threats, persuasion, or bribes."[66]

On the international plane, anarchist thought has been one of the intellectual streams that merged with other ideological, nationalist, and religious forces to produce the problem of transnational terrorism in the latter part of the twentieth century. The phenomenon of terrorism is as old as the various forms of tyranny, oppression, and injustice, which through the ages have bred feelings of revolutionary resentment and rage against governments, economic institutions, and other entities that individuals and groups have been determined to change or to destroy by violent means. Only since the mid-1950s, however, has terrorism come to be regarded as a significant factor within the international system. Theorists are far from agreement concerning the nature and causes of terrorism, given its multiple manifestations, and they have not yet been able to determine in a satisfactory way what its impact has been on the behavior of governments and the state system.[67] (See the section on "Terrorism" in Chapter 8.)

THE NORMATIVE THEORY
OF JUST WAR IN THE NUCLEAR AGE

Most of the older theories discussed in Chapter 1 and in this chapter had a *normative* dimension. Anyone who says that A is better than B or that to do this is better than to do that is making a normative judgment. Normative theory is more *qualitative,* in the sense of traditional values than is positivist–empiricist–behavioralist theory, which stresses a *quantitative,* value-free approach in the social sciences. The former deals with a moral, ethical, political, legal, or strategic *ought,* and not merely with the factual *is.* The theorists treated thus far advised governments, rulers, and diplomats (whether optimists or pessimists) to think and act in certain ways that they regarded as better, with respect to decisions for war and peace; the obligation to obey international law, fulfill treaties, and keep faith with others (whether for moral reasons or out of utilitarian motives of enlightened self-interest); and the advisability of coping with an anarchic world by relying on the balance of power or on international peacekeeping organizations. As we show in the next chapter on theories of imperialism, both the Marxists and non-Marxists who excoriated capitalist exploitation of non-Western peoples ("core versus periphery") and the liberals who worked for the political emancipation and self-determination of colonial territories and oppressed populations were theorizing in a normative manner, as do those in more recent decades who have analyzed *dependencia,* demanded international distributive justice, and focused concern on such problems as world poverty and hunger, the economics of arms and development, human rights and the pollution of the environment—all these were or are taking normative positions in their recipes for what is better, or what is right. With the end of the Cold War, there has been a resurgence of interest in normative approaches to international relations—in worthwhile human values, ideals, and goals to be pursued by governments. It would be a mistake, however, to conclude that realists, who have a healthy respect for the phenomenon of power relations, ignore the normative or value implications of theory. They were especially compelled to face up to those implications during decades of debate about the morality of nuclear weapons, war, and deterrence.

Chris Brown has noted that the concept of just war has to be "one of the only areas of contemporary moral philosophy where an essentially medieval theoretical construction still has common currency."[68] There are some who would argue that such a concept has no place in modern international theory because it is a philosophical and theological doctrine, not a theory based on the empirical methods of science. Such a criterion of exclusion, if rigidly applied, would involve setting aside as irrelevant virtually all normative approaches to international theory. Yet the just war idea was central to the thinking of the founders of modern international law. They grudgingly accepted the fact that the doctrine of sovereignty in an anarchical system left it to every state to judge the justice of its own cause when making the decision to go to war (*ius ad bellum*), but they insisted that international law imposes on states certain limits with regard to the conduct of war (*ius in bello*). It is granted that every government in its war propaganda trumpets the justice of its cause—a phenomenon that lends itself to empirical study and analysis, especially as to credibility.

The appeal to justice is an important part of the politics of war, for it affects such things as public support, the morale of fighting forces, the ability to hold allies, and the popularity and fate of governing elites. Despite what seemed to be a virtual moratorium on moral and ethical judgments during World War II (especially with regard to the obliteration bombing of cities), the debate over the morality of warfare has been revived with considerable vigor since the Nuremberg and Tokyo war-crimes trials and the advent of nuclear-weapons technology. Moreover, the intellectual–political controversy in the United States during the Vietnam War and the military buildup preceding the Persian Gulf War ("Desert Storm") was carried on largely within the framework of traditional just-war criteria. To a lesser extent, echoes of the traditional standards were heard in the debates about the wisdom of military intervention for humanitarian purposes in Bosnia and of threatening to invade Haiti in 1994 to oust a military junta and install an elected president.

Several writers have argued that, given the destructive power of modern military technology, the conditions of a just war—specifically, the requirement that the amount of force employed must be proportionate to the political objectives sought—can no longer be validated. Nuclear pacifists contend that, even though it may have been theoretically possible to justify the resort to force by states in earlier periods, nuclear war cannot be deemed politically or morally justifiable under any circumstances, no matter how unjust the aggression being defended against. The inhuman consequences of modern warfare have prompted increasing numbers of ethicists and theologians to raise again the ancient questions as to whether waging war is ever compatible with the Christian conscience.[69]

Pacifist arguments are widespread and well-known: During the Cold War, nuclear conflict was said to threaten not only mutual extinction for nations party to more than a minimal nuclear exchange, but also to pose grave dangers of widespread radioactive fallout, genetic mutations, and nuclear winter for large segments of humanity. In view of the superpowers' large nuclear stockpiles, it was highly unlikely that a nuclear exchange could have been controlled and kept limited. The strategy of nuclear deterrence was based on an uncertain, overly optimistic assumption that governmental decision makers can be expected to act rationally in crisis. (See Chapter 9 on "Rational Deterrence" and Chapter 11 on "Rationality and Decision-Making Theory.") A nuclear arms race, even if it did not lead inevitably to war, nevertheless piled up an overkill capability, wasting resources that could have been channeled into development, and producing a climate of neurotic fear. Prior to the end of the Cold War and the beginning of substantial nuclear disarmament in the late 1980s and the 1990s, some writers were so appalled by these dismal prospects that they advocated unilateral disarmament and nonviolent resistance as the only escape from disaster.[70]

Nevertheless, despite the potential horrors of modern warfare and frequent distortions of the just-war notion throughout history as mere political propaganda, modern proponents of the theory insist that the traditional mode of rational ethical analysis—one that seeks to chart a middle course between the extremes of pacifism and bellicism—cannot be discarded. Weapons technology cannot be allowed to exploit all scientific possibilities and develop according to its own dialectic but must be subjected to a moral analysis of power and its limits. Writers in this vein have included Paul Ramsey, John Courtney Murray, Robert W. Tucker, Richard A. Falk, William V. O'Brien, James Turner Johnson, Michael Walzer, and others.[71] The general consensus of just-war writers (apart from Walzer, discussed separately later in this chapter) can be summed up in the following propositions:

1. In the absence of effective international peacekeeping institutions, the moral right of states to resort to war under certain circumstances cannot be denied. Within the self-help international system, it is probable that states will continue to feel constrained at times to resort to the use of military force. An ethical doctrine to govern and limit war, therefore, remains essential.

2. Although aggressive war (which was permitted under the traditional doctrine to punish offenses and to restore justice) is no longer considered a lawful means available to states for the vindication of violated rights, there still exists the right to wage defensive war against aggression and to give aid to another party who is a victim of aggression.[72]

3. Modern military technology cannot be allowed to render entirely meaningless the traditional distinction between combatant forces and innocents even in strategic war. Even when the state has the moral right to wage war (*ius ad bellum*), there is an obligation to adhere to the law governing the means used in war (*ius in bello*).[73]

The debate over war and morality will go on indefinitely. Pacifists of various persuasions, absolutist or relativist, will argue that it is either logically absurd or ethically monstrous to analyze warfare in terms of rationality or justice. Other theorists will contend that in a global system that lacks an effective global peacekeeping–peace-enforcement authority—that is, an international force organized in support of international justice—independent governments and other political entities are likely to be disposed from time to time to resort to the use of force, and that the world will be better off if those who advise governments—regardless of whether they are pacifists or just-war theorists—can have recourse to an intellectually credible code of rational, moral, civilized behavior that enjoins decision makers to observe humane limits in their strategizing. Despite frequent assertions that the just-war doctrine has become obsolete in a nuclear era of unlimited destructive capability, there have been numerous instances of limited conventional and unconventional warfare, as well as of efforts to develop new systems of advanced weapons technology, to which the traditional analysis of the conditions required for the moral justification of deterrence and force remains quite relevant and—what is more—is still applied with remarkable frequency in the public political debate.[74] Moreover, writers on the religious left who sought during the 1970s to develop theologies of liberation and revolution appropriated some of the elements of the just-war doctrine, even while shifting the presumption of justice away from incumbent governments (attempting to maintain internal peace and order) to insurgent revolutionary groups (attempting to overthrow incumbent governments that they deemed oppressive).[75]

Perhaps no student of the just war has dealt more intricately with the paradox confronted by strategists and moralists in the nuclear age than Michael Walzer. The human mind seems unable to devise a coherent conceptual framework—political policy, strategic doctrine, and operational military plan—that neatly combines effective deterrence with workable defense, and that is widely acceptable on grounds of rationality, credibility, and morality. Walzer reminds us that superpower governments are deterred from risking even conventional war, not to mention limited nuclear war, by the specter of ultimate horror—the danger that it might escalate to an uncontrollable nuclear exchange. In an era of plentiful nuclear stock-piles, he says, any imaginable strategy is likely to deter a central war between the giants. Once we understood what the strategists of deterrence were saying, it became unnecessary to adopt any particular strategy for fighting a nuclear war.[76] (Many strategic theorists, of course, would deny this.) It was deemed sufficient merely to pose the ultimate nuclear threat. Deterrence is frightening in principle when we stop to ponder the ultimate, but in actuality, deterrence is easy to live with because it has been a bloodless strategy. It causes no pain or injury to its hostages, unless they stop to think it through, which not many people do. Walzer puts distance between himself and most just-war theorists when he propounds the view that all nuclear war is immoral.[77]

In the Cold War era, the debate among ethicists shifted subtly from one involving the morality or immorality of war and strategic policy to one that pitted the immorality of large-scale nuclear war against the probability that nuclear war might occur and spin out of control. Virtually all moral theologians and philoso-phers have long agreed that, if nuclear deterrence should break down, carrying out the strategy of assured destruction (which is described in Chapter 9) would consti-tute a moral evil of historically unprecedented magnitude. Concerning that strate-gy itself, writers who deal with the ethics of strategy were in serious disagreement on four points:

1. What was the intention underlying the strategy of assured destruction? Was it the good intention of preventing nuclear war or the reprehensible inten-tion to wreak catastrophic death and destruction in retaliation? If the two intentions are combined in one, how is it to be judged?
2. Was it possible to distinguish the public threat embodied in a strategic deterrent policy, designed to prevent war, from the plan that would actual-ly be executed if the deterrent failed? (This question also caused problems for strategic analysts, government policymakers, and military leaders who were concerned with keeping the threat credible.)
3. For purposes of moral evaluation, could we predicate the intention of a government, just as we would of an individual in a legal case? In matters of governmental policy, especially in a pluralist constitutional democratic sys-tem, who could be held responsible for intending to do what?
4. Was it morally permissible, for the sake of preserving peace, to confront the adversary with a strategic threat that would be immoral to execute?

A compelling argument can be made that the more frightful the threat, the more effective it should be as a deterrent, provided that it is credible. That is why the strategy of assured destruction was considered so politically successful, and also why it was so roundly condemned by many church leaders and other moralists who fixed their attention on the implicit, conditional intention embodied in it to destroy urban population and industrial complexes. Some argued that it was justi-fiable to hold nuclear weapons for purposes of deterrence, but that these weapons could never be used in war. This argument contravened the requirement of deterrent credibility, because it deprived deterrence of an operational doctrine. (Whether it is possible for a democratic government to have one doctrine for deterrence and a more limited one in case of deterrence failure is debatable.)

Presumably, any effort to render the threat less immoral and more limited might also seem, at least logically, less effective as a deterrent (even though some would argue that this could enhance its credibility—i.e., its certainty of being applied). When U.S. defense officials appeared to be considering responses to aggression more measured than all-out massive retaliation with strategic nuclear missiles—for example, limited nuclear options, selective targeting, counterforce rather than countercity strategies, battlefield or tactical nuclear weapons, horizontal escalation, or conventional deterrence—they were often criticized by moralists for making nuclear war less unthinkable or more likely to occur as a result of escalation. Thus, indirectly, the moralists, whether wittingly or not, have been indicating their concern with regard not only to the morality of deterrence but also to its effectiveness. Even though they might not condemn every conceivable use of nuclear weapons, and might reluctantly approve the possibility that retaliatory use in a limited and discriminating manner against military targets could be theoretically justified, nevertheless the moralists exhibited a great deal of skepticism that a nuclear war could be kept limited, regardless of efforts to control it. Fearing the escalatory process, they generally opposed any first use of nuclear weapons.[78]

The prolonged debate about the morality of nuclear war, which has passed through several phases, has served amply to demonstrate that the concept of deterrence, which constitutes an important theoretical development in the international relations of the twentieth century, represents something quite new in history. It seems to defy adequate evaluation in terms of the two traditional Western categories of thought on the subject of war and peace—just war and pacifism—and requires a unique, rather paradoxical mode of ethical analysis.

The Cold War ended, of course, without nuclear weapons having been used and with the only instances of their employment having been against Japan in the closing days of World War II. In place of the deterrence relationship that evolved during the Cold War, the prospect loomed that weapons of mass destruction—nuclear, biological, and chemical—would be proliferated to larger numbers of states, and possibly to nonstate actors as well. Theories that had been focused on bipolar deterrence needed to be adapted to take account of such changes, as discussed in Chapter 9. At the same time, the proliferation of weapons of mass destruction gives rise to ethical questions, including the appropriate basis for deterring the employment of such systems by a regional actor such as Iraq. What would be the appropriate U.S. response in the event that Saddam Hussein had used chemical or biological weapons against Israel or Saudi Arabia during the 1990–1991 Gulf War? Having given up its own biological and chemical weapons programs, the United States retained a nuclear retaliatory option, as well as a sophisticated conventional response capability. At the same time, the post–Cold War era holds increasing potential for armed conflict by actors other than states, with such nonstate entities possibly in possession of weapons of unprecedented lethality. Such changing parameters for the conduct of warfare raise numerous questions about why armed conflict occurs and the means by which it can be deterred or otherwise prevented. In the global-conflict setting of the years leading into the twenty-first century, these questions encompass not only how wars come about but also how, or even whether, normative theories such as those set forth in this chapter, developed in the Western world, will be applicable or acceptable in a world of unprecedented paradigmatic diversity and complexity.

NOTES

1. Noteworthy samples published since 1980 include Francis A. Beer, *Peace Against War: The Ecology of International Violence* (San Francisco, CA: Freeman, 1981); Bruce Bueno de Mesquita, *The War Trap* (New Haven, CT: Yale University Press, 1981); Robert G. Gilpin, *War and Change in World Politics* (Cambridge, England: Cambridge University Press, 1981); Seyom Brown, *The Causes and Prevention of War* (New York: St. Martin's, 1987); Geoffrey Blainey, *The Causes of War*, 3rd ed. (New York: Free Press, 1988); Melvin Small and J. David Singer, eds., *International War: An Anthology* (Chicago, IL: Dorsey Press, 1989); Greg Cashman, *What Causes War? An Introduction to Theories of International Conflict* (New York: Lexington Books, 1993); John A. Vasquez, *The War Puzzle* (Cambridge, England: Cambridge University Press, 1993); Claudio Cioffi-Revilla, "Origins and Evolution of War and Politics," *International Studies Quarterly*, 40 (1) (March 1996), 1–22; and several articles in *International Studies Quarterly*, *World Politics*, *American Political Science Review*, *Journal of Conflict Resolution*, and *International Security*, which are cited later in this text.

2. Michael Howard, *The Causes of War and Other Essays* (Cambridge, MA. Harvard University Press, 1983) pp. 7–22, quoted at p. 14. J. David Singer has noted that, with the possible exception of Jean de Bloch's *Future of War* (1899), which predicted with surprising accuracy what the next European war would look like, and Pitirim Sorokin, whose 1937 work *Social and Cultural Dynamics* correlated war with cycles in cultural patterns, Quincy Wright's *A Study of War* (Chicago, IL: University of Chicago Press, 1992) and Lewis Richardson's studies of the statistics of arms races, published in 1960 on the basis of earlier research (and discussed in Chapter 8) mark the first traceable efforts to bring scientific method to bear on international conflict. He adds, while physical phenomena had been studied in an essentially scientific fashion for several centuries, and biological phenomena for nearly a century, social phenomena had remained largely the domain of theological speculation, moral imperative, and conventional folklore. "Accounting for International War: The State of the Discipline," *Journal of Peace Research*, XVIII(1) (1981), 1. Singer's judgment may be a bit unfair to the philosophers and social, political, and legal theorists who reflected prior to the twentieth century on the problem of war without employing quantitative methodologies and whose views can hardly be dismissed as conventional folklore. It is correct, nevertheless, to say that the sustained effort to study wars in a systematic, scientific way, employing the methods of the behavioral disciplines, did not get under way until after the First World War.

3. Donald Kagan, *On the Origins of War and the Preservation of Peace* (New York: Doubleday, 1995), pp. 1–11; 569.

4. Lewis A. Coser, *The Functions of Social Conflict* (New York: Free Press, 1956), p. 3.

5. H. L. Nieburg, *Political Violence* (New York: St. Martin's, 1969).

6. Seymour Martin Lipset has noted that both Tocqueville and Marx emphasized the necessity for conflict among social units, and Lipset defines the existence of a moderate state of conflict as another way of defining a legitimate democracy. *Political Man: The Social Bases of Politics* (Garden City, NY: Doubleday-Anchor, 1963), pp. 7 and 71. Conflict is an essential aspect of growth, one that we can neither fully control nor prevent, nor should we wish to do so. H. L. Nieburg, op. cit., pp. 16–17. Human existence without conflict is unthinkable. Conflict gives life much of its meaning, so that its elimination, even if attainable, would not be desirable. Jerome D. Frank, "Human Nature and Nonviolent Resistance," in Quincy Wright et al., eds., *Preventing World War III* (New York: Simon & Schuster, 1962), p. 193. Kenneth Boulding has suggested that in a given situation there may be too much or too little conflict, or an optimal amount, which lends to life a certain dramatic interest. *Conflict and Defense* (New York: Harper & Row, 1962), pp. 305–307.

7. Quoted in Abram Kardiner and Edward Preble, *They Studied Man* (New York: New American Library Mentor Books, 1963), p. 102. Elsewhere, Emile Durkheim wrote, "Social facts do not differ from psychological facts in quality only: *they have a different substratum*; they evolve in a different milieu; and they depend on different conditions. . . . The mentality of groups is not the same as that of individuals; [the group mentality] has its own laws." Introduction to S. A. Solvay and J. K. Mueller, *The Rules of Sociological Method*, 2nd ed., trans. G. E. G. Catlin, ed. (New York: Free Press, 1938), p. xix (Emphasis in original).

8. See Reuben Osborn, *Freud and Marx* (London: Victor Gallancz, 1937), and *Marxism and Psycho-Analysis* (London: Barrie and Rockliff, 1965).

9. See, for example, the collection of essays from various social-science disciplines in Elton B. McNeil, ed., *The Nature of Human Conflict* (Englewood Cliffs, NJ: Prentice-Hall, 1963); also J. David Singer, "Man and World Politics: the Psycho-Cultural Interface," *Journal of Social Issues*, XXIV (July 1968), 127–156.

10. Michael Haas, *International Conflict* (New York: Bobbs-Merrill, 1974), p. 4.

11. Stephen Withey and Daniel Katz, "The Social Psychology of Human Conflict," in Elton B. McNeil, ed., *The Nature of Human Conflict* (Englewood Cliffs, NJ: Prentice-Hall, 1965), p. 65.

12. Herbert C. Kelman, "Social-Psychological Approaches to the Study of International Relations," in Herbert C. Kelman, ed., *International Behavior: A Social-Psychological Analysis* (New York: Holt, Rinehart and Winston, 1965), pp. 5–6. See also the references to the work of Werner Levi in Chapter 7 on the microcosmic theories of war.

13. See M. Jane Stroup, "Problems of Research on Social Conflict in the Area of International Relations," *Journal of Conflict Resolution*, IX (September 1965), 413–417. See also Coser, op. cit., pp. 15–38; Jesse Bernard, "Parties and Issues in Conflict," *Journal of Conflict Resolution*, I (June 1957), 111–121; and Raymond W. Mack and Richard C. Snyder, "The Analysis of Social Conflict: Toward an Overview and Synthesis," ibid., I (June 1957), 212–248. For the argument that Talcott Parsons's structural–functional approach, relegating conflict to the realm of the abnormal, deviant, and pathological, renders itself incapable of explaining social change and conflict, see Ralf Dahrendorf, "Toward a Theory of Social Conflict," *Journal of Conflict Resolution*, II (June 1958), 170–183. According to Dahrendorf, Parsonians focused attention on problems of adjustment rather than of change. For them, social conflict was essentially disruptive and dysfunctional. Dahrendorf, in his sociology, stresses change rather than persisting configurations, conflict rather than consensus. He presents his postulates not to overturn the Parsonian view, but rather to complement it with an organic model of different emphases. He believes that neither model alone, but only the two taken syntheti-

cally, can exhaust social reality and supply us with a complete theory of society in its changing as well as in its enduring aspects. See Georg Simmel "Conflict," trans. Kurt H. Wolff, in *Conflict and the Web of Group Affiliations* (New York: Free Press, 1955). Simmel wrote: "Just as the universe needs love and hate—that is, attractive and repulsive forces—in order to have any form at all, so society, too, in order to attain a determinate shape, needs some quantitative ration of harmony and disharmony, of association and competition, of favorable and unfavorable tendencies." Ibid. p. 15. Even in relatively hopeless situations, the opportunity to offer opposition can help to render the unbearable bearable: "Opposition gives us inner satisfaction, distraction and relief, just as do humility and patience under different psychological conditions" (p. 19). See Lewis Coser, ed., *Georg Simmel* (Englewood Cliffs, NJ: The Free Press, 1955), pp. 1–77. See also R. C. North et al., "The Integrative Functions of Conflict," *Journal of Conflict Resolution,* IV (September 1960), 355–374; Lewis A. Coser, "Some Social Functions of Violence," *Annals of the American Academy of Political and Social Science,* CCCLXIV (March 1966), 8–18; and Charles Lockhart, "Problems in the Management and Resolution of International Conflicts," *World Politics.* XXIX (April 1977), 370.

14. See the excellent chapter on "Ancient China," in Frank M. Russell, *Theories of International Relations* (New York: Appleton, 1936); Mousheng Lin, *Men and Ideas: An Informal History of Chinese Political Thought* (New York: John Day, 1942); Arthur Waley, *Three Ways of Thought in Ancient China* (London: Allen and Unwin, 1939 Anchor edition, 1956); H. G. Creel, *Chinese Thought from Confucius to Mao Tse-tung* (New York: New American Library, 1960), especially pp. 51–53, 113–121, and 126–130; and Ch'u Chai and Winberg Chai, eds., *The Humanist Way in Ancient China: Essential Works of Confucianism* (New York: Bantam, 1965). Jacques Gernet pointed out that Mo-Ti's followers sought to avoid wars but were willing to defend by force of arms cities subject to unjust attack. *A History of Chinese Civilization,* trans. J. R. Foster (Cambridge, England: Cambridge University Press, 1983), p. 88.

15. For further discussion of historical Indian attitudes toward war, see D. MacKenzie Brown, *The White Umbrella: Indian Political Thought from Manu to Gandhi* (Berkeley: University of California Press, 1953), especially Part I; U. N. Goshal, *A History of Hindu Political Theories* (London: Oxford University Press, 1923); A. L. Basham, "Some Fundamentals of Hindu Statecraft," in Joel Laurus, ed., *Comparative World Politics: Readings in Western and Pre-Modern Non-Western International Relations* (Belmont, CA: Wadsworth, 1964), especially pp. 47–52; and the chapter on "Ancient India," in Frank M. Russell, op. cit.; Norman D. Palmer, "Indian and Western Political Thought: Coalescence or Clash?" *American Political Science Review,* XLIX (September 1955), 747–761; George Modelski, "Kautilya: Foreign Policy and International System in the Ancient Hindu World," *American Political Science Review,* LVIII (September 1964), 549–560.

16. John Burnet, *Greek Philosophy: Thales to Plato* (New York: Macmillan, 1961), pp. 72–74; Bertrand Russell, *A History of Western Philosophy* (New York: Simon and Schuster, 1945), p. 42.

17. Plato, *The Republic,* trans. F. M. Cornford (New York: Oxford University Press, 1945), Book II.

18. Aristotle, *Politics,* trans. Ernest Barker (Oxford, England: Oxford University Press, 1946), Books VI anad VIII.

19. Thucydides, *The Pelopponesian War,* trans. Rex Warner (Harmondsworth, England: Penguin, 1954), p. 56. For Pericles, see ibid., pp. 118–121.

20. Coleman Phillipson, *The International Law and Custom of Ancient Greece and Rome* (London: Macmillan, 1911), Vol. II, pp. 192–195.

21. Ibid., Vol. II, pp. 329–343.
22. Ibid., Vol. II, p. 223.
23. F. R. Cowell, *Cicero and the Roman Republic* (Harmondsworth, England: Pelican Books, 1956), pp. 41–43.
24. Hamilton A. R. Gibb, *Mohammedanism: An Historical Survey* (New York: New American Library, 1955), pp. 57–58. Majid Khadduri has written two fine expositions of the subject: *War and Peace in the Law of Islam* (Baltimore, MD.: Johns Hopkins Press, 1955) and "The Islamic Theory of International Relations and Its Contemporary Relevance," in J. Harris Proctor, ed., *Islam and International Relations* (New York: Praeger, 1965), pp. 24–39; Bernard Lewis, "The Return of Islam," in Michael Curtis, ed., *The Middle East Reader* (New Brunswick, NJ: Transaction Books, 1986), especially pp. 79–82; Abdulaziz A. Sachenida has pointed out that *jihad* is better translated as "internal struggle" or "spiritual effort," rather than "holy war," but agrees that Islam approves war for both defensive and offensive purposes "to bring about the kind of world that the Qu'ran envisions." James Turner Johnson and John Kelsay, eds., *Cross, Crescent and Sword: The Justification and Limitation of War in the Western and Islamic Tradition* (New York: Greenwood, 1990), p. 39.
25. D. Mackenzie Brown, op. cit., p. 143.
26. For the beliefs and practices of the Israelites in the ages of the prophets and judges, before the rise of political kings, see Exodus 15:1–21; Deuteronomy 20:1–20 and 23:15; Joshua 1:19, 2:23, 3:510 and 6:119; Judges 7:2–22 and 2 Samuel 5:24. See also Everett F. Gendler, "War and the Jewish Tradition," in James Finn, ed., *A Conflict of Loyalties* (New York: Pegasus, 1968); George Foot Moore, *Judaism* (Cambridge, England: Cambridge University Press, 1966), Vol. 2, pp. 106–107; Roland de Vaux, *Ancient Israel: Its Life and Institutions* (New York: McGraw-Hill, 1961), pp. 213–267; "War," article in the *Jewish Encyclopaedia* (London: Funk and Wagnall's, 1905), Vol. 12, pp. 463–466; Y. Yarden, "Warfare in the Second Millenium B.C.E." in Benjamin Manzar, ed., *The History of the Jewish People* (New Brunswick, NJ: Rutgers University Press, 1970); and "Peace (*Shalom*)," article in *The Encyclopaedia Judaica* (Jerusalem: Keter Publishing Company, and New York: Macmillan, 1971), Vol. 13, pp. 274–282. For the later themes of love, justice, and peace, see the books of Isaiah, Jeremiah, Hosea, and Amos.
27. In the New Testament scriptures, see Matthew 26:7 and 52; Luke 14:31–33 and 22:38. See also John Cadoux, *The Early Church and the World* (Edinburgh: T & T Clark, 1925), pp. 36 and 51–57; Roland H. Bainton, *Christian Attitudes Toward War and Peace* (Nashville: Abingdon Press, 1960), chaps. 4, 5, and 6; Peter Brock, *Pacifism in Europe to 1914* (Princeton, NJ: Princeton University Press, 1972), pp. 3–24; Edward A. Ryan, S. J., "The Rejection of Military Service by the Early Christians," *Theological Studies*, 13 (March 1952); Knut Willem Ruyter, "Pacifism and Military Service in the Early Church," *Cross Currents*, 32 (Spring 1982); Joan D. Tooke, "The Development of the Christian Attitude Toward War Before Aquinas," Chapter 1 in *The Just War in Aquinas and Grotius* (London: SPCK, 1965); G. I. A. D. Draper, "The Origins of the Just War Tradition," *New Blackfriars* (November 1964); F. Homes Dudden, *The Life and Times of Saint Ambrose* (Oxford, England: Clarendon Press, 1945), Vol. 2, pp. 538–539; *Saint Augustine, The City of God*, trans. Demetrius B. Zema, S. J. and Gerald G. Walsh, S. J. (New York: Fathers of the Church, 1950), Book 4, Chapter 15; and Book 19, Chapter 12; James E. Dougherty, *The Bishops and Nuclear Weapons: The Catholic Pastoral Letter on War and Peace* (Hamden, CT: Archon Books, 1984), pp. 18–42.
28. St. Thomas Aquinas, "Summa Theologica," 22ae, Question 40, Article 1 in Aquinas, *Selected Political Writings*, trans. J. G. Dawson (Oxford, England: Blackwell, 1948), p.

159; Joan D. Tooke, op. cit., pp. 21–29; James E. Dougherty, *The Bishops and Nuclear Weapons,* op. cit., pp. 42–47.

29. James Turner Johnson, *The Just War Tradition and the Restraint of War: A Moral and Historical Inquiry* (Princeton, NJ: Princeton University Press, 1981); Frederick Russell, *The Just War in the Middle Ages* (Cambridge, England: Cambridge University Press, 1975); E. B. F. Midgley, *The Natural Law Tradition and the Theory of International Relations* (New York: Barnes and Noble, 1975), pp. 62–93; James R. Childress, "Just War Theories," *Theological Studies,* 39 (September 1978). Because medieval society exalted cavalry over infantry, only a limited number of full-fledged warriors was available. Given the low level of the armor-making arts, the fully equipped mounted knight represented a considerable investment. Monarchs lacked the financial and organizational resources to raise and maintain large professional armies. Europe, with population sparse and agricultural methods poor, was usually preoccupied with basic problems of survival. Furthermore, the intricate feudal network of land–loyalty relationships gave rise to many conflicts of fealty among vassals and lords. In a society of delicately balanced bargaining relationships, wars were frequent, but they were waged on a small scale for strictly limited objectives. See Henri Pirenne, *Economic and Social History of Medieval Europe* (New York: Harcourt Brace Jovanovich, 1937); Joseph R. Strayer and Rushton Coulborn, *Feudalism in History* (Princeton, NJ: Princeton University Press, 1956); F. L. Ganshof, *Feudalism* (London: Longmans, 1952); and Richard A. Preston, Sydney F. Wise, and Herman O. Werner, *Men in Arms: A History of Warfare and Its Interrelationships with Western Society* (New York: Praeger, 1962), chaps. 6 and 7. For an account of the rules of warfare laid down by the Catholic Church during the twelfth century under the "Truce of God" and the "Peace of God," see Arthur Nussbaum, *A Concise History of the Law of Nations* (New York: Macmillan, 1954), p. 18.

30. Gwynne Dyer, *War* (New York: Crown, 1985), p. 60.

31. See Francisco de Victoria, *De Indis et De Iure Belli Relectiones,* trans. John P. Bate (Washington, DC: Carnegie Endowment for International Peace, 1917); Francisco Suarez, *De Triplici Virtute Theologica,* Disp. VIII, "De Bello," in *Selection from Three Works* (Oxford, England: Clarendon, 1925); Balthazar Ayala, *Three Books on the Law of War, the Duties Connected with War and Military Discipline* (Washington, DC: Carnegie Institute, 1912); Emmerich Vattel, *Le Droit des Gens* (Washington, DC: Carnegie Institute, 1916); and Albericus Gentilis, *De Iure Belli,* trans. John C. Rolfe (Oxford, England: Clarendon, 1933).

32. John U. Nef, *War and Human Progress* (Cambridge, MA: Harvard University Press, 1950), pp. 250–259; Richard A. Preston et al., *Men in Arms,* chap. 9; Dyer, op. cit., p. 67.

33. Paul Hazard, *European Thought in the Eighteenth Century,* trans. J. Lewis May (New York: World, 1963), p. 18.

34. Kingsley Martin, *French Liberal Thought in the Eighteenth Century,* 2nd ed. (New York: New York University Press, 1954), chap. XI.

35. Jean-Antoine-Nicolas de Caritat, Marquis de Condorcet, *Outlines of an Historical View of the Progress of the Human Mind,* 1794. Excerpts from an English translation of 1802 in Hans Kohn, *Making of the Modern French Mind* (Princeton, NJ: Van Nostrand Anvil Books, 1955), pp. 97–98.

36. Candide, chap. 3, in Edmund Fuller, ed., *Voltaire: A Laurel Reader* (New York: Dell, 1959), pp. 13–14.

37. William Penn, *Essay Toward the Present and Future Peace of Europe,* reprinted in Frederick Tolles and E. Gordon Alderfer, eds., *The Witness of William Penn* (New York: Macmillan and Company, 1957), pp. 140–159; Abbé de St. Pierre, *A Project for*

Making Peace Perpetual in Europe, reprinted in C. E. Vaughan, ed., *Political Writings of Jean-Jacques Rousseau: Volume 1* (Cambridge, England: University Press, 1915), pp. 364–87; Jean-Jacques Rousseau (London: Constable Publishers, 1917); *A Lasting Peace through the Federation of Europe and the State of War,* trans. C. E. Vaughan; Immanuel Kant, *Perpetual Peace* (New York: Liberal Arts Press, 1957); and Jeremy Bentham, *Plan for a Universal and Perpetual Peace,* reprinted in Charles W. Everett, *Jeremy Bentham* (London: Weidenfeld and Nicolson, 1966), pp. 195–229.

38. Dyer, op. cit., pp. 68–72. The death toll in the Revolutionary and Napoleonic wars came to 4 million, most of them soldiers. The total number killed was only half that of the Thirty Years War, when most of the deaths were civilian, caused by famine, plague, murder, and socioeconomic breakdown. Ibid., p. 72.

39. See Henry A. Kissinger, *A World Restored—Europe After Napoleon: The Politics of Conservatism in a Revolutionary Age* (New York: Grosset and Dunlap Universal Library, 1964). See also Charles Breunig, *The Age of Revolution and Reaction* (New York: W. W. Norton, 1970), chaps. 3–5.

40. David W. Zeigler, *War, Peace and International Politics,* 4th ed. (Boston: Little, Brown, 1987), chap. 1, "The Wars for German Reunification"; Gordon A. Craig, *Germany 1866–1945* (New York: Oxford University Press, 1978), chap. 1.

41. In the American Civil War, 622,000 soldiers died. That total was greater than the combined total for U.S. military personnel in the two world wars, plus Korea and Vietnam, although the population of the country was much larger in the 1980s than in the 1860s. Gwynne Dyer, op. cit., p. 77.

42. R. A. Preston et al., *Men in Arms: A History of Warfare and Its Interrelationships with Western Society,* 4th ed. (New York: Holt, Rinehart and Winston, 1979), chap. 15, "Approach to Total Warfare."

43. Dyer, op. cit., pp. 7–8, 150; Preston et al., op. cit., pp. 244–245, 250–253; Barbara Tuchman, *The Guns of August* (New York: Dell, 1962), pp. 91–95.

44. Jonathan Dymond, *An Inquiry into the Accordancy of War with the Principles of Christianity and an Examination of the Philosophical Reasoning by Which It Is Defended,* 3rd ed. (Philadelphia: Brown, 1834).

45. Norman Angell, *The Great Illusion: A Study of the Relation of Military Power to National Advantage* (New York: Putnam's, 1910), p. 71. One of the arguments employed by Angell to prove that economic prosperity can be separated from military capability was that the national bonds of small nonmilitary states were sought after by investors as more secure than bonds of the larger military powers. In rebuttal to Angell, J. H. Jones of the University of Glasgow pointed out that it was the military expenditures of the larger powers that created the conditions of international stability and security on which smaller nations depended, in *The Economics of War and Conquest* (London: King and Son, 1915), p. 25. For a skeptical critique of the view that railways, steamships, and international commerce promote friendship among nations and were responsible for long periods of peace in nineteenth-century Europe, see Geoffrey Blainey, *The Causes of War* (New York: Macmillan–Free Press, 1973), especially chap. 2, "Paradise Is a Bazaar."

46. Norman Angell, ibid., p. 335. For Herbert Spencer's view that war is too costly and destructive for industrial societies, see his *Principles of Sociology* (New York: Appleton, 1898), Vol. II, pp. 568–642. George Liska's views are discussed in chap. 4.

47. Karl von Clausewitz, *On War,* trans. O. J. Mathhias Jolles (New York: Modern Library–Random House, 1943), pp. 5, 30, 34; cf. also Sir Basil H. Liddell Hart, "The Objective in War," in B. Mitchell Simpson, ed., *War, Strategy and Maritime Power* (New Brunswick, NJ: Rutgers University Press, 1977), p. 33 and Hans Rothfels,

"Clausewitz," in Edward Mead Earle, ed., *Makers of Modern Strategy* (Princeton, NJ: Princeton University Press, 1943), pp. 93–94.

48. Clausewitz, *On War,* p. 9, held that the abstract object of disarming the enemy "by no means universally occurs in practice, nor is it a necessary condition to peace." Ibid., p. 20. See also Sun Tzu, *The Art of War,* trans. and with Introduction by Samuel B. Griffith (Cambridge, England: Clarendon Press, 1963), pp. 40–45.

49. G. W. F. Hegel, "Philosophy of Right and Law," paragraph 324, in Carl J. Friedrich, ed., *The Philosophy of Hegel* (New York: Random House–Modern Library, 1953), p. 322.

50. "What is good? All that enhances the feeling of power, the Will-to-Power, and power itself in man. What is bad? All that proceeds from weakness. What is happiness? The feeling that power is increasing—that resistance has been overcome. Not contentment, but more power; not peace at any price, but war; not virtue, but efficiency. The weak and the botched shall perish: first principle of our humanity. And they ought even to be helped to perish. What is more harmful than any vice? Practical sympathy with all the botched and the weak—Christianity." From "The Twilight of the Idols (1888)," in Geoffrey Clive, ed., *The Philosophy of Nietzsche* (New York: New American Library, 1965), p. 427. See also Chris Brown, *International Relations Theory: New Normative Approaches* (New York: Columbia University Press, 1992), pp. 59–69. Brown discusses two English idealists, T. H. Green and Bernard Bosanquet, who were influenced by Hegel but reached different conclusions from his (pp. 68–69).

51. William James, *Human, All Too Human,* Vol. I (1878), pp. 372–373. According to William James, peaceful activities involving a challenge to strenuous exertion and sacrifice could serve as a substitute for war in providing the "social vitamins" generated by war. The philosopher–psychologist recognized that war and the military life met certain deep-rooted needs of societies and summoned forth human efforts of heroic proportions. He did not think it possible to attenuate the proclivity to war until these same energies could be redirected—for example, by training young men to fight not other human beings but such natural forces as diseases, floods, poverty, and ignorance. If the nation is not to evolve into a society of mollycoddles, youth must be conscripted to hardship tasks to "get the childishness knocked out of them." See William James, "The Moral Equivalent of War," in his *Memories and Studies* (London: Longmans, 1912); and *A Moral Equivalent for War* (New York: Carnegie Endowment for International Peace, 1926). Later, Aldous Huxley was to popularize the hypothesis that many people find an exhilaration in war because their peacetime pursuits are humiliating, boring, and frustrating. War brings with it a state of chronic enthusiasm, and "life during wartime takes on significance and purposefulness, so that even the most intrinsically boring job is ennobled as 'war work'." Prosperity is artificially induced; newspapers are filled with interesting news; and the rules of sexual morality are relaxed in wartime. However, Huxley, writing just before World War II, conceded that the conditions of modern war have become so appalling that not only the civilians on the home front, but "even the most naturally adventurous and combative human beings will soon come to hate and fear the process of fighting." *Ends and Means* (New York: Harper & Row, 1937). Excerpted in Robert A. Goldwin et al., eds., *Readings in World Politics* (New York: Oxford University Press, 1959), pp. 13–14.

52. Friedrich Meinecke, *Machiavellism: The Doctrine of Raison d'État and Its Place in Modern History* (New York: Praeger, 1957), p. 371 and ff. in chap. 14.

53. Heinrich von Treitschke, *Politics* (New York: Macmillan, 1916), II, 595.

54. "We have learned to perceive the moral majesty of war through the very processes which to the superficial observer seem brutal and inhuman. The greatness of war is

just what at first sight seems to be its horror—that for the sake of their country men will overcome the natural feelings of humanity, that they will slaughter their fellow-men who have done them no injury, nay whom they perhaps respect as chivalrous foes. Man will not only sacrifice his life, but the natural and justified instincts of his soul;. . . here we have the sublimity of war." Ibid., pp. 395–396.

55. Quoted in Frank M. Russell, op. cit., p. 245.

56. Alfred Thayer Mahan, *Armaments and Arbitration* (1912), p. 31. Quoted in Charles D. Tarlton, "The Styles of American International Thought: Mahan, Bryan, and Lippmann," *World Politics*, XVII (July 1965), 590. The foregoing summary of Mahan is based largely on Tarlton's analysis.

57. Vilfredo Pareto, *The Mind and Society,* trans. A. Bongiorno and A. Livingston (New York: Harcourt Brace 1935), Vol. IV, pp. 2170–2175 and 2179–2220; Gaetano Mosca, *The Ruling Class,* trans. H. D. Kahn (New York: McGraw-Hill, 1939). For interesting and valuable assessments of both Pareto and Mosca, see Parts III and VI of James Burnham, *The Machiavellians: Defenders of Freedom* (New York: John Day, 1943).

58. Holmes glorified war as a romantic adventure and as a necessary corrective for the irresponsible and sybaritic tendencies of modern youth. See Edward McNall Burns, *Ideas in Conflict: The Political Theories of the Contemporary World* (New York: Norton, 1960), p. 54.

59. Oswald Spengler, *The Decline of the West,* trans. Charles F. Atkinson (New York: Knopf, 1926–1928), 2 vols.; and *The Hour of Decision,* trans. Charles F. Atkinson (New York: Knopf, 1934).

60. See A. James Gregor, *The Fascist Persuasion in Radical Politics* (Princeton, NJ: Princeton University Press, 1974); Anthony James Joes, *Fascism in the Contemporary World: Ideology, Evolution, Resurgence* (Boulder, CO: Westview, 1978), chap. 3; H. S. Harris, *The Social Philosophy of Giovanni Gentile* (Urbana: University of Illinois Press, 1960).

61. Irving Louis Horowitz, ed., *The Anarchists* (New York: Dell, 1964), from the editor's introduction, p. 22.

62. See the excerpt from Thomas G. Masaryk, in Horowitz, ed., ibid., pp. 469–473.

63. Irving Louis Horowitz, op. cit., pp. 44–55.

64. Georges Sorel, *Reflections on Violence* (New York: Macmillan, 1961), pp. 77–79, 115. See his chap. 2, "Violence and the Decadence of the Middle Classes." See also Part IV, Sorel: "A Note on Myth and Violence," in James Burnham, op. cit.; and William Y. Elliott, *The Pragmatic Revolt in Politics: Syndicalism, Fascism and the Constitutional State* (New York: Howard Fertig, 1968), pp. 111–141.

65. Irving Louis Horowitz, op. cit., pp. 53–54; Francis W. Coker, *Recent Political Thought* (New York: Appleton, 1934), chap. VII, especially pp. 223–225.

66. Quoted in Daniel Bell, *The Cultural Contradictions of Capitalism* (New York: Basic Books, 1976), p. 6. Contemporary terrorists often select at random, for kidnapping or murder, typical members of the group or class they seek to terrorize (e.g., business personnel, diplomats, air travelers, or restaurant diners). See Edward Hyams, *Terrorists and Terrorism* (New York: St. Martin's, 1974); Paul Wilkinson, *Political Terrorism* (New York: Wiley, 1974); and J. Bowyer Bell, "Trends on Terror: The Analysis of Political Violence," *World Politics*, XXIX (April 1977), 476–488.

67. See J. Bowyer Bell, "Explaining International Terrorism: The Elusive Quest," in Charles W. Kegley, Jr., ed., *International Terrorism: Characteristics, Causes, Controls* (New York: St. Martin's Press, 1990), pp. 178–184.

68. Chris Brown, *International Relations Theory: New Normative Approaches* (New York: Columbia University Press, 1992), p. 132.

69. For a representative sample of the voluminous literature reflecting these attitudes, see Roland H. Bainton, *Christian Attitudes Toward War and Peace* (Nashville: Abingdon Press, 1960); John C. Bennett, ed., *Nuclear Weapons and the Conflict of Conscience* (New York: Scribner's, 1962); Gordon Zahn, *An Alternative to War* (New York: Council on Religion and International Affairs, 1963); James Finn, ed., *Peace, the Churches and the Bomb* (New York: Council on Religion and International Affairs, 1965); Donald A. Wells, *The War Myth* (New York: Pegasus, 1967); James W. Douglass, *The Non-Violent Cross* (New York: Macmillan, 1968); John H. Yoder, *Politics of Jesus* (Grand Rapids, MI: Erdmans, 1972); Gene Sharp, *The Politics of Non-Violent Action* (Boston: Sargent, 1973); Joseph Fahey, *Justice and Peace* (Maryknoll, NY: Orbis Books, 1979); Thomas Merton. *The Non-Violent Alternative* (New York: Farrar, Straus and Giroux, 1980), and Thomas Merton. *The Church and the Bomb: Nuclear Weapons and the Christian Conscience*, A report of a working party under the chairmanship of the Bishop of Salisbury (London: Hodder and Stoughton, 1982).

70. See Erich Fromm, "The Case for Unilateral Disarmament," in Donald G. Brennan, ed., *Arms Control, Disarmament and National Security* (New York: Braziller, 1961), pp. 187–197; Mulford Q. Sibley, "Unilateral Disarmament," in Robert A. Goldwin, ed., *American Armed* (Chicago: Rand McNally, 1961), pp. 112–140; Gordon Zahn, op. cit.

71. Paul Ramsey, *War and the Christian Conscience* (Durham, N.C.: Duke University Press, 1961) and *The Limits of Nuclear War* (New York: Council on Religion and International Affairs, 1963); John Courtney Murray, *Morality and Modern War* (New York: Church Peace Union, 1959); Richard A. Falk, *Law, Morality and War in the Contemporary World,* Princeton Studies in World Politics No. 5 (New York: Praeger, 1963); Robert W. Tucker, *The Just War* (Baltimore: Johns Hopkins University Press, 1960) and *Just War and Vatican II: A Critique* (New York: Council on Religion and International Affairs, 1966); William V. O'Brien, *Nuclear War, Deterrence and Morality* (Westminster, MD: Newman Press, 1967), and *The Conduct of Just and Limited War* (New York: Praeger, 1981); Michael Walzer, *Just and Unjust Wars* (New York: Basic Books, 1977); James T. Johnson, *Just War Tradition and the Restraint of War* (Princeton, NJ: Princeton University Press, 1981).

72. O'Brien, *Nuclear War, Deterrence and Morality,* pp. 34–41.

73. Ibid., pp. 23–26 and chap. 5, "Morality and Nuclear Weapons Systems."

74. See Ralph B. Potter, *War and Moral Discourse* (Richmond, VA: John Knox Press, 1969); Robert Ginsberg, ed., *The Critique of War* (Chicago: Regnery, 1969); Richard A. Wasserstrom, *War and Morality* (Belmont, CA: Wadsworth, 1970); Morton A. Kaplan, ed., *Strategic Thinking and Its Moral Implications* (Chicago: University of Chicago Center for Policy Study, 1973); James T. Johnson, "The Cruise Missile and the Neutron Bomb: Some Moral Reflections," *Worldview,* 20 (December 1977); Robert L. Phillips, *War and Justice* (Oklahoma City: University of Oklahoma Press, 1984); John D. Jones and Marc F. Griesbach, eds., *Just War Theory in the Nuclear Age* (Lanham, MD: University Press of America, 1985); William V. O'Brien and John Langan, S. J., eds., *The Nuclear Dilemma and the Just War Tradition* (Lexington, MA: D. C. Heath, 1986).

75. For the debate over the theology of liberation and the morality of revolutionary violence, see the October 1968 issue of *Worldview,* devoted to "Revolution and Violence"; Gustavo Guttierez, "Liberation and Development," *Cross Currents,* 21 (1971); Philip E. Berryman, "Latin American Liberation Theology," *Theological Studies,* 34 (December 1973); Guenter Lewy, *Religion and Revolution* (New York: Oxford University Press, 1974), especially chap. 20; Francis P. Fiorenza, "Political Theology and

Liberation Theology," in Thomas M. McFadden, ed., *Liberation, Revolution and Freedom: Theological Perspectives* (New York: Seabury Press, 1975); Gustavo Guttierez, *A Theology of Liberation,* trans. Caridad Inda and John Eagleson (Maryknoll, NY: Orbis Books, 1978); Dennis P. McCann, *Christian Realism and Liberation Theology* (Maryknoll, NY: Orbis Books, 1981); and Quentin L. Quade, ed., *The Pope and Revolution: John Paul II Confronts Liberation Theology* (Washington, DC: Ethics and Public Policy Center, 1982).

76. Michael Walzer, op. cit., p. 278.

77. Ibid., p. 274. Chris Brown defends Walzer against what he regarded as patronizing British critics of Walzer's book, who called his philosophical grasp of the issues shallow and his notion of morality platitudinous. In Brown's view, Walzer's book is the best current work on the subject. *International Relations Theory: New Normative Approaches,* op. cit., p. 136.

78. Concerning the ethics of the strategy of nuclear deterrence, see (in addition to the works cited in Notes 69, 71, and 74): Geoffrey Goodwin, ed., *Ethics and Nuclear Deterrence* (New York: St. Martin's Press, 1982); German Grisez, "The Moral Implications of a Nuclear Deterrent," *Center Journal,* 2 (Winter 1982); Francis X. Winters, S. J., "Nuclear Deterrence Morality: Atlantic Community Bishops in Tension," *Theological Studies,* 43 (September 1982); John Langan, "The American Hierarchy and Nuclear Weapons," ibid.; David Hollenbach, S. J., "Nuclear Weapons and Nuclear War: The Shape of the Catholic Debate," ibid. (December 1982); *The Challenge of Peace: God's Promise and Our Response,* U.S. Catholic Bishops' Pastoral Letter on War and Peace, Text in *Origins,* NC Documentary Service 13 (May 19, 1983); L. Bruce van Voorst, "The Churches and Nuclear Deterrence," *Foreign Affairs,* 61 (Spring 1983); Albert Wohlstetter, "Bishops, Statesmen and Other Strategists on the Bombing of Innocents," *Commentary* (June 1983); Donald L. Davidson, *Nuclear War and the American Churches: Ethical Positions on Modern Warfare* (Boulder, CO: Westview, 1983); Jim Castelli, *The Bishops and the Bomb: Waging Peace in the Nuclear Age* (Garden City, NY: Doubleday-Image, 1983); Michael Novak, *Moral Clarity in the Nuclear Age* (Nashville, TN: Thomas Nelson, 1983); Philip F. Lawler, ed., *Justice and War in the Nuclear Age* (Lanham, MD: University Press of America, 1983); Judith A. Dwyer, S. S. J., ed., *The Catholic Bishops and Nuclear War* (Washington, DC: Georgetown University Press, 1984); James E. Dougherty, *The Bishops and Nuclear Weapons* (Hamden, CT: Archon Books, 1984), especially chaps. 5 and 6; Bruce M. Russett, "Ethical Dilemmas of Nuclear Deterrence," *International Security,* 8 (Spring 1984); Michael Fox and Leo Groarke, *Nuclear War: Philosophical Perspectives* (New York: Peter Land, 1985); George Weigel, *Tranquillitas Ordinis: The Present Failure and Future Promise of American Catholic Thought on War and Peace* (New York: Oxford University Press, 1987); *The Nuclear Dilemma,* Statement of the Commission on Peace, Episcopal Diocese of Washington, 1987. The more technical questions of deterrence strategy, the controllability of nuclear war, a NATO policy of no first use, the possibility of substituting conventional for nuclear deterrence, and related issues are discussed in Chapter 9. See also Robert K. Tucker, *The Nuclear Debate: Deterrence and the Lapse of Faith* (New York: Holmes and Meier, 1985).

Chapter
6

Theories of Imperialism and the Economic Causes of International Conflict

*I*n the study of the essential conditions for world peace and the causes of international conflict, economic factors have held a position of considerable importance. Implicit, if not explicit, in many theories of international relations is the assumption that rising living standards and national economic growth contribute to peace among nations. In nineteenth-century liberal thought, writers such as Adam Smith, John Stuart Mill, and Richard Cobden considered free trade to be a guarantor of peace. Free trade would create a division of labor based on international specialization in an international economy in which nations were so interdependent as to make virtually impossible the resort to war. (A more elaborate form of the theory of interdependence has gained prominence in the fourth quarter of the twentieth century.[1]) The growth of individual and national prosperity was expected, then and since, to divert public attention from military ventures because of the potentially disruptive effects of such ventures on economic growth and prosperity. In marked contrast to the proponents of free trade based on economic competition, other writers have argued that free competition is a principal determinant of international conflict and exploitation. Notable among these have been theorists in the Marxist–Leninist, neo–Marxist, *dependencia,* and some socialist schools of thought.

There is a widespread disposition to explain all international political relations by reference to forces associated with the quest for economic gain or advantage, although this explanation is more often gratuitously asserted than scientifically demonstrated. The most significant trends in world politics and the most significant decisions of governments are said to be traceable to such economic forces as capitalist financial institutions and complex, powerful MNCs. At times, it has been difficult to sort out incompatible rhetorical charges—on the one hand ruthless competition among the major industrialized trading centers (now the European Union, the North American Free Trade Area, and Japan and/or the Pacific Rim), and on the other hand sinister collusion of those regions of the North to exploit the poorer, less developed countries of the global South. (This admittedly is a simplified caricature of an increasingly complex world economy, but that is how the rhetoric often distorts the reality and compounds the problem of achieving a calm, dispassionate approach to theory where politics and economics meet.) The polemical tone was maintained throughout most of the Cold War, characterized as it was by fierce and rather futile debates over the relative merits of free-market economies versus centrally directed socialist economies—futile for four decades because there could be no authoritative decision before Soviet Communism collapsed in the years 1989–1991.

A leading economist of the left, Robert Heilbroner, who had long argued that the system of advanced capitalism suffered from a terminal illness, announced in 1989 that the contest was over and that capitalism had won. Yet at the same time, he criticized the triumphant economic model for its tendency to produce cyclical gluts, intractable poverty, and glaring disparities of income. Heilbroner expressed doubt "that the triumph of capitalism means its assured long and happy life or that the defeat of socialism means its ignominious exit from history," for although centralized planning has proved disastrous, both politically and economically, socialism stands for a commitment that seems to him unattainable under capitalism— "above all, the moral, not just the material, elevation of humankind."[2] This would seem to indicate that for at least some intellectuals, the failure of the Soviet experiment does not spell the end of Marxist socialist theory.* Marxist socialist theory was for nearly a century and a half an important weltanschauung; it had a powerful impact on modern history. The fact that it is currently out of fashion, and that the market economy is now universally popular, does not justify ignoring a long-lived theoretical explanation of the causes of international conflict.

Central to Marxist theories of imperialism and war is the assumption (rejected by the authors of this book) that all international issues are reducible to issues of economic gain rather than political power. The strength of such an assumption, dubious as it may be, lies in the considerable influence of the philosophical system propounded originally by Karl Marx and Friedrich Engels, as well as of the pronouncements, whether consistent or contradictory, of their numerous socialist and communist descendants. Generations of academic and journalistic theoreticians, as well as would-be political practitioners, who never lived under a communist or a socialist regime, have expounded an essentially Marxist analysis of the world.[3] Large numbers of otherwise bourgeois teachers, students, politicians, and writers, and even businesspeople have adopted an economic interpretation of history based at least in part on Marxian analysis. In nearly all the developing countries, elites long took for granted the validity of Lenin's notion of imperialism, and this

---

*Two points might be kept in mind: (1) Most intellectuals and students in the West and in the developing world learned about Marxist and neo-Marxist theories from Western writers and university teachers, not from hidebound dullards in Moscow who studied and taught the ideology in an uninspiring, dogmatic manner. It was centralized planning Soviet-style that collapsed, not Marxian socialist ideology. (2) By the mid-1990s, former communists had been returned to power as a result of elections in several Central-Eastern European countries.

powerfully influenced their attitude toward the West. The main elements of Marxist theory date back to 1848. Yet the theory showed a remarkable survivability into the final quarter of a century that has often proved brutally critical of abstractions inherited from the past.

MARXIST THEORY

Marxism is an admixture of metaphysics (dialectical materialism), theory of history (economic determinism), economic and sociological science, political ideology, theory and strategy of revolution, social ethics, and an eschatological moral theology that looks toward a secular salvation: the advent of a classless social order of perfect justice, in which conflict ceases and the psychology of a new human is generated. Marx, more than any other individual, strengthened the idea that conflict arises inevitably out of the life-and-death struggle of socioeconomic classes. Capitalism is the bondage from which people strive to be liberated, and this liberation will be accomplished through knowledge of the inexorable dialectical laws of historical–social change. Up to now, class conflict has been the motor of social change. Once class conflict comes to an end with the establishment of communism, social change will occur only as a result of rational planning, debate, and decision making.

Karl Marx (1818–1883) evolved a theory of history based on dialectical materialism, in which the system of economic production determines the institutional and ideological structures of society.[4] Whoever controls the economic system also controls the political system. Marx and Engels' study of history and of nineteenth-century Britain led them to conclude that each period contains clashing forces—a dialectic—from which a new order emerges. "In ancient Rome, we have patricians, knights, plebeians, slaves; in the Middle Ages, feudal lords, vassals, guild-masters, journeymen, apprentices, serfs; in almost all of these classes, again, subordinate gradations."[5] All history is the history of class struggle between a ruling group and an opposing group, from which comes a new economic, political, and social system. Marx's model for the study of society and its transformation contains a thesis (ruling group) and an antithesis (opposing group), which clash and produce a synthesis (a new economic, political, and social system).

Like the systems that preceded it, capitalism contains the seeds of its own destruction. Marx believed that the growing impoverishment of the working class—the proletariat—would lead to a revolution to overthrow the ruling capitalist class. The lower strata of the middle class are absorbed into the proletariat because they do not have the capital to compete on the scale of their more fortunate confreres, and their specialized skills become worthless as a result of new methods of production. As the ranks of the proletariat increase, the struggle with the bourgeoisie grows in intensity. Initially the struggle is conducted by individual members of the exploiting capitalist class. Marx envisaged a series of clashes of increasing intensity between the proletariat and the bourgeoisie, until the eruption of a revolution, finally resulting in the overthrow of the bourgeoisie.

In Marx's doctrine of surplus value, the socially useful labor that produces a commodity is considered to be the only measure of its worth. Capitalists themselves produce nothing. Instead, they live like parasites from the labor of the producing class. The capitalist pays the laborer a subsistence wage and keeps the rest. According to Marx, the vast mass of the population is reduced to wage slavery in a capitalist society. The proletariat produces goods and services for which it receives little or no return. In a capitalist system, the bourgeoisie, which controls the means of production, exploits the worker and widens the gap—the surplus value—between the price paid workers for their labor and the price obtained by the bourgeoisie in the marketplace.[6]

The coming clash between the capitalist, bourgeois class (thesis) and the proletariat (antithesis) was expected to lead to a socialist order. There would be a period of extensive government controls over production and distribution until the last vestiges of capitalism were removed. Marx predicted the withering away of the state with the development of a communist economic, political, and social order. Anarchists, as we saw in Chapter 5, despised Marxist socialists for advocating a dictatorship of the proletariat as a ruthless necessity before the state withered away, if it ever would.

Orthodox Marxists view all political phenomena, including imperialism and war, as projections of underlying economic forces. All forms of consciousness are subordinated to the economic. Religious, humanitarian, political, cultural, and military-strategic motives for any kind of power relationship between a stronger and a weaker community are explained by the Marxist as rationalizations designed to disguise the economic substructure. This has been essentially true throughout history, but it becomes most apparent in the era of capitalism. Marx and Engels declared,

> The bourgeoisie . . . has left no other bond between man and man than naked self-interest, than callous cash payment. It has drowned the most heavenly ecstasies of religious fervor, of chivalrous enthusiasm, of philistine sentimentalism, in the icy water of egotistical calculation. . . . The bourgeoisie has stripped of its halo every occupation hitherto honored and looked up to with reverent awe. It has converted the physician, the lawyer, the priest, the poet, the man of science, into its paid wage-laborers.[7]

Marx had a vision of peace—the peace of the self-alienated person restored as a result of the "negation of the negation," the revolutionary self-appropriation by the proletariat, taking that which rightfully belongs to itself.[8] In his earlier years, he may have preferred or hoped that the inevitable victory of socialism could be achieved through a nonviolent working out of the dialectic. As he grew older, however, Marx's youthful philosophical idealism gave way to the thought modes of a frustrated, impatient, professional revolutionary. John Plamenatz put it as follows:

> Logically, violence, the shedding of blood, is no essential part of revolution as Marx and Engels conceived it. True, they thought there would be violence when the proletariat took over power, in most countries if not in all. They even at times, I suspect, took pleasure in the thought that there would be.
>
> They were not very gentle persons; nor did they believe, as certain other socialists and communists of their day did, that violence is wrong or that it corrupts those who

use it. But all this takes nothing away from the point I am making: revolution, as Marx and Engels conceived of it, does not necessarily involve violence.[9]

It was Lenin, coming out of a tradition of Russian revolutionary conspiratorial activity that had become a mirror image of the czarist oppressiveness it fought, who more than anyone else imparted to twentieth-century Marxist communism its predilection for violence and terror. Lenin was reacting in part against the revisionism of such German Marxists as Karl Kautsky (1854–1938) and Eduard Bernstein (1850–1932), who realized that some of Marx's predictions had gone awry and that the achievement of socialism might be a long, gradual process utilizing education, psychological intimidation, and the ballot box. Lenin insisted that the appeal of violence was inherent in the makeup of the true revolutionary, and that the bourgeois state cannot be replaced by the proletarian state through a withering away but, as a general rule, only through a violent revolution, because capitalists will never relinquish their dominant position peacefully.

Although Marx fully appreciated the worldwide scope of capitalist operations for acquiring raw materials and for marketing manufactured goods, he himself did not elaborate a theory of imperialism. This task was left to his twentieth-century intellectual heirs—Rudolph Hilferding (1877–1941), a German Social Democrat; Rosa Luxembourg (1870–1919), a German Socialist; and, of course, Lenin.

HOBSON ON IMPERIALISM

Curiously enough, most of the clues to the communist theory of imperialism in this century were provided by the English economist John A. Hobson (1858–1940). Hobson, an Oxford graduate, was a journalist, essayist, and university lecturer who had been influenced toward liberalism by John Stuart Mill and toward the science of society by Herbert Spencer. Attracted to idealist, humanitarian, and ethical causes of social reform, he became a self-designated religious and economic heretic, and gravitated toward a Fabian-type socialism as he grew increasingly disenchanted with what he called "mechanized capitalism." During the Boer War, he went to South Africa as a correspondent for *The Manchester Guardian*. His coverage of that conflict, which he saw as a concoction of diamond monopolists and other economic exploiters, moved him further in the direction of an anticapitalist, antimilitarist polemic that was not free of anti-Semitic overtones. In any event, it is not too much to say that Hobson practically invented the modern theory of imperialism, and he did a great deal to create an intellectual–moral revulsion against it in the English-speaking world.[10] (Liberal opinion in the United States was already manifesting a guilt feeling over Cuba and Pacific expansionism in the wake of the Spanish–American War.[11])

More than 60 years later, two scholars would conclude that "the worldwide misinterpretation of the Boer War as a capitalist plot . . . became the basis of all subsequent theories of imperialism."[12] The very word *imperialism,* which had hitherto been invoked proudly to imply what Britain had contributed toward civilizing the parts of the world once or still controlled by Britain—the rule of law, parliamentary institutions, a rational administration of civil servants with some sense of public responsibility (hitherto a rather rare phenomenon in many regions), and a conviction of the worth and rights of human beings (even rarer)—became in England "a recognized symbol of a strong moral revulsion on the part of a minority with Liberal, Radical, and Labour leanings, or with strong religious scruples."[13]

Hobson argued that imperialism results from maladjustments within the capitalist system, in which a wealthy minority oversaves, while an impoverished or bare-subsistence majority lacks the purchasing power to consume all the fruits of modern industry. Capitalist societies are thus faced with the critical dilemma of overproduction and underconsumption. If capitalists were willing to redistribute their surplus wealth in the form of domestic welfare measures, there would be no serious structural problem. The capitalists, however, seek instead to reinvest their surplus capital in profit-making ventures abroad. The result is imperialism, "the endeavor of the great controllers of industry to broaden the channel for the flow of their surplus wealth by seeking foreign markets and foreign investments to take off the goods and capital they cannot sell or use at home."[14]

Hobson was aware that there were noneconomic factors at work in late nineteenth-century European expansion abroad—forces of a political, military, psychological, and religious–philanthropic character. He insisted, however, that the essential ingredient in imperialism is finance capitalism, which galvanizes and organizes the other forces into a coherent whole:

> Finance capitalism manipulates the patriotic forces which politicians, soldiers, philanthropists and traders generate; the enthusiasm for expansion which issues from these sources, though strong and genuine, is irregular and blind; the financial interest has those qualities of concentration and clear-sighted calculation which are needed to set imperialism at work.[15]

In Hobson's view, imperialism in the case of Britain had not been necessary to relieve population pressure, for Britain was not overpopulated, and its growth rate at the turn of the century was declining toward a stationary level. Furthermore, he noted, British people did not seem at all anxious to resettle in most areas of the Empire acquired after 1870.[16]

Hobson condemned late nineteenth-century imperialism as irrational and as bad business policy for the nation as a whole, even though it was rational and profitable for certain groups—bourse participants, speculative miners, engineers, the shipbuilding and armaments industrialists, exporters, contractors to the military services, and members of the aristocratic classes, who sent their sons to be officers in the army, navy, and colonial service.[17] Although the economic activities of these groups constituted but a small fraction of Britain's total enterprise, the groups benefiting from imperialism were well organized for advancing their interests through political channels. Imperialism, said Hobson, involves enormous risks and costs to the nation, compared with its relatively meager results in the form of increased trade, and hence the rationale for it must be sought in the advantages it brings to special groups within the society: "To a larger extent every year Great Britain is becoming a nation living upon tribute from abroad, and the classes who enjoy this tribute have an ever-increasing incentive to employ the public policy, the public purse, and the public force to extend the field of their private investments."[18] E. M.

Winslow (1896–1966), evaluating the significance of Hobson's study, concluded, "No other book has been so influential in spreading the doctrine of economic imperialism."[19] Later, Lenin clearly acknowledged his indebtedness to Hobson's work.

Hobson anticipated the later Leninist attack on capitalist profiteering as a major factor in causing international war. Policies of aggressive imperialism and war lead to vast arms budgets, public debts, and the fluctuation of the securities values from which the skilled financier benefits most. "There is not a war, a revolution, an anarchist assassination, or any other public shock, which is not gainful to these men; they are harpies who suck their gains from every new forced expenditure, and every sudden disturbance of public credit."[20] To be sure, Hobson is not saying here that the capitalists are responsible for the wars from which they profit. Almost certainly he would not contend that capitalists lurked behind every anarchist assassin. Nonetheless, the unmistakable thrust of his reasoning, later made more explicit by Lenin, was that if the behavior of capitalists is primarily motivated by the desire to gain profits, and if certain segments of capitalist society can profit from imperialistic wars, then these elements can be expected to bend every effort to bring about war when the circumstances call for it.

LENIN: IMPERIALISM AND INTERNATIONAL CONFLICT

Rosa Luxembourg, a theoretical German socialist, closely followed Hobson's analysis, while Rudolph Hilferding sought to refine it by attributing the export of capital to the operation of cartel and monopoly systems that limit domestic investment possibilities. The best-known theorist of imperialism in modern times, of course, was Lenin. The architect of the Bolshevik Revolution was neither the scholar nor the original thinker that Hobson was. In addition to borrowing ideas from Hobson, Lenin relied on Hilferding's analysis of the role of monopoly capitalism:

> Imperialism is capitalism in the stage of development in which the dominance of monopolies and finance capital has established itself; in which the export of capital has acquired pronounced importance; in which the division of the world among the international trusts has begun; in which the division of all territories of the globe among the great capitalist powers has been completed.[21]

Lenin derived monopoly capitalism, which he equated with imperialism, from four factors: (1) the concentration of production in combines, cartels, syndicates, and trusts; (2) the competitive quest for sources of raw materials; (3) the development of banking oligarchies; and (4) the transformation of the old colonial policy into a struggle for spheres of economic interest in which the richer and the more powerful nations exploit the weaker ones. Thus, Lenin took strong exception to Karl Kautsky's thesis that imperialism was merely the preferred policy of capitalist states; for Lenin, imperialism was inevitable. Moreover, in the Leninist interpretation, the receipt of monopoly profits by the capitalists of certain industries enables them to corrupt the workers in those industries, who for the sake of a higher standard of living ally themselves with the bourgeoisie against their fellow workers of the exploited, imperialized countries.

Because finance capitalism is the source of imperialism, it also becomes for Marxist–Leninists the principal source of international wars in the capitalist era, or at least the only source in which they are interested. If there are other sources of conflict, Marxists prefer not to call much attention to them. Hobson had conceded that there are primitive instincts in the human race that played a part in nineteenth-century imperialism—the instinct for the control of land, the nomadic habit that survives as love of travel, the spirit of adventure, the sporting and hunting instincts, and the lust of struggle, which in the age of spectator sports is transformed into gambling on the outcome of athletic games and which is transformed into jingoism during war.[22] Nonetheless, Hobson circumvented the theoretical difficulty implicit in the plurality of factors merely by accusing the dominant classes in capitalistic societies of advancing their own interests by playing on the primitive instincts of the race and channeling them into imperialistic ventures.

Lenin's contribution to communism was twofold. First, he imparted an organizational theory in which the communist party became the "vanguard of the proletariat" to hasten the coming of the revolution that Marx had foreseen as inevitable. Second, drawing heavily on the aforementioned work of Hobson, Lenin developed a theory of imperialism that ranks as the principal communist theory of international relations in a global system consisting of capitalist states.[23]

Looking back on the history of Europe in the decades after Marx published his *Communist Manifesto,* Lenin concluded that the proletariat would not revolt spontaneously, as Marx had believed, against the ruling bourgeoisie. In his famous tract entitled *What Is to Be Done?* Lenin held that a strong, tightly knit, highly motivated party of professional revolutionaries was essential to the success of the revolution against the capitalist order. To Lenin, the communist party, the vanguard of the proletariat, was the most class-conscious, devoted, and self-sacrificing part of the proletariat.[24] Lenin held that the party must be centralized or hierarchical. It must be based on *democratic centralism*—that is, the party must provide for discussion and debate of issues before a decision was taken, while adopting iron-clad discipline in executing policy after a decision had been made.

Lenin saw imperialism as a special, advanced stage of capitalism. In capitalist systems, competition is eventually replaced by capitalist monopolies.[25] Imperialism is the monopoly stage of capitalism. The countries that are the principal exporters of capital are able to obtain economic advantages based on the exploitation of peoples abroad. Moreover, the greater the development of capitalism, the greater the need for raw materials and markets, and hence the greater the scramble for colonies. The establishment of political control over territories overseas is designed to provide a dependable source of raw materials and cheap labor and to guarantee markets for the industrial combines of advanced capitalist countries. Lenin held that imperialist policies would enable capitalist powers to stave off the inevitable revolution, because conditions of the domestic proletariat would be ameliorated by the exploitation of the working class in colonial territories.

Writing in the spring of 1916, nearly two years after the outbreak of World War I, Lenin viewed the history of the previous generation as a struggle among the advanced capitalist powers for the control of colonies and markets. Capitalist countries have formed alliances for the exploitation of the underdeveloped areas. Especially in East Asia and Africa, the imperialist powers had claimed territories and spheres of influence. Their alliances are only breathing spells between wars. Because of the ultimate dependence of capitalist economic systems on overseas markets and resources, international conflict is endemic in a world of capitalist states. The elimination of capitalist states, Lenin concluded, was the essential precondition to abolishing international conflict.

For Lenin, capitalism had developed at its own pace in each country—earlier in Holland, England, and France; later in Germany and the United States; and later still in Japan and Russia. Lenin was of the opinion that by his time, the cartels had virtually completed the process of parceling out the territories of the world for exploitation. Because the planet had already been divided up, further expansion by some capitalists could occur only at the expense of other capitalists, and thus capitalistic imperialism would provoke international wars.[26] Stalin, remembering the Allied intervention in Russia at the end of World War I, regarded the capitalist West with suspicion and hostility, and he spoke often of those outside plotting aggression against the Soviet Union. Nonetheless, in his famous "last thesis," issued on the eve of the 1952 meeting of the Communist Party of the Soviet Union, Stalin argued that the frightful clashes that Lenin had predicted between the capitalist and socialist camps were no longer inevitable, because such a war would jeopardize the very existence of capitalism. Stalin then went on to declare that contradictions within the capitalist systems made the recurrence of war among capitalist states inevitable.[27]

LENIN, STALIN, AND WAR

Orthodox Leninist–Stalinist reasoning led inescapably to the conclusion that modern war is a function of capitalist imperialism; that if war should occur between the two systems it would be as a result of capitalist aggression, and it would lead to the destruction of capitalism and the universal triumph of socialism; and that in an all-socialist world, once the dangers of capitalist encirclement had been eliminated, war would disappear. Stalin declared, "In order to destroy the inevitability of wars, it is necessary to destroy imperialism."[28] Of course, he was not necessarily implying that the socialist camp must someday try to destroy the imperialist camp by carrying out an aggressive military attack across national boundaries. He was, if anything, a cautious, conservative strategist; he certainly was not calling for a socialist holy war against a technologically superior Western state system. Both he and his successor, Khrushchev, propounded the thesis that capitalist encirclement must eventually give way to socialist encirclement. Khrushchev is rather widely thought to have had a better appreciation than did Stalin of the implications of nuclear-weapons technology for the inevitability-of-war problem, inasmuch as he formally recognized that general nuclear war could very well destroy not only capitalist society but communist society as well. Thus, while pursuing limited-risk arms-control agreements with the capitalist West in order to render more manageable the strategic-military environment as reflected in international armaments competition, while continuing to develop Soviet military capabilities, both strategic and tactical, Khrushchev and his successors (prior to Gorbachev) lent at least propaganda and at times tangible military and political support to so-called wars of national liberation in the Third World—forms of warfare considered both just in terms of socialist ideology and safe from the standpoint of strategic analysis in an era of mutual nuclear deterrence.[29]

MARXIST–LENINIST THEORY SINCE THE 1950s

The history of international relations since World War II has not dealt too kindly with the Leninist theory of imperialism. That theory is hard-pressed to explain Soviet communist imperialism in Eastern Europe. Stalin's last thesis concerning the inevitability of war within the capitalist camp cannot be validated unless we stretch his meaning to include arguments about trade wars and competitiveness in the global economy which have never led to military conflict.

Even long before the collapse of the Soviet Union and its empire, the communist state system itself had been torn by serious conflicts. Soviet troops had suppressed the workers' revolt in East Germany in 1953 and crushed the Hungarian uprising in 1956. When Czechoslovakia in 1968 experienced the liberation stirrings known as the "Prague Spring," it had elicited a response in the form of an invasion by the armed forces of five Warsaw Pact countries. Leonid Brezhnev subsequently justified the action by enunciating the Soviet doctrine that bore his name:

> The CPSU has always been in favor of every socialist country determining the concrete forms of its development along the road to socialism, taking into account the specific character of national conditions. But we know, comrades, that there are also general laws of socialist construction, deviations from which could lead to deviations from socialism as such. And when internal and external forces hostile to socialism try to turn the development of any socialist country back toward a capitalist restoration, when a threat arises to the cause of socialism in that country, a threat to the security of the socialist community as a whole, that is no longer a problem only for the people of the country in question, but a general problem, the concern of all socialist states.[30]

Throughout the decade of the 1960s, the relationship between the Soviet Union and the People's Republic of China (PRC) had become increasingly polarized over several issues—ideological purity, support for world revolution, foreign development assistance, nuclear proliferation, territorial disputes as a result of old unequal treaties, and the foolhardiness of socialist states entering into disarmament and arms-control negotiations with capitalist states while the latter remained militarily powerful. (This last point was the orthodox Leninist position.[31]) In 1969, when U.S.–Soviet Strategic Arms Limitation Talks (SALT) were getting underway at a time of rising Sino–Soviet tension and hostilities along the Amur-Issuri Rivers, Mao Zhedong decried the collusion of the imperialist powers, both capitalist and socialist. Within a few years, as the United States prepared to disengage from Southeast Asia, the leadership of the PRC concluded that the growth of Soviet military power was becoming a greater danger than a waning U.S. imperialist power, and it began to warn Japan and other Asian states against Soviet hegemonic aims within their region.[32] Although the Sino–Soviet relationship became less confrontational in the 1980s, Beijing continued to regard Moscow as the primary threat to world peace, largely as a result of what was perceived to be its effort to encircle and contain China through political–military moves in Mongolia and along their common border, in Afghanistan and Southeast Asia, and in the growth of the Soviet Pacific Fleet, as well as the deployment of intermediate-range missiles in the Far East.[33] Some Marxists continued to explain Soviet interventions in Eastern Europe and Vietnam in terms of a moral struggle between the forces of good and evil, of socialism and capitalism. However, such explanations grew feeble with time, after the Soviet-backed Cuban intervention in Angola after 1975, the Vietnamese invasion of Cambodia in December 1978, the PRC attack on Vietnam in February 1979, and the Soviet invasion of Afghanistan in December 1979. The last-named military intervention led to mounting domestic discontent within the Soviet Union and alienated much of the Islamic world, much as the U.S. war in Vietnam had aroused anti-American sentiment in many Western and developing countries.

The closing years of the Brezhnev era (1980–1982) saw a subtler form of Soviet imperialism. When the Polish worker movement known as Solidarity (*Solidarnosc*) extracted from the government several concessions that seemed to threaten communist control, the Kremlin conducted military maneuvers along the Polish border. This fanned Polish fears of an invasion and paved the way for a declaration of martial law in late 1981, which precluded the necessity of overt Soviet intervention. The Andropov–Chernenko interregnum (1982–1985) was a transitional period of floundering, unstable leadership, without precedent in Soviet history. It was marked by frustrating stalemate in East–West arms-control negotiations, strident polemics about the military balance in Europe, frantic concern in Moscow over President Reagan's Strategic Defense Initiative (SDI),[34] and a spreading impression that the Soviet Union was approaching an internal crisis. The dramatic reversal of Soviet imperialism initiated by Mikhail Gorbachev is treated subsequently in this chapter.

CRITICS OF THE ECONOMIC THEORIES OF IMPERIALISM

Modern critics of the economic theories of imperialism have taken strong exception to the conclusions of Hobson, Lenin, and their followers on grounds of both semantics and economic–political analysis. Generally speaking, the semantic attack has taken the shape of an accusation that the followers of Lenin have been so obsessed by an ideological aversion to finance capitalism as to confuse a particular historical manifestation of the imperialistic impulse with a much more comprehensive sociological political phenomenon—what St. Augustine called the *animus dominandi*—which has assumed many different shapes throughout history.

Early in the Cold War, the most important critic of the Hobson–Leninist theory of imperialism as a terminological perversion for narrow polemical purposes was Hans J. Morgenthau. Morgenthau lamented the application of the term *imperialism* to any foreign policy that the user of the term found objectionable, and he urged the post–World War II generation of university students to accept an objective, ethically neutral definition of imperialism as "a policy that aims at the overthrow of the status quo, at a reversal of the power relations between two or more nations."[35] He denied that every increase in the international power of a nation is necessarily imperialistic. Moreover, he warned against the disposition to regard every foreign policy that aims conservatively at maintaining an already existing empire as imperialistic when the term should be properly reserved for the dynamic process of changing the international status quo by acquiring an empire.[36] The economic interpretation of imperialism, contends Morgenthau, errs in the attempt to build a universal law of history on the limited experience of a few isolated cases. Such a theory, in his view, ignores the problem of precapitalist imperialism (including the ancient empires of Egypt, Assyria, Persia, and Rome; Arab imperialism of the seventh and eighth centuries; the European Christian imperialism of the Crusades; and the personal empires of such leaders as Alexander the Great, Napoleon, and Hitler).[37] Moreover, Morgenthau contended that the theory fails to provide a convincing explanation even of capitalist-age imperialism in the *belle époque* of imperialism, 1870 to 1914.

In the following summary of arguments against the Hobson–Lenin interpretation, the Morgenthau refutation is joined with that of several other prominent theorists, including the French political sociologist Raymond Aron; the Austrian economist Joseph A. Schumpeter (1883–1950), who taught at Harvard University; the American diplomatic historian William L. Langer (1896–1978); and the American economist Jacob Viner (1892–1970), as well as with the findings of more recent scholars who have uncovered several anomalies in the Hobson–Lenin hypothesis.[38]

1. The followers of Marx, Hobson, and Lenin were said to confuse a particular historical manifestation of the imperialistic impulse with a much more comprehensive, multifaceted political–sociological phenomenon that has assumed many different shapes throughout history. The turn-of-the-century economic theory of imperialism is seen as a distortion, insofar as it subordinates international politics to international economics, both rigidly and superficially. Economic interests are frequently only a rationalization for a nation's will-to-power. Jacob Viner argued that in most cases

> the capitalist, instead of pushing his government into an imperialistic enterprise in pursuit of his own financial gain, was pushed, or dragged, or cajoled, or lured into it by his government, in order that, in its relations with the outside world and with its own people this government might be able to point to an apparently real and legitimate economic stake in the territory involved which required military protection.[39]

2. Schumpeter insisted that imperialism cannot be reduced to the mere pursuit of economic interest when history is replete with examples of societies "that seek expansion for the sake of fighting, victory for the sake of winning, dominion for the sake of ruling."[40] Wars are not fought in order to realize immediate utilitarian advantages, even if these are the professed purpose. Imperialism rather is "the objectless disposition on the part of a state to unlimited forcible expansion."[41] Like nationalism, it is irrational and uncon-

scious, a calling into play of instincts from the dim past. Imperialism, in short, is an atavism in the social culture. If one wants to trace it to economic roots, it should be attributed to *past* rather than present relations of production. Undoubtedly it is the ruling classes in any state who make the decisions for war, but it is not the business bourgeoisie who constitute the principal foreign-policy decision makers in the modern world; it is the vestigial aristocratic classes of an earlier regime who still fill the important governmental, diplomatic, and military posts.[42]

3. Notwithstanding the *devil theory of war,* which traces the causality of war to munitions makers and others who stand to reap financial gain from its outbreak, capitalists as a whole are not given to bellicosity. Because war involves the irrational and the unpredictable, whereas capitalism thrives best on rational foresight and planning in a stable international environment, most capitalists are partisans of peace rather than of war, simply because those who suffer from the disruption of war greatly outnumber those who profit from it.[43] Competitive enterprise in the capitalist system, according to Schumpeter, absorbs tremendous amounts of human energy in purely economic pursuits, leaving little excess to be worked off in war and even less tendency to welcome war as a diversion from unpleasant activities or from boredom.[44] Capitalist society creates the sociological basis for a substantial popular opposition to war and armaments, as well as to socially entrenched professional armies. Before the age of capitalism, pacifist principles had been taken seriously in the West only by a few minority religious sects. Modern pacifism as a significant political movement emerges only in capitalist society in which organized parties produce peace leaders, peace slogans, and peace programs, along with a popular aversion to imperialism and popular support for arbitration of disputes, disarmament, and international organization. (The question of whether war is becoming obsolete is taken up in Chapter 9. See the section, "The End of the Cold War.")

4. Hobson's theory has not stood the test of critical examination. The examples given by him for the fateful influence of capital investments overseas—South African mines and Chinese concessions—proved of ephemeral significance.[45] The effort to produce a universal theory on the basis of such scant evidence leads to several glaring anomalies in regard to what it leaves unexplained. According to that theory, the most advanced capitalist nations should have been the most expansionist and colonialist in the era of the highest development of monopolies and finance capitalism. Actually, Europe's acquisition of colonial territories in the late nineteenth and early twentieth centuries was less extensive than in the period from the sixteenth to the eighteenth centuries. European settlements in North and South America involved genuine colonization; European imperialism in Asia and later in Africa did not, except for relatively small areas. The logical corollary of the Lenin–Hobson theory is that less capitalist states should be less imperialist and colonialist. Yet Portugal, backward among capitalist countries, was a leading colonial power. In contrast, Sweden and Switzerland, two states profoundly imbued with the capitalist spirit, exhibited no instinct whatever for imperial-colonial ventures.[46]

Schumpeter pointed to the United States, a developing country in the first half of the nineteenth century and a rapidly rising capitalist power after the American Civil War (1861–1865). According to the theory, the United States should have tried to seize its two resource-rich but militarily weak neighbors, Mexico and Canada, but it did not do so.[47] Finally, the theory ignores the role of Western capital in making Japan an independent power of formidable proportions by the early twentieth century and of the United States' postwar policy of rebuilding Western Europe's and Japan's ability to compete in world markets.

5. It can be noted, in refutation of Hobson's underconsumption–oversavings hypothesis, that the export of surplus capital was not absolutely essential for growth; as revisionist Marxists such as Karl Kautsky and Eduard Bernstein realized, the capitalists were not playing Marx's "iron law of wages" game to bring about the increasing "immiseration" of the workers; actually the workers' standard of living was on the rise, and domestic purchasing power was increasing in real terms, as a consequence of trade-union activity and the enfranchisement of larger numbers of people.[48] During the period from 1870 to 1914, more capital moved into England than out of it, and three quarters of the capital exported from Britain did not come from monopoly companies but consisted of loans to governments and government-guaranteed public utilities.[49] Colonies were not as important in the trade and investment patterns of the capitalist countries as the theory indicated. No more than 10 percent of France's overseas investments prior to 1914 were directed to the Empire.[50] Apart from India, the colonies, especially those in Africa, were not a source of much profit to Britain. Aron writes, "The two nations which during the half century before the First World War conquered the largest territories, France and Great Britain, were also the nations which, economically, least needed to acquire new possessions."[51] Most of the capital exported from the advanced capitalist countries during that period went to other industrially advanced countries, or else to such countries as Russia that were just beginning to develop industrially—and that France was anxious to build up for political–strategic reasons against Germany.

6. Lenin's contention that imperialism, as he defined it, is the principal cause of war in the capitalistic era has not stood up well under the scrutiny of scholars. The major wars since 1870 have not been fought primarily for economic motives. The Boer War in South Africa and the Chaco War between Bolivia and Paraguay (1932–1935) were, but not the Franco–German War, the Spanish–American War, the Russo–Japanese War, or the Turko–Italian War, and certainly not the two World Wars, the Arab–Israeli Wars, the Korean War, the Indo–Chinese War, the Indo–Pakistani Wars over Kashmir and Bangladesh, or the Vietnam War (even though leftist critics of the war in the West sometimes tried unconvincingly to reduce the Southeast Asian conflict to a capitalist–imperialist plot, mainly because the

United States was identified as the leader of the capitalist–imperialist system).[52] A better case can be made for the Persian Gulf War of 1991, in which Western states had concerns over future access to Middle East oil, but the elements of Iraqi aggression versus international law, intra–Arab politics, the security of Israel, and other factors were also involved.

Against the background of World War I, Aron assigns a central place to Anglo–German rivalry, especially the naval arms race, but he denies that this had much to do with capitalism. The British were aware that Germany represented a threat to their prosperity, but they also knew that each country was the best customer of the other's goods. If capitalist imperialism had been the main motive for England's going to war in 1914, then the country should have arrayed itself against its major competitor since the turn of the century—the United States.[53] That such a course of action was unthinkable should serve to cast some doubt on the explanatory power of the Leninist–Stalinist theory. Coming to more recent times, no one has ever bothered to try making a case for economic imperialism as the cause of the Korean War; such a task must strike even the most single-minded Marxist as futile. Kenneth Boulding wrote that any economic benefits the United States might have hoped to derive from the Vietnam War would hardly be worth the cost of waging that war for one day.[54] In the Arab–Israeli conflict since 1948, anyone who wishes to prove that American policy has been based on considerations of economic imperialism is hard-pressed to explain why the United States has supported Israel, even at the risk of alienating the oil-producing Arab states.

Michael Doyle suggested that earlier theorists of imperialism—notably Hobson, Lenin, and Schumpeter—were less interested in producing scholarly explanations of a particular phenomenon in international relations than they were in presenting either a political condemnation or defense of capitalism.[55] Doyle defined *imperialism* as "the actual process by which empires are formed and maintained," and *empire* as "a system of interaction between two political entities, one of which, the dominant metropole, exerts political control over the internal and external policy—the effective sovereignty—of the other, the subordinate periphery."[56] He distinguishes *empire* from two commonly encountered forms of international equality: (a) *hegemony*, in which one power controls or influences the foreign but not the internal policy of other states; and (b) *dependence*, a condition under which a state finds itself limited by constraints on its economic, social, and political autonomy.[57] He denies that the forces driving and shaping imperialism are either primarily economic or primarily military; rather, they are economic, military, political, social, and cultural. "Both the opportunities that give rise to imperialism and the motives that drive it are to be found in a fourfold interaction among metropoles, peripheries, transnational forces, and international systemic incentives."[58] Whereas Hobson, Lenin, and Schumpeter trace the causes to the metropoles—the desire for financial profit, the necessities of monopoly capital, the atavistic impulses of military elites—others, such as John Gallagher and Ronald Robinson, see the roots of imperialism in the crises of weak, vulnerable societies on the African, Asian, and Latin American peripheries. Benjamin Cohen, Kenneth Waltz, A. J. P. Taylor, Morton Kaplan, Edward Gulick, and other theorists of power explain imperialism as a normal concomitant of the structural dynamic implicit in an international system in which stronger states engage in a power-balancing process by exerting their sway over weaker states.[59]

Doyle notes that anomalies often arise when we try to assess the elements of political and economic control in our study of empires and imperialism. For the half-century from 1890 to the outbreak of World War II, *empire* implied conquered territory while *imperialism* reflected a deep disposition within the metropolitan society. Following postwar decolonization, *imperialism* was transmuted into *neoimperialism* or *neocolonialism*—terms that meant continued economic control by the West of territories that had been granted formal political–legal independence. (The concepts, of course, are Marxist in inspiration.[60]) In Doyle's view, the legal acquisition of territory does not necessarily imply effective control. From 1882 until 1914, Egypt was still legally part of the Ottoman Empire, yet it was completely controlled by Britain. Finally, political control does not inevitably produce economic exploitation; the metropolitan country brings, as well as takes. It is erroneous to assume that inequality of power must lead to exploitation, as the long, friendly relationship between England and Thailand amply demonstrated.

MODERN MARXISTS AND THE THIRD WORLD

Contemporary Marxist writers who adhere, however vaguely, to the Leninist theory of imperialism often charge that Western colonialism suppressed the economic, social, and political development of the countries that now constitute the Third World, and that the West is still to blame for the poverty of those countries. Khrushchev had contended that the economic advances made by some Western countries were due to the underdevelopment of Asia, Africa, and Latin America. Western governments were faulted for having failed during the era of colonial rule to introduce central economic planning in their territories and to promote the growth of indigenous industry with protective tariffs. André Gunder Frank has denied that underdevelopment is attributable to the survival of archaic institutions and capital shortages in regions isolated from the mainstream of world history. "On the contrary, underdevelopment was and still is generated by the very same historical process which also generated economic development: the development of capitalism itself."[61]

Marxists generally accuse the West—or the world capitalist system—of keeping the poor countries in a position of subordination, dependence, or bondage by limiting investments to the extractive (raw materials) industries and by Westernizing, subjugating, and bribing the new elites who have an interest in modernizing their societies. Before the period of decolonization, the Marxists predicted that once the colonial territories had gained political independence, they would become masters of their own economic destiny, and thus the capitalists would fight to the end to prevent them from achieving self-government because that would spell the collapse of the capitalist system. Marx himself saw capital penetration and imperialism as progressive forces, bringing civilization and capitalism, which he held to be the necessary prerequisites to socialism.

Most of Europe's remaining colonies had gained their independence by the 1960s. The Western capitalists had not fought effectively to hold them as colonies. The British and the Belgians—if not the French, the Dutch, and the Portuguese—seemed almost eager at times to get rid of their empires, as if the empires were millstones around their necks.[62] Conflict did indeed attend the independence of some imperial possessions—Algeria, Indonesia, Cyprus, the Congo, Kenya, India, and Pakistan (due, in the latter cases, to historic religious divisions in the subcontinent)—yet more than forty colonial territories in Asia and Africa achieved status as independent states with relatively little or no violence. Furthermore, because the standard of living of the masses in the Western capitalist states had been alleged by the Marxists to be artificially high because it had long been based on the exploitation of native populations, disimperialism should have led to a perceptible decline in the West's standard of living, but this did not occur. To the contrary, the formation of the European Economic Community (now the European Union) ushered in a period of unprecedented economic growth and prosperity during the decade of decolonization.

Despite the steady movement of Asia and Africa toward political decolonization, the Soviet Union frequently warned that the Western nations were seeking new forms for keeping the peoples of economically underdeveloped countries in a state of permanent dependence.[63] Official communist theory singled out the European Economic Community as an instrument of neocolonialism, against which the new states had to be particularly on their guard.[64] Following independence, development in Third World countries continued pretty much as before. It did not spurt ahead dramatically. This historic reality of the process of decolonization and its aftermath necessitated further modification of Marxist–Leninist theory. Political independence for the former colonies was portrayed as a sham, because it led to no significant improvement in their economic status. The poor countries, said the Marxists, were still locked into the capitalist system and were being impoverished by its iron law of prices. This new explanation offset the failure of the prediction that the capitalists would fight tenaciously to hold on to their colonies: The capitalists knew that they would have no difficulty continuing their economic domination.

Thomas E. Weisskopf noted several factors at work within the world capitalist system, which, in his view, reinforce the subordination of poor to rich countries:

- Rising elites in the poor countries are persuaded to emulate the consumption patterns of the bourgeoisie in the rich countries and to create a demand for Western imports that satisfy elite consumers without contributing to economic development.
- The brain drain of scientists, engineers, managers, and other technically educated professionals from poor to rich countries increases the dependence of the less developed countries (LDCs) on the industrialized regions.
- Foreign private enterprise perpetuates the conditions that made foreign capital indispensable and discourages the growth of host-country knowledge, technology, skills, and incentives that would enhance its independence.
- Western capitalists create a labor aristocracy in the poor countries by paying a smaller number of skilled workers higher wages rather than paying a larger number of unskilled workers lower wages.[65]

Marxists have generally held that the affluence of Western society has not been due to human energy, scientific inventiveness, technological proficiency, managerial and organizational efficiency, economies of scale, and a climate of political freedom in which economic decisions, while subject to public-policy regulations, can be taken without excessive constraints being imposed by bureaucratic central planners. Instead, they have explained that affluence is attributable in large measure to the exploitation by European and American capitalism of the peoples of Asia, Africa, and Latin America—an exploitation in which even the bourgeois workers of the West participated. To offset the paradox of the continued rise in the West's standard of living when it should have declined after the loss of empire, Marxists laid increasing emphasis on the argument that the Western economies were being artificially stimulated by the arms race.

The notion that colonial exploitation was replaced by the arms race did not stand up under serious scrutiny. The United States, which, compared to the European nations, had a very meager overseas empire, would undoubtedly have become the principal military defender of Western civilization after World War II regardless of developments in the colonial world. The Western European nations, which renounced rather enormous colonial holdings, consistently allocated a lower percentage of their gross national product to defense than did the United States, and the case could be made that the West German, French, and Japanese standards of living rose more rapidly than that of the United States during the Cold War.

Among Marxist theorists in the post–World War II period who sought to link imperialism closely with American foreign policy, Harry Magdoff was one of the leading writers. Magdoff took issue with those who held that political aims and national security, rather than economic imperialism, were the prime motivators of United States foreign policy. Such people, said Magdoff, rely on the argument that foreign trade and investment make up such a small part of the GDP of the United States (less than 5% in the case of total exports) that economic factors could not possibly determine American foreign policy. Magdoff denied that the size of ratios was by itself an adequate indicator of what motivates foreign policy. He further argued that the stake of American business abroad is many times larger than the volume of merchandise exports. He estimated that the size of the foreign market for all United States firms (domestic and those owned abroad) came to about two fifths of the domestic output of all farms, factories, and mines. He saw foreign economic activity as of growing importance to this country and its national-security policy, usually justified in political–military terms:

> The widespread military bases, the far-flung military activities, and the accompanying complex of expenditures at home and abroad serve many purposes of special interest to the business community: (1) protecting present and potential sources of raw materials; (2) safeguarding foreign markets and foreign investments; (3) conserving commercial sea and air routes; (4) preserving spheres of influence where United States business gets a competitive edge for investment and trade; (5) creating new foreign customers and investment opportunities via foreign military and economic aid; and, more generally, (6) maintaining the structure of world capitalist markets not only directly for the United States but also for its junior partners among the industrialized nations.[66]

The Norwegian theorist Johan Galtung viewed trade relationships between European and Third World countries as characterized by a threefold structural dominance—the already mentioned vertical division of labor, plus two additional means of perpetuating the exploitative status quo: (1) *fragmentation* (the relative absence of horizontal economic relationships among the developing countries); and (2) *penetration* (which involves the growth, previously alluded to, of economic, educational, cultural, and other relationships between local rising elites in Third World countries and the former metropolitan powers).[67] Galtung faulted the European Community for permitting the Associated States of Africa to produce only such processed goods as will no longer be competitive with European Community exports. Even by granting "Associated" status and selective tariff preferences to certain African states, he declares, the European Community gives them a privileged position vis-à-vis the rest of the Third World, and thus fragments the "Group of 77" in UNCTAD (the United Nations Conference on Trade and Development).[68] Galtung, not a Marxist, in his structural theory of imperialism, employed several of the same categories of thought as do the Marxists. Unlike Lenin, however, Galtung regarded any system of core–periphery relations in which the states are unequal as imperialistic.[69]

CRITIQUE OF THE NEO-MARXISTS

Marxists and others who blame the West for the poverty of the LDCs have been roundly criticized for oversimplifying the situation. No matter how much good may be done, it is always easy (and usually true) to say that more should have been done. Nonetheless, to blame the European governments for failing to carry out a higher degree of development in their empires when they held the responsibility, says P. T. Bauer, is to "overstate the potentialities of state power as an instrument of economic progress."[70] Actually, Bauer insists, colonial status was not incompatible with economic development. Whereas there had been virtually no economic growth in Africa before the Europeans arrived, between 1890 and 1960 West African trade (particularly for the Gold Coast and Nigeria) increased by a factor of 100 or more. According to Bauer,

> It is highly probable that over the last century or so the establishment of colonial rule in Africa and Asia has promoted, and not retarded, material progress. With relatively little coercion, or even interference in the lives of the great majority of the people, the colonial governments established law and order, safeguarded private property and contractual relations, organized basic transport and health services, and introduced some modern financial and legal institutions. The resulting environment also promoted the establishment or extension of external contacts, which in turn encouraged the inflow of external resources, notably administrative, commercial, and technical skills, as well as capital. . . . It is unlikely (though this cannot be proved conclusively) that in the absence of colonial rule, the social, political, and economic environment in colonial Africa and Asia would have been more congenial to material progress.[71]

Bauer makes the telling observation that the African states not subject to Western imperialism—Liberia and Ethiopia—are today more economically backward than their neighbors that had been colonized.[72] The relationship between the West and the colonial peoples was far from being one-sidedly exploitative. With Western domination came literacy and education, hospitals, hygiene, sanitary methods, and at least a rudimentary knowledge of science and technology. The political impact of the West on the colonial lands was in some respects greater than the economic impact. The concepts of independence, self-determination, freedom, and sovereign equality that the peoples of Asia and Africa employed with great effect after World War II to express their political aspirations were, as Hans Kohn pointed out, borrowed from the Western political vocabulary by native leaders who had received their university education in Western countries.[73]

Other non-Marxist analysts have argued persuasively that there is no necessary relationship between poverty and the reliance of Third World countries on extractive and agricultural industries. Posing a serious challenge to the fundamental assumptions of this particular iron-law thesis are the anomalies of Australia and New Zealand. Taking issue with Galtung, Andrew Mack writes:

> The economic exchange relationships which link Australia and New Zealand with the rich industrialized countries are precisely those which Galtung held not only characterize Third World/EC relationships but which are also the root cause of the former's underdevelopment. Both countries depend on the export of primary commodities . . . characterized by nonexistent or very low degrees of processing. On the other hand, both countries depend on imports which are typically highly processed. . . . In other words, both countries lie at the lower end of the vertical division of international labor. . . . Yet both countries have experienced steady economic growth and a significant degree of domestic industrialization. This is indeed an anomaly which Galtung's theory cannot explain.[74]

Marxist analysts seem to believe that whatever capitalists do constitutes exploitation. At the same time, they condemn Western governments and entrepreneurs for not having done more to help the colonial territories and their successor independent states. Seldom do Marxists spell out what capitalists ought to have done for Third World economic development and failed to do. Perhaps Marxists cannot do this, for the more active capitalists are, the more exploitative they are—by definition. Marxists also assume that the socialist system, by definition, cannot be exploitative. Here they prefer to ignore the Soviet Union's postwar record in Eastern Europe. For many years, elites in the LDCs were strongly attracted to the Soviet model of economic development. Since the fragmentation of the USSR, many of those same elites have been extolling the virtues of the market economy and seeking capitalist investment.

More recently, Jack Snyder has studied the strategic myths constructed by parochial domestic interests and bureaucratic groups to rationalize their imperialistic policies. Hobson and Lenin had pointed to the concentrated interests of monopoly capitalists as the driving force, while the costs of expansionist policies were passed on to the general society in the form of taxation. To the contrary, Snyder contends that the specific groups that benefit from imperialist policies are not powerful enough to shape state policy, whereas the larger segments of the population (for example, a majority of democratic electorates), which are politically capable of influencing governmental policies, lack significant motivation because for them the benefits of imperialism are too diffuse to serve as springs of action. The elites who do perceive benefits, says Snyder, form coalitions and develop strategic myths, which link state security to expansion. After examining five cases of overexpansion—Germany from Bismarck to Hitler, Japan between the two world wars, Britain in the nineteenth century, and the Soviet Union and the United States during the Cold War—he concluded that overexpansion is less extreme and less likely in democratic societies that industrialize early, where elite interests are more diffuse, and where the climate of free exchange of ideas militates against official strategic mythmaking. Germany and Japan, both highly cartelized systems in the interwar period, showed the greatest tendency toward overexpansion. They also underwent industrialization later than the democracies. The Soviet Union, a centralized system that was the latest of the five to industrialize, ruled by a unified elite with a common ideology and interests, fell between the cartelized and democratic systems with regard to overexpansion.[75]

· Soviet postwar imperialist expansion into Eastern Europe initially provided economic advantages (looted industrial and agricultural production, exploited technology and labor skills, an expanded area for the command economy, etc.).[76] When Moscow sought to expand its influence in the Third World during the Khrushchev years, it was highly selective in targeting (and trumpeting) a very limited amount of foreign aid to ten countries.[77] Most of the aid sent abroad to the Third World (North Korea, Egypt, North Vietnam, Algeria, Libya, Syria, Iraq, Cuba, Somalia, Ethiopia, and Angola) came from its most efficient industrial sector—military production. Neglect of consumer goods was one of the chief legacies of the Stalinist era.

According to Jack Snyder, Stalin's system of a "militant Communist Party and a command economy geared toward autarkic military production" had been the outgrowth of a paranoid fear of capitalist intervention. The institutions Stalin put in place to meet the foreign threat he perceived hung on as atavisms under his successors up to the time of Gorbachev.[78] By the time Gorbachev came to power in 1985, he was painfully aware of the dismal condition to which the Soviet Union had sunk—political ossification, economic inefficiency, technological obsolescence, incompetence, and corruption wherever he looked. Whereas Western economies had undergone continuous progressive reform since World War II, the Soviet economy had steadily stagnated. Apparently convinced that the Communist Party, the Soviet State, and the centralized economy all had to undergo profound transformation if the USSR was to survive as a modern world power in the twenty-first century, he immediately set about dismantling an authoritarian and increasingly bankrupt imperial system in an advanced stage of erosion.

His new thinking, including *glasnost* (openness and greater freedom of information) and *perestroika* (restructuring and reform) had a more immediate effect on Soviet foreign and defense policy than on the domestic economy.[79] His moves toward democratization in the form of contested elections and an easing of restrictions on the media unleashed a wave of ethnonational forces, which had long been suppressed, as well as debates about the legal rights of the republics, which threatened the stability of the Soviet Union. Not only did he extricate the armed forces from the disastrous intervention in Afghanistan but he also withdrew them from Central Eastern Europe and set the stage for the dissolution of the Warsaw Pact. His willingness to agree to startling reductions in both nuclear and conventional capabilities met with the initial grudging approval of the military, insofar as the cuts seemed to contribute to enhanced security. The armed forces were also in favor of economic reforms aimed at preserving the nation's power position. The military, however, became more anxious over abandoning the empire's security buffer zone and allowing the reunification of Germany. Meanwhile, Gorbachev had to temporize between those who demanded faster and more radical economic reforms and the entrenched party bureaucrats who were intransigent in opposition to all changes.

After the aborted military coup in August 1991, from which Boris Yeltsin emerged as the popular democratic hero, both the Communist Party and the Soviet Union disintegrated by the end of the year. Gorbachev had indeed unhinged the imperialist machine built by Lenin and Stalin. Realists were taken by surprise because no imperialist power had ever carried out such an uncharacteristic reversal. Gorbachev did what he considered necessary to save the system; it was partially the free choice of a remarkable political leader, but it was a choice of necessity, imposed by the internal failure of a decadent regime no longer able to compete after a half century of Cold War, nuclear deterrence, and the aspirations of people for freedom.[80]

The concern of states adjacent to Russia over the possibilities of future expansionist policies have not been entirely attenuated since the collapse of the Soviet communist empire. For decades, Western analysts debated about the distinctions, differences, and relative weights of the ideology-driven imperialism of the Soviet Union and the more traditional variety inherited from the tsars. Post–Cold War Russia has not abandoned all its former heavy-handed methods, as the violent attack on the Congress of People's Deputies; military interventions in the Crimea, Ossetia, Abkhazia, Georgia, and Tajikistan; and the suppression of Chechnya's move toward autonomy have demonstrated. The popular appeal of Russian chauvinists and antireform communists who seek an ethnically pure state and a restored empire does not reassure Russia's newly independent neighbors, such as the Baltics, Ukraine, and Kazakhstan. The reluctance of Ukraine's parliament to renounce the nuclear missiles on the nation's territory, which delayed Russian compliance with arms-control agreements, was due largely to uncertainty about the country's future security. The impotence and prolonged frustration of the United Nations, NATO, and the European Union in dealing with the Bosnian crisis, compared with the steady support of Moscow for the Serbs—as a manifestation of historic pan-Slavism—added to the unease. The Visegrad countries of Central-Eastern Europe—Poland, Hungary, the Czech Republic, and Slovakia—have sought to improve their security outlook through admission to the European Union and NATO. Russia has opposed such a development, except on the unlikely condition that it too will be admitted with special privileges. In sum, reports of the demise of Russian imperialism may be premature.[81]

IMPERIALISM AS POLITICAL SLOGAN

Imperialism remained a principal slogan or shibboleth of world politics prior to the last decade of the twentieth century. The Leninist theory has often been called narrowly Eurocentric, but the term took on a universal applicability after World

War II. All of the leading powers employed it to describe the policies of their rivals. Arab nationalists railed against British and American–Zionist imperialism in the Middle East. It was inevitable that the activities of United States oil companies in the Middle East and fruit companies in Latin America should be labeled prime examples of imperialism, and that trade agreements between the European Community Union and its Associated States of Africa and Asia should be characterized as instruments of neo-imperialism. The Indonesian leader Sukarno and other Third World neutralists, in the late 1950s, excoriated the West for having subjugated all the peoples living along the imperialist highway from the Atlantic Ocean to the Indian Ocean and the South China Sea.[82] Until the late 1960s, when the Soviet Union replaced the United States as Beijing's principal enemy, Mao Zhedong, adhering to a hard Stalinist line, made imperialism the main slogan in China's propaganda war against the United States. One development after another—Mossadeq's nationalization of the Anglo–Iranian Oil Company (1951), the defeat of French forces at Dien Bien Phu (1954), Nasser's takeover of the Suez Canal Company (1956), Castro's ascent to power (1960), the U.S. withdrawal from Vietnam (1975), the overthrow of the Shah of Iran, and the victory of the Nicaraguan Sandanistas (1979)—each was hailed throughout the Second and Third Worlds as a historic triumph over Western imperialism.

Most Western theorists of international relations, as well as Western political leaders, regarded the Soviet domination of Eastern Europe as imperialism, even though Third World intellectuals were not greatly exercised over the Soviet suppression of the Hungarian uprising in 1956. Kenneth E. Boulding wrote,

> It is quite impossible to explain modern imperialism in economic terms. The only possible exception to this, paradoxically enough, is the socialist imperialism exercised by the Soviet Union on Eastern Europe and especially on East Germany after the Second World War. The Soviet Union probably extracted more goods from East Germany in the ten years after the Second World War than Britain did in two hundred years from India, and this was pure tribute.[83]

The neutralists of the Third World, for three decades after World War II, seemed to take it for granted, as many had earlier, that imperialists are people who come in ships from distant lands. Those who could impose their dominance simply by marching armies across borders were for a long time excluded from the definition of imperialists. It was the People's Republic of China, which itself had engaged in some imperialistic adventures against India and Tibet, that began to accuse the Soviet Union of imperialism in a manner credible to leftist elites in the Third World. While trying to replace the Soviet Union as the leader of the forces of world revolution, Mao first accused Soviet leaders of revisionism, bourgeoisification, and betrayal of the revolution, through arms-control collusion with capitalist imperialists. Later the Chinese leaders condemned capitalist and socialist imperialism in one breath. Later still, they began to indicate that they regarded the socialist imperialism of the Soviet Union as a greater threat than the capitalist imperialism of the United States, and they acted as if they would welcome a tacit alliance with the enemy farther away against the enemy nearer. At the same time, they encouraged the strengthening of NATO, urged Europe to unite, and warned the West not to take a Soviet-promoted détente too seriously. In July 1978, the foreign ministers of more than 100 nonaligned states, meeting in Belgrade, hinted for the first time that they were becoming more worried about Soviet expansion, especially in Africa, than they were about a waning Western imperialism.[84]

Nevertheless, despite its many theoretical deficiencies and failures of prediction and practice—for example, several countries organized along Marxist communist lines have found it harder to feed themselves than they did before—Marxism continued for a long time to exercise a worldwide appeal as a vehicle for the expression of criticism, resentment, and protest against the complexities and frustrations of contemporary social reality.[85] According to Adam B. Ulam, the Hobson–Leninist theory of imperialism, "because of its simplicity, because of its psychological appeal and because of the undoubted depredations and brutalities that accompanied the process of colonization," retained its influence by enabling the disadvantaged of the world to express their rage and to disturb the conscience of a guilt-ridden West.[86]

In the final analysis, the Leninist theory of imperialism did a disservice to the developing nations of the non-Western world. The simplistic, polemical urge to blame all or most of those countries' troubles on the exploitation of a few capitalistic states, as Anthony James Joes noted, diverts the attention of planners who take the ideological explanation seriously from examining carefully the obstacles posed to modernization by indigenous political, cultural, economic, and geographic factors. The theory was also self-serving to some Third World leaders, said Joes, for "it exculpates dogmatic theorists, incompetent windbags, epauleted megalomaniacs, and 'village tyrants' from all responsibility for the deplorable condition of their suffering countrymen even after two decades—or two centuries or two millennia—of political independence."[87]

THE NORTH–SOUTH DEBATE

Since the early 1970s, political practitioners and academic theorists have been arguing that economic problems rival the traditional security concerns of nations and that world politics has become increasingly meshed with issues of trade, aid, and monetary affairs. Many went so far as to contend, years before the end of the Cold War, that the North–South debate, which focuses on structural inequities in the international economy, had supplanted the East–West security preoccupation as the most urgent issue on the global agenda, at least in the eyes of more than two-thirds of the countries of the world. The Third World, with persistent vehemence, condemned the arms race between the First (Western) World and the Second (Soviet Socialist Bloc) World (not including Communist China) and pressed hard within the United Nations for disarmament of the nuclear-weapons powers as a principal means of freeing up what the Third World regarded as resources wasted on the dangerous chimera of deterrence—resources that could be reallocated to international development.[88]

It is gross oversimplification to identify the Northern industrial countries with "the rich" and the Southern less developed countries with "the poor." Both within and among states of the North we can note economic disparities—for example, between the northern part of Italy and the Mezzogiorno in the south, or between the slums and the suburbs of many cities in the United States, or between Portugal and Greece on the one hand and the more affluent northwestern Europe on the other. After the oil-price rise of the early 1970s, the Third World was divided into two worlds, one of which was adversely affected by the increased cost of oil imports required for industrial and agricultural development, and a Fourth World that includes some countries that can, thanks to OPEC pricing and production policies, boast per-capita incomes higher than those of a few Northern countries. Several of the more than 100 states that identify themselves with the South are themselves newly industrializing countries (NICs) with labor-intensive economies, the manufacturing exports of which have proved highly competitive in international markets against countries that enjoy a higher standard of living.° Finally, the gap between the wealthy and the poverty-stricken classes in the urban areas and countries of the South is often more glaring than in the North or in the global economic system as a whole between North and South. Indeed, Third World voices that are most scathing in their condemnation of the Western industrialized nations for consuming three quarters of the world's resources to satisfy one quarter of its population often condone glaring inequalities in the class structures of their own societies, which they usually blame on the capitalist West.[89]

After all the caveats have been noted, no one can deny that the bulk of humankind living in the 100 countries (outside North America, West Europe, Japan, East Europe, OPEC, and the NICs) with the lowest per-capita incomes is substantially much worse off in material terms (although perhaps not culturally or psychologically or spiritually) than the people who live in the 40 countries with the highest income levels. Analysts have been pointing to the unequal relationship between the richer and the poorer nations for decades. Some prefer to ignore the glaring differences that exist, but no intelligent person can disagree with the grim statistical comparisons that have been recited so many times that most people in the industrialized countries have grown virtually immune to them.

Not surprisingly, the perspectives of the global problem adopted by the North and South are poles apart. In 1976, Mahbub ul Haq, the Pakistani Director of Policy Planning and Program Review at the International Bank for Reconstruction and Development (the World Bank) in Washington, summed up the two points of view as follows:

> The poor nations are beginning to question the basic premises of an international order that leads to ever widening disparities between the rich and poor countries and to a persistent denial of equality of opportunity to many poor nations. They are, in fact, arguing that in the international order—just as much as within national orders—all distribution of benefits, credits, services, and decision-making gets warped in favor of a privileged minority and that this situation cannot be changed except through fundamental institutional reforms.
>
> When this is pointed out to the rich nations, they dismiss it casually as empty rhetoric of the poor nations. Their standard answer is that the international market

---

°These include Argentina, Brazil, Mexico, India, South Korea, Taiwan, the Philippines, Hong Kong, Singapore, and, more recently, Malaysia and Thailand.

mechanism works, even though not too perfectly, and that the poor nations are always out to wring concessions from the rich nations in the name of past exploitation. They believe that the poor nations are demanding a massive redistribution of income and wealth which is simply not in the cards. Their general attitude seems to be that the poor nations must earn their economic development, much the same way as the rich nations had to over the last two centuries, through patient hard work and gradual capital formation, and that there are no shortcuts to this process and no rhetorical substitutes. The rich, however, are "generous" enough to offer some help to the poor nations to accelerate their economic development if the poor are only willing to behave themselves.[90]

The World Bank official went on to draw an analogy between the global poor and the poor strata within a national society, for whom the market mechanism ceases to function equitably because the wealthy classes can bend the market to their will, while the poor lack the power to influence its decisions. "This is even more true at the international level," he adds, "since there is no world government and none of the usual mechanisms existing within countries that create pressures for redistribution of income and wealth."[91] Churches, philosophers, theologians, social theorists, and others may argue with forceful eloquence that the fortunately situated peoples of this world have a high moral obligation to help those much less fortunate. They are undoubtedly right. Even certain courageous politicians agree, despite the fact that such a message is never popular with taxpayers in democratic parliamentary countries (and it was practically never heard preached in the socialist bloc). People in affluent Western societies can exhibit extremely generous impulses when it comes to helping people whom they know in circumstances of chronic hardship (at home) or emergency needs (at home and abroad). It has never been easy for any government, however, to generate much enthusiasm for sustained, long-range, well-planned, and massive programs of international development assistance. Regardless of what the *moral* obligations of nations may be, there exists no effective world public authority to enforce the obligation by translating it into policy.

The Theory of Dependencia

Most of the LDCs have emerged in the latter half of the twentieth century from a past in which either political colonialism, economic imperialism, or both predominated. Whereas all Western industrial countries and Japan experienced some problems in the transition from traditional to modern societies, for most of them the process was gradual and phased over a longer period. Many Third World countries, suddenly caught up in rapid social change, have felt revolutionary pressures as a result of the modernization process. Most of them manifest glaring inequities in patterns of accumulated wealth and annual income distribution. Most suffer from high or above-average rates of population growth, infant mortality, malnutrition or hunger, contagious disease, and illiteracy, as well as inadequate programs of education, health, and welfare. Throughout the Third World, planning for coherent economic development is hampered by shortages of technical–administrative expertise, political instability, inflation, unfavorable terms of trade (because of dependence on the export of a few primary products and the import of costly capital and manufactures, plus large-scale indebtedness to foreign banking institutions, whether national or international), and pressures for consumption that more often than not outstrip domestic productivity.

Dependency theory originated during the 1970s as one school of structural–globalist thought, the object of which was to explain the gap between the rich and the poor nations of the world. It was developed largely by Latin American analysts of the Economic Commission on Latin America (ECLA), and was quickly adopted by UNCTAD-oriented writers who were not satisfied with the explanations of those who attributed the development failure of Third World societies to the assumption that religious–cultural traditions acted as a bulwark against modernization. The basic thesis of the *dependentistas* is that dependency differs from the dependence that most contemporary scholars have in mind when they refer to an interdependent world, even when they acknowledge inequities in interdependent relationships. James Caporaso distinguished the two concepts as follows:

> The dependence orientation seeks to probe and explore the symmetries and asymmetries among nation-states. This approach most often proceeds from a liberal paradigm which focuses on individual actors and their goals and which sees power in decisional terms. The individual actors are usually internally unified states which confront the external environment as homogeneous units. . . . The dependency orientation, on the other hand, seeks to explore the process of integration of the periphery into the international capitalist system and to assess the developmental implications of this peripheral capitalism. This approach proceeds from a *structuralist* paradigm which focuses on the class structure and international capital, and the role of the state in shaping and managing the national, foreign, and class forces that propel development within countries. The dependency framework, in other words, explicitly rejects the unified state as actor as a useful conceptual building block of theory.[92]

In the view of dependency theorists, the relationship between the Northern core and the Southern periphery, far from being a relationship of mutual-interest cooperation, connotes both the subordination of the latter to the former and the exploitation of the latter by the former. Thus, in the eyes of *dependentistas,* the poor countries do not lack capital and lag behind the rich because they lie outside or on the edge of the capitalist world but rather because they have been integrated into the international class structure of the capitalist system. In this respect, dependency theory is essentially a variant of the neo-Marxist perspective on the situation facing the erstwhile colonial territories. Tony Smith characterized dependency theory as follows:

> Put briefly, it holds that economic processes are the basic structural force of history, and that over the last several centuries it has been northern capitalism (first in its mercantile, then in its free trade, later in its financial, and today in its multinational guises) that has been history's locomotive. Those lands and peoples are "dependent" that are not "autonomous" (a favorite word of many of these writers that is never rigorously defined . . .) in the face of these external economic forces. . . .
>
> The major criticism to be made of dependency theory is that it exaggerates the explanatory power of economic imperialism as a concept to make sense of historical change in the south. Too much emphasis is placed on the dynamic, molding power of capitalist imperialism and the socioeconomic forces in league with it locally; too little

attention is paid to political motives behind imperialism or to the autonomous power of local political circumstances in influencing the course of change in Africa, Asia and Latin America.[93]

Samuel and Arturo Valenzuela criticized the "modernization perspective" that economists, anthropologists, sociologists, and political scientists had developed in the postwar period to explain the failure of new nations to reach the economic takeoff point following an infusion of Western foreign aid. Such a perspective, in their view, was an outgrowth of the tradition–modernity dichotomy of nineteenth-century European sociology that saw culture itself, resistant to change, as the main obstacle to economic modernization. Traditional societies are marked by ascription, not achievement; by social status and not individual effort; and by an extended kinship structure rather than the nuclear family. Such societies manifest little occupational specialization and social mobility, a highly stratified system of upward deference, and an emphasis on elitism and hierarchical authority. By contrast, the features of modern society are conceptually quite different—indeed, polar opposites: high rates of social mobility; a complex occupational system; a predominance of secondary over merely primary economic activities (i.e., manufacturing and service industries beyond agriculture and mining); differentiated political, legal, and social structures; and an institutionalized capacity for change, rather than a rigid pattern calculated to preserve immemorial social, religious, and cultural values. Western modernizationists were faulted for assuming that unless traditional societies could learn to innovate and adopt Western ideas, techniques, organizational methods, incentives, and institutions—a whole new set of attitudes and way of life—they must continue to languish on the fringe of poverty.

Dependency theorists, note the Valenzuelas, reject the modernizationist assumption that genuine development can result only through an appropriate response to stimuli from exogenous sources according to the uniquely successful Western model, as if development and Westernization were identical processes. These theorists also reject the notion that the national society is the proper unit of analysis in this context. The Valenzuelas argue that different levels in the transition from tradition to modernity cannot explain differences in levels of economic growth achievement. Nations and regions can be analyzed only by reference to their locus in the world political–economic system—whether they are closer to the core or to the periphery. This is a central tenet running through all dependency literature. Dependency literature, unfortunately, is marred by such imprecise or inelegant concepts as "associated-dependent development," "inwardly [or outwardly] directed development," "global historical–structural processes," the "operationalization of dependency," and "diachronic analysis."[94]

Before and after World War II, several developing countries, especially in Latin America, tried to reduce their dependency on the industrialized capitalist system by pursuing a strategy of import substitution. Governments encouraged indigenous industries with high protective tariffs. Earnings from agricultural exports were used to pay for the importation of needed capital equipment, while a variety of policies discouraged the importation of consumer goods that would henceforth be produced at home. This import-substitution strategy promoted development for a while, until it required large-scale borrowing by governments to finance heavy industrial enterprises that, in restricted domestic markets, were unable to produce at efficient economies of scale. Such firms often enjoyed so much protection and public assistance as to become virtual monopolies unable to face competition.[95]

A number of developing countries have become substantial producers of manufactures. The NICs include South Korea, Taiwan, Argentina, Brazil, India, the Philippines, Hong Kong, Singapore, Mexico, Venezuela, Thailand, and Malaysia. In some cases, the NICs themselves have become major exporters, even to such countries as the United States. Stephen Haggard compared the East Asian strategy of export-led industrialization with the import-substitution strategy of several Latin American countries, and he found the former notably more successful in terms of national economic independence, equity of income distribution, and qualify-of-life indices.[96] Dependency theorists admit that MNCs have been attracted to these countries, but it is because of cheaper labor costs and, in many cases, shorter supply lines for raw materials. Nevertheless, the *dependentistas* contend, such development as does occur is not really autonomous but is dictated by the global requirements of the world capitalist system. Neo-Marxists and dependency theorists prefer to emphasize the continued subordination of this semiperiphery to the core and ignore the fact that some entire countries are now better off than before.[97]

The success of the oil-producing countries in quadrupling the price of their product convinced many political leaders, along with their advisers, that the Third World could employ various forms of commodity power as leverage against what they regarded as the oppressive global liberalism of the industrialized West. They believed that they could flex their muscles through their voting power in the United Nations General Assembly, UNCTAD and UNCLOS III (the Third U.N. Conference on the Law of the Seas), and through their suasive rhetoric in the IMF and the World Bank. Their objectives were to speed up the pace of their own economic development and to shift the pattern of income distribution—less for the rich and more for the poor nations. By no means were all Third World states agreed on what had to be done, because of the divergences of interest that had become obvious within their own ranks—for example, between oil exporters and oil importers, between coastal and landlocked states, between agricultural-commodity-dependent states and the NICs. Generally, however, there was widespread agreement in what was termed the New International Economic Order (NIEO) that the North must

A. ensure a quickened rate of technology transfer (for most Third World countries were afraid that the technology gap would continue to widen rather than narrow);

B. improve the terms of trade for the South and expand trade preferences for its manufactures;

C. multilateralize foreign economic development assistance to insulate it against the attachment of political strings that often accompanied bilateral transactions;

D. negotiate with UNCTAD and other Third World groups commodity-price-stabilization agreements to protect primary products exported to the North against wide price fluctuations in the world market;

E. impose more stringent controls on First World capital investment abroad and on the operations of MNCs;

F. grant debt relief by rescheduling or canceling Third World indebtedness to Northern banks and other North-dominated international financial institutions;

G. accept price indexation, under which the prices of Third World primary products exported to the First World would be linked to the prices of manufactured goods imported from it; and

H. accept a new international legal regime for the high seas that would recognize the mineral resources of the ocean bed as the common heritage of humankind and require that a portion of any economic benefits resulting from the exploitation of those resources by the technologically advanced First World go into an international fund for Third World development.

The South made no progress with the NIEO as such. The North was willing to hear it discussed but refused to negotiate it. Modest progress has been made, however, toward the partial fulfillment of certain NIEO demands. Technology has moved to the NICs, which now produce textiles, clothing, shoes, steel and steel goods, machine tools, autos, radios and other audio equipment, toys, chemicals, medical supplies, and basic appliances—many items that the North, with high-cost labor, can no longer turn out efficiently. The North has approved a Generalized System of Preferences (GSP) for the manufactured (but not agricultural) exports of the South, and the European Union has granted, in the Lomé Convention, trading arrangements that discriminate in favor of the Third World. The IMF, the World Bank, and Northern private banks have become more sensitive to balance-of-payments and debt problems of Third World countries. Some oil producers, able to identify with the poor states and unable to absorb all their petrodollar wealth, initiated aid programs. The subsequent experience of OPEC from the late 1970s amply demonstrated that the solidarity of the South was becoming fragmented, along with its commodity power.

Stephen D. Krasner has shown that LDCs pursue simultaneously several different objectives in the international system, some of which may strike Western observers as inconsistent. He divides Third World political behavior into two general categories. The first he calls "relational power behavior," which accepts existing regimes and works through established economic institutions such as the IMF and the World Bank in order to alleviate foreign-exchange difficulties and capital shortages, or through bilateral channels to conclude tax treaties and orderly marketing agreements. Such an approach may involve hard bargaining and reluctant submission to unpleasant conditions (e.g., debt-service charges and pledges to reduce imports). The second type of political behavior, says Krasner, is "meta-power behavior," which aims at restructuring international regimes—altering institutions, rules, principles, values, and norms in favor of the weaker, poorer, more vulnerable states. The LDCs, lacking material-power capabilities (although these are growing in many areas), have relied more on political rhetoric and their voting power as formally equal sovereign communities in international organizations to effect fundamental changes in the way the international economy operates. Up to now, as we have seen, the changes have been far from fundamental in the eyes of the Third World, but there have been substantial changes, and the process of change will undoubtedly continue, more through the exercise by the South of relational power rather than metapower.[98]

Multinational Corporations (MNCs)

One of the important aspects of the North–South debate pertains to the MNCs. Whether the multinationals on balance have benefited or exploited host countries in the South has long been a subject of bitter controversy, but the debate has become somewhat less polemical and more economically complex of late. It should be realized first of all that well over two thirds of the foreign affiliates of MNCs headquartered in the First World (that is, the United States, Western Europe, and Japan) also happen to be located in First World rather than in Third World countries. The United States accounts for about a quarter of all MNCs; Britain and West Germany, another quarter. Approximately three quarters of all First World foreign investments are in First World countries.[99] More than half of all U.S. direct foreign investment is located in five industrialized countries (Britain, Canada, Germany, Switzerland, and the Netherlands).[100]

By 1988, the annual volume of sales of the 10 largest MNCs was greater than the gross domestic product (GDP) of more than 130 developing members of the United Nations.[101] It has usually been inferred from this that MNCs can readily interfere, directly or indirectly, in the economic and political life of host countries, and even exercise a dominating influence in poorer Third World countries. Exactly how economic capabilities of foreign corporations translate into domestic political power in either industrially advanced or less developed countries is seldom spelled out in specific terms, but rather it is readily assumed by those who take it for granted that politics is subordinate to economics. Corporations can, of course, serve the foreign-policy interests of their host governments, just as they can contravene those interests. They can engage in intelligence-gathering activities; they can intervene legally or illegally in the domestic political affairs of the host (for example, by trying to influence the outcome of elections, or persuading the host government to alter certain policies); and they can pressure the parent state government to pursue legislatively enacted and foreign diplomatic policies that will promote the interests of MNCs, regardless of the consequences for host countries. The number of documentable cases, however, is not large enough to justify the elaboration of a general universally valid theory.

It is possible to present a balanced assessment of the positive and negative aspects of MNCs—their economic benefits and costs to the host countries.[102] Advocates argue that MNCs have served as a principal means of satisfying the overwhelming desire of most countries in the world to attract foreign investment capital and technological know-how. The initial inflow of capital improves the balance-of-payments picture; brings in advanced technology not available domestically; creates jobs locally; effects savings on research and development; enhances the technical, productive, and organizational–managerial skills of indigenous personnel; and exerts a continuing positive effect on the balance of payments, both by elevating the host country's export capacity and by manufacturing for domestic consumption, thereby saving what would be spent on comparable imports. MNCs also introduce, through their own personnel policies, higher standards of wages, housing, and social welfare, which eventually affect other segments of society.

Critics contend that MNCs are nothing but instruments of neocolonialist, profit-seeking capitalism, which absorb more local capital than they bring in from abroad; transfer in older, obsolescing technology that has become less efficient under the higher-cost labor conditions of the First World and that often has little relevance to the real needs of poorer countries; take advantage of local cheap labor while excluding host-country nationals from higher-paying technical-skill and management positions; reap higher profits than they could in their parent countries, by locating where national taxes are low; import from parent-country affiliates instead of purchasing locally; and manipulate international differences in prices, licensing, interest rates, and other economic factors for their own advantage, and with minimal consideration for the economic interests of the host country.

Joan Edelman Spero (from whom the foregoing balance sheet was largely drawn) has trenchantly described how Third World governments manifested a learning curve in their response to MNCs, as local elites developed technical, legal, managerial, and financial expertise. They also became aware that once MNCs had become established, the host country's bargaining power became stronger than it had been when the country was seeking to attract foreign investment. The host country could gradually adopt laws and administrative regulations to bring the corporations under greater control. Original investment agreements become subject to later revision on more favorable terms for the host country, especially as the number of foreign investors competing for entry into the South increases.[103] In really tough bargaining confrontations, the threat of expropriation may become more credible than the threat of disinvestment. At any rate, many governments within the Southern periphery have become confident that they can hold their own in dealing with the MNCs; that local control or ownership patterns are improving over time; and that most MNCs, even though they may take more than they give on current account, are becoming useful instruments of development and channels of ingress–egress into the global economic system.

The Capitalist World Economy

Related to, yet different from, the theory of *dependencia* is the broader school of thought that looks beyond the current problems of the Third World in an effort to understand the uneven development of the world capitalist system as a whole, in its various political, economic, and social aspects, and to fit the historical evolution of each country or region into a global spatiotemporal perspective encompassing the capitalist world economy since the sixteenth-century transition from feudalism. The principal spokesperson for this weltanschauung is Immanuel Wallerstein.

Wallerstein's analysis is essentially neo-Marxist, but he combines elements of realism and Marxism. He shares with such realists as Kenneth Waltz and

Hedley Bull the view that the international system is characterized by anarchy— the absence of a single global political authority. It is precisely this condition that makes it impossible to regulate the capitalist mode of production across national boundaries. Consequently, there emerges an international economic division of labor consisting of a central core of powerful, industrially advanced capitalist states; a periphery made up of weak states, kept on a level of technological underdevelopment and subordinated to the status of provider of raw materials for the core; and a semiperiphery of states, the economic activities of which are a mixture in between those of core and periphery—those usually called "NICs."

Wallerstein avoids the excessive and exclusive emphasis that classical Marxists have placed on the class struggle. He recognizes the important roles played within the capitalist world economy by nation-states; ethnic, religious, racial, and linguistic groups; and even households. He realizes that the competition of bourgeoisie and proletariat has the effect of strengthening the state because both classes, regardless of whether they pursue exploitative status quo, reformist, or revolutionary strategies, work consciously or unconsciously to enhance the functional powers of government. Wallerstein readily concedes that the international distribution of power among states shifts constantly as one historic period gives way to another. In the end, however, he is more Marxist than realist when he insists that the balance of power is a function of economic processes that transcend purely national boundaries—such as those, for example, by which the United States replaced Britain as the world's premier power in the early decades of the twentieth century.[104]

Christopher Chase-Dunn, following Wallerstein, inquired into the relationship between economic and political processes within the capitalist system. Some Marxists, he observed, joined such realists as Waltz and Modelski in reacting against the economism of Wallerstein by reemphasizing the autonomy of political factors, the interstate system, and geopolitical processes. Chase-Dunn contended that the interstate system and the capitalist mode of production and wealth accumulation are not only interdependent, but also integrally unified. He attributes the separation of politics and economics in the past to the fact that economic phenomena seem more regular and more determined by mechanistic laws, whereas the order of political phenomena seems to be more influenced by free will and therefore less predictable. He notes that Adam Smith and his followers also attributed the separation to the public–private dichotomy, the state being equated with the public realm and economic activity with the private. Chase-Dunn rejects both the explanations of the separation and the separation itself.

Whether states pursue free enterprise and trade policies or impose strict controls over the economy depends on their position within the capitalist world-economy. (In this regard, Chase-Dunn agreed essentially with Wallerstein's assumption that socialist states cannot escape from the fact that, like it or not, they are a part of the capitalist world economy and cannot isolate themselves from it, try as they might.) Hegemonic core states possessing productive advantages, along with peripheral states dominated by capitalist producers of cheap-labor goods for export to the core, both support free trade. Less favorably situated core states and semiperipheral states (NICs) seeking to improve their position relative to the core are usually characterized by centralized direction of the economy and protectionist policies. Chase-Dunn elaborated on Wallerstein's view that the global system is anarchic. The capitalist world economy prefers to preserve this condition and opposes the emergence of a single power capable of acting as a universal hegemony or world state. Rival states engage in a balance of power that operates to prevent the establishment of a worldwide monopoly state strong enough to impose controls on the global economic order, for capitalism could not then survive.[105] According to this theory, the liberal, decentralized state (such as the United States and Britain) was primarily a product of economic forces, especially the desire for unlimited material self-aggrandizement by capitalist entrepreneurs, rather than the fulfillment of a deep-rooted human spiritual impulse for freedom, equality, and dignity intrinsic to Western civilization, itself the outgrowth of Judeo-Christian, Greco-Roman ideas and ideals.

Post-Marxist Critical International Theory

Although Marxist theory as such has been widely rejected, we have witnessed the emergence of a form of post-Marxist critical theory. As described and elaborated by Andrew Linklater,[106] realism, rationalism, and revolutionism represent the three principal traditions of international-relations theory. Realism emphasizes a struggle for power and security; rationalism stresses the level of order achievable by states under conditions of anarchy; and revolutionism attaches primacy to the promotion of human emancipation within a context of realizing the fullest human potential. Taken together, these traditions, first described by Martin Wight, as Linklater acknowledges, coexist and contend with each other, although the revolutionist or emancipatory is superior and constitutes what Linklater terms *critical international theory*. Radically differing from each other, these dominant perspectives provide a sequence of successively more adequate approaches to theoretical development, of which critical international theory, based on revolutionism, constitutes the highest of the three traditions.

Among the most influential of the revolutionist theories was Marxism. Although Marxism purported to be a theory of emancipation, Linklater points out, Marx and many of his followers failed to understand the potential for totalitarian oppression and domination within Marxism itself. Linklater refers extensively to the Frankfurt School, and in particular to the writings of Jürgen Habermas, whose work has been of central importance to critical theory as such and, therefore, to critical international theory. Under the tutelage of Habermas, the essential tenet of the Frankfurt School is that human reason provides the basis for emancipation. In this regard, so the argument goes, Marx contended that the circumstances under which history is normally made are inherited and transmitted from the past. The issue, for Marx and for critical theory, is how to free human beings from the dead weight of the past, including political, social, and economic institutions within which they are oppressed. For the Frankfurt School, humans have within themselves the capacity, through reason, to produce fundamental or revolutionary change. Nevertheless, Marx's optimism about the outcome of the class struggle allegedly blinded him to the capacity of the state, as in the case of the Third Reich or the Soviet Union, under fascism or communism, to dominate whole societies.

Accepting Marx's essential premise that humans can be liberated from historical circumstances, the Frankfurt School asserts that oppression is not reducible simply to class domination based on control of the means of production. Other forms of domination exist, such as those based on gender, race, religion, ethnicity, or nationalism. Therefore, emancipation encompasses the analysis of other phenomena extending beyond what Marx saw as the proletariat's quest for control of the means of production within Marxian dialectical materialism. According to Linklater, the struggle for emancipation, which is the focus of critical international theory, makes necessary a rejection of the idea that class conflict has been responsible, in dialectical fashion, for advances in political and social development. The struggle for emancipation has been conducted, as Habermas also suggested, in arenas and spheres other than that of control of the means of production. Thus the determinants of history cannot be reduced to economics or technology, however important such factors may be in shaping the state, the nature of warfare, and culture.

The struggle for military power as a basis for the extension of political control over space, a central realist tenet, appear to be at least as important as Marx's emphasis on the means of production in shaping international behavior. Therefore, according to Linklater, both realism and Marxism have a place in constituting a critical international theory which, in addition, must address and answer questions related to how to establish emancipatory political communities as the essential basis for human change, progress, and revolutionism.

THE POST–COLD WAR GLOBAL ECONOMY

In recent decades, international political economists have divided their field into three broad schools of thought—liberal, Marxist, and realist.[107] Liberals look on politics and economics as two separate dimensions. Politics is a public affair; economic activity proceeds according to natural laws that are determined by the sum total of myriad private choices of production and consumption, saving and investment. The typical nineteenth-century liberal believed that if the economy could be insulated against interference by governments, then the creative energies of individuals seeking their own good in a laissez-faire environment would maximize the wealth of nations, as if under the guidance of an invisible hand, as Adam Smith had put it in 1776. Free trade in a market unfettered by the artificial regulations of bureaucrats would ensure prosperity and peace for all.

Whereas orthodox liberals contend that neither politics nor economics should or does dominate the other, Marxists, neo-Marxists, and realists agree that the two orders are closely related and interpenetrate each other. Marxists and realists part company, however, in assigning dominance to one or the other. Realists, as we have seen, see nation-states as the primary actors, which subordinate economics to their quest for power. Joan Edelman Spero argued that the political system shapes the economic system, that political concerns often shape economic policy, and that international economic relations are really political relations.[108] As mentioned previously, the Communist Party of the Soviet Union preached an ideology of economic dominance, but in practice invariably gave priority to the political–military goals for which central economic planning was the means. Perhaps we can see Spero's point as equally applicable to nonsocialist countries by contemplating the interplay of political and economic factors in the domestic and foreign policies of those countries. For example, during the Cold War, for security and political reasons, Western governments imposed penalties on their domestic industries by prohibiting the export of a broad range of technological products to communist countries. An even clearer example is to be found in the trade wars of the 1990s between the forces of the free international market and those of protectionism among the European Union, Japan, the North American Free Trade Area (NAFTA), and the Asia Pacific Economic Cooperation (APEC) countries.

Protectionism has a long history, much longer than that of free trade. Plato, Aristotle, and the medievalists advocated economic self-sufficiency as an ideal for the political community.[109] In the early days of nation-states and capitalism, the preference was for a policy of state-directed trade, known as "mercantilism," aimed at the enhancement of state power and wealth. The classical liberal economists later carried the day with their argument that the most efficient location of manufacturing production is ensured by the law of comparative advantage in a climate of free trade. The old view of comparative specialization, however, cannot explain the fact that trading partners often export and import the same products. Governments frequently manipulate free-market forces in response to pressure from special interest groups that have sufficient domestic political clout. Many of these groups are undoubtedly acting out of their own economic and political motivations, but there is such a diversity of pressures in modern democratic states (political, economic, moral, etc.) that it requires a sophisticated political process to determine their priority. Governments apply strategic trade-policy instruments to promote the national interest (e.g., by maintaining the viability of an industry vital to defense or promoting technological innovation), to stabilize or enhance the national economy (e.g., by forestalling the loss of industry, a rise in the unemployment rate, a wider trade gap, or a currency devaluation), or to protect a specific domestic group (e.g., by providing subsidies to farmers, negotiating export restraints or import quotas, or taking unilateral action to penalize dumping). Ever since World War II, the United States has been the chief proponent of the global free-trade ideology, yet for political reasons (foreign or domestic), it has at times pursued managed-trade policies.[110]

The question of which is the determinant factor in international relations—politics or economics—is one of the most important issues in international-relations theory. No one can reasonably doubt that economics is of growing salience to international politics, but no matter how important economic considerations may become within the global system, they cannot—and should not be allowed to—replace political values, goals, and interests in the architectonic thinking of policymakers. In sum, the authors of this text, while fully recognizing the close reciprocal relationship between international politics and international economics, do not accept either the Leninist or the neo-Marxist explanation of imperialism. We are more impressed, intellectually and scientifically, with the realist than the liberal philosophy of the relation between politics and economics.

NOTES

1. The literature on this subject was influenced by Robert O. Keohane and Joseph S. Nye, *Power and Interdependence: World Politics in Transition* (Boston: Little Brown, 1977); 2nd ed. (Glenview, IL: Scott, Foresman, 1989).
2. Robert L. Heilbroner, "Triumph of Capitalism," *The New Yorker* (January 23, 1989), 88–109, quoted at 108–109.
3. These included Karl Kautsky and Eduard Bernstein (Germany); G. D. H. Cole, R. H. Tawney, Sidney and Beatrice Webb, Harold J. Laski, and Clement Attlee (England); Jules Guesde, Jean Jaurès, and Leon Blum (France); and Daniel DeLeon, Harry W. Laidler, Norman Thomas, Morris Hillquit, and Herbert Marcuse (United States). One could also list several Christian socialists, utopian socialists, anarchists, recent revisionist historians, and advocates of a variety of New Left causes.
4. For a detailed examination of this concept, see Gustav A. Wetter, *Dialectical Materialism: A Historical and Systematic Survey of Philosophy in the Soviet Union* (New York: Praeger, 1963).
5. Karl Marx and Friedrich Engels, *Manifesto of the Communist Party* (New York: International Publishers, 1932), p. 9.
6. See Karl Marx, *Capital: A Critique of Political Economy* (New York: Random House Modern Library, n.d.), especially chaps. 1, 7, 9, 11, 12, 16, 18, and 24 for Marx's most extensive treatment of the concept of surplus value.
7. Karl Marx and Friedrich Engels, *Manifesto of the Communist Party,* p. 11.
8. See Robert C. Tucker, *The Marxian Revolutionary Idea* (New York: Norton, 1970) and *Philosophy and Myth in Karl Marx* (Cambridge, England: Cambridge University Press, 1972); Vendulka Kubalkova and Albert Cruickshank, *Marxism and International Relations* (Oxford, England: Clarendon Press, 1985).
9. John Plamenatz, *Man and Society: Political and Social Theory, Vol. II: Bentham Through Marx* (New York: McGraw-Hill, 1963), p. 310. Hannah Arendt notes in a similar vein that Marx was aware of the role of violence in history but deemed it less important than the contradictions inherent in the old society in bringing about the old society's end, in *On Violence* (New York: Harcourt Brace Jovanovich, 1969), p. 11.
10. See Philip Siegelman's Introduction to J. A. Hobson, *Imperialism: A Study* (Ann Arbor: University of Michigan Press, 1965). Hobson's work was originally published in London by George Allen and Unwin in 1902. Subsequent references are to the 1965 edition.
11. Foster Rhea Dulles, *America's Rise to World Power, 1898–1954* (New York: Harper & Row, 1954), chaps. 2 and 3.
12. Richard Koebner and Helmut Dan Schmidt, *Imperialism: The Story and Significance of a Political Word, 1840–1960* (New York: Cambridge University Press, 1964), p. 249. For a discussion of the anti-Semitic theme in Hobson's thought, see pp. 226–228. George Lichtheim notes that the American Founding Fathers, both Federalists and Republicans, had no qualms about calling the federal union an empire, and that in nineteenth-century England, both Liberals and Tories employed the term *imperialism* for its popular appeal. *Imperialism* (New York: Praeger, 1971), chaps. 4, 5, and 6.

For a thorough analysis of British "imperialism of free trade," see William Roger Louis, ed., *Imperialism: The Robinson and Gallagher Controversy* (New York: New Viewpoints, 1976).

13. Richard Koebner and Helmut Dan Schmidt, *Imperialism,* p. 233.

14. J. A. Hobson, *Imperialism: A Study* (Ann Arbor: University of Michigan Press, 1965), p. 85.

15. Ibid., p. 59.

16. Ibid., pp. 41–45. Later, Italy and Germany employed the argument concerning population pressure to justify their quest for colonies in Africa prior to World War I, and the Japanese did likewise in their Manchurian venture in the early 1930s. However, in all the cases where the lebensraum argument was employed, subsequent movement of population to the conquered areas proved negligible. See N. Peffer, "The Fallacy of Conquest," in *International Conciliation* (New York: Carnegie Endowment for International Peace, No. 318, 1938).

17. J. A. Hobson, op. cit., pp. 46–51.

18. Ibid., pp. 53–54.

19. E. M. Winslow, *The Pattern of Imperialism* (New York: Columbia University Press, 1948), p. 106.

20. J. A. Hobson, op. cit., p. 58.

21. V. I. Lenin, *Imperialism: The Highest Stage of Capitalism* (New York: International Publishers, 1939), p. 89. See the section, "Imperialism and Capitalism," by Alec Nove, "Lenin as Economist," in Leonard Schapiro and Peter Reddaway, eds., *Lenin: The Man, the Theorist, the Leader* (New York: Praeger, 1969), pp. 198–203.

22. "Jingoism is merely the lust of the spectator, unpurged by any personal effort, risk, or sacrifice, gloating in the perils, pains, and slaughter of fellow-men whom he does not know, but whose destruction he desires in a blind and artificially stimulated passion of hatred and revenge. . . . The arduous and weary monotony of the march, the long periods of waiting, the hard privations, the terrible tedium of a prolonged campaign play no part in his imagination; the redeeming factors of war, the fine sense of comradeship which common personal peril educates, the fruits of discipline and self-restraint, the respect for the personality of enemies whose courage he must admit and whom he comes to realize as fellow-beings—all those moderating elements in actual war are eliminated from the passion of the Jingo. It is precisely for these reasons that some friends of peace maintain that the two most potent checks of militarism and of war are the obligation of the entire body of citizens to undergo military service and the experience of an invasion." Hobson, op. cit., p. 215.

23. For the complete works of Lenin, see V. I. Lenin, *Collected Works* (Moscow: Foreign Languages Publishing House, 1963), 44 vols. For a biographical account of Lenin's life, see Louis Fischer, *The Life of Lenin* (New York: Harper & Row Colophon Books, 1965); Robert Payne, *The Life and Death of Lenin* (New York: Simon & Schuster, 1946); Stefan T. Possony, *Lenin: The Compulsive Revolutionary* (Chicago: Regnery, 1964); Christopher Hill, *Lenin and the Russian Revolution* (London: English Universities Press, 1961); Bertram D. Wolfe, *Three Who Made a Revolution* (Boston: Beacon, 1955).

24. See V. I. Lenin, *Collected Works,* Vol. V, pp. 425–529.

25. V. I. Lenin, *Imperialism: The Highest Stage of Capitalism,* op. cit., pp. 16–30.

26. Lenin, *Collected Works,* op. cit., Vol. XIX, pp. 87 and 104.

27. Bernard Taurer, "Stalin's Last Thesis," *Foreign Affairs,* XXXI (April 1953), 374.

28. Ibid., p. 378.

29. See Herbert S. Dinerstein, *War and the Soviet Union* (New York: Praeger, 1959), pp. 68–69, 80–81; Frederick C. Barghoorn, *Soviet Foreign Propaganda* (Princeton, NJ: Princeton University Press, 1964), pp. 92–93; Frederic S. Burin, "The Communist Doctrine of the Inevitability of War," *American Political Science Review*, LVII (June 1963), 352–354; Walter C. Clemens, Jr., "Ideology in Soviet Disarmament Policy," *Journal of Conflict Resolution*, VIII (March 1964), 17–20.

30. Statement to the Fifth Congress of the Polish United Workers' Party, November 12, 1968. L. I. Brezhnev, *Following Lenin's Course: Speeches and Articles* (Moscow: Progress Publishers, 1972).

31. Allen S. Whiting, "Foreign Policy of Communist China," in Roy C. Macridis, ed., *Foreign Policy in World Politics*, 3rd ed. (Englewood Cliffs, NJ: Prentice-Hall, 1967), pp. 223–263; "The Disarmament Issue in the Sino–Soviet Dispute: A Chronological Documentation," Appendix in Alexander Dallin et al., *The Soviet Union, Arms Control and Disarmament* (New York: School of International Affairs, Columbia University, 1964), pp. 238–276; Walter C. Clemens, Jr., *The Arms Race and Sino–Soviet Relations* (Stanford, CA: Hoover Institute on War, Revolution and Peace, 1968), pp. 13–68; William E. Griffith, *Cold War and Co-existence: Russia, China and the United States* (Englewood Cliffs, NJ: Prentice-Hall, 1971).
Lenin wrote in 1916: "Only *after* the proletariat has disarmed the bourgeoisie will it be able, without betraying its world-historical mission, to throw all armaments on the scrap heap; and the proletariat will undoubtedly do this, but *only when this condition has been fulfilled, certainly not before.*" Passage from Lenin's *War Programme of the Proletarian Revolution,* quoted in PRC Letter of June 14, 1963 (italic emphasis in original). In Walter C. Clemens, Jr., *The Arms Race and Sino–Soviet Relations,* op. cit., p. 227.

32. Alistair Buchan, "A World Restored?" *Foreign Affairs* (July 1972); W. A. C. Adie, "China's Strategic Posture in a Changing World," in *Royal United Services Institute and Brassey's Defence Yearbook 1974* (London: Brassey's Annual, 1974); John Gittings, *The World and China 1922–1972* (New York: Harper & Row, 1974), pp. 261–263; Francis O. Wilcox, ed., *China and the Great Powers: Relations with the United States, the Soviet Union and Japan* (New York: Praeger, 1974); Allen S. Whiting, "Foreign Policy of Communist China," in Roy C. Macridis, ed., op. cit., 7th ed. (Englewood Cliffs, NJ: Prentice-Hall, 1989), pp. 251–297.

33. Steven I. Levine, "China in Asia: The PRC as a Regional Power," in Harry Harding, ed., *China's Foreign Relations in the 1980s* (New Haven, CT: Yale University Press, 1984), pp. 117, 124; and Jonathan D. Pollack, "China and the Global Strategic Balance," ibid., pp. 157, 166–169.

34. See Benjamin Lambeth and Kevin Lewis, "The Kremlin and SDI," *Foreign Affairs*, 66 (Spring 1988), 755–770.

35. Hans J. Morgenthau, *Politics Among Nations: The Struggle for Power and Peace,* 4th ed. (New York: Knopf, 1966), p. 42. This definition has been carried in all six editions of the book since 1948.

36. Ibid.

37. Ibid., p. 47. Cf. Raymond Aron, *Peace and War: A Theory of International Relations,* trans. Richard Howard and Annette Baker Fox (New York: Praeger, 1968), p. 259.

38. Raymond Aron, *The Century of Total War* (Boston: Beacon, 1955), chap. 3, "The Leninist Myth of Imperialism," especially p. 59; Morgenthau, *Politics Among Nations,* op. cit., pp. 47–50; William L. Langer, "A Critique of Imperialism," *Foreign Affairs,* XIV (October 1935), 102–115.

39. Jacob Viner, "International Relations Between State-Controlled Economies," in *Readings in the Theory of International Trade*, American Economic Association (Philadelphia: Blakiston, 1949), Vol. IV, pp. 437–458.

40. Joseph A. Schumpeter, *Imperialism and Social Classes*, trans. Heinz Norden, ed. Paul M. Sweezy (Oxford, England: Basil Blackwell, 1951), p. 5.

41. Ibid., p. 6.

42. Morgenthau, *Politics Among Nations*, op. cit., pp. 48–49.

43. Ibid., pp. 84–85. Kenneth E. Boulding has reiterated Schumpeter's view that imperialism was a form of social lag and, from an economic standpoint, unprofitable to the point of being a fraud. "Reflections on Imperialism," in David Mermelstein, ed., *Economics: Mainstream Readings and Radical Critiques*, 2nd ed. (New York: Random House, 1970), p. 201.

44. Joseph A. Schumpeter, *Imperialism and Social Classes*, op. cit., pp. 89–96. Schumpeter's own analysis of imperialism did not go unchallenged. He was faulted for defining imperialism as both "objectless" and "forcible," the expression of a warrior-class social structure that fights only because it is geared for fighting. He therefore excluded from the meaning of imperialism whatever is not due to a warrior-class social structure. Murray Greene, "Schumpeter's Imperialism—A Critical Note," *Social Research* (*An International Quarterly of Political and Social Science*), XIX (December 1952), 453–463. Greene took issue with Schumpeter's thesis that because capitalism is rationalistic, it is antithetical to imperialism, militarism, and armaments.

45. Richard Koebner and Helmut Dan Schmidt, *Imperialism*, op. cit., p. 255.

46. Hans J. Morgenthau, op. cit., p. 47.

47. Joseph A. Schumpeter, op. cit., p. 57.

48. Andrew Mack, "Theories of Imperialism: The European Perspective," *The Journal of Conflict Resolution*, 18 (September 1974), 518.

49. Ibid., where Mack cites as authorities two Marxist critiques of the Leninist theory; Michael Barratt Brown, "A Critique of Marxist Theories of Imperialism" and Harry Magdoff, "Imperialism Without Colonies," in Roger Owen and Bob Sutcliffe, eds., *Studies in the Theory of Imperialism* (London: Longmans, 1973).

50. Raymond Aron, *Peace and War: A Theory of International Relations*, op. cit., p. 261. See also William Langer, "A Critique of Imperialism," op. cit., p. 105.

51. Raymond Aron, *Peace and War*, op. cit., pp. 262–263.

52. Hans J. Morgenthau, pp. 46-47; Aron, *The Century of Total War*, op. cit., pp. 59–62. Referring to the Spanish-American War, Eugene Staley wrote, "The causes of this war, and of the expansionism exhibited in connection with it, have been laid at the door of private investment interests—on the whole, erroneously. Their role was slight compared with that of the interests of the 'yellow' press and of other internal influences in American life which made for chauvinism." *War and the Private Investor* (Chicago: University of Chicago Press, 1935), p. 433. Most diplomatic historians who studied the origins of World War I, including Sidney Bradshaw Fay, G. P. Gooch, A. J. P. Taylor, Bernadotte E. Schmitt, Nicholas Mansergh, and Raymond Sontag, have listed imperialistic rivalry (in its political more than its economic aspects) as one of the background causes of that war, but less important than the interaction of the European alliance systems and nationalisms in a framework dominated by balance-of-power thinking, security apprehensions generated by militarism and armaments competition, and the condition of international anarchy— that is, the absence of organization adequate to ensure peaceful settlement of disputes.

53. Raymond Aron, *The Century of Total War*, op. cit., p. 65; Aron, *Peace and War*, op. cit. p. 267. One additional anomaly might be mentioned. Canada took part in the Boer War, World Wars I and II, and the Korean War, not because its capitalistic interests

were at stake in those wars but because Canada was part of a political empire (the British Empire, Commonwealth and the U.S. NATO alliance) in which the empire leader made the decision for war and Canada followed out of a sense of political loyalty. Gernot Kohler, "Imperialism as a Level of Analysis in Correlates-of-War Research," *The Journal of Conflict Resolution,* 19 (March 1975), 48.

54. Kenneth E. Boulding, "Reflections on Imperialism," op. cit., p. 202.
55. Michael W. Doyle, *Empires* (Ithaca, NY: Cornell University Press, 1986), p. 12. See also pp. 20 and 24.
56. Ibid., p. 12.
57. Ibid., pp. 12–13. Doyle notes that what characterizes empire is control of both foreign and domestic policy. Where only foreign policy is controlled, he uses the term *hegemony.* Ibid., p. 40.
58. Ibid., p. 19.
59. Ibid., pp. 25–28. Cf. also John Gallagher and Ronald Robinson, "The Imperialism of Free Trade," *Economic History Review,* 2nd ser., 6(1) (1953), 1–15; Benjamin Cohen, *The Question of Imperialism* (New York: Basic Books, 1973); David Fieldhouse, *Economics and Empire, 1830–1914* (London: Weidenfeld and Nicholson, 1973); and Tony Smith, *The Pattern of Imperialism* (New York: Cambridge University Press, 1981).
60. Michael W. Doyle, *Empires,* op. cit., pp. 31–33. On this point, see A. P. Thornton, *Doctrines of Imperialism* (New York: Wiley, 1963), p. 4, and J. Woodis, *Introduction to Neo-Colonialism* (New York: International Publishers, 1971), p. 56.
61. André Gunder Frank, "The Development of Underdevelopment," in Robert I. Rhodes, ed., *Imperialism and Underdevelopment: A Reader* (New York: Monthly Review Press, 1970), p. 9.
62. Boulding, "Reflections on Imperialism," op. cit., p. 201.
63. Nikita S. Khrushchev, *For Victory in Peaceful Competition with Capitalism* (New York: Dutton, 1960), pp. 33, 628–629, and 750–751.
64. See also G. Mirsky, "Whither the Newly Independent Countries?" *International Affairs* (Moscow), XII (December 1962), 2, 23–27.
65. Thomas E. Weisskopf, "Capitalism, Underdevelopment and the Future of the Poor Countries," in David Mermelstein, ed., op. cit., pp. 218–223.
66. Harry Magdoff, "The American Empire and the U.S. Economy," chap. 5 in *The Age of Imperialism* (New York: Monthly Review Press, 1969). Reprinted in Robert I. Rhodes, ed., op. cit., pp. 18–44; see especially pp. 18–29.
67. Johan Galtung, *The European Community: A Superpower in the Making* (London: Allen and Unwin, 1973).
68. Speaking of Europe as the economic center, Galtung wrote, "Fragmentation means that whereas the center is well coordinated, even unified in the European Community, the periphery, the developing countries, are split in many ways." Ibid., p. 76. Economists who study the underdeveloped lands typically point out that the foreign trade of countries within the African, Arab, and Latin American regions is largely extraregional; usually less than 10 percent is intraregional.
69. John Galtung, "A Structural Theory of Imperialism," *Journal of Peace Research,* 8(2) (1971), 81–117.
70. P. T. Bauer, "The Economics of Resentment: Colonialism and Underdevelopment," *The Journal of Contemporary History,* 4 (January 1969), p. 59.
71. Ibid., p. 56.
72. Ibid.
73. Hans Kohn, "Reflections on Colonialism," in Robert Strausz-Hupé and Harry W. Hazard, eds., *The Idea of Colonialism* (New York: Praeger, 1958), pp. 6–14.

74. Andrew Mack, "Theories of Imperialism," op. cit., p. 526.

75. Jack Snyder, *Myths of Empire: Domestic Politics and International Ambitions* (Ithaca, NY: Cornell University Press, 1991).

76. See Jan Wszelaki, *Communist Economic Strategy: The Role of East Central Europe* (Washington, DC: National Planning Association, 1959).

77. The Soviet economic offensive was aimed largely at Egypt, India, Syria, Ethiopia, Guinea, Yemen, Afghanistan, Burma, Ceylon, and Indonesia. *Significant Issues in Economic Aid,* Staff Paper of the International Industrial Development Center, Stanford Research Institute, Palo Alto, CA, 1960.

78. Jack Snyder, "The Gorbachev Revolution: A Waning of Soviet Expansionism?" *International Security,* 12 (Winter 1987/1988), 94.

79. Mikhail Gorbachev, *Perestroika: New Thinking for Our Country and the World* (New York: Harper & Row, 1987). Gorbachev was not willing to renounce the mission of the Communist Party, to allow freedom of expression to be carried too far, or to abandon the basic principles of Marxist socialism. "More socialism means more democracy, openness and collectivism in everyday life, more culture and humanism in production, social and personal relations among people, more dignity and self-respect for the individual." Ibid., p. 33. In short, for him, socialism required liberalization and more democracy. See also Stephen M. Meyer, "The Sources and Prospects of Gorbachev's New Political Thinking on Security," *International Security,* 13 (Fall 1988), 124 ff; David Holloway, "Gorbachev's New Thinking," and Robert Legvold, "The Revolution in Soviet Foreign Policy," *Foreign Affairs,* 68 (America and the World 1988–1989), 66–81, 82–98.

80. See Seweryn Bialer and Michael Mandelbaum, eds., *Gorbachev's Russia and American Foreign Policy* (Boulder, CO: Westview Press, 1988); Jerry F. Hough, *Russia and the West: Gorbachev and the Politics of Reform* (New York: Simon & Schuster, 1988); F. Stephen Larrabee, "Gorbachev and the Soviet Military," *Foreign Affairs,* 66 (Summer 1988), 1002–1026; Robert G. Kaiser, "The U.S.S.R. in Decline," *Foreign Affairs,* 67 (Winter 1988/1989), 97–113; Gail W. Lapidus, "Gorbachev's Nationalities Problem," *Foreign Affairs,* 68 (Fall 1989), 92–108; Richard Pipes, "The Soviet Union Adrift," *Foreign Affairs,* 70 (America and the World 1990–1991), 70–87; Elie Abel, *The Shattered Bloc: Behind the Upheaval in Eastern Europe* (Boston: Houghton Mifflin, 1990); Robert G. Kaiser, "Gorbachev: Triumph and Failure," *Foreign Affairs,* 70 (Spring 1991), 16–174; Seweryn Bialer, "The Death of Soviet Communism," *Foreign Affairs,* (Winter 1991/1992), 166–181. Virtually all the works cited agree essentially that Gorbachev was a brilliant political leader who realized that the nation, the party, and the ideology were badly in need of renovation and democratization, but who underestimated the magnitude and consequences of the task. Unable to control the forces he unleashed, he lost credibility, and in the end, he destroyed the system he had set out to save and strengthen.

81. See Ronald D. Asmus, Richard L. Kugler, and F. Stephen Larrabee, "Building a New NATO," *Foreign Affairs,* 72 (September/October 1993), 28–40; Owen Harries, "The Collapse of 'The West'," *Foreign Affairs,* 41–53 (in which the author argues that NATO expansion eastward would ignore Russian strategic sensitivities over its historic security zone and arouse chauvinist reactions); Dimitri Simes, "The Return of Russian History," *Foreign Affairs,* 73 (January/February 1994), 67–82; Zbigniev Brzezinski, "The Premature Partnership," *Foreign Affairs,* (March/April 1994), 67–82; Jacob W. Kipp, "The Zhirinovsky Threat," *Foreign Affairs,* (May/June 1994), 72–86; Carl Bildt, "The Baltic Litmus Test," *Foreign Affairs,* (September/October 1994), 72–85.

82. Koebner and Schmidt, *Imperialism,* op. cit., pp. 321–322.

83. Kenneth E. Boulding, "Reflections on Imperialism," op. cit., p. 202.

84. Flora Lewis, "Superpower Proxy Wars and the Difficulty of Remaining Non-aligned," *New York Times,* July 31, 1978. p. 6. See also David Andelman, "Non-aligned Nations End Divisive Talks; Plan Club Meeting," also *New York Times,* July 31, 1978, p. 1.

85. Robert G. Wesson, *Why Marxism? The Continuing Success of a Failed Theory* (New York: Basic Books, 1976).

86. Adam B. Ulam, *The Bolsheviks* (New York: Macmillan, 1965), p. 311. See also P. T. Bauer, op. cit., pp. 57–58.

87. Anthony James Joes, *Fascism in the Contemporary World: Ideology, Evolution, Resurgence* (Boulder, CO: Westview, 1978), p. 103.

88. See United Nations Centre for Disarmament, *The Relationship Between Disarmament and Development* (New York: United Nations, 1982); Saadet Deger and Somnath Sen, "Disarmament, Development and Military Expenditure," *Disarmament* (a periodic review by the United Nations), 13(3) (1990).

89. See William C. Olson and David S. McLellan, "Population, Hunger and Poverty," in the book they coedited with Fred A. Sondermann, *The Theory and Practice of International Relations,* 6th ed. (Englewood Cliffs, NJ: Prentice-Hall, 1983), p. 270.

90. Mahbub ul Haq, *The Third World and the International Economic Order,* Development Paper No. 22 (Washington, DC: Overseas Development Council, 1976). Reprinted in Olson, McLellan, and Sondermann, eds., op. cit., pp. 325–326.

91. Ibid., p. 326.

92. James Caporaso, "Dependence and Dependency in the Global System," *International Organization,* 32 (Winter 1978), 2.

93. Tony Smith, "The Logic of Dependency Theory Revisited," *International Organization,* 35 (Autumn 1981), 756–757. Smith became less unsympathetic to dependency theory a few years later, conceding that it had prompted those in the mainstream to think in broader, more complex and normative terms about Third World development. "Requiem or New Agenda for Third World Studies," *World Politics,* XXXVII (July 1985).

94. Samuel Valenzuela and Arturo Valenzuela, "Modernization and Dependency: Alternative Perspectives in the Study of Latin American Underdevelopment," *Comparative Politics,* 10 (July 1978), 535–557. The Valenzuelas make it clear that they are criticizing the modernization perspectives of such writers as Sir Henry Maine, Ferdinand Tönnies, Emile Durkheim, Max Weber, Robert Redfield, Harry Eckstein, David Apter, Daniel Lerner, Neil J. Smelser, Alex Inkeles, Cyril Black, Gabriel Almond, James S. Coleman, Talcott Parsons, Seymour Martin Lipset, Kalvin H. Silvert, and others. Other representative works on dependency theory include Fernando Henrique Cardozo and Enzo Faletto, *Dependency and Development in Latin America* (Berkeley: University of California Press, 1979), and André Gunder Frank, *Crisis in the Third World* (New York: Holmes and Meier, 1981). For a critical view of dependency theory, see Tony Smith, "The Underdevelopment of Development Literature: The Case of Dependency Theory," *World Politics,* 31 (January 1979). See also James A. Caporaso, "Industrialization in the Periphery: The Evolving Global Division of Labor," *International Studies Quarterly,* 25 (September 1981), 351. See also David B. Yoffie, "The Newly Industrializing Countries and the Political Economy of Protectionism," *International Studies Quarterly,* 25 (December 1981).

95. Thomas D. Lairson and David Skidmore, *International Political Economy: The Struggle for Power and Wealth* (New York: Harcourt Brace, 1993), pp. 202–204. They conclude that the import-substitution strategy "may once have played a necessary role in

jumpstarting the process of development." Many observers now think that its "rigidities and inefficiencies . . . have more recently served to hinder growth and development." Ibid., p. 204.

96. Stephen Haggard, *Pathways from the Periphery: The Politics of Growth in Newly Industrializing Countries* (Ithaca, NY: Cornell University Press, 1990).

97. A full compendium of NIEO proposals over a 30-year period was compiled by Alfred George Moas and Harry N. M. Winton, librarians of the United Nations Institute for Training and Research (UNITAR): *A New International Economic Order, Selected Documents, 1945–1975,* 2 vols. (New York: United Nations, 1977). See also Jagdish N. Bhaghwati, ed., *The New International and Economic Order: The North–South Debate* (Cambridge, MA: MIT Press, 1977); Karl P. Sauvant and Hajo Hasenpflug, eds., *The NIEO: Confrontation or Cooperation Between North and South* (Boulder, CO: Westview Press, 1977); J. S. Singh, *A New International Economic Order* (New York: Praeger, 1977); D. C. Smyth, "The Global Economy and the Third World: Coalition or Cleavage?" *World Politics,* 29 (April 1977); Robert L. Rothstein, *Global Bargaining: UNCTAD and the Quest for a New International Economic Order* (Princeton, NJ: Princeton University Press, 1979); Edwin Reuben, ed., *The Challenge of the New International Economic Order* (Boulder, CO: Westview Press, 1981); Jeffrey A. Hart, *The New International Economic Order: Cooperation and Conflict in North–South Economic Relations* (New York: St. Martin's Press, 1983); Craig N. Murphy, "What the Third World Wants: An Interpretation of the Development and Meaning of the New International Economic Order Ideology," *International Studies Quarterly,* 27 (March 1983); and Stephen D. Krasner, *Structural Conflict: The Third World Against Global Liberalism* (Berkeley: University of California Press, 1985).

98. Stephen D. Krasner, "Transforming International Regimes: What the Third World Wants and Why," *International Studies Quarterly,* 25 (March 1981). For additional discussions of North–South economic relations and the obstacles to achieving the NIEO, see Roger D. Hansen, *Beyond the North–South Stalemate,* for the Council on Foreign Relations (New York: McGraw-Hill, 1979); John Gerald Ruggie, ed., *The Antinomies of Interdependence* (New York: Columbia University Press, 1983); Robert O. Keohane, *After Hegemony: Cooperation and Discord in the World Political Economy* (Princeton, NJ: Princeton University Press, 1984); and David A. Lake, "Power and the Third World: Toward a Realist Political Economy of North–South Relations," *International Studies Quarterly,* 31 (June 1987) pp. 217–234.

99. See Commission on Transnational Corporations, "Supplementary Material on the Issue of Defining Transnational Corporations," United Nations Economic and Social Council, March 23, 1979, pp. 8 and 11; Commission on Transnational Corporations, *Transnational Corporations in World Development: A Re-examination* (New York: United Nations, 1981), p. 286. Joan Edelman Spero has concluded that more than 95 percent of recorded direct foreign investment flows from countries that are members of the Organization of Economic Cooperation and Development (OECD), and that about three quarters of this total is invested in other OECD countries. *The Politics of International Economic Relations,* 3rd ed. (New York: St. Martin's Press, 1985), p. 134. John R. Oneal and Frances H. Oneal, after comparing the rates of investment return in two groups of countries—LDCs and industrialized—concluded that dependence results in systematic exploitation. "Hegemony, Imperialism and the Profitability of Foreign Investments," *International Organization,* 42 (Spring 1988), 373.

100. John R. Oneal, "Foreign Investment in Less Developed Regions," *Political Science Quarterly,* 103 (Spring, 1988), 137–138.

101. World Bank, *World Development Report 1990* (Oxford, England: Oxford University Press, 1990), pp. 182–183.

102. Among the earlier assessments of the pros and cons of MNCs, see Samuel Hunting-ton, "Transnational Organizations in World Politics," *World Politics,* 25 (April 1973), and John Diebold, "Multinational Corporations: Why Be Scared of Them?" *Foreign Policy,* (12) (Fall 1973); Raymond Vernon, *Sovereignty at Bay* (New York: Basic Books, 1971), and Robert Gilpin, "Three Models of the Future," *International Organization,* 29 (Winter 1979). For later assessments of the impact of MNCs on Third World countries, see Joan Edelman Spero, op. cit., chap. 8; and Thomas D. Lairson and David Skidmore, *International Political Economy: The Struggle for Power and Wealth* (New York: Harcourt Press, 1993), pp. 256–261.

103. For an account of how the Third World countries have adjusted, see Joan Edelman Spero, op. cit., pp. 285–287. Edith Penrose has argued that the presence of MNCs in Third World countries is likely to strengthen the governments of those countries polit-ically and to improve their capabilities over time to control the foreign corporations. "The State and Multinational Enterprises in Less-Developed Countries," in Jeffrey A. Frieden and David A. Lake, eds., *International Political Economy: Perspectives on Global Power and Wealth* (New York: St. Martin's Press, 1987).

104. Immanuel Wallerstein, "The Future of the World Economy," in Terrence K. Hopkins and Immanuel Wallerstein, eds., *Processes of the World System* (Beverly Hills, CA: Sage Publications, 1980). Wallerstein's theory is to be found in two volumes: *The Modern World System I: Capitalist Agriculture and the Origins of the European World Economy in the Sixteenth Century* (New York: Academic Press, 1974), and *The Modern World System II: Mercantilism and the Consolidation of the European World-Economy, 1600–1750* (New York: Academic Press, 1980). See also his *Capitalist World-Economy* (Cambridge, England: Cambridge University Press, 1979).

105. Christopher Chase-Dunn, "Interstate System and Capitalist World-Economy: One Logic or Two?" *International Studies Quarterly,* 25 (March 1981). See the other arti-cles in this special issue on "World System Debates," edited by W. Ladd Hollist and James N. Rosenau. Cf. also William R. Thompson, Christopher Chase-Dunn, and Joan Sokolovsky, "An Exchange on the Interstate System and the Capitalist World-Economy," *International Studies Quarterly,* 27 (September 1983).

106. Andrew Linklater, *Beyond Realism and Marxism: Critical Theory and International Relations* (New York: St. Martin's Press, 1990); see especially pp. 1–34; 165–172.

107. See, for example, Jeffrey A. Frieden and David A. Lake, eds., *International Political Economy,* especially. pp. 1–17; Paul R. Viotti and Mark V. Kauppi, *International Relations Theory, Realism, Pluralism, Globalism* (New York: Macmillan, 1987); Kenneth Waltz, *Theory of International Relations* (Reading, MA: Addison-Wesley, 1979); and the works by Stephen Krasner, Immanuel Wallerstein, Christopher Chase-Dunn, Michael W. Doyle, and others cited in this chapter. Rajan Menon and John R. Oneal have reviewed the debate about imperialism in terms of socialist and capitalist theo-ries, realist theories, and the theory of imperialism as a result of lateral development pressure, as expounded by Nazli Choucri and Robert North (treated in Chapter 8); "Explaining Imperialism: The State of the Art as Reflected in Three Theories," *Polity* (Winter 1987) 169–193.

108. Spero, op. cit., pp. 8–12.

109. Stephen C. Neff, *Friends but No Allies: Economic Liberalism and the Law of Nations* (New York: Columbia University Press, 1990), pp. 11–20.

110. Robert Kuttner, "Managed Trade and Economic Sovereignty," in Frank J. Macchiaro-la, ed., *International Trade: The Changing Role of the United States,* Proceedings of the American Academy of Political Science, 37(4) (1990), 37–53, especially 37–44. For a comparison of foreign trade and domestic economic policies of Japan and the Unit-ed States, which casts light on why each country considers itself an advocate of free

trade and the other a proponent of managed trade, see Samuel Kernell, ed., *Parallel Politics: Economic Policymaking in Japan and the United States* (Washington, DC: Brookings Institution, 1991). See also Cletus C. Coughlin et al., "Protectionist Trade Policies: A Survey of Theory, Evidence and Rationale"; Robert Baldwin, "The New Protectionism: A Response to Shifts in National Economic Power"; and Alison Butler, "Environmental Protection and Free Trade: Are They Mutually Exclusive?" all in Jeffrey A. Frieden and David A. Lake, *International Political Economy: Perspectives on Global Power and Wealth,* 3rd ed. (New York: St. Martin's Press, 1994).

Chapter
7
Microcosmic Theories of Violent Conflict

HUMAN MOTIVATIONS AND CONFLICT

In his significant work *Man, the State and War,* Kenneth N. Waltz distinguished three images of international relations, or levels of analysis, in terms of which we usually try to analyze the causes of war. According to the first image, war is traceable to human nature and behavior.[1] Partisans of the second image seek the explanation of war in the internal structure of the state, and this group includes both liberals (who believe that democracies are more peaceful than dictatorships) and Marxist–Leninists (who believe that capitalist states foment war, while socialism leads to peace). The third image postulates the causes of war in the condition known to the classical political theorists (including Kant, Spinoza, Rousseau, and, in modern times, Waltz himself and other realists and neorealists discussed in Chapter 2) as international anarchy—that is, the absence of those instruments of law and organization that would be efficacious for peacekeeping. In other words, according to Waltz's third image, a deficiency in the state system makes it necessary for each state to pursue its own interests and ambitions, and to act as judge in its own case when it becomes involved in disputes with another state, thereby making the recurrence of conflict, including occasional wars, inevitable and giving rise to the expectation of war as a normal feature of the state system.[2] It is a provocative thought—that the nonexistence of something (an effective peace enforcer) might be a cause of something else, namely, war. In this chapter, we are concerned initially with the first-image explanations of conflict—those microcosmic theories pertaining to individual human nature and behavior. In Chapter 8, we address the macrocosmic theories that deal with larger social and political forces.

The historian is usually interested in the specific and unique events that lead to the outbreak of a particular war. The theorist of international relations cannot ignore the concrete circumstances in which wars occur; these have to be taken into account in the theory. However, the theorist seeks to go beyond specific wars in an effort to explain the more general phenomenon of *war* itself—that is, large-scale fighting or other acts of violence and destruction involving the organized military forces of different states. The causality of international war may be, and probably is, related at least in part to the causality of other forms of violent political conflict, such as civil war, revolution, and guerrilla insurgency; but international war is a specific phenomenon, different from the others, and it requires a specific explanation of its own. Waltz eschews the first two images and prefers the third.

Waltz, in his treatment of first-image theorists, noted that both optimists and pessimists, utopians and realists, agree in diagnosing the basic cause of war as human nature and behavior, but disagree in their answers to the question of whether that nature and behavior can be made to undergo a sufficient change to resolve the problem of war.[3] It is doubtful that either the traditionalists or the behavioral scientists will ever be able to isolate a single dominating causal factor adequate for explaining all violent conflict. Human life is much too diverse and complex to permit such an explanation. A more reasonable presumption is that all forms of violence, whether individual or social, have in common a few explanatory factors, related to what we refer to here as human nature. Microcosmic and macrocosmic theories of human aggression, violence, and war cannot be neatly separated from each other. International war cannot be adequately explained solely by reference to biological and psychological explanations of individual aggressiveness, nor can the latter phenomenon be comprehended purely internally, without reference to social factors. In all fields that study human social behavior, micro and macro approaches must be appropriately blended.

MODERN STUDIES OF MOTIVATIONS AND WAR

In the twentieth century, social scientists have turned increasingly toward motives, reasons, and causal factors that may be operative both in individual human beings and in social collectivities, even though people are not immediately aware of them and do not become consciously aware of them except as a result of scientific observation and methodical analysis. Why do individuals behave aggressively? Why do states and other groups or actors wage wars? The two questions are related, but they are not the same. The former pertains to the inner springs of action within individual human beings, the latter to the decision-making processes of national governments. Violent revolution constitutes yet another phenomenon, different from individual aggressiveness, which is rooted in the biological–psychological characteristics of human beings, and from international war, which is a highly politicized and institutionalized form of learned social behavior. Revolution itself, insofar as it requires organization, leadership, ideology and doctrine, propaganda, planning, strategy, tactics, communications, recruits and supplies, and very often a diplomacy for the acquisition of foreign support, assumes a highly politicized character with the passage of time. Thus, it requires more of a *macrocosmic* than a *microcosmic* analysis. (See the section "Revolution and War" in Chapter 8.)

Psychological (especially social psychological) factors alone might go far to explain instances of anomic[4] violence, such as a food or language riot in India, an outbreak of fighting at a sports event, or a racial disorder at a public beach. However, even in these cases, social psychologists would be wary of "the fallacy of the single factor," and social scientists would argue that some instances of apparently anomic violence might involve an element of political organization and can be adequately comprehended only when placed in their total sociological and political context. In all cases of social violence, it is probably wise to assume the presence of multiple explanatory factors.

The phenomenon of international war is the most complex and difficult of all to explain. It is impossible to describe the causes of war purely in terms of individual psychology, as if it were a case of psychic tensions within individuals mounting to the breaking point and then spilling over into large-scale conflict. Analogies between psychologically based explanations of aggression by individuals and explanations of international war confront yet another problem. In the case of war, those who make the momentous decision to lead a state into war do not themselves do the fighting on the battlefield, even though in an age of total war, the distinction between the battlefield and the home front has sometimes been blurred beyond distinction. Conversely, those who actually engage in battle are likely to have had little or nothing to do with the actual decision to fight. Feelings of hostility, moreover, might indeed be widespread within a nation vis-à-vis another nation and yet war might be averted by astute stateleadership. By the same token, a government can lead a people into a war for which there is little enthusiastic support, if not overt opposition. On this subject, Werner Levi suggests,

> When for instance will certain natural traits or psychological drives find outlets in war, and when in something more peaceful? . . . What these explanations fail to do is to indicate how these human factors are translated into violent conflict involving all citizens, regardless of their individual nature, and performed through a highly complex machinery constructed over a period of years for just such a purpose.
>
> There is always the missing link in these fascinating speculations about the psychological causes of war between the fundamental nature of man and the outbreak of war. . . . Usually, the psychological factors and human traits can be classified as conditions of war more correctly than as causes.[5]

BIOLOGICAL AND PSYCHOLOGICAL THEORIES

Conflict has an inside and an outside dimension. It arises out of the internal dimensions of individuals acting singly or in groups, and also out of external conditions and social structures. At all levels of analysis, larger organized aggregates of human beings affect smaller aggregates and individuals, and vice versa. Individuals and groups are in constant interaction. Which is more important, the larger or the smaller? Scientists from the many disciplines interested in conflict will probably never be able to agree on an answer to this fundamentally important question. The only available solution to this dilemma is to regard social situations and individual inner processes as an organic whole.

Peter Corning has noted that without an understanding of the evolutionary and genetic aspects of behavior, we cannot fully comprehend the inner principles by which human life is organized, and that social scientists must attend increasingly to the interaction between the organism and the environment.[6] Within recent years, a controversial new field has made its appearance in academe—sociobiology. *Sociobiologists* study the genetic roots of social behavior in insects, animals, and human beings, and seek to bridge the gap between the genetic inheritance of individuals on the one hand and social processes and institutions on the other. The founder and most prominent exponent of the new discipline, Edward O. Wilson, professor of science at Harvard and expert on insect societies, postulates that in place of a general aggressive instinct (treated later in this chapter), there are particular patterns of aggressive behavior that have been adapted by various species to ensure their survival in the Darwinian evolutionary scheme. Wilson identified eight categories of aggressive behavior among living beings, some innate, some learned. He analyzes human social evolution primarily in biological rather than in cultural terms. The new field is seen as somewhat pretentious in its effort to combine *ethology* (the study of animal behavior) with sociology and its tendency to make wide-sweeping assertions about the genetic basis of behavior.[7]

All living organisms have certain fundamental, species-specific biological requirements. "These needs include a reasonably pure atmosphere, numerous nutritional requirements, fresh water, sleep, . . . shelter and clothing (or, more generally, maintenance of body temperature), health care, including sanitation, physical security, procreation, and the nurture and training of the young."[8] Over the world as a whole, the greater part of all economic activity is devoted to meeting basic biological needs. Among humans, biological needs quickly shade off into higher psychological needs that are often even more difficult to satisfy—sense of belonging, self-esteem and prestige, self-actualization, and so forth.[9] Much of the political and economic competition and conflict among human societies is traceable to the fact that the demand for things required to satisfy biological and psychological needs always exceeds the supply.[10] This does not necessarily lead to the conclusion that nature is "red in tooth and claw" and that violent aggression and war are inescapable among human societies. Several biologists have insisted that fitness for survival dictates cooperation and mutual aid at least as often as aggressive conflict.[11]

INSTINCT THEORIES OF AGGRESSION

The key microcosmic concept developed by biologists and psychologists for the explanation of conflict is *aggression*. Normally, we think of aggression as a form of violent behavior directed toward injuring or killing a human being, or damaging or destroying a nonhuman entity. Some writers have distinguished between *hostile aggression*, the aim of which is to inflict injury, and *instrumental aggression*, the purpose of which is to secure extraneous rewards beyond the victim's suffering. This distinction has been criticized as misleading by Albert Bandura, who argues that most acts of hostile aggression serve ends other than the mere production of injury, and hence are instrumental.[12] Bandura defines aggression as behavior that results in personal injury (either psychological or physical) or in destruction of property, but he insists on the importance of the "social labeling process"—that is, on social judgments that determine which injurious or destructive acts are to be called "aggressive." Neither the surgeon who makes a painful incision nor the bulldozer operator who razes a condemned building is accused of committing aggression.[13]

Do human beings carry within their genetic or psychic structures an ineradicable instinct or predisposition for aggression? Given the way in which the debate about instinctive behavior has developed in the twentieth century, it is useful to examine first the positions taken earlier by certain psychologists. Generally, psychologists have long agreed that aggression is to be understood in some sort of stimulus–response framework. A basic issue that arose in their field early in this century was whether aggressive tendencies are innate, instinctual, and ever-present in humans, or whether they appear only as a result of externally produced frustration.

Leading figures identified with the instinct theories of aggression during the early decades of the century were William James (1842–1910) and William McDougall (1871–1938). McDougall, the leading British psychologist of his day, considered instinct as a psychophysical process inherited by all members of a species; it was not learned, but it could be modified by learning. McDougall took issue with the psychoanalysts who considered the aggressive impulse as ever-present in humans and constantly seeking release. McDougall insisted that the "instinct of pugnacity," as he called it (1 of the 11 he identified), became operative only when instigated by a frustrating condition.[14] He did not look on human aggressiveness as a built-in impulse constantly seeking release.

The most famous and most controversial of the instinct theories was that of the so-called death instinct, put forth by Sigmund Freud. Originally, Freud was inclined to the view that aggression results from frustration, especially the frustration of the sexual impulses.[15] After World War I, however, Freud postulated the existence in the human being of a fundamental *eros*, life instinct, and a fundamental *thanatos*, death instinct. In no other way was the Austrian psychoanalyst able to explain why millions of men went to their death on the battlefield between 1914 and 1918.[16] For Freud, all instincts were directed toward the reduction or elimination of tension, stimulation, and excitation. The motivation of pleasure-seeking activity is to attain an unstimulated condition—a sort of nirvana or absence of all desire. Death involves the removal of all excitation. Hence all living things aspire to "the quiescence of the inorganic world."[17] Nonetheless, people go on living despite the death instinct, because the life instinct channels the annihilative drive away from the self toward others. Aggressive behavior thus provides an outlet for destructive energies that might otherwise lead to suicide. According to this hypothesis, the recurrence of war and conflict becomes a necessary periodic release by which groups preserve themselves through diverting their self-destructive tendencies to outsiders.[18]

Most contemporary psychologists reject Freud's hypothesis of the death wish as the basis for aggression theory. Professor Leonard Berkowitz called it "scientifically unwarranted"[19] and deficient from the standpoint of positivist logic and modern experimental science. He maintained that Freudian theory attributes the cause of present behavior to a future goal—that is, the reduction or removal of excitation. He also argued that research performed with animals negates the validity of the notion that all behavior is aimed at the reduction of tension, inasmuch as "organisms frequently go out of their way to obtain additional stimulation from their external environment."[20] It should be remembered that Freud never adduced any compelling body of evidence in support of his hypothesis; hence, there is no scientific need to disprove it.[21] Freud fails to explain the causes of war.

ANIMAL-BEHAVIOR STUDIES

In recent decades, one of the most rapidly advancing branches of biological science, as we have noted, has been *ethology*—the study of animal behavior in all its aspects, with particular emphasis on the four basic animal drives of reproduction, hunger, fear, and aggression.

Human behavior and animal behavior are quite dissimilar; in some respects, though, they may be analogous, and a comparison of basic similarities and subtle differences can help us to avoid oversimplified single-factor explanations. From a knowledge of animal behavior, we cannot directly infer anything about human behavior. "Work on one species," according to Elton B. McNeil, "can serve as a model only for the formation of hypotheses about other species."[22] Thus, although an examination of animal studies can furnish no direct proof as to the way human beings act, it can suggest fruitful areas for future research. The principal caveats to remember, of course, are that humans are vastly more complex than even the most highly developed animals, that the computing organism of the human nervous system lends itself to almost unlimited learning and adaptation, and that, above all, human beings exist in a moral–spiritual order.

The causes of aggressive behavior in animals are relatively few. Males, for example, fight over food, females, and territory; females do so to protect the young. All exhibit hostility when strange members of their own species are introduced into their midst, when others make off with objects toward which they have become possessive, and when their expectations have been first aroused and then frustrated. Researchers have found that there is a relationship between aggressiveness and the production of the male hormone (even though in a few species, the female is more aggressive than the male); that within a species, some breeds may be more aggressive than others; that the so-called instinctive targets of aggression (such as the mouse as target for the cat) appear to be more a matter of learning than of heredity; that fighting within a species may produce intricate patterns of submission and dominance; that an animal will fight rather than be deprived of status; that repeated success in fighting can make an animal more aggressive; and that various forms of electrical, chemical, and surgical interventions into the brain can produce predictable alterations in animal aggressiveness.[23] Studies have also indicated that the same principles of learning on which the stimulation of conflict behavior is based may be applied in reverse, as it were, to control and reduce the aggressive urge.[24]

Recent feminist approaches to international-relations theory have emphasized the implications of gender differences for conflict behavior. Do women and men have different interests, perspectives, and motivations, based solely or even largely on gender? Is gender more important than class or national identity in defining the basis for conflict? Are women more—or perhaps less—innately prone than men to aggressive action? What is most apparent in addressing such questions is the obvious fact that wars have been waged, won or lost, and studied almost exclusively by men. Although decisions about war in advanced, democratic societies are no longer exclusively the preserve of men, it remains the case that men still heavily influence how and whether wars will be fought and concluded.

According to feminist writings, gender has been of crucial importance in sustaining military activities. Militarism has been more fully associated with men than with women. Writers such as Spike Peterson and Cynthia Enloe go so far as to ask whether militarism in the absence of masculinism is possible, suggesting that the two are clearly intertwined.[25] The idea of armed combat is a male characteristic if only because of the fact that men, rather than women, historically compose political–military decision-making units, as well as the ranks of armed combatants. Therefore, militarism helps to sustain male dominance. Although men are the principal actors in military situations, feminist writers assert, major effects of their military actions are felt by women, who compose the civilian populations increasingly targeted in modern warfare. There are gender-differentiated effects resulting from war. Women are affected in ways that differ from men. For example, women care for those who are disabled by war. Women, as well as children, become refugees and noncombatant casualties. To what extent, feminist writers ask, has the domination of international relations by men both shaped the conflict setting and defined the security agenda? What would have been different in the absence of such control? Is it a paradox that women seek equality in the military?

John Paul Scott denies that there is any physiological evidence pointing to a spontaneous instinct for fighting within the body. "There is, however, an internal physiological mechanism which has only to be stimulated to produce fighting."[26] As Scott sees it, aggression is the result of a learning process in which the motivation for fighting is increased by success; the longer success continues, the stronger the motivation becomes. Scott therefore roots the aggressive impulse in physiological processes but demands a stimulus from the environment and rejects the concept of self-activation.

Generally speaking, biologists have been less reluctant than psychologists to speak of instinct—not so much as an explanation of an inherited pattern of behavior (through genetic transmission) as a short-hand description of those behavior differences that are determined by the interaction of heredity and environment.[27] However, most biologists now prefer the term *innate behavior* over the older term *instinct*.

LORENZ: INTRASPECIFIC AGGRESSION

Konrad Lorenz, of the Max Planck Institute of Behavioral Physiology, studied more than 40 species of fish, dogs, birds, rats, deer, and farmyard animals, and he concluded that aggression is something very different from the destructive principle of the Freudian death wish. For Lorenz, aggression is an instinct, which under natural conditions helps to ensure the survival of the individual and the species.[28] The typical aggressive instinct, he says, occurs among members of the same species, not between members of different species; in short, it is *intra*specific rather than *inter*specific, and it is best illustrated by the tenacity with which a fish, mammal, or bird will defend its territory against others of its own species. It thereby serves a species-preserving function, in the Darwinian sense, by spacing members of a species over the available habitat instead of bunching together excessively. Nonaggresive species do not form love bonds, but all species that exhibit bond behavior for mutual protection of mating partners and safe rearing of the young are highly aggressive toward territorial neighbors, perhaps because the sexual and family bond must overcome the tendency toward repulsion of others at the very heart of the individual's territory, where intraspecific aggression ought to be strongest.[29] The aim of the aggressive urge, Lorenz insists, is to ward off the intruder, possess the female, or protect the brood, not to exterminate fellow members of the species. He described a phenomenon that he termed *ritualization of aggression*, a fixed motor pattern involving a ceremonialized series of menacing gestures to ward off interloping members of the same species without resort to actual violence.[30]

According to Lorenz, several animal species have developed some remarkable aggression-inhibiting mechanisms or appeasement gestures. The wolf, for example, bares its neck to the fangs of a victorious foe, giving the latter pause and the former time to leave. Lorenz laments that weak creatures (such as doves, hares, and chimpanzees) that normally lack the power to kill a foe of their own size and can rely on fleeing have not been under pressure to develop inhibitions against killing their own kind. He places humans in the same category (apart from their invention of technological weapons), and deems them particularly dangerous because of this combination, but he does not think, as some writers do, that humans are uniquely vicious as killers of their own kind.[31] He has no doubt that humans are vastly more advanced and complex than all other primates, but he warns that the very faculties of conceptual thought and verbal speech that elevate them to a level above all other creatures pose the risk of extinction to humanity.[32] Lorenz recognized that there is a subtle relationship between the two factors of adaptation—innate behavior and learning in the environment. From studies of aggression in certain species of fish, dogs, birds, rats, deer, and farmyard animals, Lorenz concluded that aggression is something very different from the destructive principle expressed in Freud's hypothetical thanatos. According to Lorenz, aggression, the effects of which are frequently equated with those of the death wish, is an instinct like any other, and in natural conditions, it helps just as much as any other to ensure the survival of the individual and the species.[33] (One may hope that this is the central meaning implicit in the ending of the Cold War.)

Lorenz has been criticized by analysts who see nurture as more important than nature as a determinant of behavior. Erich Fromm rejects the theory of all instinctivists who stress the innate character of aggression (including Lorenz's relatively benign form) as traceable to conservative or reactionary attitudes. In his view, such a theory absolves human beings of a sense of responsibility for self-destructive, belligerent behavior, and it offers little hope for lasting peace and democracy.[34] Behavioral psychologist B. F. Skinner and anthropologist Ashley Montagu also take issue with Lorenz. While admitting that there is such a thing as instinct in human beings, they contend that as a component of behavior, it is much less important than conditioning and learning.[35] Social-learning theorist Albert Bandura faults Lorenz for weak scholarship, for errors of fact and questionable interpretations, and for failing to differentiate inborn patterns of behavior from those resulting from experimental learning.[36] Fellow ethologists have criticized Lorenz not only for extrapolating from his animal studies to humans, but also for reaching allegedly wrong conclusions about animals in general after having studied a relatively small number of species.[37]

Other biological factors appear to have some relationship to human aggressive behavior. Prolonged hunger or chronic malnutrition is likely to affect the operations of the brain and other organs, as well as the energy, judgment, and behavior of humans. Francis A. Beer, however, probably goes too far when he suggests that Third World governments, possessing advanced military technology and faced with mass starvation, may threaten, provoke, or launch nuclear war over the issue of hunger.[38] In all likelihood, it is not the *leaders* of states experiencing mass starvation who themselves will be hungry. Therefore, especially in cases of authoritarian or totalitarian regimes, the impact of hunger on collectivities of *individuals* may be irrelevant to decisions by *leaders* to start a war. Here again, we confront the conceptual problem of inferring behavior at the state level from the motivations, interests, and behavioral patterns of individuals.

Still other writers have suggested that conditions of human overcrowding can cause hyperirritability, fighting, and interference with all normal behavior patterns.[39] Moreover, it has been plausibly argued that an international crisis can be a stress-inducing stimulus for political leaders and decision makers (even though some may feel a sense of elation in the midst of crisis pressures), and that their performance under stress may be significantly affected by such factors as health, age, fatigue (especially sleep deprivation), circadian and diurnal rhythms, and the intake of tranquilizing drugs or other medication. Other examples could be drawn from the field of biopolitics, but these few will serve to illustrate the variety of ways in which biological factors are said to have a bearing on human conflict behavior and political decision making.[40] (See Chapter 11.)

FRUSTRATION–AGGRESSION THEORY

Most psychologists today trace individual aggression to some form of frustration. The frustration–aggression theory is a relatively old one, suggested at one time or another by McDougall, Freud, and others. It received its modern scientific expression in the work of John Dollard and his colleagues at Yale University, who began with the assumption that "aggression is always a consequence of frustration" and that frustration always leads to some form of aggression. They defined frustration as "an interference with the occurrence of an instigated-goal response at its proper time."[41] When a barrier is interposed between persons and their desired goals, extra energy is mobilized, which flows "over into generalized destructive behavior."[42] Deprivation that is unimportant to the individual differs from a threat to a life goal; only the latter, said Abraham Maslow, causes frustration.[43] According to the Dollard study, aggression does not occur if the deprivation is unperceived. Not every frustrating situation produces overt aggression. Acts of aggression may be inhibited if they are expected to lead to punishment. The frustrating barrier-target may be physically, psychologically, or socially immune to attack—stronger, vested with an aura of authority, sacred in character, capable of retaliating with socially approved punishment, or otherwise rendered invulnerable. In such cases, direct aggression may give way to indirect aggression, which may be displaced toward a target not responsible for the original frustration, converted into imagining or wishing injury to the target, or turned inward regressively, in self-castigation, self-injury, or, in the most extreme case, suicide. Any act of aggression is supposed to produce *catharsis*—that is, a release of aggressive energy and a reduction in the instigation to aggression.[44]

Like most theories, this one has been criticized and modified since it was formulated in the early 1940s. Psychologists are now widely agreed that frustration may be worked off with different types of responses, one of which is aggression, and that there are other causes of aggression besides frustration.[45] Some argue that frustration exerts no significant influence as a source of aggression, when compared with social-learning factors.[46] Psychologists are still far from agreement as to whether the frustration–aggression nexus is a simple and virtually automatic stimulus–response pattern or whether such emotional states as anger and fear must be or can be interposed. Similarly, there is disagreement as to whether additional cues, releasers, or other triggering stimuli must be present for aggression actually to occur. What constitutes a frustration is not a completely objective matter; it often depends on cognition and interpretation by the individual.[47] Various types of frustrations may lead to different kinds of aggressive reactions.[48] Although it may be relatively easy to see the operation of the frustration–aggression syndrome in children, it is considerably more ambiguous in adults.

The frustration–aggression theory appeals to the common sense of most people, who know from personal experience that they have at times felt aggressive urges after being frustrated. There can be little doubt of its utility when it is applied to certain limited and simpler aspects of individual and small-group behavior. Its use, however, is not appropriate for extrapolating from relatively simple stimulus–response experiments to an explanation of more complex modes of human action, at the much broader level of collective social behavior. The Dollard group sought to explain the lynching of blacks by whites in the American South earlier in this century and the scapegoating of Jews in Nazi Germany as due to the displacement of aggression flowing from economic frustration. They did this without offering any substantiating evidence that such a transfer can in fact be made.[49] The Dollard study suggested that even the Marxist theory of the class struggle depends implicitly on the frustration–aggression principle.[50]

Shifting the analysis of frustration from the plane of the individual to that of the society gives rise to a major level-of-observation, or level-of-analysis, problem. Although it may be quite easy to see the frustration–aggression hypothesis validated in experiments with individuals, it is more difficult to verify the hypothesis at the level of large-group behavior. The time factor is quite different. Individuals react quickly to frustration. Social-psychological phenomena, apart from the behavior of a crowd that is deliberately incited to violence, usually develop at a slower rate. Frustrating situations are perceived more slowly; the perceptions are less uniform and the interpretations more diverse; the extended time frame provides greater opportunity for individuals to adjust; the variety of responses is broader for large groups than for individuals; responses to frustrating situations are likely to vary according to the cultural values of different groups within the social structure; and, perhaps most importantly, a whole complex of external sociological (rather than internal psychological) factors pertaining to crowd behavior contributes toward determining the response to frustration. Hence, it may be possible to verify the frustration–aggression hypothesis in the behavior of smaller, unstructured groups (e.g., such anomic outbursts as the rioting of an unorganized mob), but it is much more difficult, and perhaps impossible, to apply the theory in any precise way to the behavior of larger, more highly institutionalized social entities.[51]

Furthermore, it should be emphasized that most exponents of the frustration–aggression explanation are careful to exclude learned aggression from the scope of their theory. Learned aggression is important to remember in any consideration of organized conflict (such as war, revolution, ethnic conflict, and guerrilla insurgency), in which training for aggressive conduct plays a significant role. The organized warfare that is characteristic of human societies requires a high degree of social learning and does not flow from individual aggressiveness.

SOCIALIZATION, DISPLACEMENT, AND PROJECTION

The frustration–aggression school has attempted to move from the individual to the social level more by logical inference than by experimentation. The principal conceptual mechanisms by which the transfer is made are the socialization of aggression, displacement, and projection. Psychologists hold that the process of acquiring social habits invariably gives rise to frustrations, inasmuch as every forced modification of spontaneous behavior from childhood to adulthood interferes with goal responses.[52] Frustration–aggression patterns are culture-bound; both the factors that make for frustration in human beings and the directions in which aggressive impulses are turned—or the targets of aggression—will depend largely on the values of the specific cultural system. Every society imposes social controls on the spontaneous behavior of individuals. Thus, every social system produces in its members frustrations that might eventually lead to fear, hatred, and violent aggression. Every culture must develop its own solution to the problem of socially managing the aggressive impulses of its members.[53] The socialization of aggression takes place in all human societies, attenuating hostile action among members of the in-group by directing aggressive impulses against out-groups.[54]

A child who is frustrated by the decision of a parent may seek release by substituting a different object of aggression, such as a toy, a piece of furniture, a sibling, another child in the neighborhood, a teacher, a pet, or a neighbor's property. The repression of hostile impulses from the level of consciousness can help in the displacement process by allowing the individual to forget the identity of the original source of the frustration.[55] Repression can lead to projection, which involves attributing to, and exaggerating in, others the unfavorable qualities and malicious motives that one is reluctant to recognize in oneself. Individuals seek to reduce their guilt feelings by projecting their intolerable thoughts and feelings to others. Once they have fastened on their target, perceptual distortion sets in; everything in the target's behavior confirms and justifies their suspicions.[56]

It is quite common for psychologists, especially social psychologists, to cite the frustration–aggression–displacement syndrome as the explanation of hostile attitudes toward scapegoat groups within a society and toward foreign nations.[57] However, it is not clear how the leap is made, or even whether it can logically be made, from individual psychological theory to the analysis of attitudes and behavior at the level of large sociological entities, even if children do assimilate the attitudes and prejudices of parents and other adults toward so-called enemy groups. In a different vein, Marc Howard Ross has found that, whereas affectionate child-rearing practices and close child–parent ties are associated with cooperative attitudes and a low propensity to violence, harsh socialization practices and male gender identity conflict (often the result of child–father distance) tend to increase hostile attitudes and aggressive behavior.[58]

The mechanism by which individual psychic attitudes and complexes of a quasi-pathological character are translated into the concrete political decisions of leaders building up toward the actual outbreak of organized conflict has not yet been adequately defined and described, much less experimentally tested, in a manner intelligible to political scientists. Undoubtedly, the frustrations of human beings form an important part of the total matrix out of which social conflict arises. The presence of widespread frustration would seem to lend a conflict potential to any social situation. It might be said to constitute a prerequisite or a necessary condition, at least for some forms of collective aggression.[59] Nevertheless, we do not understand the relationship between childhood frustration experiences (with their accompanying effects on personality) and adult sociopolitical attitudes. The frustration–aggression–displacement syndrome alone cannot supply both the necessary and the sufficient conditions for collective aggression on a large scale. Frustration might supply the potential for conflict, but a trigger mechanism is required, and the potential must somehow be organized and given specific direction.

One of the most glaring deficiencies in the frustration–aggression–displacement theory is its failure to explain adequately why particular foreign groups are selected as targets of displaced aggression, especially when alternative targets are available.[60] At various times, it has been suggested that they are chosen because they are visible, because they are different and strange, because they have been traditionally mistrusted and disliked, or because they are most feared. At the level of international relations, the selection of conflict targets has much more to do with macrocosmic factors—political, economic, ideological, and sociocultural—than with the inner frustrations of individuals.

Social-learning theorist Albert Bandura cites anthropological evidence that in some cultures, aggression is not the typical response to frustration. He contends that the definition of frustration has become so broad as to lose meaning because it may include not only interfering with the achievement of desired goals, but also personal insults, subjection to pain, deprivation of rewards, and experience of failure. He sees frustration as only one, and not necessarily the most important, factor affecting the expression of aggression. He agrees that the threat of punishment, on the other hand, is more complex than originally believed. Convinced of the great complexity of human responsiveness in various situations, Bandura sets forth a sophisticated and somewhat intricate theory of aggressive behavior based not on inner impulses or drives, but on social learning, social contexts and roles, response-feedback influences, modeling and reinforcement, and the learned ability to assess the rewarding and punishing consequences of any given action.[61]

LEARNED AGGRESSION AND MILITARY TRAINING

Those who have pondered the causes of war seem at times unable to make up their minds whether the frequency and ferocity of war in history are due to the fact that human beings like to fight, or whether most people actually hate to go to war but perform their soldierly duties out of a sense of obligation to serve their country, or to make a sacrifice for preserving ideals and loved ones, or simply because they are coerced by conscription or peer pressures, conditioned to fight during military training, and frightened at the prospect of death if they do not kill first.[62] Within two consecutive pages of a single work, we are told, somewhat contradictorily, not only that people are naturally inclined to do battle, and to hurl themselves with profound passion into war on slight or nonexistent pretexts, but also that human beings find the sight of the gore of warfare so utterly repugnant because resistance to killing is rooted in their whole psychic history, that hatred of the enemy is difficult to inculcate.[63]

Bandura has shown that the conversion of socialized individuals into effective military combatants requires a carefully conceived and executed training program. People who have been brought up to abhor killing as immoral and criminal must be made to accept killing in war as justified. Only in this way can they escape the self-condemnation consequent on taking human life in battle.[64] The soldier is taught that he or she is fighting for family and friends, for country and civilization, for a cherished way of life and moral values, and perhaps for other high ideals—for example, in defense of religion, democracy, freedom, or lasting peace.[65] Recruits to military service must be completely reoriented from familiar civilian ways. They are issued new, distinctive clothing and are indoctrinated with new beliefs and modes of behaving. Many behavioral patterns are regulated in accordance with a military code of discipline, under which automatic compliance with orders is expected. Soldiers are given an intensive, practical training in the techniques of warfare, designed to inculcate a host of survival and combat skills, familiarize them with equipment and tactics, reduce the fear of battle, and enhance fighting-unit solidarity, morale, and coordination.[66]

Despite the assertion of many social scientists that human beings kill enthusiastically for abstract ideas and theories, those who have made a careful, systematic study of the biological and psychological impulses to aggression do not argue that the typical soldier, in waging war, is working out any sort of aggressive instinct or frustration–aggression–displacement syndrome. If politically organized communities really thought that human beings are as innately aggressive as some intellectuals take them to be (perhaps thereby passing judgment on themselves rather than on humanity), societies in all probability would long ago have felt some need at the end of a war to devote a significant effort to the retraining of ex-soldiers to peacetime life—at least comparable to the kind of training required to inculcate a warlike spirit. A minority of veterans may be psychologically disturbed and prone to violent behavior as a result of wartime experiences,[67] but most veterans seem able to manage the transition from war to civilian life without special conditioning programs. This is a rather hopeful sign.

◆

LEARNING, IMAGES, AND INTERNATIONAL CONFLICT

Social psychologists and others have long wondered how human beings (leaders, elites, publics) form their attitudes about the world and other nations. Following World War II, UNESCO (United Nations Educational, Scientific and Cultural Organization) called for an inquiry into the influences that predispose to international aggressiveness on the one hand and to nationalistic hostility and aggressiveness on the other. Hadley Cantril urged governments to become aware of the state of mind of the people with whom it must deal at home and abroad—their feelings and aspirations, frustrations and fears, customs and traditions.[68] (This is difficult enough for scholars who focus on one country in which they have lived for a long time; it is a formidable task indeed for the staff of a bureaucratic structure such as a foreign office or intelligence agency to become familiar with nearly all countries in the international system and to transmit this knowledge efficiently to political decision makers, as needed.) More than a decade earlier, Harold Lasswell had suggested a more narrow (but not necessarily more manageable) approach. Lasswell took Thucydides's three basic motives of human action—fear, interest, and honor—and renamed them safety, income, and deference. Following such European sociologists as Gaetano Mosca, Vilfredo Pareto, and Karl Mannheim, Lasswell stressed the importance of studying the attitudes and behavior not of the masses but of the elites, and he advocated a type of war-preventive politics that would probe the psychological and social roots of the personal insecurity of key leaders who can provoke foreign crises and make moves that lead to war.[69] Some leaders at times have displayed what Karen Horney identified as a neurotic search for glory, in which individuals confuse their real selves with an idealized self-image that demands personal triumph and visible success, perhaps to vindicate humiliations experienced earlier in life.[70]

More recently, Bernard Susser has written,

Whatever the methodological difficulties it poses, the psychological approach to politics is inevitable, and irreplaceable. There would be virtually universal agreement, for example, that Lyndon Johnson's character is critical for understanding the United States' role in the Vietnam War. Who would wish to disavow the intimate link between Hitler's psychopathology and the phenomenon of national socialism? Could we consider severing Stalin's personal idiosyncrasies from the great purges of the 1930s or Saddam Hussein's from the Gulf Crisis of 1990–1991? Would anyone seriously contend that the dramatic power needs exhibited by many political leaders are explicable without psychological categories? In short, the psychological aspect of political behavior is manifest and critical even though our ability to get at it with precision and reliability leaves much to be desired.[71]

The images that individuals and societies form of foreign cultures, peoples, nations, and leaders are a product of diverse sources: folklore; childhood experiences; attitudes of parents and teachers, churches and school systems; newspapers, magazines, and books read (by dwindling numbers); information, ideas, and impressions received from radio, movies, and television; opinions and prejudices of peer groups (co-workers, professional associates, friends, and acquaintances); and the particular goals and policies of political parties, organized interests, governmental leaders, official elites, and agencies. In modern democratic states, the question is still open as to whether elites or the voting masses play the more determinative role in forming modal national images of foreign countries, from friendly allies to dangerous enemies. Even this question is a misleading simplification, given the complexity of the interactive process in modern systems of political communication, marked by positive and negative feedback (see Chapter 3; the question of whether democracies are less war-prone than nondemocratic states is treated at some length in Chapter 8).

Kenneth Boulding, an economist rather than a psychologist, noted that the behavior of complex political organizations is determined by decisions that are in turn the functions of the decision maker's image. The image is a product of messages received in the past—not a simple accumulation of messages but a highly structured piece of informational capital. Every nation is a complex of the images of the persons who think about it; hence, the image is not one but many. The images of the decision makers are more important than the images of the masses. For both groups, impressions of nationality are formed mostly in childhood and usually in the family group. He dismisses as a fallacy the notion that the image is imposed by the powerful on the masses. According to Boulding, the folk-image is a mass image, shared by rulers and ruled alike.[72]

That last statement about the folk image may seem a bit archaic, especially for industrially advanced societies, but it may still be quite valid for less developed communities, and perhaps not entirely inapplicable to any country. Nevertheless, it is probably the case that wherever audiovisual technology spreads, the masses become more vulnerable to propagandistic manipulation by those capable of controlling the media—charismatic leaders, governments, opinion-molding elites, and financial interests. In democratic states, all the influential forces are rarely found to be moving in the same direction: There is much competition and conflict among political ideologies and parties, as well as divergent economic, social, and cultural interests. Moreover, increasingly frequent attitude surveys show that public opinion can shift substantially within relatively short periods of time. The picture is further complicated by the fact, acknowledged by most social scientists, that image formation often reflects a process of selective perception, misperception, and perceptual distortion.[73] In an era when the human mind is inundated daily with new information, people tend to take shortcuts and simplify their images of the world by fitting new data into their existing mental schemas, and by filtering out facts that run counter to their existing prejudices while incorporating those that reinforce well-entrenched stereotypes.[74]

The notion of mirror images became popular during the Cold War and was based on the assumption that the people of two countries involved in a prolonged hostile confrontation develop fixed, distorted attitudes that are really quite similar. Each group of people sees itself as virtuous, restrained, and peace-loving, and views the adversary nation as deceptive, imperialistic, and warlike. Arthur Gladstone described it in this way,

> Each side believes the other to be bent on aggression and conquest, to be capable of great brutality and evil-doing, to be something less than human and therefore hardly deserving respect or consideration, to be insincere and untrustworthy, etc. To hold this conception of the enemy becomes the moral duty of every citizen, and those who question it are denounced. Each side prepares actively for the anticipated combat, striving to amass the greater military power for the destruction of the enemy. . . . The approaching war is seen as due entirely to the hostile intentions of the enemy.[75]

According to social psychologists, the perception of the enemy, even though it may be erroneous, can help to shape reality and bring on the self-fulfilling prophecy: When suspicions run high, a defensive move by one side may look provocative to the other, evoking from the latter a further defensive reaction that serves only to confirm the suspicions of the former.[76] Urie Bronfenbrenner argued that American and Soviet citizens believed essentially the same things about each other's societies: *They* were the aggressors, *their* government exploited and deluded the people, the mass of *their* people were not really sympathetic to the regime, *they* could not be trusted, and *their* policy verged on madness.[77] Even within the restricted context of Soviet–American relations, the concept of the mirror image had some serious problems. In some hands, it led to pseudocorollaries:

1. The social and political values of the two sides were scarcely distinguishable from each other.
2. Neither party could properly be cast in the role of aggressor or defender.
3. Both sides were equally right, equally wrong, and equally responsible for pursuing policies that produced international tensions.
4. The reduction of image distortion could be accomplished with equal ease on both sides.

The advocates of mirror-image theory often made some effort to dissociate themselves from these illogical inferences. Ralph K. White warned, "The proposition that 'there is probably some truth on both sides' should be distinguished from the quite different proposition that there is probably an equal amount of truth on both sides."[78] Urie Bronfenbrenner called attention to an important asymmetry:

> It proved far easier to get an American to change his picture of the Soviet Union than the reverse. Although showing some capacity for change, Soviet citizens were more likely than Americans to cling to their stereotypes and to defend them by denial and displacement. . . . Soviet society would reveal a stronger predilection . . . for black-and-white thinking, moral self-righteousness, mistrust, displacing of blame to others, perceptual distortion, and denial of reality.[79]

The concept of the mirror image in international relations was logically related to a number of suggestions put forth at that time for reducing the hostility of the Cold War, as well as the risks of hot war between the superpowers, through unilateral initiative by one side, designed to reduce international tensions and evoke reciprocal gestures of cooperation from the other side. The basic idea, of course, was that the process of relating tensions, no less than the process of exacerbating them, is a reaction process, and that if one side can bring itself to break the vicious circle and take the initiative by making friendly gestures and concessions, the behavior of the other will sooner or later change for the better.[80]

AGGRESSION DIVERSION AND REDUCTION

Social psychologists often point out that the expression of aggression within a society may be either covert or overt. Physical aggression may be eschewed in favor of verbal aggression; that is, murder, suicide, and other forms of violence may be rather rare, while the culture sanctions malicious gossip and slander as means of retaliating against those one dislikes. Elton B. McNeil pointed out that a relationship appears to exist between a high amount of freedom for the overt expression of aggression and a low degree to which it will take covert forms, and vice versa.[81] Political scientists have long been aware of the safety-valve theory.

Societies may develop culturally acceptable ways of either reducing or working off aggressive impulses. In the search for social aggression inhibitors or aggression reducers, one might logically look to such areas of life as religion, politics, business, sports, and education. In each one of these dimensions, we find ourselves faced with ambiguities that prevent us from drawing definite conclusions. Religions that preach a doctrine of love and renunciation of self may significantly lessen the aggressiveness of those adherents who take the doctrine seriously, who apply it not selectively but universally, and who are sufficiently disciplined to follow it in practice. Yet throughout history, religious differences themselves have often contributed to the occurrence and the ferocity of war.

In the realm of politics, one might argue that, in comparison to authoritarian or totalitarian regimes, democratic states should be less aggressive because they provide a variety of outlets through which political frustrations can be released—free speech and press, election campaigning, voting, lobbying for a law, or organizing a protest. There is something to this safety-valve theory of democratic government, but the democratic milieu also permits aggressive individuals and parties to play on xenophobic attitudes and propagate nationalistic policies, whereas in more tightly controlled societies, the promotion of nationalism and the organization of demonstrations are much closer to being government monopolies. (see "Democracies, War, and Peace," in Chapter 8). In free-market economies, business enterprise undoubtedly siphons off a considerable amount of creative aggression. However, although most businesspeople prefer the conditions of peace and order for making their rational profit calculus, some may support trade, investment, and other economic policies that increase international tensions. A minority might even hope to gain from war, or engage in activities abroad, which arouse anti-imperial resentment and tensions that can lead to international conflict (see Chapter 6).

Behavioral and other scientists interested in controlling aggression have wondered whether a society might diminish its funds of pent-up aggressive energy by diverting them into harmless channels such as organized athletic contests. There is no clear consensus on the subject. According to Konrad Lorenz, all human sport is a form of ritualized fighting. Even though it contains an aggressive motivation absent in most animal play, it helps to keep people healthy, and its main function consists in the cathartic discharge of aggression. Thus, it provides a release for that dangerous form of collective militant enthusiasm that underlies aggressive nationalism.[82] D. O. Hebb and W. R. Thompson suggest that sports may be a useful means of creating and working off an optimum amount of frustration and thus of contributing to social stability.[83] Jerome Frank calls attendance at such spectator sports as prizefights and professional football games a vicarious discharge of aggression. He admits, however, that body-contact sports often involve inflicting pain and may arouse anger and hostility, but he notes that the games themselves require the development of self-discipline to control the expression of anger.[84] Lorenz, Frank, and others have perceived much good in the Olympics as an exercise in promoting international cooperation and good sportsmanship,[85] although it cannot be denied that the Olympic Games have often been politicized—for example, being converted into an arena of international hostility (Berlin in 1936), violent conflict (Munich in 1972), protest over South Africa's apartheid (Montreal in 1976), and intricate diplomatic maneuvering and boycott to express political opposition to the host country's policies (Moscow in 1980 and Los Angeles in 1984).[86]

Within recent years, writers have expressed concern that under some circumstances, sports may get out of hand, possibly exacerbating both the aggressive impulses of individual players and spectators, and international tension, ill will, and hostility.[87] If there is such a thing as a fund of pent-up aggressive energy (a hypothesis never proven), competitive sports could represent on balance a healthy safety valve because most sports contests are conducted peaceably, and the losers, if they are good sports, do not harbor lasting grudges. International sports competition, if approached purely as sports in a spirit of fair play, can contribute to strengthening international good will and amity. However, sports contests, no less than religion and trade, are neutral from a political standpoint, and they do not necessarily lead to peace, especially if governments, ideological movements, political organizations, or ethnic partisans attempt to exploit them for ends that have little to do with sports.[88] In the final analysis, we cannot be certain whether sports attenuate or stimulate aggression within individuals and among nations. The answer cannot be generalized but must be given for each event, and it probably depends less on the athletes themselves than on such factors as prevailing national or racial issues, the crowd behavior of fans, and media coverage.

The area to which a great many psychologists and social-learning theorists attach their hopes for reducing human aggressiveness and fostering international standing is education. Changes in regard to education have been urged at two distinct levels. The first pertains to basic modifications in the method of rearing children, aimed at reducing the level of frustration, the modeling of violence, and the display of aggression within a society. Some theorists who associate warlike cultures with asceticism, celibacy, and strict codes of sexual behavior advocate greater sexual permissiveness.[89] In medieval Europe, however, the celibate priestly class was forbidden to take part in warfare, and the knights who did fight were usually far from celibate. Francis of Assisi and most gentle, peaceful saints lived an ascetic life, and Gandhi insisted on chastity and ascetic practices as a precondition for his *satyagraha* (soul force) pacifism.

Some psychologists trace the problem to the readiness of parents to mete out physical punishment to children; they urge parents to be more tolerant of children's desire to express themselves.[90] Still others argue that it is unhealthy to bottle up feelings of rage and anger, and that the ventilation of aggression can have a therapeutic effect, despite warnings to the contrary by experimental psychologists.[91] Recent decades have produced increasing demands, not just from social psychologists, for (a) eliminating the violence in the mass media in order to decrease the incidence of violent behavior by imitation, and (b) banning the manufacture of toy guns.[92] The foregoing proposed remedies involve considerable cultural or social changes that may not be acceptable or easy to achieve. This represents a case of saying that if human beings behaved differently from the way they do, they would be less aggressive. There is no way of knowing, however, whether these changes—assuming that they could be achieved—would be relevant to the propensity toward international war.

The second proposed change pertains to the realm of formal educational efforts, calculated to attenuate international hostility and conflict by promoting understanding among societies. Theorists have long taken it for granted that courses in school that increase the student's knowledge about foreign cultures and countries—as well as international teacher, student, and cultural exchange programs that facilitate personal contacts and learning experiences across political boundaries—are bound to contribute to the growth of international good will and the strengthening of international peace.[93] However, Kenneth N. Waltz has questioned whether misunderstandings among peoples of diverse cultural backgrounds have anything to do with the occurrence of most wars. "Conversely," he asks, "does understanding always promote peace, or do nations sometimes remain at peace precisely because they do not understand each other well?"[94] We probably cannot assume that increased communication leads inevitably to improved understanding, or that understanding necessarily makes for cooperation rather than conflict.

OTHER PSYCHOLOGICAL THEORIES

In addition to frustration–aggression and social-learning theories, there are several other psychological theories of conflict with which the student of international relations should be familiar. These often serve to complement and in some cases to modify the theories treated in the foregoing sections. They include the studies of Allport, Klineberg, and others on such phenomena as bias, prejudice, and stereotypes, and the part played by educational and mass communications systems in the shaping of intergroup attitudes.[95] The student should be conversant with the phenomenon that Frenkel-Brunswik calls the "intolerance of ambiguity," the tendency of human beings to reduce uncertainties and contradictions perceived as frustrating or anxiety-producing by reducing social reality to nice, neat, dichotomous categories—black and white, good and bad, friend and foe.[96] Adorno and his colleagues attempted to correlate a high degree of nationalistic feeling with an authoritarian personality that is characterized by neuroticism—an exaggerated fear of weakness, unquestioning submissiveness to authority, a heavy emphasis on conventional behavior, a conservative idea of a masculine–feminine dichotomy, and a preference for autocratic, punitive child-rearing methods.[97] A quarter-century later, two social psychologists, aware that the authoritarian-personality hypothesis had received some harsh criticisms, reported that they had found evidence of a distinct type (of political leader) who displayed a consistent preference for belligerence and possessed certain recognizable personality traits, which they related to the notion of compensatory masculinity and the archetype described by the Adorno group.[98]

Many writers have sought to probe the murky area of the influence that the personality of national leaders may have on their foreign-policy decisions. Michael P. Sullivan, after reviewing a fair sample of the voluminous literature on the subject, reaches the judicious conclusion that the personality characteristics or attributes of political leaders must undoubtedly have some effect, at various times, on foreign-policy decisions, but we are still far from sure what types of behavior can be accounted for by personality factors. The field of personality psychology was defined by Gordon Allport and Ross Stagner in the late 1930s. Allport postulates a distinct personality, a unity of self, independent of the social environment; Stagner integrated the two more closely. Psychologists and social psychologists have not yet fully agreed on how to bridge the gap between the independent and the integrative approaches.[99]

Also significant for understanding certain aspects of national and international politics is Erich Fromm's thesis concerning the desire of the modern human being to escape the burdens of freedom. Feeling alone and powerless in the face of gigantic entities and social forces that individuals cannot control, we are, according to Fromm, tempted to dissolve ourselves in the omnipotent state, to identify entirely with the state, and to seek satisfaction vicariously in the fortunes of the larger collectivity—to seek an "escape from freedom." Ready to submit to power within our nation, we want our nation to assert itself at the expense of the weak beyond its borders.[100] These psychological interpretations of political behavior cannot be examined here in detail; however, it should be obvious to the reader that if either national leadership groups or large segments of their publics should lapse into pronounced forms of the neuroticism these theories describe, it could have a profound impact on the international behavior of states.

Related to Frenkel-Brunswik's "intolerance of ambiguity" is the psychological theory of cognitive dissonance and consistency advanced by Leon Festinger.[101] Stated simply, this theory refers to the normal tendency of the individual to reduce inconsistencies that may arise in the knowledge concerning the person's values, environment, and behavior. Inconsistency might be reduced by modifying any one of the three. Festinger presents the fertile example of the mental processes and rationalizations that a chain smoker may go through to reduce cognitive dissonance by reconciling the values of health, long life, and love of family with the personal addiction to cigarettes that makes behavior modification the most difficult course to pursue.

The normal tendency of the individual to shift from cognitive dissonance to consistency may have significant implications for the study of conflict at the level of international relations, even though this is not empirically demonstrable. If it is operative at all, it will probably be within the minds of key decision makers. A hypothetical example may illustrate the point. In the Cold War, leaders of a nation might have been convinced ideologically that permanent security could not be achieved until the adversary had been destroyed by war. However, with the growth of nuclear-weapons stockpiles, leaders were compelled to realize that direct hostilities between the two rival powers would have proven mutually suicidal. Leaders, therefore, reduced cognitive dissonance by restructuring their knowledge patterns concerning the world situation, focusing on such notions as "the balance of terror," "gradual convergence of social systems," "mutual deterrence," "limited adversary relationship," and so forth.

Other situations likely to produce cognitive dissonance among foreign-policy decision makers could include, for example, the desire to control inflation, thereby increasing unemployment, or the desire of OPEC countries to raise the price of oil without stimulating Western efforts to seek alternative energy sources, or the attempt to use nuclear civilian energy without abetting the proliferation of national nuclear-weapons capabilities and polluting the human environment with waste materials from reactors.

The theory of cognitive dissonance might also cast light on the phenomenon of internal revolution within a society. It is often suggested that when human beings perceive an intolerably wide gap between their social ideals and the operating reality of the existing political system, they become alienated from the latter and seek to reduce their inner dissonance by gravitating toward revolutionary organization for the purpose of restructuring the external environment according to their ideal vision. In revolutionary situations, of course, many individuals will hover precariously on the borderline between continuing to grant the system minimal or passive support and withdrawing from the system to oppose it actively by violence. This is partly a matter of weighing prospective rewards and punishments and thus falls under the heading of what psychologists call "approach–avoidance conflict" within the individual, in which the antagonistic tendencies are both sufficiently strong to produce ambivalent or neurotic behavior.[102]

For more than half a century, social psychologists and other behavioral scientists have been exhorting enlightened governments to pursue behavioral–scientific approaches calculated to enhance international cooperation and to prevent war through educational programs, cultural exchanges, new methods of child/citizen training, conditioning of public attitudes toward peace through the media, screening out certain types of personalities in the process of selecting leaders, and so on. Unfortunately, their ability to show specific concrete results from their efforts remains quite limited. In the industrially advanced nations of the world, developments in modern weapons technology have had the effect of making war increasingly abhorrent to elites and publics alike. Education at all levels, the mass media, and a wide variety of institutions and organizations, from churches and political parties to ecological and antiwar groups, have played a significant part in transforming popular psychological attitudes toward war, as well as the traditional readiness of diplomats and political leaders to threaten or order the use of military force. Nevertheless, there are still areas of the world where large-scale violence and war remain possible and capable of serving as tinderboxes for dangerous international conflagrations. Even among the "most highly civilized and economically developed" societies, future wars cannot be ruled out with certainty. Perhaps some consolation can be derived from the thought, not at all implausible, that without the combination of all the aforementioned efforts, the situation might well be far worse than it is.

CONCLUSION: MICROCOSMIC THEORIES IN PERSPECTIVE

The various theories discussed in this chapter—biological, psychological, social learning, personality types, and so on—have been presented here in their clear, pristine form for the purpose of helping to explain the sources from which contemporary theories are evolving. Students are strongly encouraged to go back to the original theories, to trace these through subsequent modifications, including tendencies toward convergence, and to formulate their own syntheses, based on reflection, analysis, and insights.

However important first-image causes of war may be—and no one denies their importance—we may never completely understand the factors that operate, consciously or unconsciously, at the personal level, and how drives and motives on the part of individuals are translated into group and institutional behavior, much less into the public policies of states that make for peace or war. This chapter has shown how complex are the biological and psychological foundations of politics. Both traditional and behavioral social scientists have ample reason to avoid simplified explanations. Some peace researchers and theorists may go too far in dismissing valid biological and psychological explanations of human aggressiveness a bit too hastily in their understandable effort to discredit the war-in-our genes hypothesis. In 1986, a group of behavioral scientists from 12 countries meeting in Spain issued the "Seville Statement," which included the following assertions:

> It is scientifically incorrect to say that we have inherited a tendency to make war from our animal ancestors. Warfare is a peculiarly human phenomenon and does not occur in other animals. . . . It is scientifically incorrect to say that war or any other violent behavior is genetically programmed into our human nature. It is scientifically incorrect to say that in the course of human evolution there has been a selection for aggressive behavior more than for other kinds of behavior. . . . It is scientifically incorrect to say that humans have a "violent brain". While we do have a neural apparatus to act violently, there is nothing in our neurophysiology that compels us to. It is scientifically incorrect to say that war is caused by "instinct" or any single motivation. . . . We conclude that biology does not condemn humanity to war, and that humanity can be freed from the bondage of biological pessimism. Violence is neither in our evolutionary legacy nor in our genes.[103]

The Seville Statement on Violence (SSV) has been criticized by ethologists as narrow in focus, incomplete in formulating issues, and naïve and simplistic in its message. The critics have sought to correct what they regard as an inadequate view of the biology of aggression embodied in the SSV, which—they seem to suggest—

implies that animals are predominantly aggressive creatures from whose modes of behavior humans must dissociate themselves totally. They argue that peacemaking is not unique to humans and that aggression is not something necessarily always to be avoided and condemned because it can serve adaptive as well as maladaptive functions.[104]

In summary, it is uncertain and even questionable that biological and psychological mechanisms within the individual that pertain to aggressive behavior can explain intersocietal warfare. To the extent that such a relationship exists, it is probably indirect rather than direct, and it may be rather remote at some times and more proximate at other times. Innate aggressive urges or drives may feed or reinforce belligerent political attitudes and may give them an emotional basis. In the case of some individuals, highly developed inner aggressiveness may make them easier to train for fighting and killing in war. Aggressive impulses frequently indulged rather than controlled might contribute to a short temper in a political leader and dispose the leader to resort readily to force in order to solve a problem that might be managed adequately through negotiation. Conversely, personality factors can also make another leader vacillate and procrastinate in a state of Hamlet-like indecision until either war becomes inevitable or peace prevails by default. Nonetheless, despite these and several other linkages that could be drawn, it would be inaccurate to conclude that innate biological and psychological drives are the cause of war or peace. They probably constitute one of the important necessary conditions for the emergence of aggressive discontents among individual leaders, elite groups, and masses that make the recurrence of war a possibility throughout human history. By themselves, however, they do not constitute a *sufficient* condition of war. Fortunately, there is no compelling reason to think that humanity is being pushed inexorably toward war by some innate biological–psychological urge to aggress. War is a matter for political decision, which can be the result of rational as well as irrational processes.

NOTES

1. Kenneth N. Waltz, *Man, the State and War: A Theoretical Analysis* (New York: Columbia University Press, 1959), chaps. 2 and 4.
2. Ibid., chap. 6. The anarchic character of the international system is discussed in chap. 1, pp. 60–62. See also Waltz "War and Expectation of War," chap. 7 in Vernon Van Dyke, *International Politics,* 2nd ed. (New York: Appleton, 1966); Gordon W. Allport, "The Role of Expectancy," in Hadley Cantril, ed., *Tensions That Cause War* (Urbana: University of Illinois Press, 1950); and Werner Levi, "On the Causes of War and the Conditions of Peace," *Journal of Conflict Resolution, IV* (December 1960), 411–420. Levi notes that war should be traced not to any specific factor but to a constellation of factors. Ibid., p. 418.
3. Kenneth N. Waltz, *Man, the State and War,* op. cit., pp. 18–20.
4. The word *anomic* here refers to a condition of normless violence flaring up rather unexpectedly.
5. Werner Levi, op. cit., p. 415. See statement by Herbert C. Kelman: "Any attempt to conceptualize the causes of war and the conditions for peace that starts from individual psychology rather than from an analysis of the relations between national-states is

of questionable relevance"; "International Relations: Psychological Aspects," in *International Encyclopedia of the Social Sciences* (New York: Macmillan, 1968), Vol. 8, p. 76. See also Seymour Feshbach and Adam Fraczek, *Aggression and Behavior Change: Biological and Social Processes* (New York: Praeger, 1979).

6. Peter Corning, "The Biological Basis of Behavior and Some Implications for Political Science," *World Politics*, XXIII (April 1971), 339–340.

7. The founder of sociobiology is Edward O. Wilson, a professor of science and curator of entomology at Harvard University, who outlined the field in *Sociobiology: The New Synthesis* (Cambridge, MA: Harvard University Press, 1975). Since 1975, several works have appeared either attacking or defending the field or presenting the debate. These include David P. Barash, *Sociobiology and Behavior* (New York: Elsevier, 1977); Arthur L. Caplan, ed., *Sociobiology Debate* (New York: Harper & Row, 1978); Michael S. Gregaroy et al., eds., *Sociobiology and Human Nature: An Interdisciplinary Critique and Defense* (San Francisco: Jossey-Bass, 1978); George W. Barlow and James Silverberg, eds., *Sociobiology: Beyond Nature–Nurture* (Boulder, CO: Westview, 1979); James A. Schellenberg, *The Science of Conflict* (New York: Oxford University, 1982); and James H. Fetzer, ed., *Sociobiology and Epistemology* (Boston: D. Reidel, 1985).

8. Peter A. Corning, op. cit., pp. 339–340. See Thomas Landon Thorson, *Biopolitics* (New York: Holt, Rinehart and Winston, 1970); the essays in Albert Somit, ed., *Biology and Politics* (Paris: Mouton, 1976); and Roger D. Masters, "The Biological Nature of the State," *World Politics*, XXXV (January 1983). Cf. also additional references in Note 39.

9. Abraham H. Maslow, *Motivation and Personality* (New York: Harper & Row, 1954), pp. 80–98. (A second edition was published in 1970.) Maslow argues that basic physical and safety needs demand satisfaction before the higher psychological needs emerge.

10. Robert C. North has shown that the shortages or scarcities that give rise to political conflict are due not only to objective physical causes (such as entropy) but also to psychological perceptions and anticipations of demand in excess of supply. "Toward a Framework for the Analysis of Scarcity and Conflict," *International Studies Quarterly*, 21 (December 1977), 569–591; see also David Novick et al., *A World of Scarcities: Critical Issues in Public Policy* (New York: Halsted, 1976).

11. See William Etkin, *Social Behavior from Fish to Man* (Chicago: University of Chicago Press, 1967), p. 33; George Gaylord Simpson, *The Meaning of Evolution* (New Haven, CT: Yale University Press, 1967), p. 222; Theodosius Dobzhansky, *Mankind Evolving* (New Haven, CT: Yale University Press, 1962), p. 134.

12. Albert Bandura, *Aggression: A Social Learning Analysis* (Englewood Cliffs, NJ: Prentice-Hall, 1973), p. 3.

13. Ibid., p. 5. Also, Corning, following the approach of the Committee on Violence of the Stanford University School of Medicine, defines aggressiveness as encompassing the entire spectrum of assertive and attacking behaviors found in humans and other animal species. "It includes overt and covert attacks, self-directed attacks, displacement attacks, dominance behavior, defamatory acts, and the motivational and emotional components of any determined attempt to accomplish a task"; op. cit., p. 345. Rollo May notes that, besides being physical, aggression may also be psychological, intellectual, spiritual, or economic. It may employ as its weapons words, artistic symbols, gestures, ad hominem arguments, insults, or even prolonged silence calculated to hurt or punish. *Power and Innocence: A Search for the Sources of Violence* (New York: Norton, 1972), pp. 148–152.

14. William McDougall, *An Introduction to Social Psychology* (Boston: Luce, 1926), especially pp. 30–45. See also his *Outline of Psychology* (New York: Scribner's 1923), pp. 140–141.
15. Sigmund Freud, *A General Introduction to Psychoanalysis,* trans. G. S. Hall (New York: Boni and Liveright, 1920), pp. 170–174.
16. See Urpo Harva, "War and Human Nature," in Robert Ginsberg, ed., *The Critique of War* (Chicago: Regnery, 1969), p. 48. "Aggression and necrophilia are seen as the two deep sources from which war derives its motive energies"; ibid., p. 49.
17. Sigmund Freud, *Beyond the Pleasure Principle* (New York: Bantam, 1958), p. 198.
18. "Why War?" in a letter from Sigmund Freud to Albert Einstein, written in 1932. Text in Robert A. Goldwin et al., *Readings in World Politics* (New York: Oxford University Press, 1950). After describing the death instinct, Freud wrote, "The upshot of these observations . . . is that there is no likelihood of our being able to suppress humanity's aggressive tendencies. . . . The Bolshevists, too, aspire to do away with human aggressiveness by ensuring the satisfaction of material needs and enforcing equality between man and man. To me this hope seems vain." Then, paradoxically, he added that "complete suppression of a man's aggressive tendencies is not an issue; what we may try is to divert it into a channel other than that of warfare." Ibid., p. 29. This last statement seems to parallel William James's quest for a "moral equivalent" of war. See also Freud's *Civilization and Its Discontents* (New York: W. W. Norton, 1962), pp. 65–69.
19. Leonard Berkowitz, *Aggression: A Social-Psychological Analysis* (New York: McGraw-Hill, 1962), p. 8; Rollo May, op. cit., p. 155. For a statement by one of Freud's own students rejecting his instinctivist theory of aggression, see Erich Fromm, *The Anatomy of Human Destructiveness* (New York: Holt, Rinehart and Winston, 1973).
20. Leonard Berkowitz, *Aggression,* op. cit., pp. 9–10. Human beings actively seek an optimum level of frustration. Cf. D. O. Hebb and W. R. Thompson, "The Social Significance of Animal Studies," in Gardiner Lindzey, ed., *Handbook of Social Psychology* (Reading, MA: Addison-Wesley, 1954). Reprinted in Leon Bramson and George W. Goethals, eds., *War: Studies from Psychology, Sociology, Anthropology* (New York: Free Press, 1968), p. 53.
21. Contemporary psychoanalytic writers have adhered to the aggressive instinct theory. A few, such as Karl Menninger, retain the notion of death instinct. Others, such as Heinz Hartmann, Ernst Kris, and Rudolph Maurice Loewenstein continue to postulate an aggressive instinct but do not trace it to the death wish. Still others, including Otto Fenichel, have shifted back toward the frustration explanation of aggression. See Berkowitz, op. cit., pp. 11–12.
22. See McNeil's chapter, "The Nature of Aggression," in Elton B. McNeil, ed., *The Nature of Human Conflict* (Englewood Cliffs, NJ: Prentice-Hall), 1965, p. 15. Peter A. Corning has warned that it "would be fallacious to make an unqualified identification between any given human behavior and apparently similar behavior in lower animals"; op. cit., p. 331.
23. Students of animal behavior–physiology are producing some interesting insights into the problem of aggression, but they would be the first to admit difficulties in interpreting their data and to caution against the hasty application of their findings to the more mysterious realm of human affairs. A useful summary of findings on animal aggression can be found in McNeil, op. cit., pp. 15–27.
24. John Paul Scott, *Animal Behavior* (Garden City, NY: Doubleday Anchor Books, 1963), pp. 121–122. One should note that if human aggressiveness is to be reduced or inhibited, it will have to be by way of learning because the avenues of electrical, hormonal, chemical, and surgical interventions into the human body are of necessity quite limited.

25. V. Spike Peterson, "Security and Sovereign States: What Is at Stake in Taking Feminism Seriously?" in V. Spike Peterson, ed., *Gendered States: Feminist (Re)Visions of International Relations Theory* (Boulder, CO, and London: Lynne Rienner Publishers, 1992), pp. 31–64. In the same volume, see also Rebecca Grant, "The Quagmire of Gender and International Security," pp. 83–97; Cynthia Enloe, *Bananas, Beaches and Bases: Making Feminist Sense of International Politics* (Berkeley: University of California Press, 1990).

26. John Paul Scott, *Aggression* (Chicago: University of Chicago Press, 1958), p. 62; Leonard Berkowitz, *Aggression,* op. cit., p. 15.

27. John Paul Scott, *Animal Behavior,* op. cit., pp. 153–155.

28. Konrad Lorenz, *On Aggression,* trans. Marjorie Kerr Wilson (New York: Bantam, 1967), p. x.

29. Ibid., pp. 28–32 and 161–164. This is the concept popularized, perhaps too simplistically, especially in its application to humans, by Robert Ardrey, as the "territorial imperative." Robert Ardrey, *The Territorial Imperative* (New York: Atheneum, 1966), p. 103; see also pp. 47, 110–117, as well as his book *African Genesis* (New York: Dell, 1967), p. 174. For severe criticisms of Ardrey's work on territoriality as unscientific, see Geoffrey Gorer, "Ardrey on Human Nature," *Encounter,* 28 (June 1967), and the essays by R. L. Holloway, Jr., P. H. Klopfer, Geoffrey Gorer, and J. H. Crook, in M. F. Ashley Montagu, ed., *Man and Aggression,* 2nd ed. (New York: Oxford University Press, 1973).

30. Konrad Lorenz, op. cit., pp. 54–65, 69–81, and 99–110. He gives the familiar example of the ceremonial inciting by the female duck, who will charge menacingly toward an enemy couple until, frightened by her own boldness, she suddenly hurries back to her own protective drake to refurbish her courage before the next hostile foray. Thus, without actually joining battle, she delivers her warning message. Ibid., p. 127. See also pp. 72–74, 122–132, and 232–233.

31. For a further elaboration of Lorenz's views concerning the implications of biological findings for a knowledge of human social behavior, see "A Talk with Konrad Lorenz," Magazine Section, *The New York Times* (July 5, 1970). Lorenz's widely cited example of the wolf who submissively exposes his jugular vein to the adversary was later dismissed as having been based on faulty observation. R. Schenkel, "Submission: Its Features and Frustrations in the Wolf and Dog," *American Zoologist,* 7 (1967), 319–329. Most biologists, however, still subscribe to the concept of aggression-inhibiting mechanisms.

32. Konrad Lorenz, op. cit., p. 233–234. See also Jerome D. Frank, *Sanity and Survival: Psychological Aspects of War and Peace* (New York: Random House Vintage Books, 1968), pp. 42–45 in his chap. 3, "Why Men Kill—Biological Roots." R. L. Holloway, Jr., suggests that the averting of eyes, cringing, and shedding of tears may serve an inhibiting or appeasing function in humans, even though they are quite weak. "Human Aggression: The Need for a Species-Specific Framework," *Natural History,* LXXVI (December 1, 1967), 41.

33. Alec Nisbett, *Konrad Lorenz: A Biography* (New York: Harcourt Brace Jovanovich, 1976), pp. 171–172.

34. Erich Fromm, "The Erich Fromm Theory of Aggression," Magazine Section, *The New York Times* (February 27, 1972), 74, and "Man Would as Soon Flee as Fight," *Psychology Today,* 7 (August 1973), 35–45. A similar criticism may be found in Ralph L. Holloway, Jr., "Human Aggression: The Need for a Species-Specific Framework," op. cit., 41.

35. See B. F. Skinner, *Beyond Freedom and Dignity* (New York: Knopf, 1971), in chap. 1, "A Technology of Behavior"; Meredith W. Watts, "B. F. Skinner and the Techno-

logical Control of Social Behavior," *American Political Science Review*, LXIX (March 1975).

36. Albert Bandura, *Aggression: A Social Learning Analysis* (Englewood Cliffs, NJ: Prentice-Hall, 1973), pp. 16–31. See also T. C. Schneirla, "Instinct and Aggression," in Ashlex Montagu, ed., op. cit., p. 61.

37. These criticisms are documented in Stephen D. Nelson, "Nature/Nurture Revisited. I: A Review of the Biological Bases of Conflict," *Journal of Conflict Resolution*, 18 (June 1974), especially pp. 296–302, and in Samuel S. Kim, "The Lorenzian Theory of Aggression and Peace Research: A Critique," in Richard A. Falk and Samuel S. Kim, eds., *The War System: An Interdisciplinary Approach* (Boulder, CO: Westview, 1980), pp. 82–115.

38. Francis A. Beer, *Peace Against War: The Ecology of International Violence* (San Francisco: W. H. Freeman, 1981), p. 304.

39. George M. Carstairs, "Overcrowding and Human Aggression," in Hugh Davis Graham and Ted Robert Gurr, eds., *Violence in America, Report to the National Commission on the Causes and Prevention of Violence*, June 1969 (New York: New American Library, 1969), pp. 730–742. Cf. also Jonathan Freedman, *Crowding and Behavior* (San Francisco: Freeman, 1975); Susan Seagart, *Crowding in Real Environments* (Sage: Beverly Hills, CA: 1976); and Larry Severy, ed., *Crowding: Theoretical and Research Implications* (New York: Humanities Science Press, 1979).

40. Thomas C. Wiegele, "Decision-Making in an International Crisis: Some Biological Factors," *International Studies Quarterly*, 7 (September 1973), 295–335, and *Biopolitics* (Boulder, CO: Westview, 1979); Meredith Watts, ed., *Biopolitics: Ethological and Physiological Approaches* (San Francisco: Jossey-Bass, 1981); Gerald W. Hopple and Lawrence Falkowski, *Biopolitics, Political Psychology and International Politics* (New York: St. Martin's, 1982).

41. John Dollard, Leonard W. Doob, Neal E. Miller, et al., *Frustration and Aggression* (New Haven, CT: Yale University Press, 1939), p. 7. For another basic work in the field, see Norman R. F. Maier, *Frustration: The Study of Behavior Without a Goal* (New York: McGraw-Hill, 1949). The psychological concept of frustration has held up well. See Abram Amsel, *Frustration Theory* (New York: Cambridge University Press, 1992).

42. Ross Stagner, "The Psychology of Human Conflict," in Elton B. McNeil, ed., *The Nature of Human Conflict*, p. 53.

43. Abraham H. Maslow, "Deprivation, Threat and Frustration," *Psychological Review*, XLVIII (6) (1941); reprinted in J. K. Zawodny, ed., *Man and International Relations, Vol. 1: Conflict* (San Francisco: Chandler, 1966), pp. 17–19.

44. John Dollard et al., *Frustration and Aggression*, op. cit., pp. 39–47. According to a later reformulation of the concept of catharsis, aggressive action was thought to have three possible separable effects: reducing, increasing, or producing no observable change in the level of aggressive response. S. Feshback, "Aggression," in P. H. Mussen, ed., *Carmichael's Manual of Child Psychology* (New York: Wiley, 1970); pp. 159–259. Cited in Albert Bandura, op. cit., p. 37.

45. Elton B. McNeil, "Psychology and Aggression," *Journal of Conflict Resolution*, III (September 1959), 204; Leonard Berkowitz, *Aggression*, op. cit., p. 29.

46. Leonard Berkowitz, ibid., p. 30.

47. For an elaboration of these first two points, see Leonard Berkowitz, ibid., pp. 32–48.

48. Sanford Rosenzweig, "An Outline of Frustration Theory," J. McV. Hunt, ed., *Personality and the Behavior Disorders* (New York: Ronald, 1944), pp. 381–382. Elton B. McNeil, following Rosenzweig, says, "The privation of being born into poverty poses

a series of frustrations for the individual; but his reaction to them differs considerably from his responses to being deprived of wealth, once he has possessed it"; "Psychology and Aggression," op. cit., p. 203.

49. John Dollard et al., *Frustration and Aggression,* op. cit., p. 2.

50. The Yale group noted that "when Marxists have described the dynamic human inter-relationships involved in the class struggle and in the preservation and destruction of the state, they have introduced unwittingly a psychological system involving the assumption that aggression is a response to frustration." Ibid., p. 23. The frustrating agents, of course, are the bourgeoisie, and the aggressive response by the frustrated proletariat is the organization of a class that finally carries out a revolution. However, most sociologists, including Marxist ones, would not use the term *frustration* except metaphorically and in a social context, not in the same sense in which psychologists use it. See also pp. 44, 151–153 and 153–158 on prejudice against blacks and Jews.

51. Sociologists distinguish between the behavior of small groups and that of large groups. Herbert Blumer has called attention also to the differences between collective behavior (even by fairly large groups) in an undefined or unstructured situation and organized social behavior that follows culturally prescribed norms. "Collective Behavior," in J. B. Gitter, ed., *Review of Sociology: Analysis of a Decade* (New York: Wiley, 1957), pp. 130, 199. Neil J. Smelser, while modifying some of Blumer's ideas, agrees with the aforementioned distinction: "Collective behavior . . . is not institutionalized behavior. According to the degree to which it becomes institutionalized, it loses its distinctive character." *Theory of Collective Behavior* (New York: Free Press 1963), p. 8. It is interesting to note that Smelser, in his chapter on "The Hostile Outburst," makes no mention of the frustration–aggression hypothesis in his efforts to explain aggression in society. Ibid., pp. 222–269.

52. John Dollard et al., *Frustration and Aggression,* op. cit., pp. 55–76.

53. Martin Gold, "Suicide, Homicide and the Socialization of Aggression," in Bartlett H. Stoodley, ed., *Society and Self: A Reader in Social Psychology* (New York: Free Press, 1962), pp. 281–282.

54. Robert R. Sears, Eleanor Maccoby, and Harry Levin, "The Socialization of Aggression," in Eleanor E. Maccoby, Theodore M. Newcomb, and Eugene L. Hartley, eds., *Readings in Social Psychology* (New York: Holt, Rinehart and Winston, 1958), pp. 350–352.

55. Elton B. McNeil, "Psychology and Aggression," op. cit., p. 212. Albert Bandura notes that the fear of punishment produces an inhibiting or deterrent effect and causes the displacement of aggression from similar to dissimilar targets; *Aggression,* op. cit., pp. 34–35. E. F. M. Durbin and John Bowlby contended that the conflict within the child arising out of the fear of punishment is an important source of aggressiveness in the adult because aggression can be controlled but not destroyed. The boy, instead of striking his father, whom he fears, strikes a smaller boy, whom he does not fear. Disguised aggression has made the boy into a bully. In the same way, revolutionaries who hate ordered government, nationalists who hate foreign policies, and individuals who hate bankers, Jews, or their political opponents may be exhibiting characteristics that have been formed by the suppression of simple aggression in their childhood education. Durbin and Bowlby, *Personal Aggressiveness and War* (New York: Columbia University Press, 1939), excerpted in J. K. Zawodny, *Man and International Relations, Volume 1: Conflict* (San Francisco: Chandler Publishing Company, 1966) p. 97.

56. McNeil, "Psychology and Aggression," op. cit., p. 213; Ross Stagner, op. cit., pp. 55–56.

57. Stagner, ibid., p. 54; and Ralph K. White, "Images in the Context of International Conflict," in Herbert C. Kelman, ed., *International Behavior: A Social Psychological Analysis* (New York: Holt, Rinehart and Winston, 1965), pp. 267–268.

58. Marc Howard Ross, "Childrearing and War in Different Cultures," in Francesca M. Cancian and James William Gibson, eds., *Making War/Making Peace: The Social Foundations of Violent Conflict* (Belmont, CA: Wadsworth, 1990), pp. 51–63.

59. Albert Bandura, *Aggression,* op. cit., p. 170.

60. Leonard Berkowitz, op. cit., pp. 139, 149, and 193–264; cf. also his "Concept of Aggressive Drive," in Leonard Berkowitz, ed., *Advances in Experimental Social Psychology* (New York: Academic Press, 1965), Vol. 2, p. 312.

61. Albert Bandura, *Aggression,* op. cit., pp. 29–30, 32–36, 44.

62. For a fascinating account and analysis of how soldiers in battle face the prospect of imminent death, see J. Glenn Gray, *The Warriors: Reflections on Men in Battle* (New York: Harper, 1967), especially pp. 100–121, and John Keegan, *The Face of Battle* (New York: Penguin) 1983.

63. Donald A. Wells, *The War Myth* (New York: Pegasus, 1967), pp. 174–175. Within two pages of his text, Wells first suggests that "war is not so natural or so psychologically grounded in human nature as we have been led to believe," but then arrives at what appears to be an opposite conclusion: "The emptiness of the reasons men verbalize for war suggests that war really does not rest on any rationale. . . . After all, if people didn't like to fight," he concludes, "there are no good reasons why they should do so much of it." Ibid., pp. 176–177. For a rather depressing and not entirely convincing picture, see William Broyles, Jr., "Why Men Love War," in Cancian and Gibson, eds., *Making War/Making Peace,* op. cit., 29–37. This first appeared in *Esquire.* For quotations from various authors reflecting ambiguity with regard to the attractiveness and repulsiveness of war, killing, and confrontation with death in combat, see David P. Barash, *Introduction to Peace Studies* (Belmont, CA: Wadsworth, 1991), pp. 150–156.

64. Albert Bandura, *Aggression,* op. cit., p. 99.

65. Raymond Aron has noted that, as modern warfare technology has grown more frightful, industrially advanced societies have, by articulating ever more grandiose statements of war aims, sought to inspire their citizens to sustain the hardships and sacrifices of war. *The Century of Total War* (Boston: Beacon, 1955), p. 26.

66. John H. Faris, "The Impact of Basic Combat Training," in Nancy Goldman and David R. Segal, eds., *The Social Psychology of Military Service* (Beverly Hills, CA: Sage, 1976), pp. 14–15.

67. Francis A. Beer, *Peace Against War,* op. cit., p. 128, and his documentation on p. 339.

68. Hadley Cantril, *The Human Dimension: Experiences in Policy Research* (New Brunswick, NJ: Rutgers University Press, 1967), pp. 16, 156, and quoted at pp. 127–128. See also Hadley Cantril, ed., *Tensions That Cause Wars* (Urbana: University of Illinois Press, 1950), p. 7; Hadley Cantril and William Buchanan, *How Nations See Each Other* (Urbana: University of Illinois Press, 1953).

69. Harold D. Lasswell, *World Politics and Personality Insecurity* (New York: McGraw-Hill, 1935), pp. 3, 207, and 237. For the results of a study of foreign ministers as a small but strategically important segment of the world elite, made up of persons who exhibit a set of background similarities, who share some values regarding world order and professional diplomatic conduct, and who interact with each other enough to develop some friendships as a basis for elite cohesion, see George Modelski, "The World's Foreign Ministers: A Political Elite," *Journal of Conflict Resolution,* XIV (June 1970), 135–175. See also William T. R. Fox and Harold D. Lasswell, "The Study of

World Politics," in Arnold A. Rogow, ed., *Politics, Personality, and Social Science in the Twentieth Century* (Chicago: University of Chicago Press, 1969), pp. 376–377.

70. Karen Horney, *Neurosis and Human Growth* (New York: W. W. Norton, 1950), pp. 21–27.

71. Bernard Susser, "Psychology and Politics," in Susser, ed., *Approaches to the Study of Politics* (New York: Macmillan, 1992), p. 356.

72. Kenneth E. Boulding, "National Images and International Systems," *Journal of Conflict Resolution*, III (June 1959), 120–131. This and the previous quotations are on pp. 121–122. See also his book, *The Image: Knowledge in Life and Society* (Ann Arbor: University of Michigan Press, 1956); Ole R. Holsti, "The Belief System and National Images," *Journal of Conflict Resolution*, 16 (September 1962) 244–252 and "Cognitive Dynamics and Images of the Enemy," *Journal of International Affairs*, 1(21) (Summer 1967); 16–39 and Robert Jervis, *The Logic of Images in International Relations* (Princeton, NJ: Princeton University Press, 1970).

73. Robert Jervis, *The Logic of Images in International Relations* (Princeton, NJ: Princeton University Press, 1970), and *Perception and Misperception in World Politics* (Princeton, NJ: Princeton University Press, 1976).

74. Pamela J.Conover and Stanley Feldman, "How People Organize the Political World," *American Journal of Political Science*, 28 (February 1984), 95–126; John Hurwitz and Mark Peffley, "How Are Foreign Policy Attitudes Structured?" *American Political Science Review*, 81 (December 1987), 1099–1120.

75. Arthur Gladstone, "The Conception of the Enemy," *Journal of Conflict Resolution*, III (June 1959), 132.

76. Ross Stagner, "The Psychology of Human Conflict" in Elton B. McNeil, ed., *The Nature of Human Conflict*, op. cit., p. 46.

77. Urie Bronfenbrenner, "The Mirror Image in Soviet–American Relations: A Social Psychologists's Report," *Journal of Conflict Resolution*, XI (September 1967), 325–332; Charles E. Osgood, "Analysis of the Cold War Mentality," *Journal of Social Issues*, XVII(3) (1961), 12–19.

78. Ralph K. White, "Images in the Context of International Conflict," in Kelman, ed., op. cit., p. 240.

79. Urie Bronfenbrenner, "Allowing for Soviet Perceptions," in Roger Fisher, ed., *International Conflict and Behavioral Science, The Craigville Papers* (New York: Basic Books, 1964), p. 172.

80. See, for example, the discussion of "Graduated and Reciprocated Initiative in Tension-Reduction, (GRIT)" in Charles E. Osgood, *An Alternative to War or Surrender* (Urbana: University of Illinois Press, 1962), and his "Questioning Some Unquestioned Assumptions About National Defense," *Journal of Arms Control, I* (January 1963), 213. Cf. also Arthur I. Waskow, *The Limits of Defense* (Garden City, NY: Doubleday, 1962), chap. 4.

81. Elton B. McNeil, ed., *The Nature of Aggression*, op. cit., p. 35.

82. Konrad Lorenz, op. cit., pp. 271–272.

83. D. O. Hebb and W. R. Thompson, op. cit., p. 53.

84. Jerome D. Frank, op. cit., pp. 75, 87–88.

85. Konrad Lorenz, op. cit., p. 272; Jerome D. Frank, op. cit., pp. 88, 241.

86. Wilson Carey McWilliams, "The Political Olympics," *Worldview* (July 1984). See also Harry Edwards, *The Sociology of Sport* (Homewood, IL: Dorsey Press, 1973).

87. See Parton Keese, "Violence in Sports: What It Could Mean," *The New York Times* (January 26, 1975), Section 5, p. 1; Lowell Miller, "World Cup Or World War?" *The New York Times* (May 21, 1978), Section 6, p. 20.

88. For an interesting discussion of the implications of international athletic contests for diplomatic recognition, political protest, propaganda, and state prestige, as well as interstate cooperation and conflict, see Andrew Strenk, "The Thrill of Victory and the Agony of Defeat: Sport and International Politics," *Orbis,* 22 (Summer 1978), 453–469.

89. Elbert Russell, *Human Aggression,* Paper presented at Canadian Peace Research Institute Summer School, Grindstone Island, Ontario, July 18, 1973; James W. Prescott, "Body Pleasure and the Origins of Violence," *The Bulletin of the Atomic Scientists,* XXXI (November 1975), 10–20.

90. Prescott, Ibid.; Jerome D. Frank, *Sanity and Survival,* op. cit., 68–69, 283. Bandura, however, while agreeing that punishment may have unfavorable consequences if it is excessive, ill-timed, erratic, or administered in a spirit of vengeance without providing constructive direction, nevertheless argues that punishment can, under certain conditions, effectively modify undesirable behavior; *Aggression: A Social Learning Analysis,* op. cit., pp. 289, 304–308.

91. See Leonard Berkowitz, "The Case for Bottling Up Rage," *Psychology Today* (July 1973), 24, 31.

92. Jerome D. Frank, op. cit., pp. 72–74, 283–284; Bandura, op. cit., pp. 266–286. Bandura dismisses the disclaimers that because behavior is determined by multiple factors, it is unfair to place blame on the mass media and that aggressive modeling affects only people who are already disturbed or predisposed to aggression. He argues that in the face of abundant experimental evidence for observational learning, continued equivocation on the aggressive modeling impact of television on both children and adults cannot be justified. Ibid., pp. 266–271; see also Bandura "Toy Guns: Do They Fan Aggression?" *The New York Times* (June 16, 1988). Section C, p. 1. Psychologists were reported debating whether toy guns encourage violent behavior among youngsters or acquaint them with the horrors and death of war. Government officials have often blamed toy guns for actual deaths when police officers mistook them for real weapons.

93. See, for example, Ithiel DeSola Pool, "Effects of Cross-National Contact on National and International Images," in Herbert C. Kelman, ed., *International Relations: A Social-Psychological Analysis* (New York: Holt, Rinehart and Winston, 1964), pp. 106–129.

94. Kenneth N. Waltz, *Man, the State and War,* op. cit., p. 48.

95. Gordon W. Allport, *The Nature of Prejudice* (Reading, MA: Addison-Wesley, 1954); and Otto Klineberg, *The Human Dimension in International Relations* (New York: Holt, Rinehart and Winston, 1964).

96. Else Frenkel-Brunswik, "Intolerance of Ambiguity as an Emotional and Perceptual Personality Variable," *Journal of Personality,* XVIII (September 1949), 108–143; and "Social Tensions and the Inhibition of Thought," *Social Problems,* II (October 1954), 75–81.

97. T. W. Adorno, Else Frenkel-Brunswik, Daniel J. Levinson, and R. N. Sanford, *The Authoritarian Personality* (New York: Harper & Row, 1950). For criticisms of the hypothesis, cf. Richard Christie and Marie Jahoda, eds., *Studies in the Scope and Methods of the Authoritarian Personality* (Glencoe, IL: Free Press, 1954).

98. S. Griedlander and R. Cohen, "The Personality Correlates of Belligerence in International Conflict," *Comparative Politics,* 7 (January 1975).

99. Michael P. Sullivan, *International Relations: Theories and Evidence* (Englewood Cliffs, NJ: Prentice-Hall, 1976), pp. 26–40. See also Alexander L. George, "Assessing Presidential Character," *World Politics,* XXVI (January 1974) 234–282.

100. Erich Fromm, *Escape from Freedom* (New York: Holt, Rinehart and Winston, 1941), pp. 21, 22, 141–142 and 164–168.

101. Leon Festinger, *A Theory of Cognitive Dissonance* (Stanford, CA: Stanford University Press, 1957), and *Conflict, Decision and Dissonance* (Stanford, CA: Stanford University Press, 1964). Festinger's theory has been accepted by most psychologists and has "become part of the warp and woof of the field." See Harold B. Gerard's "Retrospective Review" of Festinger in *Contemporary Psychology,* 39 (November 1994), 1013–1017.

102. Judson S. Brown, "Principles of Intrapersonal Conflict," *Journal of Conflict Resolution,* I (June 1957), 137–138. For a different perspective of how psychological factors in the personal background of a political leader may affect the leader's decision to become a revolutionary, see E. Victor Wolfenstein, *Violence or Non Violence: A Psychoanalytic Exploration of the Choice of Means in Social Change,* Monograph Series, (Princeton, NJ: Center for International Studies, Princeton University, 1965).

103. The Seville Statement on Violence (SSV) is excerpted in David P. Barash, *Introduction to Peace Studies* (Belmont, CA: Wadsworth, 1991), pp. 140–141. Barash identifies the view that "war is in our genes" disproportionately with right-wing and promilitary persons but presents no evidence for such an association. Ibid., p. 140.

104. James Silverberg and J. Patrick Gray, eds., *Introduction to Aggression and Peacefulness in Humans and Other Primates* (New York: Oxford University Press, 1992).

Chapter
8

Macrocosmic Theories of Violent Conflict: International War

W e now turn to those who theorize about war at the macro level—the level of societies, nation-states, and the global system. Here we examine insights into large-scale social-structural violence that can be obtained from the work of anthropologists, sociologists, political scientists, and international-relations specialists. Whereas the microanalysts look within the individual member of the species for unconscious, aggressive drives, and tend to be somewhat skeptical of consciously articulated motives for social and international conflict, macroanalysts in general take seriously statements of conscious, verbal motives and reasons for people's resort to violence within, between, and among societies. They regard such statements as particularly important for explaining why specific conflicts break out between specific parties at specific times. They ascribe a certain validity to the dictum of Thucydides: If you want to know why people are fighting a war, ask them and they will tell you.

Social scientists, especially most sociologists and anthropologists, who adopt a macro approach to human phenomena tend to regard conflict as a normal concomitant of group existence, not as the disruptive, dysfunctional, or even pathological condition most psychologists take it to be. Those sociologists who follow Talcott Parsons in emphasizing social adjustment, common-value orientation, and system maintenance are an exception. More interested in social order than in social change, in social statics than in social dynamics, the Parsonians consider conflict as a disease with disruptive and dysfunctional consequences. However, most European sociologists from Karl Marx to Georg Simmel and Ralf Dahrendorf, and most American sociologists in the pre-Parsonian era (e.g., Robert E. Park, John W. Burgess, William Graham Sumner, Charles H. Cooley, E. A. Ross, and Albion W. Small) and some in recent decades (e.g., Jesse Bernard and Lewis A. Coser) have viewed conflict as serving positive social purposes.[1] Even violent conflict sometimes is seen as a useful means of resolving disputes within society and between societies. Political scientists, economists, and game theorists, along with most rational political leaders, usually prefer to evaluate specific conflicts on the basis of probable or actual outcomes—that is, by weighing the gains of conflict in terms of values at stake versus the risks and cost of the conflict.

For conflict-as-functional theorists, conflict not only integrates, but also helps to establish group identity, clarifies group boundaries, and contributes to group cohesion. Nearly every sociologist and anthropologist postulates some degree of in-group hostility for the out-group. When there are many out-groups, the political scientist can cast light on the question of why a particular one may be singled out at a particular time as the target of hostility. Historians of nationalism often describe the importance of the external *bête noire* in the formative period of a nation's consciousness. The prime example in American history is the role played by Britain in the early formative period of national feeling. Beyond this well-known phenomenon, some social theorists contend that even within groups, discord and opposition help to hold the groups together by providing inner relief and making the unbearable bearable.[2] Thus, many thinkers in modern times accept conflict as "the central explanatory category for the analysis of social change or progress."[3]

INSIDE VERSUS OUTSIDE DIMENSIONS OF CONFLICT

Many social theorists since Machiavelli have taken it for granted that a significant relationship exists between conflict *within* societies and conflict *between* societies. This gives rise to one of the most durable yet hard-to-confirm hypotheses in social-conflict theory. The relationship can be formulated in two ways: (1) internal conflict varies inversely with external conflict; and (2) domestic cohesion correlates positively with involvement in foreign wars. Political rulers in all ages, faced with growing troubles and turmoil at home, have apparently been tempted to provoke foreign military adventures as a diversionary tactic.

William Graham Sumner advanced the theory that groups seek internal unity, for strength in competition with external enemies; that the sentiments of peace and cooperation inside the group are complementary to sentiments of hostility toward outside groups; and that societies that experienced frequent and fierce wars developed governments and legal systems, while the whole societal system became more firmly integrated.[4] William James, too, saw war as "the gory nurse that trained societies to cohesiveness" in ancient times.[5]

Uncertainty over tenure of power among ruling elites, according to Richard Rosecrance, may make war more probable by bringing aggressive military and political personalities to the fore.[6] Clyde Kluckhohn writes, "If a nation's intra-group aggressions become so serious that there is danger of disruption, war, by displacing aggression against another group, is an adjustive response from the point of view of preserving national cohesion."[7] Students of primitive tribes have noted that where warfare once served those groups as a safety-valve institution, and intrasocietal aggressiveness was siphoned off by directing considerable hostility toward the outside world to promote the integration of the society, modernization and peace have led to community fission.[8] Georg Simmel noted the reciprocity between social–political centralization and the aggressive impulse to war. War promotes inner cohesiveness, yet internal political centralization increases the probability that external release of tensions will be sought through war. According to Simmel, "War with the outside is sometimes the last chance for a state ridden with inner antagonisms to overcome these antagonisms, or else to break up indefinitely."[9]

Geoffrey Blainey, on the contrary, rejects what he calls the "scapegoat theory" of war, despite its undoubted universal glow in the eyes of political scientists, historians, and anthropologists. Although admitting that more than half of all international wars from 1823 to 1937 studied by him were immediately preceded by serious disturbances in one of the fighting nations, he concluded that scapegoat theorists rely on dubious assumptions—for example, that war can be blamed on one side, that strife-torn nations are more likely to initiate war, and that every mild disturbance poses a threat of disintegration in the absence of war. If scapegoat theorists read the evidence of political history more carefully, he observed, they would cease to overlook two important facts: (1) The troubled nation can more easily suppress internal discontent if it does not become involved in international war; and (2) an external foe, seeing turmoil within a country as a sign of weakness, is more likely to try to exploit the situation by making war.[10]

The empirical evidence for the reciprocal relationship between internal and external conflict is not as conclusive as it once seemed. Studies conducted in the 1960s and 1970s, using quantitative methods to prove or disprove the correlation, produced ambiguous results.[11] Bruce Bueno de Mesquita and David Lalman have concluded, "We do not know . . . whether the expectation of high domestic costs makes nations more or less likely to shun violent escalation of crises."[12] In 1992, Randolph M. Siverson and Harvey Starr rendered this summary opinion:

> The relationship between internal and external factors in the explanation of international politics and foreign policy may be seen as an academic equivalent to the quest for the Holy Grail—many have searched for it; the search has taken place over long periods of time and in diverse research areas. . . . Many signs point to the reality of such internal–external linkages, but a systematic connection has been hard to demonstrate consistently.[13]

Nevertheless, despite the difficulty of establishing a simple, generalized correlation, political and other social scientists will probably continue to be intrigued by the theory for its utility in explaining such types of cases, and to inquire into the similarities and dissimilarities of the types of cases in which it appears valid and those in which it does not. Several international-relations writers in the 1960s and 1970s noted a correlation between periodic thaws in U.S.–Soviet relations (e.g., in 1956, 1967, and 1973) and a loosening of the cohesion of their respective alliances.[14] There is no need to interpret the traditional theory to mean that external conflict always militates in favor of increased social cohesion or that in the prolonged absence of external conflict, internal disintegration necessarily occurs. Both domestic and international politics are too complicated and subtle for such facile rules of thumb.

Well-integrated communities are held together by more than fear, hostility, and external conflict. Shared beliefs and values, as well as the expectation of mutual benefits from living together, can be important factors making for cohesion. What the theory asserts is that external conflict can be one significant factor, but certainly not the only one. If the process of internal consensus–disintegration has progressed too far, involvement in a foreign conflict might hasten rather than reverse that progress. France became internally divided during the Algerian conflict, as did the United States during the Vietnam War, and the Soviet Union as a result of its intervention in Afghanistan. Any effort to correlate internal and external conflict behavior is likely to be inconclusive if it ignores such crucial variables as the degree of consensus that exists concerning the priority values of the political system and the societal beliefs about what is at stake in the conflict.

In World War II, when the American people were almost unanimous in supporting the war against Germany and Japan, the press gave little if any coverage to those who resisted. In sharp contrast, the Vietnam War found the American people deeply divided over the nature of the conflict (whether an international or a civil war), the purpose of U.S. involvement (to fulfill a treaty commitment, contain communism, preserve Vietnamese national independence, or establish a balance of power in Asia), and the extent to which developments in Southeast Asia could jeopardize the U.S. national interest. Instead of waging all-out war, the United States imposed limits on the conduct of its own military operations, partly because of criticism and opposition from intellectuals, students, pacifist groups, the media, many politicians and substantial segments of the public—all of whom were increasingly confused and frustrated by a costly war effort that seemed futile. Moreover, President Johnson was torn between his domestic and his foreign priorities—building the "Great Society" and prosecuting the war against a small country that was able to mobilize its resources fully to achieve victory. The relation between internal and external conflict can be evaluated only within a total political context that varies greatly from case to case. Although empirical studies in this area thus far leave much to be desired, it would seem that the theory of an inverse linkage between intrasocietal and extrasocietal conflict needs greater refinement and more differentiated research by students of international relations.[15]

LESSONS FROM PRIMITIVE AND OTHER SOCIETIES

The experience of primitive societies is not directly relevant for understanding contemporary international relations. Modern technologically advanced civilizations are not lineal descendants of primitive cultures. Ever since the age of discovery and exploration four centuries ago, Western philosophers and social theorists have been fascinated by primitive ways of social organization and life, and they have sought to gain from them insights into the problems of civilization, including war. In earlier times, when there were abundant cases of societies unaffected by contact with the West, there were practically no trained scientific observers, and many superficial or erroneous conclusions were drawn. (Hobbes, Locke, and Rousseau, for example, apparently thought that the Indians of North America lived in a "state of nature," without government.) In the nineteenth century, as the science of cultural anthropology developed, the purity or authenticity of most primitive cultures had been diluted by the importation of Western religious and social beliefs, ideas, and practices. Considerable care must be exercised, therefore, in the interpretation of primitive institutions and customs.

Anthropologists avoid striving for a single generalization—for example, that primitives are basically warlike or that they are basically peaceful. Some primitives are extremely belligerent and always spoiling for a fight; others are almost exclusively peaceful. Clyde Kluckhohn writes,

> Organized offensive warfare was unknown in aboriginal Australia. Certain areas of the New World seem to have been completely free from war in the pre-European period. . . . What is absolutely certain at present is that different types of social order carry with them varying degrees of propensity for war. The continuum ranges from groups like the Pueblo Indians who for many centuries have almost never engaged in offensive warfare to groups like some Plains Indians who made fighting their highest virtue.[16]

Where the word for war as a form of socially organized aggression or fighting is not even a part of some primitive languages—for example, of the Eskimos and the Andaman Islanders—we must hesitate to attribute this to the inherently peaceful character of the people, especially because they are in no proximate contact with well-defined societies. For technologically undeveloped societies, war, like violent crime, is usually a function of physical proximity. Prior to the era of the airplane and the missile, only maritime countries possessed the capabilities to mount offensive warfare at a distance.[17] In fact, even in recent decades, most international wars have been waged between those communities that usually have the most frequent occasions and perhaps the strongest reasons for fighting—territorially adjacent states.

It would seem that the experience of most primitive societies is similar to that of many modern civilized states: They know alternating periods of war and peace, except that primitive wars (or raids) are more frequent and of shorter duration. Nearly all primitive societies seek to minimize *internal* violence by developing systems of law calculated to prevent the application of the *lex talionis,* which permits vindictive retaliation by individual victims of crime, from escalating out of control.[18] Nonetheless, most of these societies are willing from time to time to resort to external violent behavior for purposes they consider important. Andrew P. Vayda has pointed out that war among primitives serves as a regulating variable for the achievement of several different functions:

1. To remove inequalities in the possession of, or access to, certain economic goods and resources (land, camels, horses, water, hunting grounds, etc.) through redistribution;
2. To regulate such demographic variables as population size, sex ratios, and age distribution (as a result of war casualties), obtaining new sources of food and taking women and others captive;
3. To regulate relations with other groups (i.e., to deter certain types of undesirable behavior in the future by avenging and punishing offenses or wrongs committed); and
4. To regulate psychological variables (anxiety, tension, and hostility) that are adverse to in-group cohesion by directing them outward.[19]

Some anthropologists stress singular explanatory variables, such as the desire to avenge insults[20] or the determination to protect the tribal reputation against charges of weakness and cowardice that may invite attack.[21]

Vayda's analytic scheme synthesizes psychological, demographic, economic, and social variables, in which the regulation of each one depends on the regulation of another. He refrains from insisting that his hypotheses about primitive war could be applied to warfare between civilized states. Moreover, he admits that more extensive data are needed to validate the hypotheses, and that some of the data needed are difficult to obtain.[22]

Finally, it is worth noting that primitive societies do not become involved in conflict over differing patterns of socioeconomic organization (e.g., private or communal property systems), probably because such societies do not develop elaborate sentiment structures or ideologies over such things. In some cases, the ferocity of conflict between neighboring primitives is attenuated by common religious beliefs, by endogamy (the practice of seeking wives from other tribes, thereby establishing blood ties), by imposing certain limits on warfare, by the conclusion of peace treaties and the exchange of hostages, and occasionally even by substituting *cold war* (the shouting of epithets and insults) for physical combat. However, Vayda concedes that such intercommunity ties as intermarriage, commerce, and beliefs in common descent do not constitute a guarantee against the outbreak of hostilities.[23]

OTHER INSIGHTS FROM THEORISTS OF SOCIETY

According to Alvin and Heidi Toffler, conflict can be traced to what they term the *massive changes* that periodically transform societies. Writing about the "general crisis of industrialism" in 1970, the Tofflers pointed to the dramatic changes that accompanied the end of industrial civilization and the dawn of a new postindustrial era.[24] To describe the inherent dynamism of such a transition, the Tofflers used the metaphor of colliding waves of history in which civilizations clash with each other, unleashing powerful conflicting crosscurrents. The world is in the midst of a deepening division among three "distinct, differing, and potentially clashing civilizations."[25] The waves described by the Tofflers include (First Wave) agrarian societies, the production and wealth-generation base of which is agricultural, and the societal structures of which are premodern, with populations living at primitive, subsistence levels, and with little or no change from how their ancestors lived; (Second Wave) industrial-age civilization based on factory production resulting from the Industrial Revolution and giving rise to unprecedented urbanization, mass education, mass media, and dramatic changes in family and other social structures; and (Third Wave) postindustrial society based on information-age technologies with a quickening pace of technological and cultural change. The Tofflers point out that First Wave societies provide agricultural products and minerals, while the Second Wave sector is the source of cheap labor and mass production. The Third Wave nations are distinguished by the extent to which they sell information, engage in innovation, and are the source of a broadening range of services, including military protection, such as that provided by the United States and other high-tech nations for Kuwait and Saudi Arabia during the Persian Gulf War.

Although Third Wave societies will remain dependent on First and Second Wave societies for markets and resources, Third Wave partners will have a greater range of interaction with each other than with members of the First or the Second Waves. As a result, the Tofflers foresee rising tensions between Third Wave civilizations and the First and Second Waves. They point to the destabilizing conflicts, including wars, that marked the clash between agrarian and industrial societies as the Industrial Revolution unfolded and spread from its point of origin to other parts of the world. They suggest that in every industrializing country there were conflicts, often violent, between Second Wave industrial interests and First Wave groups such as landowners. Millions of people were thrust into factories and sprawling cities from the agrarian existence they and their forebearers had led for centuries. The strikes, civil disturbances, nationalist uprisings, and wars sparked by the collision between the agrarian–industrial waves can be expected to have their counterpart in the Third Wave era, and perhaps to be intensified by the accelerating pace and magnitude of postindustrial change.

Just as the clash between the first two waves produced a change in the center of gravity of world power to the industrialized world in Europe and North America and away from the Ottoman Empire, the locus of global power for the future will be determined by the outcome of the information revolution. The leading Third Wave societies will be the future major powers, just as the basis for a Second Wave great-power status was defined by industrial development. The net effect, assert the Tofflers, will be to produce a twenty-first-century global system in which the arena in which future conflicts will be waged will be shaped by fundamental differences among the types of units in their connectivity with each other, in the speed of change to which they are subjected, and in their respective interests, including survival requirements. Conflicts will arise from increasing economic gaps among the three waves, as well as the likely efforts by the Third Wave to establish global hegemony, as Second Wave societies did with respect to premodern societies in previous eras.

In sum, according to the Tofflers, we are in the midst of historic change from a world based on agrarian and industrial societies to a system that includes, as its most dynamic element, the postindustrial, information-age Third Wave. The conflicts of the future will be the result of efforts by states to position themselves in this emerging three-tiered setting. The wars that will be fought, the Tofflers assert, will differ from those of the past, as a result of the impact of information-age technologies. Such technologies will dominate the digitized battlefield, while a multiplicity of transborder electronic networks will create new spatial relationships and conflict dimensions. Unlike agrarian states, Third Wave societies will have no need to acquire new territories or even as in the industrial Second Wave, to have direct control over natural resources. Their principal requirement, in addition to energy and food, will be access to knowledge that is convertible to wealth. Specifically, this translates into control of databases and telecommunications networks, or cyber-spaces, together with access to markets for information-based services.

Anthropologists and sociologists have formulated a great many hypotheses and partial theories relating to social conflict. It is not possible to examine all of them. Most of these hypotheses and theories have been suggested only in passing, without ever being subject to any thorough, systematic development and rigorous testing. All that can be done here is to present in summary form a sample of better-known hypotheses and theories, some of which are the stock-in-trade of so many writers that they cannot properly be attributed to any one.

1. Organized and collective fighting is distinct from individual, sporadic, and spontaneous acts of violence. The latter are antecedents of homicide and civil disorder, but not of war.[26] For anthropologists and sociologists, large-scale conflict and war arise more out of social structures and conditions than they do out of biological urges or psychological states. Warfare, said Margaret Mead, is a cultural invention, not a biological necessity.[27] William Graham Sumner argued that war originates from a struggle between groups, not between individuals.[28] Bronislaw Malinowski held that war is not primeval or biologically determined, and it makes its appearance late in human evolution. "Human beings never fight on an extensive scale under the direct influence of an aggressive impulse," Malinowski declared,[29] thereby severing the connection between psychological pugnacity and culturally determined fighting. Most cases of violent action are seen as the result of purely conventional, traditional, and ideological imperatives. Malinowski further stated, "All types of fighting are complex cultural responses due not to any direct dictates of an impulse, but to collective forms of sentiment and value."[30] David Bidney has criticized Malinowski for adhering too rigidly to the view that war played no significant part in the earlier stages of human development. For Bidney, war can be an agent of cultural change and can bring about significant alterations in social structure.[31]

2. Discussion of international conflict in the abstract lacks cogency. Social scientists should not analyze the behavior of nations without reference to the intervening variable of culture, warn Margaret Mead and Rhoda Metraux, who cite as an example the impossibility of understanding conflict in Lebanon while ignoring the role of religious communities.[32] If Soviet behavior during the Cold War was to be at all intelligible and predictable, they suggested, one must understand the Russian preoccupation with the full use of strength, insistence on testing the limits, and willingness to be guided by them. "For example, in a situation in which Englishmen, Americans, and Russians are involved as participants, it is useful to know that the English regard compromise as a positive outcome, that Americans regard compromise negatively, and that Russians define behavior which, in English and American eyes, would be regarded as compromise, as a necessary and quite admirable strategic retreat after having put forth all available strength."[33]

3. The basic attitudes and values of societies are deeply embedded in an intricate system of cultural institutions and processes. Hence they cannot be easily or quickly changed. Clyde Kluckhohn has offered this advice to reformers: "Make haste slowly is usually a good motto for those who wish to institute or direct social change. Because of the enormous tenacity of non-logical habits, the hasty attempt to alter intensifies resistance or even produces reaction."[34]

4. In recent decades, many social psychologists and political scientists have sought to minimize the misleading and potentially dangerous consequences of stereotyped thinking in an era of mass communications, so they have become skeptical concerning the concept of national character; in contrast, anthropologists are more inclined to attribute a certain validity to it, provided that it is handled with appropriate care.[35]

5. Anthropologists and sociologists are for the most part suspicious of psychopolitics or psychohistory—the efforts to explain policy decisions made by such leaders as Wilson, Hitler, Stalin, de Gaulle, or Zhedong in terms of childhood experiences or psychological characteristics.[36] They do not, of course, deny that key individuals might play an important political role in the making of crucial conflict decisions, but they are disposed to explain those decisions in terms of social rather than psychological factors. (Although psychohistory has sometimes been severely criticized, it continues to have its defenders.[37])

6. Ethnocentrism, the overvaluation of one's own group in comparison with other groups, is virtually a universal phenomenon.[38]

7. The relative persistence of cultural patterns does not mean that nations are incapable of undergoing significant behavioral changes over time. Many writers have called attention to the striking alteration in the political outlook and behavior of Germany and Japan, and the substitution of democratic constitutional systems for dictatorial–militarist regimes, following defeat in World War II. These extreme cases might prompt us to formulate a trauma theory of rapid, fundamental social change. More gradual and more complex was the change in the world view, and the conception of its own role, that Britain underwent as a result of the profound political–technological–strategic shifts set in motion by the two world wars.

8. All through history, from the time Archimedes went to a mountaintop near the sea and used a glass to focus the rays of the sun on the sails of an enemy ship, down to our own days of nuclear warheads, laser beams, and information-age warfare, war and technological change have been closely related. Preparations for war and waging war itself bring science, technology, industry, and medicine into cooperation with governments for purposes of military research and development, which may have spin-off applications in nonmilitary dimensions. Scholars have shown how inventions from the canning of food and the sewing machine through chemicals down to jet engines, radar, nuclear energy, rockets, electronic communications, and blood plasma received their initial impetus from the military needs of the state.[39]

9. Some anthropological hypotheses may appear to be contradictory but actually are not. We are told, for example, that both differences and similarities of peoples may lead to bitter conflicts. Substantial differences of an ethnic, linguistic, religious, racial, cultural, or ideological character are easily perceived and thus can give rise to animosity and a sense of threat, especially when different groups are physically close to each other, yet unequal in political and economic power. Differences that have been politically muted or controlled for a long time within a single nation may flare up and generate pressures for separatism or autonomy (e.g., Quebec in Canada, the

Scots in the United Kingdom, the Walloons and the Flemish in Belgium, and the Basques in Spain).[40] On the other hand, it has often been noted that the closer the parties are together in belief systems, the more intense a conflict between them is likely to be.[41] Thus conflict is particularly intense when a group that was previously united undergoes schism and both groups henceforth claim to be the authentic heirs to the tradition. Examples include Catholic and Protestant Christians, Sunni and Shi'i Muslims, and Stalinists and Trotskyites.

10. Conflict may be studied by reference to the pattern of communications between the parties and the language employed in the conflict. As the conflict is developing, communication between the parties declines and intra-party communication (and cohesion) intensifies. Maximum conflict intensity coincides with minimal communication between the parties, as well as with intragroup propaganda of maximum hostility against the enemy. Changes in patterns of communication and propaganda usually signal a change in conflict intensity and a movement toward conflict resolution. Every conflict has its unique structure, arising out of the nature of the parties, the issues at stake, the circumstances in which the conflict is waged, and the particular dynamic according to which it develops. In analyzing any specific conflict, a knowledge of the particular features of that conflict is just as important as, if not more important than, generalized knowledge of conflict processes.

REVOLUTION AND WAR

The phenomenon of revolution, quite separate from that of war, belongs properly to the study of the internal politics of states, and thus to the subfield of comparative politics rather than to international relations. In the late 1960s, American social scientists, largely in response to the Vietnam War, became preoccupied with the problem of revolutionary wars of guerrilla insurgency and national liberation in the Third World. Once nuclear deterrence had greatly reduced the likelihood of direct military hostilities among the major powers and those aligned with one of the principal rivals, it appeared that military strategists had shifted their attention to a dimension of conflict in which such factors as nation-building, alienation, rising socioeconomic expectations, the dislocating effects of development and modernization, the breakdown of traditional mechanisms of social integration, ideological propaganda, and communications media played a more important part than did advanced weapons technology. Because the Soviet Union was favorably disposed to support disputes considered to be just wars of national liberation, whereas Western governments usually felt compelled to support incumbent regimes in those countries where they had political, economic, and military interests, several of the gray-area wars in Asia, Africa, and Latin America were drawn into the vortex of the Cold War between the two superpowers and their alliance systems. Notable among these were the upheavals in Laos, Cambodia, Vietnam, Indonesia, the Philippines, Malaya, Somalia, Eritrea, Ethiopia, Mozambique, Angola, Algeria, the Western Sahara, Cyprus, Cuba, Nicaragua, and El Salvador. The United States, the Soviet Union, Britain, France, and Communist China at various times intervened in some of these and other so-called revolutionary insurgencies by providing not only political, diplomatic, and economic support but also military assistance in the form of advisers, training, equipment, weapons, and military forces.

Revolution is an old concept in social theory. Classical political writers were intensely interested in the problems of cyclical change, efforts to overthrow governments by violence, and the moral–political justifications of revolution. They usually attributed revolutionary pressures to an intolerable discrepancy between people's desires and their perceived situation, leading to irreconcilable disagreement over how and by whom society ought to be politically organized. It is necessary to distinguish between genuine political revolutions and other phenomena that are often called by the same name—for example, the coup d'etat (including palace revolts by rival relatives of a monarch, the illegal prolongation of a leader's term of office, military coups, and other relatively sudden seizures of power by small groups of high-status individuals);[42] various forms of peasant, urban, religious, and other short-lived uprisings; and political breaking away, known as secession (provincial, colonial, ethnic, or religious). None of these need have the remotest connection with revolutionary change, says Mark N. Hagopian, who defines revolution as "an acute, prolonged crisis in one or more of the traditional systems of stratification (class, status, or power) of a political community, which involves a purposive, elite-directed attempt to abolish or to reconstruct one or more of said systems by means of an intensification of political power and recourse to violence."[43]

Revolutions are often connected in one way or another with wars, and thus are of more than passing interest to international theorists. An understanding of revolutionary behavior and of the leaders who mobilize and give political direction to collective frustration–aggression enables us to differentiate between internal revolution and international war.[44] Moreover, revolution is often fraught with significant implications and consequences for the international system, and thus provides a salient case of linkage between domestic and foreign politics. This certainly holds for the large-scale, historic, true revolutions, such as the French, Bolshevik, Chinese, Cuban, and Iranian revolutions. To a lesser extent, the linkage applies also to smaller-scale revolutionary insurgencies and guerrilla wars such as the aforementioned (Laos, Angola, Nicaragua, etc.), which, although they arise out of internal causes, often become internationalized as a result of indigenous motives (seeking outside support) and/or the interests of external states in intervening.

According to Stephen M. Walt, "studying the international effects of revolutionary change is an obvious way to compare the merits of systemic and unit-level explanations of state behavior."[45] He calls revolutions "watershed" events in international politics, inasmuch as they "cause abrupt shifts in the balance of power, place alliance commitments and other international agreements in jeopardy, and provide inviting opportunities for other states to improve their positions."[46] Most of the literature on revolutions, he laments, focuses on either their causes or their domestic consequences (see Note 42), whereas a study of the foreign policies of revolutionary states can show how systemic forces modify revolutionary behavior and how unit-level factors (e.g., a revolutionary regime) may change the impact of normal systemic restraints on the action of states.[47] Basing his findings on a study of ten cases—France (1789), Mexico (1910), Russia (1917), Turkey (1919), China (1949), Cuba (1959), Ethiopia (1974), Cambodia/Kampuchea (1975), Iran (1978), and Nicaragua (1979)[48]—Walt concludes that revolutions increase the pressures that lead to war. He regards three popular explanations as inadequate, even though they may be partially valid in particular cases:

1. Revolutionary regimes cause war because they insist on exporting their dogmatic, radical, and aggressive ideologies. (He cites five of the ten cases in which postrevolutionary wars were initiated by other than the revolutionary states.)
2. Postrevolutionary wars arise out of the domestic political situation, when contending factions exploit foreign wars to advance their own ends, or the revolutionary leaders promote foreign conflict to rally popular support, justify repressive policies, and provide a scapegoat to distract from continuing domestic ills. (Leaders are just as likely to prefer consolidating their power by focusing on domestic problems rather than by risking all in a foreign war.)
3. Personality traits of revolutionary leaders—ruthlessness, arrogant self-confidence to the point of recklessness, the need to maintain a heroic image, and so on—impel them to provoke foreign conflicts. (Walt rejects the concept of a revolutionary personality as imprecise, inconsistent, and extremely difficult to relate either logically or empirically to the concrete foreign-policy situations that are conducive to war or peace.)[49]

Neither is Walt satisfied with an explanation based on the neorealist balance-of-power theory of Kenneth N. Waltz, in which security is the highest goal of states and the distribution of power capabilities is the primary explanatory variable. Because revolutions may alter the balance of power, they create opportunities for either the revolutionary regimes or other states to improve their own positions.[50] Walt demurs, arguing that states do not rush to war merely because the balance of power has changed; they must also expect that rushing to war will make them more secure. Walt abandons balance-of-power theory in favor of a balance-of-threat theory, in which threat is a matter of both offensive power and intention.

> In addition to changing the overall balance of power and making it more difficult for states to measure it accurately, revolutions also reduce each side's ability to assess the other's intentions with confidence. Indeed, revolutions encourage both sides to believe that the other's intentions are even more hostile than they are. . . . Each side thus fears that it is vulnerable to ideological challenge, yet each also tends to believe that its opponents are vulnerable as well. . . .[51]
>
> Although balance-of-power theory emphasizes the importance of security, it is not the aggregate balance of power that drives states to war. Rather, it is each side's perception of threat. These perceptions arise both from systems-level and unit-level factors. Revolutions alter the balance of threats by changing the distribution of power, by increasing perceptions of hostility, and by increasing perceptions of an offensive advantage. The problem is exacerbated by uncertainty regarding each of these factors and by

the other dynamics that encourage both sides to view the other as especially hostile and dangerous.[52]

Whereas Walt treats the relationship between revolution and war as explicable within the realist framework, Harvey Starr suggests that such a relationship casts doubt on the realist assumption of Kenneth N. Waltz that international systemic behavior is rather independent of what happens *within* states. In Starr's view, the earlier writings of Rummel and Tanter on the systematic relationships between internal and external conflict lacked theoretical specification, and their flaws in logic and research design—pertaining to case selection and time periods covered—led to problems of validity and failed to demonstrate the connection between internal and external conflict.[53] Starr, however, seems to agree essentially with Walt in this passage:

> We must first differentiate between the ways in which revolution could lead to war and the ways in which war could lead to revolution. Looking at revolution-to-war, two basic relationships emerge—in what ways revolution would lead a state to attack another, or in what ways revolution would make a state an attractive *target* for another state. War-to-revolution may be based upon war as an agent of change, as a factor in the growth of domestic discontent . . . in the weakening of government legitimacy and/or strength, or . . . in the changing resource base of opposition groups. Whether a war is won or lost must also be factored into the war-to-revolution relationship.[54]

Starr cites George Tsebelis's notion that decision makers play multiple games in multiple arenas, where "any of the actor's moves has consequences in all arenas" and where "an optimal alternative in one arena (or game) will not necessarily be optimal with respect to the entire network of arenas in which the actor is involved."[55] To put Starr's theory as simply as possible: Governments require resources in order to survive and remain viable in the face of internal opposition and external threat; leaders can try to extract the needed resources from either domestic or foreign sources; thus they must engage in a two-level game, estimating internal versus external risks and internal versus external defense capabilities.[56] Starr notes that both Karl W. Deutsch's integration theory (see Chapter 10) and Nazli Choucri and Robert North's international lateral-pressure theory (treated later in this chapter) indicate that governments find themselves in a constant quest for resources, and that many other scholars in recent decades have focused on this search for resources.[57] Lateral-pressure processes play a significant part in the theories of hegemonic war of Gilpin and of power transition (or differential rates in the growth of nations' power) of A. F. K. Organski and Jacek Kugler (both of which are discussed later herein). Harvey Starr adds that revolution can also produce a significant effect on differential rates of power growth or decline, and he concurs with Stephen Walt's complaint that this phenomenon has not received the explicit recognition it deserves in the war literature.[58]

THE INTERNATIONALIZATION OF INTERNAL WAR AND LOW-INTENSITY CONFLICT

In nearly every historical age, the existence of revolutionary conditions within states has led to intervention by strong foreign powers.[59] Weaker revolutionary forces seek to augment their chances for success by inviting outside aid, usually from revolutionary or expansionist powers. Several considerations help to determine the location of revolutionary conflict. Insurgents are disposed to establish bases in regions with a record of previous revolutionary activity or sentiment.[60] They want access to major political targets, as well as economic self-sufficiency. They are anxious to secure a base in zones of weak political control, not easily accessible to and penetrable by government forces. Hence, they are attracted to provinces not served efficiently by road, rail, and air transport and to terrain that, although lending cover to small guerrilla bands, proves hostile to the movement of larger and more cumbersome conventional military forces—mountains, jungles, forests, river deltas, swamplands, and deserts. Not only physical geography but also political geography enters the picture. Whenever possible, insurgents usually find it advantageous to establish headquarters, training camps, and supply routes close to or across the borders of friendly or neutral countries. The guerrillas may then seek legal sanctuary or political haven when subjected to hot pursuit, thus compelling incumbent government forces to incur international censure if they carry their punitive action to the area of retreat. Moreover, borderlands are frequently zones of ethnic heterogeneity and diversity of political loyalties, factors that revolutionaries may find helpful. Logistical considerations always loom large. Sources and routes of foreign supply are extremely important factors in the political geography of guerrilla revolution.

During the period of the Cold War, the two principal powers committed to a reversal of the international status quo strongly supported "national liberation warfare" (as the Soviet Union called it) or "people's war" (as the Chinese called it). These modes of indirect conflict were relatively safe methods of carrying on the international revolutionary movement, compared with the more dangerous methods of direct confrontation with what was then unquestionably a nuclear-superior West. If one superpower intervened in a Third World internal war, the other usually felt some temptation, pressure, or tendency to do likewise in support of the opposite side. In the 1960s, the United States, the Soviet Union, and China intervened at various times in Third World insurgencies, particularly in Asia. In the 1970s and subsequently, Asia and Africa were arenas of competition among the three major military powers. It was not at all uncommon to find, in such areas as Angola, Zimbabwe (formerly Rhodesia), and Eritrea, two or three competing revolutionary organizations, each with a different ethnic or religious base, as well as incumbent regimes—all supported by different outside major powers, or pairs of them. In the 1980s, Afghanistan and Central America constituted principal areas of competitive superpower intervention. The situation has changed substantially since the end of the Cold War.

During the period of superpower confrontation, virtually every conflict that occurred within the purview of news-gathering agencies became an item in the competitive environment of international relations. Revolutions and insurgencies produced demonstrations in distant foreign countries to support one side or protest against the other. The world communications net was fully exploited in the globalization of localized conflict, as revolutionary and guerrilla organizations sought to acquire some semblance of international personality and thus to win foreign support in the forms of money, arms, diplomatic backing, popular sympathy, and other kinds of assistance. The process by which the Palestine Liberation Organization (PLO) achieved recognition by the United Nations General Assembly was a classic case in point. Many other internal conflicts were drawn into the vortex of world politics when they became items in the decision-making or deliberative processes of national movements, the United Nations, and such regional alliances as NATO (e.g., Algeria), the Organization of American States (e.g., El Salvador), and the Organization of African Unity (e.g., the Western Sahara). Some conflicts were internationalized when anti-status-quo causes were taken up by political parties, churches, peace groups, and ethnic, religious, and ideological affiliates.

In some cases, conflict outcomes were determined largely by internal factors, such as the morale, training, leadership and strategic–tactical doctrines of revolutionary and governmental forces, as well as their ability to utilize the media and otherwise influence elites and masses. In other cases, external factors such as large-scale arms aid, training and advice, political support, and economic assistance may have been decisive. As Karl W. Deutsch observed more than three decades ago, if outside resources constitute the main capabilities committed to the struggle on both sides, then it is appropriate to speak of war by proxy—an international conflict between two foreign powers, fought out on the soil of a third country; disguised as conflict over an internal issue of that country; and using that country's human and natural resources and territory as means for achieving preponderantly foreign goals.[61] In such a case, local parties to the conflict lose the power of initiative and control to a complex international process of strategic planning, diplomatic bargaining and negotiation, and political–military decision making—a process in which the local parties within the conflict-ridden nation may play only a subordinate client role. In the 1970s, several scholars began to examine this nexus between the internal and the external causes of revolutionary conflict in the Third World. This reflected a recognition of the increasing significance of state-supported and, in some cases, state-sponsored insurgency, terrorism, and other forms of low-intensity conflict. Previous studies purporting to identify the causes of internal war had emphasized the importance of indigenous factors, while giving only scant attention to the impact of forces and influences from outside the area of conflict. What tended to be overlooked was the degree to which foreign powers could contribute to the growth and expansion of revolutionary insurgent and terrorist movements through the provision of various kinds of military, political, and economic assistance.[62]

Bard O'Neill, Mark Hagopian, Thomas Greene, and Mostafa Rejai, among others, raised questions about this oversight in the scholarly analysis of internal war or low-intensity conflict.[63] They argued that while the initial causes or preconditions of internal war remain predominantly attributable to indigenous political, economic, and social developments, an important factor that could contribute to the growth of insurgent and terrorist movements to a more advanced stage is the presence of assistance from governments external to the conflict. In the late 1970s and 1980s, the examination of external factors proceeded in several directions. This included an assessment of the strategy and tactics of the Soviet Union and its allies and surrogates as they related to this form of conflict. For example, Stephen

Hosmer and Thomas Wolfe, Bruce Porter, and Joseph Whelan and Michael Dixon surveyed Soviet involvement in low-intensity conflicts throughout the Third World and documented the ways in which it had evolved and escalated. While noting that from the inception of the Soviet regime, the Communist Party of the Soviet Union (CPSU) leadership had identified an almost symbiotic relationship between itself and national liberation movements in the Third World, they attributed the increase in both the level of support and the number of movements receiving assistance to several factors, including

1. Military parity with the United States;
2. An enhanced Soviet capacity to project power and to supply arms and other conflict technology well beyond its borders;
3. The sharpening of active measures, including propaganda, disinformation, agents of influence, international fronts, and related instruments of political and psychological warfare;
4. The declining willingness of the United States to maintain active security commitments in the Third World, as exemplified by its withdrawal from Vietnam, and its subsequent hesitancy, perhaps due to neo-isolationist tendencies, to become as directly involved in foreign conflicts as it had been during the period when it played the role of world police officer; and
5. An increasing number of states and political organizations willing to cooperate with the Soviet Union for the purposes of fundamentally transforming the structure of the international system.[64]

Some specialists concentrated on the specific political and military instruments utilized by the USSR and its allies and surrogates to assist revolutionary insurgent and terrorist movements. For example, John Dziak and John Collins examined the paramilitary role played by the intelligence and security services of the Soviet bloc.[65] John Copper, Daniel Papp, and W. Scott Thompson focused on arms transfers, other kinds of military assistance, and force-projection capabilities.[66] Yet other scholars concentrated on the ways in which propaganda, psychological operations, and political warfare te chniques were employed by the Soviet bloc as part of its overall strategy for aiding revolutionary groups with tactics operationalized and integrated to advance the legitimacy of movements pursuing revolutionary warfare strategies.[67] Decades earlier, Paul Linebarger, William Daugherty, Morris Janowitz, Daniel Lerner, Harold Lasswell, and Jacques Ellul, to name the most prominent, had produced major studies on political and psychological warfare as instruments of statecraft.[68] While the 1970s saw a marked decline in the attention paid by scholars to political, psychological, and paramilitary measures as tools of foreign policy, the 1980s witnessed a rekindling of interest in the topic.[69] Of special interest to Uri Ra'anan, Dennis Bark, and Richard Shultz was the role of Soviet allies and surrogates in providing external support to internal war.[70] They argued that Soviet surrogates appeared to be quite specialized in the tasks and missions they undertook, and that the degree of Moscow's control of influence seemed to vary with and depended on the ideological, political, geographical, and economic nature of the client state itself.

The role of Western countries, particularly the United States, in low-intensity conflicts in the Third World likewise received considerable scholarly and public-policy attention during the 1980s.[71] However, the literature has been marked by considerable disagreement in defining the parameters of low-intensity conflict. At minimum, specialists such as Sam Sarkesian, Stephen Hosmer and George Tanham, and David Dean have argued that low-intensity conflict, as it relates to U.S. foreign and national security policy, includes counterinsurgency, insurgency (resistance movements), counterterrorism, contingency operations (e.g., rescue, raids, and demonstration), and peacekeeping.[72] This subject, as it relates to policy studies, has generated a lively debate, which can be seen by contrasting the works of Sam Sarkesian, Frank Barnett et al., and Richard Shultz with those of Michael Klare and Peter Kornbluh, D. Michael Shafer, and John Prados. Beyond these broader studies of policy and strategy there also is an extensive literature on each of the specific subcategories of low-intensity conflict, including several case studies.[73]

During the Cold War, revolutionary insurgent warfare was among the most prominent forms of low-intensity conflict. Those who employed it combined ancient guerrilla tactics with political, ideological, and psychological means to seize government power and transform political systems. In the 1990s, factions and movements that adopt religion and ethnicity as their ideological basis are employing insurgent and other low-intensity strategies (including terrorism). The pace of ethnic and religious conflict began to pick up in the late 1970s and early 1980s.[74] However, it has escalated in the aftermath of the Cold War and, according to several specialists, will continue to do so in the coming years.[75] These internal conflicts are a serious source of international instability today and a cause of much of the ungovernability that now affects an increasing number of states, many of which can no longer contain demands for autonomy from internal minorities. The growth and spread of such conflicts within states, their seeming ability to leap national boundaries in acts of terrorism, and the dangers of the escalation of these conflicts through the proliferation of both conventional arms and weapons of mass destruction mean that threats arising from ethnic and religious strife cannot be ignored. It is clear from a review of past and present ethnic–religious upheavals that a great deal remains to be learned about the nature of the underlying causes and what, if anything, can be done in response.

A number of different nonstate actors are adopting the methods of political violence associated with low-intensity strategies and tactics. They include ethnic factions, various kinds of religious radicals, militias, secessionists, international criminal organizations, and terrorists and insurgents. They are having, and undoubtedly will continue to have, an increasingly destabilizing impact on specific geographic regions. In fact, according to David Fromkin, it may be that these various forms of low-intensity conflict will result in a "testing time for the modern state system. . . . The overarching issue, as the twenty-first century may come to see it, will not be one cause against another, or one power against another, but order versus anarchy."[76] In other words, there will be a growing global ungovernability—an inability of governments to govern, to provide domestic security, or to maintain the integrity of their boundaries and institutions. This threat and its effects will result in escalating instability in states in various regions of the world, as well as in international economic, political, and security structures. Thus, low-intensity conflict may have a fundamental impact on the international system and its viability as we enter the twenty-first century.

Finally, as during the Cold War, there are international linkages that characterize post–Cold War low-intensity conflict. These linkages exist both between states and the various nonstate actors noted previously and among these nonstate actors themselves. The surge in ethnic conflict has engendered an increase in secessionist movements and nation-state disintegration. Additionally, state support for secessionists reveals that such movements have access to more outside backing at the end of the twentieth century than they did in the past.[77] State support for religious movements is also increasing. The rise of transnational Islamic radicalism and the cooperation between Islamic factions and states is illustrative.[78] There is also evidence of expanding ties between ethnic and religious groups and organized crime. Criminal organizations search out opportunities in the midst of ethnic conflict, and ethnonational movements likewise find advantages in their associations with organized crime. It has become increasingly clear that ethnonationalist and religious groups are taking advantage of international organized crime to purchase arms, share information, and finance operations.

Among the best known of these groups are the Sendero Luminoso ("Shining Path") in Peru, the National Liberation Army and the Revolutionary Armed Forces (FARC) in Colombia. Another case in point is Hezbollah in Lebanon. Since the mid-1980s, it has become involved in drug trafficking as a way of financing its operations. The Hezbollah provides production and transshipment protection to criminal organizations and charges fees for false documents used by couriers.[79] A second example is the Kurdish Workers Party (PKK), which operates from bases in eastern Turkey and northern Iraq. The PKK has links to Iran, Iraq, and Syria, and trains in Lebanon's Beka'a Valley. It also raises funds through various associations with criminal organizations and involvement in criminal activities.[80] Both Hezbollah and the PKK have challenged existing state power in Lebanon and Turkey, as well as that of Israel in southern Lebanon.

In short, notwithstanding the dissolution of the Soviet Union and the end of the Cold War, the study of internal war and low-intensity conflict within the theory and practice of international relations will continue to be of importance in the years ahead. It will, however, be cast in a very different form, in light of the fundamental changes that the global system has been undergoing in the 1990s.

INTERNATIONAL TERRORISM

International terrorism as a form of low-intensity conflict has been a cause of concern to governments in recent decades. The phenomenon cuts across many levels of analysis, from the psychological states of individuals through the sociology of groups to the internal factional politics within states to the governments of targeted countries and of states that support, sponsor, host, train, and shelter terrorist organizations. Terrorist activity takes many different forms—bombings, kidnappings, assassinations, hijackings, violations of diplomatic immunity, the holding of hostages, and so on. It may reflect a variety of motivations—national liberation, irredentism, and secession (e.g., among Irish, Basque, Armenian, Palestinian, and Kurdish nationalists); ideological goals of the left and right (Marxist–Leninists and Fascists); Latin American drug cartels against rival parties, incumbent governments, police forces, MNCs, capitalism, and socialism; fundamentalist and/or revolutionary religious rage against implacable enemies (e.g., Iranian Islam against the "Great Satan," the Hindu–Moslem rivalry over the Ayodhya temple in India, and Islamic fundamentalist efforts to destabilize such secular Arab governments as Egypt, Algeria, and Tunisia, and conservative pro-Western monarchies in Saudi Arabia and Jordan). It is not surprising, therefore, that theorists have had a difficult time defining international terrorism, suggesting effective strategies to contain its spread, and assessing its impact on state behavior and the international system.

Terrorists can hurt weak governments more than those of the great powers, although they can frustrate and embarrass the latter by making them look impotent despite their superior power. Western governments have ostracized Iran, Libya, Syria, and Iraq for sponsoring and supporting terrorist activity, and they have sought to punish these countries with a spectrum of retaliatory policies. Economic sanctions are often ineffective, and military reprisals involve a danger that established governments will be equated with terrorists for harming innocent people. Several governments have improved their cooperation for dealing with terrorists (e.g., pooling information, tightening border controls, and extraditing accused terrorists). It has not been possible, however, to develop coherent international legal standards in this area because of the diffuse nature of the phenomenon, the difficulty of defining and proving state sponsorship, and the fact that many Third World countries resent Western covert operations and are sympathetic toward at least some terrorist causes. An effective, agreed response is not to be expected because political, cultural, and religious attitudes toward the legal and moral justification of using force and violence vary widely within the international community.

It is not unreasonable to conclude that, notwithstanding particular conspiratorial explanations, we shall probably never arrive at a single, coherent theory of international terrorism, nor a universally acceptable solution to it. Terrorism poses a challenge to governments, for not only democratic but all governments are expected to protect their citizens. The hard fact of life, however, is that terrorists injure or kill innocent citizens much more than they damage governments. Up to the present, strong governments have remained relatively impervious to the threats and demands of terrorists, and the latter cannot point to many clear successes in accomplishing their avowed objectives. Stable governments have usually refused to negotiate until terrorist acts are ended—sometimes only after many decades of suffering, when other social, political, psychological, economic, and technological forces have altered the total situation.[81]

POLITICAL SCIENCE AND THE CAUSES OF WAR

Among political scientists, some can be found who are partial to their own single-factor explanations of war, but most are likely to be wary of theories that trace wars to one overriding cause, whether inner biological–psychological urges, the profit

motives of capitalist imperialists, arms races, or alliances. Recalling the fate of earlier predictions that the replacement of monarchies by republics would lead to a
more peaceful world, political scientists are careful about postulating a precise
connection between the form of government and the propensity to go to war. Political scientists are not for the most part easily impressed by the proposals of those
who, diagnosing a single cause of war, prescribe a single panacea for it—universal
socialism, free trade, universal brotherhood of good will, a radical new approach to
education, world government, complete disarmament, maximum military preparedness, or standing firm at all times. Each is woven into a multidimensional
framework, and some may be more important than others as a means of reducing
the likelihood of specific wars.[82]

Quincy Wright, in his pioneering and comprehensive survey of the subject,
stressed the multiple causality of war and warned against simplistic approaches to
the problem: "A war, in reality, results from a total situation involving ultimately
almost everything that has happened to the human race up to the time the war
begins."[83] In his monumental study, which cannot adequately be summarized here,
Wright put forth a four-factor model of the origins of war, corresponding to the levels of technology, law, social–political organization, and cultural values. Karl W.
Deutsch, in his preface to a reissue of Wright's classic work, wrote of these levels,

> Whenever there is a major change at any level—culture and values, political and social
> institutions, laws, or technology—the old adjustment and control mechanisms become
> strained and may break down. Any major psychological and cultural, or major social
> and political, or legal, or technological change in the world thus increases the risk of
> war, unless it is balanced by compensatory political, legal, cultural, and psychological
> adjustments.[84]

According to yet another writer, Clyde Eagleton,

> War is a means for achieving an end, a weapon which can be used for good or for bad
> purposes. Some of these purposes for which war has been used have been accepted by
> humanity as worthwhile ends; indeed, war performs functions which are essential in
> any human society. It has been used to settle disputes, to uphold rights, to remedy
> wrongs; and these are surely functions which must be served. . . . One may say, without
> exaggeration, that no more stupid, brutal, wasteful, or unfair method could ever have
> been imagined for such purposes, but this does not alter the situation.[85]

Nations resort to force to enhance their security by extending or preserving
power, control, and influence over their environment—over the territory, populations, governments, and resources of societies with which they are in contact. In
earlier times, nations were primarily concerned about disputes and contests of
strength with neighbors that were geographically proximate or were more remote
yet reachable by maritime or overland transport. In modern times, developments
in military and communications technology, as well as in international trade,
investment, and monetary matters, have gradually forced a diplomacy that was—
until two centuries ago—confined largely to Europe to become global in outlook.
Conventional political science, based on a knowledge of modern history, has compiled an impressive inventory of conscious reasons why governments have decided
to go to war:

- To gain dominion over territory
- To enhance security
- To acquire wealth and/or prestige
- To preserve (by defending or extending) ethnic, cultural, and religious identity and values
- To preserve or extend dynastic interests
- To weaken a foreign foe
- To gain or hold a colonial empire
- To spread a political ideology
- To prevent secession and national dissolution or territorial loss
- To intervene in foreign conflicts (whether to honor a treaty obligation, support a friendly government, overthrow an unfriendly one, aid in a liberation struggle, etc.)
- To maintain alliance credibility
- To preserve or restore a balance of power and to thwart the hegemonial aims of another power
- To protect a vital economic interest abroad
- To uphold the principle of freedom of the seas
- To fill a power vacuum (before someone else does)
- To fight a small war now rather than a larger one later, or a preventive war that can be won now against a growing power that would pose a greater threat later
- To carry out reprisals against governments for past injuries inflicted
- To protect endangered nationals
- To defend national honor and avenge a grave insult

Even this list is not exhaustive. There are many types of wars—personal, feudal, dynastic, national, civil, revolutionary, religious, ideological, imperialistic, and anticolonial, as well as alliance wars, local and general wars, proxy wars, limited wars, and total wars. The motives for which political communities go to war change over time. Four hundred years ago, Europe was torn by a series of ferocious wars over religious issues. Most Europeans today would regard such a *casus belli* as unthinkable. (Nonetheless the mixing of political and religious issues can still flare up in virulent form, as in the Ulster conflict, the civil war in Lebanon, the war between Iran and Iraq, the conflicts between Sikhs and Hindus, between Sri Lankan Buddhist Sinhalese and Hindu Tamils, or among Serbs, Croats, and Muslims in the former Yugoslavia.)

Political scientists generally insist, therefore, that we cannot understand the causes of war exclusively in terms of biological, psychological, or other behavioral factors, but instead we must always return to the level of political analysis to find out why a particular government regards certain foreign governments as allies and others as adversaries. It is out of a matrix of political communications—involving politicians and diplomats, the public, the press, the military, socioeconomic elites, special interest groups in the foreign policymaking process—that governments define their goals, interests, policies, and strategies, weighing the likely consequences of acting or not acting in specific situations, as well as the prospects of success or failure in invoking force. The findings of the behavioral scientists can serve as valuable illuminators to our understanding of the causes of war, provided that we place them in perspective as partial explanatory factors within the larger international political context in which those who wield the power of decision opt either to go to war or to refrain from it.[86]

Violent encounters between organized political communities may have myriad origins. The ground, sea, or air forces of two adversary societies might suddenly and spontaneously find themselves involved in hostile skirmishes without an authoritative political decision having been made by either government, or one government might order a unit of its armed forces to contrive a military confrontation with a unit of the adversary's forces merely to gauge the psychopolitical reaction without intending war. In an era of advanced military technology, many analysts worried all through the Cold War era about the possibility of accidental or unintentional war, as if nuclear war might be triggered automatically by an incident of technical malfunction.[87] Political scientists and other macrotheorists call attention to the fact that, so far as historical evidence goes, the initiation of war is a matter of conscious, deliberate choice, not of decisionless outbreak.[88]

A number of writers who have dwelt on the concept of inadvertent war have focused on the crisis of July 1914 as a powerful example of how interlocking mobilization schedules (in that case with the Schlieffen Plan as their linchpin) can help trigger the outbreak of war. The lesson often drawn was that in the age of nuclear missiles, preemptive strike or launch-on-warning strategies might overwhelm political leaders in time of crisis, lead to a loss of control, and precipitate an unintended war—one that no one wanted.[89] Marc Trachtenberg rejects the relevance of the 1914 case for the theoretical possibility of inadvertent nuclear war. While conceding that the mechanism of interlocking mobilization plans clearly existed, he contends that it cannot be blamed as a cause of World War I, for the precise reason that the prominent decision makers understood fully in advance how the system worked and that a decision for preemptive mobilization was really a decision for war. Mobilization was seen as the initial phase of an option for war undertaken with eyes wide open. After reviewing the empirical evidence, he denies that Europe's political leaders were ignorant of military matters, ordered mobilization light-heartedly, and stumbled blindly and unwillingly into war. He also rejects the explanation that stateleaders were under irresistible pressure to act quickly, were not really free decision makers, and had surrendered their control of events to the military. Most of the significant political and military decision makers, while dreading war, had—according to Trachtenberg—concluded that war was inevitable before they ordered mobilization.[90]

THE SCIENTIFIC STUDY OF WAR

As we saw in Chapter 1, quantitative analysis is often associated with a behavioral rather than a traditional or postmodernist approach to international theory. Moreover, realists and neorealists are often assumed to be wedded to the traditional state-centric, power-oriented paradigm. Such categorizations are not entirely accurate. Neither traditionalists nor behavioralists, neither realists nor idealists, neither deductive nor inductive theorists can claim a monopoly of scientific methodology. Most modern scientific studies of war, including the statistical analyses conducted since the early 1960s, have been related, wittingly or not, directly or indirectly, positively or negatively, to the dominant realist paradigm of an anarchic international system.

The term *anarchy* in this context carries no connotation of chaos, as it often does in popular discourse. As noted in Chapter 2, it simply implies that there is no international political authority invested with a legitimate monopoly of force capable of enforcing peace, protecting states against aggression, and guaranteeing that their rights will not be violated. The international system, in short, is not the same kind of political system as is the modern, efficient, sovereign nation-state. The collective-security experiment undertaken through the Covenant of the League of Nations was a failure: the motto of the Three Musketeers ("One for all, and all for one") could not be universalized among states. Although the United Nations has been more successful, its mixed record of peacekeeping and preventive diplomacy over the past half-century (examined later in this chapter) gives states little reason to expect any escape from a security dilemma, which continues to compel states' reliance on self-help to defend themselves and their vital interests in a dangerous world.

Thus for the title of his text, Robert J. Lieber has drawn on a line from Thomas Hobbes's *Leviathan:* "Hereby it is manifest, that during the time when men live without a common power to keep them in awe, they are in that condition which is called war."[91] Since World War II, realists and neorealists have not been so pessimistically Hobbesian as to think that all states, or even all great powers, are necessarily disposed at all times toward aggressive expansion. In any given historical age, it is probable that a number of governments prefer to pursue peaceful policies and avoid violent conflicts, so long as those that might conceivably pose a threat to them do likewise. Yet in every era since antiquity—of city-states, empires, kingdoms, and modern nation-states—some organized political communities have perceived an advantage of gain in going to war, and others have perceived threats to their security. The anticipations of gain may have been shrewd or unfounded; the threats perceived may have been real or imaginary. The fact remains that wars have recurred throughout history. Wars can bring such disastrous consequences that the likelihood or even the possibility of credible future threats to the security of states induces most governments—except a happy few that feel remote from harm's way—to make prudent preparations for war in peacetime.

The perception of threat, therefore, becomes a matter of importance to political scientists. For one state to perceive another as a threat, it must see the latter as having both the *capability* and the *intent* to block goal attainment or to jeopardize national security.[92] J. David Singer, for whom national security rather than abstract ideology constituted *the* categorical imperative in United States and Soviet foreign policy during the Cold War, suggested that two powers that find themselves in a relationship of rivalry or hostility will each be inclined to "interpret each other's military capability as evidence of military intent," and he reduced the perception of threat to the quasi-mathematical formula of Estimated capability × Estimated intent.[93] Singer hastened to assert that the Soviet Union was more concerned over the British or French nuclear capabilities than was the United States, indicating that the mere possession of nuclear weapons does not furnish, in the absence of political differences between parties, a basis for apprehension.

Raymond L. Garthoff warned against possible fallacies in any effort to estimate and impute intentions. Among common examples of fallacious reasoning, he cited the following:

1. Because overestimating the enemy's intentions merely costs dollars, whereas underestimating can cost lives, when in doubt, it is best to assume the worst.
2. Because it is impossible to read intentions accurately, it is safer to estimate measurable military capabilities and assume an intention to maximize those capabilities.
3. Assume that the adversary's strategic perceptions and ways of thinking are either the same as your own or necessarily always different. (Garthoff advises that both pitfalls should be avoided.)
4. Assume that the leaders of the adversary nation either never mean what they say or always mean what they say. Both assumptions are unfounded.

Estimating intentions, he concluded, is difficult enough without allowing such fallacies as the foregoing to enter into the process.[94]

Throughout the period of the Cold War, most theorists who grappled with the causes of war proceeded from the realist premise that states cannot escape from the security dilemma. Since the 1980s, a growing number of theorists have been dissatisfied with the realist paradigm. These theorists have sought to demonstrate that the ostensible reasons why governments in the past have opted for war were often at odds with the presuppositions of the realist rational-actor model. They have hoped to contribute toward the emergence of a new paradigm in which cooperation among increasingly interdependent states becomes so dominant over conflict that, first, the industrially advanced powers and, eventually, all states will abjure war in favor of nonviolent, mutually constructive competition. In the remaining parts of this chapter, we examine a variety of contending approaches to the causes-of-war puzzle—realist–neorealist and neoliberal, traditionalist, and quantitative–behavioralist. In our view, all can qualify as scientific. It is up to the reader to weigh the different theories and to decide whether the old paradigm will survive, give way to a new one, or be merged in a synthesis the shape of which cannot yet be discerned.

THE CORRELATES OF WAR PROJECT AND STATISTICAL ANALYSES OF WAR

The age-old quest for an understanding of the causes of war has culminated in the collection of a vast amount of quantitative data. The first task, of course, was to compile an accurate inventory of wars in the modern era. Notable among the pioneering efforts in this field during the 1930s were the works of Pitirim A. Sorokin,[95] Quincy Wright,[96] and Lewis F. Richardson,[97] although Richardson's research did not become well known until several years after the Second World War. (Further references to the work of Sorokin, Wright, and Richardson are made subsequently in connection with the relation between armaments and war, reaction processes, and cyclical theories of conflict.) Since the 1960s, J. David Singer, Melvin Small, and others have built on the earlier studies, refining definitions, improving the collection of statistical data, and conducting continuous research on factors associated with war in the Correlates of War (COW) Project.[98] The closing quarter of this century has witnessed a considerable growth of interest in statistical studies of war, building on Richardson's work, discussed in this chapter, designed to relate the probability of war's occurrence with arms races, alliances, power transitions, the expected utility of war in the decision-making processes of leaders and governments, and other relevant factors. Up to the present, the statistical methodologies have produced no startling surprises, and few conclusive or unambiguous results, but they have brought a certain amount of scientific precision to the subject and have drawn some valid and insightful distinctions among factors that, in the past, were sometimes lumped together uncritically in the general explanations offered by realists. The statistical studies have also raised new questions, which challenge neorealists to probe their own assumptions more deeply and carefully in order to refine and strengthen their theories. (This should not be taken to imply an adversarial relation between quantifiers and neorealists; several quantifiers proceed from realist premises regarding the behavior of states in the international system.)

Singer and Small realized that the raw data available to scholars on the phenomenon of war left much to be desired. They began, therefore, by compiling an inventory of information on the frequency, magnitude, severity, and intensity of international wars in the period from the end of the Napoleonic Wars (1815) to 1945, subsequently changing the initial date to 1816 and updating to 1965 and then 1980.[99] The period covered appeared to them to be manageable with respect to the availability of reliable historical sources, systemic continuity, and a sufficiently long time span to show permutations in the occurrence of violence. It was expected that other researchers would be able to take their data as a convenient point of departure, and many did.

It should be made clear that the collection of data on wars is not theory (i.e., explanation) but rather description of the historical evidence on which inductive theory must be based. Kenneth Waltz, a leading deductive neorealist theorizer, has argued trenchantly that quantitative analysis in general and the COW Project in particular—based on the accumulation of statistical information—will be likely to lead to errors of induction, not significant new knowledge, unless guided by theory; without theory, one does not know what data to generate or how to test properly.[100] John A. Vasquez, in an extensive review of the COW findings by scholars within and outside the project (including not only Singer and Small, but also Michael Wallace, Bruce Bueno de Mesquita, James Lee Ray, Alan Ned Zabrosky, Zeev Maoz, Russell Leng, Wayne Ferris, Randolph Silverson, Charles Kegley, Jack Levy, Manus Midlarsky, and others), cites criticisms that the project has been too inductive and insufficiently theoretical; that it has failed to offer an explanation of war or provide firm support for a particular set of hypotheses about war; and that its findings have been complex, unclear, and sometimes contradictory.[101] While not

disagreeing with Waltz that without some theoretical assumptions, a research analyst does not know where to begin, Vasquez defends Singer and Small on the
grounds that time and funding constraints compelled them to focus on such critical variables as alliances and national capability, both of which have always been
deemed significant by realists. Vasquez sums up the difference between Singer
and Waltz:

> Singer does not profess to know what regularities of behavior pervade world politics,
> and therefore he has nothing to explain until he has documented the regularities that
> do in fact exist. Waltz, on the other hand, knows what the regularities are (indeed, he
> may find them somewhat obvious), and sees his main purpose as explaining why they
> occur. . . . Are the regularities and "laws" Waltz wants to explain really known, and are
> they "laws," or, as Singer would argue, merely untested propositions? Can the use of
> the scientific method bring to light heretofore unknown relationships? If the scientific
> study of war is to be vindicated, it will have to produce a set of empirical generaliza-
> tions for which it has adduced new evidence and which, at least in some cases, reveal
> relationships previously not recognized.[102]

Vasquez agrees with Waltz at least to as the extent that the quantitative study of war
accumulates increasing numbers of data and begins to suggest empirical generalizations, the need for a more conscious theoretical perspective will grow.

One must start with a clear definition of the phenomenon being investigated.
What do we mean by "war"? Vasquez is partial to Hedley Bull's definition: "War is
organized violence, carried on by political units against each other."[103] He finds it
useful because it encompasses all forms of collective violence that is focused and
directed, not merely random, and it excludes nonviolent conflicts; it is formulated
in a way that can be dealt with readily by political scientists, historians, anthropologists, sociologists, and others; and it has no biased theoretical content. Vasquez
notes that it is not limited specifically to interstate war, which is the object of most
international-relations research. He then focuses attention on the COW Project,
which has provided "the most thorough and influential quantitative data set on
war."[104] The COW Project used the following precise yet arbitrary operational definition: "An international war is a military conflict waged between (or among)
national entities, at least one of which is a *state,* which results in at least 1000 battle deaths of military personnel."[105] This, too, is free of theoretical preconceptions,
and it produces a data set that can be used to test hypotheses based on different
theoretical preconceptions.[106]

Wright had defined wars as "all hostilities involving members of the family of
nations, whether international, civil, colonial or imperial, which were recognized as
states of war in the legal sense or involved 50,000 troops."[107] Richardson identified
"deadly quarrels" only (including violent incidents that were nonmilitary) according to the logarithm to the base ten of the total number of deaths.[108] Singer and
Small, writes Vasquez, reviewed the lists of Wright and Richardson but eliminated
as non-wars incidents that failed to meet the COW criteria because of the "inadequate political status of the participants" or because there were fewer than 1,000
battle deaths. Singer and Small distinguished between interstate and extrasystemic
(imperial and colonial) wars, and they collected data on both types. They found the
data for *interstate* wars more complete and accurate, because the Western imper-

ial powers did not bother to keep body counts for peoples not recognized as independent members of the international diplomatic community. Moreover, any war with fewer than 1,000 casualties was excluded. (Precision in defining the universe under study requires strict adherence to rigid coding; the problem of the numerical threshold would be the same if they had selected 500 as the cutoff point.) They counted a total of 118 international wars between 1816 and 1980—67 of them interstate and 51 extrasystemic.[109]

Small and Singer found that international war appears to be neither waxing nor waning, but that extrasystemic wars have naturally declined in frequency toward the zero point, as colonial empires have been liquidated. Whether they focused on frequencies, magnitudes, severities, or intensities, they did not find appreciably more or less war in any given period; once they took into account the expanding number of states in the system, international war did not appear to be on the rise or the decline.[110] Not surprisingly, most of the wars in the period after 1815 were fought by major or important middle powers. Largest numbers of casualties, in descending order, were sustained by Russia, Germany, China, France, Japan, England, Austria-Hungary, Italy, and Turkey. In about three quarters of the cases, states initiating wars were victors, but this proved most valid for major power attacks on minor powers, less so for minors versus minors, and not at all for major powers attacking major powers (where initiators won three and lost six wars).[111]

An alternative set of data to that of the COW Project was developed by Jack S. Levy, who was interested in working from a much longer time base, back to 1495, and in confining his inventory to great-power wars, which have been of chief importance for international relations:

> They have generally been history's most destructive conflicts and have had the greatest impact on the stability of the international system. For the most part, the interaction of the Great Powers determines the structure and evolution of the system and serves as the basis for most of our theories of international politics.[112]

Great powers are defined as those that play major roles with respect to security issues, possess high levels of capabilities (especially military), and receive de facto recognition of their status by being admitted to major international conferences and diplomatic activities of principal players in the system. Levy identifies 14 such powers entitled to such status at one time or another in the period 1495–1975. He counts only wars fought between the military forces of 2 or more great powers, involving at least 1,000 battle deaths, or an annual average of 1,000, among the powers. Levy excluded civil, imperial, and colonial wars (except for the Russian Civil War, in which outside powers intervened).[113] He counted 64 wars that met his definitional terms from 1495 to 1975, the Korean War being the last. Under his criteria, the Arab–Israeli wars of 1948, 1956, 1967, and 1973; the Vietnam War; the Iran–Iraq War; the Desert Storm Persian Gulf War in 1991 to reverse the Iraqi seizure of Kuwait; the Falklands War of 1982; and the ethnic wars in the former Yugoslavia in the 1990s would not qualify for the list because they did not involve great powers fighting each other, even though the numbers of casualties in these wars were high. Levy's principal purpose was to cast light on the widely held belief that the probability of war between the superpowers was diminishing as its potential destructiveness increased by examining the record over nearly five centuries. Using a combination of frequency counts and percentages, regression analysis, and rank-order correlation analysis, he found that war among great powers has been declining significantly in frequency but becoming increasingly serious in extent, magnitude, severity, intensity, and concentration in space and time—in every dimension except duration, which has remained relatively constant.[114]

ARMS RACES, ALLIANCES AND WAR

During the period between the two world wars, virtually all the historians who examined the origins of World War I cited among its chief causes military preparations and the formation of alliances (discussed later in this chapter), with other prominent causes being nationalism, imperialistic rivalry, propaganda and the role of the press, and the condition of international anarchy (that is, the absence of a mechanism for settling interstate disputes peacefully). Here we take up the question of whether the competitive acquisition of arms is more likely to escalate to war or to be conducive to peace through deterrence. The classical maxim of the ancient Roman writer Vegetius, *si vis pacem, para bellum* ("If you want peace, prepare for war"), has always been a favorite of realists.

Frederick L. Schuman, noting that pacifists have long believed that arms lead to war and disarmament to peace, wrote, "In reality, the reverse is more nearly true: war machines are reduced only when peace seems probable, the expectation of conflict leads to competition in armaments, and armaments spring from war and from the anticipation of war."[115] Hans J. Morgenthau delivered this terse dictum: "Men do not fight because they have arms. They have arms because they deem it necessary to fight."[116] Michael Howard has suggested that weapons can be used for essentially four purposes: to deter an adversary from resorting to war, to defend oneself should deterrence fail, to wage aggressive warfare, or to engage in political intimidation. As such, weapons, the implements of conflict, are neutral instruments to be employed by the defender or the aggressor.[117] Michael D. Wallace has called the evidence cited by the preparedness school anecdotal and idiosyncratic, and he has argued that an arms race between two states is strongly associated with escalation to full-scale hostilities when they are involved in disputes.[118]

Richardson's Reaction Processes

Before reviewing the debate among the quantitative theorists during the last quarter of a century, it is advisable to look at the work of the English physicist–mathematician Lewis Fry Richardson, whose ideas were posthumously given currency among American political scientists after 1957.[119] Using linear differential equations, Richardson sought to analyze the armaments acquisition policies of two rival parties within the framework of a mutual stimulus–response or action–reaction model.[120] He reduced the rate of change in the military budgets of rival states to the following equations:

$$\frac{dx}{dt} = ky - ax + g$$

$$\frac{dy}{dt} = lx - by + h$$

where

x = the armaments of Country A

t = time

k = a positive constant standing for A's perception of the menace

a = a positive constant representing "the fatigue and expenses of keeping up defenses"

g = a constant standing for A's grievances against B

$y, l, b,$ and h = corresponding values for Country B[121]

Dina A. Zinnes has pointed out that Richardson's focus was not, strictly speaking, a search for the cause of war, since he did not specifically consider wars in his models, but merely sought to describe processes that precede and may produce some—we would say few—modern wars.[122] What Richardson put forth was a purely theoretical model of the way two rival states interact in the military-expenditures dimension. Country A is stimulated by B's arms accumulation, and what A does by way of reaction serves as a further stimulus to B, but each country is constrained by its own total amount of arms and the effects of an increase of armaments on its own economy. Like all purely theoretical models, it is a highly simplified one in which the only two variables are the unique geostrategic requirements of each party, the military preparedness or vulnerability of allied countries, and whether the rivals are pursuing initiative–aggressive or reactive–defensive policies. According to Richardson, the interactive process can be either stable or unstable. Nations, like individuals, usually behave toward others as others behave toward them. If both nations are xenophobic and mutually hostile, the reaction coefficient will be greater than one. Let us assume that each feels secure only with a 10 percent margin of superiority over the other. The accumulation of 100 units of arms on one side (A) will stimulate the other (B) to accumulate 110; this will provoke A to aim at 121, and in turn B will insist upon 133, and so on, in an indefinite escalation characteristic of an unstable system in which the acquisition lines move away from the equilibrium point. Conversely, as two parties attenuate their hostility and turn toward increased friendliness and cooperation, their reaction coefficient will be less than one, they will de-escalate their rates of military expenditure, and their arms acquisition lines will converge toward a balance of power.[123]

Zinnes, who manifests considerable admiration for the pioneering research of Richardson, concedes that his basic model "is exceedingly naïve in its assumptions, and perhaps also extremely narrow in its substantive concern."[124] She justifies devoting a great amount of attention to it on the grounds that it stimulated the efforts of many others to develop extensions, modifications, and refinements of mathematical arms-race models and to apply Richardson's interaction processes to other fields.[125]

Richardson's basic model, it should be stressed, is more a purely theoretical construct than a hypothesis that can be empirically tested in the complex laboratory of history. The model has been criticized by Martin Patchen[126] on the grounds that it cannot explain more than a small portion of international behavior. Some of Richardson's modifications of his basic model fit the data for the military expenditures of France and Russia and of Germany and Austria in the period between 1909 and 1914. His equations are less neatly applicable to the period prior to World War II, when the reluctance of the Western democratic states to modernize their military establishments encouraged the anti-status-quo dictatorships to increase their armament rate and to become more aggressive in their foreign policies, rather than constraining them.

What the Richardson model tells us is that if two rivals are engaged in an unbridled and constantly escalating arms race, then they are interacting in this one dimension in a tension-increasing manner, and this may indicate that they will end up at war sooner or later unless they alter their course because arms-acquisition policies usually reflect other basic disagreements. His equations cannot enable us to predict when the tensions become so great that the breaking point is reached.[127] Even the data from the period prior to World War I do not prove that the arms race caused that war, but only that it was one of the several contributing factors.

No simplified mathematical model can take into account the great variety of factors that affect the course of international relations and modify action–reaction processes, perhaps leading one party to change more rapidly than the other, or one to misinterpret what the other is doing and to react in a manner not in accordance with the model. This, of course, is a shortcoming not only of the Richardson model, but also of all single-factor explanations. It is difficult to say how many there have been in this century. Richardson was interested only in three arms races—before 1914, before 1939, and after 1945. Other writers (considered in a subsequent section) have examined larger numbers of arms races. Nor can we always measure arms races merely by reference to levels of military spending, even after correcting for economic fluctuations to obtain constant currency units over a period of time. A technological breakthrough might enable a country to enhance its overall military capabilities at lower costs.[128] Conversely, it is quite conceivable, in a period of steady inflation and rising costs, that a nation's overall military capabilities would deteriorate despite modestly rising budgets.

Studies of Arms Races and War

An arms race is not easy to define. Certainly not every arms increase in every dyad of nations constitutes an arms race. There must be some sort of reaction process involving two states that are capable of harming each other. An increase due to competitive pressure from a foreign rival is one thing, whereas an increase that results from purely domestic factors (for example, a national policy of economic priming of the pump through the defense budget, an effort to placate a disgruntled military, or a strategy by an incumbent government to ward off opposition-party criticism in an election campaign) is quite another. Must the period of abnormal growth (however defined) meet a minimum time requirement beyond the initial sharp acceleration?

Michael Wallace, using COW Project data (1816 to 1965), and limiting his definition to armaments competition between powers of comparable capability, studied only great-power disputes that escalated to war (that is, disputes between great powers or between a great power and a minor power allied militarily with a great power).[129] Wallace set as his criteria a 10-year period and an annual average bilateral growth rate of 10 percent.[130] Others had different criteria. Paul Diehl specified an annual military expenditure of 8 percent and a minimum of 3 years.[131] T. C. Smith was willing to consider any interactive increase in the quality or quantity of military equipment or personnel where the competition lasted at least 4 years and involved palpable mutual hostility. (Obviously, differences in definitional criteria can be expected to produce different results.) A question arises as to how one can measure the intensity of rivalry or hostility that enables an arms race to qualify. Must the two rival governments make clear in their public statements that they suspect each other, hate each other, and target each other as enemies? Rather inexplicably and implausibly, T. C. Smith perceived an arms race between France and Germany during 1961–1977, despite their joint membership in the Atlantic Alliance and oft-avowed rapprochement.[132]

Wallace was primarily concerned with determining whether arms races lead to war, or somehow contribute to the onset of war. He carefully avoided arguing that military acquisitions by themselves are likely to provoke hostilities. "Some other factor or factors must lead nations into a dispute or confrontation of sufficient severity that the military dangers created by the arms race are transformed from chronic irritants into acute threats to national survival."[133] In other words, he saw serious disputes as theoretical preconditions to war. The statistical evidence he gathered was rather impressive, indicating that disputes preceded by arms races escalated to war in 23 out of 28 cases, while disputes not preceded by arms races escalated to war only 3 out of 71 times; this represented a better than 91 percent confirmation of his hypothesis.[134]

Randolph M. Siverson and Paul F. Diehl cast a shadow of doubt on Wallace's findings with the following observation: "Determining whether or not arms races increase the likelihood of war is exceedingly difficult unless the researcher knows the probability, ceteris paribus, or escalation in the absence of competition."[135] They also asked whether research can identify all the arms races that do not lead to war, and they cited a study by Diehl and Kingston, which indicated that arms competition does not increase the likelihood that rival nations will become involved in disputes.[136] They also criticized Wallace for ignoring the impact of alliances on the diffusion of war. If nations are drawn into a war as a result of alliance ties, it is not appropriate to counter such entries into war as caused by previous arms buildups, even though the latter may not be irrelevant to alliance and war-entry decisions.[137] Siverson and Diehl summarize their extensive review of the pertinent literature by noting that the earlier absolutist position on when arms races escalate to war must be carefully qualified with regard to the type of arms race and other surrounding conditions that may be decisive.[138] (The related question as to when arms competition can prevent war is examined in the discussion of deterrence in Chapter 9.)

Studies of Alliances and War

No less than in the case of military preparedness, political scientists have been divided over the question of whether alliances between states are more likely to contribute to peace or to bring on war. Some writers have argued that they increase security fears and tensions, thereby generating hostility and exacerbating conflicts; others view alliances as having a stabilizing and war-deterring effect. Certainly, alliances are closely associated with wars, because they come fully into play in wartime, but whether they can be credited with preventing wars or blamed for causing them is harder to say.

Singer and Small attempted to correlate the amount of war in the international system with the number of alliances in the system. Thus, they sought to determine whether alliance aggregation is a reliable predictor to the occurrence of war. They began with a theoretical model that might be characterized as the diplomatic equivalent of Adam Smith's "invisible hand"—a mechanism whereby the freedom of all nations to interact with each other as national interests dictate would redound to the stability and advantage of the whole international community. It would appear logical, then, that alliances, by reducing the interaction opportunities and freedom of choice of states, would increase polarization and the chances of war within the system. Under this line of reasoning, a highly polarized system should produce a high incidence of war. This is essentially the hypothesis tested by Singer and Small in a series of bivariate correlations between several alliance indicators and the magnitude, severity, and frequency of war, allowing time lags of 1, 3, and 5 years from the formation of the alliance to the onset of war. Over the whole period surveyed, from 1815 to 1945, they found no significant correlation. However, when they divided the period into two parts—nineteenth and twentieth centuries—they found two contrary patterns. For the nineteenth century, the correlation between gross-alliance aggregation and the frequency, magnitude, and severity of war was strongly negative. For the twentieth century, the same correlation was even more strongly positive—up to the end of World War II.[139]

Singer and Small, however, were unable, on the basis of their data, to explain why alliances appeared to be more successful in deterring war or limiting its magnitude in the nineteenth century than in the first half of the twentieth century. Traditionalists had long realized that there was a considerable difference between international relations in post-Napoleonic Europe and the subsequent century of total war. John A. Vasquez clearly recognized this:

> In the nineteenth century, alliances more frequently aimed to prevent war between major states by coming to an understanding about how to deal with major issues . . . [or] to keep any war that did occur limited. This claim seems to hold for the two most peaceful periods in the nineteenth century—the Concert of Europe era from 1816 to 1848 and the Bismarckian era from 1871 to 1895. . . . [Alliances] did not pose any threat to the existing major states, since they reflected a consensus and a set of under-

standings among major states . . . [Thus] these alliances did not give rise to arms races.[140]

Jack S. Levy, in his study of great-power wars over the period 1495–1975 found that, apart from the nineteenth century (which was exceptional), the majority of alliances were followed within five years of their formation by wars involving at least one of the allies (but not necessarily all members of the alliance). During the nineteenth century, no great-power wars were initiated within that five-year period.[141] Charles W. Ostrom, Jr., and Francis W. Hoole found in a similar vein that alliance formation correlates positively with an increased probability of war within a three-year period, after which the danger of war's occurrence declines.[142] Vasquez, however, hesitates to regard alliances as causes of war. He cites Levy's finding that from the sixteenth to the twentieth century, only 26 percent of wars, on average, were preceded by an alliance involving one of the parties.[143] He also notes that actors often enter into alliances because they anticipate the danger of war due to other causes, and that while states intend to increase their relative military power by forming an alliance, they often fail to achieve the purpose because they bring on the creation of a counteralliance.[144]

Relying on a study by Randolph Siverson and Joel King, both of whom were outside the COW Project but used its data, Vasquez agrees that alliances can act as a contagion mechanism for the spread and expansion of war. The fewer the alliances within a system, the smaller the wars, and vice versa.[145] (Here, the data of Siverson and King do little more than confirm statistically what logic dictates.) Later work by Benjamin Most, Harvey Starr, and Randolph Siverson identified shared geographic borders as a second interaction opportunity, which can rival alliances as contributing to the contagion effect or spatial diffusion of war. They suggest that small-scale wars may be more likely to spread through alliances.[146] Vasquez, who has conducted extensive reviews of the literature, suspects that alliances in general are not conducive to peace, but he is cautious in ascribing causality to them:

> Alliances are probably more responsible for the severity, magnitude, and duration of war than for its onset. Since there is often an interval between the alliance and the outbreak of war, it is a legitimate inference that alliances do not directly cause war, but help to aggravate a situation that makes war more likely. They may do this in two ways: by promoting an atmosphere that polarizes the system and by encouraging arms races.[147]

Vasquez attached importance to both arms races and polarization as factors related to the problem of alliances and war. Referring to the work of Nazli Choucri and Robert North on lateral pressures (discussed in the next section of this chapter) and a later study by Wallace, Vasquez argues that between 1903 and 1914, there was a dynamic interactive pattern between alliances and arms races, as mutual perceptions of threat fed on each other.[148] Conceding that several writers on polarization came up with inconsistent findings, Vasquez was partial to those of Wallace, who uncovered curvilinear relationships indicating that (1) wars of the greatest magnitude and severity correlate with systems of maximum polarization (two blocs) and minimum polarization (no blocs); (2) a moderate amount of war, or no war, is associated with moderate polarization (multipolarity); and (3) moderate crosscutting (links across blocs) reduces the intensity of war, while very low and very high crosscutting links increase it.[149] Vasquez also concurred with the findings of Bruce Bueno de Mesquita and Alan Ned Sabrosky that increases in systemic tightness (polarization) induce stepped-up military preparations and make for wars of greatest magnitude, severity, and duration.[150]

Vasquez makes World War I a classic model showing how alliances can be an important contributor toward war. He is perhaps on less firm ground when he relies on selective qualitative literature and links the formation of NATO to the outbreak of the Korean War as a case "supporting the generalization that alliances are followed by war."[151] NATO was intended as an instrument of containment in Europe—a means of reassuring the West Europeans that peace could be preserved by a democratic alliance capable of balancing Soviet power and making the cost of any war too high for rational politics. There was no war in the geographic area covered by NATO from its founding until the collapse of the Soviet Union.

Vasquez often seems critical of the balance-of-power policy, as in this passage: "There is no clear reason why a balance of power should produce peace in the nineteenth century, but war in the twentieth: A scientific explanation that captures the causes of war should be fairly generalizable and not shift so radically from one century to the next."[152] This does not seem to be an adequate formulation of the issue, for it appears to equate the balance-of-power policy exclusively with alliances while ignoring other cultural, historical, social, and political factors (including an intelligent diplomacy of restraint) which can make the policy work in one era, while their absence or distortion contributes to its failure in another. Moreover, it is too much to speak of the pre–World War I bipolar alliance situation as characteristic of the twentieth century. The period between the two world wars was not marked either by balance-of-power policies or by an alliance system of the status-quo democracies against the revisionist totalitarian or authoritarian states. For the second half of the twentieth century, the situation has been in sharp contrast with the first half. Whereas most of the 16 members of NATO and 7 members of the Warsaw Treaty Organization (which was dissolved in 1991), or their predecessor states, had been participants in both world wars, no member of either alliance system has become involved in a military conflict with a member of the opposite alliance. Moreover, former Warsaw Pact members have received partial admission to NATO in the form of the alliance's consultation procedures within the Partnership for Peace, while criteria have been developed for the eventual full membership that is widely sought by former Warsaw Pact states such as Poland, Hungary, the Czech Republic, and the Slovak Republic, to mention just a few. Vasquez has produced in *The War Puzzle* one of the most comprehensive and valuable surveys of the voluminous literature on the subject, but he scarcely mentions the deterrence of war, which was the purpose of the North Atlantic alliance and its counteralliance, and which ultimately proved to be its outcome over nearly half a century, despite prolonged and intense arms competition, which nevertheless was kept under political restraint.

NATIONAL GROWTH AND INTERNATIONAL VIOLENCE

Writing on the relationship between domestic development and war, Nazli Choucri and Robert North contend that the processes of national growth themselves are likely to lead to expansion, competition, rivalry, conflict, and violence.[153] Selecting World War I as a test case, they analyzed long-range trends over the period from 1870 to 1914. They applied econometric techniques over time and across six major powers (Britain, France, Germany, Italy, Russia, and Austria-Hungary) to a variety of aggregate data—demographic, economic, political, and military—as well as interactions among those countries. Choucri and North did not focus their attention on such discrete events as the assassination of the Archduke or the Russian decision to mobilize, nor did they focus on the personality of key leaders, but rather they focused on the dynamics of population and technological growth, changes in trade and military expenditures, the conflict of national interests, and patterns of colonial activity, alliance formation, and violence behavior. These are the variables, wrote Choucri and North, that produce changes in the international system conducive to crisis and war. In their view, the probability of war is not significantly lowered by good will alone, by deterrence strategy, or by détente and partial arms limitations.[154]

Choucri and North devote a great deal of effort to explaining their methodology, apologizing for the lack of statistical significance in many of the correlations, and pointing out the deficiencies of data in the book, which they call a progress report on the initial phases of their research.[155] Here we are principally interested in the explanatory theory on the basis of which they proceed, which can be summarized as follows. As noted in Chapter 4. Choucri and North hypothesize that a growing population experiences an increasing demand for basic resources. As technology becomes more advanced, the greater will be the kinds and quantity of resources required by the society. If these demands are not met, the development of new capabilities will be sought, and if these cannot be attained within the nation's boundaries, lateral pressures will be created to attain them beyond the boundaries. Lateral pressure may be expressed through commercial activities, the building of navies and merchant fleets, the dispatch of troops into foreign territory, the acquisition of colonial territory or foreign markets, the establishment of military bases abroad, and in other ways. In a subsequent reaffirmation of their basic hypothesis, the authors added the quest for investment areas and sources of cheap labor; the extension of religious, educational, and scientific activities; uses of the continental shelf, seabed, and outer space; and international migrations as manifestations of lateral pressures.[156] A country is not absolutely determined to obtain satisfaction of its needs beyond its territory. It might be content with less and mind its own business, but most modern industrialized countries manifest strong lateral pressures in some form.

The expansion of one country's lateral pressure may be acquiesced in or resisted by other countries. All lateral pressure contains a potential for international conflict. As interests grow, it is usually assumed that they require protection. This means military expenditures and an increased sense of competition or rivalry. One colonial power is likely to feel threatened each time another acquires new territory. Alliances are formed both to enhance national capabilities and to moderate conflicts of interest among some parties, even though these alliances may arouse the suspicion of others, prompt the formation of a countervailing coalition, and contribute to exacerbation of international conflict, as the process of antagonizing tends to become mutual.[157] The study partially validates the Richardson reaction-process hypothesis, but it also modifies the hypothesis in certain important respects because the data show that arms increases are sometimes better explained by domestic growth factors than by international competition.[158]

The most important finding to emerge from the study is that domestic growth (measured by population density and per-capita national income) is a strong determinant of national expansion, and that both domestic growth and national expansion are linked to military expenditures, alliances, and international violence. Such a finding, in the view of Choucri and North, has ominous implications for the conventional wisdom concerning the gap between the strong, rich nations and the poor, weak nations. For a long time, there was a widely shared assumption that by narrowing this gap through technological and economic growth, the probability of conflict and war would be lessened. This assumption now seems dubious.[159] In the end, Choucri and North raise somber questions about the ability of populous societies, equipped with highly destructive military technology, to live together on a planet that now offers little room for further lateral expansion and increasingly limited opportunities for growth. If uninhibited growth and aggressive competition might lead to international violence on a massive scale, Choucri and North ask, might not the severe curtailment of growth lead just as surely to disaster?[160] Nearly a decade after publishing the book in which they set forth their lateral-pressure explanation of international conflict, North and Choucri reiterated the hypothesis in an assessment of the economic and political factors that enter into the bargaining and leverage of domestic and international actors. All forms of lateral pressure, they assert, are ultimately traceable to individual needs, wants, desires, demands, and capabilities. The mix of leverages that states employ may lead to various outcomes—cooperation, competition, and conflict, producing peace or war.[161]

Others have accepted the Choucri–North notion of lateral pressures as their point of departure in explaining international conflict. Richard K. Ashley, for example, assumes that human beings act according to a dialectical process to reduce the gap between what is and what ought to be. Thus, they interact with their environment in an unending competition for scarce resources. Ashley stresses demographic, technological, and economic factors, both within nations and in their interactions. He seems to make economic expansion the crucial factor generating international conflict, as population growth and technological progress produce ever-mounting demands for satisfaction. When the expanding demands of countries intersect, and cooperative solutions cannot be worked out, military conflict may very well result.[162] It should be noted, however, that in revisiting their theory, Choucri and North observe cautiously that lateral pressure itself "seldom triggers a war."[163] It can at times lead to cooperation. The intersections most likely to turn violent are those where fear, distrust, and hostility already exist or where one party interprets the leveraging activities of another as negative, threatening, coercive, or overtly violent.[164]

The work of Choucri and North, of Ashley, of Most and Starr, and of several other scholars since the mid-1960s who have analyzed the war problem, is useful, in that it calls attention to the fact that state policies for peace and war are determined not only by what goes on within the domestic political systems but also as a result of interacting with other states. States can interact with other states, whether friendly or adversary, without necessarily becoming involved in the kinds of rigid action–reaction processes that Richardson and some of his most orthodox disciples have in mind when they speak of arms races. Arms competition is, in a real sense, a form of bargaining and leverage building that need not end in war, and that might lead to a more stable relationship marked by a relaxation of arms competition and a tendency to shift the competition to other (say, economic or diplomatic) foreign-policy modes. The decision for war cannot be entirely isolated and attributed exclusively to one state—at least not in all cases. War is often the culmination of a dyadic rather than a purely unilateral process. It may be somewhat misleading, therefore, to investigate the attributes of single nation-states in an effort to discover which ones are more inherently aggressive or war-prone than others.[165]

POWER AS DISTANCE AND POWER TRANSITION

We turn next to relative levels of power (or power as distance between two actors) and to the dynamism of shifts in power relationships. From the standpoint of theory, it is intriguing to ask which is more conducive to war—equality or inequality of power—and whether the probability of war increases or decreases as equality is approached. At first glance, one might deem it logical to assume that as two rival states move toward equality, they should be able to deal with each other more fairly and even-handedly. Certainly one of the most commonly stated assumptions underlying United States–Soviet relations during the era of the strategic-arms negotiations between 1969 and the late 1980s was that strategic parity was a prerequisite of stable mutual deterrence and of progress in arms limitation. The question, however, must be probed carefully.

A. F. K. Organski was among the first to call attention to the danger that the probability of war may increase during a period of power transition.[166] Perceptible inequality of power makes it foolish for the weaker side to initiate a war, while the stronger side need not be apprehensive. This is borne out by the experience of India and Pakistan following the Bangladesh War of 1971. Prior to that conflict, the two subcontinent neighbors lived in an almost constant fear of—and readiness for—war for a quarter-century. After Pakistan's population, territory, and resources were substantially reduced and India tested a nuclear explosive device, Pakistan's resentment ran high, but little could be done to alter the ituation, and both the probability and fear of an Indo-Pakistani War in the proximate future declined markedly.[167] One of Organski's principal objections to the classical balance-of-power theory (which he agreed had some validity in an earlier period) was that it presupposes a relatively stable distribution of power among units and an ability of prudent leaders of state to act in time to compensate for disturbances in the balance—for example, by entering an alliance. In the twentieth century, industrial technology permits the occurrence of rapid shifts of power that perhaps cannot be prevented. Balances are unstable because they are not durable. As power parity is approached, two rivals may become increasingly nervous about the balance and sensitive to fluctuations within it, thereby increasing the danger of war. As the challenger overtakes the erstwhile leader, its more rapid growth rate may breed an excess of self-confidence and tempt it to seek complete victory.[168] The converse danger is that the dominant power, viewing apprehensively the expanding capabilities of its rival, may go to war to defeat the latter while it can.

Inis L. Claude succinctly expressed the ambiguity of the situation: If an equilibrium means that either side may lose, it also means that either side may win.[169] Michael P. Sullivan has suggested that the relationship between approaching equality may be curvilinear:

> The more equal two countries are, the greater the probability of conflict, except that at some point the opposite process, as suggested by Claude, begins to operate: high equality stifles aggressive tendencies because of the fifty–fifty chance of losing. Gross inequality would have either low probability of conflict or low conflict; the greater the equality, however, the greater the chance of conflict and, if conflict does break out, the greater the chance of high levels of conflict. When two powers are exactly equal, however, the probability of conflict drops off and if conflict does occur, it will be low level.[170]

In our view, the process of making a decision to war cannot be reduced to a probability based on a mere quantitative comparison of power between rivals. Much may depend on the attitude and outlook of the two states, the nature of their political systems, the hostility or friendship that marks their relationship, the extent to which their vital interests clash, the degree to which the dominant power accepts and accommodates its policies to the expanding power of the challenger, and so forth.[171] A timid preponderant power might lose its competitive spirit, whereas the challenger, though gaining, is still substantially weaker in terms of military power but stronger in ideology, morale, and self-confidence. Accommodation by the satisfied power may either appease the dissatisfied power, making it more patient and cooperative, or serve only to whet its appetite and make it more aggressive. We cannot therefore predict the point at which the opposite process begins to operate, nor can two powers know when they are exactly equal.

One of the most controversial aspects of the debate about arms races and escalation to war is the one attributing high danger to power transition. As we noted earlier, A. F. K. Organski has long been identified with the hypothesis that the probability of war increases as the power gap narrows, especially as a rival revisionist challenger comes closer to equalizing the capabilities of the once stronger guardian of the status quo. He has continued to adhere to this view in the book he co-authored with Jacek Kugler, *The War Ledger.* They write that war is caused by differences in rates of growth among the great powers and, of particular importance, the differences in rates between the dominant nation and the challenger that permit the latter to overtake the former.[172] This would seem to conform to strategic logic, since the leading power grows more edgy and may be tempted to strike preventively, while the secondary power, aware of this temptation, may initiate war to gain the advantage of a surprise first strike.

In a later retrospective analysis, Kugler and Organski reaffirmed their basic thesis. Power-transition theory, they noted, views the international system not as anarchic but as a hierarchically organized order in which actors accept their position based on relative power distribution. The power-transition model postulates a dominant nation, great powers, and a potential future challenger. Alliances are stable when most great powers are satisfied and support the dominant nation. Most dissatisfied nations are weak middle or smaller powers. The United States, Japan, and Europe are alone strong enough to maintain global stability against Russia and China.[173] "Instability is likely only during periods of relative parity among potential competitors. As a dissatisfied great nation approaches parity by growing in power more rapidly than the dominant nation, instability increases and so does the probability of conflict."[174] The theory of Kugler and Organski is thus in sharp contrast to that of Morgenthau, Kissinger, and Waltz, who hold out for a balance of power based on the assumption of power maximization as the goal of states and coalition diplomacy (whether voluntary as a matter of choice or involuntary as a matter of necessity) to prevent hegemony. Most theories relating to the initiation of war run into paradoxes, dilemmas, and anomalies when it comes to dealing with nuclear deterrence, as we show in Chapter 9.

CAPABILITY, RISK, EXPECTED UTILITY, AND PROBABILITY OF WAR

Bruce Bueno de Mesquita has taken issue with a basic assumption of realpolitik theorists—namely, that the probability of war involving specific key states depends on the distribution of power among those states. The realists, as we have noted previously, are not entirely agreed among themselves concerning power distribution and war probability. Some think that peace is best ensured when power is in equilibrium; others think that peace is most likely when those states favoring a peaceful status quo possess a preponderance of power. Bueno de Mesquita casts doubt on both the Kissinger view that an equal balance of power is a precondition of peace and lowers the probability of war between the two principal powers[175] and the hypothesis of Organski and Kugler that the probability of war among individual key states decreases as the inequality in the power distribution (or "power distance") increases.[176] Bueno de Mesquita similarly dismisses the comparable hypotheses of Zinnes et al. and Claude relating the low probability of war to equality or inequality in the distribution of power among coalitions of key states.[177]

Bueno de Mesquita concedes that the probability of achieving success in war is almost a certain function of relative power capabilities. If power is taken in its most comprehensive sense, this must be the case. The distribution of power, however, whether real or perceived, is not the only determinant of whether political decision makers choose war or peace. In any conflict situation, individual decision makers on both sides may assess differently the utility (values) that attach to the possible outcomes of a given war (expanding, maintaining, or losing power for their state). Any given probability of success (expressed in rough percentages) may be sufficient for some leaders but not for others to undertake the risks of war.

Assuming that the probability of success in war does correlate highly with the power of one nation or a coalition of nations relative to that of the adversary, and assuming further that whether leaders are risk accepting or risk averse is independent of the actually prevailing power distribution, Bueno de Mesquita constructs nine hypothetical international systems with varying distributions of strong and weak states and varying risk-taking orientations among decision makers. He analyzes each of the nine deductive models, covarying calculations of the probability of success, the actors' expected utility of war, and the actors' risk-security levels. He also reviews Singer's COW Project, empirical studies flowing from it, and the theoretical debate (Deutsch and Singer vs. Waltz).[178] He concludes that no particular distribution of power has exclusive claim as a predictor of peace or war, either in theory or in the empirical record of the period 1816–1965.[179]

In his investigations, some systems marked by power predominance support Organski and Kugler; others, in which the probability of war decreases as the distribution of power approaches equality, lend weight to the Kissinger hypothesis. In short, the distribution of power alone, without reference to another crucial variable—the risk-taking propensity of individual decision makers—"is not systematically associated with the incidence of war," and decision makers who presume, perhaps too simplistically, that either a power equilibrium or a power predominance is essential to peace may be "acting on false, incomplete, and potentially lethal premises."[180] He laments the tendency of those who analyze war probability to focus almost exclusively on capability differentials and to neglect the factor of risk-taking orientation among governing leaders. The principal exception to this tendency, he adds significantly, is to be found in strategic analysts of deterrence, who pay a great deal of attention to the unwillingness of ruling elites to run great security risks of initiating war in the nuclear age, but he fails to elaborate on this extremely important exception.

In three subsequent articles during the 1980s, Bueno de Mesquita (once in collaboration with David Lalman) continued to develop his expected-utility model of international conflict. Assuming that the probability of escalation of a dispute increases monotonically with leaders' expectation of gain in comparison with the expected costs of conflict, he revised his earlier theory and discovered an improved statistical ability to discriminate between disputes that escalated to warfare and those that did not in Europe between 1816 and 1970. He showed that leaders, faced with a decisional problem of whether to challenge an adversary to alter the adversary's policies, estimate the relative utility of success and failure. Leaders who have adopted foreign policies that leave them near the extreme of their possible range of vulnerability are assumed to be more willing to accept risks than those who have diminished their vulnerability to external threats. "Differences in risk-taking propensities are viewed as the source of variations in actor perceptions."[181] Bueno de Mesquita and Lalman concluded that a continuous theory linking expected-utility estimates to conflict escalation provides a powerful tool for the future analysis of international conflict, both at the level of individual decision makers and at the level of systemic action.[182]

At this point, it may be useful to go back to our discussion in Chapter 1 about the difference between inductive and deductive theory. Most of the scientific studies of war summarized thus far have been of the inductive, empirical, quantitative (statistical) variety. Bruce Bueno de Mesquita's expected-utility theory represents a deductive approach to the study of international conflict. He admits its limitations and distinguishes between formal mathematical models and less formal but more detailed studies of particular events.

> Formal models are not intended to illuminate the rich details and texture of events. Rather, they are designed to specify a simplified, ordered view of reality that reveals internally consistent and externally useful general principles. Formal models are not a substitute for rich information about the events studied. Rather, they are designed to specify a simplified, ordered view of reality. But they can complement the richness of detail, providing more order and strengthening the ability to generalize. In doing so, formal models do sacrifice details for breadth and specificity for generality. When combined with expert knowledge, a powerful synergy results in which the level of insight is often greater than can be gleaned from expert judgment or formal models alone.[183]

(We refer again to Bueno de Mesquita's theory in Chapter 11 on decision making.)

Expected-utility theory, Bueno de Mesquita insists, can account for behaviors that appear to be anomalous. He has shown that allies are more likely to wage war (but not severe wars) against one another than are enemies.[184] He attributes to great powers a high expectation of being able to influence the outcome of conflicts among small states, as the United States had in Vietnam.

> As the perceived probability of success in war, the utility for success can decrease and still satisfy the critical threshold level of expectation at which one is willing to commit troops to combat. This means that great powers have a higher probability of fighting in wars whose outcome is not of great significance to them than do lesser powers. Weaker powers cannot rationally engage in such wars. They are limited to fighting in disputes in which they perceive their stakes to be quite large.[185]

The lesson he draws from this is that opponents of the Vietnam War, instead of arguing that U.S. vital national interests were not involved, should have questioned Johnson's and then Nixon's perceived probability of success.[186]

John Vasquez agrees with Bueno de Mesquita that, despite long-held realist beliefs to the contrary, the thrust of empirical analysis to date suggests that capability or differences of power are unrelated to the onset of war in any significant causal sense. Instead, it appears that capability and differences in power are related to the type of war that is fought and not to whether there will be peace or war."[187] Vasquez constructs a typology in which he separates wars of rivalry from wars of opportunity. The former are waged between equals, and "are more oriented to the logic of the balance of power and prey to its deficiencies, such as mutual fear, suspicion and insecurity, arms races and preventive war."[188] Wars of opportunity are fought between unequals, when the stronger side perceives utility in starting a war. The contrasting logic of the two situations can become linked if a weak state manages to ally with one of two strong rival powers. Wars of rivalry are more likely than wars of opportunity to become total. Vasquez also distinguishes between dyadic wars and the general wars of the great powers, "which grow out of wars that were initiated in the expectation that they would be limited," but which could not be confined to the initial parties. He finds expected-utility theory less applicable to these complex wars than to dyadic wars. He concurs with Wallace and Bueno de Mesquita "that alliance-making that leads to polarization produces wars of the highest magnitude, severity and duration," although he is quick to add that the "reason for this is not fully explained in the literature."[189] In his very plausible explanation of the consequences of polarization, Vasquez shows convincingly that there are points where behaviorists and traditional scholars can find common ground in realistic deductive reasoning.[190] Vasquez himself has done much in his efforts to bridge the gap between quantitative and qualitative knowledge about the war phenomenon.

A great deal of analysis remains to be done before we can fully understand the interrelationship between the onset of war and the myriad factors that may contribute to it—alliances and arms races, power transitions, the utilitarian calculations of governmental decision makers, cyclical phenomena in the global political and economic systems, multipolarity, bipolarity, and unipolarity, and so forth. J. David Singer admits that "the reproducible findings of the research to date hardly point in one clear direction" because political scientists have not sufficiently specified their theoretical models and may have overlooked an important variable that could resolve apparent anomalies.[191]

This latter observation highlights a problem that persistently plagues social scientists who employ statistical correlations and regression analysis. The problem was identified in the late nineteenth century by the English mathematician, Sir Francis Galton, who worked in genetics, psychometrics, and anthropology. Galton warned that in any effort to correlate two variables, one must strive to make sure that they are not both dependent on a third factor that would make the correlation spurious.[192] Instead, both variables may be skewed by a third factor of which the investigator is unaware. The monumental difficulty in the field of international relations, as in all the social sciences, is that it is never possible to isolate a dependent and an independent variable in the real world as completely as one can isolate them for correlation in the mind. Almost all statistical correlations are vulnerable to criticism for one methodological deficiency or another. Investigators may use different databases, modify the COW Project or Levy databases to suit special purposes, employ different classification (definitional) schemes, and interpret findings differently. Most analysts are well aware of these difficulties.

We do not wish to convey the impression that the scientific study of war has been marching off in too many divergent directions to produce any coherent theory. Several theorists, by building on the pioneering work of Sorokin, Richardson, Wright, Singer and Small, and Levy, even while pursuing distinctive approaches, have found some points of intersection with each other. Those who study the effects of arms races do not ignore the part played by alliances and shared borders in the initiation of war. Theorists who deal with the diffusion of war through the interaction opportunity of alliances and shared borders realize that when allies and neighbors refrain from entering an ongoing war, this may have to be explained by reference to the expected-utility calculations of governmental decision makers. We show other points of intersection in the remaining portions of this chapter, which are devoted to cyclical and long-cycle theories of the occurrence of war, and the increasingly impressive hypothesis that democratic states do not go to war with each other. Analysts are under mounting internal compulsion and external pressure to seek linkages between their own and other theories because they share a growing realization that war is a phenomenon of multiple causes, not single factors. Yet at the same time, they are aware that powerful theories do not lie in the compilation of ever-longer lists of possible causes, but rather in explanatory theories that are parsimonious—that is, simple, readily comprehensible, and capable of being applied to and verified in a broad range of cases. We cannot expect, however, to formulate for the complex social universe general laws that operate with the precision and certainty of physical laws.

CYCLICAL AND LONG-CYCLE THEORIES OF WAR

Efforts to determine whether there is a war–peace cycle in the international system have been made since the mid-1930s by several analysts—Pitirim A. Sorokin, Quincy Wright, Lewis F. Richardson, Arnold Toynbee, J. David Singer and Melvin Small, Gaston Bouthoul, Jacques Ellul, Alec L. Macfie, Geoffrey Blainey, Jack Levy, Robert Gilpin, Immanuel Wallerstein, George Modelski, William R. Thompson, Joshua Goldstein, Lois W. Sayrs, Edward Mansfield, and others. The implication of all cyclical theories is that wars inevitably occur at periodic intervals, which are more or less regular, or at irregular intervals when several clearly identifiable, contributing conditions (necessary and sufficient) converge. While a few of the studies conducted thus far agree with each other in limited respects, most of them have produced widely varying outcomes because they have employed different databases (including different definitions of *war*), different time periods, and different ways of interpreting the results. The cyclical patterns for which evidence has been perceived range in length from 20 years to 2 centuries. Sorokin counted 862 European wars in the period 1100–1925—an average of more than 1 per year![193] Richardson, who lumped major international and domestic violence together, identified 317 incidents between 1820 and 1949.[194] (These totals were comparable to those later compiled by Singer and Small, who discovered 367 such incidents between 1815 and 1945.)[195] Richardson wondered whether the cycle might correspond to the time needed for a new generation to forget the suffering and cost of the previous war, but neither he nor Sorokin could ever discern much of a pattern. Quincy Wright, who estimated that there were about 200 wars between 1480 and 1941, concluded that major wars are followed by periods of peace lasting about 50 years.[196]

Arnold Toynbee found what appeared to him to be a general cycle of war and peace, lasting on the average a little more than a hundred years. Whereas Richardson had suggested that the immunity to war might tend to wear off in two decades or so following a bloody war, Toynbee more hopefully thought that terribly costly wars bred peace settlements (Westphalia, 1648; Utrecht, 1713; Vienna, 1815; Versailles, 1919) that would endure for fairly long periods among the leading powers—except for short, minor wars such as the Crimean and Franco-Prussian during the beneficent Concert of Europe between the protracted Napoleonic Wars and the outbreak of war in 1914.[197] Blainey made short shrift of Toynbee's warweariness explanation of the cycle. Writing as a historian of particular wars—not at all as a scientific–quantitative theorist—Blainey noted that war weariness, which is virtually impossible to measure empirically in any event, did not help to preserve the peace of Europe in the late 1930s. Indeed, its manifestations in the form of pacifism and appeasement in the Western democracies may have helped to bring on World War II:

> Toynbee himself was puzzled that the Second World War should have come at a time when, according to his theory, mental immunity against war should still have been high. At least he tried to face the dilemma; he confessed that either his theory was jeopardized or else human nature must have changed. Like most of us in a similar quandary, he plumped for his theory. The Second World War, he suggested, was "manifestly something contrary to human nature."[198]

Theorists have been intrigued by the possibility that the periodicity of war may be related to worldwide economic cycles. Two French social analysts, Gaston Bouthoul and Jacques Ellul, pointed in a Marxist vein to the unemployment problem, which becomes severe in certain phases of the economic cycle, as a factor provoking the outbreak of war: "the plethora of young men [surpasses] the indispensable tasks of the economy."[199] Conversely, Blainey relied on a 1938 study by Macfie to hypothesize a link between the optimism that usually accompanies an expansive upswing in a nation's economy and the increased readiness of a government to initiate war because its costs can then be more easily borne. Macfie's study had been quite narrow in scope: He had examined the outbreak of 12 wars in the very limited period 1850–1914.[200] William R. Thompson could discover no such correlation as Macfie had postulated, but subsequently several analysts (including Thompson) have sought to link wars with the upswing phase of the economic K-waves first described in the 1920s by Nikolai D. Kondratieff (discussed later).[201]

In a sense, all recurring phenomena may be considered cyclical, but the problem in the social universe is that nearly all cycles appear to be irregular. (Exceptions can be cited, of course, such as periods between elections fixed by a constitution.) More than a quarter of a century ago, Small and Singer defined the task as one of delineating the phenomenon under examination from the background noise:

> Although cycles are not apparent when we examine the amount of war beginning in each year or time period, a discernible periodicity emerges when we focus on measures of the amount of war under way. That is, discrete wars do not necessarily come and go with regularity but with some level of interstate violence always present; there are distinct and periodic fluctuations in the amount of that violence.[202]

For more than a decade, George Modelski, William R. Thompson, and others have been seeking to find greater cyclical regularity in long cycles of approximately a century. To do this, they have had to draw on a much longer historical record of the modern world system—back to 1494, not merely the Singer–Small list of wars since 1816. They have distinguished what they call "global wars" from lesser conflicts that show up on an inventory of wars in general, most of which did not produce any significant change in the structure of the international system. They define *global wars* as those "that determine succession struggles and usher in new leaders of the global political system and new phases of highly concentrated global reach capabilities."[203] These capabilities in the past took the form of sea power (and more recently sea–air power), which permits the emerging global leader to project political, military, and economic influence so effectively as to dominate the international system. Modelski and Thompson discern a pattern whereby the system passes through four characteristic phases over the course of about a century: *Macrodecision* (global war), marked by severe and widespread violence, which settles the issue of leadership; *Implementation* (world-power phase) in which one nation-state is able to act as global leader and implement new programs; *Agenda setting* (delegitimation phase), when questions are raised about the legitimacy of the world leader, and new problems enter the global agenda; *Coalitioning* (or deconcentration phase), in which the power of the world leader declines to a low point, and new coalitions are organized by one or more challengers (perhaps formerly allied with the global leader).[204] Spain challenged Portugal. France challenged the Netherlands. France and Germany challenged Britain a century apart. After helping Britain repel the challenge of 1914–1918, the United States emerged from World War II as the global leader facing an early challenger in the USSR.[205] (Note: Most primary challengers do not become successor global leaders.)

According to this model, the international system is not always anarchic. For a substantial portion of the cycle following global war, the world leader dominates a unipolar system—the most stable of all systems. However, such a stable system does not last. It gives way to a bipolar and ultimately a multipolar (deconcentrated) system, which is least stable. The Modelski–Thompson analysis fits Toynbee's war-and-peace cycle (based on the balance-of-power model) only imperfectly, because Toynbee's general wars are not really decisive.[206]

The long-cycle approach comes closer to Gilpin's hegemonic-war theory and Wallerstein's neo-Marxist world-capitalist-economy model, which covers five centuries. Gilpin focuses on the uneven growth of power among nations (not merely economic, but all changes in transportation, communication, industrial technology, population, military capabilities, etc.), which may alter a nation's perception of the cost–benefit ratio of trying to alter the international status quo. His analysis helps to explain how the "hegemon" eventually declines, due to expanding costs of maintaining dominance in the system while various economic, technological, and military advantages and innovations shift to other nations once deemed inferior by obsolescent criteria.[207] (Gilpin is discussed in Chapter 2.)

Wallerstein has presented a more strictly economic case for the achievement of hegemonic status in the world economy by three powers—the Netherlands in the 1600s, Britain in the 1800s, and the United States in the mid-1990s. Wallerstein associates the rise and fall of hegemonic powers with phases of expansion and contraction (or stagnation) in the world economy. The global wars that produced the three hegemonic states just mentioned each lasted about 30 years (e.g., 1914–1945).[208] (Wallerstein is discussed in Chapter 6.) More is said subsequently concerning the relationship between the occurrence of war and economic cycles.

Modelski and Thompson suggest that their long-cycle theory offers a rich framework for solving or at least ameliorating some of the research puzzles debated by scholars in recent decades. In answer to the question whether bipolar or multipolar systems are more stable, long-cycle theory nominates unipolarity as most stable and multipolarity as least. Whereas Singer found evidence to support both sides of the question as to whether war is more likely in a situation of preponderance or parity, long-cycle theory postulates a consistently negative correlation between preponderance and warfare. According to the long-cycle theory, the search for an answer to the causes-of-war riddle becomes less significant—at least for global wars. Such theorists as Blainey, Vasquez, Bueno de Mesquita, Singer and Small, and others who study the causes of wars in general, including both larger and lesser wars, do not deserve to be dismissed as lightly as long-cycle theorists are wont to put them aside. Modelski and Thompson, however, would relieve them of the necessity of looking for the causes of global wars, which occur almost regularly, somewhat like elections on a global political calendar for the purpose of macrodecision making—choosing a new leader when the older one has declined to a point of inability to preserve a stable international system in the face of deconcentration.[209]

Modelski and Thompson do not rely on, but find some resonance in, Charles F. Doran's power-cycle theory, which focuses on the cycle of nation-state power and its role as the underlying dynamic of international politics (discussed in Chapter 2). According to Doran, since the sixteenth century, 12 states have passed through the curve of relative power, even if only for a short time. In addition to the 8 states mentioned by Modelski and Thompson, Doran counts Austria-Hungary, Italy, Japan, and China. Rising states enter, and declining states exit the great-power subsystem, depending on their dynamic relative power, which is a function more of behavior than of capabilities per se.[210] What matters is not merely the growth, maturation, and decline of a state's power measured in absolute statistical criteria (such as GNP, production of basic industrial power elements, or military spending), but the ratio of a state's total power relative to that of others in the system at a given time.

Doran identifies four critical points along the generalized curve of relative power, the dynamics of which are applicable to all states in the central system. Two are turning points (at the low point, where relative power begins to increase, and at the high point, where it starts to decline), and two inflection points (one on the rising side and one on the declining side, where acceleration gives way to deceleration). It is at these four critical points, says Doran, that we find clues to changes in a state's power position and international political role. Such changes may involve abrupt, unpredictable inversions in the dynamics of the power cycle, which upset the normal expectations of governmental planners and decision makers.[211] Doran concludes that the "power cycle dynamic contains the causal mechanism explaining *why, when,* and *how* the propensity is highest for major powers to initiate wars that become extensive."[212] (Doran's "extensive wars" are essentially the same as what others call "hegemonic," "systemic," and "global" wars.) Decision makers usually extrapolate straight-line projections of past experience into the future; the four critical points signal a new trajectory for state power, which may imply a transformation of the system, require painful adjustments, and give rise to misperceptions and anxiety for which both the state and the system are jointly responsible.[213]

> Because passage through a critical point on a single nation's power cycle is difficult for that nation and for the system to assimilate and increases the likelihood of major war, the roughly simultaneous passage of several states through critical points on their respective curves (with multiplicative as well as additive effects) is certainly much more difficult for the system to absorb.[214]

Doran finds some points of convergence between his relative-power-cycle theory and theories advanced by Organski and Kugler on power transition, Levy on the motivation of dominant states to block challengers, Gilpin on the cost-versus-benefit calculation of the effort to alter the status quo, as well as others, but he rejects the notions of determinism implicit in theories, which presume either the demise of the nation-state or the irreversibility in the decline of a nation's relative power position. Moreover, he postulates no deterministic outcome or inevitable connection between a change in a state's relative power position and the outbreak of war, for the impetus to war may be either catalyzed or constrained.[215]

The debate over long cycles in the occurrence of war remains unsettled. Modelski at one point (1981) suggested that there may be a relationship between his century-long cycle between systemic macrodecisions and a pair of Kondratieff's 50-year cycles in the economic order (25 years of upswing and 25 years of downswing),[216] but by the end of the 1980s, he did not press the point too vigorously.[217] Edward Mansfield, noting a surprisingly low correlation, in two different data sets (those of Wright and of Singer and Small), between the numbers of wars breaking out in particular years, finds variations in the relationship between Kondratieff price-fluctuation cycles and hegemony on the one hand and the incidence of war on the other.[218] After comparing those two data sets of wars in general with Jack Levy's data set on wars involving a great power since 1495,[219] Mansfield concludes that "hegemony does not seem to be associated consistently with either a decrease or an increase in wars with major-power participants, although it does appear to be strongly associated with a greater incidence of all types of war."[220] If Kondratieff cycles really exist, he adds, "they seem to have more influence on the incidence of war among smaller powers than among major powers"—not a comforting thought (he notes) to those who hold that interdependence necessarily enhances the probability of peace.[221]

Terry Boswell and Michael Sweat, employing time-series regression analysis and comparing three conceptions of hegemony—economic efficiency in the world economy (Wallerstein), global reach via sea power (Modelski and Thompson), and relative total power of states (Gilpin, Organski, and Kugler)—investigated the effects of hegemonic transition, long waves ("Kondratieffs"), and imperial expansion on the intensity of major wars during the period 1496–1967. They concluded that *resource* theory provides a better explanation than long-wave theory for the causal connections between economic expansion and the size of major wars. "Wars are larger during expansion periods because great powers can amass larger armies, sustain prolonged conflicts, and reap greater benefits from plunder than when the world economy is stagnating."[222] In their view, state leaders are likely to be more optimistic about the uniqueness and relative value of their nations' internal resources during long periods of economic expansion. "Beyond resource considerations, theories of long waves and major wars are not, in our estimation, either logically plausible or empirically supported."[223] They are particularly contemptuous of Marxist crisis theories, which predict major wars during periods of economic stagnation.

Some analysts have sought to save the appearances for the theory of long cycles by eliminating the need for regularity in their periodicity. Joshua S. Goldstein, for example, has contended that "just as Newtonian physics is subsumed by a more general relativistic physics, so fixed-period cycles constitute only one category of social cycles more broadly defined."[224] Cyclical phenomena in the social universe need not have a fixed repeating relationship with calendar time "as defined by the rotation of the planet we inhabit."[225] He contends that "periodicity is not appropriate to the social world . . . [where] phenomena are not well defined by physical laws of mechanical motion." Because he defines a cycle as a repeating sequence that involves a causal mechanism, Goldstein's cycle time can vary from one cycle to another. Periodicity is "only the superficial aspect of the cycle—the essence of a cycle is a (sometimes unknown) inner dynamic that gives rise to repetition."[226]

Lois W. Sayrs, too, defends the long cycle in international relations, despite what she calls mounting evidence against it. In her view, those who reject the long-cycle hypothesis do so because they make linear-model assumptions about the shape of the cycle, which are not applicable to nonlinear processes, where the cycle occurs at irregular intervals. Like Goldstein, she recognizes that the war cycle is most likely not periodic, and thus she does not specify a priori its length, shape, amplitude, or frequency.[227] Whereas Modelski has suggested a relation between global wars and *pairs* of Kondratieff waves (gradual upswings and downswings in the global economy occurring at 50-year intervals), for a century-long cycle,[228] Sayrs finds a cycle of approximately 21 years (12 on the upswing and 9 on the downswing).

Taking sharp issue with Goldstein (and implicitly with Sayrs), Nathaniel Beck insists that "models based on cycles of fixed periods are appropriate for the social sciences, and that only fixed period models are meaningful models of cyclic phenomena."[229] Beck insists that spectral analysis is the best standard method of studying the cyclic behavior of series, and he notes "an extensive international relations literature using spectral analysis that almost invariably finds no evidence for long cycles."[230] In Beck's view, without periodicity and a regular sine wave, the cycle is unpredictable and therefore nonexistent for all practical purposes. Despite disagreements, controversies, and inconsistencies (or contradictions), the theoretical and statistical debates about war cycles are bound to continue. Some will see cycles that others deny. There the question lies, not quite peacefully at rest.

DEMOCRACIES, WAR, AND PEACE

One of the most intensively debated questions among international-relations theorists in recent years pertains to the hypothesis linking democracy to peaceful international relations. Stated in its crudest and least credible form, the hypothesis runs as follows: "Liberals tend to be pacifists; liberal governments prefer negotiation to war (as do their publics); liberal democracies pursue peaceful foreign policies." Even Immanuel Kant, to whom such simplified beliefs are often uncritically attributed, never held that "republics" (the term he used in contrast to autocratically ruled states) did or should refrain from going to war under all circumstances. In fact, Kant took it as normal that liberal republics, seeing themselves threatened by aggression from nonrepublics (unconstrained as they are by representation and respect for the rights of others), would remain in a state of war with the latter and be obliged to go to war against them from time to time. According to Michael Doyle's interpretation of Kant's views, liberal governments are compelled to suspect the foreign policies of nonliberal states as no less aggressive and unjust than their domestic policies.[231] Kant looked forward to a "pacific federation" of liberal republics, "an enduring and gradually expanding federation likely to prevent war." Doyle quotes Kant's 1795 work, *Perpetual Peace:*

> It can be shown that this idea of federalism, extending gradually to encompass all states and thus leading to perpetual peace, is practicable. . . . For if by good fortune one powerful and enlightened nation can form a republic (which is by nature inclined to seek peace), this will provide a focal point for federal association among other states. These will join up with the first one, thus securing the freedom of each state in accordance with the idea of international right, and the whole will gradually spread further and further by a series of alliances of this kind.[232]

Several other liberal and utilitarian writers of the late eighteenth and mid-nineteenth centuries—Adam Smith, Jeremy Bentham, Herbert Spencer, John Stuart Mill, and so on—shared the conviction that capitalist economics and the rise of industrial societies reinforced the tendency of constitutional, parliamentary governments to pursue peaceful foreign policies, simply because rational *homo oeconomicus* realizes that war does not pay, and that laissez-faire and free-trade policies can produce their beneficial effects only in a predictable commercial environment of international peace. In the early twentieth century, Woodrow Wilson preached that world public opinion and a partnership of democratic states were essential prerequisites to international peace, while Norman Angell reiterated the optimistic view that war would become increasingly obsolescent as publics and governing elites could see how unprofitable it is.[233]

Modern democratic peace theorists do not claim that democracies are less war-prone than nondemocratic states, but rather that they rarely if ever go to war against each other. That is a very different proposition, one anticipated by Kant. The phenomenon was first publicized by Small and Singer in 1976.[234] Later, Paul Diehl called the no-war thesis "axiomatic," as applied to genuinely democratic states, even though they are not inhibited from going to war against authoritarian or totalitarian dictatorships that pursue provocative, aggressive foreign policies.[235] As we show later, there is not full agreement concerning how to define a "democratic state," or exactly how many states fall into that category today. If the phenomenon was not statistically noteworthy until the last quarter of this century, presumably it is because democracies were few and far between prior to World War II; geographically distant states are less likely to fight than contiguous ones; the democracies generally enjoyed greater political and economic stability; and leading democratic states were aligned against German autocracy in World War I, Axis totalitarianism in World War II, and Soviet Communism after World War II.[236] Only two of the least democratic members of NATO (Greece and Turkey at the time) fought each other over Cyprus. Despite problems with the hypothesis, Jack S. Levy has asserted that "the absence of war between democracies comes as close as anything we have to an empirical law in international relations."[237] Michael W. Doyle, who lists more than 50 democratic states at present, finds no wars waged between democratic dyads for more than 150 years.[238] Nicholas G. Onuf and Thomas J. Johnson note that advances in communications technology, together with unprecedented levels of prosperity and the liberal preoccupation with human rights, tolerance, and diversity, contribute to and expand a cosmopolitan perspective. This is most manifest in democracies, the dominant values of which reflect domestic and international peace.[239]

Granted that the statistical evidence is impressive, is there something in the nature of democratic states that makes them inherently peaceful? Rudolph Rummel once argued that democratic or libertarian states are less war prone than other states.[240] His analysis has been faulted for covering too limited a time period.[241] Rummel subsequently conceded that democracies may not be less war-prone once they are involved in a military confrontation, but that they are less likely to enter into such confrontations.[242] Here we are concerned with the more precise hypothesis that democracies do not fight each other.

Can this be explained with political logic? Kant contrasted monarchies and republics. Monarchs do not personally feel the costs of war and lose no privileges by waging it; republican peoples directly suffer the disastrous human and economic consequences of war and thus are more hesitant about going to war unless it is to promote freedom, protect their private property, or come to the aid of republican allies against nonrepublican foes. Liberal states, Kant believed, are more inclined to observe international law and to respect the rights of others. "As culture grows and men gradually move towards greater agreement over their principles, they lead to mutual understanding and peace."[243] Free speech and the effective communication of accurate conceptions of foreign societies, Doyle notes, also foster the growth of peace among states with similar cultural attitudes and political institutions: "Domestically just republics, which rest on consent, then presume foreign republics to be also consensual, just, and therefore deserving of accommodation."[244] Kant apparently foresaw that both institutional and cultural factors would contribute to a sense of mutual security and the gradual growth of a unique zone of peace among liberal states.

In a similar vein, Carol R. Ember, Melvin Ember, and Bruce Russett, citing recent studies testing alternative hypotheses with proper statistical controls, have concluded,

> Even when controls for physical proximity, alliances, wealth, economic growth, and political stability are incorporated into the analysis, there still remains an independent explanatory role for democracy. . . . In short, people in a democracy perceive themselves as autonomous, self-governing people who share norms of live and let live; they respect . . . others who are also perceived as self-governing. . . . They will also know that the institutional constraints, and the need for public debate in the other democracy, will prevent a surprise attack and so eliminate their own incentives to launch a preemptive strike. Two democratic states—each constrained from going to war and anticipating the other to be similarly inhibited—are likely to settle their conflicts without resort to war.[245]

Questions continue to be raised, even by analysts who are friendly to the hypothesis and who wish to clarify how the unwillingness of democratic people to go to war is translated into governmental policy, inasmuch as modern democracies never put the decision for war to a popular referendum. Bruce Bueno de Mesquita and David Lalman have lamented our scant understanding of how domestic attitudes (especially of opposition) produce an impact on foreign-policy decisions. "We do not know, for instance, whether the expectation of high domestic costs makes nations more or less likely to shun violent escalations of crises."[246] Whereas cultural factors affect general public attitudes toward foreign democracies, making them seem more trustworthy, reasonable, and amenable to negotiation, it is the institutional structure of democratic states that constrains or inhibits the governmental elites who make the decisions for war. "No modern democracy," T. Clifton Morgan and Sally Howard Campbell have noted, "puts a decision for war to a vote of the entire electorate."[247] They add, however, that a jingoistic population can push a government toward war. (The Spanish–American War, in which case a "yellow press" stirred public emotions, provides a clear example.)

Morgan and Campbell identify three principal types of decisional constraints. First, leaders who face the prospect of a popular election must worry more than dictators about incurring the wrath of voters. Second, institutionalized political competition within the state affects the decision-making process; a vigorous political-party opposition constitutes a significant constraint on an incumbent government. Third is the degree to which a leader must share decision-making power with other individuals or institutions (cabinet members, legislature, the military, etc.). Their conclusion is that we should expect to find the least war proneness not merely among popularly elected governments but also among those facing the most severe decisional constraints.

They point out that many nondemocracies are also affected by decisional constraints: Authoritarian leaders might be answerable to a junta capable of overthrowing them, and might face factional opposition. Moreover, states do not face an equal number of decisions for war in a given year; thus an instance of dispute involvement is a more appropriate unit of analysis than a nation-year in which wars were or were not being waged.[248] In the end, they admit that the empirical data do not provide clear support for their theoretical argument because their analyses uncovered no "strong statistically significant relationships linking high levels of domestic political constraints to a low probability of war."[249] By way of interpreting their ambiguous results, they suggest that "the causal mechanism associating democracy with war-proneness operates through political culture rather than domestic political structure," and that their initial assumption—heads of state are more likely to opt for war than those they govern, but they are pushed toward peace by domestic constraints—now seems questionable.[250] In their view, democracy "does not appear to be a force for peace in any straightforward, uniform or consistent fashion."[251]

Christopher Layne examined in depth four historic cases in which democratic states were involved in disputes that brought them to the brink of war—the United States and Britain in the Trent affair (1861) and the Venezuela crisis (1895–1896), France and Great Britain in the Fashoda crisis (1898), and France and Weimar Germany in the Ruhr crisis (1923).[252] If democratic peace theory is valid, he argues, it should provide a satisfactory explanation of why serious crises between democratic states produced threats of war, jingoistic outbursts of public opinion, ultimata, and big-stick diplomacy rather than a desire for mutual accommodation. In all four cases, Layne contends, war was finally averted by a near miss, but that in all four cases realpolitik rather than democratic peace theory provides the explanation of the outcome. The determining factors, as is normally the case among great powers in the international anarchic system, were rational calculations by governments concerning prestige, national interest, the power equation, the possibility that other powers might exploit the dispute, and so on. Layne concludes that "democratic peace theory's causal logic has only minimal explanatory power."[253] He remains unimpressed with the logical case for institutional and cultural constraints on the foreign policies of democratic states. Because the theory's deductive logic lacks explanatory power, he calls for further analysis of the empirical evidence:

> The statistical evidence that democracies do not fight each other seems impressive but in fact it is inconclusive, because the universe of cases providing empirical support . . . is small, and because several important cases of wars between democratic states are not counted for reasons that are not persuasive.[254]

Layne cites with approval the findings of a fellow skeptic, David E. Spiro, who criticizes Doyle for failing to perform any probability analyses to determine the statistical significance of zero wars since 1816 among the states he lists as liberal. Spiro argues, on the basis of his own statistical analysis, that random chance is a better predictor of the absence of war among the states in question than is democratic-peace theory. He has serious problems with the ways the advocates of that theory "select definitions of the key terms of democracy and war, . . . the methods they choose for statistical analysis . . . and operationalization of variables that undergo contortions before they yield apparently significant results."[255] In Spiro's view, "the absence of wars between democracies would not be a confirmation of this theory, unless we were also able to prove that democracies fought fewer wars with non-democracies."[256] He notes that Zeev Maoz and Michael W. Doyle disagree for two thirds of the nations that either or both list as democratic, regarding either the nature or years of democracy.[257] He faults Doyle, Russett, and others for arbitrary classifications (ignoring ancient democracies, women's suffrage, and slavery, and disagreeing over other criteria, such as degree of participation, competitiveness of executive recruitment, restraints on the chief executive, political stability, domestic oppression of individual rights, etc.).[258] Spiro finds that the criteria for determining what was and what was not an interstate war are hardly less arbitrary than those used for defining whether a state was democratic at a given period.[259] Spiro seems to commend Maoz and Russett for restricting their analysis to the period 1946–1986 because this enabled them to use contemporaneous standards (which did not change fundamentally over the four decades) for deciding which nations are liberal, thus avoiding the "shifting threshold [which] is much more of a problem for studies that consider longer sweeps of history."[260] (For the analysis of Maoz and Russett, see the latter part of Spiro's article.)

David A. Lake adds an interesting postcript to the debate, noting "the propensity of democracies to win the wars that they do fight," a paradox, in view of the problems of cumbersome decision making and proneness to stalemate or paralysis often associated with the democratic conduct of foreign policy.[261] Lake employs a complex microeconomic theory of the state as a profit-maximizing firm that trades services for revenues. The state is the monopoly provider of protection against external threats; this is the state's foremost service. Because even high levels of defense spending seldom create feelings of total security, the state as monopoly provider can control the quantity of protection supplied and charge whatever the market will bear, whether at a normal profit level or at a supernormal profit level, which he calls "rent." States can artificially increase the demand for and the price of protection through extortion or racketeering, or by exaggerating foreign threats, supplying incomplete information and false propaganda. State "rent seeking" creates an imperialist bias in foreign policy, which leads to expansionism and war proneness; this is greater in autocracies than in democracies where individual citizens have better opportunities to assess the foreign threat level, monitor the state's performance, criticize its strategic policies, and control its rent-seeking behavior. Lake has no difficulty finding congruence between his own economic explanation of the difference between democratic and autocratic states with regard to rent-seeking and the political theories of Kant and Doyle, summarized earlier concerning the reasons for wars between democratic and autocratic states.[262] Lake's more original contribution pertains to the democracies' propensity for victory in war. He argues that democratic states, earning fewer rents,

> tend (1) to create fewer economic distortions, possess greater national wealth, and devote more resources to security; (2) to enjoy greater societal support for their policies and therefore a greater extractive capacity; and (3) to form overwhelming counter-coalitions against expansionist autocracies.[263]

According to Lake's list of 26 wars fought from 1816 to 1988 between democracies and autocracies, the former have won 21 (81%) and lost 5 (19%).[264]

Maoz and Russett call the democratic-peace result "probably one of the most significant nontrivial products of the scientific study of world politics"—perhaps "the basis of far more important insights into the workings of the international political world in modern times."[265] What they find most striking is the fact that democracies, although they cannot be shown to be less conflict-prone than nondemocratic states, do not fight each other. They ask whether this is more attributable causally to a *normative* model of behavior, in which domestic political norms are externalized in relations with other states, or to a *structural* model, in which the process of mobilization for war is considerably more difficult and cumbersome in democratic states. They contrast democracies, where internal conflicts are resolved through compromise rather than elimination of opponents, with nondemocracies, where coercive or violent outcomes are more likely. In the normative model, democracies deal with one another to resolve conflicts in a nonviolent manner of reasonable accommodation, according to democratic values; conflicts between democratic and nondemocratic states are dominated by nondemocratic norms because nondemocratic states tend to force the issue by taking advantage of the moderation inherent in democracies. In the structural model, the complexity of the democratic process makes leaders reluctant to mobilize to wage war except as a last necessary resort; two democratic parties to a conflict take sufficient time to pursue processes that enable diplomats to work out nonmilitary solutions. Conversely, nondemocratic leaders are under fewer structural constraints to mobilize for war, less concerned about public opinion, and thus in a better position to escalate the conflict quickly to a level of violence.

The authors admit that the two models are extremely difficult to distinguish conceptually, and that cost–benefit calculations of war are different for richer democracies than for poorer nondemocracies.[266] After extensive theoretical analysis of the normative–cultural and structural–institutional models, Maoz and Russett conclude that both models "provide reasonably good explanations of why democracies rarely fight each other, but that the normative model is somewhat more robust than the structural."[267] In drawing out the implications, they suggest that newly created democracies in transition may still experience some interstate conflict, but that the spread of democracy may make for a more stable international system, one in which norms and rules become more peaceful and accommodating, reflecting the internal cultural and political values of systems in which governments are popularly controlled.[268] Conversely, Edward Mansfield and Jack Snyder, on the basis of a recent study, warned that states in transition to democracy are two thirds more likely over the course of a ten-year period to fight wars than those undergoing no regime change.[269]

The debate over the relative war proneness of top-down (nondemocratic) versus bottom-up (democratic) political systems will undoubtedly continue. Even granting the persuasiveness of the statistical evidence that democracies have not fought each other during the past century and a half, it is legitimate to wonder whether this trend will remain firm in the twenty-first century, when the number of democratic states is likely to increase,[270] becoming a larger proportion of the total universe of states, especially if we reach a situation of conflict over scarce resources, as well as over trade, monetary, environmental, and other economic policies that might severely test what now strikes many analysts as the closest approximation to a valid empirical law in international relations.

NOTES

1. See Georg Simmel, "Conflict", trans. Kurt H. Wolff, in *Conflict and the Web of Group-Affiliations* (New York: Free Press, 1964), pp. 15–38; Jesse Bernard, "Parties and Issues in Conflict," *Journal of Conflict Resolution,* I (March 1957); and Ralf Dahrendorf, "Toward a Theory of Social Conflict," trans. Anatol Rapoport, *Journal of Conflict Resolution,* II (June 1958). Dahrendorf, a German sociologist, argues that when certain social–structural arrangements are given, conflict is bound to arise. He traces the responsibility for the shift of emphasis within the field of sociology from social conflict to social stability to Talcott Parsons and Parsons's structural–functional approach to the study of society. (For a discussion of the work of Parsons and structural–functionalism, see Chapter 3.) This approach contains the following implicit postulates: (1) Every society is a relatively persisting configuration of elements. (2) Every society is a well-integrated configuration of elements. (3) Every element in a society contributes to its functioning. (4) Every society rests on the consensus of its members. Dahrendorf believes that this social-equilibrium conception of society is not compatible with the serious study of conflict. The foregoing postulates not only fail to explain change and conflict, but they also exclude these phenomena altogether. When confronted with instances of conflict, the structural–functional school treats them as abnormal, deviant, and pathological. In contrast to the structural–functional theory, Dahrendorf offers four different postulates: (1) Every society is subjected at every moment to change; change is ubiquitous. (2) Every society experiences at every moment social conflict; conflict is ubiquitous. (3) Every element in a society contributes to its change. (4) Every society rests on constraint of some of its members by others. Dahrendorf's postulates are not presented to replace the Parsonian view, but rather to complement it. The two organic models together, he suggests, would exhaust social reality, and a synthesis of the two would supply us with a complete theory of society in both its enduring and its changing aspects. Dahrendorf, ibid., especially pp. 173–175.
2. Georg Simmel, op. cit., pp. 16–20.
3. Lewis A. Coser, *The Functions of Social Conflict* (Glencoe, IL: Free Press, 1964), p. 8. Western theorists as far apart in their fundamental premises as Saint Augustine and Karl Marx regarded conflict as the motor of social change. See Robert A. Nisbet, *Social Change and History: Aspects of the Western Theory of Development* (New York: Oxford University Press, 1969), pp. 76–90.
4. William Graham Sumner, *War and Other Essays* (New Haven, CT: Yale University Press, 1911), excerpted in Leon Bramson and George W. Goethals, eds., *War: Studies from Psychology, Sociology, Anthropology,* rev. ed. (New York: Basic Books, 1968), pp. 210–212.
5. William James, "The Moral Equivalent of War," *Memories and Studies* (London: Longman, 1912) p. 23.
6. Richard N. Rosecrance, *Action and Reaction in World Politics* (Boston: Little, Brown, 1963), pp. 255, 304–305.
7. Clyde Kluckhohn, *Mirror for Man: A Survey of Human Behavior and Social Attitudes* (Greenwich, CT: Fawcett World Library, 1960), p. 173. See also Stephen Withey and Daniel Katz, "The Social Psychology of Human Conflict," in Elton B. McNeil, ed., *The Nature of Human Conflict* (Englewood Cliffs, NJ: Prentice-Hall, 1965), p. 81; and Nicholas S. Timasheff, *War and Revolution* (New York: Sheed and Ward, 1965), chap. 5.

8. Robert F. Murphy, "Intergroup Hostility and Social Cohesion," reprinted from *American Anthropologist,* LIX (6) (December 1957), 1018–1035, in J. K. Zawodny, ed., *Man and International Relations* (San Francisco: Chandler, 1966), pp. 602–603. R. F. Maher has reached a similar conclusion from his study of tribes in New Guinea. See Robert A. LeVine, "Socialization, Social Structure and Intersocietal Images," in H. C. Kelman, ed., *International Behavior: A Sociological Analysis* (New York: Holt, Rinehart and Winston, 1965), p. 47. For the case of the Teton Indians, supporting a comparable hypothesis in an obverse form, see Elton B. McNeil, "The Nature of Aggression," in McNeil, ed., op. cit., p. 37.

9. Georg Simmel, op. cit., p. 93; see also pp. 88–89. M. Mulder and A. Stemerding have shown that a group faced with a threat becomes cohesive and highly tolerant of strong leadership. "Threat, Attraction to Group, and Need for Strong Leadership," *Human Relations,* XVI (November 1963), 317–334.

10. Geoffrey Blainey, *The Causes of War* (New York: Free Press, 1973), pp. 71–86. (Same pp. in 3rd edition, published in 1988.)

11. Rudolph J. Rummel concluded that foreign-conflict behavior is generally unrelated to domestic-conflict behavior, "Dimensions of Conflict Behavior Within and Between Nations," *General Systems Yearbook,* VIII (1963), p. 24. In a subsequent replication, Raymond Tanter similarly found little positive relationship. "Dimensions of Conflict Behavior Within and Between Nations, 1958–1960," *Journal of Conflict Resolution,* X (March 1966), 65–73. Later still, in a study of the U.S. domestic scene during the Vietnam War, Tanter suggested a positive correlation between a foreign war that continues without apparent success and the incidence of domestic turmoil. "International War and Domestic Turmoil," in *Violence in America, A Report to the National Commission on the Causes and Prevention of Violence,* prepared by Hugh Davis Graham and Ted Robert Gurr (New York: New American Library, 1969). Jonathan Wilkenfeld, utilizing political variables analyzed by Philip M. Gregg and Arthur S. Banks "Dimensions of Political Systems," *American Political Science Review,* 59 (September 1965), 602–614, rearranged the nations of the world into three political-type groups (personalist, centrist, and polyarchic), and he concluded that there is a relationship between domestic- and foreign-conflict behavior if the type of political regime is taken into account; "Domestic and Foreign Conflict Behavior of Nations," in William D. Coplin and Charles W. Kegley, Jr., eds., *Analyzing International Relations: A Multimethod Introduction* (New York: Praeger, 1975), pp. 96–112. See also Karen Rasler, "War, Accommodation and Violence in the United States, 1890–1970," *American Political Science Review,* 80 (September 1986); Ole R. Holsti and James N. Rosenau, *American Leadership in World Affairs: Vietnam and the Breakdown of Consensus* (Winchester, MA: George Allen & Unwin, 1984).

12. Bruce Bueno de Mesquita and David Lalman, "Domestic Opposition and Foreign War," *American Political Science Review,* 80 (September 1990), 747.

13. Quoted from a 1992 paper by Randolph M. Siverson and Harvey Starr in Harvey Starr, "Revolution and War: Rethinking the Linkage Between Internal and External Conflict," *Political Research Quarterly,* 47 (June 1994), 481.

14. See Herbert S. Dinerstein, "The Transformation of Alliance Systems," *American Political Science Review,* LIX (September 1965), 589–601. Emile Benoit says that membership in a common defense alliance against an agreed potential aggressor is a powerful integrating factor, and "the reduced fear of such external aggression seems to have been a major factor in slowing down the European Economic Community . . . not only weakening the international alliance, but encouraging conflicts, internal dissidence, and secessionist movements within individual countries." "Kenneth Boulding

as Socio-Political Theorist," *Journal of Conflict Resolution,* XXI (September 1977), 557.

15. Jack S. Levy concludes, "Whereas the theoretical and historical literature suggests the importance of the diversionary use of force by political elites to bolster their internal political positions, the quantitative empirical literature in political science has repeatedly found that there is no consistent and meaningful relationship between the internal and external conflict behavior of states"; "The Diversionary Theory of War: A Critique," in Manus I. Midlarsky, ed., *Handbook of War Studies* (Boston: Unwin Hyman, 1989), p. 282. Levy goes on to observe that "the scapegoat hypothesis or diversionary theory of war is not the same as the relationship between internal and external conflict"; ibid., p. 283.

16. Clyde Kluckhohn, *Mirror for Man,* op. cit., p. 48. According to Alexander Lesser, the concept of war does not appear among Andaman Islanders, aboriginal Australians, Mission Indians, Aruntans, Western Shishonis, Semangs, and Todas; "War and the State," in Morton Fried et al., *War: The Anthropology of Armed Conflict and Aggression* (Garden City, NY: Natural History Press, 1968), p. 94. In contrast, the Yanomamo, who live along the Orinoco River in Venezuela and Brazil, believe that humans are inherently fierce and warlike. Their entire culture is geared to the development of belligerence—threats, shouting, duels, wife-beating, a strong preference for male children, and encouraging the young to strike their elders; Napoleon A. Chagnon, "Yanomamo Social Organization and Warfare," in Fried et al., ibid., pp. 109–159, especially pp. 124–133.

17. Lewis F. Richardson showed that between 1820 and 1945, the number of foreign wars with more than 7,000 war dead correlated with the number of bordering neighbors for 33 countries studied; *Statistics of Deadly Quarrels* (Pittsburgh, PA: Boxwood Press, 1960), p. 176. See also James Paul Wesley, "Frequency of Wars and Geographical Opportunity," *Journal of Conflict Resolution,* 6 (September 1962) 387–389.

18. See Robert Redfield, "Primitive Law," in Paul Bohannan, ed., *Law and Warfare: Studies in the Anthropology of Conflict,* American Museum Sourcebooks in Anthropology (Garden City, NY: Natural History Press, 1967), pp. 3–24.

19. Andrew P. Vayda, "Hypotheses About Functions of War," in Morton Fried et al., op. cit., pp. 85–89. According to J. P. Johansen, the Maoris of New Zealand sometimes resolved intragroup tensions by having a member of the tribe commit an act of violence against another tribe, thereby provoking a retaliation that would reestablish group unity; cited by Andrew P. Vayda, "Maori Warfare," in Paul Bohannan, ed., *Law and Warfare,* op. cit., p. 380. William T. Divale, "An Explanation for Primitive Warfare: Population Control and the Significance of Primitive Sex Ratios," *The New Scholar* (2) (1970), 173–192; Marvin Harris, "Ecology, Demography and War," in his *Culture, Man and Nature* (New York: Thomas Crowell, 1971), pp. 200–234.

20. See, for example, Kaj Birket-Smith, *Primitive Man and His Ways* (New York: New American Library, 1963), pp. 67 and 195.

21. Anthony F. C. Wallace has observed that for the Iroquois, the symbolically arousing stimulus that preceded mobilization for war was a report that a kinsman had been slain and a survivor was calling for revenge; "Psychological Preparations for War," in Robert F. Murphy et al., eds., *Selected Papers from The American Anthropologist 1946–1970* (Washington, DC: American Anthropological Association, 1976), pp. 175–176.

22. Andrew P. Vayda, op. cit., pp. 89–91.

23. Andrew P. Vayda, "Primitive Warfare," in D. Sills, ed., *International Encyclopedia of the Social Sciences,* XVI (NY: Crowell Collier and Macmillan, Inc., 1968), p. 468.

24. Alvin and Heidi Toffler, *Future Shock* (New York: Bantam, 1970). By the same authors, *Powershift* (New York: Bantam, 1990); *Previews and Premises* (New York: William Morrow, 1983); *The Third Wave* (New York: Bantam, 1980).

25. Alvin and Heidi Toffler, *War and Anti-War: Survival at the Dawn of the Twenty-first Century* (Boston: Little, Brown and Company, 1993), especially pp. 18–25.

26. Bronislaw Malinowski, "An Anthropological Analysis of War," in Bramson and Goethals, eds., op. cit., p. 209.

27. Margaret Mead, "Warfare Is Only an Invention, Not a Biological Necessity," in Bramson and Goethals., eds, ibid., pp. 269–274.

28. William Graham Sumner, "War," reprinted from *War and Other Essays* (1911), in Bramson and Goethals, eds., ibid., p. 209.

29. Bronislaw Malinowski, op. cit., pp. 255 and 260.

30. Ibid., p. 260.

31. David Bidney, *Theoretical Anthropology* (New York: Schocken, 1967), pp. 231–232 and 361–362.

32. Margaret Mead and Rhoda Metraux, "The Anthropology of Human Conflict," in McNeil, ed., op. cit., p. 122.

33. Ibid., p. 128.

34. Clyde Kluckhohn, op. cit., p. 213.

35. Alex Inkeles, "National Character and Modern Political Systems," in Francis L. Hsu, ed., *Psychological Anthropology* (Homewood, IL: Dorsey, 1961), pp. 171–202.

36. See, for example, Margaret G. Hermann and Thomas W. Milburn, *A Psychological Examination of Political Leaders* (New York: Free Press, 1977).

37. David E. Stannard denounced the psychoanalytic approach to history for overstressing childhood experience and failing to pass empirical tests; *Shrinking History: On Freud and the Failure of Psychohistory* (New York: Oxford University Press, 1980). Rudolph Binion, in a review of that work, defended psychohistory as "a discipline in its own right, independent of the Freudianism from which it is derived". *American Historical Review* (April 1981), 370.

38. Otto Klineberg, *The Human Dimension in International Relations* (New York: Holt, Rinehart and Winston, 1964) p. 95.

39. See Lewis Mumford, *Technics and Civilization* (New York: Harcourt Brace, 1934); J. F. C. Fuller, *Armament and History: A Study of the Influence of Armament on History from the Dawn of Classical Warfare to the Second World War* (London: Eyre & Spottiswoode, 1945); William F. Ogburn, ed., *Technology and International Relations* (Chicago: University of Chicago Press, 1949); John U. Nef, *War and Human Progress* (Cambridge, MA: Harvard University Press, 1950; New York: Norton, 1968); Bernard Brodie and Fawn Brodie, *From Cross-bow to H-bomb* (New York: Dell, 1962).

40. See, for example, Paul R. Brass, ed., *Ethnic Groups and the State* (Totowa, NJ: Barnes and Noble, 1985). One should not overlook the fact that those multiethnic societies that are most violence-prone are usually characterized by perceived and objectively measurable political and economic inequality. See Christopher Hewitt, "Majorities and Minorities: A Comparative Survey of Ethnic Violence," *Annals of the American Academy of Political and Social Sciences*, (433) (September 1977), 150–160. For an explanation as to why Scottish, Quebecois, and Basque ethnonationalist movements have not enjoyed striking success, see Edward A. Tiryakian and Ronald Rogowski, eds., *New Nationalisms of the Developed West* (Boston: Allen & Unwin, 1985).

41. Georg Simmel, op. cit., pp. 43–48; Lewis Coser, op. cit., pp. 67–72. See reference to Jesse Bernard in Note 1 supra.

42. Edward Luttwak, *Coup d'Etat: A Political Handbook* (Harmondsworth, England: Penguin, 1969); William G. Andrews and Uri Ra'anan, eds., *The Politics of the Coup*

d'Etat (Princeton, NJ: Van Nostrand, 1969); Morris Janowitz, *Military Institutions and Coercion in the Developing Nations* (Chicago: University of Chicago Press, 1977); Amos Perlmutter and Gavin Kennedy, *The Military in the Third World* (New York: Charles Scribner's Sons, 1974); Amos Perlmutter, *The Military and Politics in Modern Times* (New Haven, CT: Yale University Press, 1977); Robert W. Jackman et al., "Explaining African Coups d'Etat," *American Political Science Review,* 80 (March 1986) pp. 225–250.

43. Mark N. Hagopian, *The Phenomenon of Revolution* (New York: Dodd, Mead, 1974), p. 1.

44. Earlier editions of this book carried an extensive discussion of revolution. Those interested in its causes, nature, ideology, strategy, leadership, characteristic phases, and consequences should consult the standard works on the subject: Crane Brinton, *Anatomy of Revolution* (New York: Norton, 1938; Random House, 1965), a study of four successful revolutions (English, American, French, and Russian); Alexis de Tocqueville, *The Old Regime and the French Revolution,* originally published in French in 1856, trans. by Gilbert Stuart (Garden City, NY: Doubleday-Anchor, 1955); Hannah Arendt, *On Revolution* (New York: Viking, 1965), an analysis of the phenomenon as marked by a pathos of novelty, a notion that the course of history is about to begin anew; Chalmers Johnson, *Revolutionary Change* (Boston: Little, Brown, 1966); James H. Meisel, *Counterrevolution: How Revolutions Die* (New York: Atherton, 1966), in which it is argued that every revolution dies in overorganization, terror, oppression, the restoration of the old order, or sheer boredom and final alienation; Karl Leiden and Karl M. Schmitt, *The Politics of Violence: Revolution in the Modern World* (Englewood Cliffs, NJ: Prentice-Hall, 1968); Peter Calvert, *Revolution* (New York: Praeger, 1970); Ted Robert Gurr, *Why Men Rebel* (Princeton, NJ: Princeton University Press, 1970), in which the author identifies the frustration–aggression mechanism as the primary source of the human capacity for violence, and economic deprivation in the Third World as a major precondition of violent civil conflict; James C. Davies, ed., *When Men Revolt and Why* (New York: Free Press, 1971), in which Davies presents a useful J-curve theory, which suggests that the danger of revolutionary conflict becomes more acute when a society on the long-term path toward development suddenly experiences an economic downturn, which frustrates popular expectations; John Dunn, *Modern Revolutions* (Cambridge, England: Cambridge University Press, 1972); David Wilkinson, *Revolutionary Civil War* (Palo Alto, CA: Page-Ficklin, 1975); Melvin Lasky, *Utopia and Revolution: On the Origins of a Metaphor* (Chicago: University of Chicago Press, 1976), a work which highlights the causal role of utopian rhetoric; Bruce Mazlish, *The Revolutionary Ascetic: Evolution of a Political Type* (New York: Basic Books, 1976); Mostafa Rejai, *The Comparative Study of Revolutionary Strategy* (New York: McKay, 1977); Charles Tilly, *From Mobilization to Revolution* (Reading, MA: Addison-Wesley, 1978); Anthony Burton, *Revolutionary Violence: The Theories* (New York: Crane, Russak, 1978); James Billington, *Fire in the Minds of Men: Origins of the Revolutionary Faith* (New York: Basic Books, 1980); William H. Friedland et al., *Revolutionary Theory* (Totowa, NJ: Allenheld, 1982); N. K. O'Sullivan, *Revolutionary Theory and Political Reality* (New York: St. Martin's Press, 1984); Seymour Martin Lipset, *Revolution and Counterrevolution: Change and Persistence in Social Structure* (New Brunswick, NJ: Transaction Books, 1987). Noteworthy articles include James C. Davies, "Toward a Theory of Revolution," *American Sociological Review,* 27 (February 1962) 5–18; Lawrence Stone, "Theories of Revolution," *World Politics,* 18 (January 1966) 159–176; and Jack A. Goldstone, "Theories of Revolution," *World Politics,* 32 (April 1980) 425–453.

45. Stephen M. Walt, "Revolution and War," *World Politics,* 44 (April 1992), 321.

46. Ibid.
47. Ibid., 322. Walt notes that there are several excellent case studies, but very few theoretical works on the international implications of revolutionary change. He cites Peter Calvert, *Revolution and International Politics* (New York: St. Martin's, 1984); and Kyung-Won Kim, *Revolution and International System* (New York: New York University Press, 1970). Earlier, George Modelski had asserted that every internal war creates a demand for foreign intervention. "The International Relations of Internal War," in James N. Rosenau, ed., *International Aspects of Civil Strife* (Princeton, NJ: Princeton University Press, 1964), p. 20. See also Richard Little, *Intervention: External Involvement in Civil Wars* (Totowa, NJ: Rowman and Littlefield, 1975). Foreign intervention in revolutions and other internal conflicts would seem to be a characteristic of state behavior in the international system, but Walt's approach to this subject is more theoretical than the earlier studies.
48. Walt, "Revolution and War," 325.
49. Ibid., 325–330.
50. Ibid., 330–332.
51. Ibid., 332–333.
52. Ibid., 360.
53. Harvey Starr, "Revolution and War: Rethinking the Linkage Between Internal and External Conflict," *Political Research Quarterly*, 47 (June 1994), 481–486.
54. Ibid., 482.
55. George Tsebelis, *Nested Games* (Berkeley, CA: University of California Press, 1990), pp. 7–8.
56. Starr, op. cit., 486–487.
57. Starr cites Charles Tilly, *Coercion, Capital and European States, AD 990–1990* (Oxford, England: Basil Blackwell, 1990); Hedley Bull and Adam Watson, eds., *The Expansion of International Society* (Oxford, England: Oxford University Press, 1984); Michael Mastanduno, et al., "Toward a Realist Theory of State Action," *International Studies Quarterly*, 33 (December 1989), 457–474.
58. Starr, op. cit., 489–490.
59. "That every internal war creates a demand for foreign intervention," writes George Modelski, "is implicit in the logic of the situation"; "The International Relations of Internal War," in James N. Rosenau, ed., *International Aspects of Civil Strife* (Princeton, NJ: Princeton University Press, 1964), p. 20. See Richard Little, *Intervention: External Involvement in Civil Wars* (Totowa, NJ: Rowman and Littlefield, 1975); Peter Calvert, *Revolution and International Politics* (New York: St. Martin's Press, 1984).
60. Robert W. McColl, "A Political Geography of Revolution: China, Vietnam and Thailand," *Journal of Conflict Resolution*, I (June 1967), 153–167.
61. See Karl W. Deutsch, "External Involvement in Internal War," in Harry Eckstein, ed., *Internal War: Problems and Approaches* (New York: Free Press, 1964), pp. 100–110, especially p. 102.
62. Ekkhart Zimmerman, *Political Violence, Crises, and Revolution* (Cambridge, MA: Schenkman, 1983); Jack A. Goldstone, "Theories of Revolution," *World Politics* (April 1980) 425–453.
63. Bard O'Neill, William Heaton, and Donald Alberts, eds., *Insurgency in the Modern Age* (Boulder, CO: Westview Press, 1980); Mark Hagopian, *The Phenomenon of Revolution* (New York: Dodd, Mead, 1974); Thomas Greene, *Comparative Revolutionary Movements* (Englewood Cliffs, NJ: Prentice-Hall, 1974); Mostafa Rejai, *The Comparative Study of Revolutionary Strategy* (New York: David McKay, 1977).

64. Stephen Hosmer and Thomas Wolfe, *Soviet Policy and Practice Toward Third World Conflicts* (Lexington, MA: Lexington Books, 1983); Bruce Porter, *The USSR In Third World Conflicts* (London: Cambridge University Press, 1984); Joseph Whelan and Michael Dixon, *The Soviet Union in the Third World: Threat to World Peace* (New York: Pergamon-Brassey's, 1986).

65. John Dziak, "Military Doctrine and Structure," in Uri Ra'anan, Robert L. Pfaltzgraff, Jr., Richard Shultz, Ernst Halperin, and Igor Lukes, eds., *Hydra of Carnage: International Linkages of Terrorism* (Lexington, MA: Lexington Books, 1985); *Chekisty, A History of the KGB* (Lexington, MA: Lexington Books, 1987); John Collins, *Green Berets, SEALS, and Spetsnaz: U.S. and Soviet Special Military Operations* (New York: Pergamon-Brassey's, 1987).

66. John F. Copper and Daniel S. Papp, eds., *Communist Nations' Military Assistance* (Boulder, CO: Westview Press, 1983); W. Scott Thompson, *Power Projection* (New York: National Strategy Information Center, 1978).

67. Richard Shultz, *The Soviet Union and Revolutionary Warfare: Principles, Practices, and Regional Comparisons* (Stanford, CA: Hoover Institution Press, 1988); Uri Ra'anan et al., eds., op cit.; Dennis Bark, ed., *The Red Orchestra* (Stanford, CA: Hoover Institution Press, 1986); Walter Laqueur, ed., *The Patterns of Soviet Conduct in the Third World* (New York: Praeger Press, 1983). Shultz examines four specific instances in his thorough evaluation of Soviet successes and failures in the period from the late 1960s to the mid-1980s.

68. Paul Linebarger, *Psychological Warfare* (Washington, DC: Infantry Journal Press, 1948); William Daugherty and Morris Janowitz, eds., *A Psychological Warfare Casebook* (Baltimore, MD: Johns Hopkins University Press, 1958); Daniel Lerner, ed., *Propaganda in War and Crisis* (New York: Stewart Publishers, 1950); Harold Lasswell et al., *Language of Politics* (New York: Stewart Publishers, 1949); Jacques Ellul, *Propaganda: The Formation of Men's Attitudes* (New York: Alfred A. Knopf, 1965).

69. Richard Shultz and Roy Godson, *Dezinformatsia: Active Measures in Soviet Strategy* (New York: Pergamon-Brassey's, 1984); Paul A. Smith, Jr., *On Political Warfare* (Washington, DC: National Defense University Press, 1988); Carnes Lord, ed., *Psychological Warfare in U.S. Strategy* (Washington, DC: National Defense University Press, 1988); Donald Brown, *International Radio Broadcasting* (New York: Praeger, 1982); Ladislav Bittman, *The KGB and Soviet Disinformation* (New York: Pergamon-Brassey's, 1985) and *The New Image-Makers: Soviet Propaganda and Disinformation Today* (New York: Pergamon-Brassey's, 1988).

70. Ra'anan et al., eds., op. cit.; Bark, ed., op. cit.; Shultz, *The Soviet Union and Revolutionary Warfare* and "Soviet Use of Surrogates to Project Power into the Third World," *Parameters* (Autumn, 1986) 32–42.

71. The term *low-intensity conflict* began to be used by U.S. national-security specialists in the second half of the 1970s. See George Tanham et al., "United States Preparation for Future Low-Level Conflict," *Conflict,* (12) (1978) 1–20; Sam Sarkesian and William Scully, eds., *U.S. Policy and Low Intensity Conflict* (New Brunswick, NJ: Transaction Books, 1981). The terminology may have been borrowed from the British specialist, Frank Kitson; see Kitson, *Low Intensity Operations* (Harrisburg, PA: Stackpole, 1971).

72. Sam C. Sarkesian, *The New Battlefield* (Westport, CT: Greenwood Press, 1986); Stephen Hosmer and George Tanham, *Countering Covert Aggression* (Santa Monica, CA: Rand Corporation, 1986); David Dean, ed., *Low Intensity Conflict and Modern Technology* (Maxwell Air Force Base, AL: Air University Press, 1986). See also U.S. Army Training and Doctrine Command Pamphlet 52544, *U.S. Army Operational*

Concept for Low Intensity Conflict (Fort Monroe, VA: Army Training and Doctrine Command, 1986).

73. Sarkesian, op. cit.; Frank Barnett, Hugh Tovar, and Richard Shultz, eds., *Special Operations in U.S. Strategy* (Washington, DC: National Defense University Press, 1984); Richard Shultz, "Discriminate Deterrence and Low Intensity Conflict: The Unintentional Legacy of the Reagan Administration," *Conflict* (June 1989) 21–44; Michael Klare and Peter Kornbluh, *Low Intensity Warfare* (New York: Pantheon, 1988); D. Michael Shafer, *Deadly Paradigms* (Princeton, NJ: Princeton University Press, 1988); John Prados, *President's Secret Wars* (New York: William Morrow, 1986); A. J. Bacevich, James D. Hallums, Richard H. White, and Thomas Young, *American Military Policy in Small Wars: The Case of El Salvador* (New York: Pergamon-Brassey's, 1988). For other studies, see Collins, *Green Berets, SEALS, and Spetsnaz,* op. cit., Richard Shultz, Robert L. Pfaltzgraff, Uri Ra'anan, William Olsen, and Igor Lukes, eds., *Guerrilla Warfare and Counterinsurgency: U.S. Soviet Policy and the Third World* (Lexington, MA: Lexington Books, 1988); David Charters and Maurice Tugwell, eds., *Armies in Low Intensity Conflict* (Ottawa, Canada: Department of National Defense, 1985); Ian F. W. Beckett and John Pimlott, eds., *Armed Forces and Modern Counterinsurgency* (New York: St. Martin's Press, 1985); William Burgess, "Iranian Special Operations in the Iran–Iraq War," *Conflict* (August 1988); Richard H. Shultz, Jr., Robert L. Pfaltzgraff, Jr., and W. Bradley Stock, *Roles and Missions of Special Operations Forces in the Aftermath of the Cold War* (Ft. Bragg, NC: United States Special Operations Command, 1995).

74. Donald Horowitz, *Ethnic Groups in Conflict* (Berkeley: University of California Press, 1985); and Ted Robert Gurr, *Minorities at Risk: A Global View of Ethnopolitics* (Washington, DC: U.S. Institute of Peace, 1993). See also Robert L. Pfaltzgraff, Jr., and Richard H. Shultz, Jr., eds., *Ethnic Conflict and Regional Instability: Implications for U.S. Policy and Army Roles and Missions* (Carlisle, PA: Strategic Studies Institute, U.S. Army War College, 1994).

75. Gurr, *Minorities at Risk,* op. cit., Richard H. Shultz, Jr., and William J. Olson, *Ethnic and Religious Conflict: Emerging Threat to U.S. Security* (Washington, DC: National Strategy Information Center, 1994); Myron Weiner, "Peoples and States in the New Ethnic Order?" *Third World Quarterly,* (2) (June 1992) 317–334; Paul Weaver, "Flashpoints," *Jane's Defense Weekly* (January 11, 1992), 53; Vladimir Kolossov, *Ethno-Territorial Conflicts and Boundaries in the Former Soviet Union* (Durham, England: University of Durham, International Boundaries Research Unit, 1992).

76. David Fromkin, "The Coming Millennium: World Politics in the Twenty-First Century," *World Policy Journal* (Spring, 1991), 4.

77. Alexis Heraclides, *The Self-Determination of Minorities in International Politics* (London: Frank Cass, 1991); Heraclides, "Secessionist Minorities and External Involvement," *International Organization* (Summer, 1990) 341–378; Joseph Rothchild, *Ethnopolitics* (New York: Columbia University Press, 1981).

78. Nikki R. Keddie and Farah Monian, "Militancy and Religion in Contemporary Iran," in Martin Marty and R. Scott Appleby, eds., *Fundamentalisms and the State* (Chicago: University of Chicago Press, 1993) pp. 511–528; Graham Fuller, *The Center of the Universe: The Geopolitics of Iran* (Boulder, CO: Westview, 1991); John Esposito, ed., *The Iranian Revolution: Its Global Impact* (Miami: Florida International University Press, 1990); Martin Kramer, "Hezbullah: The Calculus of Jihad," in Marty and Appleby, eds., *Fundamentalisms and the State,* op. cit.; Abdulaziz Sachedina, "Activist Shi'ism in Iran, Iraq, and Lebanon," in Marty and Appleby, eds., *Fundamentalism Observed* (Chicago: University of Chicago Press, 1991); Mark Juergensmeyer, *The New Cold War? Religious Nationalism Confronts the Secular State* (Berkeley: University of California Press, 1993).

79. Shultz and Olson, *Ethnic and Religious Conflict: Emerging Threat to U.S. Security,* op. cit., p. 32.

80. Ibid.

81. For a full discussion of the problem, see Charles W. Kegley, Jr., ed., *International Terrorism: Characteristics, Causes, Controls* (New York: St. Martin's Press, 1990); Peter C. Sederberg, *Terrorist Myths: Illusion, Rhetoric, and Reality* (Englewood Cliffs, NJ: Prentice-Hall, 1989); Shireen T. Hunter, "Terrorism: A Balance Sheet," *Washington Quarterly,* 12 (Summer 1989) 17–29; Robert Oakley, "International Terrorism," *Foreign Affairs,* 65 (Summer 1987); Walter Laqueur, "Reflections on Terrorism," *Foreign Affairs,* 65 (Fall 1986) 86–100.

82. Dean G. Pruitt and Richard C. Snyder, eds., *Theory and Research on the Causes of War* (Englewood Cliffs, NJ: Prentice-Hall, 1969), pp. 4–5.

83. Quincy Wright, *A Study of War,* Vol. I (Chicago: University of Chicago Press, 1942), p. 17. See also Vol. II, p. 739, where he asserts that war has "politico-technological, juroideological, socioreligious and psychoeconomic causes." Wright's classic was reprinted in 1983.

84. Karl W. Deutsch, "Quincy Wright's Contribution to the Study of War: A Preface to the Second Edition," *Journal of Conflict Resolution,* XIV (December 1970), 474–475.

85. Clyde Eagleton, *International Government,* rev. ed. (New York: Ronald, 1948), p. 393. See Quincy Wright on "The Political Utility of War," in *A Study of War,* Vol. II, op. cit., pp. 853–860.

86. For a thoughtful and critical analysis of the contributions behavioral scientists had made prior to 1959 toward the control of interstate violence, see Kenneth N. Waltz, *Man, the State and War* (New York: Columbia University Press, 1958), pp. 42–79. Waltz anticipated the conclusion reached here—namely, that the behaviorists must take into greater account the political framework of war–peace issues. See also L. L. Farrar, Jr., ed., *War: A Historical, Political and Social Study* (Santa Barbara, CA: ABC-Clio, 1978); Geoffrey Blainey, *The Causes of War,* 3rd ed. (New York: Free Press, 1988); and Manus I. Midlarsky, *On War: Political Violence in the International System* (New York: Free Press, 1975).

87. See Franklyn Griffiths and John C. Polanyi, eds., *The Dangers of Nuclear War* (Toronto, Canada: University of Toronto Press, 1979); Richard Ned Lebow, *Between Peace and War: The Nature of International Crisis* (Baltimore, MD: Johns Hopkins University Press, 1981); Daniel Frei, with the collaboration of Christian Catrina, *Risks of Unintentional Nuclear War,* United Nations Institute for Disarmament Research (Totowa, NJ: Allenheld, Osmun, 1983).

88. See Theodore Abel, "The Elements of Decision in the Pattern of War," *American Sociological Review,* VI (December 1941), 853–859.

89. See, for example, Thomas C. Schelling, *Arms and Influence* (New Haven, CT: Yale University Press, 1966), pp. 221–225; Graham T. Allison, Albert Carnesale, and Joseph Nye, Jr., eds., *Hawks, Doves and Owls: An Agenda for Avoiding Nuclear War* (New York: Norton, 1985), pp. 30, 43, and 210; Richard Ned Lebow, *Nuclear Crisis Management: A Dangerous Illusion* (Ithaca, NY: Cornell University Press, 1987), pp. 24–26, 32–35, 109–113.

90. Marc Trachtenberg, "The Meaning of Mobilization in 1914," *International Security,* 15 (Winter, 1990–1991), 120–150. Cf. the follow-up correspondence by Jack Levy, Thomas J. Christensen, and Marc Trachtenberg, "Mobilization and Inadvertence in the July Crisis," *International Security,* 15 (Summer 1991), 189–203.

91. Robert J. Lieber, *No Common Power: Understanding International Relations* (New York: HarperCollins, 1995). The quotation following his title page is from Chapter 13 of *Leviathan.*

92. "Motives and Perceptions Underlying Entry into War," Introduction to Part 2 in Pruitt and Snyder, eds., *Theory and Research on the Causes of War,* (Englewood Cliffs, NJ: Prentice-Hall, 1969) pp. 22–26.

93. J. David Singer, "Threat Perception and National Decision-Makers," in Pruitt and Snyder, eds., op. cit., pp. 39–42.

94. Raymond L. Garthoff, "On Estimating and Imputing Intentions," *International Security,* 2 (Winter 1978), 22–32. See Richard Pipes, "Why the Soviet Union Thinks It Could Fight and Win a Nuclear War," *Commentary,* 64 (July 1977), 21–34; Paul H. Nitze, "Deterring Our Deterrent," *Foreign Policy* (25) (Winter 1976–1977), 195–210; "Soviet Strength and Fears," Report by the Center for the Study of Democratic Institutions in *World Issues* (October–November 1977), 22–30; Bernard Brodie, "The Development of Nuclear Strategy," *International Security,* 2 (Spring 1978), 65–83; and Stanley Sienkiewicz, "SALT and Soviet Nuclear Doctrine," *International Security,* 2 (Spring 1978), 84–100.

95. Pitirim A. Sorokin, *Social and Cultural Dynamics* Vol. 3, (New York: American Book, 1937). *Fluctuation of Social Relationships, War and Revolution,* Vol. 3 (Englewood Cliffs, NJ: Bedminster Press, 1962).

96. Quincy Wright, *A Study of War* (Chicago: University of Chicago Press, 1942), 2 vols.

97. Lewis F. Richardson, *Statistics of Deadly Quarrels* (Pittsburgh, PA: Boxwood, 1960).

98. John A. Vasquez, "The Steps to War: Toward a Scientific Explanation of Correlates of War Findings," Review Article, *World Politics,* XL (October 1987), 109–110. This article has often been cited in the literature as an excellent and comprehensive account of the COW Project and the follow-on research that it stimulated.

99. The primary database for the COW Project is to be found in J. David Singer and Melvin Small, *The Wages of War, 1816–1965: A Statistical Handbook* (New York: Wiley, 1972). Their original research was updated and refined in J. David Singer, ed., *The Correlates of War.* Vol. I. *Research Origins and Rationale* (New York: Free Press, 1979); ibid., Vol. II. *Testing Some Realpolitik Models* (New York: Free Press, 1980); Melvin Small and J. David Singer, *Resort to Arms: International and Civil Wars, 1816–1980* (New York: Free Press, 1980); and Melvin Small and J. David Singer, "Patterns of International Warfare, 1816–1980," in the book they edited, *International War: An Anthology and Study Guide* (Homewood, IL: Dorsey Press, 1985), pp. 7–19.

100. Kenneth N. Waltz, *Theory of International Politics* (Reading, MA: Addison-Wesley, 1979), pp. 8–13.

101. John A. Vasquez, "The Steps to War: Toward a Scientific Explanation of Correlates of War Findings," 111.

102. Ibid., pp. 113–114.

103. Hedley Bull, *The Anarchical Society* (New York: Columbia University Press, 1977), p. 184; quoted in John A. Vasquez, *The War Puzzle* (Cambridge, England: Cambridge University Press, 1993), p. 23.

104. Vasquez, *The War Puzzle,* op. cit., p. 25.

105. J. David Singer and Melvin Small, *The Wages of War, 1816–1945,* op. cit., p. 37. This definition was used in subsequent updating studies.

106. Vasquez, *The War Puzzle,* op. cit., p. 26.

107. Wright, *A Study of War,* op. cit., p. 636.

108. Richardson, *Deadly Quarrels,* op. cit., p. 6.

109. Vasquez, *The War Puzzle,* op. cit., pp. 26–28. The list of 118 international wars is in Small and Singer, "Patterns of International Warfare, 1816–1980," op. cit., pp. 9–12.

110. Small and Singer, "Patterns," op. cit., p. 13.

111. Ibid., pp. 14, 17.

112. Jack S. Levy, "Historical Trends in Great Power War, 1495–1975," *International Studies Quarterly,* 26 (June 1982), 278–300, quoted at p. 279.

113. Ibid., 283–286.

114. Ibid., 278–279, 286, 290–291. These correlations were reaffirmed in Jack S. Levy and T. Clifton Morgan, "The Frequency and Seriousness of War: An Inverse Relationship?" *Journal of Conflict Resolution,* 28 (December 1984), 731–749.

115. Frederick L. Schuman, *International Politics,* 5th ed. (New York: McGraw-Hill, 1953), p. 230.

116. Hans J. Morgenthau, *Politics Among Nations: The Struggle for Power and Peace,* 4th ed. (New York: Knopf, 1967), p. 392.

117. Michael Howard, *The Causes of Wars* (Cambridge, MA: Harvard University Press, 1983), chap. 3, "The Strategic Approach to International Relations."

118. Michael D. Wallace, "Arms Races and Escalation: Some New Evidence," *Journal of Conflict Resolution,* 23 (March 1977), 316; and "Armaments and Escalation," *International Studies Quarterly,* 26 (March 1982), 37–56.

119. In 1957, Anatol Rapoport wrote a special monograph issue of *The Journal of Conflict Resolution,* devoted exclusively to the work of Richardson. Richardson was first noted for his scientific work in the field of meteorology, for which he was selected as a fellow in the British Royal Society in 1926. His experience in meteorology influenced his method of research on arms races and war. Recognizing the difficulty of predicting even the next day's weather by using as many as 60,000 computers of that era, he was nevertheless convinced that events that seem to be governed by chance (such as weather) are subject to natural laws and therefore predictable, provided that sufficient data can be processed. See Anatol Rapoport, "Lewis Fry Richardson," *International Encyclopedia of the Social Sciences,* (New York: Free Press, 1968), Vol. 13, p. 514.

120. Lewis F. Richardson's principal work on the mathematics of arms races is *Arms and Insecurity: A Mathematical Study of the Causes and Origins of War* (Pittsburgh, PA: Boxwood Press, 1960). In another work, *Statistics of Deadly Quarrels* (Chicago: Quadrangle, 1960), he classified deadly quarrels between states on the basis of the number of persons killed, and he examined the frequency of war between dyads of states, the length of wars and peace intervals, the pattern of war repetitions, the probability that allies and enemies group themselves similarly in subsequent wars, and the correlation between the incidence of wars and such factors as geographical proximity, population, religion, and language.

121. Lewis F. Richardson, *Arms and Insecurity,* op. cit., pp. 13–15.

122. Dina A. Zinnes, *Contemporary Research in International Relations* (New York: Free Press, 1976), p. 332. She adds that "while it is probably fair to say that an underlying assumption of the arms race models is that they provide a possible explanation for processes that appear to result in some wars, it must be admitted that Richardson does not formally link defense expenditure and the outbreak of war in any of the arms race models which he constructs"; ibid., p. 332. This is an extremely important point to keep in mind, inasmuch as so many writers who have not studied Richardson as carefully as Zinnes has, or perhaps have not even read him, have often cited his research as demonstrating scientifically and conclusively that arms races lead to wars. The student trained in mathematics will find a complete exposition and analysis of Richardson's basic model in Zinnes, op. cit., pp. 333–369. Michael D. Intriligator and Dagobert L. Brito admit that Richardson-type models can be criticized as mechanistic because they treat arms races from outside instead of inside the minds of decision makers, and thus they ignore strategic considerations; "Richardson Arms Race Models" in Manus I. Midlarsky, ed., *Handbook of War Studies* (Boston: Unwin Hyman, 1989), p. 226.

123. See Dina A. Zinnes, op. cit., pp. 339–354; Kenneth Boulding, *Conflict and Defense* (New York: Harper & Row, 1962), pp. 19–40; and Robert C. North, Richard A. Brodie, and Ole R. Holsti, "Some Empirical Data on the Conflict Spiral," *International Peace Research Society Papers,* 1 (1964), 1–14.

124. Dina A. Zinnes, op. cit., p. 369.

125. Dina A. Zinnes devotes chap. 15 to the work of Quincy Wright, Kenneth Boulding, Dean Pruitt, and several others; ibid. For the description of an effort to apply the Richardson model to arms negotiations, see P. Terrence Hopmann and Theresa C. Smith, "An Application of a Richardson Process Model: Soviet–American Interactions in the Test Ban Negotiations, 1962–1963," *Journal of Conflict Resolution,* XXI (December 1977), 701–726.

126. Martin Patchen, "Models of Cooperation and Conflict: A Critical Review," *Journal of Conflict Resolution,* XIV (September 1970), 389–408.

127. John V. Gillespie, Dina A. Zinnes, and others have noted that Richardson's model contains no decision calculus. "The equations are merely a description of what people would do if they did not stop to think"; "An Optimal Control Model of Arms Race," *American Political Science Review,* LXXI (March 1977), 226–244, quoted at p. 226. Later, Dina Zinnes and Robert G. Muncaster concluded from a model of hostility dynamics that it is possible to predict the time when war will occur and the level of hostility necessary to provoke its onset; "The Dynamics of Hostile Activity and the Prediction of War," *Journal of Conflict Resolution,* 28 (June 1984), 187–229. See also J. David Singer, "Confrontational Behavior and Escalation to War, 1816–1980: A Research Plan," *Journal of Peace Research,* 19(1) (1982).

128. David W. Zeigler, citing Samuel P. Huntington, writes, "In the 1860s the British replaced their wooden ships with ironclad ships in response to French innovation, yet they spent less on their navy in these years than they had in preceding ones." *War, Peace and International Politics,* 4th ed. (Boston: Little, Brown, 1987), p. 206.

129. Michael D. Wallace, "Arms Races and Escalation," *Journal of Conflict Resolution,* 23 (March 1979), 3–16.

130. Ibid., 5, 13.

131. Paul F. Diehl, "Arms Races and Escalation: A Closer Look," *International Studies Quarterly,* 20 (June 1983), 205–212.

132. T. C. Smith, "Arms Race Instability and War," *Journal of Conflict Resolution,* 24 (June 1980), 253–284. Cited in Randolph M. Siverson and Paul F. Diehl, "Arms Races, the Conflict Spiral, and the Onset of War," in Manus I. Midlarsky, ed., *Handbook of War Studies* (Boston: Unwin Hyman, 1989), p. 198.

133. Michael D. Wallace, "Arms Races and Escalation," op. cit., 5.

134. Ibid., 14–15.

135. Siverson and Diehl, op. cit., in Note 132, p. 198.

136. Paul F. Diehl and J. Kingston, "Messenger or Message? Military Buildups and the Initiation of Conflict," *Journal of Politics,* 49 (December 1987), 789–799. Cited by Siverson and Diehl, op. cit., p. 207. Erich Weede identified three periods of substantial length (1852–1871, 1919–1938, and from 1945 onward) when the escalation of disputes was nil, regardless of high or low arms-race indices. "Arms Races and Escalation," International Studies Quarterly, 27 (June 1980), 233–235.

137. Siverson and Diehl, op. cit., pp. 207–211, cite Michael Altfeld, "Arms Races?—and Escalation?" *International Studies Quarterly,* 27 (June 1983), 225–231; Michael Altfeld and Bruce Bueno de Mesquita, "Choosing Sides in Wars," *International Studies Quarterly,* 23 (March 1979); Paul F. Diehl (see Note 131); Randolph M. Siverson and Joel King, "Alliances and the Expansion of War, 1815–1965," in J. David Singer and Michael Wallace, eds., *To Auger Well* (Beverly Hills, CA: Sage, 1979), pp. 37–49.

138. Siverson and Diehl, op. cit., p. 212.

139. J. David Singer and Melvin Small, "Alliance Aggregation and the Onset of War, 1815–1945," in J. David Singer, ed., *Quantitative International Politics* (New York: Free Press, 1968), pp. 247–286. Reprinted in J. David Singer, ed., *The Correlates of War: I. Research Origins and Rationale* (New York: Free Press, 1979), pp. 225–264.

140. John A. Vasquez, *The War Puzzle,* op. cit., pp. 170–171.

141. Jack S. Levy, "Alliance Formation and War Behavior: An Analysis of the Great Powers, 1495–1975," *Journal of Conflict Resolution,* 25 (December 1981), 581–613.

142. Charles W. Ostrom, Jr., and Francis W. Hoole, "Alliances and War Revisited: A Research Note," *International Studies Quarterly,* 22 (June 1978), 215–236.

143. John A. Vasquez, p. 120, citing Jack S. Levy, "Alliance Formation and War Behavior," op. cit., p. 599. According to Levy's table, ibid., 18, 14, 35, and 25 percent of wars in the sixteenth, seventeenth, eighteenth, and nineteenth centuries, respectively, were preceded by alliances, compared with 60 percent in the twentieth century.

144. Vasquez, "The Steps to War," op. cit., pp. 120–121.

145. Siverson and King, "Alliances and Expansion of War," (see Note 37), cited in Vasquez, "The Steps to War," op. cit., 121–122.

146. Benjamin A. Most, Harvey Starr, and Randolph M. Siverson, "The Logic and Study of the Diffusion of International Conflict," in Manus I. Midlarsky, ed., *Handbook of War Studies* (cf. Note 132), pp. 111–139, especially pp. 133–134.

147. Vasquez, "The Steps to War," op. cit., 123.

148. Vasquez, *The War Puzzle,* op. cit., pp. 172–173. He cites Wallace, "Polarization: Towards a Scientific Conception," in Alan Ned Sabrosky, ed., *Polarity and War* (Boulder, CO: Westview Press, 1985), pp. 110–111; and Nazli Coucri and Robert C. North, *Nations in Conflict* (San Francisco, CA: W. H. Freeman, 1975), pp. 106–111, 117.

149. Vasquez, "The Steps of War," op. cit., 123–125, where he summarizes Wallace, "Alliance Polarization, Cross-Cutting, and International War, 1815–1964," *Journal of Conflict Resolution,* 17 (December 1973), 575–604. Charles W. Kegley, Jr., and Gregory A. Raymond found in this same article of Wallace's a possible compromise between Waltz on bipolarity and Deutsch and Singer on multipolarity in their debate over which is more stable; "Alliance Norms and War," *International Studies Quarterly,* 26 (December 1982), 572–595.

150. Vasquez, "The Steps of War," op. cit., 125–128. He cites Bruce Bueno de Mesquita, "Systemic Polarization and the Occurrence and Duration of War," *Journal of Conflict Resolution,* 22 (June 1978), 241–267; and Alan Ned Sabrosky, "Alliance Aggregation, Capability Distribution, and the Expansion of Interstate War," in Sabrosky, ed. (cf. Note 148), pp. 148, 151, 181. Vasquez reaffirms and develops his views on polarization in *The War Puzzle,* pp. 251–258, 261–262.

151. Vasquez, *The War Puzzle,* op. cit., p. 173.

152. Ibid., p. 154.

153. Nazli Choucri and Robert C. North, *Nations in Conflict: National Growth and International Violence* (San Francisco: W. H. Freeman, 1975).

154. Ibid., p. 2.

155. Ibid., p. 278.

156. See ibid., pp. 15–17, and their later work, "Lateral Pressure in International Relations: Concept and Theory," in Manus I. Midlarsky, ed., *Handbook of War Studies* (Boston: Unwin Hyman, 1989), pp. 289–326, especially p. 295.

157. Choucri and North, *Nations in Conflict,* op. cit., pp. 17–22.

158. Ibid. The authors also found that increases in the military budget of one country might be due to a rival expansion in a nonmilitary area; see chap. 13, "Military Expenditures," ibid.

159. Ibid., p. 284.

160. Ibid., pp. 285–286. The authors point out that actions taken in one part of a system, to relieve distress, may produce unexpected consequences in another part, and that policies aiming at desirable short-term outcomes may often involve a high long-term price.

161. Robert C. North and Nazli Choucri, "Economic and Political Factors in International Conflict and Integration," *International Studies Quarterly,* 27 (December 1983), 451–453, 459.

162. Richard K. Ashley, *The Political Economy of War and Peace* (London: Francis Pinter; New York: Nichols, 1980).

163. Choucri and North, "Lateral Pressure in International Relations," (see Note 156), p. 296.

164. Ibid., pp. 296–297.

165. Benjamin A. Most and Harvey Starr, "Conceptualizing War: Consequences for Theory and Research," *Journal of Conflict Resolution,* 27 (March 1983), 154–157.

166. A. F. K. Organski, *World Politics* (New York: Knopf, 1958), chap. 12; (2nd ed., 1968), chap. 14.

167. See G. S. Barghava, *India's Security in the 1980s* (London: International Institute of Strategic Studies; Adelphi Paper No. 125, Summer 1976), pp. 5–6. Erich Weede has found that overwhelming or ten-to-one preponderance is favorable to the prevention of war. "Overwhelming Preponderance as a Pacifying Condition Among Contiguous Asian Dyads, 1950–1969," *Journal of Conflict Resolution,* XX (September 1976), 395–411.

168. A. F. K. Organski, op. cit., 1958, pp. 319–320; 1968, pp. 357–359. The hypothesis that lethal international violence between pairs of contiguous states is more probable if the two states are equally powerful was substantiated in an empirical study of a brief five-year period. See David Garnham, "Power Parity and Lethal International Violence, 1969–1973," *Journal of Conflict Resolution,* XX (September 1976), 379–391.

169. Inis L. Claude, *Power and International Relations* (New York: Random House, 1962), p. 56.

170. Michael P. Sullivan, *International Relations: Theories and Evidence* (Englewood Cliffs, NJ: Prentice-Hall, 1976), pp. 166–167.

171. John W. Burton has argued that Japan resorted to a policy of force in the 1930s because other powers were not prepared to make the adjustments necessary to allow Japan to develop through access to international markets; *Peace Theory: Preconditions of Disarmament* (New York: Knopf, 1962), p. 9.

172. A. F. K. Organski and Jacek Kugler, *The War Ledger* (Chicago: University of Chicago Press, 1980), p. 61.

173. Jacek Kugler and A. F. K. Organski, "The Power Transition: A Retrospective and Prospective Evaluation," in Manus I. Midlarsky, ed., *Handbook of War Studies* (see Note 156), pp. 171–194, especially pp. 172–174.

174. Ibid., p. 175.

175. Bruce Bueno de Mesquita, "Risk, Power Distributions, and the Likelihood of War," *International Studies Quarterly,* 25 (December 1981). The author's major book-length work is *The War Trap* (New Haven, CT: Yale University Press, 1980). The article cited and other articles written since 1980 contain refinements of his major work. See also his "Systemic Polarization and the Occurrence and Duration of War," *Journal of Conflict Resolution,* 22 (June 1978), 241–267; "The Costs of War: A Rational Expectations Approach," *American Political Science Review,* 77 (June 1983), 347–357; and "The War Trap Revisited: A Revised Expected Utility Model," *American Political Science Review,* 79 (March 1985), 157–177. With additional refinements, he says, "the

revised version . . . is a powerful tool for integrating many extant hypotheses about conflict" and he expresses confidence that his approach may yield "significant, lawlike generalizations about the initiation, escalation and termination of international conflict." Ibid., pp. 156, 172.

176. Ibid.

177. Ibid. Cf. Dina A. Zinnes et al., "Capability, Threat and the Outbreak of War," in James A. Rosenau, ed., *International Politics and Foreign Policy: A Reader in Research and Theory* (New York: Free Press, 1961).

178. See the discussion on Waltz and Deutsch/Singer in Chapter 4; see also J. David Singer et al., "Capability Distribution, Uncertainty and Major Power War, 1820–1965," in Bruce Russett, ed., *Peace, War and Numbers* (Beverly Hills, CA: Sage Publications, 1972).

179. Singer et al., ibid., p. 541.

180. Ibid., p. 567.

181. Ibid., p. 564. For a fuller elaboration of Singer's views on the risk orientation of leaders, see Bueno de Mesquita's *The War Trap*, op. cit., and Bueno de Mesquita's *Strategy, Risk, and Personality in Coalition Politics* (Cambridge, England: Cambridge University Press, 1976). In a penetrating and moderately critical review of Bueno de Mesquita's *The War Trap*, R. Harrison Wagner observed that the author provides only limited evidence concerning the tendency of leaders to maximize expected utility, and no evidence, one way or the other, on the question of how theories of individual rational choice can explain the foreign-policy decisions of states; "War and Expected Utility Theory," *World Politics,* XXXVI (April 1984), 423.

182. Bruce Bueno de Mesquita and David Lalman, "Reason and War," *American Political Science Review,* 80 (December 1986), 11–19. Their analysis was an outgrowth of ideas in Bruce Bueno de Mesquita, "The Costs of War: A Rational Expectations Approach" and "The War Trap Revisited" (see Note 175).

183. Bruce Bueno de Mesquita, "The Contribution of Expected-Utility Theory to the Study of International Conflict," in Manus I. Midlarsky, ed., *Handbook of War Studies* (see Note 132), p. 148.

184. Bueno de Mesquita, *The War Trap,* op. cit., p. 162.

185. Bueno de Mesquita, "The Contribution of Expected Utility Theory," op. cit., p. 147.

186. Ibid. John G. Stoessinger contrasted the nineteenth century, when initiators of war usually won, with the twentieth, when they did not; *When Nations Go to War* (New York: St. Martin's Press, 1974), p. 219.

187. John A. Vasquez, "Capability, Types of War, Peace," *Western Political Quarterly,* 39 (June 1986), p. 313.

188. Ibid., p. 322.

189. Ibid., p. 315.

190. Ibid., p. 324.

191. J. David Singer, "System Structure, Decision Processes, and the Incidence of International War," in Manus I. Midlarsky, ed., *Handbook of War Studies,* pp. 17–18.

192. Urs Luterbacher, "Last Words About War?" *Journal of Conflict Resolution,* 28 (March 1984), 167–168. For other works on war correlations, see Jack S. Levy, "Misperceptions and the Causes of War," *World Politics,* XXXVI (October 1983) 76–99, and "Theories of General War," *World Politics,* XXXVI (April 1985) 344–374; Randolph M. Siverson and Michael P. Sullivan, "The Distribution of Power and the Onset of War," *Journal of Conflict Resolution,* 27 (September 1983) 473–494; Randolph M. Siverson and Michael R. Tennefoss, "Power, Alliance and the Escalation of International Conflict, 1815–1965," *American Political Science Review,* 78 (December 1984) 1057–1069; George Modelski and Patrick Morgan, "Understanding Global War," *Journal of Con-*

flict Resolution, 29 (September 1985) 391–417; Paul A. Anderson and Timothy J. McKeown, "Changing Aspirations, Limited Attention, and War," *World Politics,* XL, (1) (October 1987) 1–29.

193. Pitirim A. Sorokin, *Fluctuation of Social Relationships, War and Revolution* (New York: American Book Company, 1937), Vol. 3 in his three-volume series, *Social and Cultural Dynamics,* p. 283.

194. Lewis F. Richardson, *Statistics of Deadly Quarrels* (Pittsburgh, PA: Boxwood, 1960), chap. 2.

195. J. David Singer and Melvin Small, "Alliance Aggregation and the Onset of War, 1815–1945," in J. David Singer, ed., *Quantitative International Politics* (New York: Free Press, 1968), pp. 247–286.

196. Quincy Wright, *A Study of War,* 2 vols. (Chicago: University of Chicago Press, 1942), Vol. 1, p. 651.

197. Toynbee covers the period from 1494 down to 1945. *A Study of History,* 12 vols., Vol. 9 (London: Oxford University Press, 1954), pp. 250–255.

198. Geoffrey Blainey, *The Causes of War* (New York: Free Press, 1973; 3rd ed., 1988), p. 8.

199. Bouthoul's view is cited with approval by Jacques Ellul in his *The Technological Society* (New York: Random House-Viking Books, 1964), p. 137.

200. Blainey, *The Causes of War,* op. cit., pp. 91–96.

201. William R. Thompson, "Phases of the Business Cycle and the Outbreak of War," *International Studies Quarterly,* 26 (June 1982) 301–311. See also his "Uneven Economic Growth, Systemic Challenges, and Global Wars," *International Studies Quarterly,* 27 (September 1983) 341–355, and Raimo Vayrynen, "Economic Cycles, Power Transitions, Power Management and Wars Between Major Powers," *International Studies Quarterly,* December 1983 389–418. Small and Singer tentatively mentioned the possibility of a 15-to-20-year cycle, but they fixed the cycle at irregular intervals between 20 and 40 years.

202. Melvin Small and J. David Singer, "Patterns in International Warfare," *The Annals* (Collective Violence), No. 391 (September 1970), 147–148. The authors cite Frank H. Denton and Warren Phillips, who derived from the data of Wright, Sorokin, and Richardson a cycle of wars every 30 years since 1680. "Some Patterns in the History of Violence," *Journal of Conflict Resolution,* XII (June 1968), 182–195.

203. George Modelski and William R. Thompson, "Long Cycles and Global War," in Manus I. Midlarsky, ed., *Handbook of War Studies* (Boston: Unwin Hyman, 1989), pp. 23–54, quoted at p. 36. See also George Modelski and Patrick Morgan, "Understanding Global War," *Journal of Conflict Resolution,* 29 (December 1985), 473–502; George Modelski, *Long Cycles in World Politics* (Seattle, WA: University Press, 1987); William R. Thompson, "Polarity, the Long Cycle, and Global Power Warfare," *Journal of Conflict Resolution,* 30 (December 1986), 587–615; and *On Global War: Historical–Structural Approaches to World Politics* (Columbia, SC: University of South Carolina Press, 1988).

204. Modelski and Thompson, "Long Cycles and Global War," op. cit., p. 24.

205. Ibid., table on p. 25.

206. Ibid., pp. 28–29.

207. Ibid., pp. 30–31. Here the authors rely on Robert Gilpin's *War and Change in World Politics* (New York: Cambridge University Press, 1981). See the discussion on this topic in "The International System: Cyclical Theories and Historical-Structural Theories of War," chap. 9 in Greg Cashman, *What Causes War? An Introduction to Theo-*

ries of International Conflict (New York: Lexington Books, 1993), especially pp. 254–257.

208. Immanuel Wallerstein, *The Politics of the World Economy* (Cambridge, England: Cambridge University Press, 1984), pp. 37–46. Cited in Modelski and Thompson, op. cit., pp. 31–32.

209. Modelski and Thompson, op. cit., pp. 34–42.

210. Charles F. Doran, "Power Cycle Theory of Systems Structure and Stability: Commonalities and Complementarities," in Manus I. Midlarsky, ed., *Handbook of War Studies,* op. cit., pp. 82–110, cited at pp. 85–87. "International relations are . . . the resultant of foreign policy influences operating both on the 'horizontal chessboard' of short-term strategic calculation and balance and on the 'vertical plane' of long-term upward and downward movement along the state cycles of differential change in power and role." Ibid., p. 83.

211. Ibid., p. 88. See also Doran's "War and Power Dynamics: Economic Underpinnings," *International Studies Quarterly,* 27 (December 1983), 419–441; "Systemic Disequilibrium, Foreign Policy Role, and the Power Cycle: Challenges for Research Design," *Journal of Conflict Resolution,* 33 (September 1989), 371–401.

212. Doran, "Power Cycle Theory . . . " in Midlarsky, ed., op. cit., p. 103.

213. Ibid., p. 90.

214. Ibid., p. 91.

215. Doran, "War and Power Dynamics: Economic Underpinnings," op. cit., 431–438.

216. George Modelski, "Long Cycles, Kondratieffs and Alternating Innovations: Implications for U.S. Foreign Policy," in Charles W. Kegley, Jr., and Patrick McGowan, *The Political Economy of Foreign Policy Behavior* (Beverly Hills, CA: Sage, 1981). For the economic theory, see Nikolai D. Kondratieff, "Long Waves in Economic Life," originally published in 1926, *Review of Economic Statistics,* 17 (November 1935), 195–215; *The Long Wave Cycle,* from the Russian version of 1928 (New York: Richardson and Snyder, 1984); Joshua S. Goldstein, "Kondratieff Waves as War Cycles," *International Studies Quarterly,* 29 (December 1985) 411–444.

217. See Modelski and Thompson, "Long Cycles and Global War," op. cit., 27.

218. Edward Mansfield, "The Distribution of Wars over Time," *World Politics,* 41(1) (October 1988), 44.

219. Jack Levy, *War in the Modern Great Power System, 1945–1975* (Lexington, KY: University of Kentucky Press, 1983).

220. Mansfield, op. cit., 44.

221. Ibid., 45.

222. Terry Boswell and Mike Sweat, "Hegemony, Long Waves and Major Wars: A Time Series Analysis of Systemic Dynamics, 1496–1967," *International Studies Quarterly,* 35 (June 1991), 123–149, quoted at 144.

223. Ibid., 145.

224. Joshua S. Goldstein, "The Possibility of Cycles in International Relations," *International Studies Quarterly,* 35 (December 1991), 477–480. Both quotations at 477.

225. Joshua S. Goldstein, *Long Cycles* (New Haven, CT: Yale University Press, 1988), p. 176.

226. Goldstein, "The Possibility of Cycles . . . ," op. cit., 478; and *Long Cycles,* op. cit., p. 177.

227. Lois W. Sayrs, "The Long Cycle in International Relations: A Markov Specification," *International Studies Quarterly,* 37 (June 1993), 215–237, especially 216–218.

228. George Modelski, "Long Cycles, Kondratieffs and Alternating Innovations," in Charles W. Kegley, Jr., and Patrick McGowan, eds., *The Political Economy of Foreign Policy Behavior* (Beverly Hills, CA: Sage, 1981).

229. Nathaniel Beck, "The Illusion of Cycles in International Relations," *International Studies Quarterly,* 35 (December 1993), 455–476, quoted at p. 456.

230. Ibid.

231. Michael W. Doyle, "Liberalism and World Politics Revisited," in Charles W. Kegley, Jr., ed., *Controversies in International Relations Theory: Realism and the Neoliberal Challenge* (New York: St. Martin's, 1995), p. 102. This draws on Doyle's earlier important article, "Liberalism and World Politics," *American Political Science Review,* 80 (December 1986), 1151–1169, which is cited by virtually all who have written subsequently on the subject. See also Wade L. Huntley, "Kant's Third Image: Systemic Sources of the Liberal Peace," *International Studies Quarterly,* 40 (1) (March 1996), 45–76. For another perspective, see John R. Oneal, Frances H. Oneal, Zeev Moaz, and Bruce Russett, "The Liberal Peace: Interdependence, Democracy, and International Conflict, 1950–1985," *Journal of Peace Research,* 33 (1) (1996), 11–28. See also Henry S. Farber and Joanne Gowa, "Polities and Peace," *International Security,* 20 (2) (Fall 1995), 123–146; and Ido Oren, "The Subjectivity of the 'Democrative' Peace: Changing U.S. Perceptions of Imperial Germany," *International Security,* 20 (2) (Fall 1995), 147–184.

232. Doyle, in Kegley, ed., op. cit., p. 95. The quotations are taken from *Kant's Political Writings,* ed. by Hans Reiss and trans. by H. B. Nisbet (Cambridge, England: Cambridge University Press, 1970), pp. 105, 104.

233. Kenneth N. Waltz, *Man, the State and War* (New York: Columbia University Press, 1959), pp. 83–114.

234. Melvin Small and J. David Singer, "The War-Proneness of Democratic Regimes," *Jerusalem Journal of International Relations,* 1 (Summer 1976), 50–69.

235. Paul Diehl, "Arms Races and Escalation: A Closer Look," *Journal of Peace Research,* 20(3) (September 1983), 205–112, and "Armaments Without War: An Analysis of Some Underlying Effects," *Journal of Peace Research,* 22(3) (September 1985), 249–259.

236. Carol R. Ember, Melvin Ember, and Bruce Russett, "Peace Between Participatory Polities: A Cross-Cultural Test of the 'Democracies Rarely Fight Each Other' Hypothesis," *World Politics,* 44 (July 1992), 574–575.

237. Jack S. Levy, "Domestic Politics and War," in Robert J. Rotberg and Theodore K. Rabb, eds., *The Origin and Prevention of Major Wars* (Cambridge, England: Cambridge University Press, 1989), p. 88.

238. Michael W. Doyle, "Liberalism and World Politics Revisited," op. cit., pp. 89–92.

239. Nicholas G. Onuf and Thomas J. Johnson, "Peace in the Liberal World: Does Democracy Matter?" in Charles W. Kegley, Jr., ed., *Controversies in International Relations Theory: Realism and the Neoliberal Challenge* (New York: St. Martin's Press, 1995), pp. 192–193. For another perspective, see John R. Oneal, Frances H. Oneal, Zeev Maoz, and Bruce Russett, "The Liberal Peace: Interdependence, Democracy and International Conflict, 1950–1985," *Journal of Peace Research,* 33 (1) (1996), 11–28.

240. Rudolph Rummel, "Libertarianism and International Violence," *Journal of Conflict Resolution,* 27 (March 1983), 27–71.

241. S. Chan, "Mirror, Mirror on the Wall . . . Are the Democratic States More Pacific?" *Journal of Conflict Resolution,* 28 (December 1984), 617–648; and Eric Weede, "Democracy and War Involvement," *Journal of Conflict Resolution,* 28 (December 1984), 649–694.

242. Rudolph Rummel, "Libertarian Propositions on Violence Between and Within Nations," *Journal of Conflict Resolution* 29 (September 1985), 419–455. Zeev Maoz and Nasrin Abdolali, in an extensive replication of earlier studies, reached the "robust conclusion" that there is no link between regime type and war at the national level of analysis, but that "dyadic analyses generally provide clear support" for the hypothesis that joint political and economic freedom is inversely related to conflict involvement; "Regime Types and International Conflict, 1816–1976," *Journal of Conflict Resolution,* 33 (March 1989), 30.

243. Immanuel Kant, *Perpetual Peace,* quoted by Michael W. Doyle, op. cit., p. 99, from Reiss, ed., p. 114.

244. Michael W. Doyle, op. cit., p. 99.

245. Carol R. Ember, Melvin Ember, and Bruce Russett, op. cit., 575–577. Like most analysts, they see consistent evidence that, in dyadic relationships with nondemocratic dictatorships, democracies can be swept along by war fever.

246. Bruce Bueno de Mesquita and David Lalman, "Domestic Opposition and Foreign War," *American Political Science Review,* 84 (September 1990), 747.

247. T. Clifton Morgan and Sally Howard Campbell, "Domestic Structure, Decisional Constraints, and War: So Why Kant Democracies Fight?" *Journal of Conflict Resolution,* 35 (June 1991), 189.

248. Ibid., 190–195.

249. Ibid., 206.

250. Ibid., 208.

251. Ibid., 210.

252. Christopher Layne, "Kant or Cant: The Myth of the Democratic Peace," *International Security,* 19 (Fall 1994), 5–49.

253. Ibid., 38.

254. Ibid., 38–39. Layne complains that the democratic peace theorists treat all dyads equally, whereas "a dyad is significant only if it represents a case where there is a real possibility of two states going to war"—that is, having the opportunity and capability and reason to do so (p. 39). He also criticizes them for excluding Wilhelmine Germany, which he says was autocratic in domestic politics (as Doyle admits) but no less democratic than Britain and France with respect to the aristocratic nature of its foreign policymaking process (which was in all three countries insulated from parliamentary control and criticism) (pp. 41–44).

255. David E. Spiro, "The Insignificance of the Liberal Peace," *International Security,* 19 (Fall 1994), 51.

256. Ibid., 53.

257. Ibid., 56.

258. Ibid., 55–56.

259. Ibid., 56.

260. Ibid., 58. On the difficulties of defining *democracy* and measuring the degree to which the newer democracies meet the criteria, see Doh Chull Shin, "On the Third Wave of Democratization," *World Politics,* 47 (October 1994), 135–170.

261. David A. Lake, "Powerful Pacifists: Democratic States and War," *American Political Science Review,* 86 (March 1992), 24.

262. Ibid., 28–30.

263. Ibid., 30.

264. Ibid., 31. The statistical evidence, including reasons for including or excluding certain wars, is discussed over pp. 31–33.

265. Zeev Maoz and Bruce Russett, "Normative and Structural Causes of Democratic Peace, 1946–1986," *American Political Science Review,* 87 (September 1993), 624–638, quoted on p. 624. On this point, they cite previous work by Levy, Ray, and Russett. Throughout the article, they make points previously made by Maoz, Chan, Abdolali, Doyle, Lake, Rummel, and others cited previously.

266. Ibid., 625–627.

267. Ibid., 636.

268. Ibid., 636–637.

269. Edward Mansfield and Jack Snyder, "Democratization and War," *International Security,* 20 (Summer 1995), 5–38, especially p. 12.

270. Some of those who are skeptical of the "democracies-don't-fight" hypothesis fear that it will buttress the Wilsonian belief that "making the world safe for democracy" ought to be a central focus of post–Cold War U.S. foreign policy, justifying intervention abroad to expand the zone of democratic peace from Haiti to East Central Europe to the former states of the Soviet Union. See Layne, "Kant or Cant: The Myth of Democratic Peace," op. cit., 46–49. See also Scott Gates, Torbjörn L. Knutsen, and Jonathon W. Moses, "Democracy and Peace: A More Skeptical View," *Journal of Peace Research,* 33 (1) (1996), 1–10.

Chapter
9

Theories of Deterrence

No single concept dominated international strategic theory during the four decades of the Cold War so much as that of nuclear deterrence. Since the mid-1980s, there has been much discussion about conventional deterrence, a subject of growing importance in the aftermath of the Cold War and in an era marked by reductions in the size of the largest nuclear arsenals. It should be noted, however, that the term *deterrence* is a product of the nuclear age. It did not appear in the literature of international relations or strategic theory prior to World War II. Previously (since the latter part of the nineteenth century), it had been common for legal theorists, following the Utilitarian philosopher Jeremy Bentham, to justify punishment as a means of deterring people from criminal behavior. Since the development of nuclear weapons, wrote Bernard Brodie, "the term has acquired not only special emphasis but also a distinctive connotation."[1] Robert Jervis called deterrence theory "probably the most influential school of thought in the American study of international relations," perhaps because most American scholars accepted realism and found the theory congenial.[2]

The nuclear-weapons component is not essential to the definition. Alexander L. George and Richard Smoke wrote, "In its most general form, deterrence is simply the persuasion of one's opponent that the costs and/or risks of a given course of action he might take outweigh its benefits."[3] Glenn Snyder defined it as a combination of stick and carrot: "One deters another party from doing something by the implicit or explicit threat of applying some sanction if the forbidden act is performed, or by the promise of a reward if the act is not performed."[4] The bulk of the literature on deterrence, with only a few exceptions, which are noted later, has focused on the threat of punishment, while the prospect of reward has often been ignored. Nonetheless, when understood in either sense, the idea of deterrence is a very old one. One can find examples of the idea in the writings of Thucydides and Machiavelli, even though they never used the term. The balance-of-power system that prevailed in Europe for a century after the Napoleonic Wars was essentially a technique for the management of power in which state leaders usually sought to make war unprofitable. Deterrence was implicit in such signaling or warning communications as the dispatch of naval forces, the exchange of military observers, or the conclusion of alliances, but it came to mean more in the nuclear age, when it took on the character of an explicit threat of heavily damaging retaliation.[5]

As we show subsequently, those who use statistical or comparative case-study methods to test hypotheses about deterrence success and failure must rely on the history of conventional deterrence cases. Nevertheless, because the great debate for decades turned on the issue of nuclear deterrence, and because it was that strategic policy that gave rise to the more recent studies of deterrence success and failure, it is important to understand how that idea came to loom so large after World War II—at first in the policy sciences and then in the early stages of theoretical development.

HISTORICAL BACKGROUND

The generally acknowledged pioneer theorist of strategic deterrence was Bernard Brodie, a former Yale professor who became an analyst at the RAND Corporation. Brodie pondered the new international reality within months of the Hiroshima and Nagasaki bombings. He wrote, "Thus far the chief purpose of our military establishment has been to win wars. From now on its chief purpose must be to avert them. It can have almost no other useful purpose."[6] Brodie overstated his case in that last sentence quoted, but subsequent history substantiated the main point he was trying to make at the dawn of the nuclear age—at least so far as strategic, all-out war was concerned. He considered the atomic bomb, as it was then called, the "absolute weapon," and any war waged with such weapons the greatest of catastrophes, one to be avoided at almost any cost. Deterrence was to be accomplished by convincing potential aggressors (assuming their decision-making rationality) that the gains to be achieved by deliberately resorting to nuclear war on a sizable scale could never outweigh the costs of embarking on such a course. At that time, of course, the United States possessed an atomic monopoly, but atomic scientists had no doubt that the Soviet Union would test a similar weapon within about five years. (It did so in 1949.) It is important to emphasize at the outset that the concept of nuclear deterrence rests on the assumption that modern government policymakers, before opting for war, normally perform the kind of cost-to-gains ratio analysis of which economic theorists have long been fond, and which underlies Bruce Bueno de Mesquita's expected-utility theory, discussed in Chapters 8 and 11.

The theory of deterrence did not emerge suddenly; rather, it evolved gradually and was developed in stages (or what Jervis calls "waves").[7] During the period when the United States enjoyed a monopoly on atomic weapons (1945–1949), there was no systematic strategic theory of deterrence. It was preceded by the policy of *containment,* based on a concept recommended by George F. Kennan.[8] The policy of containment as a response to the threat of Soviet expansion did not involve any specific military doctrine for supporting the policy. In fact, Kennan neither emphasized nor ruled out military means of containment, but he assumed that they were part of the panoply of diplomatic instruments, along with political and economic leverages available.[9] True, the idea was gradually taking shape in many quarters that the very existence of atomic weapons had radically altered the character of warfare and would—everyone hoped—preclude henceforth the waging of all-out war. The Soviets, however, did not yet possess such weapons. Among American military planners in the Truman years, it was taken for granted that if general war should break out between the United States and the Soviet Union, the former would achieve victory, as in World War II, by relying on its long-range bomber force, the principal difference being that the planes would carry the new absolute weapons rather than conventional bombs.[10] Still recuperating from heavy losses in World War II, the Soviet Union hardly appeared ready to become embroiled in all-out war with the world's only nuclear power, the United States.

It was under the impact of certain developments and perceptions in the early 1950s that Western analysts began to sharpen and refine their theories of nuclear deterrence. These developments and perceptions included the Korean War; the growing awareness that two powers would soon possess substantial arsenals of nuclear weapons (both atomic and thermonuclear); and an apprehension that the Western countries, having carried out rapid military demobilization after World War II, were inferior to the Communist bloc in conventional forces and probably would find it politically and economically difficult to match the Communist states at that level for a global application of the containment policy over the long haul.

The Korean War produced a strategic literature devoted to the concept of limited war. The costly, prolonged, and ambiguous conflict in East Asia had proved highly frustrating to the American people, who had become accustomed in this century to fighting all-out war to total victory and unconditional surrender of the enemy. Even though the Soviet Union was not prepared for general war at the time (and the People's Republic of China was less so), the United States, under strong political pressure from its European allies to contain the conflict, and unwilling to become involved in a large-scale ground war on the Asian mainland, imposed severe limits on its military operations. It refrained from employing atomic weapons (despite its near monopoly) and from bombing beyond the Yalu River, and it prevented the forces of Chiang Kai-shek's Nationalist government on Formosa (as Taiwan was then still known) from joining the United Nations' police action. Against General Douglas MacArthur's declaration that "in war there is no substitute for victory," the advocates of limited war argued that in the emerging nuclear era, wars must be kept nonnuclear, and war aims must be strictly limited. In their view, it was essential to devise ground rules for preventing war from escalating, even if this meant an agonizingly bitter struggle that resulted only in stalemate.[11]

The debate over nuclear deterrence began in earnest after the Eisenhower Administration enunciated the doctrine known as "massive retaliation." The United States would no longer feel constrained to fight an indefinite number of costly and protracted limited wars of the Korean variety without resort to nuclear weapons. According to Secretary of State John Foster Dulles, "Local defenses must be reinforced by the further deterrent of massive retaliatory power. . . . The way to deter aggression is for the free community to be willing and able to respond vigorously at places and with means of its own choosing."[12] It is important to keep in mind that the doctrine proclaimed by Dulles was not at all identical with the policy of deterrence that emerged gradually throughout the 1950s; rather, it was only an early, crude, and controversial application of the concept of deterrence, and it soon came in for much criticism. The Air Force had been arguing for strategic nuclear forces vastly superior to those of the USSR, such that the United States could prevail in a strategic exchange.

President Eisenhower, however, as a fiscal conservative concerned about the economics of deterrence and defense over the long haul, was convinced that superiority and a counterforce capability (to destroy enemy forces before they could inflict heavy damage on the United States and its allies) would be too expensive. Such an approach would undermine the notion that nuclear weapons provided an economically efficient substitute for large conventional forces. Eisenhower settled for the concept of strategic sufficiency, which presupposed the maintenance of large, yet not unlimited, nuclear forces—a posture midway between strategic superiority and minimum deterrence. "This strategy," wrote Jerome H. Kahan, "did not merely reflect a doctrinal choice but represented a bureaucratic compromise between those who argued that America had too much strategic power and those who argued that it had too little."[13] Even with such a policy, the United States enjoyed de facto strategic superiority over the USSR for many years, but the U.S. government never seriously considered the option of preventive war during the period when it could have achieved a decisive victory.

Within a relatively short time, the credibility of the Dulles doctrine as an effective bulwark against Communist expansion—except in the case of large-scale attack against Western Europe—was being questioned by several critics. The doctrine of massive retaliation implied that the United States would reply to a future Communist attack on such in-between areas as Asia, as well as on NATO territory, with nuclear strikes by the Strategic Air Command against the Soviet Union and/or China. William W. Kaufmann raised objections against such an operational policy. Although conceding that the United States possessed the capacity for carrying out long-range strikes, he questioned whether the policy met the fundamental requirements of effective deterrence when considering the problem of making intentions *credible*. Kaufmann gave his reasons:

> They [the Communist leaders] would see that we have the capability to implement our threat, but they would also observe that, with their own nuclear capability on the rise, our decision to use the weapons of mass destruction would necessarily come only after an agonizing appraisal of costs and risks, as well as of advantages. . . . Korea and Indochina are important symbols of our reluctance, not only to intervene in the peripheral areas, but also to expand the conflicts in which we have become engaged. . . . Finally, the state of domestic and allied opinion provides them with ample reason to believe that the doctrine would be, if not a case of outright bluff, at the very most a proposal that would still have to undergo searching and prolonged debate before becoming accepted policy.[14]

Paul Nitze, who had served earlier as Director of the Policy Planning Staff in the Department of State, criticized the Dulles pronouncement by distinguishing between a purely *declaratory policy*, designed for a psychological or a political purpose, and an *active policy*, which lends itself realistically to implementation. Nitze contended that the Dulles doctrine contained too wide a gap between what was declared and what could be done.[15] In the mid-1950s, Western strategic analysts sought to tone down the doctrine of massive retaliation and to reduce the gap between rhetoric and reality by speaking of "graduated deterrence." The term was

not a particularly apt one, insofar as it implied that deterrence itself can be graduated. One can argue that aggression either is or is not deterred, but that the application of military force can be graduated once aggression has occurred. The exponents of graduated deterrence suggested that the Western deterrent would be
more credible if the West's inferior conventional posture were to be compensated
for by a doctrine calling not for massive retaliation but for the minimum amount of
nuclear force needed to discourage, repel, or defeat aggression—entailing the use
of tactical nuclear weapons against the Communist heartland.[16]

Convinced that total nuclear war would destroy all political and social values,
Brodie rejected those approaches to strategic planning that might increase the
probability of nuclear war—preventive war, striking preemptively when war
seemed imminent, and massive retaliation.[17] He linked the strategy of deterring
general war to the complementary principle of limiting those military conflicts that
might break out from time to time.[18] He was sure that the U.S. government would
not deliberately start a nuclear war and deemed it essential to persuade potential
aggressors that they could never gain a significant advantage by striking first.[19] The
only way to do this, he argued, was to ensure the survivability of forces that would
be capable of wreaking devastating damage on an aggressor in retaliation:

> For one thing, it [the policy of deterrence] uses a kind of threat which we feel must be
> absolutely effective, allowing for no breakdowns ever. The sanction is, to say the least,
> not designed for repeating action. . . . Deterrence now means something as a strategic
> policy only when we are fairly confident that the retaliatory instrument on which it re-
> lies will not be called upon to function at all. Nevertheless, that instrument has to be
> maintained at a high pitch of efficiency and readiness and constantly improved . . . at
> high cost.[20]

Brodie saw no serious problem of the credibility of U.S. deterrent policy with
regard to a direct, strategic nuclear attack on the United States, since no adversary,
plotting a first strike, could count on the inability, much less the unwillingness, of
U.S. leadership to retaliate. The crucial problem, in his view, arose from the likelihood that the adversary would find it hard to believe that the United States would
ever retaliate massively in cases of less than massive aggression because no government would risk resorting to nuclear weapons unless vital national interests
were gravely threatened. Yet he hastened to caution that it would be a tactical mistake to give the enemy an advance assurance that nuclear war is so unthinkable as
to be impossible, for this might tempt the foe to make the wrong prediction and
inadvertently precipitate total nuclear war by taking an ill-conceived gamble.[21]
Although he did not admire massive retaliation as an operative doctrine, he did not
object to allowing the enemy to think that this was the American policy when the
United States enjoyed nuclear superiority.

He was more worried about those who would place "less reliance upon deterrence of vast retaliatory power" and who would resort to the use of tactical nuclear
weapons in local wars. Dulles himself, stung by criticisms of his massive retaliation
stance, appeared willing to move in this direction in 1957, and Brodie had misgiv-
ings about a shift that might increase the risk of nuclear war's occurrence.[22] Even
in the early days of deterrence theory, there were subtleties in the debate as to

whether it was possible to distinguish clearly between strategic and tactical nuclear weapons, whether such a theoretical distinction could be maintained under actual combat conditions, and whether a war involving nuclear weapons of any sort—tactical or strategic—could be kept limited. Questions such as these came up repeatedly in the theoretical debate about deterrence during the period of the Cold War.

As we noted earlier, Brodie's thinking profoundly influenced his cotheorists of deterrence at RAND. Albert Wohlstetter, for example, agreed wholeheartedly on the need for a survivable nuclear retaliatory force. Recognizing that weapons technology undergoes constant dynamic change, he argued trenchantly that deterrence required the construction of an invulnerable second-strike capability to inflict an unacceptable level of damage in a retaliatory blow against any aggressor who would try to carry out a surprise first strike against the deterrer. Writing after the USSR had launched the first earth-orbiting satellite in 1957, Wohlstetter pointed out that impending technological developments would render strategic weapons more vulnerable to surprise attack and that deterrence credibility could henceforth be maintained only through the dispersal, mobility, and protection (or hardening) of nuclear missile systems.[23] Fixed, unprotected missiles above ground could not serve a second-strike role because they were vulnerable to a first strike and would thus appear to be provocative first-strike weapons. If both sides retained such forces, the international situation would be characterized by a condition of trigger-happy nervousness and instability in time of crisis, when each side might be tempted to seek the undoubted advantages of a first strike.

Brodie concurred on the need for expensive technological innovation to maintain up-to-date deterrence, because he knew that stable mutual deterrence could not be achieved once and for all with any given level of state-of-the-art weapons technology. He did, however, think that Wohlstetter's analysis concerning the requirements of deterrence was too exclusively technological and failed to take into account relevant political and psychological factors.[24] Although he respected Herman Kahn's technical competence and the originality of his imaginative war scenarios,[25] Brodie regarded Kahn as unwarrantedly optimistic in thinking that the United States could survive a thermonuclear war.[26]

For more than a quarter-century, Brodie was a consistent advocate of credible deterrence through the maintenance of a survivable second-strike retaliatory capability, but he remained skeptical of most proposals for policies, weapons systems, conventional buildups (or counterinsurgency buildups), and strategic and tactical options that might tempt policymakers to plunge incautiously into conflict situations with a potential for escalation to nuclear war. "One effective way of keeping out of trouble is to lack the means of getting into it."[27] By no means did he regard nuclear weapons as useless. Their most important use is to inhibit large-scale military hostilities with potentially catastrophic consequences.[28]

While the United States enjoyed strategic nuclear superiority, virtually no one doubted its ability to deter a direct attack on itself. Many, as we have seen, doubted the credibility of a policy that threatened the use of nuclear retaliation against Communist aggression in such peripheral (or "gray") areas as Asia and the Middle East. (It is much harder for a nation to maintain a credible threat that it will run the grave risk of nuclear war for the sake of allies just as it would for its own vital national interests or survival.) The most serious question was whether Western Europe, given its political, economic, and cultural importance, fell into a special geographic category. Could the United States protect Europe through indirect or extended deterrence? Whether the Soviet Union under Stalin had any serious plans to fill the postwar power vacuum in Europe by resorting to military force has remained debatable even in the post–Cold War era. What is certain is that in the years after 1945, responsible leaders in Western Europe were deeply concerned over the region's vulnerable condition. According to historian Michael Howard, Europeans were more worried about their own political, economic, and military weakness than over any specific, imminent threat of attack from a Soviet Union suffering from at least comparable exhaustion and destruction. What they needed, says Howard, was *reassurance* more than *deterrence*. He suggests that the Marshall Plan, by sharply contrasting the economic recovery prowess of the West with the bleak prospects for improvement in the East, might have been perceived as a threat to Moscow's ability to maintain control of Eastern Europe; and this, in turn, he says, may have provoked behavior (such as the Berlin blockade and the Czech coup) that connoted aggressive designs westward.[29] Stalin's seizure of Eastern Europe had been quite ruthless; the United States had quickly demobilized its wartime military strength, leaving only a modest-sized occupation force in Germany and Austria; large Communist parties in France and Italy were acting like disciplined subversives, loyal to Moscow's party line.

West Europeans were not reassured by America's economic aid alone; many feared that the restoration of their industrial and agricultural capacity, far from enhancing their security, might make Western Europe a more inviting target. Being the historical inventors of and staunch believers in the balance of power, they wanted from the United States an assurance that would eliminate whatever temptation the Soviet Union might have to attack. The result was the Atlantic Alliance. The allied governments, after calculating (at the Lisbon meeting of 1951) the high costs of matching formidable Soviet conventional forces in a traditional balancing process, decided to pursue their policy of containment by relying on what Prime Minister Churchill and President Eisenhower (the former NATO Supreme Allied Commander) regarded as a cheaper and more effective strategy of nuclear deterrence.[30] This proved to be an excellent deal for the Europeans, reducing their defense burden costs below what they would have otherwise been, but, as Michael Howard notes, it meant "that the credibility of the deterrent posture depended on a continuing American nuclear ascendancy over the Soviet Union. . . . (and) that the peoples of Western Europe effectively abandoned responsibility for their own defense."[31] For reasons of national dignity, the British and French governments, determined to preserve a semblance of military independence, developed strategic nuclear forces of their own, even though this involved defense budgets of 4 percent of GDP rather than about 3 percent for all other Continental allies. These national nuclear forces were not militarily significant at first. In fact, their credibility was often ridiculed, but they were politically important to the two countries, and they eventually became impressive enough to complicate U.S.–Soviet arms-control diplomacy.

THE THEORETICAL DEBATE

There were certain essential propositions on which most of the advocates of nuclear deterrence were in fundamental agreement—most of the time. However, they could seldom engage in discourse, spoken or written, without finding points of divergence. Some critics, of course, rejected outright the strategic policy and strategy of nuclear deterrence, as well as the theory on which it was supposed to be based. At this point, it is useful to summarize those essential propositions on which there was a near-consensus among those realists who found this concept of deterrence intellectually compelling:

1. The principal purpose of nuclear weapons is not to wage but to preclude large-scale war among the major powers—not only nuclear war but also conventional war with a serious potential for escalation to the nuclear level.
2. Nuclear deterrence cannot be expected to prevent most forms of conflict—brushfire wars or guerrilla insurgencies, civil wars, local international wars, or ethnic genocide in areas where a nuclear power has no vital interests or where its nuclear threat would lack credibility and relevance.
3. Effective deterrence requires constant and costly technological innovation (modernization) in order to maintain international strategic stability through the planned updating of secure, invulnerable, second-strike capabilities. (By the mid-1960s, there was a widespread assumption among strategic analysts that the superpowers either had achieved or were moving deliberately toward stable mutual deterrence as a result of dispersing and protecting land-based ICBMs and sea-based SLBMs.[32]
4. Deterrence is as much a psychological-political concept as a military-technological one. Because its success depends on the perceptions and evaluations that go on in the decision-making minds of a potential aggressor, credibility is always a principal requirement. A threat is most credible when it appears to be based on an adequate military capability to inflict "an unacceptable level of damage," coupled with a clear intention and determined political will to use it punitively. Henry Kissinger wrote,

   > From the point of view of deterrence a seeming weakness will have the same consequences as an actual one. A gesture intended as a bluff but taken seriously is more useful as a deterrent than a bona fide threat interpreted as bluff. Deterrence requires a combination of power, the will to use it, and the assessment of these by the potential aggressor. Moreover, deterrence is a product of those factors and not a sum. If any one of them is zero, deterrence fails.[33]

5. To be effective, a deterrent capability cannot be kept secret. A certain amount of knowledge about it must be communicated to the adversary. If one side deploys additional weapons or modernizes its weapons arsenal in total secrecy, then it has not really upgraded the effectiveness of its deterrent force. (For a discussion of strategic communication, see the section on Thomas C. Schelling in Chapter 11.) At any given time, of course, governmental policymakers may feel comfortable with their estimates of the exist-

ing military situation. All governments carry on intelligence-gathering activities and expect others to do likewise. Different departments and agencies of a government may disagree among themselves concerning intelligence estimates. Individuals may fear inadequate data, contradictions in the data, deliberate deception or distortion of data, and interpretations of the data that are deemed unduly optimistic or pessimistic. Although deterrence requires that some knowledge be communicated to the other side, transmitting too much intelligence might weaken the deterrent if it were to facilitate planning an attack.[34]

6. Deterrence and defense are conceptually quite distinct. Yet for practical planning purposes, they are inextricably related. A nuclear power relies on deterrence to prevent a nuclear attack on its own or its allies' vital interests, but it also needs conventional defense capabilities to protect against non-nuclear military threats to its vital interests in areas of the world where a nuclear deterrent is highly incredible.

Thus the advent of nuclear weapons did not by any means prompt either governments or military advisers to conclude that military power (nuclear or conventional) had lost its utility, as Walter Millis[35] and other writers suggested. Klaus Knorr, Barry Blechman and Stephen Kaplan, Laurence Martin, and Robert Gilpin, as well as others, noted that military forces, both nuclear and conventional, would continue to cast a shadow of power capable of influencing the political behavior of states, even though they might not be used in combat; that conventional wars might still be waged with significant international consequences while remaining below the level of the nuclear threshold, and that the implicit threat of escalation to the nuclear level could serve as a powerful deterrent to conventional aggression in some areas.[36] Martin argued trenchantly that the strategic nuclear balance between the two superpowers had produced a widespread but unwarranted belief that nuclear weapons can have no function beyond neutralizing each other in the framework of nuclear deterrence, and that the inaccurate assumption concerning the uselessness of nuclear weapons for positive purposes had helped to shape both elite and popular attitudes toward the utility of military force in general.[37] In his view, nuclear weapons could be said to possess considerable utility because they provide "the only firm assurance of immunity from attack and the only reliable guarantee against extreme pressure from other, blackmailing, nuclear powers."[38] He also made a convincing case that nuclear weapons, combined with adequate conventional defenses, can deter a Soviet attack by superior conventional forces on U.S. allies in Europe, even if such an attack did not threaten the survival of the United States.[39] We return later to the issue of deterrence versus defense in NATO Europe.

7. The proponents of deterrence were fairly well agreed on their basic albeit sometimes esoteric and acronym-ridden terminology. They distinguished between *preventive war* (premeditated to be carried out at a time of the attacker's own choosing) and *preemptive war* (resorted to by a government

under the pressure of a conviction that the outbreak of nuclear war is imminent and that it must strike first rather than forfeit to the adversary the undoubted advantages of executing a disarming blow). They also distinguished between a *countervalue* strategy (under which the adversary's population centers are targeted) and a *counterforce* strategy (which aims at destroying the adversary's strategic weapons sites and other military capabilities). They defined *strategic weapons* as those of intercontinental range (long-range bombers, ICBMs, and SLBMs); *tactical weapons* as those of short-range used on the battlefield; and *theater weapons* as those of intermediate range in Europe (e.g., Soviet SS-20s, and NATO Tomahawk cruise missiles). The situation has changed since the disintegration of the Soviet Union, and attention is paid toward the end of this chapter to deterrence in the post–Cold War era. A distinction, too, was drawn between a deterrent strategy of massive retaliation or Defense Secretary Robert McNamara's assured destruction, which may implicitly involve the threat of all-out use of nuclear weapons (or "spasm response"), and the damage-limiting strategy of actually using nuclear weapons with restraint in military operations once deterrence has failed and war has broken out. (See the following discussion on "Dilemmas of Deterrence.")

Earlier students of international-relations theory had to be familiar with such basic concepts of nuclear strategy and also with the various factors that entered into the calculus of deterrence and defense capabilities—multiple warheads, hardening, dispersal and mobility, warning times, effectiveness of surveillance, C^3 systems (command, control, and communication), reliability and guidance-system accuracy of missiles, and the characteristics of various types of weapons. Yet the architects of nuclear strategy based on mutual assured destruction (MAD) continued to warn that serious thought should not be given to the possibility of deterrence failure, for this might increase the probability of its failure by making nuclear war appear less unthinkable.

The concept of mutual deterrence is, in a sense, the classical notion of balance of power in modern guise. Many writers, including Bernard Brodie, Hedley Bull, Henry A. Kissinger, Robert Bowie, Robert Osgood, Donald G. Brennan, Thomas C. Schelling, and Herman Kahn treated mutual deterrence, stable deterrence, balanced deterrence, and stable arms balance in terms remarkably reminiscent of earlier treatises on the balance of power, and these writers reflected a keen awareness of the same difficulties that plagued the older theory. It has often been said that the balance of power does not provide a good theoretical basis for foreign-policy decision making because it is uncertain (because there are no reliable criteria for measuring comparative power) and because it is unreal (because nations, feeling uncertain, are not content to aim at achieving a balance, but seek instead a margin of superiority or a unilaterally favorable balance of power). Thus, political leaders and their advisors have always had difficulty in determining whether stable mutual deterrence describes a condition that exists or prescribes a course that should be pursued, whether it is an objective situation best achieved automatically by the continued efforts of both sides to attain superiority in military technology or whether it is a policy requiring a cooperative conscious quest for parity by rival governments.

DILEMMAS OF DETERRENCE

Even theorists impressed by the power of the nuclear deterrence idea realized that it gave rise to serious intellectual difficulties, dilemmas, and self-contradictions: Deterrence presupposes rational decision-making processes within the bureaucratic governments of industrially advanced powers, which are supposed to act according to expected-utility models and cost–benefit calculations.[40] Because the capitalist and communist states were said to subscribe to ideologies based on rational behavior, both superpowers appeared to fit the category of rational actors, capable of making cool, clear-headed choices after weighing the pros and cons of alternative courses of action. Yet as thousands of warheads accumulated in their nuclear arsenals, it became increasingly difficult to believe that rational political leaders could seriously threaten retaliation on a large scale.

Even though assured destruction seemed logically to be the surest way to hold an adversary at bay and prevent war, American theorists and political decision makers were motivated to make the strategy of nuclear deterrence appear more credible by probing the possibilities of so-called flexible response, limited nuclear options, selective counterforce targeting, and demonstration uses of nuclear weapons (the nuclear shot across the bow) simply, as Kenneth N. Waltz put it, "to remind everyone—should anyone forget—that catastrophe threatened." Raymond Aron, Glenn H. Snyder, Richard Rosecrance, Leon Wieseltier, and others distinguished between a deterrent threat of devastating damage posed before the start of a war and the response actually made after hostilities break out.[41] Nevertheless, many deterrence strategists warned against thinking seriously about the failure of deterrence, fearing that this might increase the likelihood of its failing.

Waltz sought a middle view, based on practical political experience, between the twin pessimistic positions that deterrence cannot possibly work and that the failure of deterrence must necessarily lead to mutual superpower incineration. Drawing a stark contrast between the logic of nuclear weapons and that of conventional weapons, Waltz returned to the original theorem of Brodie—that pure nuclear deterrence precludes the need for an elaborate defense. One need not build up large, expensive conventional forces to convince the aggressor that the cost of victory on an invaded territory is too high; all that is needed is to persuade the potential attacker that the risk of having certain, quick, and catastrophic destruction inflicted on its own territory is too frightful. "The absolute quality of nuclear weapons sharply sets a nuclear world off from a conventional one."[42] Moreover, successful deterrence does not require a MAD strategy of destroying cities along with a sizable portion of the adversary's population and economic–industrial base. In the nuclear age, the threat to use only a small amount of force is sufficient, "because once the willingness to use a little force is shown, the adversary knows how easily more can be added."[43] We might say that Waltz advocated minimal deterrence, not with respect to the size of the force, but with respect to the punishment to be threatened as the initial response to attack.

Thus, the second dilemma of deterrence arose from the fact that, as military technology becomes more complex, uncertainties in the minds of strategic planners and political decision makers increase. The deployment of each new generation of advanced weapons systems makes it more difficult to calculate the strategic balance and the possible effects of a nuclear exchange. Does the compounding of uncertainty (which occurs in spite of computers) seem likely to strengthen or to weaken the condition of mutual deterrence?

Robert E. Osgood aptly described the part played by uncertainty in the delicate and fragile calculus of deterrence—a calculus that involves a process of mutual mind reading in an effort to second-guess an opponent with respect to intentions, values assigned to an objective, estimated costs and effectiveness of certain actions, and the probability of specific interactive responses. He noted that up to a point, the element of uncertainty in nuclear deterrence, taken together with the frightful implications of miscalculation, may contribute to caution and restraint, and thus to international stability. Nonetheless, he warned against an excessive reliance on uncertainty:

> It leads to a kind of strategic monism that relies too heavily upon the undeviating self-restraint and low risk-taking propensities of statesmen. It ignores the provocative effect of the fearful uncertainties and risks, to breed unwarranted confidence in the regularity and predictability of that balance, which in turn diminishes the restraints upon military action.[44]

Later, Stanley Sienkiewicz named uncertainty as the central problem in contemporary strategic analysis. A nuclear aggressor planning an attack does not know whether the potential victim will launch vulnerable retaliatory forces as soon as it is clear that an attack is underway, nor can the aggressor predict how the enemy's command and control system will function and how well the retaliatory forces will operate. Sienkiewicz concluded that the greater the operational uncertainty associated with the forces of both sides—particularly with those that have first-strike capabilities—the greater the crisis stability of the strategic nuclear balance.[45]

The superpowers remained preoccupied with the fine points of the military balance at the strategic level. New developments in the fields of ballistic missile defense, multiple independently targeted reentry vehicles (MIRVs), and several other significant areas of advanced military technology prompted writers throughout the 1960s to express concern over the possibility that the international strategic situation, viewed in objective mathematical terms, would become unstable. It was suggested that a ballistic missile defense, if deployed to protect a nation's population centers, might arouse an adversary's fears that the nation was enhancing its first-strike option by preparing to blunt the retaliatory blow; MIRVs were looked on by some as means of increasing the number, penetrability, and accuracy of warheads, and thus of threatening to eliminate a large part of a land-based ICBM force on which the ability to carry out assured destruction in retaliation heavily depended. Some analysts discerned an action–reaction relationship in superpower armaments competition: If one side insisted on deploying a ballistic missile defense to protect its strategic missiles, the other allegedly would probably develop MIRVs in order to compensate with augmented offensive power, and might actually overcompensate, thus prompting the first party both to speed up its strategic defense efforts and also eventually to develop MIRVs.[46] Essentially similar arguments, appropriately updated, were revived in the 1980s by the critics of proposals for strategic space-based defense, treated subsequently in this chapter.

The strategic theorists were not always consistent. Some of them opposed ballistic missile defense on the grounds that it was technically and militarily of low effectiveness against incoming missiles, and at the same time criticized it because it would allegedly be highly destabilizing. Some argued that if the Soviets insisted on deploying their own antimissile missiles, it would be much cheaper and more effective for the United States to upgrade its offensive capabilities by deploying MIRVs; they later argued against MIRVs because they were destabilizing, would set the arms race into an upward spiral, and would not substantially improve the security of the United States or the effectiveness of the deterrent, since they would supposedly provoke the Soviet Union into a compensatory effort.[47]

RATIONALITY VERSUS IRRATIONALITY

More serious criticisms of deterrence theory came from those troubled by doubts about the assumption of policymakers' rationality on which it heavily depends. Some of the most astute analysts of deterrence, who grudgingly supported it in its nuclear form, given the absence of politically feasible and available alternatives during the Cold War, nevertheless felt constrained to point out its shortcomings, ambiguities, and contradictions. The leading figure in this group was Robert Jervis, who found it odd that so many analysts tended to rely on deductive logic while ignoring the emotions and perceptions of decision makers. Participants in international rivalries and conflicts, he warned, seldom have an adequate understanding of each other's perspectives and goals. The receiver, therefore, often misses or misinterprets signals that appear perfectly clear to the sender.

Jervis raised such questions as these: Are the psychological attitudes and decisional processes similar for challengers and defenders of the status quo? Is the defender capable of understanding the challenger's fears that the defender may constitute a security menace? Do both parties view the credibility of threats symmetrically? Can leaders know the intentions of the other side, and predict how it will respond? Are both sides equally concerned about its reputation for living up to its commitments? (In Jervis's view, the United States was much more sensitive on that score than the Soviet Union.) In short, he saw decision makers as burdened with "unmotivated biases"—beliefs, images, preconceptions, and other cognitive predispositions. Yet he did not entirely discount the assumption of deterrence rationality. "The fact that people are not completely rational does not automatically vitiate this approach."[48]

As we show in Chapter 11, a number of theorists have questioned the assumption that modern governments are rational actors. Greg Cashman has summarized the impediments to rational decision making within bureaucratic organizations: (1) Not all decision makers are completely rational in terms of the national interest; some at all levels may act out of subconscious psychological needs. (2) Misperception may thwart an accurate image of the international situation. (3) In crisis situations, leaders may have to make decisions under conditions of stress and lack of sleep. (4) The quality or quantity of information required for rational decisions may be lacking. (5) The time available may be limited, not used efficiently, or shortened by a desire for speedy action. (6) The ability to predict likely outcomes of various policy options in time of crisis is often imperfect. (7) Performing adequate cost–benefit analysis on all feasible alternatives is a daunting task within other given constraints. (8) Individuals within various advising and decision-making groups vary in their rational assessments of policy options, preferred means, and likely outcomes.[49]

The foregoing list of problems indicates that even when governmental bureaucracies want to formulate rational policy in time of crisis, they may be unable to make optimum decisions, in spite of Max Weber's optimistic thesis that bureaucracies cancel out the personal values, goals, and psychological idiosyncrasies of individuals and institutionalize rational procedures in decision making on behalf of the state.[50] Beyond the difficulties faced by rational bureaucracies, some theorists discern more fundamental deficiencies. Christopher Achen, for example, rejects deterrence theory as logically incoherent.[51] Jervis, too, has held that "a rational strategy for the employment of nuclear weapons is a contradiction in terms."[52] Jervis also finds the theory wanting because it is derived from the experience, culture, and values of the West—in short, it is ethnocentric. It rests on the assumption that while nations may pursue contrary goals, they all share the same basic behavioral patterns, and it fails to "consider that people from other cultures might develop quite different analyses."[53] Patrick M. Morgan noted that "classic criticisms of deterrence theory turn on the charge that governments simply lack the necessary rationality to make it work, that they are particularly subject to irrationality in times of intense crisis or actual attack."[54] It has become commonplace to regard nuclear deterrence as an irrational game of "Chicken" (described in Chapter 12).[55]

Frank C. Zagare has tried to square the circle between rational and irrational decision making by distinguishing between "procedural" and "instrumental" rationality. The former is what most Western thinkers (including critics of nuclear-deterrence theory) have usually meant by rational (based on a sensible cost–benefit calculus). According to Zagare, procedural rationality requires omniscience and excludes misperceptions, as well as psychological and emotional deficiencies. In Western civilization, rational action has normally been taken to mean action that is predictable, prudent, reasonable, and appropriate in the light of dominant social values and preferences. Zagare does not say this, but this seems to be what he means by procedural rationality. Instrumental rationality, in his view, is something more limited. The instrumentally rational player is one who has a logically consistent order of preferences on which choices are based, regardless of whether they impress others as rational on ethical, strategic, political, or moral grounds. Thus, Hitler and Khomeini are fitted under the canopy of instrumental rationality: One understands their behavior simply by understanding their goals.[56] "The individual decisionmakers analyzed by rational choice theorists can be, at one and the same time, rational in the limited instrumental sense, and irrational in the sense of the proceduralist."[57] Compare this with the judgment of Ole R. Holsti, who held out for the more traditional interpretation of what constitutes rationality: Although the assumptions of deterrence are valid in most times and circumstances, nevertheless deterrence does presuppose rational and predictable decision processes. He warned, therefore, that no system of deterrence

> is likely to prove effective against a nation led by a trigger-happy paranoid, or by some-one seeking personal or national self-destruction or martyrdom, or by decision makers willing to play a form of international Russian roulette . . . or by those who regard the loss of most of their nation's population and resources as a reasonable cost for the achievement of foreign-policy goals.[58]

Jervis observes that the theory does not demand *total* rationality to be valid. He does not agree with Patrick Morgan when Morgan cites a basic paradox—namely, that the classic deterrence theory may be counterproductive if it always seeks to enhance the confidence of governments in their ability to remain perfectly cool and deliberate in times of crisis. Jervis moves closer to one of the most sophisticated theorists of deterrence, Thomas C. Schelling, in the following passage:

> The paradox is not as great as Morgan thinks. There is an irreducible minimum of un-predictability that operates, especially in situations which engage a state's highest val-ues. Thus, even though there is no rational argument for a countercity response to a Soviet attack on the United States or Western Europe, the mere possibility may be an effective deterrent. . . . it is bizarre for a state to maintain its security by making its ad-versaries believe that it is prepared to bring about the end of its civilization. This pol-icy makes more sense when we consider threats that leave something to chance: it can be rational to threaten, and carry out, a move that increases slightly the danger of an all-out war, while it would be completely irrational to launch an attack. Indeed, much of deterrence rests on the fact that both sides know that events are not entirely under their control.[59]

The "threat that leaves something to chance" was an invention of Thomas Schelling. The fear of things getting out of hand was Schelling's favorite method of solving the credibility problem. "A response that carries some risk of war can be plausible, even reasonable at a time when a final, ultimate decision to have a gener-al war would be implausible or unreasonable."[60] While the fear of irrational action can strengthen deterrence, an excess of rationality might lead to an unwanted war, according to Jervis, if one rational party initiates a crisis or decides to stand firm in the conviction that the other is bound to retreat, while the latter calculates that it can make one more last safe move because the former is thought to be rational enough to back down. The status-quo or defending power may fear the domino effects of retreating in a crisis, including the impact of such behavior on third-party allies and on the self-confidence of the aggressive party in future confrontations. Beyond the dangers of misunderstanding, misperception, and misjudgment, there also lurks the danger of the accidental and the irrational, either of which can cause things to go wrong or to get out of hand, thus interfering with the neat, calculable operation of deterrence prescribed by the intellectual theory of deterrence.

In the final analysis, Jervis, following Brodie and Schelling, is more interested in achieving deterrence through manipulating the level of risk than through acquiring a military capability for the escalation dominance favored by Paul Nitze. Jervis sees deterrence through the acceptance of a spectrum of risks as preferable to deterrence through a spectrum of planned violence:

> The first problem with the escalation dominance logic is that a state confident of winning at a given level of violence may be deterred because it judges the cost of fighting at that level to be excessive. On the other hand, even if defense cannot succeed, the threat to defend can deter if the other side thinks that the status quo power is sufficiently strongly motivated to fight for a losing cause. Nuclear weapons have not changed the fact that defeating an enemy is not worthwhile if the costs entailed are greater than the gains.
>
> . . . It is not correct to claim that the threat to escalate will be credible only if it is believed the action will bring a military victory; one must consider the price that both sides would have to pay. Thus, the U.S. might deter a Soviet invasion of Western Europe by threatening to use tactical nuclear weapons even if the Soviets believed that they could win such a war.[61]

Frank C. Zagare concluded from his studies that "we are ignorant about the conditions under which statesmen are prepared to fight or capitulate, that is, we do not as yet have an understanding of the forces which give rise to the preferences of the players."[62] Nonetheless, because each player, when contemplating change in the status quo, is uncertain about the opponent's preferences, and whether the opponent may be instrumentally rational (and perhaps self-programmed to execute the threat), Zagare took successful deterrence (if credible) to be likely although not certain.[63]

The Limits of Deterrence

In one of Jervis's definitions of deterrence as a theory "about the ways in which an actor manipulates threats to harm others in order to coerce them into doing what he desires," he seems to confuse *deterrence* with *compellence,* although he is well aware that there is a considerable difference between trying to dissuade an adversary from undertaking an action you want to prevent and trying to compel the other party to take some positive action that you want done. The threat of nuclear punishment can be used to deter, but hardly to compel, except perhaps to reverse a dangerous process already set in motion that might conceivably lead to nuclear war (e.g., removing Soviet missiles from Cuba during the Cuban Missile Crisis of 1962).[64] A threat to employ U.S. strategic nuclear superiority in the 1950s to force the Soviet Union to withdraw from Eastern Europe would have lacked any semblance of credibility or political–strategic prudence. Jervis himself admits that deterrence theorists "present reasonable arguments about why compellence is usually more difficult than deterrence,"[65] but he expresses doubt that it is easier to deter than to compel in all circumstances, especially if the aggressor decides to risk taking the initiative:

> It has been said that the state trying to change the status quo is in a weaker bargaining position because it can drop its demand without raising the danger that the status-quo power will raise new demands. But it is hard for the latter to retreat without damaging its ability to stand firm against demands for further changes; therefore, it should be

able to prevail. There is a difficulty with this argument, however. One must look at what each side will gain if it prevails. Here the very advantage just ascribed to the status-quo power turns out to be a disadvantage. What the aggressor can gain is not limited to the specific issue, but includes an increased chance of prevailing in future attempts to alter the status quo. The status-quo power, by contrast, gains only a temporary respite.[66]

Jervis criticized deterrence theory on the grounds that "it says little about how to change . . . an adversary or to determine whether changes have taken place."[67] As a guide for stateleaders, it tells them how to maintain a hostile, mutually dangerous relationship, but not how to alter the situation. Thus, "it provides a greater help in understanding crises than in understanding long-run disputes," but it offers no advice on how to avoid crises or how to decide whether the national interests at stake are sufficient to warrant the resort to military force; and it is inadequate because it fails to take into account that "successful accommodation usually requires at least some change in the values and goals of both sides."[68] Jervis charges further that deterrence theory neglects the role of rewards and compromises in the resolution of confrontational crises because "it is simpler to ignore outcomes that are not clear-cut" and because realist scholars who dominate the field assume that promises of rewards are less potent than threats of punishment in influencing the behavior of states.[69]

A decade after Jervis published his criticism, Paul Huth and Bruce Russett reiterated the view that not only the negative threat of punishment or sanctions but also the positive offer of rewards or inducements constitutes a logical part of rational deterrence theory, and they lament the fact that this latter aspect has been so long neglected or considered—for example, by Richard Ned Lebow and Janice Gross Stein—as an alternative to deterrence theory.[70] The debate between the two pairs of scholars is considered subsequently, in connection with efforts to test deterrence empirically.

Deterrence and the Arms-Reaction Process

Was the U.S.–Soviet nuclear-weapons competition from the late 1940s to the late 1980s an arms race, embodying the sort of action–reaction process that had been described by Richardson (discussed in Chapter 8)? Those who were not merely skeptical about certain aspects of deterrence theory but deeply and emotionally opposed to the concept of deterrence and the nuclear strategy based on it were often inclined to think that every addition to the superpowers' arsenals was bound to increase the probability of war. They accepted the conventional wisdom that "no weapon has ever been invented that was not eventually used." They ignored the fact that both superpowers retired and replaced earlier generations of nuclear missiles without ever employing them in war. (Nuclear weapons might be used in the future, but they were not used in a military conflict between the United States and the Soviet Union, although both sides used the possession of these weapons for the political–psychological purpose of deterrence.)

There were occasional calls for minimum or finite deterrence, accompanied by assurances that modest-sized forces—much smaller than those in existence—would be quite sufficient to deter nuclear war. That may have been true, but in the context of the Cold War, such a judgment was politically irrelevant. Both super-powers carried on more or less steady competition in the research and development, production, and deployment of advanced weapons. Each side had to make sure that it had enough for adequate deterrence, given the uncertainty factor discussed earlier and the lack of progress toward negotiated arms reduction before the late 1980s. Barry Nalebuff summarized the dilemma:

> The theory of minimal nuclear deterrence highlights the degree of cooperation that two mutually suspicious countries can achieve. If perfect monitoring and enforcement of agreements were somehow available, then both sides would have great incentives to reduce their weapon supplies. But there is no supreme enforcer. . . . Without monitoring and enforcement, the noncooperative solution becomes unstable at low levels of arms. . . . At low enough levels, at least one side will have an incentive to break any agreement and attempt to achieve a dominant position. The rational fear of a violation puts a limit on how far one can trust an opponent to disarm rather than attack.[71]

Albert Wohlstetter argued in 1974 that over a nine-year period 1962–1971, there had not really been an arms race—that the United States, still strategically superior, instead of overreacting to Soviet arms programs (as required by the Richardson process model discussed in Chapter 8), had underreacted with self-confidence and restraint, reducing constant dollar expenditures on strategic weapons by two thirds.[72] U.S. defense budgets continued to decline after the end of the Vietnam War (which had absorbed a substantial fraction of U.S. expenditures in the latter part of the period studied by Wohlstetter). In contrast, the Soviet Union, which was not a participant in the Vietnam War except as a supplier at much lower cost, not much more than 10 percent of the American commitment, devoted the bulk of its military budget to acquiring new capabilities, with seemingly little regard for resource constraints.[73]

After a quarter century in which the United States had enjoyed virtually unquestioned strategic superiority, the late 1970s and early 1980s produced a growing perception throughout the West that, in view of Soviet heavy multiple-warhead strategic missiles (intercontinental) and multiple-warhead intermediate-range missiles in the European theater, the global strategic and theater balance was tilting gradually in favor of the Soviet Union.[74] U.S. and NATO problems were exacerbated by the fact that the two superpowers (regardless of their actual strategic intentions) maintained very different public strategic doctrines in their official governmental statements and military literature concerning what they would do in the event of deterrence failure. The United States adhered to a second-strike strategy in the event of a direct attack on itself; it would never initiate a first strategic strike on the USSR. (U.S. strategy for its extended deterrent in Europe is discussed later.) The Soviet Union, which was undoubtedly no less interested than the United States in deterring nuclear war, made it fairly clear that if nuclear war should ever appear to be imminent, it would pursue a preemptive first-strike strategy.[75]

Granted that strategic doctrine is not the same as theory, differences in doctrine nevertheless certainly influenced and complicated the theoretical debate. Matters were not helped by the fact that Washington was sometimes too explicit and at other times too vague in promulgating official policy, while Moscow placed a high premium on secrecy, as a United Nations document noted:

The concept of military doctrine is used in somewhat different ways by the major military powers. . . . Soviet nuclear doctrines are generally not as openly expressed as is the case in the United States. Soviet thinking on the subject to a large extent has to be deduced from very general statements, from military force dispositions, and from Soviet military writing.[76]

Many Western analysts, therefore, were skeptical as to whether the Soviet Union accepted the concept of mutual deterrence as understood in the West. Those who believed that the Soviet Union was an inherently expansionist power bent on the eventual achievement of global hegemony took one approach to the Soviet threat; those who considered the Soviet Union a traditional nation-state given to revolutionary rhetoric but increasingly defensive in outlook took quite another. Even the former group divided between those who thought that the leadership in Moscow strongly preferred a psychopolitical strategy that prescribed the avoidance of a decisive, frontal military encounter at all costs and those who were convinced that Moscow was seeking military superiority for a strategic first strike. Up to the mid-1970s, most American strategic analysts hoped that Soviet planners could gradually be persuaded to adopt American theories of deterrence and arms control.

The most crucial issue in the strategic debate was the relationship between deterrence and a war-fighting capability. Those who followed along the path marked out by Bernard Brodie held that the only purpose of possessing stockpiles of nuclear weapons is to deter nuclear war or any war with a potential for escalating to the nuclear level. For this school of thought, nuclear war must remain unthinkable, and nuclear weapons must never be used. The mere existence of nuclear weapons should be sufficient to dissuade the opponent from carrying out a strategic-nuclear first strike against the United States or large-scale conventional aggression against Western Europe. Jervis and others argued that nuclear superiority did not matter.[77]

Others, following more along the lines suggested by Herman Kahn and Albert Wohlstetter, argued that deterrence, to be most credible and effective, requires an operational doctrine and a perceived capability for fighting, winning, surviving, and recovering from a nuclear war. This type of strategy presupposes the achievement of strategic military superiority, involving invulnerable (hardened, dispersed, and/or mobile forces), a damage-limiting capability (to destroy the adversary's nuclear weapons before they could be used), active antimissile and passive civil defenses, a highly efficient and survivable C^{3}I system (command, control, communications, and intelligence) for early warning and battle management, an arsenal of reliable missiles and warheads accurate enough to kill hardened targets, all combined with the political will and psychological readiness to strike first.[78] The debate over nuclear deterrent strategy was never finally settled before the global situation began to undergo a fundamental transformation in the late 1980s. (More is said about this later.)

It is worth stressing, however, that the U.S.-Soviet arms race—if that is what it was—did not escalate to war, despite the many fears expressed from the late 1970s until well into the 1980s that the Soviet Union was trying to overtake the United States in strategic military power. Two Dutch scholars, Hank Houweling and Jan Siccama, provided a theoretical basis for the fears by concurring with the Organski–Kugler hypothesis (discussed in Chapter 8) that war occurs when a powerful challenger overtakes a formerly powerful dominant nation, and they argued that this would hold true in the nuclear as in the prenuclear age.[79] Concern over Soviet heavy multiple-warhead missile deployments, after the SALT I Accord had allegedly codified strategic parity, led U.S. defense officials (including James Schlesinger in the Nixon Administration and Harold Brown in the Carter Administration) to raise questions as to how certain the United States could continue to be about the maintenance of an assured-destruction capability, that is, the ability to inflict an unacceptable amount of damage in retaliation after a surprise first strike. Schlesinger called for "limited nuclear options" and "selective targeting";[80] Brown adopted a "countervailing strategy," which was widely interpreted as a sign that the United States was regearing from deterrence to war-fighting plans.[81]

Richard L. Garwin warned strategists worried over the window of vulnerability not to advocate a policy of "launch on warning."[82] The central issues in this phase of the debate were (1) whether the adoption of a war-fighting strategy by the United States would strengthen the deterrent against war or make war more likely to occur, besides the obviously controversial issue of whether nuclear war could be won in any politically meaningful sense; and (2) whether nuclear war, should it ever begin, could be limited and controlled below the level of mutual extinction of the superpowers and the destruction of a large part of the human race and its civilizations. The answer to the first question is highly subjective, for it depends on the psychology and politics (or psychopolitical characteristics) of each individual making the judgment. Some would argue, with McGeorge Bundy, that no rational American or Soviet leader would be willing to contemplate the loss of even one or two cities for the sake of winning a foreign-policy crisis.[83] At the opposite side of the psychopolitical spectrum, some would insist that the Soviet Union, having recovered from the highly destructive World War II (in which military and civilian deaths in excess of 20 million were a hundred times greater than American losses), might be willing to place a higher price on a nuclear war that it thought, in a critical confrontation, it might win and from which it could recover.

The Controllability of Nuclear War

The second question—Can nuclear war, once begun, be limited and controlled?—is more technical. The limitation of nuclear war would require on both sides a great deal of political self-restraint as well as a highly developed system of C^3I. For instance, let us assume a very strong mutual determination to prevent uncontrollable escalation and a desire to avoid damaging the adversary's C^3I structure (despite powerful military incentives in some cases to destroy it), so that the adversary can know the intention to limit and can respond in kind. Even if we make this assumption, it was nevertheless suggested that the performance of the C^3I structure may not prove adequate to the heavy demands placed on it during a nuclear exchange because of many factors—jamming, deception, infiltration, and sabotage by *spetznaz* (special forces), or defense-suppression attacks by NATO–Warsaw Pact or U.S.–Soviet strategic forces; staffing by incompetent or poorly trained personnel who undergo psychological shock once nuclear hostilities have been initiated; improper netting and coordination of communicating units; technical equipment failures; time lags; human operating errors under conditions of extreme stress; misinterpretation of information and or orders; atmospheric and ionospheric disturbances; communications blackout effects (lasting several hours) of electromagnetic pulse (EMP) from the detonation of large thermonuclear weapons in and above the atmosphere; and other causes.[84]

Desmond Ball analyzed the vulnerabilities of C^3I systems and their implications for the control of nuclear war. He pointed out that the National Command Authority is vulnerable to attack by SLBMs, for which the warning time would be minimal. Ball described technologically more complex difficulties and failures that could arise in the operation of airborne C^3 systems of the Strategic Air Command or the Navy, affecting the communications links between command centers and ICBMs or SLBMs, or both; of satellite warning, reconnaissance, and communication systems (thereby degrading intelligence concerning what is actually happening worldwide); of the Washington–Moscow Hot Line, on which superpower emergency communications depend; and of the submarine command and control system, not because of the submarine survivability factor but rather because of the special problems associated with maintaining reliable communications with submerged submarines, properly functioning navigation systems, and the ability to use SLBMs selectively.

Ball and other analysts, including Michael Howard, Andrei Sakharov, Spurgeon M. Keeny, Wolfgang K. H. Panovsky, Ian Clark, and Robert McNamara, concluded that nuclear war could not be controlled, except perhaps for a relatively small portion of strategic nuclear forces, only for a brief period, and only in situations where the Soviet Union practiced restraint, but not in a high-level nuclear exchange in which strategically important military, political, and administrative power and C^3 centers were being destroyed at a rapid rate.[85] Soviet analysts, throughout most of the nuclear age, while insisting that the use of nuclear weapons must always be subject to political control, did not think as thoroughly about controlled or limited war as did earlier Western advocates of the concept. They envisaged simultaneous and massive blows against any and all targets capable of causing damage to the Soviet Union, not sequential, restrained, discriminating surgical strikes.

Throughout the Cold War period of intensive superpower rivalry, the world was said to be better off if principal decision makers in all nuclear-weapon states remained firmly convinced in advance of an outbreak of war that a nuclear exchange could not be limited. Such a shared conviction tended to strengthen deterrence by creating a mental block, as it were, against a deliberate choice for initiating any war containing a built-in potential for escalation to the nuclear level. This will hold true for the future. Uncertainty about controllability should compel responsible leaders to conduct themselves with consummate prudence in time of crisis—and future crises cannot be ruled out summarily.

Despite the nonproliferation regime (discussed subsequently), nuclear weapons may come into the possession of states with leaders who are less experienced, more impulsive, more prone to risk taking, and less constrained by rational processes and/or other political—cultural—moral inhibitors than those who have avoided nuclear war up to this time. Moreover, there remain ways in which nuclear war may begin unintentionally, or—more precisely—without careful premeditation by the leaders of states governed by rational bureaucracies.[86] In any event, if total deterrence should fail, responsible leaders must be ready to do whatever they can to compensate with rational decision making *after* the fact of the outbreak of war for the collapse of rational decision making *before* the fact. It will then be of the utmost urgency for political and military leaders on both sides to become convinced quickly that nuclear war can and must be limited, that city destruction must be avoided, that the C^3 networks of the adversary must be left intact for the sake of controllability, and that if nuclear weapons are introduced, their use against strictly military targets must be as discriminating as possible, with minimal collateral damage to innocent populations and civilizational structures, until the conflict can be terminated as quickly as possible on terms less disadvantageous to each side than a continuation of nuclear war would be for both and for the international community.

NUCLEAR DETERRENCE
AND CONVENTIONAL DEFENSE

The debate about controllability pertained mainly to the possibility of a limited strategic nuclear exchange between the superpowers. What about a nuclear war that did not involve intercontinental attacks but the use of nuclear weapons on the in-between battleground of Europe? Such a war might appear to be tactical and limited for the superpowers, but the Europeans would regard it as strategic, so far as their own interests were concerned. Many people, including media commentators and perhaps some theorists, were confused by the apparent contradiction in Western deterrence policy: The United States declared that it would never launch a first strategic strike, while NATO, under U.S. leadership, refused to subscribe to a no-first-use policy regarding nuclear weapons in Europe.

The U.S. pledge to defend Western Europe was quite believable when the United States enjoyed unquestioned strategic nuclear superiority. The members of the Atlantic Alliance and its integrated military organization, NATO, had no choice from the beginning but to rely on U.S. nuclear power because of the Soviet–Western conventional force imbalance and the prohibitive cost of trying to match Warsaw Pact conventional strength over the long haul.

Ideally, it is desirable to have both a high deterrent posture and a high degree of defense readiness in case deterrence fails. Such a combination of nuclear threat and war-fighting capability enhances the credibility of deterrence, for it eliminates the danger of self-paralysis in time of crisis that inheres in the possession of a capability to make only an all-or-nothing response. In contrast to the last years of the Eisenhower Administration, when the air was filled with talk about a "conventional pause," "dual-capability forces," and tactical or limited nuclear war, the Kennedy Administration, strongly influenced by Defense Secretary Robert McNamara's doctrine of flexible response, tried to separate nuclear from conventional forces and responses by time, geography, and command and control systems. The administration pursued what it regarded as the prudent and responsible way of reducing the probability of nuclear war and increasing the options available between holocaust and surrender. American policymakers believed that, in order to minimize the risk of escalation to all-out nuclear war, NATO had to reduce its reliance on tactical nuclear weapons and maintain a clear firebreak between conventional and nuclear hostilities because the distinction between tactical nuclear war and strategic or central nuclear war would be highly ambiguous and extremely difficult to maintain under actual combat conditions.[87]

West European strategists and policymakers, analyzing the situation from a very different geostrategic space and geopolitical perspective, were quite understandably of two minds on the subject. At times, they feared that in a crisis, the United States would not be willing to defend them with nuclear weapons; at other times, their fear was that it *would* be willing to do so. Most European policymakers, remembering the terrible carnage of the two world wars—"conventional" wars—preferred maximum reliance on nuclear deterrence to preclude any war at all. They certainly did not want tactical, limited nuclear war, nor did they want a purely conventional response by NATO, involving a NATO fallback and a subsequent liberation counteroffensive. (They had had a taste in World War II of what that would mean.) Some American policymakers and strategic analysts undoubtedly regarded the European attitude as illogical, unrealistic, or perhaps ostrichlike in its characteristic avoidance of thinking through the potential consequences of relying too heavily on a nuclear strategy. In the minds of many Europeans, the Americans were being too logical and too mathematical, but not sufficiently intelligent in terms of European psychology and politics. The strategy of deterrence works, Europeans argued. By taking a remote hypothesis of how deterrence might break down, and making that the basis of a new strategic doctrine for NATO, the United States, in European eyes, might increase the probability of military conflict that could eventually become nuclear. From one European perspective, flexible response involved a weakening rather than a strengthening of deterrence.

Moreover, if war was being deterred by the specter of swift, condign punishment to be inflicted on an aggressor, why should European governments, which were being urged by the Kennedy Administration and later by the Carter Administration to increase their conventional force contributions, waste resources on expensive military capabilities that were not necessary? Modest-sized conventional forces, including some from the United States on European territory, were deemed quite sufficient to serve as a tripwire for a NATO nuclear response. Thus, logic would dictate the continued effectiveness of the deterrent at a low level of actual war-fighting capability. Unfortunately, however, the danger of attack still could not be dismissed lightly.

As Frank C. Zagare asked, "given the overall stability at the highest level of general strategic deterrence, why doesn't one side or the other simply escalate to the penultimate stage of the game since, by assumption, each player is deterred in the next and last stage of the game?"[88] In other words, why could not the Soviet Union invade with conventional forces only on the assumption that each side's nuclear weapons were deterred? That option may have sounded theoretically attractive, and some military planners worried about it, but it was unrealistic for three reasons: (1) The Soviet Union, as a strategically conservative and cautious power could never be certain that NATO, unable to repel a conventional attack, would refrain from introducing nuclear weapons. Even at the height of the massive

West European antinuclear protest in the early 1980s, NATO would not renounce the possible first use of nuclear weapons, as advocated by leading American ex-policymakers,[89] because of the fear of decoupling the defense of Europe from the central strategic deterrence capabilities of the United States, thereby removing from the minds of Soviet planners the crucial uncertainty that served as the ultimate guarantee of Western Europe's defense.[90] Prominent European defense specialists argued that the problem was to deter not only nuclear war, but also war at any level in Europe.[91] They did not wish to make Europe safe for a conventional war with nonnuclear weapons that had become quite capable of decimating civilization more thoroughly than in World War II.[92] (2) Even in the improbable contingency that the United States, at a critical juncture, should decide in its own national interest not to fulfill its alliance pledge, but to withhold the use of its nuclear weapons in the European theater, there remained the possibility that Britain and/or France might invoke their own national nuclear deterrents to defend supreme national security interests.[93] (3) Moreover, despite what Western analysts generally considered a three-to-one margin of superiority in armor and other conventional force capabilities, Soviet planners may not have been as confident as some of their Western counterparts that they could penetrate NATO defenses.[94]

The effort to persuade NATO to renounce the first use of nuclear weapons in case of war in Europe must be placed in the context of the time. There was concern in many quarters that not only the U.S.–Soviet global strategic balance but also the theater balance between NATO and the Warsaw Treaty Organization was tilting ominously eastward. In the later 1970s, the Soviet Union, having achieved the formal codification of strategic parity in the Strategic Arms Limitation Talks and the SALT I Accords of 1972, began to acquire a formidable array of theater nuclear capabilities, including SS-20 land-based missile delivery systems of considerably longer range than those at the disposal of NATO. Rather than forfeit to the Soviet Union a monopoly of the right to modernize intermediate-range theater nuclear forces, NATO in December 1979 took a two-track decision to modernize its own Europe-based nuclear capabilities by deploying ground-launched cruise missiles (GLCMs) in five countries and, in Germany, Pershing-2 missiles that could reach targets in the USSR. These were to be deployed during negotiations for a European balance at lower or zero levels. The NATO governments insisted that such deployments were necessary to prevent Western Europe from being "Finlandized"—that is, made politically more sensitive to Moscow by being brought further into the shadow of its military power—and also to threaten the USSR with the prospect of symmetrical vulnerability with Western Europe while arms reductions were being negotiated.

Soviet leaders during the Andropov–Chernenko years charged that the United States and NATO were attempting to deploy on European territory weapons that would threaten Soviet strategic central systems. The early 1980s was the period when the fear that nuclear war was imminent began to reach unprecedented heights. This was paradoxical, inasmuch as the assumption of deterrence success was considerably stronger at earlier times when the size of nuclear arsenals was less formidable. These were the years when the peace, nuclear freeze, and antinuclear movements of a religious, ethical, and political character reached their highest and most emotionally intensive peaks.[95] Millions of West Europeans were no longer reassured by the American nuclear deterrent pledge, and they poured out into the streets in protest—often in anti-U.S. terms rather than anti-Soviet terms. (The Netherlands, which had been the first NATO country to welcome U.S. nuclear weapons in the late 1950s, was also the first to stage large-scale demonstrations of moral protest against them in the early 1980s.)[96] Despite what appeared to be a political crisis that threatened to split the Atlantic Alliance, NATO governments were united in their determination to retain the first-use option. Several analysts in the 1980s pointed out that Warsaw Pact conventional superiority was exaggerated and that conventional defense options were available;[97] antinuclearists argued that these would allow NATO to subscribe to a no-first-use agreement.

Richard K. Betts presented a theoretical explanation of the NATO position. While accepting the need for improving conventional capabilities, he challenged those who would rely completely on conventional deterrence. Substantial improvements in the conventional military balance might enable NATO to withstand attack, he conceded, but they would produce uncertainty rather than confidence:

> Uncertainty (about conventional outcomes or about what could motivate an enemy attack) is conducive to deterrence when buttressed by a threat of awesome punishment (nuclear retaliation) that dramatically magnifies the risks for the attacker. Without that support, extremely high confidence in conventional options, rather than uncertainty, would be necessary to provide the same degree of deterrence. . . . It is prudent to raise the probability that conventional defense would succeed, but little can be gained from dispensing with the complementary nuclear deterrent.
>
>   Pure conventional deterrence raises the danger of nuclear war by making the potential consequences of resort to conventional war less unthinkable for the attacker. As long as nuclear weapons exist, so does the danger that any war between the superpowers could escalate despite declared doctrines or actual intentions. Short of abandoning deterrence altogether, the best way to minimize the danger of nuclear war is to minimize the chance of conventional war.[98]

Several of the conventional deterrence options proposed were criticized on the grounds that they could prove to be recipes for defeat in case of war and might well increase the probability of war. John J. Mearsheimer, for example, warned that a strategy of maneuver-oriented NATO defense, falling back in one sector and thrusting forward in another, could be a formula for disaster, enabling the attacker to penetrate deeply, envelop NATO forces, and sever their lines of communications.[99] Samuel Huntington's proposal for a NATO strategy of threatening to carry out a counterattack into Eastern Europe, threatening Moscow's control of that region, was criticized as a plausible military strategy in an actual conflict situation, but it was argued that if such a political strategy were publicly adopted in peacetime, it might well be provocative and bring war closer rather than deterring it. A leading theorist of conventional deterrence, Richard Ned Lebow, also criticized the Huntington proposal, along with other strategic concepts then current for air–land battle, follow-on forces attack (FOFA), and deep-strike options, for they would have been perceived by the Soviet leaders as evidence of hostile Western intentions.

> Perhaps the greatest irony is that many American military officers and defense intellectuals are attracted to offensive strategies at a time when an effort should be made to

dissuade the Soviets from *their* commitment to the offensive. Surely if there is anything more dangerous than one side committed to an offensive strategy, it would be both sides committed to it.[100]

EMPIRICAL STUDIES OF DETERRENCE

Most of this chapter has dealt with the subject of nuclear deterrence, which is in a separate category from conventional deterrence. Nonetheless, as the previous section illustrated, there was a growing interest in the 1980s—among political and military leaders, defense intellectuals, and academic theorists—in the possibilities of conventional deterrence. This probably contributed at least indirectly to the success of the negotiations for a treaty in 1987 to eliminate intermediate-range nuclear missiles from Europe and to reduce rather than modernize short-range nuclear missiles by the end of this century. It also stimulated theorists to study historical cases of deterrence success and failure in both the prenuclear and the nuclear eras.

Raymond Aron argued that "there is no deterrent in a general or abstract sense; it is a case of knowing *who* can deter *whom, from what, in what circumstances, by what means.*"[101] Thus, according to the late political sociologist of the University of Sorbonne, deterrence must always be analyzed in specific, concrete terms. What deters one government might not deter another. What succeeds in one geographical–cultural context might fail in another. For this reason, Aron questioned the value of a certain type of strategic fiction that describes dozens of conflict situations or scenarios, reduced to simplified schemes that lack historical reality. Such writing, in Aron's view, might make stateleaders "overestimate the technical aspect of the diplomatic or military problems, and underestimate the importance of the psychological, moral, and political data" that are unique in each situation.[102] The study of actual historical cases, therefore, can be a corrective to fictional scenarios and vague generalizations; over a period of time, it contributes to a more subtle understanding of what deterrence is and what it is not; how it differs from compellence; and under what conditions it is more likely to succeed or to fail.

Successful deterrence involves a nonevent. It is difficult enough in the realm of human affairs to demonstrate why something did happen; it is impossible to prove conclusively why something did not happen. Can we be certain, for example, that the Cuban Missile Crisis did not lead to war because nuclear deterrence was successful in that case? If so, is this all that is meant by deterrence—namely, that the thing feared (nuclear war) did not occur under circumstances where it appeared to be a distinct possibility? Was either superpower strongly motivated to go to war at the time, only to be held back by an assessment of the consequences, or were both superpowers determined throughout the series of events composing that crisis to do their utmost to achieve their objectives without resorting to actual warfare? (The Cuban Missile Crisis is treated in Chapter 11, "Decision-Making Theories.") Such questions can probably never be answered with finality. The strategic theory of deterrence is not quite the same as mathematics, which proceeds by an intrinsic logical necessity of its own. The analysis of deterrence always involves debatable factors of human judgment, such as political common sense based on experience (which some might call "intuition" or a "hunch"), the interplay of individual and bureaucratic rationality, and "second-guessing," as well as risk-taking. Some scholars, however, have warned that intuitive evaluations of deterrence credibility are unreliable.[103] This, too, furnishes a strong motivation for seeking greater objectivity through the study of concrete historical cases.

Patrick M. Morgan has drawn a useful distinction between *general deterrence* and *immediate deterrence*. *General deterrence* implies a policy stance of regulating an adversary relationship and balancing power over what may be a long period of time, through maintenance of a satisfactory level of forces. Most of the time, adversaries do not regard war as imminent or proximate. *Immediate* (or *pure*) *deterrence*, in contrast, implies a specific situation in which one side is seriously considering mounting an attack, whereas the other side is preparing a threat of retaliation in order to prevent it, and both sides realize what is going on.[104]

As George and Smoke have pointed out, deterrence at the level of limited war and "sublimited"* conflict is much more complex than at the strategic level. Whether we consider the objectives of the players or the means at their disposal, the number of variables involved is greater. Each side is likely to be unsure of its own motivation and that of the other side to achieve various objectives. Deterrence of lower-level conflict is not as readily modeled as the nuclear strategy of assured destruction. The selection of the means to be employed must be subordinated to the imperative of escalation control and the political objectives of the actors in the conflict, as well as the reassurance and/or placation of allies, neutrals, and domestic opinion. At lower conflict levels, deterrence is a context-dependent problem. George and Smoke conclude that "it is dependent not upon comparatively few technical variables, known with high confidence on both sides, but upon a multiplicity of variables, many of them partially subjective, that fluctuate over time and are highly dependent upon the context of the situation."[105] This compounds the difficulty of identifying and analyzing instances of deterrence.

Paul Huth and Bruce M. Russett picked up on Morgan's definition of immediate deterrence as a situation "where at least one side is seriously considering an attack while the other is mounting a threat of retaliation in order to prevent."[106] They made an empirical study of 54 cases over the period 1900 to 1980, in an effort to determine under what circumstances immediate extended deterrence is likely to be successful in preventing attacks on third parties. The cases they identified therefore stretched over both the prenuclear and the nuclear era; they also included nuclear and nonnuclear states in the role of would-be deterrers.[107] Huth and Russett assume, for purposes of their investigation, that states are unitary (rather than pluralist bureaucratic) actors, that key decisions for war or peace are made by single decision makers or small groups, and that the decision makers operate

---

*The term *sublimited conflict* was introduced in the 1960s to refer to a broad spectrum of conflict below the level of conventional war. It included insurgency, infiltration, demonstration of force, naval blockades, and similar modes of applying pressure. It was later replaced by the term *low-intensity conflict*.

according to Bruce Bueno de Mesquita's expected-utility model in their assessment of utilities and probabilities attached to outcomes.[108]

> For the attacker, the options are holding back or pressing ahead with military force against the protégé. For the defender, the choices are accepting the consequences of the loss of the protégé or meeting the attack with substantial military force.[109]

Because the mere absence of an attack does not necessarily argue to the success of deterrence (if the attacker did not intend to attack), the proper assessment of threats and intentions becomes a matter of crucial importance and, as we show subsequently, a source of controversy among scholars.

Huth and Russett judged deterrence to be successful in 31 (or 57%) of the 54 cases they examined. They grouped their hypotheses to be tested under three categories: (1) relative military capabilities, (2) the role of past behavior in signaling current intentions—for example, did the defender back down the last time; will this make the defender more or less likely to fight this time?—and (3) the nature and extent of the military, economic, and other ties of mutual interest between defender and protégé. The third category of factors, they found, is more important than the other two in influencing the motivation, commitment, and resolve of the defender.[110]

Richard Ned Lebow and Janice Gross Stein were unable to replicate either the selection or the coding of cases in the Huth–Russett data set, and they found that only 9 out of the 54 cases qualified as immediate extended deterrence in their view.

> In thirty-seven cases, we find no evidence that the alleged attacked intended to use force or that the putative defender practiced deterrence; both are necessary to identify valid cases of deterrence. Four cases are reclassified as compellence, and the remaining four cases are ambiguous; either they are open to multiple historical interpretations, or insufficient evidence is currently available to permit confident classification and coding.[111]

Lebow and Stein fault Huth and Russett for improperly designating attacker and defender, incorrectly identifying third parties as targets of attack or deterrence, and confusing both direct with extended deterrence and deterrence with compellence—discrepancies that "reveal alarmingly low levels of cross-study reliability—between two teams of investigators classifying and coding precisely the same set of cases."[112] Of the nine cases that Lebow and Stein accepted as meeting their criteria, none of the three they coded as successes had been so designated by Huth and Russett. The latter pair subsequently defended their work and attributed the discrepancies to the use of different theoretical concepts and operational rules for identifying and selecting cases. They criticize Lebow and Stein for restricting deterrence cases to those in which the attacker has a serious intention to use force; this to Huth and Russett means a firm resolution and commitment to use force from the outset of the dispute. This is wrong, argue Huth and Russett, for it eliminates all cases of bluff and uncertainty where the potential attacker may not be certain about its own intentions until after it has proved the defender's resolve. The two pairs of scholars diverge widely over how to differentiate serious from nonserious threats.[113] Huth and Russett are accused of bias in favor of deterrence failure. The net result of the debate is a recognition that data sets for deterrence cases have a way to go before they are sufficiently refined to achieve the level of acceptability accorded to the lists of wars discussed in Chapter 8.

DISARMAMENT, ARMS CONTROL, AND DETERRENCE

Arms control and disarmament are related but distinct concepts. They overlap occasionally yet reflect divergent approaches to the arms problem. Disarmament in the strict sense involves the destruction of armaments and the prohibition against their future production. Disarmament may be partial or complete. Although substantial disarmament has become a persistent propaganda theme in the foreign-policy statements of most states, no government has ever taken seriously the utopian goal of general and complete disarmament (GCD). Arms control, presupposing that nations will continue to possess arms at levels deemed adequate for security, aims at managing them to enhance security and promote desirable political and strategic objectives, rather than allowing weapons technology to dictate policies in ways that reduce the safety and controllability of the international environment. Thus, arms-control policies typically seek to impose some kind of restraint or regulation on the qualitative design, quantitative production, method of deployment, protection, control, transfer, and planned, threatened, or actual use of military forces and weapons.

Such policies may imply collaboration between adversaries—formal agreements, tacit understandings, or informal cooperation. They may also embrace unilateral decisions that were made with the hope or expectation of reciprocal action, or unilateral decisions deemed worth making even if the adversary does not respond, simply because they enhance the stability of the deterrent, controllability, security against unintended war, and damage limitation if war should occur. Central to the thinking of most arms-control proponents is the reduction of tensions, risks, and dangers without weakening deterrence. Specific arms-control proposals, however, may have other purposes in the minds of their supporters—for example, to promote détente, to effect budget cuts, to permit a shift of resources to nondefense programs, to preserve arms-control momentum, to satisfy public opinion, and so on.[114] Finally, arms control involves partial disarmament—arms reductions that improve the security of a nation, its allies, and the international environment.

It is not the function of a text on international-relations theories to detail the provisions of diplomatically negotiated arms instruments. We limit our attention here to selected aspects of the subject, most of which have lent themselves to theorizing only to a limited degree. Take the nuclear test ban, for example. Originally, the Western powers refused to accept a cessation of nuclear testing except as an integral part of a comprehensive nuclear disarmament program, on the plausible grounds that so long as nuclear weapons were necessary for deterrence, continued nuclear testing would also be essential for keeping the deterrent technologically up to date. Later, when radioactive fallout from testing became a serious problem, the superpowers agreed to eliminate all except underground testing. Two nuclear powers, France and China, have never signed the Partial Test Ban Treaty.

The nonaligned bloc long urged a comprehensive test ban (CTB) as a means of curbing the arms race and nuclear proliferation. The superpowers, however, despite improved verification technology, continued underground detonations to proof-test the reliability of their stockpiles and to modernize their nuclear-weapons systems (offensive or defensive), while citing the nonuniversality of adherence as reasons for their inability or unwillingness to reach agreement.[115] Meanwhile, the SALT Accords of 1972, including the Antiballistic Missile (ABM) Treaty, as well as the SALT II Treaty of 1979 (which was observed even though not ratified), eliminated most ballistic defense missiles and set ceilings on strategic offensive weapons, but they brought about no reduction in the superpowers' lethal arsenals.[116] The SALT II Treaty was not ratified, but each superpower, in a display of tacit cooperation, signaled an intention to abide by its terms "so long as the other did so." (See the discussion on tacit bargaining in Chapter 12.)

The arms-control scene was fundamentally transformed in the 1980s—gradually at first but at a quickening pace—as a result of several factors: (1) President Reagan's 1983 Strategic Defense Initiative (SDI);[117] (2) NATO's deployment of intermediate-range nuclear forces (INF); (3) the rise of Gorbachev, who was anxious to avoid an outright arms race in outer space and was willing to reach an INF agreement rejected by his predecessors, and who withdrew Soviet troops from Afghanistan, manifested an interest in attenuating conflict in other regions, and adopted a more practical approach in other arms-limitation areas. Whether his new thinking—less intransigent and far more flexible than that of Brezhnev, Andropov, and Chernenko—was due primarily to the demands of internal *perestroika* cannot be known for certain, but there can be no doubt that Gorbachev's diplomacy proved remarkably successful both in Western Europe and in the United States, at a time when significant elements on both sides of the Atlantic were, for a variety of political and economic reasons, reassessing the Atlantic Alliance, as well as the need and cost of alternative strategies.

SDI had a significant impact on Soviet thinking about arms control in the Gorbachev era. Prior to the Reagan–Gorbachev Summit Meeting in Geneva in November 1985, the Soviet Union made an unprecedented announcement: It was ready to negotiate reductions of strategic nuclear weapons on the order of 50 percent if the United States would renounce SDI. (Back in 1977, it had summarily rejected President Carter's call for 25 percent cuts.) In his January 1986 plan for a world without nuclear weapons by the year 2000, Gorbachev proposed an early liquidation of Soviet and U.S. intermediate-range missiles in Europe. A year later, he agreed to unlink the INF issue from those of strategic missiles and space defense, and he accepted Reagan's "zero–zero" option of November 1981.

Meanwhile, the two superpowers converged toward mutual willingness to observe the ABM Treaty (a priority demand of the Soviet Union) by carrying on strategic-defense research and development only within its prescribed limits. Under the INF Treaty of December 1987, it was agreed that a whole important class of nuclear weapons would be eventually removed from Europe. There still remained tactical or shorter-range battlefield nuclear weapons, most of which in a future war would fall only on German territory. Naturally, the Germans wanted to get rid of all nuclear weapons in Central Europe and to cancel an earlier NATO decision to modernize some of its short-range weapons. Britain and other allies were concerned lest a totally denuclearized Central Europe foreshadow a drift by West Germany toward neutralism, perhaps as a prelude to national reunification (an unfounded fear, as later events were to show). Germany did gain a reversal of the NATO modernization decision, but NATO refused to abandon nuclear deterrence entirely and insisted that greater stability in Europe could not be achieved without substantial reductions in Warsaw Pact conventional forces.

In December 1988, Gorbachev announced sizable Soviet unilateral cuts—the beginning of a massive military withdrawal that would, within three years, bring about fundamental changes not only in the map of Europe but also in the pattern of East–West relations. Within a year, the Berlin Wall came down, a non-Communist government was ruling Poland, and Communist parties were losing their monopoly control in Hungary, Czechoslovakia, Bulgaria, and Romania. Within another year, Communist parties were changing their names almost everywhere, as others in the Eastern bloc were hailing the end of the Cold War and trying to move toward unfamiliar democratic methods and market economies. The Warsaw Pact found itself in the throes of dissolution. Most unexpectedly of all, Germany was suddenly unified peacefully—an event that, had it happened a few years earlier, would certainly have been a *casus belli.* In 1991, the Strategic Arms Reduction Talks (START) Treaty pared the strategic arsenals of the superpowers by 25–30 percent, and this was soon followed by informal reciprocal moves by Presidents Bush and Gorbachev to accelerate their negotiated cuts.

These developments, which contributed significantly to the attenuation of international tensions (and eventually to U.S. aid in the Soviet dismantling effort, aid to Soviet nuclear facilities and scientists, and the re-aiming of erstwhile adversary missiles away from each other's targets) came after Moscow's somewhat lukewarm cooperation with Washington in the Persian Gulf "Desert Storm" War in early 1991. An aborted coup in Moscow in August 1991 led to the political supremacy of Boris Yeltsin over Mikhail Gorbachev, the demise of Soviet communism, and the dissolution of the Soviet Union into its constituent republics before the end of 1991. Within the short space of three years, the international system had undergone changes at a breathtaking speed that no Western policymakers or scholars had anticipated, and that many as late as 1989 denied could happen.

THE END OF THE COLD WAR

Since the phasing out of the Cold War, 1989–1991, neorealists and neoliberals have argued over what preserved the long peace until the Soviet Union disintegrated as a failed political and economic system. Such realists as Hans J. Morgenthau, Kenneth N. Waltz in his earlier writings, Karl W. Deutsch and J. David Singer, and Richard N. Rosecrance had attributed the long peace to the structure of the international system, whether bipolar, multipolar, or a mix of the two. From 1981 onward, Waltz upgraded the role of nuclear weapons (which he had earlier depre-cated) as a factor making for stability.[118] Frank C. Zagare noted that "the majority of Western strategic thinkers hold that the existence of the U.S. nuclear deterrent is uniquely responsible for the stability of the international system since 1945."[119]

As we saw in Chapter 8, long-cycle theorists Modelski and Thompson postu-lated an extended period of global stability as a normal consequence of major-power wars, and a predictable phase in the century-long cycle through which the international system passes periodically. In their view, we should not be at all sur-prised by the long peace. Postwar periods are propitious for peace; nuclear weapons have very little to do with the phenomenon. For all practical purposes, they deny that nuclear deterrence has brought about a fundamental change in international politics. If their theory is valid, they declare, it may take another half century to determine whether nuclear weapons are as important as deterrence theorists say they are, because as part of the natural cyclical process we can expect the probability of global war to increase in the next few decades (say, up to the year 2030), as the global system moves toward its next macrodecision—the selection of a new management structure. For Modelski and Thompson, this is a regular fea-ture of the global calendar, comparable to the recurrence of elections. What is more, if the leading powers continue to carry out substantial nuclear disarmament, the next global war may be waged largely with conventional ground, naval, and air forces, with only a few nuclear weapons used selectively against military rather than urban targets.[120]

Richard Ned Lebow raised questions about the realist analysis of internation-al politics based on systemic structure. When did the bipolar world begin—in the late 1940s, before the Soviet Union developed nuclear weapons (a period that Lebow categorizes as unipolar)? In view of the realists' insistence that power involves a panoply of several different elements besides military strength (e.g., population, territory, resources, economic capability, ideology, morale, quality of government, etc.), when did the Soviet Union become a superpower? When did the bipolar system give way to multipolarity—when the Soviet Union broke up or earlier?[121] (Some analysts were perceiving a shift from bipolarity to multipolarity as early as the 1970s, identifying Japan and Western Europe as economic superpow-ers, and Saudi Arabia as a financial superpower.)

Lebow saw much of the discussion of polarity, including its definitions and measurements, as in need of greater precision. Lebow admits that Soviet policy seemed consistent with realist theories (including power-transition theory) until the late 1980s. In his view, the policy became increasingly inconsistent with those theories under Gorbachev, whose retreat from the Soviet Union's principal secu-rity zone and sphere of interest in Central and Eastern Europe "went far beyond any realist conception of retrenchment" that might be expected of a hegemonic power in economic decline.[122] Correctly or not, Lebow appears to conclude that the end of the Cold War and the demise of the Soviet communist empire may have sounded the death knell for traditional realist theories, according to which nations cannot escape the security dilemma, and also for those theories of deter-rence in which nuclear weapons constitute the most effective means of prevent-ing great-power war.[123]

The obsolescence of war has been an idea attractive to thinkers throughout history, increasingly so since the Enlightenment era. Richard Falk and Anatol Rapoport, both writing in a frankly utopian view, have discerned hopeful trends in an evolving political culture, which they see as moving away from realist premises toward the restructuring of a more humane, cooperative, law-dominated global civil society.[124] John Mueller has gone beyond Norman Angell, who (as we noted in Chapter 5) argued prior to World War I that war had become an unprofitable, suicidal, anachronistic method of resolving conflicts, from which the governments of industrial nations can derive no gain, and that war would eventually be eliminated through democratic education and the application of reason to foreign policies. In the late 1980s, Mueller set forth the thesis that war among modern nations is now "subrationally unthinkable."

> An idea becomes impossible not when it becomes reprehensible or has been renounced, but when it fails to percolate into one's consciousness as a conceivable option. . . . On the one hand, peace is likely to be firm when war's repulsiveness and futility are fully evident—as when its horrors are dramatically and inevitably catastrophic. On the other hand, peace is most secure when it gravitates away from conscious rationality to become a substantial, unexamined mental habit. . . . [War is] rejected not because it's a bad idea but because it remains subconscious and never comes off as a coherent possibility.[125]

Moreover, according to Mueller, the fundamental change in the attitudes and behaviors of nations had not been wrought by the existence of nuclear weapons; it would have occurred even had they not been invented. The number of nuclear weapons in the arsenals of the superpowers, whether 50,000 or 50, was irrelevant.[126] The governments of civilized states—remembering the human, economic, and social costs of two world wars—were sufficiently appalled at the destructiveness of modern nonnuclear weapons technology to shrink from initiating hostilities. Thus within a decade, from the late 1970s to the late 1980s, the intellectual mood of the critics of realism had swung from one extreme to the other—from gloomy pessimism to neo-utopian optimism, from regarding Armageddon as inevitable to dismissing the possibility of major-power war as unthinkable and obsolete.

Carl Kaysen, himself a realist, was inclined to concur with Mueller's basic conclusion about the obsolescence of war, if limited to modern Westernized industrial societies, but he criticized Mueller's explanation or, more precisely, his failure to explain the changes he postulates "in mental habits through socio-cultural evolution," as if war will become unthinkable and ridiculous, just as dueling and slavery did more than a century ago, and all the great industrial powers will go the way of their predecessors: Holland, Sweden, Switzerland, Spain, Denmark, and Portugal. (It is interesting to note that all the examples cited were quite Western.) Kaysen, influenced by Bruce Bueno de Mesquita's expected-utility model of war decisions, preferred to attribute modern Westernized governments' aversion to large-scale war to changes since the nineteenth century, which have made war unattractive to governing elites—changes of a political, economic, and technological character (democratic attitudes, cost-versus-benefit calculations, and the destructive power of weaponry). If war has a positive payoff, as in the Falklands/Malvinas conflict (and one could add the Persian Gulf War over Kuwait), it remains thinkable. Kaysen faults Mueller for ignoring the extent to which nuclear weapons and the risks of escalation strengthen the late twentieth-century animus toward war.[127] What is more, Mueller fails completely "to confront the traditional realist and neorealist argument that war is an inescapable feature of the anarchic international system in which independent states seek power and security . . . one of the dominant models of international relations, if not the dominant one."[128]

Stephen Van Evera explained the aversion to war as a result of "vanished and vanishing causes of war." Offensive dominance has been replaced by nuclear deterrence, which favors the defender over the aggressor. (Not all nuclear proliferation, therefore, is bad; it should be managed and limited to states that are capable of maintaining secure deterrents.) The spirit of militarism, hypernationalism, and social imperialism (characteristic of former aristocratic elites that could divert domestic discontent by provoking foreign wars) has been virtually eliminated by the process of democratization; social and economic stratification has given way to socioeconomic leveling. Aggressive states, both capitalist and revolutionary, have disappeared and have been replaced by responsible social democracies. Van Evera cites three illusory dangers: European multipolarity; a resurgence of German aggressive expansionism; and the risk that praetorian states will emerge in the East. He does admit that there are two real dangers that could spoil an otherwise peaceful picture: a breakdown of established international and domestic order in East Europe and the reappearance of nationality–minority conflicts and border disputes in that region, such as we have witnessed in the Balkans in the aftermath of the breakup of Yugoslavia and in parts of the former Soviet Union in the years following its collapse.[129]

RETHINKING DETERRENCE AFTER THE COLD WAR

Central to Cold War deterrence was the threat of U.S. nuclear retaliation, the purpose of which was to prevent, or deter, the Soviet Union from launching a nuclear or conventional attack against the United States or its allies. Nuclear forces had to be sufficiently survivable, reliable, and secure to survive a strike against the United States and subsequently to be able to retaliate against targets, based on the assets that the Soviet leadership most valued. Such deterrence, termed *assured destruction, or mutual assured destruction,* was based not on the ability to defend the United States, but instead on the capacity to deter by inflicting unacceptable levels of destruction on the adversary. It was not until the 1980s, with President Reagan's SDI, that thinking about deterrence began to embrace the concept of *defense* against nuclear weapons, or strategic defense, as a basis for deterring the use of nuclear weapons. If *both* parties to a nuclear relationship could survive— that is to say, neither could destroy the other—it was asked, would we not have achieved deterrence by our ability to preserve the United States and its allies rather than by our capacity to destroy the Soviet Union? However, offensively based deterrence—destruction of the adversary (assured destruction)—rather than defensively based deterrence (assured survival)—dominated Western deterrence thought. Military capabilities in the form of defense against ballistic missiles were rejected because it was believed they might upset a deterrence relationship deemed to be stable because it was based on mutual U.S. and Soviet vulnerability to nuclear retaliation.

Whether there would have been general war between the United States and the Soviet Union in the absence of the deterrent relationship provided by nuclear weapons will never be known with certainty. If nuclear deterrence contributed in some fashion to such superpower stability as existed for the two generations of Cold War, what are the deterrence requirements in and beyond the 1990s? To answer this question, it is essential to compare and contrast the assumptions about the conditions that framed the Cold War U.S.–Soviet deterrence relationship. These conditions include expectations about how leaders will think and behave, how they will formulate policy and execute decisions, and how they will control the military forces under their command.

According to Keith Payne, several important assumptions guided the Cold War superpower deterrence setting, contributing to stability.[130] Their absence following the collapse of the Soviet Union and the potential for proliferation in a multinuclear world enhances the need to rethink deterrence requirements for the post–Cold War era. In summary form, these Cold War assumptions included the following: (1) Rational leaderships, in the case of the United States and the Soviet Union, are capable of making decisions on the basis of cost–benefit, or risk-versus-gain, calculations and in control of the decision-making process and able to execute their decisions; (2) the ability of each side to communicate a threatened sanction effectively to an opponent is clearly understood and is regarded as decisive in developing cost–benefit calculations; (3) both parties share a level of mutual understanding and communication about behavioral expectations and about the responses that actions taken by one side will elicit from the other; and (4) the threatened retaliatory action has a level of plausibility sufficient to influence in a desired fashion the behavior of the adversary.

Rationality is a requirement for deterrence.[131] This component of deterrence does not assume that opponents necessarily share similar value structures. Instead, it means that a rational actor has a priority of preferences, engages in an ends–means calculation, and an assessment of alternative courses having different outcomes, and chooses the alternative deemed to be optimal in light of the preferred outcome. As Keith Payne suggests, behavior that is considered bizarre or horrible need not be irrational. The preference hierarchy of one leader may differ drastically from that of another leader. By this definition, such behavior would still be the result of a rational decision-making process. Thus, it is not the preferences of the leader that are the issue; it is the process by which such preferences are developed, adopted, and executed that shapes the definition of rationality.

In the U.S.–Soviet Cold War deterrence relationship, in retrospect, there evolved a level of mutual understanding within the posited conditions of deterrence just set forth. Both sides devoted extensive intelligence resources to understanding the political motivations, military strategy, decision-making structure, command and control systems, and force levels of the other. The leaderships of both sides were risk averse, apparently understanding the need to prevent crisis escalation to nuclear use—considerations deemed essential to nuclear deterrence. Such attributes enhanced deterrence to the extent that they helped reduce the prospects for misunderstanding and miscalculation. Nevertheless, the potential for deterrence failure based on escalation to the use of nuclear forces was present at least twice during the Cold War—in the Cuban Missile Crisis of 1962 and the Yom Kippur War of October 1973.

As early as January 1988, the Commission on Integrated Long-Term Strategy delivered to the Secretary of Defense and the Assistant to the President for National Security Affairs a report entitled *Discriminate Deterrence*.[132] The report noted that the next few decades will probably bring significant changes in the number of major military powers, the acquisition of advanced weapons technology by lesser powers, the impact of arms agreements on superpower forces both nuclear and conventional, and the uncertain behavior of allies and friends. All of these will modify the international environment to which policies and strategies of deterrence must be addressed:

> We should emphasize a wider range of contingencies than the two extreme threats that have long dominated our alliance policy and force planning: the massive Warsaw Pact attack on Central Europe and an all-out Soviet nuclear attack. By concentrating on these extreme cases, our planners tend to neglect attacks that call for discriminating military responses and the risk that in these situations some allies might opt out.[133]

The bipolar superpower deterrence relationship of the Cold War has been replaced by a group of states, and possibly eventually nonstate actors, in possession of nuclear and other weapons of mass destruction (biological and chemical capabilities) or having programs that may lead to the acquisition of such weapons. If the conditions posited for Cold War deterrence success cannot be met in the future, it follows that deterrence as a basis for stability is likely to be less reliable when the United States confronts countries with which it is less familiar—leaders whose value preferences are not well known or easily knowable, with whom we may have few proven channels of communications or shared basic assumptions about the relationship. The emerging structure of the international system, including the fragmentation or breakup of several existing states, the resurgence of ethnic–sectarian conflict,[134] religious fundamentalism, the potential for acquisition of weapons of mass destruction by actors other than states—all within a context in which dual use (civilian and military) technologies are more widely available—provide a formidable and complex challenge to deterrence. As the number of countries that the United States will have to deter increases, the likelihood that their leaderships will have any great familiarity with the United States will diminish. If the emerging paradigm contains a large number of states as well as nonstate actors, it follows that the operational requirements for deterrence will become more complex and therefore the possibility of deterrence failure will increase.

According to Keith Payne, the difficulties inherent in attempting to establish a reliable post–Cold War deterrence relationship are best illustrated by setting forth a checklist of questions that U.S. leaders would have to address as a necessary basis for a predictable deterrence strategy. Such questions derive from the conditions posited for deterrence success during the Cold War. Because there will be a need to deter more than one potential adversary, deterrence strategies will have to be designed for specific purposes to take into account the diverse value structures of numerous prospective regional opponents. Therefore, deterrence will have to be tailored to the particular threat situation. The need will increase for a greater understanding of how to communicate deterrence threats credibly to a larger number of adversaries, who themselves may hold a variety of opinions about the credibility of U.S. declaratory policy. It will be essential, although difficult, to establish those threats likely to be most effective, given the specific context and opponent against which deterrence is to be applied. R. James Woolsey, as Director of the Central Intelligence Agency, observed that "we have slain a large dragon. But we live now in a jungle filled with a bewildering variety of poisonous snakes. And in many ways, the dragon was easier to keep track of."[135]

If the United States is unlikely to be able to establish with multiple and diverse third parties the level of mutual understanding and effective communication necessary for confidence to be placed in a policy of deterrence, it follows that preparation for deterrence failure will become increasingly important. In the Cold War period, nuclear forces considered essential for punitive retaliation were deemed to be stabilizing, while defense systems in the form of strategic defense were criticized as destabilizing because they would allegedly lead the Soviet Union to build larger offensive forces designed to penetrate whatever defensive shield the United States might put into place. Such a conception of missile defense was based on the assumption that offensively based deterrence (assured destruction) between the United States and the Soviet Union would not fail. In the post–Cold War era, as the prospects for deterrence failure increase, the debate about defensive capabilities has intensified. This had led to an increasing interest in missile defense as a component of deterrence and as a hedge against deterrence failure in a multipolar world of state and nonstate actors. Three decades ago, Glenn H. Snyder observed that "considerations of reducing the probability of war and of mitigating its consequences must be evaluated simultaneously," and that planning for the consequences of deterrence failure is a matter of political judgment that must be weighed against the likelihood that deterrence will succeed.[136] Preparations for the failure of deterrence are essential, but such preparations should be carefully managed so as not to increase its likelihood. Thus, the end of the Cold War produced a long list of issues that establish the context for theorizing about the requirements for stability in a global system containing unprecedented numbers, types, and categories of actors. Such issues encompass deterrence of armed conflict in an era of increasing possessors of a broader range of destructive capabilities and the need to continue to theorize about the deterrence of armed conflict in the post–Cold War era.

NOTES

1. Bernard Brodie, "The Anatomy of Deterrence," *World Politics*, XXVI (January 1974), 174.
2. Robert Jervis, "Deterrence Theory Revisited," *World Politics*, XXXI (April 1979), 289.

3. Alexander L. George and Richard Smoke, *Deterrence in American Foreign Policy: Theory and Practice* (New York: Columbia University Press, 1974), p. 11.

4. Glenn Snyder, *Deterrence and Defense* (Princeton, NJ: Princeton University Press, 1961), p. 9.

5. George and Smoke, op. cit., pp. 14–16.

6. Bernard Brodie, *The Absolute Weapon: Atomic Power and World Order* (New York: Harcourt Brace, 1946), p. 76. In addition to the works cited previously, principal works on deterrence prior to 1980 include William W. Kaufmann, "The Requirements of Deterrence," in W. W. Kaufmann, ed., *Military Policy and National Security* (Princeton, NJ: Princeton University Press, 1956); Paul Nitze, "Atoms, Strategy and Policy," *Foreign Affairs,* XXXIV (January 1956); Bernard Brodie, *Strategy in the Missile Age* (Princeton, NJ: Princeton University Press, 1959); Albert Wohlstetter, "The Delicate Balance of Terror," *Foreign Affairs,* 37 (January 1959); Herman Kahn, *On Thermonuclear War* (New York: Free Press, 1960); Thomas C. Schelling, *Strategy of Conflict* (Cambridge, MA: Harvard University Press, 1960); Henry A. Kissinger, *Nuclear Weapons and Foreign Policy* (New York: Harper and Row, 1957); Herman Kahn, *Thinking About the Unthinkable* (New York: Horizon Press, 1962); Bruce M. Russett, "The Calculus of Deterrence," *Journal of Conflict Resolution,* VII (March 1963); Thomas C. Schelling, *Arms and Influence* (New Haven, CT: Yale University Press, 1966); George H. Quester, *Deterrence Before Hiroshima* (New York: Wiley, 1966); James L. Payne, *The American Threat: The Fear of War as an Instrument of Foreign Policy* (Chicago: Markham, 1970); Alain C. Enthoven and K. Wayne Smith, *How Much Is Enough?* (New York: Harper & Row, 1971); Bernard Brodie, *War and Politics* (New York: Macmillan, 1973); Richard Rosecrance, *Strategic Deterrence Reconsidered,* Adelphi Papers, No. 116 (London: Institute for Strategic Studies, 1975); Patrick M. Morgan, *Deterrence: A Conceptual Analysis* (Beverly Hills, CA: Sage, 1977).

7. Robert Jervis, "Deterrence Theory Revisited," (cf. Note 2), 291.

8. Kennan's famous "long telegram" of February 22, 1946, from Moscow to the State Department in Washington is to be found in the U.S. Department of State Series, *Foreign Relations of the United States, 1946* (Washington, DC: U.S. Government Printing Office), Vol. VI, pp. 696–709. Kennan's policy views were published in modified form in the article signed by "X," "The Sources of Soviet Conduct," *Foreign Affairs,* XXV (July 1947). Concerning George F. Kennan's background, especially his outpost service as a young diplomat in Riga, where his attitudes toward the Soviet Union were formed, see Daniel Yergin, *Shattered Peace: The Origins of the Cold War and the National Security State* (Boston, MA: Houghton Mifflin, 1978), chap 2. One of the most influential, although not uncontroverted, interpretations of Kennan's concept of containment and the meanings attached to it by various administrations is to be found in John Lewis Gaddis, *Strategies of Containment: A Critical Appraisal of Postwar American National Security Policy* (New York: Oxford University Press, 1982). See also Walter Isaacson and Evan Thomas, *The Wise Men: Six Friends and the World They Made* (New York: Simon & Schuster, 1986), pp. 238–239, 353–355, and 484–485; and Stephen M. Walt, "The Case for Finite Containment," *International Security,* 14 (Summer 1989), 5–50.

9. John Lewis Gaddis, op. cit., pp. 39–40.

10. Donald M. Snow, *Nuclear Strategy in a Dynamic World* (University Alabama: University of Alabama Press, 1981), p. 50; Richard Smoke, *National Security and the Security Dilemma,* 2nd ed. (New York: Random House, 1987), p. 53. See also Samuel P. Huntington, *The Common Defense: Strategic Programs in National Politics* (New York: Columbia University Press, 1961), pp. 33–47.

11. Alexander L. George and Richard Smoke, op. cit., pp. 23–27; Richard Smoke, op. cit., pp. 77–82. For a thorough examination of the theory of limited war, see Henry A. Kissinger, *Nuclear Weapons and Foreign Policy* (New York: Harper, 1957); Robert E. Osgood, *Limited War* (Chicago, IL: University of Chicago Press, 1957); Klaus Knorr and Thornton Read, eds., *Limited Strategic War* (New York: Frederick A. Praeger, 1962); Robert E. Osgood, *Limited War Revisited* (Boulder, CO: Westview Press 1979).

12. Excerpts from Dulles, Address to the Council on Foreign Relations, New York, January 12, 1954, in *The New York Times*, January 13, 1954. Dulles published a clarification of his views in "Policy for Security and Peace," *Foreign Affairs*, XXXII (April 1954). For an account of the alarm raised by some of Dulles's statements, see Louis J. Halle, *The Cold War as History* (New York: Harper & Row, 1967), pp. 276–282. For a later retrospective account, cf. Samuel F. Wells, "The Origins of Massive Retaliation," *Political Science Quarterly*, 96 (Spring 1981).

13. Jerome H. Kahan, *Security in the Nuclear Age: Developing U.S. Strategic Arms Policy* (Washington, DC: Brookings Institution, 1975), p. 34.

14. William W. Kaufmann, "The Requirements of Deterrence," op. cit., pp. 23–24.

15. Paul Nitze, Atoms, "Strategy and Policy," *Foreign Affairs*, XXXIV (January 1956), 188–198.

16. See Sir Anthony Buzzard et al., "The H-Bomb: Massive Retaliation or Graduated Deterrence?" *International Affairs* (London), XXXII (April 1956); and Arnold Wolfers, "Could a War in Europe Be Limited?" *Yale Review*, XLV (Winter 1956).

17. Bernard Brodie, *Strategy in the Missile Age* (Princeton, NJ: Princeton University Press, 1959), chap. 7.

18. Ibid., pp. 268–269.

19. Ibid., p. 271.

20. Ibid., pp. 272–273. As early as 1945, Brodie had observed that in the atomic age, American security made it essential "to take measures to guarantee to ourselves in case of attack the possibility of retaliation in kind." *The Absolute Weapon*, op. cit., 76.

21. Brodie, *Strategy in the Missile Age*, op. cit., p. 274.

22. Ibid., pp. 261–263.

23. Albert Wohlstetter, "The Delicate Balance of Terror," *Foreign Affairs*, XXXVIII (January 1959), 211–234.

24. Bernard Brodie, *War and Politics* (New York: Macmillan, 1973), p. 380. Brodie did not agree that the balance of terror was as *delicate* as Wohlstetter implied. "Many things are technologically feasible that we have quite good reason to believe will not happen"; ibid. Brodie's observation is correct. Nevertheless, military planners and strategic policymakers within the governments of the superpowers always showed keen concern over the need for constantly modernizing nuclear-weapons technology. The Harvard Nuclear Study Group placed the modernization of the strategic triad at the very top of its agenda for avoiding nuclear war. Graham T. Allison, Albert Carnesale, and Joseph S. Nye, Jr., eds., *Hawks, Doves and Owls: An Agenda for Avoiding Nuclear War* (New York: W. W. Norton, 1985), p. 21.

25. Herman Kahn's principal work was *On Thermonuclear War* (Princeton, NJ: Princeton University Press, 1960).

26. Bernard Brodie, *War and Politics,* op. cit., pp. 419–420.

27. Ibid., p. 126.

28. Ibid., chap. 9, "Nuclear Weapons: Utility in Nonuse."

29. Michael Howard, "Reassurance and Deterrence," *Foreign Affairs*, 61 (Winter 1982/1983), 310.

30. For an excellent summary of the development of British and U.S. official deterrence policy, including the view that the United Kingdom was the first to subscribe to it, thanks to Marshal of the Royal Air Force, Sir John Slessor, then Chairman of the Chiefs of Staff, see Michael Howard, *The Classical Strategists*, Adelphi Papers No. 54 (London: International Institute for Strategic Studies, February 1969), especially pp. 20–30.

31. Michael Howard, "Reassurance and Deterrence," op. cit., p. 312.

32. Thomas C. Schelling and Morton H. Halperin, *Strategy and Arms Control* (New York: Twentieth Century Fund, 1961), 50–54; Morton H. Halperin, *Contemporary Military Strategy* (Boston, MA: Little, Brown, 1967), pp. 19–20; Jerome H. Kahan, op. cit. p. 271. Soviet strategists appeared less interested than their American counterparts in a second strike strategy. The USSR did not achieve a significant degree of invulnerability of missile forces until the 1970s.

33. Henry A. Kissinger, *Nuclear Weapons and Foreign Policy* (cf. Note 6), p. 12.

34. For an excellent account concerning the efforts of the American intelligence community to monitor and predict the development of Soviet nuclear forces, as well as the debates over the reliability of various estimates, see Lawrence Freedman, *U.S. Intelligence and the Soviet Strategic Threat*, 2nd ed. (New York: Macmillan, 1986). See also Robert L. Pfaltzgraff, Jr., Uri Ra'anan, and Warren H. Milberg, eds., *Intelligence Policy and National Security* (London: Macmillan, 1981); Christopher Andrew and David Dilks, eds., *The Missing Dimension: Governments and Intelligence Communities* (London: Macmillan, 1984); and Jeffrey Richelson, *The U.S. Intelligence Community* (Cambridge, MA: Ballinger, 1985). Noteworthy earlier works include Sherman Kent, *Strategic Intelligence for American World Policy* (Princeton, NJ: Princeton University Press, 1966), and Lyman B. Kirkpatrick, *The Intelligence Community* (New York: Hill and Wang, 1973).

35. Walter Millis, *A World Without War* (Santa Barbara, CA: Center for Democratic Institutions, 1961).

36. Klaus Knorr, *On the Uses of Military Power in the Nuclear Age* (Princeton, NJ: Princeton University Press, 1966), and "On the International Uses of Military Force in the Contemporary World," *Orbis,* 21 (Spring 1977), 5–28; Barry M. Blechman and Stephen S. Kaplan, *Force Without War: U.S. Armed Forces as a Political Instrument* (Washington, DC: Brookings Institution, 1978); Laurence Martin, *Strategic Thought in the Nuclear Age* (Baltimore, MD: Johns Hopkins University Press, 1981); Robert Gilpin, *War and Change in World Politics* (Cambridge, England: Cambridge University Press, 1981).

37. Laurence Martin, op. cit., p. 5.

38. Ibid.

39. Ibid., p. 9.

40. See Sidney Verba, "Assumption of Rationality and Non-rationality in Models of the International System," in Klaus Knorr and Sidney Verba, eds., *The International System: Theoretical Essays* (Princeton, NJ: Princeton University Press, 1961); R. Harrison Wagner, "Deterrence and Bargaining," *Journal of Conflict Resolution,* 26 (June 1982), 329–358; Frank C. Zagare, "Rationality and Deterrence," *World Politics,* XLII(2) (January 1990), 238–260. Zagare cites Stephen J. Brams, Marc Kilgour, Bruce Bueno de Mesquita, and William Riker, among others who postulate rational behavior in their models of deterrence, 238. For the rational-actor model and Bueno de Mesquita's expected-utility model, cf. Chapters 8 and 11 in this volume.

41. Raymond Aron, *The Great Debate: Theories of Nuclear Strategy,* trans. Ernest Pawel (Garden City, NY: Doubleday, 1965), pp. 32–33; Glenn H. Snyder, *Deterrence and*

Defense: Toward a Theory of National Security (Princeton, NJ: Princeton University Press, 1961), pp. 3–16, 33–40; Richard Rosecrance, *International Relations: Peace or War?* (New York: McGraw Hill, 1974), p. 284; Leon Wieseltier, "When Deterrence Fails," *Foreign Affairs*, 63 (Spring 1985), 827–847. Wieseltier rejected the hidden apocalyptic premise in much thinking about nuclear deterrence: It "implies that the end of deterrence will be the same as the end of history. More specifically, it implies that once any nuclear weapons are used, all nuclear weapons will be used. . . . It implies, too, that immediately after deterrence fails, from the moment that a nuclear weapon is fired, there will be nothing left to save"; ibid., 829.

42. Kenneth N. Waltz, "Nuclear Myths and Political Realities," *American Political Science Review*, 84 (September 1990), 732. For a debate on the deterrent effects of nuclear weapons, see Scott D. Sagen and Kenneth N. Waltz, *The Spread of Nuclear Weapons: A Debate* (New York and London: W. W. Norton, 1995). See also L. Brito Dagobert and Michael D. Intriligator, "Proliferation and the Probability of War," *Journal of Conflict Resolution*, 40 (1), March 1996), 206–214.

43. Sagen and Waltz, ibid., p. 734. "Deterrence," Waltz held, "depends on what one *can* do, not on what one *will* do"; ibid., p. 733.

44. Robert Osgood, "Stabilizing the Military Environment," in Dale J. Hekhuis et al., eds., *International Stability* (New York: Wiley, 1964), p. 87; A. R. Hibbs, "ABM and the Algebra of Uncertainty," *Bulletin of the Atomic Scientists*, XXIV (March 1968), 31–33; D. G. Brennan, "Uncertainty Is Not the Issue," ibid., 33–34.

45. Stanley Sinkiewicz, "Observations on the Impact of Uncertainty in Strategic Analysis," *World Politics*, XXXII (October 1979), 98–99. See also the references in the text, and in Note 98, regarding the views of Richard K. Betts on the role of uncertainty in NATO's nuclear deterrent. Benjamin Lambeth noted that "a great deal of uncertainty remains about Soviet strategic uncertainty. There is much we do not know (and cannot know) about how Soviet leaders would act in the face of a major test. Uncertainty can cut two ways, depending on how the Soviet leadership perceives the risks and stakes of a situation. It could either make them hesitant or provide a powerful incentive for the leaders to seize the initiative and try to dominate the outcome before it is too late." "Uncertainties for the Soviet War Planner," *International Security*, 7 (Winter 1982–1983), 164–165.

46. For a representative sampling of the literature, see Carl Kaysen, "Keeping the Strategic Balance," *Foreign Affairs*, XLVI (July 1968), 665–675; Harold Brown, "Security Through Limitations," and Donald G. Brennan, "The Case for Missile Defense," both of which are in *Foreign Affairs*, XLVII (April 1969), pp. 422–432 and 443–448, respectively; and J. W. Fulbright et al. "Missiles and Anti–Missiles: Six Views," *Bulletin of the Atomic Scientists*, XXV (June 1969), 20–28; William R. Kintner, ed., *Safeguard: Why the ABM Makes Sense* (New York: Hawthorne, 1969); Abram Chayes and Jerome B. Weisner, eds., *ABM: An Evaluation of the Decision to Deploy an Anti-Ballistic Missile System* (New York: Harper & Row, 1969); Morton H. Halperin, "The Decision to Deploy the ABM: Bureaucratic and Domestic Politics in the Johnson Administration," *World Politics*, XXV (October 1972), 62–95.

47. U.S. Defense Secretary Robert McNamara regarded ballistic missile defense as technically and militarily ineffective, potentially destabilizing at least on the American side, and much more costly than MIRVs to saturate Soviet ballistic-missile defense.

48. Robert Jervis, chap. 1 and 2, in the book he edited with Richard Ned Lebow and Janice Gross Stein, *Psychology and Deterrence* (Baltimore, MD: Johns Hopkins University Press, 1985), especially pp. 3–12, 18–19; quoted at p. 5. Jervis adds that "in an uncertain world the utility of the rationality postulate is not undermined by the profu-

sion of cases in which the policy turns out to have been ill designed"; ibid., 6. He refers here to cases of conventional deterrence.

49. Greg Cashman, *What Causes War? An Introduction to Theories of International Conflict* (New York: Lexington Books—Macmillan, 1993), pp. 79–81.

50. Max Weber, *Economy and Society,* Vol. II, edited by Guenther Roth and Claus Wittich (Berkeley: University of California Press, 1978), pp. 973–976.

51. Christopher H. Achen, "A Darwinian View of Deterrence," in Jacek Kugler and Frank C. Zagare, eds., *Exploring the Stability of Deterrence* (Denver, CO: University of Denver School of International Studies, 1987). See also Christopher H. Achen and Duncan Snidal, "Rational Deterrence Theory and Comparative Case Studies," *World Politics,* 41 (January 1989), 143–69.

52. Robert Jervis, *The Illogic of American Nuclear Strategy* (Ithaca, NY: Cornell University Press, 1984), p. 19.

53. Robert L. Jervis, "Deterrence Theory Revisited," *World Politics,* XXXI (April 1979), 295.

54. Patrick Morgan, *Deterrence: A Conceptual Analysis,* 2nd ed. (Beverly Hills, CA: Sage, 1983), p. 13.

55. See Steven J. Brams, *Game Theory and Politics* (New York: Free Press, 1975), chap. pp. 12, 46.

56. Frank C. Zagare, "Rationality and Deterrence," *World Politics,* LXII(2) (January 1990), 238–260, cited at 241–242.

57. Ibid., 243.

58. Ole R. Holsti, *Crisis, Escalation, War* (Montreal: McGill-Queens University Press, 1972), pp. 8–9.

59. Robert L. Jervis, "Deterrence Theory Revisited," op. cit., pp. 299–300.

60. Thomas C. Schelling, *Arms and Influence* (New Haven, CT: Yale University Press, 1966), pp. 37–38.

61. Robert Jervis, "Deterrence Theory Revisited," op. cit., 302. See also Lisa J. Carlson, "A Theory of Escalation and International Conflict," *Journal of Conflict Resolution,* 39(3) (September 1995), 511–534.

62. Frank C. Zagare, "Rationality and Deterrence," op. cit., 258.

63. Ibid., 269. See also George W. Downs, "The Rational Deterrence Debate," *World Politics,* 41 (January 1989), 225–237.

64. Kennedy's ability to persuade Khrushchev to withdraw Soviet missiles from Cuba in 1962 was due not only to U.S. strategic superiority prevailing at the time, but also to U.S. local conventional military superiority in the region of critical confrontation. On the difference between deterrence and compellence, see Patrick M. Morgan, op. cit., 31; Thomas C. Schelling, *Arms and Influence,* op. cit., pp. 69–91; and the concluding chapter of Alexander George et al., *The Limits of Coercive Diplomacy* (Boston, MA: Little, Brown, 1971).

65. Robert L. Jervis, "Deterrence Theory Revisited,"op. cit., 297.

66. Ibid., 298.

67. Ibid., 292.

68. Ibid., 293.

69. Robert L. Jervis, "Deterrence Theory Revisited," op. cit., 295–296, 304. Jervis developed his analysis without substantial modification in the book he edited with Richard N. Lebow and Janice Gross Stein, *Psychology and Deterrence* (Baltimore, MD: Johns Hopkins University Press, 1985), and in "Rational Deterrence: Theory and Evidence," *World Politics,* 41 (April 1989), 183–207.

70. Paul Huth and Bruce Russett, "Testing Deterrence Theory: Rigor Makes a Difference," *World Politics,* 42 (July 1990), 466–501, especially 469–471; Richard Ned

Lebow and Janice Gross Stein, "Rational Deterrence Theory: I Think, Therefore I Deter," *World Politics,* 41 (January 1989), 208–224; and "Deterrence: The Elusive Dependent Variable," *World Politics,* 42 (April 1990), 336–369.

71. Barry Nalebuff, "Minimal Nuclear Deterrence," *Journal of Conflict Resolution,* 32 (September 1988), 411–425, quoted at 423–424.

72. Albert Wohlstetter, "Is There a Strategic Arms Race?" *Foreign Policy,* 15 (Summer 1974), 320; and "Rivals but No Race," *Foreign Policy,* ibid., 16 (Fall 1974), 48–81. Another analyst, after studying U.S. and Soviet arms expenditures over a longer period (1948–1970), attributed U.S. increases to changes in military technology, while the Soviet Union kept expanding productive capabilities at a more stable level of military technology; W. Ladd Hollist, "An Analysis of Arms Processes in the United States and the Soviet Union," *International Studies Quarterly,* 21 (September 1977), 503–528. See also Miroslav Nincic, *The Arms Race* (New York: Praeger, 1982).

73. John C. Lambelet made a persuasive case that all governments, regardless of their ideological and political goals, finally must confront the limits imposed by available resource restraints; "Do Arms Races Lead to War?" *Journal of Peace Research,* 12(2) (1975), 123–128.

74. See the following publications of the International Institute for Strategic Studies (London): *The Military Balance* for 1974–1975, pp. 4; for 1978–1979, pp. 3–4; for 1979–1980, pp. 3–4; and *Strategic Survey* for the following years: 1977, pp. 10–11; 1978, p. 6; 1979, 2, 4; and 1980–1981, pp. 3–6.

75. Fritz Ermarth, "Contrasts in American and Soviet Strategic Thought," *International Security,* 3 (Fall 1978), 138. Robert Legvold contended that while the United States had a doctrine of deterrence based on bargaining theory, the Soviet Union had no theory of deterrence, only a science of war, and regarded the sophisticated subtleties of the American strategic debate as rationales for using nuclear weapons. "Strategic 'Doctrine' and SALT: Soviet and American Views," *Survival,* 21 (January–February 1979). Soviet strategists probably did not believe that the United States would abide by its own professed second-strike doctrine in a crisis. One school of tough-minded American analysts inclined to the position that Soviet political and military leaders, while wishing to avoid general nuclear war at all costs, preferred active to passive deterrence, involving a war-fighting, war-winning, and war-recovery capability. See also Richard Pipes, "Why the Soviet Union Thinks It Could Fight and Win a Nuclear War," *Commentary,* 64 (July 1977), 21–34; John Erickson, "The Chimera of Nuclear Deterrence," *Strategic Review,* VI (Spring 1978), 11–17; Paul Nitze, "Assuring Strategic Stability in an Era of Détente," *Foreign Affairs,* 54(2) (January 1976,) 207–32; Dimitri K. Simes, "Deterrence and Coercion in Soviet Policy," *International Security,* 5 (Winter 1980–1981), 80–103. According to Leon Gouré, the Soviet strategy of deterring war by preparing to wage it requires a much greater interest on the part of military planners in problems of civil defense and postattack recovery than has been shown since the early 1960s by their American counterparts; *War Survival in Soviet Strategy: USSR Civil Defense* (Miami: Center for Advanced International Studies, University of Miami, 1976). Cf. also David Holloway, *The Soviet Union and the Arms Race* (New Haven, CT: Yale University Press, 1983), pp. 176–177.

76. United Nations General Assembly, *Comprehensive Study on Nuclear Weapons* (A/35/392) (New York: United Nations, 1980), pp. 94, 103.

77. Robert L. Jervis, "Why Nuclear Superiority Doesn't Matter," *Political Science Quarterly,* 94 (Winter, 1979–1980), 626–633. R. Harrison Wagner criticized the Jervis article on the grounds that Jervis based his analysis too much on the game of "Chicken," which Wagner deemed irrelevant to the problem of deterrence; "Deterrence Bargaining," *Journal of Conflict Resolution,* 26 (June 1982). Wagner argued that a strategy of limited nuclear exchange is a more potent deterrent than the threat of all-out

retaliation; ibid., 356. Barry M. Blechman and Robert Powell pointed out that the possession of nuclear superiority in the early 1950s probably helped President Eisenhower in his efforts to bring the Korean War to an end in 1953, but that the threats and decisions of that era have little if any relevance in the later period, when both superpowers possess nuclear capabilities ample and secure enough to withstand a first strike and still inflict devastating retaliatory destruction on the opposing society. Blechman and Powell, "What in the Name of God Is Strategic Superiority?" *Political Science Quarterly,* 97 (Winter 1982–1983), 601–602. See also Hans Bethe, "Meaningless Superiority," *Bulletin of the Atomic Scientists,* 37 (October 1981).

78. See Colin Gray, "Nuclear Strategy: The Case for a Theory of Victory," *International Security,* 4 (Summer 1979); Colin S. Gray and Keith Payne, "Victory Is Possible," *Foreign Policy,* 39 (Summer 1980). Donald W. Hanson, criticizing Colin Gray's thesis, wrote, "It is one thing to insist that deterrence can fail, as it surely could, and to argue that nuclear weapons may have to be used: that is, to posit the need for a viable employment doctrine. But it is quite another thing to claim that, because the need is there, it must be the case that a strategy for victory and survival also exists"; "Is Soviet Strategic Doctrine Superior?" *International Security,* 7 (Winter 1982–1983), 83. One might plausibly argue that military theoreticians and planners have a certain psychological need to propound a goal of victory for the sake of strategic logic and the morale of military forces, simply to avoid a sense of utter futility of a prolonged period of deterrence, and this need not be dangerous so long as the military remains under the control of rational political leaders who can calculate the political consequences of nuclear war. In any event, Hanson makes a point in positing the need for a viable employment doctrine. Michael Howard, a leading British theorist, has made the case that the West does not need a war-fighting capability, not for the purpose of trying to gain an impossible mutually annihilative victory, but one that will "set on victory for our opponent a price he cannot possibly afford to pay": "On Fighting a Nuclear War," *International Security* 5 (Spring 1981), 16. In sum, for all sensible advocates of deterrence, the only victory lies in preventing nuclear war.

79. Hank Houweling and Jan Siccama, "Power Transitions as a Cause of War," *Journal of Conflict Resolution,* 32 (March 1988), 87–102. They noted that Organski and Kugler, in *The War Ledger,* (Chicago: University of Chicago Press, 1980) had found great-power wars preceded by power transitions but Organski and Kugler had not tested to determine whether power transitions were always followed by wars. Using different measurements of power and a longer list of wars, they concluded that power transitions were significant predictors of wars.

80. *Report of the Secretary of Defense to the Congress on the FY 1975 Defense Budget* (U.S. Government Printing Office, March 4, 1974), pp. 35–41.

81. Excerpts from address by Defense Secretary Harold Brown, Naval War College, Newport, Rhode Island, August 20, 1980 "Brown Says ICBM's May be Vulnerable to the Russians Now," in *The New York Times* Section A, p. 1, August 21, 1980. According to Walter Slocombe, this country's doctrine had never been "based simply and solely on reflexive massive attacks on Soviet cities and population," despite widespread misconceptions to that effect in the past. He asserted that "previous administrations, going back almost two decades, recognized the inadequacy of a strategic targeting doctrine—a plan for use of weapons if deterrence failed—that would give us too narrow a range of employment options." He added that the "unquestioned attainment of strategic parity by the Soviet Union has underscored what was clear long before—that a policy based only on massive retaliation against Soviet cities is an inadequate deterrent for the full spectrum of potential Soviet aggressions"; "The Countervailing Strategy,"

International Security, 5 (Spring 1981), 19. During the debate that accompanied the writing of the Catholic Bishops' Pastoral Letter on War and Peace discussed in Chapter 5, National Security Adviser William P. Clark issued a statement that said in part: "For moral, political and military reasons, the United States does not target Soviet civilian population as such. . . . We do not threaten the existence of Soviet civilization by threatening Soviet cities." Defense Secretary Caspar Weinberger submitted a parallel statement. Quoted in the Pastoral Letter, note 81.

82. Richard L. Garwin, "Launch Under Attack to Redress Minuteman Vulnerability?" *International Security,* 4 (Winter 1979–1980). Albert Carnesale, Paul Doty, and others in the Harvard Nuclear Study Group also doubted that the Soviet Union would ever attack the U.S. land-based ICBM force alone (which carry fewer than a quarter of all American strategic nuclear warheads), on the expectation that the President of the United States would choose neither to launch the ICBMs on warning nor to retaliate with submarine-launched missiles after a Soviet attack on the Minuteman force. In short, the Harvard Group considered a Soviet attack on Minuteman alone unlikely; *Living With Nuclear Weapons* (New York: Bantam Books, 1983), p. 52. See also Albert Carnesale and Charles Glaser, "ICBM Vulnerability: The Cures Are Worse Than the Disease," *International Security,* 7 (Summer 1982).

83. McGeorge Bundy, "To Cap the Volcano," *Foreign Affairs,* 48 (October 1969), 9.

84. Desmond Ball, *Can Nuclear War Be Controlled?* Adelphi Papers No. 169 (London: IISS, Autumn 1981), pp. 9–14. See also Desmond Ball, "U.S. Strategic Forces: How Would They Be Used?" *International Security,* 7 (Winter 1982–1983). See also Michael Howard, "On Fighting a Nuclear War," op. cit.; Andrei Sakharov, "The Danger of Nuclear War," *Foreign Affairs,* 61 (Summer 1983), especially 1009–1011; Spurgeon M. Keeny and Wolfgang K. H. Panovsky, "MAD vs. NUTS: The Mutual Hostage Relationship of the Superpowers," *Foreign Affairs,* 60 (Winter 1981–1982); Ian Clark, *Limited Nuclear War* (Princeton, NJ: Princeton University Press, 1982); and Robert S. McNamara, "The Military Role of Nuclear Weapons," *Foreign Affairs,* 62 (Fall 1983).

85. Desmond Ball, *Can Nuclear War Be Controlled?* pp. 30–35; Raymond L. Garthoff, "Mutual Deterrence and Strategic Arms Limitation in Soviet Policy," *Strategic Review,* 10 (Fall 1982), 36–51; Richard Pipes, "Soviet Strategic Doctrine: Another View," ibid., 52–57; Gerhard Wettig, "The Garthoff–Pipes Debate on Soviet Strategic Doctrine: A European Perspective," *Strategic Review,* 11 (Spring 1983), 68–78; and Jonathan S. Lockwood, *The Soviet View of U.S. Strategic Doctrine* (New Brunswick, NJ: Transaction Books, 1983), especially chaps. 8 and 9; Klaus Knorr, "Controlling Nuclear War," *International Security,* 9 (Spring 1985), 79–98.

86. See Daniel Frei, with the collaboration of Christian Catrina, *Risks of Unintentional Nuclear War,* United Nations Institute for Disarmament Research (Totowa, NJ: Allenheld, Osmun, 1983).

87. See the references to Thomas C. Schelling in Note 32; Bernard Brodie, *War and Politics* (New York: Macmillan, 1973), pp. 396–412; Laurence M. Martin, "Changes in American Strategic Doctrine—An Initial Interpretation," *Survival,* XVI (July/August 1974); Michael J. Brenner, "Tactical Nuclear Strategy and European Defense: A Critical Reappraisal," *International Affairs* (London), LI (January 1975); *Tactical Nuclear Weapons: European Perspectives,* Stockholm International Peace Research Institute (London: Taylor and Francis, 1978).

88. Frank C. Zagare, "Rationality and Deterrence," *World Politics,* XLII(2) (January 1990), 256. Zagare notes that Robert Powell similarly suggests that escalation would not occur because both sides would be afraid of things getting out of control. "Crisis

Bargaining, Escalation, and MAD," *American Political Science Review*, 81 (September 1987), 717–735.

89. McGeorge Bundy, George F. Kennan, Robert S. McNamara, and Gerard Smith, "Nuclear Weapons and the Atlantic Alliance," *Foreign Affairs*, 60 (Spring 1982), 753–768.

90. Vincenzo Tornetta, "The Nuclear Strategy of the Atlantic Alliance and the 'no-first-use' debate," *NATO Review* (September–October 1982). See also François de Rose, "Updating Deterrence in Europe: Inflexible Response?" *Survival*, XXIV (January–February 1982), 19–23; and Henry A. Kissinger, "Strategy and the Atlantic Alliance," *Survival* XXIV (September–October, 1982), 194–200. For a contrary view, see Michael Carver, "No First Use: A View From Europe," *Bulletin of Atomic Scientists*, 39 (March 1983), 22–27.

91. Karl Kaiser, Georg Leber, Alois Mertes, and Franz-Joseph Schulze, "Nuclear Weapons and the Preservation of Peace: A Response to an American Proposal for Renouncing the First Use of Nuclear Weapons," *Foreign Affairs*, 60 (Summer 1982), 1157–1170.

92. John Keegan noted that conventional war waged with modern high-tech weaponry could produce horrors virtually indistinguishable from those of a limited war waged with low-yield nuclear weapons against military targets. "The Specter of Conventional War," *Harper's* (July 1983), 8, 10–11, 14.

93. See Peter Nailor and Jonathan Alford, *The Future of Britain's Deterrent Force*, Adelphi Papers No. 156 (London: IISS, Spring 1980); *Future United Kingdom Strategic Nuclear Deterrent Force* (London: Her Majesty's Stationery Office, July 1980). During the 1980s, plans to modernize the British and French strategic nuclear forces enhanced their deterrent credibility. See David S. Yost, *France's Deterrent Posture and Security in Europe: Parts I and II,* Adelphi Papers No. 194 and 195 (London: IISS, Winter 1984/85); John Prados, Joel S. Wit, and Michael J. Zagurek, Jr., "The Strategic Nuclear Forces of Britain and France," *Scientific American*, 255 (August 1986), 33–41.

94. John J. Mearsheimer, "Why the Soviets Can't Win Quickly in Central Europe," *International Security*, 7 (Summer 1982), 38–39.

95. See Bruce van Voorst, "The Churches and Nuclear Deterrence," *Foreign Affairs*, 61 (Spring 1983), 827–852; Jeffrey Boutwell, "Politics and the Peace Movement in Germany," *International Security*, 7 (Spring 1983), 72–93; Frits Bolkestein, "Neutralism in Europe: The Dutch Qualm Disease," *The Economist*, June 5, 1982, 43–45; and the essays in James E. Dougherty and Robert L. Pfaltzgraff, Jr., eds., *Shattering Europe's Defense Consensus: The Antinuclear Protest Movement and the Future of Europe* (Washington, DC: Pergamon-Brassey's, 1985).

96. Clay Clemens, "The Antinuclear Movement in the Netherlands: A Diagnosis of Hollanditis," in James E. Dougherty and Robert L. Pfaltzgraff, Jr., eds., *Shattering Europe's Defense Consensus,* op. cit.

97. See, for example, John J. Mearsheimer, "Manuever, Mobile Defense, and the NATO Central Fronts," *International Security*, 6 (Winter 1981), 104–23; and "Why the Soviets Can't Win Quickly in Central Europe," (Note 94), 3–40; Samuel P. Huntington, "Conventional Deterrence and Conventional Retaliation in Europe,"*International Security*, 8 (Winter 1983–1984), 32–56; General Bernard W. Rogers, "Greater Flexibility for NATO's Flexible Response," *Strategic Review*, XI (Spring 1983), 11–19. Samuel Huntington contended that NATO's traditional forward defense strategy of pure denial was not sufficient to deter, for it eased the aggressor's task of weighing the costs and gains of attack. He urged NATO to break out of its Maginot Line mentality,

and seek to deter with a nonnuclear threat of retaliatory offensive attacks into what were then East Germany and Czechoslovakia. "Conventional Deterrence and Conventional Retaliation in Europe," *International Security,* 8 (Winter 1983–1984), 32–56. The Report of the European Security Study (ESECS), *Strengthening Conventional Deterrence in Europe: Proposals for the 1980s* (New York: St. Martin's Press, 1983) concluded that deterrence could be enhanced through the development, acquisition, and deployment of emerging technologies—target-acquisition capabilities, precision-guided munitions (PGMs), etc. See also Barry R. Posen on NATO's conventional ability to prevent the Warsaw Pact forces from making a clean armored breakthrough. "Measuring the European Conventional Balance," *International Security,* 9 (Winter 1984–1985), 47–88.

98. Richard K. Betts, "Conventional Deterrence: Predictive Uncertainty and Policy Confidence," *World Politics,* 37 (January 1985), 153–179, quoted at 154–155.

99. John J. Mearsheimer, "Manuever Moble Defense and the NATO Central Front," *International Security,* 6 (Winter 1981). See also his *Conventional Deterrence* (Ithaca, NY: Cornell University Press, 1983), and "Nuclear Weapons and Deterrence in Europe," *International Security,* 9 (Winter 1984/1985).

100. Richard Ned Lebow, "The Soviet Offensive in Europe: The Schlieffen Plan Revisited?" *International Security,* 9 (Spring 1985), 78. See also Fen Osler Hampson, "Grasping for Technical Panaceas: The European Conventional Balance and Nuclear Stability," *International Security,* 8 (Winter 1983/1984), 57–82.

101. Raymond Aron, "The Evolution of Modern Strategic Thought," in *Problems of Modern Strategy: Part One,* Adelphi Papers No. 54 (London: Institute for Strategic Studies, February 1969), p. 9.

102. Ibid.

103. Claudio Cioffi-Revilla, "A Probability Model of Credibility: Analyzing Strategic Nuclear Deterrent Systems," *Journal of Conflict Resolution,* 27 (March 1983), 73–108.

104. Patrick M. Morgan, *Deterrence,* op. cit., pp. 28–43.

105. George and Smoke, *Deterrence in American Foreign Policy,* op. cit., p. 49.

106. Morgan, *Deterrence: A Conceptual Analysis,* op. cit., p. 30. Quoted by Huth and Russett in article cited in Note 107.

107. Paul Huth and Bruce Russett, "What Makes Deterrence Work? Cases from 1900 to 1980," *World Politics,* 36 (July 1984), 496–526.

108. Huth and Russett cite Bueno de Mesquita, *The War Trap* (New Haven, CT: Yale University Press, 1981), pp. 27–29. The expected-utility model is discussed in Chapters 8 and 11.

109. Huth and Russett, op. cit., 499. They later published a revised and expanded data set covering the period from 1885 to 1983 in "Deterrence Failure and Crisis Escalation," *International Studies Quarterly,* 32 (March 1988), 29–45. See also Paul Huth, "Extended Deterrence and the Outbreak of War," *American Political Science Review,* 82 (Summer 1988), 423–444; and his *Extended Deterrence and the Prevention of War* (New Haven, CT: Yale University Press, 1988).

110. Huth and Russett, "What Makes Deterrence Work?" op. cit., 523–524. The finding that the possession of nuclear weapons had little influence on the outcome should have caused no surprise because the authors exclude cases of direct deterrence between comparable nuclear powers (e.g., the Cuban Missile Crisis), and in the 1956 Suez Crisis, the United States sided with the Soviet Union against two most important U.S. allies for reasons of Middle East policy.

111. Richard Ned Lebow and Janice Gross Stein, "Deterrence: The Elusive Dependent Variable," *World Politics,* 42 (April 1990), 336–369, quoted at 337. They also note at

340 that Huth and Russett in their 1988 article eliminated 16 of their original cases, added 13 new ones, and recoded 5 of the 38 they retained, without offering explanations.

112. Lebow and Stein, ibid., 340. See also their "Rational Deterrence Theory: I Think, Therefore I Deter," *World Politics,* 41 (January 1989), 208–224.

113. Paul Huth and Bruce Russett, "Testing Deterrence Theory: Rigor Makes a Difference," *World Politics,* XLII(4) (January 1990), 466–501, especially 469 and 478–483.

114. For the variety of meanings of the term *arms control,* see Donald G. Brennan, ed., *Arms Control, Disarmament, and National Security* (New York: Braziller, 1961); Hedley Bull, *The Control of the Arms Race* (New York: Praeger, 1961), pp. 168–169; Thomas C. Schelling and Morton H. Halperin, op. cit.; J. David Singer, *Deterrence, Arms Control and Disarmament* (Columbus: Ohio State University Press, 1962); Richard N. Rosecrance, ed., *Dispersion of Nuclear Weapons* (New York: Columbia University Press, 1964); David V. Edwards, *Arms Control in International Politics* (New York: Holt, Rinehart and Winston, 1969); Franklin A. Long and George Rathjens, eds., *Arms, Defense Policy and Arms Control* (New York: W. W. Norton, 1975); Bernard Brodie, "On the Objectives of Arms Control," *International Security,* 1 (Summer 1976), 17–36. Philip Towle, *Arms Control and East West Relations* (New York: St. Martin's Press, 1983); Coit D. Blacker and Gloria Duffy, eds., *International Arms Control,* 2nd ed. (Stanford, CA: Stanford University Press, 1984); Wolfram F. Hanreider, ed., *Technology, Strategy and Arms Control* (Boulder, CO: Westview Press, 1986).

115. For background narrative and text of the Treaty Banning Nuclear Weapons Tests in the Atmosphere, in Outer Space and Under Water, see *Arms Control and Disarmament Agreements: Texts and Histories of Negotiations,* 1982 edition (Washington, DC: U.S. Government Printing Office, 1982), pp. 34–47. See also *The Nuclear Test Ban Treaty, Report of the Committee on Foreign Relations,* U.S. Senate, September 3, 1963; Harold K. Jacobson and Eric Stein, *Diplomats, Scientists and Politicians: The United States and the Nuclear Test Ban Negotiations* (Ann Arbor: University of Michigan Press, 1966); Donald G. Brennan, "A Comprehensive Test Ban: Everybody or Nobody," *International Security,* 1 (Summer 1976), 92–117; Donald R. Westervelt, "Candor, Compromise and the Comprehensive Test Ban," *Strategic Review,* V (Fall 1977), 33–44; Paul Doty, "A Nuclear Test Ban," *Foreign Affairs,* 65 (Spring 1987), 750–770; Frank von Hippel et al., "A Low Threshold Nuclear Test Ban," *International Security,* 12 (Fall 1987), 135–51; Steve Fetter, "Stockpile Confidence Under a Nuclear Test Ban," *International Security,* 12 (Winter 1987/1988), 132–167; J. Carson Mark, "Do We Need Nuclear Testing?" *Arms Control Today,* 20 (November 1990), 12–17; Diane G. Simpson, "Nuclear Testing Limits: Problems and Prospects," *Survival,* 33 (November/December 1991), 500–516.

116. The literature on the SALT process and the SALT I Accords and the SALT II Treaty is voluminous. Full texts and official backgrounds of SALT I and SALT II are in *Arms Control and Disarmament Agreements: Texts and Histories of the Negotiations* (Washington, DC: United States Arms Control and Disarmament Agency, 1990), pp. 150–176 and 261–300. See William R. Kintner and Robert L. Pfaltzgraff, Jr., eds., *SALT: Implications for Arms Control in the 1970s* (Pittsburgh, PA: University of Pittsburgh Press, 1973); George W. Rathjens, "The SALT Agreements: An Appraisal," *Bulletin of the Atomic Scientists,* 38 (June 1972), 8–10; John Newhouse, *Cold Dawn* (New York: Holt, Rinehart and Winston, 1973); Mason Willrich and John B. Rhinelander, eds., *SALT: The Moscow Agreements and Beyond* (New York: Free Press, 1974); Richard Burt, "The Scope and Limits of SALT," *Foreign Affairs,* 56 (July 1978),

751–770; James E. Dougherty, "SALT: An Introduction to the Substance and Politics of the Negotiations," in Paul H. Nitze et al., eds., *The Fateful Ends and Shades of SALT* (New York: Crane, Russak, 1979), pp. 1–36; Strobe Talbott, *Endgame: The Inside Story of SALT II* (New York: Harper & Row, 1979); Raymond L. Garthoff, "Mutual Deterrence and Strategic Arms Limitation in Soviet Policy," *International Security*, 3 (Summer 1978), 112–147; McGeorge Bundy, "Maintaining Stable Deterrence," *International Security*, 3 (Winter 1978/1979), 5–16; Michael Nacht, "In the Absence of SALT," ibid, 126–137; and Andrew Pierre, "The Diplomacy of SALT," *International Security*, 5 (Summer 1980).

117. "President's Speech on Military Spending and New Defense," *The New York Times*, Section A, p. 20 March 24, 1983. The address has been reprinted in several anthologies of nuclear-age issues. Extensive series of articles on SDI and space defense appeared in *The New York Times*, Series, "Weapons in Space: The Controversy Over Star Wars," March 3, 4, 5, 6, 7, and 8, Section A, p. 1; all 1985; and *The Christian Science Monitor*, Scott Armstrong and Peter Grier Series, "Star Wars: Will It Work?" November 4, p. 28; November 5, p. 20; November 6, p. 20; November 7, see page; November 8, p. 18; all 1985. For criticisms of space-based defense, see Richard L. Garwin et al., *The Fallacy of Star Wars* (New York: Random House, 1984); Hans Bethe et al., "Space Based Ballistic Missile Defense," *Scientific American*, 251 (October 1984), 39–49; McGeorge Bundy et al., "The President's Choice: Star Wars or Arms Control," *Foreign Affairs*, 63 (Winter 1984/1985), 26–78; Charles L. Glaser, "Do We Want the Missile Defenses We Can Build?" *International Security*, 10 (Summer 1985), 25–57. A well-balanced treatment of the technical issues may be found in Harold Brown, "Is SDI Technically Feasible?" *Foreign Affairs—America and the World 1985*, 64(3) (1986), 435–454. The most thorough technical study in the public domain is *Ballistic Missile Defense Technologies* (Washington, DC: Congress of the United States, Office of Technology Assessment, September 1985). See also Joseph S. Nye, "Arms Control After the Cold War," *Foreign Affairs*, 68 (Winter 1989/1990), 42–64; Brad Roberts, "Arms Control and the End of the Cold War," *The Washington Quarterly* (Autumn 1992), 39–56; Ivo H. Daalder, "Future of Arms Control," *Survival*, 34 (Spring 1992), 51–73.

118. Morgenthau's text, *Politics Among Nations*, Fifth edition, (NY: Alfred Knopf, 1973) and Waltz's text, *Theory of International Politics*, (Reading, MA: Addison-Wesley Publishing Company, 1979) both of which attributed stability to a bipolar structure, were discussed in Chapter 2. The views of Deutsch and Singer on multipolarity were treated in Chapter 3, along with Rosecrance's critique and preference for a bimultipolar model. For Waltz's later views on the role of nuclear weapons, see *The Spread of Nuclear Weapons: More May Be Better*, Adelphi Paper No. 171 (London: International Institute for Strategic Studies, 1981), pp. 3–8; and "The Emerging Structure of International Politics," *International Security*, 18 (Fall 1993), 44–79. All of these are summarized in Richard Ned Lebow, "The Long Peace, the End of the Cold War, and the Failure of Realism," in the Symposium on the End of the Cold War and Theories of International Relations, *International Organization*, 48 (Spring 1994), especially 252–255. See also Kenneth N. Waltz, "Nuclear Myth and Political Realities" (see Note 42 in this chapter).

119. Frank C. Zagare, "Rationality and Deterrence" (see Note 40), 48.

120. George Modelski and William Thompson, "Long Cycles and Global War," in Manus I. Midlarsky, ed., *Handbook of War Studies* (Boston: Unwin Hyman, 1989), pp. 41–42, 50–51.

121. Lebow (see Note 118), 255–259. He interprets Waltz's 1993 article (see Note 42) to mean that the "international system remains bipolar even after the breakup of the Soviet Union"; Lebow, ibid., 254.

122. Lebow, ibid., 260–268, quoted at 262.

123. Ibid., 276–277. For different realist interpretations, see Daniel Deudney and G. John Ikenberry, "The International Sources of Soviet Change," *International Security,* 16 (Winter 1991–1992), 74–118, and Stephen M. Walt, "The Renaissance of Security Studies," *International Relations Quarterly,* 35 (June 1991), 211–239. Walt notes a widespread belief that the end of the Cold War has lessened the risk of war but doubts that this is a permanent condition, for "as the war in the Persian Gulf reminds us, military power remains a central element of international politics, and failure to appreciate its importance invariably leads to costly reminders," 222.

124. See Richard Falk, *Explorations at the Edge of Time: The Prospects for World Order* (Philadelphia, PA: Temple University Press, 1992), especially pp. 146, 196, and 227; and Anatol Rapoport, *Peace: An Idea Whose Time Has Come* (Ann Arbor, MI: University of Michigan Press, 1992), especially pp. 107–108, 150, and 199.

125. John Mueller, *Retreat from Doomsday: The Obsolescence of Major War* (New York: Basic Books, 1989), p. 240.

126. Ibid., p. 94. See also Mueller's article, "The Essential Irrelevance of Nuclear Weapons: Stability in the Postwar World," *International Security,* 13 (Fall 1988), 55–79.

127. Carl Kaysen, "Is War Obsolete? A Review Essay," *International Security,* 14 (Spring 1990), 42–64, especially 43, 44, 46, 48, 62–63.

128. Ibid., 47. George Liska, in a similar vein, noted that conflict and war are still regarded as natural, even necessary, to give history a push in the proper direction. *The Ways of Power: Patterns and Meaning in World Politics* (Cambridge, MA: Basil Blackwell, 1990), p. 228.

129. Stephen Van Evera, "Primed for Peace: Europe after the Cold War," *International Security,* 15 (Winter 1990/1991), 7–57. For a lively debate about the long peace in Europe and the continued need for military defense, NATO and deterrence, see John J. Mearsheimer, "Back to the Future: Instability in Europe after the Cold War," *International Security,* 15 (Summer 1990), 5–56; Stanley Hoffmann, Robert O. Keohane, and John J. Mearsheimer, "Back to the Future, Part II: International Relations Theory and Post–Cold War Europe," *International Security,* 15 (Fall 1990), 191–199; and Bruce M. Russett, Thomas Risse-Kappen, and John J. Mearsheimer, "Back to the Future, Part III: Realism and the Realities of European Security," *International Security,* 18 (Winter 1990/1991), 216–222.

130. For an extended discussion of Cold War/post–Cold War deterrence issues reflected in this section, see Keith B. Payne, "Deterrence and U.S. Strategic Force Requirements After the Cold War," *Comparative Strategy* (July–September 1992), 269–282; Keith B. Payne and Lawrence Fink, "Deterrence: Gambling on Perfection," *Strategic Review* (Winter 1989), 25–40; Keith B. Payne, "Proliferation, Deterrence, Stability and Missile Defense," *Comparative Strategy,* 13(1) (January–March 1994), 117–130; and Keith B. Payne, *Missile Defense in the 21st Century: Protection against Limited Threats* (Boulder, CO: Westview Press, 1991), especially pp. 113–125; Lewis A. Dunn, "Deterring the New Nuclear Powers," *The Washington Quarterly,* 17(1) (Winter 1994), 5–25; Robert L. Pfaltzgraff, Jr., "Nuclear Weapons: Doctrine, Proliferation, and Arms Control," in Richard Shultz, Roy Godson, and Ted Greenwood, eds., *Security Studies for the 1990s* (Washington, DC: Brassey's [US], 1993), pp. 141–179.

131. In addition to the works cited in Notes 48–63 and 65–69, see Frank C. Zagare and D. Marc Kilgour, "Asymmetric Deterrence," *International Studies Quarterly,* 37 (1993), 1–27.

132. Fred C. Iklé, Albert C. Wohlstetter, Henry Kissinger, et al., *Discriminate Deterrence, Report of the Commission on Integrated Long-Term Strategy* (Washington, DC: U.S. Government Printing Office, January 1988).

133. From the *Commission's Summary of Findings and Recommendations,* ibid., p. i.
134. Since World War II, scores of ethnic conflicts have claimed considerably more than 10 million lives and have been extremely difficult, often impossible, either to deter or to control. Donald L. Horowitz has produced a comprehensive study of such conflicts, many of which have a potential for causing international tension and drawing major powers into confrontation; *Ethnic Groups in Conflict* (Berkeley, CA: University of California Press, 1985).
135. Paul Quinn-Judge, "With Soviet Threat Gone, U.S. Focuses on World Full of Snakes," Boston Globe, March 17, 1993, Section A., p. 20.
136. Glenn H. Snyder, *Deterrence and Defense: Toward a Theory of National Security* (Princeton, NJ: Princeton University Press, 1961), p. 4.

Chapter
10

Theories of International Cooperation and Integration

COOPERATION AND INTERNATIONAL INTERACTION

From its beginnings, the focus of international-relations theory has been the study of the causes of conflict and the conditions for cooperation. States that constitute the principal actors of the international system themselves display patterns of internal conflict and cooperation. The factors that contribute to their cohesiveness (e.g., nationalism), or to their fragmentation (e.g., ethnic conflict), are of central theoretical importance. Thus, the study of political relationships, within or among states, encompasses conflict and cooperation. Even in the anarchic society posited by classical realists and their neorealist successors, states achieve their security goals by both cooperative and conflictual means. Therefore, theories of cooperation, together with theories of conflict, form the necessary basis for a comprehensive theory of international relations.

The theoretical literature on the cooperative dimension of political relationships is extensive. Cooperation may occur as a result of adjustments in behavior by actors in response to, or in anticipation of, the preferences of other actors. Cooperation can be negotiated in a bargaining process that is explicit or tacit. Cooperation may be the result of a relationship between a stronger actor and a weaker party.[1] Hegemonic powers may provide stability that enhances the security and economic well-being of lesser states in the form of *Pax Britannica* of the nineteenth century or the more recent *Pax Americana*. The hegemonic power provides a basis for mutual gains in the form of expanding markets or military protection.[2]

Cooperation has been defined as a set of relationships that are not based on coercion or compellence and that are legitimized, as in an international organization such as the United Nations or the European Union.[3] State actors develop cooperative relationships within international organizations and within international regimes, defined as agreed rules, regulations, norms, and decision-making procedures, within which states seek to resolve issues and around which actor expectations converge. How and why states define their interests in terms that include participation in formal institutions at the international level or as part of international regimes, as well as coalitions and alliances, provides a major arena for theory building. To what extent do actors shape the institutional arrangements that are developed for cooperative purposes? By the same token, how do the institutions themselves affect the interactive behavioral patterns of their members? These questions are the object of ongoing theoretical debates, as we have noted in Chapters 2 and 3.

Cooperation may arise either from a commitment on the part of the individual to the welfare of the collectivity or as a result of perceived self-interest. The classical model for understanding the basis for cooperative behavior in pursuit of self-interest is found in the Prisoner's Dilemma game, discussed in Chapter 12, in which the two prisoners, each held in isolation from the other, have an incentive either to cooperate or defect. If they cooperate, in the sense that neither confesses to the crime, both may be freed for lack of evidence. If one confesses in the hope of a plea bargain, the other will receive a heavier sentence than the one who confesses. Under what conditions, therefore, does each have an incentive to cooperate with the other in pursuit of self-interest? By the same token, Jean Jacques Rousseau's game of "Stag Hunt" sets forth a model in which the stag is most likely to be captured if all participants in the chase work together in pursuit of their common goal.[4] If one or more participants defect, say to chase a rabbit, the stag is more likely to escape. Thus, with cooperative behavior, the stag will be subdued, and all will benefit in the form of a good meal. In both the Prisoner's Dilemma and the Stag Hunt, the key to cooperative behavior lies in the extent to which each person believes that the others will cooperate. In the absence of such an assumption about others, none of the participants is likely to do so. Thus, the central issue for a theory of cooperation, based on self-interest, is the extent to which the mutual rewards arising from cooperation can supplant a conception of interest based on unilateral action and competition. The problem may be illustrated by reference to the case in which two states maintain international trade barriers. If both remove such obstacles, each will benefit. If one nation gets rid of trade restrictions unilaterally, the other has an incentive to enter the new markets thereby provided while keeping its own domestic market closed to imports. Again, the issue is how to develop a theory of cooperation in situations, as Robert Axelrod suggests, in which self-interest is pursued in the absence of a central authority capable of enforcing cooperative behavior.[5]

Because international cooperation necessarily takes place in a decentralized setting lacking effective institutions and norms between or among culturally differentiated and geographically separated units, the need to overcome problems of inadequate information about the motivations and intentions of the various parties is substantial. Of central importance for a theory of cooperation is the extent to which the incentives for, or benefits from, cooperation can be seen to outweigh the incentives to act unilaterally. The frequent repetition of interactions, the development of greater communication and transparency between states in the form of exchanges of information about the objects of cooperation, and the development of even rudimentary institutions in which such cooperative patterns can be realized represent ingredients in a theory of cooperation based on self-interest in an anarchic international system.[6]

The theoretical discussion of international cooperation encompasses relationships between two states or relationships among larger numbers of units, known as multilateralism. Although cooperative arrangements emerge frequently between two states, a major focus of international cooperation has been multilateral. According to John Gerard Ruggie, *multilateralism* is defined as an "institutional form that coordinates relations among three or more states on the basis of generalized principles of conduct."[7] Thus the term *multilateral* so defined refers to generalized principles of conduct that may be expressed in a variety of institutional settings across a spectrum that includes international organizations, international regimes, and less concrete phenomena termed *international orders,* such as the open trading order of the late nineteenth century or in the era of the global economy of the late twentieth century. Accordingly, multilateralism, cooperation among three or more actors, may be based on a broad range of items or on specific issues. Cooperative action may take place within an institutional setting that is more or less formal, with greater or lesser numbers of agreed rules, accepted norms, or common decision-making procedures.

To return to a principal theme of this chapter, theories of cooperative behavior have as a central premise the need to understand and to develop political consensus about the basis for the institutional arrangements within which such behavior emerges and evolves. Beyond the multilateralism of international organizations, international regimes, and international actors lies the concept of political community and the process of integration by which such entities are created. What were the factors leading to the formation of the contemporary nation-state? What conditions and circumstances contribute to the building of larger integrated entities beyond the nation-state at the regional or global levels?

Integration Defined

Answers to such questions have been sought in theories of integration, another focal point of this chapter. Such theories have generally viewed integration as a *process* leading to a *condition* called "political community." For the most part, integration theorists have emphasized the integrative process at the international level as primarily consensual, or based principally on the development of shared norms, values, interests, or goals. Although political units constituting the international system within which integration takes place may have been formed by conquest, the evolution of integration beyond the nation-state is said to depend on perceived shared needs. If we begin from the basic assumption that global conquest as a basis for world order has proven impossible, it follows that the units of the international system will move toward cooperative arrangements as the basis for regional or global political community.

Although integration has been defined as a *process* leading to a form of political community, there are numerous definitions to which we turn briefly for illustrative purposes. Ernst Haas defines *integration* as a "process whereby political actors in several distinct national settings are persuaded to shift their loyalties, expectations, and political activities toward a new center, whose institutions possess or demand jurisdiction over the preexisting national states."[8] In a later work, Haas conceived of integration as referring "exclusively to a process that links a given concrete international system with a dimly discernible future concrete system. If the present international scene is conceived of as a series of interacting and mingling national environments, and in terms of their participation in international organizations, then integration would describe the process of increasing the interaction and the mingling so as to obscure the boundaries between the system of international organizations and the environment provided by their national-state members."[9]

Another integration theorist whose work is discussed in this chapter, Karl W. Deutsch, referred to political integration as a process that may lead to a condition in which a group of people has attained within a territory a sense of community and of institutions and practices strong enough to assure, for a long time, dependable expectations of peaceful change among its population.[10] Deutsch suggested that integration is a matter of fact, not of time.[11] He also maintained that political integration can be compared to power, for we recall that power can be thought of as a relationship in which at least one actor is made to act differently from the way that actor would act otherwise (i.e., if this power were absent).[12]

Implicit in theories of cooperation and integration, therefore, has been the need to explain such behavior in a decentralized systemic setting in which, nevertheless, there are issues said to have an impact on all or several parts of the globe.[13] Therefore, much discussion has been focused on the process by which integration takes place in a cooperative mode and, specifically, in functional arenas in which the need for such cooperative behavior is believed to exist. Such functions transcend the capacity of the nation-state to achieve satisfactory solutions by unilateral means. Therefore, states are said to have had an interest in cooperative relationships designed to find mutually acceptable solutions to common problems. The agenda of issues calling for cooperative action includes international trade, the environment, communications, migration, health, investment, transportation, and ecology. In contrast to issues of political–military security, or what is termed *high politics*, of principal concern to realist theory, this other agenda of issues is said to constitute *low politics*. Instead of focusing on the nature of conflict in an anarchic society, emphasis is placed on the circumstances in which states engage in cooperation in specific functions in which they have cooperative interests that cannot be addressed by the nation-state acting alone.

Writers on integration have several features in common. All are concerned with the process by which loyalty or attention is shifted from one point of focus to another. They share an interest in patterns of communications and transactions within units to be integrated. In general, integration theorists hold that persons adopt integrative behavior because of expectations of joint rewards for doing so or penalties for failing to do so. Initially, such expectations develop among elite groups, both in the governmental and the private sectors. Successful integration depends on people's ability to internalize the integrative process—that is, for member elites, rather than external elites, to assume the direction of an integrative process. Integration theorists emphasize the effect of integration in one sector on the ability of participating units to integrate in other sectors. Finally, it is broadly assumed that integration is a multidimensional phenomenon that encompasses the political, societal, cultural, and economic dimensions, leading to a sense of common identity and integrated community.

Functionalism and International Cooperation

Functionalism provides the essential basis for an understanding of much twentieth-century integration and cooperation theory. The work of David Mitrany (1888–1975) greatly influenced subsequent efforts to develop integration theory. Born in Romania, Mitrany spent most of his life in England, where he published in 1943 what became his most important theoretical contribution, *A Working Peace System*.[14] According to Mitrany, the world of the twentieth century was characterized by growing numbers of technical issues that could be resolved only by cooperative action across state boundaries. Such issues, whether within or among states, could best be addressed by highly trained specialists or technicians, rather than by politicians. Mitrany believed that the emergence of technical issues would lead first to the felt or perceived need for collaborative action, devoid of a political, or conflictual, content, and therefore assignable to technical experts whose approaches were essentially based on apolitical considerations.

According to Mitrany, such pressing problems could be addressed outside the politicized context of ideology or nationalism. By emphasizing cooperation in order to find solutions according to a specific need or function, Mitrany suggested, the basis would be created for a thickening web of structures and procedures in the form of institutions. Successful cooperation in one functional setting would enhance the incentive for collaboration in other fields. To the extent that tasks in specific functional arenas could be successfully completed, attitudes favorable to cooperation in other sectors would be developed. According to Mitrany, it was essential, through a cooperative learning process, to replace mutual suspicion with growing trust. Thus, functionalism contained the basis for what Mitrany termed *ramification*. In this sense, he was convinced that the process by which such cooperation came about as a result of perceived need in one functional task would in itself contribute to a change in attitudes in favor of even greater cooperation over a widening spectrum of issues. Such a process would not only broaden and deepen the sectors of cooperation, but also diminish prospects for, and eventually eliminate, war by a transformation in behavioral patterns from conflictual to cooperative. From functional cooperation would come necessary international institutions, in the form of organizations and regimes, based on multilateralism in the terminology of many of Mitrany's intellectual successors.[15]

Neofunctionalism

Neofunctionalism represents the intellectual descendant of functionalism. Its principal contribution lies in the elaboration, modification, and testing of hypotheses about integration. Much, but not all, of the focus of neofunctionalist theory is the European Union (EU) and, in particular, the process by which its institutions have been developed. Major emphasis is placed on the role of political parties and interest groups and the extent to which political elites in the units to be integrated support or oppose integration. Neofunctionalist theory, within its European Union context, attaches major importance to an integrative process leading ultimately to a federation or political union.[16] Neofunctionalist writings include works by Ernst Haas, Philippe Schmitter, Leon Lindberg, Joseph Nye, Robert Keohane, and Lawrence Scheineman.

Writing about the early post–World War II effort to integrate Western Europe, Ernst Haas examined the European Coal and Steel Community (ECSC). He postulated that the decision to proceed with integration, or to oppose it, depended on the expectations of gain or loss held by major groups within the unit to be integrated. "Rather than relying upon a scheme of integration which posits 'altruistic' motives as the conditioners of conduct, it seems more reasonable to focus on the interests and values defended by them as far too complex to be described in such simple terms as 'the desire for Franco-German peace' or the 'will to a United Europe.'"[17] Haas assumed that integration proceeds as a result of the work of relevant elites in the governmental and private sectors, who support integration for essentially pragmatic reasons, such as the expectation that the removal of trade barriers will increase markets and profits. Elites anticipating that they will gain from activity within a supranational organizational framework are likely to seek out similarly minded elites across national frontiers.

Moreover, as a result of a learning process, power-oriented governmental activities can evolve toward welfare-oriented action. As actors realize that their interests are best served by a commitment to a larger organization, learning contributes to integration. Conceptions of self-interest and welfare are redefined. Haas advances the corollary: "Integrative lessons learned in one functional context will be applied in others, thus eventually supplanting international politics."[18] Crucial to integration is the "gradual politicization of the actors' purposes which were initially considered 'technical' or 'noncontroversial.'"[19] The actors become politicized, Haas asserts, because, in response to initial technical purposes, they "agree to consider the spectrum of means considered appropriate to attain them."

To the functionalist proposition that a welfare orientation is achieved most readily by leaving the work of international integration to expert or technical groups, Haas offered two qualifications: (1) that such groups from a regional setting, such as Western Europe, are more likely to achieve integration than an organization with representatives from all over the world; and (2) that experts responsible to no one at the national level may find that their recommendations are ignored. Therefore, he suggested that expert managers of functionally specific national bureaucracies, joined together to meet a specific need, are likely to be the most effective carriers of integration.

Spillover and the Integrative Process

Central to Haas's work is the concept of *spillover*,[20] or what Mitrany called the "doctrine of ramification." In his examination of the ECSC, Haas found that among European elites directly concerned with coal and steel, relatively few persons were initially strong supporters of the ECSC. Only after it had been in operation for several years did the bulk of leaders in trade unions and political parties become proponents of the community. Moreover, such groups, as a result of gains that they experienced from the ECSC, placed themselves in the vanguard of other efforts for European integration, including the European Common Market. Thus, there was a marked tendency for persons who had experienced gains from supranational institutions in one sector to favor integration in other sectors. "Earlier decisions spill-over into new functional contexts, involve more and more people, call for more and more interbureaucratic contact and consultations, meeting the new problems which grow out of the earlier compromises."[21] Thus there was an expansive logic that contributed to spill-over from one sector to another. The process is one whereby the nations upgrade their national interests in a larger integrative setting.

In a study of the International Labor Organization, Haas developed a model that brought together the structural–functional analysis of general systems theory, and he refined the spillover concept found both in his earlier work and in Mitrany's writings in the form of the doctrine of ramification. Haas is concerned with the extent to which an international organization can transcend national boundaries and thus transform the international system. Governmental policies, the product of the interaction of national actors and their environment, constitute inputs into the international system. The organizations and accepted body of law form the structure of the international system. The structures receive inputs and convert them from tasks into actions. Collective decisions are the outputs of the international system. Such outputs may change the international environment in such a way as to produce either integrative or disintegrative tendencies within the international system. If the weak structures of the international system are inadequate to the tasks given them, their outputs enter an international environment in which national actors are predisposed either to strengthen or to weaken institutions for collaborative action at the international level. In either eventuality, the purposes (defined as consciously willed action patterns) of the actors are likely to produce new functions (defined as the results of actions that may bring unintended consequences). Purposes and functions may transform the international system by (1) producing a form of learning that enhances the original purposes of the actors and thus leads to integration; or (2) resulting in a learning experience that contributes to a reevaluation of purposes and thus leads to disintegration.[22]

The integration experience of Western Europe in the 1960s led Haas to modify further the spillover concept. Similarly, Philippe Schmitter has suggested that the spillover concept must be modified, refined, and qualified in a typology of strategic options available to actors. These include, besides spillover, *spill-around*—that is, an increase in the scope of functions performed by an integrative organization but not a corresponding growth in authority; a *buildup*—an increase in decisional autonomy and authority of an integrative organization, without entry into new issue areas; *retrenchment*—increases in the level of joint arbitration while reducing the authority of an integrative organization; and *spill-back*—a retreat both in scope of functions and authority of an integrative organization to a previous situation. Schmitter hypothesizes that "successive spill-overs or package deals" encompassing new issues, as well as less conspicuous forms of spill-around, may provide the basis for major strides toward political integration.[23]

Political Leadership: Implications for Sector Integration

Examining the European integration movement in the 1960s, Haas concluded that there had been some spillover. The progress of the European Common Market, in achieving such objectives as a common external tariff, uniform rules of competition, a freer market for foreign labor, and a community agricultural policy, had "come close to voiding the power of the national state in all realms other than defense, education, and foreign policy." Although major decisions are made by the Council of Ministers, which represents the member governments, the agreements reached have usually resulted in "increased powers for the Commission to make possible the implementation of what was decided."[24]

Despite these developments, Haas concluded that the "phenomenon of de Gaulle" was missing from his earlier integration framework. As French President in the 1960s, de Gaulle had imposed his national will on the development of European integration, setting back the development of supranational institutions in favor of intergovernmental cooperation, thus giving primacy to the nation-state. Events of the 1960s showed that "pragmatic interest politics concerned with economic welfare has its own built-in limits." This earlier work, it will be recalled, emphasized the development of expectations of gain among elites in the units to be integrated. The integrative experience of Western Europe after 1957 led Haas to conclude that interest based on pragmatic considerations—for example, expectations of economic gain—was "ephemeral," because it is not "reinforced with deep ideological or philosophical commitment," such as that found at the level of the nation-state and which Charles de Gaulle embodied in his persona and his conception of national policy. A political process that is "built and projected from pragmatic interests, therefore, is bound to be a frail process, susceptible to reversal." If it proves possible to satisfy pragmatically based expectations with modest advances in integration, support for dramatic integrative steps will be lacking. Herein, Haas admits, lies one of the important limitations of pragmatically based expectations of gain.[25]

By the mid-1970s, Haas had developed even greater reservations about the logic of incrementalism and spillover, especially in the EU context. For example, he saw no imminent prospect for a common monetary policy as the logical next step after the formation of a customs union and of EU agricultural policy. Although the issues confronting national governments had grown more complex and numerous, the likelihood that political elites would choose supranational solutions had not grown apace. Instead, Haas proposed a concept termed *fragmented issue linkage* that is said to occur "when older objectives are questioned, when new objectives clamor for satisfaction, and when the rationality accepted as adequate in the past ceases to be a legitimate guide to future action."[26]

Central to the integrative logic of functionalism, as we have seen, is the development of issues in which scientists and technicians play vitally important roles. It is appropriate, therefore, to examine the attitudes of scientific personnel in international organizations in order to ascertain their belief patterns with respect to the relationship between specialized knowledge and collective action for attaining economic, political, and social objectives, and to assess the extent to which international science and technology programs have increased in scope in relating specialized knowledge to growing economic, political, and social objectives. As Haas put it, "If we could say that a given idea, a certain discovery, or an identifiable network of specialists triggered the development of a political consensus, which in turn legitimated a new international program, we could make a definite observation about the impact of science on collective problem solving."[27]

The evidence available to Haas failed to yield findings of a positive nature. Haas and his associates interviewed 146 scientists in a large number of international organizations concerned with such fields as environmental protection, industrial development, and agriculture. The organizations included the European Community, the Organization for Economic Cooperation and Development (OECD), the World Bank, the World Health Organization (WHO), the Food and Agriculture Organization (FAO), the United Nations Environment Program, and the Global Environmental Monitoring System, to mention just a few. Despite their efforts, the researchers found little evidence of any widespread faith among those interviewed in the development of strengthened international institutions or the efficacy of comprehensive global, or regional, scientific–technical planning for the application of rational policies. Haas concluded that despite the growth of multilateral institutions and forums for deliberating scientific issues—and the ever-increasing importance of scientific knowledge in the late twentieth century—the power of international organizations to bring about change, or to compel members to alter their policies, remained weak.[28]

In summary, although Haas developed an integration framework that embodies features of systems theory and functionalism, he sought to point up some of the major limitations, as well as the potential utility of functionalism in explaining integration at the international level. Therefore, in his work on international organizations and integration, Haas provided a critique and elaboration of functionalist–neofunctionalist theory.

JOSEPH NYE AND NEOFUNCTIONALISM

Building on the work of Haas, and of Mitrany before him, several scholars have made an effort to refine neofunctionalist theories of integration. Among them is Joseph Nye, whose contribution lies in developing a neofunctionalist model based on "process mechanisms" and "integrative potential." Nye set forth a theoretical framework for analyzing the conditions for integration, drawn specifically from European as well as non-Western experiences that modified greatly the notions of politicization and spillover found in the writings of Mitrany and Haas.[29]

Nye suggested that neofunctionalist literature contains seven "process mechanisms," around which he reconceptualizes and reformulates neofunctionalist theory.

1. *Functionalist linkage of tasks, or the concept of spillover*—Nye holds that this mechanism has been applied, wrongly in his opinion, to include any sign of increased cooperation, arising, for example, from linkages, or relationships, among problems because of their inherent technical characteristics, or because of actual efforts by integrationist elites to cultivate spillover. Nye hypothesizes that "imbalances created by the functional interdependence or inherent linkages of tasks can be a force pressing political actors to redefine their common tasks."[30] However, such redefinition of tasks does not necessarily lead to an "upgrading of common tasks. The experience can also be negative."[31] Thus, if the linkage of tasks can cause spillover, it can also produce spill-back. (Nye's observation on this point may be applicable to the EU, where elites and interest groups benefited in the earlier stages of integration, but with economic growth, they later became reluctant to take additional integrative steps when growth rates dropped off. When growth rates declined as a result of the energy crisis of the 1970s, national protectionist sentiment flared up, and governments hesitated to upgrade common interests if they feared adverse effects on employment, inflation, payments, and monetary problems.)

2. *Rising transactions*—As noted elsewhere in this chapter, integration is hypothesized to be accompanied by an increase in transactions, including trade, capital movement, communications, and exchange of people and ideas. Political actors in a scheme for regional integration, faced with heavy demands on common institutions resulting from an increasing volume of transactions, may choose to deal with them on a strictly national basis, or they may decide to strengthen the common institutions. According to Nye, "Rising transactions need not lead to a significant widening of the scope (range of tasks) of integration, but to intensifying of the central institutional capacity to handle a particular task."[32]

3. *Deliberate linkages and coalition formation*—Here, Nye focuses once again on spillover, or what he terms *accentuated spillover,* in which "problems are deliberately linked together into package deals, not because of technological necessity, but because of political and ideological projections and political feasibilities."[33] Drawing heavily on the experience of the EU, Nye points to the efforts of politicians, international bureaucrats, and interest groups to create coalitions based on linked issues. Although such efforts may promote integration, they may have a negative effect if, for example, the political fortunes of a group supporting integration, or an issue identified with integration, decline. The extent to which integration can be broadened in appeal is a function of the extent to which a coalition in favor of integration enjoys widespread public support.

4. *Elite socialization*—Nye cites numerous examples of the growth of support for integration arising from elites who have participated actively in an integrative scheme. The extent to which national bureaucrats become participants in regional integration will determine the level of their socialization—deemed important because national bureaucrats are said to be wary of integration because of the possible loss of national control. However, if

the other process mechanisms considered by Nye do not facilitate integration, the socialization of elites, especially bureaucratic groups, in favor of regional integration may serve to isolate the elites from the mainstream of attitudes and of policy in their home countries.

5. *Regional group formation*—Regional integration is said to stimulate the creation, both formally and informally, of nongovernmental groups or transnational associations. Viewed in the context of both the EU and other settings, such as Central America and Africa, Nye asserts, such associations remain weak. Only the more general interests are aggregated by such groups at the regional level, whereas the more specific interests remain within the purview of national-level interest groups.[34]

6. *Ideological–identitive appeal*—The establishment of a sense of identity represents a powerful force in support of regional integration. According to Nye, "The stronger the sense of permanence and the greater the identitive appeal, the less willing are opposition groups to attack an integration scheme frontally."[35] Under such conditions, members are more likely than otherwise to tolerate short-term losses, and businesses are more likely to invest in the expectation that they will benefit, on a continuing basis, from the presence of a large market. However, the existence of rational integrative institutions may satisfy a "weak popular sense of regional identity."[36] The growth of ideological–identitive appeal within some groups may serve only to increase the opposition of insecure nationalist leaders and private-sector groups, especially if the perceived gains from integration at the regional level are uncertain.

7. *Involvement of external actors in the process*—To a greater extent than earlier neofunctionalist theory, Nye posits the importance of external actors and their active involvement in his neofunctionalist model as a part of the process mechanism. He notes the importance of outside governments and international organizations, as well as nongovernmental actors, as catalysts in regional integration schemes.

Central to Nye's neofunctionalist model is what he terms *integrative potential*—that is, the integrative conditions stimulated by the process mechanism. Here, he sets forth four conditions that are said to influence both the nature of the original commitment and the subsequent evolution of an integrative scheme.

1. *Symmetry or economic equality of units*—It matters not so much whether there exist core areas for integration or whether the prospective participants are relatively equal in size. Instead, a relationship is said to exist among trade, integration, and level of development, measured by per-capita income. Such compatibility appears to be important for regional integration. The size of potential participants, measured in total GNP, seems to be of relatively greater importance in integrative schemes among less developed states than in the case of highly industrialized countries. Nye hypothesizes, "It almost looks as if the lower the per capita income of the area, the greater the homogeneity in size of economy must be."[37]

2. *Elite value complementarity*—Nye acknowledges that the extent to which elite groups within integrating entities think alike is of considerable importance. In fact, he suggests that the higher the level of elite complementarity, the more likely the prospects for sustained impetus toward regional integration. However, he holds also that elites that have worked together effectively on a transnational basis may subsequently embrace divergent policies that are not conducive to integration.

3. *Existence of pluralism*—Functionally, specific diverse groups are said to enhance the likelihood of integration. Here, Nye points to a major difference between the West European experience and that of the Third World, where such groups are relatively absent. According to Nye, "The greater the pluralism in all member states, the better the conditions for an integrative response to the feedback from the process mechanisms."[38]

4. *Capacity of member states to adapt and respond*—This factor is said to depend vitally on the level of mutual responsiveness within the political units to be integrated into a larger regional entity. The higher the level of domestic stability and the greater the capacity of key decision makers to respond to demands within their respective political units, the more likely they are to be able to participate effectively in a larger integrative unit.

Next, Nye sets forth three perceptual conditions that are affected by the integrative process. They include (1) the perceived equity of distribution of benefits—with the hypothesis that "the higher the perceived equitable distribution in all countries, the better the conditions for further integration";[39] (2) perceived external cogency—that is, the perceptions of decision makers concerning their external problems, including dependence on exports, threats from larger powers, and the loss of status in a changing international system; and (3) low (or exportable) visible costs—the extent to which integration can be made to be perceived as relatively cost-free, especially in its initial phases—a concept, as Nye points out, that is central to neofunctionalist theory and strategy.

Finally, four conditions are likely to characterize the integration process over time: (1) *politicization*—the means by which problems are resolved and competing interests are reconciled, or the extent to which the resultant benefits are sufficiently widespread to ensure broadening and deepening support; (2) *redistribution,* with the crucial issue being the phasing of the changes in status, power, and economic benefits among groups within the integrating unit (central to the integrative process is the extent to which redistribution, benefiting some regions more than others, is compensated by growth to the benefit of the unit as a whole); (3) *redistribution of alternatives*—the extent to which, as the integrative process proceeds, decision makers face pressures to increase the level and the scope of integration and conclude that the alternatives to integration are less satisfactory; and (4) *externalization*—the extent to which members of an integrating unit find it necessary to develop a common position on issues in order to deal with nonmembers, as has happened with the EU in its various sets of negotiations with outside parties, including the United States. Nye hypothesizes that "the further integration proceeds, the more likely third parties will be to react to it, either in support or with hostility."[40]

A neofunctionalist model such as that developed by Nye provides a framework for comparing integrative processes in more developed and less developed regions of the world, and for assessing the extent to which microregional, or functionally specific, economic organizations hold potential for further development toward federations. More likely, neofunctionalist model building can provide, and has provided, more explicit theoretical propositions essential to understanding the limits, as well as the potential, of this segment of theory, both in explaining integration and in providing a strategy for advancing an integrative process.

Analyzing the roles, respectively, of macroregional political organizations—such as the Organization of American States (OAS), the Organization of African Unity (OAU), and the Arab League—and the microlevel economic organizations—including the European Union (EU), the Central American Common Market (CACM), and the East African Community (EAC)—Nye drew several tentative conclusions with respect to neofunctionalism. Microregional economic organizations are unlikely to develop into new units that encroach greatly on, or supersede, the existing nation-states. However, microregional economic and macroregional political organizations have contributed to the development of islands of peace in the world, and "their costs for world peace in terms of conflict creation have been less than their modest benefit to the world in conflict diversion."[41] Given the limited results of the regional organizations studied, the growth of multinational enterprises may be a more important trend in international organizations.

Although the impact of technology on existing political units is such as to reduce the autonomy of the nation-state, only a portion of its national powers are redistributed at the regional level. In summary, microregional economic organizations have strengthened functional links that in turn have improved relationships among members. Macroregional political organizations have played a constructive role in controlling interstate conflict among members, although such organizations were unsuccessful in cases of primarily internal conflict—a serious limitation, Nye admits, in light of the importance of such conflict in the late twentieth century.[42] Indeed, the point can be made, and has been, that in many countries of the world, the more immediate challenge to nationalist sentiment in recent decades, and especially since the end of the Cold War, comes from centrifugal subnational forces in favor of local autonomy, secession, expulsion of an unwanted group from the national domain, and the substitution of the domination of one ethnic, linguistic, or religious group for that of another.

TRANSACTIONS AND COMMUNICATIONS: IMPLICATIONS FOR SECURITY COMMUNITIES

Among the major contributors to integration was Karl Deutsch, who attempted to study the process by which political communities are formed, with major emphasis in his work on the development of indicators based on communication patterns and transaction flows. Deutsch drew on the mathematician Norbert Wiener's writings on cybernetics and on Talcott Parson's work on general systems discussed in Chapter 3. Deutsch quoted with approval the following passage from Wiener:

> The existence of social science is based on the ability to treat a social group as an organization and not as an agglomeration. Communication is the cement that makes organizations. Communication alone enables a group to think together, to see together and to act together. All sociology requires the understanding of communication.[43]

Communications among people can produce either friendship or hostility, depending on the extent to which the memories of communications are associated with more or less favorable emotions. Nevertheless, in Deutsch's scheme, political systems endure as a result of their ability to abstract and to code incoming information into appropriate symbols, to store coded symbols, to disassociate certain important information from the rest, to recall stored information when needed, and to recombine stored information entered as an input into the system. The building of political units depends on the flow of communications within the unit, as well as between the unit and the outside world.

Deutsch was concerned with the relationship between communications and the integration of political communities.[44] *Countries* are "clusters of population, united by grids of communication flows and transport systems, and separated by thinly settled or nearly empty territories."[45] *Peoples* are groups of persons joined together by an ability to communicate on many kinds of topics; they have complementary habits of communication. Generally, *boundaries* are areas in which the density of population and communications decline sharply. Diverse peoples become integrated as they become interdependent. "Wherever there is immediate interdependence, not for just one or two specialized goods or services but for a very wide range of different goods and services, you may suspect that you are dealing with a country."[46] Interdependence among nations is far lower than interdependence within nations. In fact, measured by foreign trade, Deutsch concluded that most countries were less interdependent in the mid-twentieth century when he wrote than they were in the nineteenth century, because trade, as a percentage of GNP, had declined.[47]

Deutsch's major substantive contribution to integration theory is found in work published in 1957, the focus of which was political community in the North Atlantic area. Deutsch and his collaborators examined ten cases of integration and disintegration at the national level.[48] Because these cases are examples of building political communities at the national level, the implicit assumption of this work is that generalizations derived from these comparative studies are relevant to understanding integration at the international level—that there are similarities between the process of community-building at the national level and doing so beyond the nation-state. Deutsch and his associates set forth two kinds of security communities: *amalgamated,* in which previously independent political units had formed a single unit with a common government; and *pluralistic,* in which separate governments retained legal independence. The nation-states the formation of which Deutsch and his associates studied are examples of an amalgamated security community, and the United States–Canada or France–Germany since World War II, which were included in the study, are pluralistic security communities.[49]

For the creation of an amalgamated security community in the cases that were studied, several conditions were found to be necessary: mutual compatibility of major values; a distinctive way of life; expectations of joint rewards, timed so as to come before the imposition of burdens from amalgamation; a marked increase in political and administrative capabilities of at least some participating units; superior economic growth on the part of some of the members, and the development of so-called core areas around which are grouped comparatively weaker units; unbroken links of social communication, both geographically between territories and between different social strata; a broadening of the political elite; increasing mobility of persons; and a multiplicity of communications and transactions.[50] Although the North Atlantic area, encompassing in this study for the most part the territory of the North Atlantic Treaty Organization, had not become an amalgamated security community, its members nevertheless had developed a conception of a security community in which "there is a real assurance that members of that community will not fight each other physically, but will settle their disputes in some other way."[51] Such a relationship was termed a *pluralistic security community*.

For the formation of pluralistic security communities, three conditions were found essential: compatibility of values among decision makers, mutual predictability of behavior among decision makers of units to be integrated,[52] and mutual responsiveness. Governments must be able to respond quickly, without resorting to violence, to the actions and communications of other governments. In a pluralistic security community, the member units forgo war as a means toward settling disputes.

In their study of political community and the North Atlantic area, Deutsch and his collaborators examined cases such as the Austro-Hungarian Empire, the Anglo-Irish Union, and the union between Norway and Sweden, in which political communities disintegrated. Several tentative conclusions emerged about conditions conducive to disintegration: (1) extended military commitments; (2) an increase in political participation on the part of a previously passive group; (3) the growth of ethnic or linguistic differentiation; (4) prolonged economic decline or stagnation; (5) relative closure of political elites; (6) excessive delay in social, economic, or political reforms; and (7) failure of a formerly privileged group to adjust to its loss of dominance.

The integrative process that was studied was found not to be unilinear in nature. The essential background conditions do not come into existence simultaneously, nor are they established in any special sequence. "Rather it appears to us from our cases that they may be assembled in almost any sequence, so long as all of them come into being and take effect."[53]

On the basis of findings concerning the building and disintegration of national units, Deutsch and his associates suggested that the North Atlantic area, "although it is far from integrated, seems already to have moved a long way toward becoming so."[54] An essential condition for greater integration in the North Atlantic area was said to lie in the development among countries of a greater volume of transactions and communications, especially those associated with expectations of gain and actual benefits in the form of economic growth. However, there was no clear indication of the overall level of such interaction deemed to be necessary for such integration or when the region encompassed by the study would actually achieve a higher level of integration.

Integration Theory: From the Single European Act to the Treaty on European Union and Beyond

Just as the post–World War II development of regional integration, especially in Europe, gave impetus to theory-building efforts, the further evolution of the European Economic Community from the Single European Act (SEA) of 1986 to the Treaty on European Union (TEU) signed in Maastricht, The Netherlands, in 1991, has provided the basis for theory extending beyond neofunctionalism.[55] The SEA set as a goal, since attained, the end of 1992 as the date for completing the internal market, or the removal of barriers to commerce within the European Economic Community, now called the "European Union" (EU). The TEU, which came into operation in 1993, extended qualified majority voting procedures in the Council of Ministers and established the framework for a common foreign and security policy, together with a phased movement toward a monetary union. Nevertheless, the TEU remains largely unfulfilled, and there have been serious challenges to its provisions in the form of referenda against it in Denmark, narrowly for it in France, deepening debates and reservations in the United Kingdom, and court challenges in Germany and the United Kingdom.

Taken together, these factors have provided the setting for a debate about the adequacy of existing integration theory, as well as an effort to develop alternative explanations about the present and emerging course of European integration. Studies of the SEA and TEU have generally concluded that, while integration theory developed in the previous two generations may hold elements of truth, it is inadequate in itself to account for the most recent phase. While neofunctionalist theory emphasizes the expansive logic (spillover) of sector integration leading to supranational institutions, the newer theoretical approaches attach great importance to policy convergence among major governments, notably the Federal Republic of Germany, France, and the United Kingdom.

Why, it is asked, did the interests of such states coincide at this time (the 1980s into the 1990s) to produce the intergovernmental consensus necessary for the SEA and TEU? According to Robert O. Keohane and Stanley Hoffmann, the answer lies in a conjunction of events, including the expansion of EU membership; agreement on the contributions by the United Kingdom to the EU budget (an issue that had proven deeply divisive in the late 1980s); the growing economic pressures on Western Europe from the world economy, leading to impetus for deregulation, transnational mergers, increased access to internal European markets; and political trends within member states, including the decision of the French Socialists to jettison much of their statist ideological baggage in favor of a market economy.[56] As a result, the EU has not evolved in accordance with the neofunctionalist or federalist transfer of power to supranational institutions. Instead, the EU represents a pooling or sharing of sovereignty, in which the national governments retain a dominant decision-making role. According to Keohane and Hoffmann, "The Community has a highly complex policymaking process in which formal and informal institutions at different levels in the formal structure—if in the formal structure at all—are linked by a variety of networks."[57]

Examining the SEA as a case study, Andrew Moravcsik and Daniel Cameron suggest that neofunctionalist theory alone cannot account for the SEA. Instead, the political consensus that led to the SEA was based on a combination of factors, including the internally generated momentum within the international institutions of the EC, as well as the broader support and impetus provided by national governments and domestic politics. According to Moravcsik, the SEA was at least as much the work of President Mitterrand, while France held the rotating presidency of the European Council in 1984, as it was the initiative of EC Commission President Jacques Delors.[58] Thus, the neofunctionalist theory that integration is the result of supranational and transnational coalitions that largely bypass national governments is found to be inadequate.

Moravcsik suggests instead that the SEA provides evidence of an integrative process based on intergovernmental institutionalism. In this model, the integrative process is characterized first by intergovernmental initiatives agreed on by the heads of government of EC states, based on negotiations and compromises reflecting the domestic constraints, pressures, and interests that each head of government brings to the table. Furthermore, according to Moravcsik, the Federal Republic of Germany, France, and the United Kingdom, as the largest of the EC members, have such great influence in the bargaining process that the resulting agreement represents their minimum common ground, with the exception of situations in which two of the largest members threaten to exclude the third. In Moravcsik's view, the member states, far from becoming peripheral to the supranational evolution of the institutions, place explicit limits on the transfer of sovereignty to the EC. Such patterns of intergovernmental behavior are said to explain the development of the SEA, including the efforts of member states since the early 1990s to block the development of a common monetary policy that would include an unacceptable diminution of national sovereignty.

Closely related is the study of the SEA by David Cameron, in which he contends that neofunctionalism and intergovernmentalism each provide the basis for synthesis about the integration process. In keeping with neofunctionalist theory, he observed substantial efforts on the part of domestic groups, especially business, to lobby at the supranational level (to go directly to the EC Commission), bypassing national governments. At the same time the intergovernmental dimension of the neorealist state as actor was present in the form of national interests, perspectives, and preferences that were reflected in the integrative process. According to Cameron, the SEA initiative came before the efforts by French President Mitterrand described by Moravcsik. Cameron's assertion that the European Council in 1981 requested from the Commission a draft report, submitted in 1982, that formed an important basis for the development of the internal market and itself building on a consensus, the origins of which can be traced to the late 1960s. Cameron emphasizes the importance of the European Council as "an extra-treaty manifestation of institutionalized intergovernmentalism."[59] Thus the European Council, the intergovernmental institutional manifestation of the European Community, became a political executive making it possible for member states "to act collectively not only to accelerate but also to control economic integration and supranational institution-building."[60]

Theoretical explanations of the integrative process in Europe since the SEA have encompassed efforts to relate international structural changes to the domestic political setting of European member states. According to Wayne Sandholtz and John Zysman, just as the post–World War II integration movement was the outgrowth of international structural changes, shifts in the global economy since the 1970s heightened the need for further European integration reflected in the SEA and TEU.[61] In response to transformed international economic structures, European elites, business groups such as multinational corporations (MNCs) and transnational mergers, and market-oriented political parties supported and strengthened efforts by the EC Commission to renew the drive for completing economic integration. As a process, economic integration proceeds as a result of a hierarchy of bargains, in which domestic political elites reach agreement on basic objectives, followed by subsidiary bargains, designed to achieve the agreed goals. The SEA, together with subsequent integrative efforts set forth in the TEU, represented the institutional manifestation of such bargains. The impetus toward a unified market in Europe came from essentially three groups: individual elites, governments, and the EC institutions. Although elites exerted influence on national governments, as well as on EC institutions, in the final analysis, it was the national governments that agreed to weighted majority voting in place of the single-state veto system at the EC level.

The integration process, in its European setting, has experienced what has been described as a stop-and-go pattern. According to classical realist theory and neorealist theory, the prospects for international integration are limited by diverging state interests in the anarchical self-help system. Contrasted is the utopian–neoliberal assumption that integration becomes increasingly feasible, if not even necessary, in a world of increasing interdependence. However, according to Gerard Schneider and Lars-Erik Cederman, the European Union has experienced both achievements and setbacks in what they describe as its "rocky history."[62] To focus on what has been accomplished or to emphasize the failures is to address the integrative process in incomplete fashion.

The development of the EU has taken place in a setting in which a majority seeking increases in integration has confronted a laggard state threatening to leave if its demands were not met. To the extent that such a state poses its exit threat under conditions of uncertainty, based on imperfect information, the integrationist majority cannot be certain of the laggard's actual intentions. If this is the case, the laggard state can push its threat to gain the most favorable terms possible from those members seeking to preserve the integrated entity.

In the case of the EU, as Schneider and Cederman suggest, France, Great Britain, and Denmark have used threats that often included full or partial exit to attain their goals. The integrationist members, confronting uncertainty, based on imperfect information, find themselves at a bargaining disadvantage toward the laggards. Making use of rational-choice modeling and game theory to study bargaining within the EU forward momentum and threatened withdrawals are examined as integral elements of the integration process. The laggard's ability to achieve bargaining goals is strengthened to the extent that the integrationist majority prefers a solution that keeps the obstructionist member within the organization rather than one that excludes it. Such a bargaining approach may characterize negotiations about the terms of membership for a state joining the EU, as well as the conditions under which it remains a member. For example, a potential member can strengthen its bargaining position if the integrationist majority is uncertain about its level of domestic support. The threat that the British Parliament would not approve the Maastricht Treaty if objectionable provisions on social policy were included gave British negotiators bargaining leverage in the negotiations.

Thus, information uncertainty about domestic support or opposition, including the possibility that a government even less committed to integration may come to office, enhances the laggard state's negotiating position. Although uncertainty in the form of imperfect information may be exploited by laggards, the effect may be to stall the integrative process, or at least to slow its momentum. How much the development of integration can be slowed, of course, depends also on the availability of information by the integrationist majority about the laggard and its commitment to its position. Is the laggard prepared to exit the integrative process if its demands are not met? If not, the bargaining advantage obviously lies with the integrationist majority. The ability to use models and gaming techniques, based on varying levels of information available to both sides about their respective bargaining goals and strategies represents a potential contribution to integration theory.

International Regimes

For purposes of cooperative action, states form international regimes such as the EU. Such regimes are characterized by varying levels of institutional development. According to Duncan Snidal, different types of regimes may yield different solutions to the same problems.[63] For example, states may find it more difficult in more integrated institutional regimes to embark on more cooperative actions for short-term benefit, while less formal structures may give greater flexibility to states. The result is differences in cooperative outcomes, depending on the nature of the institutional structure that constitutes the international regime. International regimes encompass issue areas as diverse as defense, trade, monetary policy, law, and food policy. Such entities are said to represent efforts within the international system to develop collaborative arrangements, by either formal or informal means. According to John Ruggie, who introduced the concept in 1975, an *international regime* is a set of mutual expectations, rules and regulations, plans, organizational energies and financial commitments, which have been accepted by a group of states.[64]

Subsequently, international regimes have been defined as principles, norms, rules, and decision-making procedures around which actor expectations converge in a given issue area.[65] Furthermore, regimes may be categorized according to function, on a continuum extending from specific or single issues to a diffuse, multi-issue level.[66] As Stephen D. Krasner suggests, international regimes have been said to consist of intervening variables standing between basic causal factors on the one hand and outcomes and behavior on the other. According to Krasner, *principles* represent "beliefs of fact, causation, and rectitude." *Norms* are standards of behavior defined in terms of rights and obligations. *Rules* are specific pre-scriptions or proscriptions for action. *Decision-making procedures* are prevailing practices for making and implementing collective choice.[67]

According to Oran R. Young, regimes consist of social institutions governing the actions of those interested in specifiable activities (or meaningful sets of activities), with the core element of regimes lying in a collection of rights and rules that are more or less extensive or formally articulated, but some such institutional arrangements will structure the opportunities of the actors interested in a given activity, and that exact content will be a matter of intense interest to these actors.[68] Included in the idea of international regimes is the decision-making process with respect to a particular form of activity. Within this process, actors may experience cognitive change or learning based on new information that may enhance or diminish the ability of actors to achieve their respective goals. Learning may lead actors to alter the means utilized to achieve a desired end, or learning may even result in changed objectives.[69] Thus, the regime concept encompasses both structural and process elements. Stated differently, inquiry focuses on questions associated with how and why regimes are established and what organizational or structural form they take, as well as the process by which decisions are made within them and the resulting outputs, together with the changes in international behavior that regimes may initiate or help to achieve.[70]

Regimes may be formal in nature, or they may consist of informal arrangements. Formal regimes may be the result of legislation by international organizations. Such regimes may possess governing councils and bureaucratic structures. Informal regimes may be based simply on a consensus of objectives and mutual interests among participants, resulting in ad hoc agreements. Regimes may be based on a conception of common interest in which collaboration represents an optimal strategy for participants. At the minimum, collaboration entails agreed rules to work together for certain goals and to abstain from certain actions. However, just as regimes may be based on common interest, they may also be the product of what Ernst Haas has termed *common aversion*. In such regimes, the actors do not agree on a jointly preferred outcome, but they do agree on the outcome all wish to avoid; such regimes merely require policy coordination, not collaboration.[71] Regimes may result from voluntary collaboration or cooperation. They may be based on the imposed will of a dominant power. Thus, we may speak of colonial or imperial regimes, or of the *ancien regime* in the prerevolutionary France of the eighteenth century.

Oran Young distinguishes between negotiated regimes characterized by explicit consent on the part of the participants and imposed regimes that are deliberately established by dominant actors who succeed in getting others to conform to the requirements of those orders through some combination of cohesion, cooperation, and manipulation of incentives.[72] Regimes may come into existence as a result of an agreement or a contract among the participants. Alternatively, regimes may be created either in evolutionary fashion or by dramatic unilateral action by one party that is accepted by others. Finally, actors who have formed one regime may engage in what Oran Young describes as a process of task expansion or spillover that will lead over time to the emergence of a more comprehensive and coherent regime.[73] In this respect, there exists a process similar to that described in neofunctionalist integration literature.

In this concept, regimes may be the result of the direct imposition of institutional arrangements on subordinate elements coerced into compliance. Imperial and feudal systems are said to be illustrative of such regimes. In an alternative conception, a dominant power may exert leadership in the formation and preservation of regimes that serve its interests but are also widely accepted in the international system. Thus Robert Keohane develops a regime concept based on hegemonic stability, cooperation, and collaboration. Focusing on the world political economy of the two generations after World War II, Keohane defines hegemony as possession of a preponderance of material resources—raw materials, sources of capital, control over markets, and a competitively advantageous position in the production of goods in great demand.[74] Central to Keohane's concept is what he terms cooperation after hegemony[75] at a time when the hegemonic power has declined in power and influence.

A large number of international regimes were formed under the leadership of the United States in the decades after World War II. What happens, it is asked, to such regimes when a hegemonic power loses its preponderant position? How and why do regimes that were formed as part of a relationship between a dominant power and lesser units endure after the hegemonic power has ceased to play a determinant role? According to Keohane, the answer lies in the fact that regimes are more easily preserved than created. In his words, "Cooperation is possible after hegemony not only because shared interests can lead to the creation of regimes, but also because the conditions for maintaining existing regimes are less demanding than those required for creating them."[76] Moreover, whether or not there exists a hegemonic power, international regimes, in Keohane's formulation, depend for their existence on perceived interests that are common or complementary in nature. As the hegemonic power's position is diminished, a growth in interaction among at least a few of the units of the regime may serve as a replacement or supplement leading to posthegemonic cooperation. International regimes arise from shared interests. The greater the incentives to cooperation, the more likely it is that such regimes will survive the decline of a hegemonic power.

Keohane draws a distinction between cooperation and harmony as the indispensable basis for the international regimes that he describes. Harmony is illustrated by the situation in which the pursuit of self-interest by all actors leads automatically to the achievement of all the participants' goals—much as in the case of the harmony-of-interest concept discussed in utopian theory (see Chapter 2). International regimes, especially those lacking formal structures, may be based simply on harmony, as with the market competition of the invisible hand of a classical economics model. However, cooperation represents a condition in which actor participants take steps to adapt their behavior to the needs of others by means of a process of policy coordination.

Harmony may exist even in the absence of communication among actors; cooperation is political in nature because it requires adjustment on the part of participants to the needs and interests of each other. Hence, cooperation does not assure that conflict is absent from the relationship. Instead, cooperation forms either a reaction to existing conflict or part of an effort to avoid future conflict. According to Keohane, the international-regime concept enhances our ability both to describe and to account for patterns of cooperation, and to understand the basis for discord. Such analysis leads Keohane to view international regimes as reflecting patterns of cooperation and discord over a period of time. Within the international-regime concept, such relationships can be treated as longer-term patterns of behavior rather than as isolated actors or events. According to Keohane, "By investigating the evolution of the norms and rules of a regime over time, we can use the concept of international regime both to explore continuity and to investigate change in the world political economy."[77]

Thus the regime, in keeping also with the concept articulated by Krasner earlier in this chapter, can be hypothesized as a set of intermediate factors, or intervening variables, that stand between the landscape of international politics, including especially the distribution of power, on the one hand, and the actual behavior of the basic entities, be they state or nonstate actors, on the other. To the extent that such actors, in a horizontally organized, decentralized international system, seek to evolve solutions to problems of disparate kinds, they form various types of international regimes. Thus, the emphasis of regime analysis is the state actor, inasmuch as regimes evolve within an international system in which power is diffused or concentrated. Regimes are found in international systems in which there is a broadly based distribution of capabilities—a balance of power—among a large number of states. Regimes exist, it has already been noted, in international systems in which, as was the case with Britain in the nineteenth century (*Pax Britannica*) or the United States in the twentieth century (*Pax Americana*), there is a hegemonic state. To the extent that such powers create a basis for peace and stability while furnishing rewards for cooperative behavior, they contribute to the formation of international regimes.

To the extent that its focus is state-centric, the regime concept draws on and contributes to neorealist theory (see Chapter 2). Classical realism holds that international behavior is based principally on interests and power, and that world politics is anarchic. The regime concept represents an effort not necessarily to reject such an assumption but instead to modify it. In the original realist formulation, states with competing interests may resort to conflict and ultimately war to achieve a resolution compatible with perceived needs. While realist theory did not reject the possibility of accommodation as a means of resolving differences, the regime concept adds an explicit and extended analysis of national interest and politics in which competitive elements produce cooperative behavior. In the regime concept, national interest is based on a calculus of benefits and costs, of perceived gains and risks inherent in complying with or violating the provisions, rules, and procedures set forth in a given international regime.

As Oran Young points out, like other social institutions, international regimes are products of human interactions and the convergence of expectations among groups of interested actors.[78] Thus, the regime concept may be viewed in part as an attempt to refine the realist idea of national interest to encompass the notion that, as Keohane suggests, cooperation is explicable even on narrowly self-interested, egoistic assumptions about the actors in world politics.[79] To the extent that contributors to the literature of regimes attribute the behavioral characteristics of members of regimes to the distribution of power among them (e.g., the study of hegemonic regimes), they adopt a structural-realist perspective. By the same token, to the extent that such theorists attempt to account for the persistence of regimes created during the period of a hegemonic power, they search for alternative explanations for the behavior of regimes.

If regime analysis draws on the realist tradition, it has equally important intellectual antecedents and links to the literature of systems and integration at the international level. According to Ernst Haas, regimes are supposed to help solve problems, but the problem itself is a function of how one manages the system in which something problematical is taking place.[80] Although they are in need of clarification in the regime literature, there exist such concepts and terms (familiar to systems theory) as type of regime structure, equilibrium, causation, adaptation, and learning. How do regimes, like systems, come into existence, adapt to changing environing circumstances, and engage in patterns of growth, preservation, and decline? As in the case of systems theory, such questions are posed in regime literature. Regimes are said to arise as expectations converge on a new focal point that, in turn, furnishes the basis for new institutional arrangements—a process familiar to students of neofunctionalist integration theory, described earlier in this chapter. Deeply embedded in the regime concept, as in systems and integration theory, is the idea of interdependence among the entities constituting the regime. The greater the level and range of interdependence, it has been hypothesized, the more extensive will be the shared interest in cooperation or collaboration, and hence the need to utilize existing regimes or to create new ones. Moreover, international regimes, in keeping with much of integration theory, are likely to enhance the prospects for increasing transnational flows, although the international regime itself may arise from the prior existence of such flows rather than being in itself a determining factor in their creation.

If the international system within which regimes are formed is state-centric, in the realist tradition, the regimes themselves may be said to represent nonstate actors, be they security systems such as NATO and the OAS, or economic arrangements such as the International Monetary Fund (IMF) or the EU. Although such entities are creations of the state system, they exist as actors, or regimes, in themselves. According to Krasner, regimes may assume a life of their own, a life independent of the basic causal factors that led to their creation in the first place.[81] Because regimes function as intervening variables, a change in the relative power of states may not always be reflected in outcomes. This is to suggest that once regimes are created, they may themselves alter the distribution of power among the entities that originally formed them—or changes in the power balance may not immediately be reflected in the structure and operation of the regime. Moreover, regimes may contribute to strengthening or weakening the capabilities of their members—for example, by transferring resources from one unit to another. As nonstate actors and entities furnishing a framework for cooperative or collaborative behavior, regimes have attracted the interest of students of integration at the international level. In sum, the regime concept represents not only an attempted refinement of realist theory but also an effort to address the basis for international collaborative structures and processes of immediate relevance to integration theory.

To what extent, it has been asked, does the concept of regimes represent an extension of the frontier of theory? Is it simply a reformulation of existing approaches? Does it furnish a long-term contribution to knowledge or instead form a fad that is likely to be cast aside by an emerging generation of scholars, just as its progenitors have rejected certain earlier approaches? According to Susan Strange, regime analysis contains several serious flaws, including an extensive emphasis on the states and an inadequate appreciation of the dynamic element of change at the international level. Its normative preoccupation is alleged to lie with the basis for order, or for the status quo, rather than with concepts such as justice. There is the criterion, familiar to realist theory as well, that the state-centric model is inadequate for the study of the complex and rapidly changing international system of the late twentieth century—even though the analysis of regimes represents in itself an effort to grapple with such phenomena. The concept of regimes has been faulted as well for its alleged lack of sufficient definitional precision. Regime has been used to describe explicitly agreed arrangements, decision-making procedures, international frameworks based on institutions, forms of cooperation lacking such institutional frameworks, and distributions of power with resulting forms of cooperation or collaboration among states relatively equal in capabilities between hegemonic and lesser powers.[82]

ALLIANCES

In the self-help systems described by classical realist and neorealist theory, states cooperate with each other in formal and informal arrangements—in alliances or coalitions—in order to enhance their security against actors perceived to pose a threat. Such cooperative relationships extend to other levels of analysis. At both the international and the domestic levels, groups are formed to enable their members to achieve a shared objective. Because such groups are disbanded when the objective for which they were created has been attained, they are far less enduring than the political communities, the formation and structure of which are of concern to writers whose work has been discussed earlier in this chapter. Alliances are designed to facilitate the attainment of goals by, as Robert L. Rothstein has suggested,

> introducing into the situation a specific commitment to pursue them; to a certain extent, it legitimizes that pursuit by inscribing it in a treaty; and it increases the probability that the goals will be pursued because the alliance creates a new status which makes it more difficult for the parties to renege on each other, not only because they would be dishonoring their commitment, and earning a reputation for perfidy, but also because their new status usually creates a response in the external world, such as a countervailing alliance, which would tend to strengthen the bonds in the original alliance. It may also stabilize a situation by forcing enemy decision-makers to throw another weight into the opposing scales.[83]

According to Robert E. Osgood, an alliance is a "latent war community, based on general cooperation that goes beyond formal provisions and that the signatories must continually estimate in order to preserve mutual confidence in each other's fidelity to specified obligations."[84] Thus, alliances have usually been formed in international contexts in which conflict, or the threat of conflict, is present.[85] Because of the historic importance of alliances in the international system, and the widespread use of coalitions by political groups intent on attaining elective office, such collaborative efforts have been the object of scholarly investigation, especially by the political realists examined in Chapter 3,[86] but also by writers concerned more specifically with the dynamics and the operation of alliances.

Among the theories of alliance behavior, we turn first to George Liska and William Riker. In their theoretical frameworks, Liska and Riker are similar in several respects. First, they agree that alliances or coalitions disband once they have achieved their objective, because they are formed essentially "against, and only derivatively for, someone or something."[87] Although a sense of community may reinforce alliances or coalitions, it seldom brings them into existence. In forming alliances to achieve some desired objective, decision makers weigh the costs and rewards of alignment. A decision to join an alliance is based on perception of rewards in excess of costs. Each country considers the marginal utility from alliance membership, as contrasted with unilateral action. Ultimately, the cohesiveness of an alliance "rests on the relationship between internal and external pressures, bearing on the ratio of gains to liabilities for individual allies."[88] Once costs exceed rewards, the decision to realign is made. According to Liska, nations join alliances for security, stability, and status. In Liska's theory, a primary prerequisite for alliance cohesion is the development of an alliance ideology. The function of alliance ideology is to provide a rationalization for alliance. In performing this function, ideology "feeds on selective memory of the past and outlines a program for the future."[89] Periodic consultation, especially between a leading member and its allies, both on procedural and substantive issues, contributes to the development and preservation of alliance ideology and thus alliance cohesion.

After victory, first, the size of the alliance or coalition must be reduced if additional gains are to accrue to the remaining participants. Second, alliances or coalitions are crucial to attaining a balance of power. In Riker's framework, the formation of one coalition contributes to the formation of an opposing coalition. When one coalition is on the verge of victory, neutral actors often join the weaker of the coalitions to prevent the stronger from attaining hegemony. If neutral members do not align themselves with the weaker side, some members of the leading coalition must shift to the weaker of the two coalitions if the system is to regain equilibrium. Equilibrium is the likely result of the existence of two "quasipermanent blocking coalitions," or the presence of such coalitions that "play the role of balancer if a temporary winning coalition sets the stakes too high."[90] In establishing his own rules for equilibrium, Riker draws on those set by Kaplan in his balance-of-power system.[91] Moreover, in relating alliances or coalitions to balance of power, Liska and Riker incorporate into their theories ideas found in realist international-relations theory.

The Optimum Size of Alliances

Liska and Riker suggest that alliance builders, if they act economically, do not form alliances haphazardly with all available allies. Instead, Liska considers the "marginal utility of the last unit of commitment to a particular ally and the last unit of cost in implementing commitments."[92] Riker stresses the "size principle," according to which participants create coalitions that are no larger than necessary to achieve their commonly shared objective. If actors have perfect information, they will form a coalition of exactly the minimum size needed to win. Without complete information, members of a winning coalition build a larger coalition than necessary to achieve their objectives; the less complete the information, the larger the coalition. This fact, which Riker observed at both the national and the international levels, contributes to the short life span of alliances or coalitions.

Liska and Riker address themselves to the question of rewards from joining an alliance or coalition. According to Liska, the gains and liabilities associated with alignment can be grouped into pairs. For example, the pair peculiar to security is protection and provocation—"the first to be derived from a particular alliance and the second producing counteraction and counteralliance." Burdens and gains, as well as potential for status enhancement and possible losses in capacity for independent action, must be balanced. Liska contended that "in order to assess a particular alignment all these factors must be compared with hypothetical gains and liabilities of other alignments, with nonalignment, or at least with a different implementation of an unavoidable alliance."[93] By contrast, in Riker's theory, actors join alliances or coalitions for several reasons: the threat of reprisal if they refuse to align themselves, to receive payments of one kind or another, to obtain promises about policy or subsequent decisions, or to gain emotional satisfaction.

Alliances usually encompass small powers, as well as great powers. Small states join alliances because they must rely fundamentally—and to an extent greater than large states—on other states. Great powers seek alignment with small states, both for the political and military gains afforded, and also in order to restrain the latter from certain actions.[94] However, smaller powers, Robert Rothstein notes, may prefer to align themselves with a less powerful state or with a combination of lesser states, rather than with a great power. Small-power alliances, however, are said to provide ineffective instruments if a state's goal is to increase its military strength. Their principal potential value lies in maintaining a local or regional status quo, or in resolving grievances among small powers without outside great-power intervention. Provided small powers can maintain agreement among themselves, they can make it difficult for a great power to intervene in their region.[95]

With its emphasis on international anarchy and competition among states, neorealist theory attaches major importance to alliances. The conditions under which alliances are formed, the issue of who allies with whom, and how this ratio of benefits and costs is calculated, is directly related to the structure of the international system. Therefore, alliance formation in a multipolar system differs substantially from what takes place in a bipolar system. According to Glenn H. Snyder, multipolar systems, encompassing three or more actors of approximately equal military power, having parallel or common interests but in possession of incomplete information about each other, have an incentive to come to the assistance of each other in the event of an attack by an outside party.[96] This situation arises from the likelihood that free riding or passing the buck may result in a power imbalance if one of the states is defeated and a hegemonic state emerges with increased power.

The logic of neorealist theory leads to the conclusion that states form alliances as a result of perceived benefits greater than the assumed costs. The relationship between benefits and costs will be determined by the relationship between one state's capabilities and those of its most likely opponents. The greater the gap between such resources on the part of one state compared with its anticipated enemies, the greater is the incentive to join an alliance. Once states join an alliance, there is an extensive and continuing bargaining process designed to maximize shared interest and to cope with security challenges posed by the enemy. Allies have the twin fears of defection and realignment, or what has been termed *abandonment* and *entrapment:* This alliance security dilemma leads states to become apprehensive that they will be abandoned in time of need by allies or that, as a result of action taken by an ally, they will be entrapped into fulfilling their alliance commitments under conditions deemed to be peripheral to their security. Glenn Snyder suggests that there is a perceived tradeoff between entrapment and abandonment in which allies seek to maintain an optimal balance. The less the dependence of a state on the alliance for its security, the greater is the state's likelihood of having flexibility of action and bargaining strength within the alliance.

In bipolar systems, alliance formation becomes a simpler process because the structure of the system provides little incentive for defection. In contrast to the multipolar system, alliances under conditions of bipolarity are established with a clear understanding of who is the adversary. Thus, the structure of the system provides little or no opportunity for states to defect. Allies of one superpower are not likely to switch alliances to ally with the opposing superpower, just as the two superpowers have no prospect of allying with each other. Although the fear of abandonment is low, there remains the contradictory apprehension about the possibility of abandonment as well as entrapment. In NATO Europe, for example, allies, worried that, far from abandoning them, the United States might resort to nuclear weapons resulting in their destruction or that U.S.–Soviet hostility outside Europe might somehow spill over into Europe. Paradoxically, however, Europeans sometimes worried that the United States might reduce its nuclear commitment to the extent that they would be abandoned, or that the U.S. extended-security guarantee, or nuclear umbrella, would be removed.

Under conditions of bipolarity, moreover, allies could assume diverse strategies and policies toward the common adversary. This included, as Glenn Snyder points out, détente with the Soviet Union on the part of NATO–European allies at a time, in the 1980s, when the United States and the Soviet Union were engaged in a more confrontational stance toward each other. The structural logic of bipolarity leads to a situation in which NATO–European states, whatever their flexibility in dealing with the Soviet Union, remained ultimately dependent on the United States for their security, while the United States could not afford to abandon its allies. Therefore, the potential for fracturing the alliance is far lower under conditions of bipolarity, given the dependency relationships and the absence of alignment alternatives, than in situations of multipolarity.

The recognition, set forth in classical-realist–neorealist theory and in work specifically on alliance systems, that states choose either to remain neutral or to join alliances to achieve security in a self-help system leaves unanswered the basic question of when and why they choose one course of action or the other. An effort has been made to address this issue in multipolar systems. In what they call strategies of "buck passing" and "chain ganging," Thomas J. Christensen and Jack Snyder suggest that, under conditions of multipolarity, the dilemmas of chain ganging and buck passing become evident. The relative equality of alliance partners in a multipolar system leads each to conclude that its security is inextricably intertwined with that of its alliance partners. Therefore, like the members of a chain gang, each alliance partner marches to war with an ally whose defeat would greatly diminish its own security. In other words, to the extent that the power balance deemed vital to an ally's own security will be upset by the defeat of an ally, the tendency will be to engage in chain-gang-like behavior. Thus, when Austria and Russia went to war, Germany had to follow its ally Austria for fear that Austria's defeat in World War I would have destroyed the European balance of power.

The same authors acknowledge that some states engage also in buck passing, in order to gain a free ride on other states' balancing efforts. Thus Britain and France failed to engage Hitler's Germany until it became apparent in 1939 that Russia and Germany would not balance each other. According to Christensen and Snyder, the explanation for chain-ganging and buck-passing lies in the extent to which states perceive themselves to be vulnerable.[97] The greater the vulnerability, the greater the propensity to align unconditionally and to defend an ally that is attacked. By the same token, the less the vulnerability of the state, the greater is the likelihood that it will pass the buck. When states concluded that they were vulnerable to the offensive capabilities of their enemies, they were prepared to engage in chain-ganging behavior. If they concluded that they enjoyed a defensive advantage, they preferred a strategy of buck-passing. If they had a choice, they opted to allow other states to assume the costs of balancing. When the offensive advantages available to other states were seen to increase vulnerability that could result in defeat in a short war, chain-ganging was chosen over buck-passing.

In a critique of this explanation and in an effort further to understand when and why states join alliances, it is suggested that security policy is based on alliances and armaments. According to James D. Morrow, the choice depends on the relative marginal cost of each option.[98] Under the assumption that the marginal cost of each new source of security increases as additional security is achieved through either armaments or alliances, states will opt for the means that is marginally cheaper. For example, the economic and political costs of increases in military capabilities may be such as to make more attractive the sharing of security burdens with allies. Alternatively, the commitments undertaken in alliances to defend allies may exceed the cost of relying solely on one's own military resources for national security. How nations make the necessary cost-effective trade-off between arms and allies is related to a combination of domestic costs and external benefits. Thus, it is suggested that a theory of alliance behavior must combine factors within the state, notably domestic political support and resource availability, with considerations framed by the international system within which alliances are formed.

Alliance Cohesion and Disintegration

Central to an understanding of international politics is the question of how states respond to threats and the role of alliances in their calculus of security needs. Do they attempt to find allies in an effort to achieve a balance against the party threatening them? Alternatively, do threatened states seek an accommodation with the power that poses the threat? According to Stephen M. Walt, the quest for a balance in order to achieve security from a threatening state is far more likely than a movement toward accommodation. The former he calls "balancing," while he refers to the latter as "bandwagoning."[99] A state that engages in a *balancing policy* allies itself with others against the prevailing threat; a state that embraces a *bandwagoning policy* aligns itself with the source of danger.[100] According to Walt, such a distinction is crucial because of the uncertainty that has often existed in the minds of scholars and policymakers alike concerning the response of states to the threats facing them.

In this respect, Walt, in discussing the raison d'être for the formation of alliances, places himself in fundamental agreement with traditional balance-of-power theory. For a state to align itself with the hegemonic power would be tantamount to placing its trust in the benevolence of the dominant state. Instead, states are likely to form alliances or alignments with other threatened states in order to assure their survival. Walt contends that not only is balancing more common than bandwagoning, but also that the stronger the state, the greater is likely to be its tendency to balance, or to ally, itself with other states in order to cope with the threat posed by the politically dominant power. Conversely, according to Walt, the weaker the state, the more likely it is to bandwagon instead of balancing. Such a condition is attributed to the fact that weak states can contribute little to the strength of a defensive coalition. Because they cannot affect the outcome in any event, such states are likely to choose the dominant side. A decision to join the weaker group in a quest for balance, contrasted with bandwagoning, will be taken if a state perceives that such action will turn a losing coalition into one that has the prospect of winning. To the extent that a state, by such a decision, actually contributes to the victory of an otherwise losing coalition, its influence is commensurately enhanced.

In Walt's formulation, the focus is what is termed a *balance of threat* rather than a *balance of power* as the basis for the formation of alliances at the international level. States join together in alliances in response to threats, not all of which may be based on the power of the opposing state. Thus, Walt places emphasis more on intention or ambition rather than simply on power itself as the basis for threat and thus for the response taken by balancing or bandwagoning states. Hence arises his preference for what is termed the balance of threat in place of the balance of power as the basic reason for alliance or alignment. Because threat perception strongly influences a decision to align as a basis for balancing, such a policy is likely to characterize behavior in peacetime, when the focus is deterrence, or in the early stages of a conflict, when the object is defeat of the power posing the greatest threat. As the outcome becomes more certain, lesser states are likely to defect from the losing side and thus to move toward a policy of bandwagoning with the victorious alliance. With the achievement of victory, the grouping that has defeated the would-be hegemonic power is itself likely to disintegrate.

To what extent, Walt also asks, is ideology likely to constitute a basis for alliance formation? States with similar political systems have often aligned with each other. According to Walt, the significance of ideology as a unifying factor in alliances diminishes as threat increases. Confronted with a serious challenge to their survival, states are likely to align with each other, with little regard for ideological differences. In such circumstances, pragmatic interests prevail over considerations of ideology. Thus, the more secure a state perceives itself to be in the international setting in which it finds itself, the greater will be its quest for ideologically similar or compatible postures in alliance choices. By the same token, states that are domestically unstable have a tendency to align themselves with ideologically similar states in order to bolster their internal legitimacy.

In their continuing quest for security, states are said to make choices between alliances and armaments. According to Michael F. Altfeld, such decisions are based on a calculus of cost—namely, what the decision makers must sacrifice in making the necessary choices.[101] To the extent that alliances permit a broader sharing of the cost of security among several parties, the burden to any one state is likely to be lower than what it would be to pay for security in the absence of an alliance. Because the means available to states are finite, the purchase of armaments, to the extent that it reduces total resources in the civilian economy, represents a cost factor to be calculated in the decision to establish or to join an alliance. Moreover, alliance membership can be expected to carry with it a reduction in the autonomy of a state as a result of the promise by each side contained in the alliance to take specific actions in the event of specific contingencies. Thus, several variables enter into the calculation with respect to alliance membership, based on the extent to which security can be achieved by a mix between greater or lesser levels of alignment or armaments.

Altfeld postulates conditions under which a government will be in equilibrium with respect to security, wealth, and autonomy. Of central importance is the marginal utility of alliance membership to the marginal utility of autonomy. Clearly related is the marginal utility of armaments to the marginal utility of domestic wealth. Stated simply, decision makers are likely to weigh the value of alliance against that of additional armaments, and to relate both alliance membership and armaments to the cost with reference to the lost autonomy, or independence of action, at the international level, and the price of additional armaments to the domestic economy. Similarly, in Altfeld's analysis, the dissolution of alliances can "be expected to occur in any of five circumstances: an increase in the marginal product of armaments; an increase in the marginal utility [of] autonomy; a decline in the marginal utility of civilian wealth; a decline in the marginal productivity of alliances; or a decrease in the marginal utility of security."[102]

Alliances represent formal expressions of commitment as a basis for cooperation. How alliances, once formed, are maintained and terminated has important implications for the stability of the international system. The failure of one party to fulfill its agreement to come to the aid of an attacked party is illustrative. Therefore, whether and to what extent allies can be relied on to live up to their treaty commitments is crucial to understanding the utility of alliances at the level of systemic stability and more immediately for member states themselves. Addressing the question of when and under what circumstances do alliances bind states together, Charles W. Kegley, Jr., and Gregory A. Raymond analyze alliances as promissory obligations in which states either honor commitments or fail to do so when changed circumstances render treaty compliance contrary to their national interests in an anarchical international setting.[103] Promissory obligations contained in alliances may strengthen or contribute to the development of normative premises in support of the binding nature of alliances. According to Kegley and Raymond, the greater the concentration of military capabilities, or polarity, within an international system, the greater the support for what they term binding promissory obligations. They also conclude that the greater the support for binding promissory obligations, the less is likely to be the frequency, scope, and intensity of international conflicts.

Addressing the question of what happens to alliances when interests diverge and the possibility of alliance disintegration increases, they suggest that such a condition tends to arise in the aftermath of major wars or in periods when the international distribution of power undergoes fundamental change. In such periods, states weigh their interests and values against the normative pressures underlying the alliance commitment. To the extent that normative standards supporting the sanctity of treaties outweigh pressures for nonfulfillment of obligations or alliance termination, the result will be the strengthening of what is called a "culture of trust." The expectation that agreements will be observed diminishes the prospect that potential aggressors will resort to war. According to Kegley and Raymond, "A diplomatic culture that condones broken promises and the breach of treaties is a culture likely to experience armed conflict." Thus alliances, to the extent that they produce or reflect normative standards based on commitment and cooperation, provide an important basis for international peace and stability.

INTEGRATION THEORY: PROBLEMS OF CONCEPTUALIZATION AND MEASUREMENT

As a theory of cooperation, integration lacks both a commonly accepted definition and a series of agreed indicators as a basis for measurement. As noted earlier, integration theorists have disagreed about the relative importance of such phenomena as supranational elites, international structures, intergovernmental action, and domestic political factors as catalysts for integration. In the absence of basic definitional and conceptual consensus, it is hardly surprising to find discord about the indicators by which integration could be measured. Where, for example, is the EU within an integration process leading to community? At what point, and in what sequence, do the various phenomena associated with integration assert themselves to produce an acceleration, or slowing, of the integrative momentum? How important is supranational institutionalism, contrasted with intergovernmental institutionalism, in the promotion of integration?[104]

Some writers, as we have seen, emphasize transaction flows such as trade and communications as indicators of integration. In the absence of adequate theory, the question remains whether a rise in transactions precedes, reinforces, results from, or causes integration. According to Haas, "the question of *when* these conditions are present is vital when we try to devise a rigorous theoretical framework to explain the causes of integration. Especially in the case of indicators based on social communication we must know whether the transactions measured among the elites to be integrated preceded the integrative process or whether they are present as a result of events that characterized the region after integration has occurred for several years. In the latter case, we have merely defined an existing community in terms of communications theory, but we have not explored the necessary steps for arriving there."[105]

It is not surprising that integration studies, using such indicators as a basis for measurement, have reached differing conclusions about the status of, and prospects for, integration, especially in Europe. In the mid-1960s, Deutsch, using transaction flows as one of his indicators to assess the level of European integration, concluded that "European integration has slowed since the mid-1950s and it has stopped or reached a plateau since 1957–1958." In part, he based this conclusion on the fact that since then, there had been no increases in transaction flows "beyond what one would expect from mere random probability and increase in prosperity in the countries concerned."[106] In support of his conclusion, Deutsch marshaled other evidence, including elite interviews and content analysis of selected key newspapers in France and Germany. Thus, in addition to transaction flows, statistical analysis of opinions expressed by elites and attention accorded in the media are said to form indicators of integration.

LIMITATIONS OF FUNCTIONALISM AND NEOFUNCTIONALISM

Functionalist theory has been the object of several kinds of criticisms and modifications, especially by neofunctionalists surveyed in this chapter. Among the alleged deficiencies of functionalism are the following: (1) that it is difficult, if not impossible, to separate the economic and social tasks from the political; (2) that governments have shown themselves unwilling to hand over to international authority tasks that encroach on the political; (3) that certain economic and social tasks do not spill over into the political sector; and (4) that the road to political integration lies through political acts of will, rather than through functional integration in economic and social sectors. Research conducted thus far has not produced agreement among students of integration about spillover or about the catalysts that initiate and sustain the integrative process. The extent to which there is a causal relationship or positive learning experience between integration in one sector and spillover to another sector (the expansive logic of sector integration) remains to be seen. Institutional changes in the EU since the SEA cannot be explained solely, or even largely, by spillover. How rapidly or extensively spillover from the intergovernmental bargain that gave impetus to the SEA and TEA will spill over to other sectors is still an open question.[107]

In another critique of functionalism, Charles Pentland concluded that, at least in light of the Western European experience since World War II, there is little evidence to suggest that technology and economic growth, in a shrinking world, by themselves will produce integration through functional cooperation. "The relation between functional need and structural adaptation, central to the theory, is 'necessary' only in the sense of being an ideal or norm, not in the sense of predetermining the direction of change."[108] Moreover, political influences and pressures have proven to be of major importance in shaping the integrative process in Western Europe. There has been little or nothing that is nonpolitical in nature in the European integration experience since World War II.

THE DEVELOPMENT OF THEORIES OF INTEGRATION AND COOPERATION

Although functionalism and neofunctionalism have provided dominant theories that have shaped integration studies, more recent work, as noted in this chapter, has emphasized the interplay between supranational institutionalism and intergovernmental institutionalism. Although entities beyond the nation-state in the form of international regimes, such as the EU, shape intergovernmental policies, states remain the principal actors of the international system. Therefore, bargains between states founded on conceptions of convergent national interest provide the indispensable basis for building supranational institutions, based not so much on the transfer of sovereignty to a new central authority as on its pooling or sharing by governments that remain powerfully engaged in the management of supranational institutions. Convergent national interest forms the basis for interstate bargains. In support of this proposition, it is suggested that the EU has evolved a supranational decision-making process that is the result of agreements, or bargains, reached at the intergovernmental level. Thus, the focus on integration in its supranational, neofunctional dimension has often contended with an emphasis on an intergovernmental, neorealist perspective. The experience of the SEA, reflected in the most recent integration literature, provides evidence of the need, as in the neoliberal–neorealist debate noted elsewhere in this volume, to achieve a synthesis. If both are present as part of a comprehensive theory of integration, the question becomes the synergism between the supranational and the intergovernmental. How does one shape the other, and in what sequence?

In other respects as well, integration is a multidimensional phenomenon. According to Joseph Nye, there is a need for integration to be broken down into economic, political, and legal components, which in turn might be divided into subtypes, each of which could be measured. "Rather than allowing us to talk about integration in general and confusing terms, this disaggregation will tend to force us to make more qualified, and more readily falsified, generalizations with the *ceteris paribus* clauses filled in, so to speak, and thus pave the way for more meaningful comparative analysis than that provided by the general schemes used so far."[109] The result, it is to be hoped, would be a theory that brings together in comprehensive fashion the key assumptions and factors that shape the integrative process leading to political community. Such a theory would cast light on how, why, and when groups are formed in order to create enduring communities, as well as immediate coalitions and, as a result, would form a basis for cooperative strategies and solutions to common problems.

NOTES

1. This literature includes Joseph Grieco, *Cooperation Among Nations* (Ithaca: Cornell University Press, 1990); Peter Haas, *Saving the Mediterranean* (New York: Columbia University Press, 1990); Kenneth A. Oye, ed., *Cooperation Under Anarchy* (Princeton, NJ: Princeton University Press, 1986); Duncan Snidal, "Cooperation Versus Prisoners' Dilemma," *American Political Science Review,* 79 (December 1985,) 932–42; Nicholas Bayne, *Hanging Together,* 2nd ed. (Cambridge, MA: Harvard University Press, 1987); Michael Taylor, *The Possibility of Cooperation* (Cambridge, England: Cambridge University Press, 1987); Oran Young, *International Cooperation* (Ithaca, NY: Cornell University Press, 1989); Harrison Wagner, "The Theory of Games and the Problem of International Cooperation," *American Political Science Review,* 70 (June 1983), 330–346; Joanne Gowa, "Anarchy, Egoism, and Third Images: The Evolution of Cooperation and International Relations," *International Organization,* 40 (Winter 1986), 174.
2. For a discussion of definitions, as well as recent literature on theories of cooperation, see Helen Milner, "International Theories of Cooperation among Nations: Strengths and Weaknesses," *World Politics,* 44 (April 1992), especially 467–470.
3. See, for example, A. J. R. Groom, "The Setting in World Society," in A. J. R. Groom and P. Taylor, eds., *Framework for International Cooperation* (London: Pinter Publishers, 1990), p. 3.
4. For an extensive discussion of the Stag Hunt and Prisoner's Dilemma models, see Robert Jervis, *"Cooperation under the Security Dilemma," World Politics,* 30, (2) (January 1978), 167–214.
5. Robert Axelrod, *The Evolution of Cooperation* (New York: Basic Books, 1984), pp. 6–7. See also David Kreps et al., "Rational Cooperation in the Finitely Repeated Prisoner's Dilemma," *Journal of Economic Theory,* 27 (August 1982), 245–252; and Michael Taylor, *The Possibility of Cooperation* (New York: Cambridge University Press, 1987).
6. See, for example, Geoffrey Garnett, "International Cooperation and Institutional Choice: The European Community's Internal Market," *International Organization,* 46(2) (Spring 1992), 533—557; Stephen D. Krasner, "Global Communications and National Power: Life on the Pareto Frontier," *World Politics,* 43 (April 1991), 336–366.
7. John Gerard Ruggie, "Multilateralism: The Anatomy of an Institution," in John Gerard Ruggie, ed., *Multilateralism Matters: The Theory and Praxis of an Institutional Form* (New York: Columbia University Press, 1993), p. 11.
8. Ernst B. Haas, *The Uniting of Europe* (Stanford, CA: Stanford University Press, 1958), p. 16.

9. Ernst B. Haas, *Beyond the Nation-State* (Stanford, CA: Stanford University Press, 1964), p. 29. (Italics in original.)

10. Karl W. Deutsch et al., *Political Community and the North Atlantic Area* (Princeton, NJ: Princeton University Press, 1957), p. 5.

11. Ibid., p. 6.

12. Karl W. Deutsch, *The Analysis of International Relations,* 2nd ed. (Englewood Cliffs, NJ: Prentice-Hall, 1978), pp. 198–199.

13. See, for example, A. J. R. Groom and Dominic Powell, "From World Politics to Global Governance—A Theme in Need of a Focus," in A. J. R. Groom and Margot Light, eds., *Contemporary International Relations: A Guide to Theory,* (London: Pinter Publishers Ltd, 1994), pp. 81–87.

14. David Mitrany, *A Working Peace System* (London: Royal Institute of International Affairs, 1943). Other works include David Mitrany, *The Progress of International Commitment* (New Haven, CT: Yale University Press, 1933).

15. For a succinct analysis of Mitrany's work, see Paul Taylor, "Functionalism: The Approach of David Mitrany," in A. J. R. Groom and Paul Taylor, eds., *Framework for International Cooperation* (London: Pinter Publishers, 1990), pp. 125–138. See also David Mitrany, "A Political Theory for a New Society," in A. J. R. Groom and Paul Taylor, *Functionalism: Theory and Practice in International Relations* (London: University of London Press, 1975), pp. 25–37; J. P. Sewell, *Functionalism and World Politics* (London: Oxford University Press, 1966); Paul Taylor and A. J. R. Groom, *Global Issues in the United Nations Framework* (London: Macmillan, 1989).

16. R. J. Harrison, "Neo-Functionalism," in A. J. R. Groom and Paul Taylor, eds., *Framework for International Cooperation* Second Edition (London: Pinter, 1994), pp. 138–150.

17. Ernst B. Haas, *The Uniting of Europe,* op. cit., 13. For an analysis of expectations of British official and nonofficial elite groups from European integration, see Robert L. Pfaltzgraff, Jr., *Britain Faces Europe, 1957–1967* (Philadelphia: University of Pennsylvania Press, 1969).

18. Robert Pfaltzgraff, Jr., *Britian Faces Europe 1957–1967,* p. 48.

19. Ernst B. Haas and Philippe C. Schmitter, "Economics and Differential Patterns of Political Integration: Projections about Unity in Latin America," *International Organization,* XVIII (Autumn 1964), 707. Reprinted in Haas and Schmitter, *International Political Communities: An Anthology* (New York: Doubleday, 1966), p. 262.

20. Haas refers to spill-over as "the expansive logic of sector integration," and suggests, "If actors, on the basis of their interest-inspired perceptions, desire to adapt integrative lessons learned in one context to a new situation, the lesson will be generalized"; *Beyond the Nation-State* (Stanford, CA: Stanford University Press, 1964), p. 48.

21. Ernst B. Haas, "International Integration: The European and the Universal Process," *International Organization,* XV (Autumn 1961), 372.

22. Ernst B. Haas, *Beyond the Nation-State,* op. cit., p. 81. According to Haas, "The major and perhaps the sole justification for using systems theory in the discussion of international politics is its ability to link the will of governments with the shape of the world to come. It is policy that produces the 'system,' though the system then goes on to constrain future policy or dictate its limits." Ernst B. Haas, *The Web of Interdependence: The United States and International Organizations* (Englewood Cliffs, NJ: Prentice-Hall, 1970), p. 106; and *Tangle of Hopes: American Commitments and World Order* (Englewood Cliffs, NJ: Prentice-Hall, 1969), pp. 10–12.

23. Philippe C. Schmitter, "A Revised Theory of Regional Integration," *International Organization,* 24(4) (1970), 846.

24. Ernst B. Haas, "The 'Uniting of Europe' and the Uniting of Latin America," *Journal of Common Market Studies,* V (June 1967), 324.

25. Ibid., 323–325.
26. Ernst B. Haas, "Turbulent Fields and the Theory of Regional Integration," *International Organization,* 30(2) (1976), 184.
27. Ernst B. Haas, Mary Pat Williams, and Don Babai, *Scientists and World Order: The Uses of Technical Knowledge in International Organizations* (Berkeley: University of California Press, 1977), p. 9.
28. Ibid., pp. 7, 352–355.
29. J. S. Nye, *Peace in Parts: Integration and Conflict in Regional Organization* (Boston: Little, Brown, 1971), pp. 56–58.
30. Ibid., p. 65.
31. Ibid., p. 66.
32. Ibid., p. 67.
33. Ibid., p. 68.
34. Ibid., pp. 71–72.
35. Ibid., p. 73.
36. Ibid.
37. Ibid., p. 80.
38. Ibid., p. 82.
39. Ibid., p. 74.
40. Ibid., p. 93.
41. Ibid., p. 182.
42. Ibid., pp. 172, 198–199; J. S. Nye and Donald Rothchild, "Ethnicity and Conflict Resolution," *World Politics,* XXII (July 1970), 597–616.
43. Quoted in Karl W. Deutsch, *The Nerves of Government* (New York: Free Press, 1964), p. 77. See Norbert Wiener, *Cybernetics* (Cambridge, MA: MIT Press, 1965).
44. In his work on nationalism, Deutsch wrote, "The community which permits a common history to be experienced as common is a community of complementary habits and facilities of communication. It requires, so to speak, equipment for a job. This job consists in the storage, recall, transmission, recombination, and reapplication of relatively wide ranges of information, and the 'equipment' consists in such learned memories, symbols, habits, operating preferences, and facilities as will in fact be sufficiently complementary to permit the performance of these functions. *A larger group of persons linked by such complementary habits and facilities of communication* we may call a people." *Nationalism and Social Communication* (Cambridge, MA: MIT Press, 1953), p. 96. (Italics in original.)
45. Karl W. Deutsch, "The Impact of Communications Upon International Relations Theory," in Abdul Said, ed., *Theory of International Relations: The Crisis of Relevance* (Englewood Cliffs, NJ: Prentice-Hall, 1968), p. 75.
46. Ibid., p. 76.
47. Ibid., pp. 84–90.
48. Deutsch et al., *Political Community and the North Atlantic Area,* op. cit., 58. They included the formation of the United States, its breakup in the Civil War, and the reunion that followed—the union of Scotland and England, the disintegration of the Anglo-Irish Union, German unification, Italian unification, the Hapsburg Empire, the union of Norway and Sweden, and the Swiss Confederation. Two other cases, the union of Wales and England and the formation of England itself in the Middle Ages, were studied less intensively.
49. Ibid. The reader may wish to refer to Chapter 1, where the point is made concerning John H. Herz's theory, to the effect that in the nuclear age, the ability of the territorial state to provide its citizens with a sense of security has been put in doubt. However, Deutsch's idea of a security community is that members of such a community do not

hold an expectation of war with each other, not that they are necessarily more secure against external attack inside than outside such a community.

50. Ibid.

51. Ibid., pp. 5–6.

52. This idea is similar to Parsons's social system, discussed in Chapter 3, in which persons develop expectations about each other's behavior. See chap. 4, pp. 143–145.

53. Deutsch et al., *Political Community and the North Atlantic Area,* op. cit., p. 70.

54. Ibid., p. 199.

55. This literature includes William James Adams, ed., *Singular Europe: Economy and Polity of the European Community After 1992* (Ann Arbor: University of Michigan Press, 1992); Robert Keohane and Stanley Hoffmann, eds., *The New European Community: Decisionmaking and Institutional Change* (Boulder, CO: Westview Press, 1991); Alberta Sbragia, ed., *Euro-Politics: Institutions and Policymaking in the "New" European Community* (Washington, DC: Brookings Institution, 1992); Dennis Swann, ed., *The Single European Market and Beyond: A Study of the Wider Implications of the Single European Act* (New York: Routledge, 1992).

56. Robert O. Keohane and Stanley Hoffmann, "Institutional Change in Europe in the 1980s," in Robert O. Keohane and Stanley Hoffmann, eds., *The New European Community: Decisionmaking and Institutional Change* (Boulder, CO: Westview Press, 1991), pp. 24–25.

57. Keohane and Hoffmann, ibid., p. 13.

58. Andrew Moravcsik, "Negotiating the Single European Act," in Robert Keohane and Stanley Hoffmann, eds., op. cit.

59. David Cameron, "The 1992 Initiative: Causes and Consequences," in Alberta Sbragia, ed., *Euro-Politics: Institutions and Policymaking in the "New" European Community* (Washington, DC: Brookings Institution, 1992), p. 63.

60. Ibid., p. 65.

61. Wayne Sandholtz and John Zysman, "1992: Recasting the European Bargain," *World Politics,* XLII(1), October 1989, 95–128.

62. Gerard Schneider and Lars-Erik Cederman, "The Change of Tide in Political Cooperation: A Limited Information Model of European Integration," *International Organization,* 48(4), (Autumn 1994), 633–662.

63. Duncan Snidal, "Coordination Versus Prisoners' Dilemma: Implications for International Cooperation and Regimes," *The American Political Science Review,* 79, (December 1985), 923–924. See also Arthur A. Stein, "Coordination and Collaboration: regimes in an Anarchic World," *International Organization,* 36(2) (Spring 1992), 299–324; Joseph S. Nye, Jr., "Nuclear Learning and U.S.–Soviet Security Regimes," *International Organization,* 41(3) (Summer 1987), 371–402.

64. John Gerard Ruggie, "International Responses to Technology: Concepts and Trends," *International Organization,* 29(3) (Summer 1975), 570.

65. Stephen D. Krasner, "Structural Causes and Regime Consequences: Regimes as Intervening Variables," in Stephen D. Krasner, ed., *International Regimes* (Ithaca, NY, and London: Cornell University Press, 1985), p. 1.

66. Donald L. Puchala and Raymond F. Hopkins, "International Regimes: Lessons from Inductive Analysis," in Krasner, ed., op. cit., p. 64.

67. Ibid., p. 2.

68. Oran R. Young, "International Regimes: Problems of Concept Formation," *World Politics,* XXXII(3) (April 1980), 332–333; Oran R. Young, *International Cooperation: Building Regimes for Natural Resources and the Environment* (Ithaca, NY, and London: Cornell University Press, 1989), pp. 12–13.

69. Joseph S. Nye, Jr., "Nuclear Learning and U.S.-Soviet Security Regimes," *International Organization,* 41(3) (Summer 1987), 371–401.

70. See, for example, Peter M. Haas, "Do Regimes Matter? Epistemic Communities and Mediterranean Pollution Control," *International Organization,* 43(3) (Summer 1989), 378–403.

71. Ernst B. Haas, "Words Can Hurt You; Or, Who Said What to Whom About Regimes," in Stephen D. Krasner, ed., op. cit., p. 27.

72. Oran R. Young, "Regime Dynamics: The Rise and Fall of International Regimes," in Stephen D. Krasner, ed., op. cit., p. 100.

73. Oran R. Young, "International Regimes: Problems of Concept Formation, *World Politics,*" XXXII(3) (April 1980), 349–350.

74. Robert O. Keohane, *After Hegemony: Cooperation and Discord in the World Economy* (Princeton, NJ: Princeton University Press, 1984), p. 32. For further discussion of hegemony and regimes, see Stephan Haggard and Beth A. Simmons, "Theories of International Regimes," *International Organization,* 41(3) (Summer 1987), 491–517; Oran R. Young, "International Regimes: Toward a New Theory of Institutions," *World Politics,* 39(1) (October 1986), 104–121.

75. Keohane, *After Hegemony,* p. 49.

76. Ibid., p. 50.

77. Ibid., p. 64.

78. Oran R. Young, "International Regimes: Problems of Concept Formation," XXXII(3) *World Politics* (April 1980), 348.

79. Robert O. Keohane, op. cit., p. 109.

80. Ernst B. Haas, "Words Can Hurt You; or, Who Said What to Whom about Regimes," in Stephen D. Kraser, ed., op. cit., p. 30.

81. Ibid., p. 357.

82. Susan Strange, "Cave! Hic Dragones: A Critique of Regime Analysis," in Stephen D. Krasner, ed., op. cit., pp. 337–354.

83. Robert L. Rothstein, *Alliances and Small Powers* (New York: Columbia University Press, 1968), p. 55.

84. Robert E. Osgood, *Alliances and American Foreign Policy* (Baltimore: Johns Hopkins Press, 1968), p. 19.

85. See "Introduction" in J. David Singer and Melvin Small, "Alliance Aggregation and the Onset of War, 1815–1945," in Francis A. Beer, ed., *Alliances: Latent War Communities in the Contemporary World* (New York: Holt, Rinehart and Winston, 1970).

86. See, for example, Hans J. Morgenthau, "Alliances in Theory and Practice," in Arnold Wolfers, ed., *Alliance Policy in the Cold War* (Baltimore: Johns Hopkins Press, 1959).

87. George F. Liska, *Nations in Alliance: The Limits of Interdependence* (Baltimore: Johns Hopkins Press, 1962), p. 12; William H. Riker, *The Theory of Political Coalitions* (New Haven, CT: Yale University Press, 1962), pp. 32–76. See also Bruce M. Russett, "Components of an Operational Theory of International Alliance Formation," *Journal of Conflict Resolution,* XII (September 1968), 285–301. For a selection of essays from the literature on alliances, see Julian R. Friedman, Christopher Bladen, and Steven Rosen, eds., *Alliance in International Politics* (Boston: Allyn & Bacon, 1970); Francis A. Beer, ed., op. cit. For a dyadic study (the United States and Italy), see Valentine J. Belfiglio, *Alliances* (Lexington, MA: Ginn Press, 1986).

88. Liska, op. cit., p. 175.

89. Ibid., p. 61.

90. William Riker, op. cit., p. 188. For another application of Riker's framework, see Martin Southwold, "Riker's Theory and the Analysis of Coalitions in Precolonial Africa," in

Sven Groennings, E. W. Kelley, and Michael Leiserson, eds., *The Study of Coalition Behavior: Theoretical Perspectives and Cases from Four Continents* (New York: Holt, Rinehart and Winston, 1970), pp. 336–350. For an effort to relate Riker's framework to balance-of-power literature, see Dina A. Zinnes, "Coalition Theories and the Balance of Power," ibid., pp. 351–368.

91. For an examination of Kaplan's rules for the balance-of-power systems, see Chapter 4.

92. George F. Liska, *Nations in Alliance,* op. cit., 27. See also George F. Liska, *Quest for Equilibrium: America and the Balance of Power on Land and Sea* (Baltimore: Johns Hopkins Press, 1977), p. 6.

93. George F. Liska, *Quest for Equilibrium: America and the Balance of Power on Land and Sea,* op. cit., p. 30.

94. Robert L. Rothstein, op. cit., p. 50.

95. Ibid., pp. 173–176.

96. Glenn H. Snyder, "Alliance Theory: A Neorealist First Cut," in Robert L. Rothstein, ed., *The Evolution of Theory in International Relations: Essays in Honor of William T. R. Fox* (Columbia, SC: University of South Carolina Press, 1991), pp. 83–103.

97. Thomas J. Christensen and Jack Snyder, "Chain Gangs and Passed Bucks: Predicting Alliance Patterns in Multipolarity," *International Organization,* 44(2) (Spring 1990), 138–168.

98. James D. Morrow, "Arms versus Allies: Tradeoffs in the Search for Security," *International Organization,* 47(2), (Spring 1993), 207–233.

99. Stephen M. Walt, *The Origins of Alliances* (Ithaca, NY, and London: Cornell University Press, 1987), p. 5.

100. Ibid., p. 17.

101. Michael F. Altfeld, "The Decision to Ally: A Theory and Test," *The Western Political Quarterly,* 37(4) (December 1984), 523–543.

102. Ibid., 528.

103. Charles W. Kegley, Jr., and Gregory A. Raymond, *When Trust Breaks Down: Alliance Norms and World Politics* (Columbia, SC: University of South Carolina Press, 1990).

104. See, for example, Joseph S. Nye, Jr., "Comparative Regional Integration: Concept and Measurement," *International Organization,* XXII (Autumn 1968), 857. For a collection of contemporary writings on integration at the international level, see, by the same author, *International Regionalism: Readings* (Boston: Little, Brown, 1968).

105. Ernst B. Haas, "The Challenge of Regionalism," *International Organization,* XII (Autumn 1958), 445.

106. Karl W. Deutsch, France, *Germany and the Western Alliance* (New York: Scribner's, 1967), pp. 218–220. Deutsch bases his findings on the Relative Acceptance Index, which purports to separate "the actual results of preferential behavior and structural integration from the mere effects of the size and prosperity of the country."

107. Robert O. Keohane and Stanley Hoffmann, "Institutional Change in Europe in the 1980s," in Keohane and Hoffmann, eds., *The New European Community: Decision-making and Institutional Change* (Boulder, CO: Westview Press, 1991), 18–20.

108. Charles Pentland, *International Theory and European Integration* (London: Faber and Faber, 1973), p. 98.

109. Joseph S. Nye, Jr., "Comparative Regional Integration: Concept and Measurement," XXII, *International Organization* (Autumn 1968), 858.

Chapter
11

Decision-Making Theories

DECISION-MAKING ANALYSIS: ITS NATURE AND ORIGINS

Decisions are, in David Easton's terminology, the outputs of the political system, by which values are authoritatively allocated within a society. The concept of decision making had long been implicit in some of the older approaches to diplomatic history and the study of political institutions. The study of how decisions are made first became the subject of systematic investigation in other fields outside of political science. Psychologists were interested in the motives underlying an individual's decisions and why some persons had greater difficulty than others in making decisions. Economists focused on the decisions of producers, consumers, investors, and others whose choices affected the economy. Business-administration theorists sought to analyze and increase the efficiency of executive decision making. In government and especially in defense planning in the 1960s, techniques known generally as "cost effectiveness" were utilized in the decision making process, such-as in regard to the acquisition of new weapons systems. Decision making was a focal point for political scientists interested in analyzing the decisional behavior of voters, legislators, executive officials, politicians, leaders of interest groups, and other actors in the political arena.[1] Thus, the study of foreign-policy decision making concentrated on one segment of a more general phenomenon of interest to the social sciences and to policymakers. Because many analysts have concerned themselves with decision making in crisis situations, the latter part of the chapter deals with that subject.

Decision making is simply the act of choosing among available alternatives about which uncertainty exists. In foreign policy, perhaps even more than in national politics—because the terrain of the former is usually less familiar—policy alternatives are seldom explicitly "given." They must often be gropingly formulated in the context of a total situation in which disagreements will arise over which estimate of the situation is most valid, what alternatives exist, the consequences likely to flow from various choices, and the values that should serve as criteria for ranking the various alternatives from most to least preferred. There are controversies both over the nature of the decision-making process and over the appropriate paradigms for its study. However, decision making has been studied not only as mere abstract choice among possible maximum-utility alternatives to decision making but also as an incremental process containing partial choices and compromises among competing organizational interests and bureaucratic pressures.

APPROACHES TO DECISION-MAKING THEORY

The decision-making approach to an understanding of international politics is not novel. Twenty-four centuries ago, the Greek historian Thucydides, in his *Peloponnesian War,* examined the factors that led the leaders of city-states to decide the issues of war and peace, as well as alliance and empire, with as great precision as they did under the circumstances confronting them. He focused not only on the conscious reasons for stateleaders' choices and their perceptions of the systemic environment—both of which are reflected in the speeches he attributes to them—but also on the deeper psychological forces of fear, honor, and interest that in varying combinations motivated them as individuals and set the prevailing tone of their particular societies. Thus, Thucydides was indeed an early student of decision making (see Note 15 in Chapter 1).

Decision-making (DM) theory identifies a large number of relevant variables, and it suggests possible interrelationships among these variables. DM theory (as we refer to it here) marks a significant shift from traditional political analysis in which writers sometimes have been prone to reify or personify nation-states as the basic actors within the international system. DM theory directs attention not to states as metaphysical abstractions, or to governments, or even to such broadly labeled institutions as "the executive," but instead seeks to highlight the behavior of the specific human decision makers who actually shape governmental policy. As Richard Snyder, H. W. Bruck, and Burton Sapin put it, "It is one of our basic methodological choices to define the state as its official decision-makers—those whose authoritative acts are, to all intents and purposes, the acts of the state. State action is the action taken by those acting in the name of the state."[2] By narrowing the subject of investigation from a larger collectivity to a smaller unit of persons responsible for decisions, DM theorists hope to make the locus of political analysis more concrete and more precise, and thus more amenable to systematic analysis. Nevertheless, it is assumed that decision makers act within a total perceived environment that includes their national political system, as well as the international system as a whole—an internal environment as well as an external environment.

Perception is assigned a central place in DM theory. When dealing with the definition of the situation, most DM theorists regard the world as viewed by decision makers to be more important than objective reality. Robert Jervis observed that the tendency toward egocentric perception makes leaders interpret their own decisions as responses to objective conditions, while attributing the actions of foreign rivals to a hostile disposition.[3] They thereby accept the distinction drawn by Harold and Margaret Sprout between the psychomilieu and the operational milieu (discussed in Chapter 2). Joseph Frankel, however, argues that DM theory must take the objective environment into account, for even though factors not present in the minds of policymakers cannot influence their choices, such factors may be important insofar as they set limits to the outcome of their decisions.[4] Similarly, Michael Brecher insists that "the operational environment affects the results or outcomes of decisions directly but influences the choice among policy options, that is, the decisions themselves, only as it is filtered through the images of decision-makers."[5]

The Decision Situation (or Occasion)[6]

Braybrooke and Lindblom suggest that decision making, although it cannot be fully identified with rational problem solving, nevertheless may be generally equated with it.[7] The question now arises as to how decision makers define the situation in relation to the problem confronting them. How do they see objects, conditions, other actors, and their intentions? How do they define the goals of their own government? What values strike them as most important, not in the abstract but insofar as they appear to be at stake in this particular situation?

Snyder observes that some situations are more highly structured than others. Some are readily grasped in their meaning, whereas others may be more fluctuating and ambiguous. The urgency of situations, or the pressure to take action, will also vary widely. Whether a problem is considered primarily political, economic, military, social, or cultural will normally have implications for how it is to be handled and by whom. It is difficult, out of the welter of opinions from professional diplomats, scholars, journalists, and others, to arrive at a relatively accurate assessment of the various trends and forces active in a foreign situation (and here foreign-policy decision making is probably more complex than is domestic, especially in times of international crisis, when the decision maker's span of attention may be stretched to the limit). Analyzing another state's intentions can be even more treacherous. Decision makers in one state, anticipating a policy initiative by their counterparts in another, may regard their own move to deter or preclude as a purely defensive response, but these measures might seem offensive to their foreign counterparts, as we noted in Chapter 8.

BUREAUCRATIC POLITICS

We have referred to the hypothesized tendency of decision makers to allow their conceptions of national interest to be colored by their perceptions of what is good for their own bureaucratic unit. The importance of bureaucracies has long been recognized by students of politics. Max Weber, without demeaning the notion of leadership, wrote, "In a modern state the actual ruler is necessarily and unavoidably the bureaucracy, since power is exercised neither through parliamentary speeches nor monarchical enunciations but through the routines of administration."[8] Although Weber wrote about the era before the 1920s, his work contains antecedents for understanding bureaucratic structures and decision making in the late twentieth century.

As Weber points out, in all advanced political systems and economies, there arise bureaucratic structures that themselves shape both the decision-making process and its outputs in the form of decisions. Modern leaders depend heavily on advisers, department and agency heads, and their bureaucratic staffs, for information about the international scene. Moreover, different policymakers often disagree in their interpretations of situations, and all bureaucracies, like governments themselves, especially in democratic political systems, constantly face budgetary constraints. Therefore, advocates of various types of foreign-policy and defense programs find themselves in competition for the allocation of scarce resources. Foreign-policy and defense programs compete not only with domestic programs (education, health, social security, agriculture, transportation, welfare, energy, construction, conservation, crime control, and urban renewal), but also with each other—various types of military–technological programs and arms transfers, force deployments, alliance diplomacy, foreign development assistance, information and cultural exchange programs, intelligence activities, support for international organizations, and the strengthening of peaceful change processes. Differing interests within and among the departments and agencies that have a role in foreign policy and national security, as well as differences among the military services, are illustrative of the bureaucratic-politics dimension of decision making.

The point can be illustrated by contrasting the views of the Departments of State and of Defense on an issue that arose in the second Reagan Administration. The issue pertained to the research, development, and testing of strategic-defense technologies amidst conflicting interpretations of the Anti-Ballistic Missile (ABM) Treaty of 1972. Secretary of State George Shultz, reflecting his department's sensitivity to diplomatic and public opinion in Europe, urged caution with respect to existing arms-control treaties, lest the European NATO allies fear that renewed Cold War tensions would dash fragile détente prospects. Secretary of Defense Caspar Weinberger, on the other hand, preferred what he called a "broad interpretation" over Shultz's "narrow interpretation" of the ABM Treaty on the grounds that strategic defense was essential to U.S. national security, which should take priority over the opinion of allies.[9] The State Department view prevailed.

Morton H. Halperin and associates showed how "politics within a government influence decisions and actions ostensibly directed outward"[10] and how the way in which officials focus on issues often depends on their bureaucratic position and perspective, meaning that the domestic objectives of bureaucrats may be more significant than the international objectives of governments. They concluded that actions or proposals by one government to influence the behavior of another government are usually based on the simple model of two individuals communicating accurately with each other, when in fact they have probably emerged from a complex bureaucratic process of pulling and hauling that is not fully understood by those who must carry out the decision. Furthermore, they asserted, the response of the foreign government is also likely to be the result of a similar bureaucratic process of pulling and hauling. (See the subsequent section, "Allison's Three Models.")

Francis Rourke has cited the law of bureaucratic inertia: "Bureaucracies at rest tend to stay at rest, and bureaucracies in motion tend to stay in motion."[11] Recent presidents have been exasperated on occasion at the slowness with which bureaucracies at rest respond to their orders, but Rourke observes that this might save a political leader from the consequences of a rash decision. Conversely, executive agencies that have been stimulated to develop certain capabilities, whether for waging combat, exploring space, negotiating arms-control agreements, or selling arms or grain abroad, may feel compelled to prove their usefulness through activity that justifies expanded budgets. Once bureaucracies gain momentum, they are difficult to slow down. Rourke points out that the irreversibility of certain types of activity by large organizations contradicts the hypothesis that policymaking in the United States moves "incrementally in one sequential step after another from initial decision to final outcome, thus permitting a discontinuance of effort or the reversal of direction at any point." He concludes that, while they can shape the views of political leaders and the public on foreign-policy issues, and often possess technical capabilities that enable them to influence the flow of events, nevertheless bureaucratic agencies compose only one part of a democratic political system. Their power ultimately depends on the willingness of others—for example, Congress and the president—to support them, accept their advice, or legitimize their activities by going along with them.[12]

Alexander L. George called attention to the fact that the executive, instead of using centralized management practices to neutralize intrabureaucratic disagreements over policy, can use a *multiple advocacy model*—a mixed system combining elements of centralized management with certain features of pluralistic participatory models to harness diversity of views and interests for the sake of enhancing rational policymaking.[13] One of the dangers of bureaucratic politics against which the executive wishes to guard is the possibility that organizational subunits might restrict competition with each other and work out compromises among themselves before the policy issues are aired at the highest level, so that the final decision is likely to be based on the preferred option that results from the internal bargaining process. Under these conditions, of course, policy options that might be viable but are unpopular with the bureaucracy are rendered unavailable as a result of unfavorable presentation or inadequate information. George warns the executive against overcentralizing and overbureaucratizing the early search and evaluation phases of policy analysis, prior to choice. In an overcentralized system, the executive might receive too narrow a range of orthodox options, based on cues transmitted, whether intentional or not, from the top down.

According to George, conflict and bargaining within the bureaucracy might contribute to a better policymaking process if it can be managed and resolved properly. He therefore espoused a multiple-advocacy model as "an integral part of a *mixed system* in which centralized coordination and Executive initiative would be required," depending on the decision maker's cognitive style and way of defining information needs, selecting advisors, and making use of them.[14] The chief executive encourages competition among bureaucratic units while reserving the power to evaluate, judge, and choose among the various policy options articulated by the advocates. George has also dealt with the constraints imposed on the policymaker by *value complexity* (the presence of multiple competing values and interests embedded in a single issue) and *uncertainty* (the lack of adequate information and of available knowledge required to assess the situation and possible outcomes).[15] The problems posed by these constraints are addressed subsequently, in the section, "The Decision-Making Process." Because the advocates compete with each other only for the executive's attention, this is a system of perfect competition, highly preferable to the imperfect competition that prevails in the bureaucratic bargaining-and-compromise model.

Although the bureaucratic-politics model has been popular among theorists since the early 1960s (see the subsequent section on Graham Allison's treatment of the Cuban Missile Crisis) and more recent analyses of this work, it has not won universal acclaim. Edward Rhodes has recently expressed skepticism of the view that states are not rational actors, but rather bureaucratic structures, the official acts of which result from a process of myopic bargaining or pulling and hauling among the parochial priorities of government agencies. He does not doubt the existence of bureaucratic politics, yet he questions whether they matter, whether they help us to understand state behavior, and whether knowledge of the bureaucratic process enables us to predict state actions any better than, or even as well as, knowledge of the ideas and beliefs that compete within governments for intellectual hegemony.[16]

MOTIVATIONS AND CHARACTERISTICS OF DECISION MAKERS

Snyder and his colleagues drew a useful distinction between two types of motivation—in-order-to motives and because-of motives.[17] The former are conscious and articulable: The decision makers are taking this particular decision *in order to* accomplish such and such an objective of the state that they serve. For example, the administration of President Johnson sought the Nonproliferation Treaty in order to promote international stability by restricting the number of states that might independently opt for the initiation of nuclear hostilities. Similarly, President Reagan chose his Strategic Defense Initiative as a means of eventually rendering nuclear weapons impotent and obsolete. *Because-of motives,* on the other hand, are unconscious or semiconscious motives or impulses arising out of previous life experience or inner values, interests, or drives of the decision maker. As we have seen in Chapter 7, however, political theorists tend to be wary of psychohistory as a means of explaining the decisions and actions of political leaders.

Most decision making theorists, like most political historians, would agree that biographical knowledge about policymakers—including their education, religion, critical life experiences, professional training, foreign travel, mental and physical health, and previous political activities—might help to cast light on the deepest motives and values of those who make specific decisions. A political leader who fought or lost a loved one in a costly war may be loath or eager to opt for war in a certain situation. However, little is known about the relationship between the total inner psychic experience of individuals and their overt policy choices in an organizational context. It is one thing to acknowledge that an individual's background is significant, especially in cases where there are unusual behavioral aberrations from what would normally be expected on the basis of the analysis of known social roles and processes. It is quite another thing, however, to draw a definite causal link between the previous psychic event (perhaps years earlier) and the present deviant action. One of the difficulties with psychohistorical explanation is that it can lend itself too easily to the workings of an overactive dramatic imagination as a substitute for rigorous analysis of real evidence.

THE DECISION-MAKING PROCESS

David Easton has defined politics as "the authoritative allocation of values for a society."[18] This, in essence, is what political decision making is all about. However, DM theorists are not in general agreement as to whether the process of political decision making is fundamentally the same as the process of nonpublic or private decision making. As political scientists, the authors of this book are strongly inclined to agree with those who postulate important differences among decisions in a family, in a university, in a business corporation, and in a government department.[19] Even though private and public decision making are both characterized by various mixes of individual and collective processes, nevertheless the frames of reference and the rules of the game exhibit rather specific properties.

Because economists and students of business administration made significant early inputs to DM theory, the theory as originally developed reflected many of the assumptions of the Enlightenment and of the Benthamite Utilitarians, with their emphasis on reason and education in the making of human social choices. It assumed a rational person who is clearly aware of all the available alternatives and who is capable of both calculating the respective outcomes of each alternative and then freely choosing according to the order of value preferences. Such assumptions have been seriously questioned in the twentieth century.

According to the classic model of decision making, policymakers make a calculation in two basic dimensions—utility and probability—and, assuming that they are rational, they will attempt to maximize the expected utility. In other words, after all the available alternatives have been surveyed and the product of weighted values and assessed probabilities has been obtained, decision makers can choose their optimal course.[20] Snyder points out that "decision-makers may be assumed to act in terms of clear-cut preferences," but that these preferences, instead of being entirely individual, derive from the rules of the organizational system, shared organizational experience over a period of time, and the information available to the decisional unit, as well as from the biographies of individuals.[21] Snyder, however, refrained from subscribing fully to the classic explanatory formula of maximization of expected utility, which had already been subject to question before he wrote his principal essay on the subject.[22]

For many decades, the Western intellectual's faith in the essential rationality of human behavior (inherited from the Enlightenment) has steadily disintegrated. Freud virtually completed the erosion process with his discoveries concerning the powerful role played in life by the unconscious. Nevertheless, political-science and international-relations students tend to assume that there are some rational elements in the political process, insofar as individuals set forth in explicit fashion their goal priorities and devise categories of means for attaining them. Moreover, even if our knowledge of the individual prompts us to postulate irrationality at times, the demands of social organization require us to grope in the direction of rationality, and to employ the criteria of rationality in order to identify and understand the irrational. The assumption of rational behavior has always been deemed to be central to the bulk of international-relations theory.[23]

However, DM theory does not necessarily assume the rationality of decision makers. Rationality is an element to be validated by empirical analysis rather than to be assumed. For example, Snyder and his associates do not differ substantially from other modern theorists of governmental decision making who have been influenced by Max Weber's concept of bureaucracy, which develops according to a rational plan. There is in the theory an assumption of purposeful behavior and explicit motivation; behavior is seen not as merely random activity. The decision-making process is said to combine rational elements; value considerations in which the rational may be synthesized with the nonrational, the irrational, or the suprarational; and such irrational or nonrational factors as the psychic complexes of the policymakers. J. David Singer, among others, pointed out that under conditions of stress and anxiety, decision makers may not act according to standards of utility that could be called rational,[24] and Martin Patchen suggested the need for greater attention to the presence of nonrational and partly conscious factors in the personalities of those who make decisions.[25] After examining both nonrational and rational models of decision making, Sidney Verba concluded that it may be useful under certain circumstances to assume that governments "make decisions as if they were following the rules of means–end rationality" and choose the alternative that enables them best to attain the ends or promote the values of the decision makers.[26]

Braybrooke and Lindblom rejected as unsatisfactory for most important decisions (i.e., those that affect significant changes in the external social world) the "synoptic conception" of decision making by which policymakers are presumed to spread out before them all their available alternatives and to measure, against their scale of preferred values, all the probable consequences of the social changes implicit in the various courses of action under consideration. This synoptic schema, in their view, simply does not conform to reality. It presupposes omniscience and a kind of comprehensive analysis that is prohibitively costly and that time pressures normally do not permit. Every solution, they asserted, must be limited by several factors, including the individual's problem-solving capacities, the amount of information available, the cost of analysis (in personnel, resources, and time), and the practical inseparability of fact and value.[27]

No one challenged the classic model of rational decision making more fundamentally, while yet remaining within a rational framework, than the eminent economist and theorist of administration Herbert Simon, who postulated a world of "bounded rationality." For the classic concept of *maximizing* or *optimizing* behavior, he substituted the notion of "satisficing" behavior. This presupposes that the policymakers do not really design for themselves a matrix that shows all available alternatives, the value pros and cons of each, and the probability assessments of expected consequences. Instead, Simon suggested, decision-making units examine alternatives sequentially until they come upon one that meets their minimum standards of acceptability.[28] In other words, people keep rejecting unsatisfactory solutions until they find one that they can agree is sufficiently satisfactory to enable them to act. (It was for this theory that Simon won the 1978 Nobel Prize for Economics.) Braybrooke and Lindblom, who are partial both to Simon's satisficing model and to Karl Popper's idea of "piecemeal engineering," suggested that pragmatic experimentalism embodies a strategy of "disjointed incrementalism." Put in its simplest form, this means that policymakers, especially in democratic states, prefer to separate their decision making problems into small segments that enable them to make incremental or marginal rather than far-reaching, profound, or irreversible choices.[29]

Decision making is not only an intellectual process involving the insight, perception, and creative intuition of policymakers, but it is also a matter of social and quasi-mechanical processes.[30] Among political scientists, Arthur Bentley and David Truman did much to stress the importance of interest groups in the decisional process, and William Riker, in his study of coalitions, suggested that decision making may depend at least partially on quasi-mechanical processes in which the actors are unconscious of their decision-making roles.[31]

ALLISON'S THREE MODELS

According to Graham T. Allison,* most foreign-policy analysts think about and explain governmental behavior in terms of the rational-actor model (also called the "classical model"), in which policy choices are seen as the more or less purposive acts of unified governments, based on logical means of achieving given objectives. The model represents an effort to relate an action to a plausible calculation.[32] Morgenthau's stateleader contemplating what the national interest calls for in a certain situation, Schelling's game theorist calculating the requirements of stable mutual deterrence or the points of saliency at which limited wars can be kept limited, Bruce Bueno de Mesquita's policymaker choosing on the basis of expected utility—all presuppose some form of rational-actor model.[33] Rational people discern clearly their objectives, the options available, and the likely consequences of each alternative choice before making their decision.[34]

"Although the Rational Actor Model has proved useful for many purposes," Allison wrote, "there is powerful evidence that it must be supplemented, if not supplanted, by frames of reference that focus on the governmental machine."[35] Allison offered two such frames of reference: an organizational-process model and a bureaucratic-politics model. In the latter, he owed a considerable intellectual debt to the writings of Max Weber. The organizational-process model envisages governmental behavior less as a matter of deliberate choice and more as independent outputs of several large organizations, only partly coordinated by government

---

*Allison's specific views on the Cuban Missile Crisis are examined in the subsequent section on that case study.

leaders. "Government leaders can substantially disturb, but not substantially control, the behavior of these organizations,"[36] which is determined primarily by standard routine operating procedures, with seldom more than gradual, incremental deviations except when a major disaster occurs.[37] The organizational-process model that Allison prefers is that of Herbert Simon, based on the concept of bounded rather than comprehensive rationality, and characterized by factoring or splitting up problems, the parceling out of problem parts to various organizational units, the type of satisficing behavior described previously, limiting the search to the first acceptable alternative, and avoidance of uncertainty or risk through developing short-run feedback and corrective procedures. Organizations operate to solve problems of immediate urgency rather than to develop strategies for coping with longer-range issues.[38]

Allison's third model, the bureaucratic-politics model, builds on the organizational-process model, but instead of assuming control by leaders at the top, the bureaucratic politics model hypothesizes intensive competition among the decision making units, and the formulation of foreign policies as the result of bargaining among the components of a bureaucracy. The players are guided by no consistent strategic master plan, but rather by conflicting conceptions of national, bureaucratic, and personal goals. Sometimes, one group may triumph over other groups committed to different alternatives. Often, however, different groups pulling in different directions produce a resultant or decisional mix that is distinct from that intended by an individual or group. The outcome depends not on the rational justification for the policy or on routine organizational procedures, but on the relative power and skill of the bargainers.[39]

Allison's three models as set forth in *Essence of Decision,* according to Jonathan Bendor and Thomas H. Hammond, exerted a considerable impact on research and teaching with regard to bureaucracy. It stimulated a generation of students to think seriously about how foreign-policy decisions are made.[40] However, Bendor and Hammond fault Allison for misinterpreting the literature of rational-choice theory, organization theory, and bureaucratic-politics theory, on which he drew for his pioneering work. In particular, Allison failed to distinguish adequately between Model II (organizational process) and Model III (bureaucratic politics); they tend to overlap each other (as many readers had noted).[41] Moreover, Allison oversimplified Model I (rational actor). The state cannot be considered merely as a single, rational actor, acting with complete information in pursuit of a single goal. Bendor and Hammond find such an assumption "odd indeed,"[42] and suggest that Allison was setting up Model I as a straw man to be knocked down.

Furthermore, Bendor and Hammond noted, decision makers in government bureaucracies are not always necessarily in pursuit of conflicting goals, as Allison and other theorists of bureaucracy seemed to assume. By taking into account the four basic variables—(1) single or multiple decision makers; (2) acting toward the same or conflicting goals; (3) with perfect or imperfect rationality; and (4) with complete or incomplete information—Bendor and Hammond come up with 12 logically possible models or typologies of policymaking.[43] They concede that some of Allison's errors are due to advances in knowledge since his writing; but some "were there from the beginning." *Essence of Decision* richly deserves its reputation, but its "continued use is . . . likely to lead to the widespread perpetuation of major misunderstandings about the nature of bureaucracy and governmental policymaking."[44]

In another recent critique of Allison's models, David A. Welch concludes that the organizational-process and bureaucratic-politics models contain propositions that do not accord with the facts of the Cuban Missile Crisis.[45] According to Welch, the existence of organizational routines was not sufficient to explain the behavior of the decision makers charged with the formidable (and dangerous) task of defusing this crisis situation. To the extent that they deemed necessary, President Kennedy and his advisors developed responses without primary concern for the routines set forth in the procedures as specified in the organizational-process model. Acknowledging that organizational routines can restrict the range of perceived options before a decision is already made, especially if the time for action is extremely short and the required response is based on a series of complex factors, Welch observes that even in military organizations not noted for peacetime strategic innovation, dramatic shifts in standard operating procedures have often taken place in the heat of battle. Similarly, in the Cuban Missile Crisis, the Executive Committee (ExComm), headed by President Kennedy, frequently overrode, circumvented, or modified organizational routines in order to facilitate the decision-making process. Nevertheless, organizational routines often do contribute to the effectiveness of decisions by setting forth necessary procedures. Therefore, Welch suggests, in each case, it should be asked whether prevailing organizational routines were more of a help or a hindrance to the achievement of goals set forth by the decision makers. On the one hand, organizational routines, including the collection and analysis of intelligence, were essential to the discovery that the Soviet Union was placing missiles in Cuba. On the other hand, the prospects for successful resolution of the crisis may have been enhanced by the ability and willingness of decision makers to reach beyond such routines in their quest for a de-escalatory strategy that served national interests.

Similarly, Welch finds the bureaucratic-politics model deficient in positing that the affiliation of decision makers is a reliable guide to understanding how they will act (or that where you sit in the bureaucracy necessarily determines where you stand on the issue.) He cites other studies that have found no relationship between bureaucratic position and policy preferences. Aside from the fact that a specific bureaucratic office itself may not have an identifiable position on every policy issue, it is not necessarily inevitable that representatives of a particular bureaucracy will be guided primarily by such a perspective even if it does exist.

According to Welch, there is evidence in support of the proposition that professional military officers (especially since the Vietnam War) have not been as willing as their civilian counterparts to advocate the use of military power as an instrument of national policy as might have been expected from a bureaucratic-politics model. After the civilian leadership has decided on the use of force, however, Welch suggests that military officers usually seek to employ greater levels of force than their civilian counterparts. Although there are numerous examples of bureaucratic politics, for example in interservice rivalries with the Army, Navy, and Air Force competing for limited budgetary resources, there are other instances in which one's place in a bureaucratic organizational chart has little bearing on decision making. In the Cuban Missile Crisis, the positions taken by ExComm members had less to do with their bureaucratic affiliation than with other factors, including the attitudes, dispositions, and values that they brought to the table.

In sum, Welch's critique of Allison's models is designed not to denigrate the importance of such paradigms, but instead to suggest the need for greater analytical refinement, as well as perhaps the development of alternative conceptual frameworks. In this light, the rational-actor model should not be abandoned because of its advantages in "clarity, parsimony, and operationalization,"[46] as shown in Allison's work. Nevertheless, rationality in the case of the Cuban Missile crisis, as Allison pointed out, was limited by organizational and bureaucratic considerations, as well as communications failures. In the final analysis, the complexity of decision making, especially in foreign-policy/national-security situations, argues for an effort to view the process through a series of different analytic paradigms, each of which may help shed light on how and why decision makers acted as they did. The question that remains unresolved relates to the most appropriate models and, of course, the extent to which decisions reflect international-systems variables or national-level variables. Here we come back to the structure–agent question discussed in Chapters 2 and 3. How do structures at the international level and within the actors, or agents, shape the decision making process?

THE REFINEMENTS OF SNYDER AND DIESING

In keeping with the emphasis of decision-making literature on international crises, Glenn H. Snyder and Paul Diesing have tested empirically three DM theories in 21 cases of crisis.[47] They included: (1) utility maximization (the classical rational theory); (2) bounded rationality (borrowed from Simon's satisficing model); and (3) bureaucratic politics (based on Weber and on Allison). Their rational-actor model, like Allison's, is based on the choice of one alternative, out of all those available, that maximizes expected utility. The bounded-rationality tradition suggests that if a choice must be made between two different values (e.g., peace and national security), there is no rational way of calculating how much of one should be sacrificed to obtain a given amount of the other. Decision makers cannot maximize; they operate under constraints and search for an acceptable course. Snyder and Diesing argue plausibly that maximizing and bounded rationality are not irreconcilable explanations but may be combined by taking either theory as basic and the other as supplementary. They also make the sensible suggestion that the bureaucratic-politics theory supplements rather than competes with the other two theories. "It focuses on the internal political imperatives of maintaining and increasing influence and power rather than on the purely intellectual problems of choosing a strategy to deal with an external opportunity or threat."[48] The problem-solving theories apply best to some cases; the bureaucratic-politics theory, to others. The former are most applicable when only one or two people are involved in the decision. When three or more people are involved, as in a committee or a cabinet, the bureaucratic-politics model—which Snyder and Diesing see as a process of forming a dominant coalition—is said to apply best.[49]

Snyder and Diesing draw an important distinction between rational and irrational bargainers in a crisis. *Rational bargainers* do not pretend to know at the very beginning of a crisis what the precise situation is, or what the relative interests, power relations, and main alternatives are. They recognize that their initial judgment may be mistaken, but they are able to correct initial misjudgment and perceive the outlines of the developing bargaining situation in time to deal with it effectively.[50] They make tentative guesses as they go along, and they constantly modify their assessments as new information is received.

Irrational bargainers, on the other hand, proceed from a rigid belief system. They are certain about the adversary's ultimate aims, bargaining style, preferences, and internal problems. They receive advice (which they seek especially from those whose opinions they value) but make their own decisions. They see themselves as the architects of the one strategy that has a chance of succeeding, and they firmly adhere to that strategy in spite of all difficulties, regardless of new incoming information. If their initial strategy was correct, irrational bargainers can be highly successful; if not, they are unlikely to realize their mistake in time to avert defeat or disaster.[51] Deception is always a problem in bargaining. Rational bargainers are open to being deceived by the opponent; irrational bargainers, by themselves. In solving the information-processing problem, a rigid image of the adversary as totally untrustworthy may be as much a hindrance as a rigid image of the adversary as totally trustworthy.[52]

Theories of the decision-making process encounter conceptual difficulties. Miriam Steiner, after analyzing comparatively the works of Snyder and Allison, concluded that each contains contradictions. Snyder claims to put human plans and purposes at the center of his conceptual framework but does not follow through consistently. "When in the interests of 'objectivity,' he attempts to outfit himself with a 'hard methodology,' he inadvertently reduces his responsible decision-makers to organizationally programmed automatons."[53] Allison, on the other hand, insists for the sake of accuracy that events be explained not teleologically in terms of goals and purposes, but scientifically in terms of causal determinants that are subject to investigation. However, into his integrated explanation, "he unwittingly introduces goals and purposes as 'the essence of decision.'"[54] Thus, neither Snyder nor Allison, in Steiner's view, succeeds in providing an approach that achieves objectives consonant with its own distinctive methodology. Instead, each begins at an opposite pole and moves in the direction of the other. Perhaps this is inevitable.

THE CYBERNETIC THEORY OF DECISION

We have seen that the classical utilitarian theory of decision making, based on the assumption of a rational weighing of value costs and value outcomes, has come under increasing criticism in recent decades. As an alternative to the traditional analytic paradigm, John D. Steinbruner has set forth the "cybernetic paradigm" as a foundation for theories and models of decision making, because the old paradigm, he contends, does not explain all the observed phenomena of decision making. He doubts that human beings normally try to analyze complex problems by breaking them down into all of their logical components (which rational theory requires them to do), or that they have access to all of the information and perform all of the calculations, especially with regard to value trade-offs (which the classical theory presupposes). Steinbruner, moreover, expresses dissatisfaction with most of the efforts the analytic school has made thus far to apply to collective decisions concepts originally developed to explain decisions by individuals.[55]

Steinbruner offers as potentially more fruitful than the analytic paradigm a cybernetic one, by which highly successful or adaptive behavior might be explained without resort to elaborate decision-making mechanisms. He begins by describing a few more or less familiar instances of simple cybernetic decisions. When worker bees locate pollen-bearing flowers at a place remote from the hive, they inform other workers of its location by engaging in a dance that contains instructions for navigating according to the angle and direction of the sun in reference to the field. In another example, practiced tennis players are cybernetic decision makers. Each time they move to meet the ball with their rackets, they select one pattern of psychomotor responses out of thousands of possible patterns, and they do it without making mathematical calculations of the speed and trajectory of the oncoming ball, their precise point of interception, the stroke they will use to hit it, and their target point in the opposite court. Steinbruner draws additional analogies pertaining to cybernetic servomechanisms in the thermostat, which keep temperature within desired bounds, the watt governor that regulates the speed of an engine, radar homing devices, the cat that changes position near the hearth as the fire grows hotter or dimmer, the retail-store manager who adjusts item prices according to volume of sales, and the cook who follows a recipe and keeps tasting when performing a sequence of culinary operations without having a clear, rational concept of the final product.

The cybernetic decision maker, in other words, deals with situations that we call "simple," but that nevertheless have a complexity of their own, by eliminating variety, ignoring elaborate calculations concerning the environment, and tracking a few simple feedback variables that trigger a behavioral adjustment. Cybernetic decision makers, believing the decision process to be a simple one, strive to minimize the calculations they must perform, whether they be mathematical or value-related. They monitor a small set of critical variables, and their principal value is to reduce uncertainty by keeping these variables within tolerable ranges. They see no need for a careful calculation of probable outcomes, which they are not likely to make in any case. The sequence of decisional behaviors is related less to an intellectual analysis of the problem at hand than to past experience, from which there emerges an almost intuitional approach to problem solving.[56]

It is relatively easy, of course, to accept the cybernetic paradigm as applied to the tennis player, the cook, or the retail-store manager, each of whom faces a small number of simple choices on each sequence. The question is whether the validity of the cybernetic paradigm is affected by the much greater complexity of decisions and heterogeneity of the actors in the foreign policy and the defense fields. Stein-bruner is convinced that the cybernetic model is applicable to highly complex deci-sions, which he defines as decisions affecting two or more values, in which there is a trade-off relationship between the values, in which there is uncertainty, and in which the decision-making power is dispersed over a number of individual actors and/or organizational units. He concedes that greater complexity entails greater variety, and that "under conditions of complexity the decision-maker must have a more elaborate response repertory if he is to retain adaptive capacity."[57] The prob-lem is solved by increasing the number of decision makers within a collectivity. Complex problems are not analyzed comprehensively by all the members of the decision making group. Instead, they are broken down into a large number of lim-ited-dimension problems, each confronted by a separate decision maker or unit. "This is the natural cybernetic explanation for the rise of mass bureaucracy."[58]

To sum up, Steinbruner relies on theories of organizational behavior to extend the cybernetic paradigm from individual decision making in relatively simple situ-ations to collective decision making designed to cope with a highly complex envi-ronment. The higher levels of organizational hierarchy do not perform the inte-grating calculations called for by the analytic paradigm. Drawing on the work of Cyert and March, Steinbruner summarizes as follows:

> Top management, in their view, focuses in sequential order on the decision issues raised by separate subunits and does not integrate across subunits in its deliberations. Decisions are made solely within the context of the subunit raising the issue. Complex problems are thus fragmented by organizations into separate components having to do with subunit organization, and the decision process at the highest levels preserves the fragmentation.[59]

Organizational theory alone is not enough, however. Steinbruner combines it with highly intricate modern theories of cognitive processes, including those devel-oped by Noam Chomsky, Ulric Neisser, Leon Festinger, Robert P. Abelson, and others. He calls attention to the consensus among cognitive theorists that "a great deal of information processing is conducted apparently prior to and certainly inde-pendently of conscious direction and that in this activity the mind routinely per-forms logical operations of considerable power."[60] Steinbruner surveys the findings of many studies relating to perception, learning, memory, inference, consistency, belief, and the ways in which the human mind either controls or copes with uncer-tainty, and he concludes that cognitive theory provides an analysis of the effects of uncertainty on the decision process that is fundamentally different from that of the analytic and cybernetic paradigms. Thus, he uses cognitive theory to modify the cybernetic paradigm, especially with regard to the subjective resolution of uncer-tainty, and to introduce into his treatment of political and organizational phenom-ena the concepts of *grooved thinking,* in which the decision maker rather simplis-tically categorizes the problems into a small number of basic types; *uncommitted thinking,* in which the decision maker who does not know what to think about the problem oscillates between groups of advisers, and may adopt different belief pat-terns at different times on the same decision problem; and *theoretical thinking,* in which the decision maker is committed to abstract beliefs, usually organized around a single value in patterns that are internally consistent and stable over time, even under conditions of uncertainty.[61] Steinbruner applied his model to a single case of governmental decision making.[62]

Clearly, Steinbruner does not regard the cybernetic–cognitive paradigm as intrinsically superior to the analytic one. Rather he suggests that the two paradigms operate as substitutes for one another in processing complex problems, and they produce different types of decisions. In our effort to understand governmental decision making under conditions of complexity and uncertainty, the cybernetic–cognitive approach may provide a coherent explanation of behavior that, in an analytic framework, appears to be stupid, absurd, incompetent, or incomprehensible, without in any way implying approval of such an outcome.[63] Zeev Maoz observed that persons with long tenure in office are less disposed to analytic choice behavior (based on rational expected utility) and more inclined toward cybernetic decision making.[64]

DECISION MAKING IN CRISIS

Since the mid-1950s, a considerable amount of literature has appeared on specific foreign-policy decisions, including many decisions made in time of crisis,* as we have noted earlier in this chapter. Until the 1970s, much of this literature was in the form of case studies of decisions telescoped in time and circumscribed as to the number of decision makers. Since that time, there has been an increasing effort to study crises on a comparative basis, in order to develop a database across time and crises, and to build a theory, or theories, drawn from such analysis. In the generation before the 1970s, the focus of crisis literature was the creation of conceptual frameworks and hypotheses that were applied to the study of one and, in some instances, more than one case study. In the 1960s, moreover, there was the beginning of an effort both to set forth alternative models and to delineate propositions for the analysis of international crisis behavior. Most notable was the work of Charles F. Hermann and Linda P. Brady, who abstracted 311 propositions concerning crisis from research completed in the 1960s.[65]

The work of this earlier period includes the decisions that led to the outbreak of World War I, the United States intervention in Korea, British intervention in the Suez crisis, and United States responses to crises in or over Berlin, Quemoy, the Bay of Pigs, and the emplacement of Soviet missiles in Cuba.[66] The study of international crisis has included examination of the role played by third parties such as the United Nations and other mediating organizations or groups.[67] There have been studies of decisions characterized by longer time frames and complex groups of actors, including legislative bodies, political parties, and governments. Such decisions, which may be of historical significance even though they were not crisis decisions in the sense used here, might pertain to such events as the French scut-

---

*The term *crisis* dates back to ancient Greek medical practice, in which it meant a life-or-death turning point. Thucydides applied the term to key points in the changing relations of peoples and states.

tling of the European Defense Community in 1954, Britain's quest over more than a decade for entry into the European Economic Community, and United States decision making concerning arms-control agreements with the Soviet Union, as well as to such policies as how greatly to support the postcommunist reform process in Russia, and how to respond to the requests of former Warsaw Pact members to be allowed to join NATO.

This type of study is often more difficult than the crisis type to cast in the mold of precise decision-making analysis because it involves a harder-to-research cumulative process that takes place in a sprawling bureaucratic labyrinth and a more comprehensive political arena over a longer time period. Such studies may encompass decision making under more or less routine circumstances. In this respect, they are likely to differ substantially from crisis decision making in such factors as the level of the policy structure at which decisions are made and the time available to do so. Let us look at three well-known case studies.

The United States' Decision to Intervene in Korea

One study, consciously designed for the purpose of applying a theoretical DM model, was Glenn D. Paige's account of seven days of United States national decision making in response to the Korean crisis. Paige reflects an awareness of the problem of applying to a single case the Snyder–Bruck–Sapin model, and of trying to verify any hypotheses merely on the basis of the Korean decision. He acknowledges that the single case produces lessons that can lead only to "a relatively low level of abstraction."[68] Paige is essentially faithful to the Snyder–Bruck–Sapin model, with its emphasis on such concepts as "spheres of competence," "motivation," "communication and information," "feedback," and the "path of action."

The Korean decision, Paige contended, can be viewed either as a unified phenomenon or as a developmental sequence of choices (of which most decision makers were aware) that contributed to a "stage-like progression toward an analytically defined outcome"—a sequence in which policymakers were apparently affected by positive reinforcement in the form of supporting UN military action, favorable editorial opinion, and congressional and international expressions of approval, as well as evidence of a temperate Soviet response.[69] Many of Paige's conclusions are stated as hypotheses that postulate relationships among the nature of the decision-making group, the perceived threat to values, the role of leadership, the quest for information, the framework of past responses, the shared willingness to make a positive response, the effort to secure international support, and so forth. Some of the propositions are novel and interesting, and some might strike the reader as slightly tedious confirmations of what might otherwise be deduced logically, but it should be remembered that the validation of apparently obvious truths, based on solid data, is essential to the scientific method and thus to the development of social-science theories.

Perception and Decision Making:
The Outbreak of World War I

The use of content analysis with a stimulus–response model represents a quite different methodological approach to the study of decision making. In their studies of the outbreak of World War I and of the Cuban Missile Crisis, Ole R. Holsti, Robert C. North, and Richard A. Brody have attempted to measure the messages exchanged during crisis situations.[70] Such an approach focuses not on interaction *within,* but rather on interaction *between* the decisional units.

The model used related perceptions to behavior (S–r: s–R). The symbol *S* is the stimulus or input behavior; it is a physical event or a verbal act. The symbol *R* represents the response action. Both S and R are nonevaluative and nonaffective; r is the decision maker's perception of the stimulus (S), and *s* is the expression of intentions or attitude. Both r and s include factors such as personality, role, organization, and system that affect perceptual variables.

The authors of the study undertook correlational analyses between the perception data and various types of hard (action) data, because they recognized that the value of content analysis depends on the relationship between the statements and the actual decisions made by stateleaders. Thus, the authors attempted to find correlations between the results of the content analysis and such actions as mobilization, troop movements, and the breaking of diplomatic relations. Other actions, such as the financial indicators—gold movements and the price of securities, which are sensitive to international tension levels—were examined. Correlating the 1914 perception data with the spiral of military mobilizations, the authors concluded that a rise in hostility preceded acts of mobilization. Stated differently, decision makers responded "to verbal threats and diplomatic moves, rather than troop movements."[71]

Among the hypotheses tested was the notion that "in a situation of low involvement, policy response (R) will tend to be at a lower level of violence than the input action (S), whereas in a high involvement situation, the policy response (R) will tend to be at a higher level of violence than the input action (S)."[72] Because the action variables, S and R, alone failed to account for the escalation of war, the intervening perceptual variables, r and s, were analyzed. No significant difference was found between the two coalitions in the s–R step. In both low- and high-involvement cases, the response action (R) was at a higher level of violence than was suggested by their leaders' statements of intent (s). Moreover, in the r–s link, there was again little difference between the Triple Entente and the Dual Alliance: In both groupings of nations, the level of hostility was perceived to be consistently greater in the other's policy (r) than in their own statements of intent (s).

However, a significant difference appeared in the S-r step, which could account for the escalation. In the low-involvement situation, r tended to be at a lower level than S, whereas in the high-involvement situation, r tended to be higher than S. Decision makers in the highly involved Dual Alliance consistently overperceived the level of violence of the threats of the Triple Entente, and they overreacted to the threats. The leaders of the less deeply involved Triple Entente underperceived the actions of the Dual Alliance. Moreover, in the later stages of the crisis, after both alliances had become highly involved, there was less difference between the two coalitions in the way actions (S) were perceived (r). The authors concluded, therefore, that intervening perceptions may perform an accelerating or a decelerating function. In this case, the S–r link served a magnifying function. "This difference in perceiving the environment (the S–r link) is consistent with the pronounced tendency of the Dual Alliance to respond at a higher level of violence than the Triple Entente."[73]

L. L. Farrar, Jr., adopts a different interpretation of the 1914 crisis. Following Theodore Abel and Bruce M. Russett, he suggests that one should not seek causes but analyze processes, beginning with the background from which the decisions of governments emerge. The final decision for war is not reached on the spur of the moment and is not triggered by the irrational motivations and emotional elements often associated with decision making under conditions of stress. Rather, it is based on a series of rational calculations that may antedate the crisis by several years. The crisis itself may be the result of precrisis decisions involving an assessment over a long period of time concerning several alternative ways of acting under a variety of circumstances. Although leaders may experience stress during the crisis, the crisis is due not to psychological tensions but to previous decisions, which are more important than personality characteristics. Farrar presents the 1914 crisis as the logical result of rational policy considerations, given the assumptions underlying the state system.[74]

The Cuban Missile Crisis

The 1962 superpower confrontation is generally regarded as the most dangerous crisis in history; it has certainly been the most thoroughly studied and analyzed, with a remarkable variety of findings and interpretations. Earlier studies[75] depended almost entirely on information from the American side; post–Cold War revelations from sources on both sides, assuming their reliability, have added to our detailed knowledge of events without always deepening our understanding of them—to the contrary, they have sometimes compounded the ambiguities and confusion.

Graham T. Allison applied each of his three previously discussed decision-making models to the crisis, concluding that they "do not settle the matter of what happened and why," but "do offer evidence about the nature of explanations produced by different analysts."[76] According to Allison, the rational-actor analyst seeks to explain the crisis in terms of strategic choices by the two superpowers. During and after the crisis, several different motives were attributed to Moscow in deciding to deploy land-based nuclear missiles for the first time beyond Soviet borders—dangerously close to the United States. It is now assumed that the two most likely Soviet goals were (1) to achieve a strategic quick fix that would redress the military imbalance[77] resulting from U.S. advances in invulnerable intercontinental ballistic missiles (ICBMs) and submarine-launched ballistic missiles (SLBMs) by quadrupling the number of nuclear warheads that could be delivered on the continental United States;* (2) to protect Cuba (newest member of the socialist camp) from an invasion that would destroy Castro's revolution and damage Moscow's reputation as leader of the world socialist camp.[78] President Kennedy interpreted the

---

*Earlier studies usually referred to doubling its capability to deliver nuclear warheads on U.S. territory. Later information indicated that the number of Soviet ICBMs deployed and operational on Soviet territory was less than originally estimated.

deployment as a prelude to a showdown over Berlin, but in the post–Cold War era, Soviet Foreign Minister Andrei Gromyko and others denied such a connection.[79] Defense Secretary Robert McNamara deprecated the motive of attempting to redress the strategic balance. He was portrayed by other members of the ExComm of the National Security Council as holding that by placing 40 missiles in Cuba, the Soviet Union had done no more than move from an unfavorable balance of 5,000 to 300 to one of 5,000 to 340 nuclear weapons.[80] In McNamara's view, Khrushchev was trying to achieve a situation symmetrical with that of U.S. Jupiter missiles in Turkey, close to Soviet borders. Most analysts now look on Khrushchev's use of the Turkish missiles issue more as justifying propaganda than as an actual motive for deployment. Was Khrushchev's decision to deploy Soviet missiles a reckless, adventurist gambit (as Mao later criticized) or a carefully calculated strategic move? Khrushchev himself admitted in his memoirs that he got the idea as early as May 1962. He discussed it fully with members of the Presidium and overcame the objections of two advisers best informed about American politics, Gromyko and Anastas Mikoyan, both of whom warned of the dangers involved. Khrushchev was determined to carry out the deployment quickly and secretly, before the U.S. midterm congressional elections in November.[81]

Allison, in his organizational-process model approach to the Cuban Missile Crisis, stressed the amount of organizational activity and degree of coordination required to move more than 100 shiploads of medium- and intermediate-range missiles, Beagle Bombers, MiG-21 interceptor aircraft, surface-to-air missiles (SAMs), cruise missiles, patrol boats, and 22,000 Soviet soldiers and technical personnel to Cuba.[82] However, American experts were puzzled that the Soviets, who could not have expected their missile sites in Cuba to escape detection by U-2s, failed to complete their radar system and SAM network prior to installing the medium-range ballistic missiles (MRBMs), and then made no attempt to camouflage the missiles until after the United States publicly disclosed what the Soviets were doing.[83] Some analysts of the rational-model school sought motives to explain the apparent inconsistencies of Soviet behavior.

Allison suggested that the anomalies might best be explained simply by assuming that large organizations do what they know how to do. SAM sites and missile sites were constructed in Cuba just as they had been in the Soviet Union, without either camouflage or hardening.[84] Other construction and phasing anomalies can be similarly explained by the characteristic problem that typically besets large organizations—lack of a strategic overview, poor coordination, delays in communication and implementation of directives, and cumbersome operating procedures. Allison also speculated that the actual Soviet decision to place missiles in Cuba may have been pressed on the Presidium by the relatively new Strategic Rocket Forces. These forces, locked into a budgetary rivalry with the Soviet Ground Forces, had been compelled to defer acquisition of ICBMs, and they worried about the strategic nuclear balance after the Kennedy Administration announced in November 1961 that not only was there no missile gap but that the United States actually enjoyed strategic nuclear superiority.[85]

On the American side, wrote Allison, the precise timing of the Cuban Missile Crisis was a function of the organizational routines and standard operating procedures of the U.S. intelligence community, for these factors determined when the crucial information reached the president. Many reports and isolated items of information had to be pieced together and analyzed before U-2 surveillance flights over Cuba were ordered, and then several more days passed while the State Department urged a less risky alternative and the Air Force and CIA carried on a jurisdictional dispute over who should fly the U-2. When a surgical air strike was being considered as a possible course of action, there was a vast discrepancy between what that term meant to President Kennedy and his White House advisers (who would have restricted it to the missile sites) and what it meant to the military (who added the missile sites to the existing contingency plan for an air strike against all Cuban storage depots, airports, and artillery batteries opposite the U.S. naval base at Guantanamo). A hastily formulated and probably erroneous military estimate that an air strike could be only 90 percent but not 100 percent effective against the missiles, of which a small number might be launched first, prompted the political leaders to eliminate the air-strike option and to concentrate on the naval blockade.[86]

Allison conceded that it is difficult to analyze Soviet decision making in the Cuban Missile Crisis in terms of the bureaucratic-politics model, but the documentation for applying this model to the United States action is abundant. After the Bay of Pigs fiasco, Kennedy was under heavy pressure from public opinion and from critics in Congress to prevent the Soviet Union from converting Cuba into an offensive base. In September 1962, when reports of the Soviet military buildup began reaching the United States, the President distinguished between defensive and offensive preparations, and he gave public assurance that the latter would not be tolerated. Administration figures denied the presence of Soviet offensive missiles, discounted the suspicions of CIA Director John McCone, and elicited from the United States Intelligence Board on September 19 an estimate to the effect that the emplacement of Soviet offensive missiles in Cuba was "highly unlikely." Early in September, a U-2 had been shot down over mainland China. Fear that another U-2 might be lost contributed to a 10-day delay after a decision was made on October 4 to carry out photograph reconnaissance flights.

Confronted with the evidence, the President was angered by Khrushchev's duplicity: "He can't do that to *me!*" Given the political environment, with congressional elections only three weeks away, earlier analysts assumed that Kennedy wished to avoid signs of weakness and to take firm, effective action, but the ExComm transcripts appear to contain no evidence to substantiate the view that the President's decisions were based on domestic political considerations.[87] It is now taken for granted that the hackneyed distinction between "hawks" and "doves" dates from this period.[88] Recommendations from Kennedy's advisers varied from doing nothing or taking a diplomatic approach to an air strike or invading the island before the Soviet missiles became operational. Allison credited Attorney General Robert Kennedy with working out a near consensus on a compromise between inaction and potentially unlimited action—the carefully calibrated response of a gradually tightening naval blockade.[89] Allison, combining the defects of the rational-actor model with the presumed characteristics of the bureaucratic-politics model, called the blockade decision "part choice and part result—a melange of misconception, miscommunication, misinformation, bargaining, pulling, hauling, and sparring, as well as a mixture of national security interests, objectives, and governmental calculations."[90]

The blockade alone did not lead to the withdrawal of Soviet missiles from Cuba. That was accomplished only after a highly ambiguous ploy—a conciliatory offer to give a United States assurance against an invasion of Cuba combined with a threat of "overwhelming retaliatory action" unless the President received immediate notice that the missiles would be withdrawn.[91] Whether the ultimatum caused the withdrawal, as the rational-actor model would argue, or whether the language of threat was a public posturing designed to screen a private deal offered by President Kennedy to Premier Khrushchev—withdrawal of Soviet missiles in Cuba in exchange for withdrawal of United States missiles in Turkey (something that Kennedy had ordered before the Cuban Missile Crisis developed and that was actually carried out a few months afterward)—Allison left in the realm of unanswered questions.[92] It now appears that Kennedy was willing to make the trade-off of the missiles in Turkey if necessary to avoid military action, despite adverse political repercussions within Turkey and NATO.[93]

Most studies of the Cuban Missile Crisis have been historically descriptive rather than theoretical. They have focused on who within the ExComm were hawks and who were doves, who advocated this or that approach, how Soviet motives and Khrushchev's moods were interpreted,° and how close to or far away from the brink of war the world came in the view of various participants. There is still disagreement over whether Soviet nuclear warheads were shipped and delivered to Cuba.[94] It is now suspected that the polarization between hawks and doves, featured in early speculative accounts, was overdrawn; all the members of ExComm stated their positions as part of a dialectic process of seeking an optimum resolution of the crisis. Irving Janis has suggested that in this instance, President Kennedy, by absenting himself periodically from the ExComm deliberations, was able to elicit a spectrum of advisory opinions for his own decision making and to avoid the kind of groupthink that had earlier contributed to the Bay of Pigs fiasco.[95] Still others have questioned whether we gain much significant new, reliable knowledge from the sort of crisis-revisited conferences that took place after the end of the Cold War, given the well-known tendency of participants to engage in personally or politically self-serving reminiscence.[96]

One of the few theoretical studies of the Cuban Missile Crisis was made as early as 1964 by Holsti, Brody, and North. Using their same interaction model described previously, they sought to find "patterns of behavior that distinguished the situation which escalated into general war (as in the 1914 crisis) from those in which the process of escalation is reversed"[97] (as in the Cuban Missile Crisis). In Cuba, in contrast to 1914, there was found to be close correspondence between the actions of the other party (S) and the perceptions of the adversary's action (r).

°Former U.S. Ambassador to Moscow Llewellyn Thompson, the only member with extensive knowledge of the Soviets, was widely regarded as the unsung hero in working toward a resolution of the crisis; Welch and Blight, "Introduction . . . ," p. 19 (See Note 87).

Here each side accurately perceived actions and responded in a like manner.[98] Such behavior differed from that of the 1914 crisis in which, at the beginning, the Dual Alliance consistently reacted at a higher level than the Triple Entente and also consistently overperceived the level of violence in actions taken by the Triple Entente. Subsequently, this difference in the S–r link between the two coalitions lessened, as both were drawn into escalation and war. From their comparative analysis of the 1914 crisis and the 1962 crisis, Holsti, Brody, and North found indications that "the more intense the interaction between parties, the more important it is to incorporate perceptual data into the analysis."[99] As was amply demonstrated in Chapter 9 on deterrence, the leaders of both the United States and the Soviet Union had compelling reasons to avoid war, even at that relatively early stage of the nuclear era, and to work toward a negotiated settlement, however ambiguous.

TOWARD A THEORY OF CRISIS BEHAVIOR

James A. Robinson has asserted that "there is no theory of crisis."[100] Nevertheless, several international-relations analysts have devoted many years of effort to acquire a better understanding of crisis behavior, to gain deeper insights into why some crises lead to war while others lend themselves to nonviolent resolution, and to ascertain why certain crises are short and others protracted in duration.[101] Others, as noted in this chapter, have attempted to develop a theory of crisis behavior that might yield systematic knowledge for the study of crisis and for crisis management and resolution. According to Michael P. Sullivan, crisis had become by the mid-1970s the most widely researched situational variable of all occasions for decision.[102]

Charles A. McClelland has noted that analysts of international-crisis behavior have focused on five approaches: (1) definition of crisis; (2) classifications of types of crisis; (3) the study of ends, goals, and objectives in crises; (4) decision making under conditions of crisis stress; and (5) crisis management.[103] An earlier, widely accepted definition of crisis developed by Robinson and Hermann had postulated three elements: (1) threat to high-priority goals of the decision-making unit, (2) restricted amount of time available for response, and (3) surprise.[104] Later studies did not deem surprise essential. According to Gilbert R. Winham, a crisis can arise "in situations ranging from a fundamental military challenge to the balance of power to an insignificant border dispute that escalates into a major confrontation."[105]

The criteria for defining crisis underwent subsequent modification. Michael Brecher and Jonathan Wilkenfeld offered the following characteristics: "a situation deriving from change in a state's internal or external environment which gives rise to decisionmakers' perceptions of threat to basic values, finite time for response, and the likelihood of involvement in military hostilities."[106] They substituted finite time for short time, included intrastate changes as potential triggers, and introduced the likelihood of military hostilities as a key element. The need for surprise was eliminated because threat situations can often be anticipated. Much depends on the quality of national intelligence and whether early warning indicators are properly routed through the bureaucracy and evaluated in a timely manner. Many critical developments, however, cannot be foreseen. Drafting a wide range of contingency plans provides no guarantee against surprise, for such plans often cannot anticipate all possible situations that may arise, especially if the other party places a premium on the strategic value of surprise. Intelligence does not always succeed; some failures of prediction are inevitable.[107]

According to Glenn Snyder, crisis has always been central to international politics—a moment of truth in which several latent elements "such as power configurations, interests, images, and alignments tend to be more sharply clarified, to be activated and focused on a single well-defined issue."[108] During the Cold War, crises between the United States and the Soviet Union were looked on as surrogates for war, rather than merely dangerous episodes that were the prelude to war and that, before the advent of nuclear weapons, might have escalated to war. Thus, the effect of nuclear weapons in the possession of the two superpowers had the effect of channeling their competition away from the ultimate (nuclear) confrontation to crisis management at levels below the nuclear threshold. "Their systemic function is to resolve without violence, or with only minimal violence, those conflicts that are too severe to be settled by ordinary diplomacy and that in earlier times would have been settled by war."[109]

According to Oran R. Young, an international crisis consists of a "set of rapidly unfolding events which raises the impact of destabilizing forces in the general international system or any of its subsystems substantially above normal [average] levels, and increases the likelihood of violence occurring in the system";[110] in turn, these events produce responses that have the effect of leading the originators of demands to additional activities; hence there is feedback. Calling crisis "international politics in microcosm,"[111] Glenn Snyder held that elements lying at the core of the international politics come fully into focus in crises. They include, in addition to conflict itself, bargaining, negotiations, force and the threat to use force, escalation and de-escalation, deterrence, alternative power configurations, interests, values, perceptions, the use (or nonuse) of international law and organization, diplomacy, and decision making.

Richard Ned Lebow called attention to the familiar differentiation between underlying long-term causes and the more immediate causes of war. The immediate causes may come into play during the tense period known as crisis, which either leads to war or to a turning away from hostilities and an easing of the situation. He acknowledged that individual case studies of crisis have generated some valuable insights, but he noted their limitations: From a single case history, one cannot determine which aspects are typical (or general) and which are unique. Following the broader approach of George and Smoke[112] and of Snyder and Diesing,[113] Lebow made a comparative study of 26 historical crises since 1898.[114] He focused on the origins and outcomes of crises, and how the crises affected the subsequent relations between the protagonists, intensifying or ameliorating the conflicts.

Lebow distinguished among crises that are manufactured to justify an already made decision for war (such as Nazi Germany vs. Poland, 1939); spin-off crises from primary conflicts, which provoke confrontations with a third party (such as Germany's 1917 policy of unrestricted submarine warfare did with regard to the

United States); and brinkmanship crises, in which one state challenges another to compel it to withdraw from an important commitment (such as the Soviet block-ade of Berlin in 1948). He concluded that acute international crises can be decisive in the choices for war or peace; that immediate causes, therefore, can be as impor-tant as underlying causes (and may affect more than just the timing of war's out-break); and that the outcome of a crisis can improve or worsen adversary relations after war has been averted. A more significant conclusion is that successful crisis management depends not only on the commitment of policymakers to avoid war, but also on an "open decision-making environment, a cohesive political elite . . . [and] cultural, organizational and personal behavioral patterns established long before the onset of any crisis."[115]

In the crisis-management literature, an effort is made to relate crisis behavior to such variables as the structure of the international system. Thus, there are numerous points of linkage between (a) theoretical constraints related to polarity and structural realism and (b) international crisis, as described subsequently in this chapter. The behavior of states in a crisis is said to be affected by the structure of the system (bipolar or multipolar) and by the nature of military technology. In this perspective, the rivalry of the United States and the Soviet Union was ordained more by structure (their power preponderance over all others) than by ideology. Snyder and Diesing agree with Kenneth N. Waltz's hypothesis that a bipolar sys-tem is more likely than a multipolar one to be stable. Such analysis accords with findings from the work of Michael Brecher, Jonathan Wilkenfeld, and Sheila Moser, discussed later in this chapter. In the bipolar system, alignments are clear, and realignments do not alter the balance of power significantly. In the multipolar system, alignments may be unclear, and shifts may be important. Because of their greater ambiguity, multipolar systems are more prone to changes in the perception of interests, to gambling or risk-taking, and to miscalculations that make crises more dangerous. The tension between bargaining among allies and bargaining between adversaries (or between restraining the ally and deterring the opponent) is more difficult to manage in a multipolar system crisis.[116] By the same token, however, crises that break out between two actors, or between two blocs of actors, in a bipolar system are likely to hold the potential for escalation to general war, or to be system dominant, rather than confined to one of the regional subsystems. A crisis can break out, however, in which superpowers are drawn into a confrontation by client states, as they were in the 1973 Yom Kippur War.

Nuclear-weapons technology has had a considerable effect on international crises by widening enormously the gap between the value of the interests in con-flict and the possible cost of war for the holders of such weapons. Nuclear powers strive to protect, and indeed to advance, their interests, but they are said to be motivated by the disaster-avoidance constraint to be more cautious and prudent in crisis management and to raise, as if by tacit consent, the provocation threshold of war, thereby increasing the range for maneuvering in crises.[117] The nuclear powers have substituted for war itself psychological force in the form of carefully managed risks of war.[118] In this respect, crisis management, including the use of a variety of instruments of statecraft and the threat, real or perceived, to use force, has become a surrogate for the actual use of military capabilities, including nuclear weapons, as we have already noted. Herein lies a linkage between crisis decision making and deterrence theory, which, as discussed in Chapter 9, encompasses both the threat of escalation, and escalation itself. The state that is able to demonstrate to its opponent the capacity to punish at a higher level of conflict—or a higher rung on the escalatory ladder—holds the potential for deterring in a crisis situation or for escalation dominance.

Crisis management, it may be inferred, is the ability of one of the parties, by credibly threatening escalation, to deter its adversary from escalation and to produce a crisis de-escalation outcome in accord with its interests. This does not mean, however, that a crisis ends only when one adversary party capitulates or backs away. A crisis may also be resolved through a process in which both contestants exercise restraint and seek a face-saving path of mutual retreat or a compromise that transforms the situation without being incompatible with the irreducible interests of either. Nor does it mean that there is universal agreement among theorists concerned with crisis behavior about the dual relationship between military power and escalation dominance, or between deterrence capabilities and crisis management.

According to Lebow, motivation is a key element in crisis behavior. His analysis of 20 crises since 1898 led him to conclude, "To the extent that leaders perceive the need to act, they become insensitive to the interests and commitments of others that stand in the way of the success of their policy." By the same token, Lebow suggests that leaders may be unwilling to commit resources at their disposal to policies that do not serve what they regard as important interests. In short, increased capabilities may not inevitably translate into policies of confrontation. As a result, leaders may discard or discount information that runs counter to the course of action on which they have embarked in support of their established goals. "In the absence of compelling domestic and strategic needs most leaders may be reluctant or unwilling to pursue confrontatory foreign policies even when they seem to hold out an excellent prospect of success."[119]

THE SYSTEMATIC STUDY
OF INTERNATIONAL CRISIS BEHAVIOR

In an effort to contribute to the development of a comprehensive theory of crisis behavior, Michael Brecher, Jonathan Wilkenfeld, and Sheila Moser assembled data about 278 international crises for the 50-year period between 1929 and 1979. Their objective, in the International Crisis Behavior Project, was to examine on a comparative basis, with the use of quantitative research, a large number of crises displaying various and differing characteristics. They sought to generate systematic knowledge about crises on a global basis. The project had as its focus crises between major powers, as well as those between major powers and smaller powers, and between smaller powers themselves. Their goal was to illuminate such dimensions of international crisis as the images and behavior of major powers, the behavioral patterns of weak actors, the role of deterrence, the bargaining between adversaries, the role of alliance partners in crisis management, the catalysts or triggering factors that produce crises, the processes and causative factors by which crises are resolved in alternative types of outcomes; and, finally, the consequences of crises for the power and status, as well as subsequent perceptions, of participant states.[120]

The authors examine crisis behavior at both the macro- and the microlevels. At the macrolevel, they address crisis behavior between or among actors. An international crisis has as its defining characteristic "disruptive interactions between two or more adversaries," accompanied by the probability of military hostilities or, if war has already broken out, the potential for an adverse change in the military balance. Furthermore, an international crisis is said to pose a challenge to the existing structure of the international system or the subsystem within which it takes place.

According to Brecher, Wilkenfeld, and Moser, moreover, it is necessary to address crisis behavior at the microlevel, from the perspective of the individual actors and their foreign policies. Therefore, they define a foreign-policy crisis as having two necessary and sufficient conditions that are derived from a change in the state's internal or external environment. These are perceptions held by the highest decision makers that there is (1) a threat to basic values, together with an awareness of finite time for response to the threat; and (2) a high probability that military hostilities will ensue. In short, at the level of the international system stand the interactive patterns between or among the crisis participants. For each of the states that are parties, there is a foreign-policy crisis. In the study of crisis management, it is possible to focus on the macrolevel—interaction between and among crisis participants—or to address the foreign-policy behavior of individual states at the microlevel. The International Crisis Behavior Project was designed to encompass both levels of analysis. In this conceptualization, there is an inextricable link between the macro- and the microlevels. A decision made or an action taken by one state elicits a response from another state, generating an interactive process that in itself makes the crisis international.

Within the 50-year period addressed by the project, it was found that crises occur in diverse geographical and strategic environments, with varying levels of participation by major powers.[121] Crises may erupt without leading to actual military hostilities, or they may be the prelude to war. In other cases, crises were found to take place as part of an ongoing conflict or war. The authors found that crises were more frequent in Asia in the period between 1929 and 1979 than in any other part of the world; such crises were longer, proportionately, than crises that took place in other regions. In contrast to the 69 crises that broke out in Asia, the Americas were the locus of 33 crises, the smallest number of any region. Europe ranked behind Asia, with 57 crises between 1929 and 1979. The crises that took place in Europe tended to be multiactor crises; those that actually led to war occurred before 1945. Ranking also behind Europe was the Middle East, with 55 crises during the 50-year period of the study. More than half of the Middle East crises had at least six actors. Most of the crises in the region came after World War II and had varying levels of U.S. and Soviet involvement.

Africa, the region containing the youngest states, most of which gained independence in the 1960s, provided the setting for 64 crises, just behind Asia. More than half of these crises formed part of protracted conflicts. In Africa, nonstate entities accounted for the largest number of triggering factors. The United States played an active role, principally political and economic, in nearly half of the post–World War II African crises. The Soviet Union took part in slightly fewer crises than the United States in Africa, although its military-related activity was greater than that of the United States.

In the International Crisis Behavior Project, the global system was divided into four polarity periods: multipolar (1929–1939); World War II (1939–1945); bipolar (1945–1962); and again multipolar (1963–1969). According to their findings, which may be read in the context of our discussion of the impact of international systemic structure on conflict (see Chapters 2–3), the multipolar system of the period after 1963 was said to be less stable than the preceding bipolar system. Multipolarity, with its diffusion of decisional centers reflecting the emergence of a large number of additional actors, resulted in a sharp increase in crises having violent break points. In the earlier multipolar decade before World War II, nearly all of the crises had the major powers as direct participants. This period ranked highest in the use of pacific techniques to achieve crisis termination—a preoccupation with appeasement as a means of war avoidance. In the subsequent period, World War II, in nearly all cases, the crisis-management techniques used were for the most part violent in nature. In the bipolar period that followed, there was a decline in the overt use of violence, and especially full-scale war, as a crisis-management technique.

In keeping with their effort to discuss crisis at the macro- and the microlevels, Brecher, Wilkenfeld, and Moser suggest a further delineation within the international system itself. Their conceptualization provides for a categorization of crises within the dominant system, such as Europe before 1945 or between East–West blocs since that time, contrasted with the several regional subsystems. Crises that break out in a subsystem such as the Middle East or Africa, with the direct participants being in the subsystem, can escalate into the dominant system. Similarly, as the authors found, crises that begin in a dominant system can spill over into a subsystem. Among their findings, they conclude that all but 64 crises had a subsystem, rather than a dominant system, as their context.

Dominant-system crises tended to be longer in duration than crises at other system levels. Dominant-system crises were more threatening, dangerous, and destabilizing than subsystemic crises because of the greater capacity of major powers for violence. The occurrence of violence in dominant-system crises was more likely to be marked by full-scale war, while serious or minor clashes were more frequent in subsystem crises. Furthermore, crises at the dominant-system level had a greater propensity than those at other levels to provide definitive outcomes, such as victory or defeat, rather than stalemate or compromise. The effectiveness of international organizations, especially the United Nations, was greater at the subsystem level than within the dominant system.

Among the phenomena studied were the types of crisis-conflict environment. Brecher, Wilkenfeld, and Moser differentiated among settings that included (1) long-term hostility between adversaries over multiple issues, leading to periodic violence resulting in protracted conflict; (2) extended wars that form part of a protracted conflict; and (3) crises that are not set within the context of any protracted conflict. They found that crises were more likely than not to occur within one or the other protracted conflict setting. The most threatening and destabilizing crises occurred within a prolonged violent conflict. In such situations, as might be expected, crisis actors were more prone to resort to violence than were their counterparts in other conflict situations. Moreover, the authors concluded that, where power discrepancies between adversaries were low, there was a greater likelihood of violent break points or triggers in the outbreak and escalation of the crisis. It is suggested that strong states facing weak adversaries find resort to violence to be less necessary than states with few or no major power disparities with their enemies. Stated differently, the most frequent type of triggering factor in crises characterized by substantial gaps in capabilities between protagonists was nonviolent in nature.

In their discussion of actor attributes or characteristics, Brecher, Wilkenfeld, and Moser concluded that in all crises, actors opted for smaller rather than larger decision-making units. The higher the level of superpower involvement, the greater is the frequency of the head of government to be the principal communicator. Furthermore, the longer a state had existed, the greater was the likelihood that its crisis decision-making unit would contain more than 10 persons. However, the basic decisional unit consisted of four persons or fewer in 51 percent of all actor cases, and in only 22 percent was the unit larger than 10 persons. It was also found that negotiation and other nonviolent techniques were more frequently employed by older states in crisis management. The more authoritarian the regime, it was found, the greater was the possibility that it would resort to violent crisis triggers. According to the data analyzed, the democratic political systems had an almost equal tendency to utilize small, medium, or large decisional units in a crisis. In contrast, authoritarian political systems, as might be expected, opted for a small decisional unit, composed of 1 to 4 persons.

PSYCHOLOGY AND DECISION MAKING

How decision makers define situations about which they must make choices leading to action has important implications for how they perceive such choices. Decision makers base decisions on images of reality that are shaped by cognition, or how decision makers think about a particular decisional situation. *Images* are generally defined as cognitive constructions or mental representations of situations, including perceptions of other actors, as well as the alternative choices that may be available in light of the goals established by decision makers. Psychologists generally agree that the process by which images are developed, as well as the relationship between images and cognition—between the stimuli that enter the brain and how the cognitive process shapes, and is shaped by, such stimuli, converting them into response—is complex.[122] How decision makers perceive reality is not easily studied because what decision makers see in any specific situation is an empirical question.

As Richard K. Herrmann and Michael P. Fischerkeller suggest, it is essential to ascertain empirically how decision makers "mentally represent the situation, understand stimuli and process their choices."[123] In other words, the causal relationships that are formed within the cognitive process consist of many elements. These may include the decision maker's philosophical beliefs about world politics, the nature and magnitude of the threat posed by an enemy, the perceived power of such an adversary, and judgments about the norms of behavior of another actors. The actions of decision makers are the result of a combination of such factors as the structure of the decisional unit, how information is received and processed, what advice the decision makers receive from their key advisers, the personality characteristics of decision makers, the political coalition they are able to form, and the nature of domestic support and opposition.

Such large numbers of causal variables, Herrmann and Fischerkeller assert, makes difficult an understanding or prediction of precisely which perceptions from this list will prevail. In their own work, these authors suggest a theory of images based on five different kinds of strategic perception. These include first, an "enemy image," the view of another actor as threatening, as set forth in the classical security dilemma described in Chapter 2. Their effort to describe a spectrum of images leads them to develop a second strategic perception, which they call a "degenerate image," in which another state is viewed as providing an opportunity to be exploited by an actor claiming cultural superiority. For example, Adolph Hitler viewed Great Britain and France, as well as the United States, as being culturally inferior to Nazi Germany. A third image is termed the "colony image," in which the target is deemed to be both weaker and culturally inferior. This accords with the Western perception of other regions during the era of European colonialism. The fourth image developed by Herrmann and Fischerkeller is the "imperialist image," which stands in sharp contrast to the colony image. In the imperialist image, a subject perceives a threat from a state that is more powerful but not culturally superior. Finally, there is the "ally image," in which one state actor perceives that the prospects for mutual gain from increasing alignment and cooperation outweigh other factors, whether they be disparities in power or in culture.

Applying this theory to an examination of conflicts in the Persian Gulf from 1977 to 1992, the authors, for example, seek to understand more fully Saddam Hussein's motives by "asking if his imagery resembled enemy, imperialist, or degenerate stereotypes of the United States, Iran, or the Arab gulf states. The first two would be consistent with a defensive and perceived-threat-based interpretation, the last with a more defensive and opportunity-based interpretation."[124] How actors respond to situations in the form of strategies depends on which of the five images forms the basis for their decisions. The authors suggest that the logic of their images leads, in the case of the target in the degenerate category, to a likely decision to initiate a direct attack. By the same token, if an actor views the target as an ally and willing, therefore, to cooperate for mutual gain, it will set forth policies based on decisions intended to increase the incentive for the ally to reciprocate. In sum, this work represents an effort to disaggregate a range of images associated with national security as a basis for understanding empirically and theoretically the cognitive dimension of decision making.

One of the most interesting aspects of crisis decision making pertains to the element of choice under pressure of time. We have already reviewed the Holsti–North–Brody study, in which perceptions of hostility in both verbal communications and action signals were shown to be important, the more so as the decision makers became more deeply engaged and involved in the crisis. Holsti has asked whether decision makers, under the stress of crisis that may require a round-the-clock watch, can be expected to be efficient in identifying major alternative courses of action, estimating the probable costs and gains of each option, discriminating between relevant and irrelevant information, and resisting premature cognitive closure and action.[125] Analysts are not in agreement on whether moderate stress improves human performance or interferes with problem solving.

Martha L. Cottam reviewed some of the major cognitive approaches employed by certain political scientists who have written on decision making—Alexander George, Nathan Leites, Ole Holsti, and others.[126] The focus of her work was on the effects of cognitive processes on political decision makers and the effects of cognitive patterns on policymakers' images of the international world, as well as their ability to adapt to changes in the political environment. Cottam agreed with Robert Jervis's view that DM studies often fail to build on earlier works, use little psychology, and do not link psychology to behavior.[127] Citing Jervis as an exception who is careful not to throw all the psychological theories into one grab-bag from which he draws a psychological model, Cottam criticizes political scientists who do not separate beliefs and cognition or distinguish between beliefs and motivations.[128] Her warning against the uncritical borrowing of psychological theory by political scientists bears repeating:

> Psychology cannot be blindly applied to political analysis. The controls of the psychological laboratory will never be available for political analysis. . . . What psychology does have to offer are very general guidelines for arguments about how people make political decisions.[129]

Cottam's particular focus was on the basic level categories used by decision makers to divide the political world—categories that facilitate the process of incoming information with maximum efficiency and minimum effort. She identified seven such images or categories typical of U.S. policymakers, based not on ideology, issue positions, or geography, but rather on such characteristic attributes of states as military capability, domestic policy, economic structure, culture, supportiveness, flexibility, and goals. The seven types by which policymakers categorize foreign states were found to be enemy, hegemonist, dependent ally of the enemy, neutral, ally, U.S. dependent, and puppet.[130]

Richard Ned Lebow suggests the importance of cognitive and motivational processes as a necessary basis for analyzing decision-making behavior under crisis conditions. Yet the relative explanatory power of cognitive and motivational models in the study of crisis decisions is not easily determined. Lebow's examination of international crises led to the conclusion that they provide competing explanations for many of the same phenomena, and notably for information distortion. For example, according to cognitive theory, decision makers seek to achieve cognitive consistency—that is to say, they are likely to interpret, incorporate, or discard information that is received as a crisis proceeds, in accordance with their existing assumptions, predispositions, and perceptions. Especially under conditions of extreme time constraints, the reluctance to reconsider a decision that has already been made is likely to be proportionate to the difficulty experienced in making it in the first place.

Such was the problem, according to Lebow, confronting Austria and other major powers in the weeks leading to the outbreak of World War I after the crisis had begun. Aside from the pressure of time, there is likely to be a reluctance, often but not always based on time constraints, under crisis conditions, to seek alternative sources of information. In the case of the United States, which in 1950 downplayed the likelihood of Chinese military intervention in the Korean War, political–military leaders "had no desire to challenge advisors who told them what they wished to hear."[131] Intelligence estimates and official policy analyses may be distorted as a result of cognitive closure. Once committed to a policy of confrontation or of high-stakes bluffing in a crisis, leaders tended to disregard information that challenged their assumptions and expectations about success. By the same token, "When initiators recognized and corrected for initial misjudgments, they usually succeeded in averting war, although this often required a major cooperative effort, as in the Fashoda and Cuban missile crises."[132]

Similarly, motivational theory, which explains misperception by reference to the emotional needs of the actors, is said to offer insights that, according to Lebow, serve to reinforce and complement findings from the cognitive model. Lebow suggests that the need on the part of decision makers to believe that the policy on which they have embarked will succeed helps to account for reluctance or unwillingness to make changes in spite of evidence to the contrary. This motivational need may itself play an important role in shaping cognitive choices. The quest for cognitive consistency is said to be related to motivational need. Thus Lebow, in his discussion of the U.S. decision to discount the prospect of Chinese military intervention into the Korean War, asks, "Did American military intelligence in Tokyo, for example, underestimate the number of Chinese in Korea because this conformed to their expectations or because it satisfied their needs? A good case can be made for either explanation."[133] It can be said that all crisis decisions give rise to situations of threat and counterthreat that produce tension within the participants, whether in the form of excitement, fear, anxiety, frustration, dissonance, or some other psychological state. A knowledge of how conditions of stress affect the solidarity and problem-solving ability of small groups may cast light on the way leaders behave at crucial decision-making junctures.

Jonathan M. Roberts has discussed somewhat anecdotally the implications for political decision making in crisis such biological factors as mental illness (cerebral arteriosclerosis, schizophrenia, paranoia, hypomania, and depression); age; impaired speech, vision, and hearing; nutritional disorders; alcoholism; lapse of memory; sleeplessness and extreme fatigue; and the effects of drugs such as stimulants.[134] It should be noted, however, that it is almost impossible to acquire accurate and reliable empirical data concerning the total health picture of key policymakers during times of international crisis. Much (but not all) research in biopolitics remains speculative and dependent on persuasive logical inference more than on strict scientific evidence.

Psychologists have designed experiments to test the effects of stress on group integration and the problem-solving efficiency of groups. It has been found, as one might expect, that individuals in groups react differently to stress. We know that for both individuals and groups, increased stress may lead to aggression, withdrawal or escape-seeking behavior, regression, or various neurotic symptoms. John T. Lanzetta has furnished the following description of his experiments with groups:

> It was found that as stress increased there was a decrease in behaviors associated with friction in the group; a decrease in the number of disagreements, arguments, aggressions, deflations, and other negative social–emotional behaviors, as well as a decrease in self-oriented behaviors. Concomitant with this decrease was an increase in behaviors which would tend to result in decreased friction and better integration of the group; an increase in collaborating, mediating, cooperating behaviors.[135]

Lanzetta suggests that the reason for this phenomenon is to be found in the tendency of group members, faced with conditions that produce stress and anxiety, to seek psychological security in the group through cooperative behavior. However, the hypothesis of group integration under stress seems to be valid only up to a point. It may be that group members provide mutual reinforcement for each other only while they expect to be able to find a solution to their common problem. Robert L. Hamblin designed an experiment that led him to suggest that group integration during a crisis will begin to decrease if no likely solution appears to be available. Cooperation is likely while it is potentially profitable, but when the members of the group meet one failure after another no matter what they do, they experience a frustration that leads to antagonism against one another. In some cases, individuals attempt to resolve the crisis problem for themselves by withdrawing and leaving the other members to work out their own solution if they can—a process tantamount to group disintegration.[136] Zeev Maoz found that decision makers do better at moderate than at high or low levels of stress.[137] Jonathan M. Roberts reached a similar conclusion, adding that a high degree of stress can improve performance for a limited time, but that the quality of decisions is likely eventually to deteriorate.[138]

Hamblin's findings may prove relevant for understanding the behavior of leadership groups in international conflict when they perceive that the tide is beginning to turn against them, regardless of which strategy or tactics they pursue. Here, however, a caveat is in order: The behavior of national or other political leadership groups is a more complex phenomenon than the behavior of a small ad hoc group playing an experimental game. The stress conditions encountered during the course of a struggle that lasts for weeks, months, or even years are much more intricate psychologically than those experienced in a 2-hour game. The internal and external settings are infinitely richer in variety, as are the values, perceptions, cross-pressures, information, and political–cultural guidelines that impinge on the decision makers. In a larger-scale and more prolonged crisis, the time factor may permit various subtle adjustment mechanisms to come into play that can never operate in a brief experiment.

One cannot deny, however, that there is some relationship between stress and problem-solving efficiency. Dean G. Pruitt, synthesizing the findings of several writers in the field, concludes that the relationship is probably curvilinear, with some stress being necessary to motivate activity, but too much stress causing a reduction in efficiency.[139] Crisis inevitably brings in its wake a foreshortened perspective, a difficulty in thinking ahead and calculating consequences, and a tendency to select for consideration only a narrow range of alternatives—those that occur most readily to the decision makers.[140] Naturally, if more time were available, a wider spectrum of choices could be evaluated, but the preciousness of time is built into the definition of crisis. Contingency planning can help, but the crisis that comes is invariably somewhat different, at least in its details, from the crisis that was abstractly anticipated in contingency plans.

Holsti lists other effects of stress uncovered as a result of empirical research: increased random behavior, increased rate of error, regression to simpler and more primitive modes of response, problem-solving rigidity, diminished focus of attention, and a reduction in tolerance for ambiguity.[141] He notes that "the common use during crisis of such techniques as ultimatums and threats with built-in deadlines is likely to increase the stress under which the recipient must operate" because they heighten the salience of the time element and increase the danger of fixation on the single, familiar approach regardless of its effectiveness in the present situation.[142] Other analysts have found that diplomatic communications transmitted during international crises that were settled peacefully (Morocco, 1911; Berlin, 1948–1949; Cuba, 1962) were characterized by greater flexibility and subtlety of distinctions, as well as by more extensive information search and usage, than were communications during crises that led to World War I in 1914 and to the Korean conflict in 1950.[143] Finally, in connection with the time variable, it should be noted that if in the past, international crises were often marked by insufficient information, in recent decades, technological conditions, combined with the desire of bureaucrats to generate and transmit vast amounts of information during crises, create the opposite danger of overloading the circuits of the decision-making system.

Other scholars in recent years have attempted to develop, as a measure of crisis decision-making behavior, what is called "voice-stress analysis."[144] Such work represents an analysis of stress levels derived from public statements of U.S. presidents, from Kennedy to Nixon, during international crises in their respective administrations. The authors suggest that much of crisis behavior consists of communications between opposing decision makers at the highest level. Statements from such leaders, even those addressed primarily to their own publics or the outside world, contain symbols and nuances that convey messages to their opposite number and furnish data for scholarly analysis. Psycholinguistics provides the basis for research into the cognitive basis for language behavior and thus for efforts to develop a measure of stress in decision makers under crisis conditions by reference to changes in speech patterns. *Stress* is defined as the "negative affect, anxiety, fear and/or biophysiological change which develops as the internal response of an individual to an external load placed on him or her by an international crisis (pathogenic agentstressor) which is perceived to pose a severe threat to one or more values of the political decision-maker."[145] By examining multiple documents such as speeches and press conferences from the 1961 Berlin, 1965 Dominican Republic, and 1970 Cambodia crises, it was possible, the authors suggest, to chart levels of stress on the part of the president as each crisis unfolded. Although they call for additional research development to advance voice-stress analysis, they conclude that prepared statements manifested the highest stress levels. Conceivably, this indicates that, at times of greatest crisis intensity and stress, decision makers are more prone than otherwise to resort to prepared, rather than extemporaneous, materials.

Last but not least, the study of crisis or other decision-making behavior by the utilization of political psychophysiology is regarded as a subarea of biopolitics, itself the use of biological indicators in the analysis of political behavior. To what extent, it is asked, do the physical–psychological conditions of decision makers contribute to, or detract from, their ability to manage crises or otherwise shape their behavioral characteristics? According to Thomas Wiegele, a "truly profound understanding of human nature must ultimately include both biological and nonbiological considerations."[146]

Groups that make the most crucial decisions in national security cases are usually limited in size—perhaps 12 to 20 persons. Irving Janis has analyzed what he calls "groupthink" and has described its characteristics. The members of a small group of decision makers often share an illusion of invulnerability that may encourage them to take extreme risks. Their self-confidence is mutually reinforcing, such that they may discount warnings or information that runs counter to their own assumptions. They often have a stereotyped and simplified view of the enemy and an unquestioned belief in their own inherent morality. They are quick to censure and drive out of circulation viewpoints that do not conform to the dominant assessments and judgments of the group, and they take the silence of dissenting or doubtful members to mean that there exists virtual unanimity in the thinking of the group.[147] It should not be taken for granted that groupthink is necessarily bad. The dominant element within the group may well be correct in its assessment of the situation and in its views on the proper course to be pursued. Furthermore, the tendency of a group to impose a dominant view on all its members—a natural social phenomenon—may produce more adverse consequences in an ideologically monolithic society than in a democratic one, and also more adverse consequences at lower bureaucratic echelons, where individuals are less independent and outspoken, than at top levels, where more powerful personalities are usually present to speak their minds.

DECISION MAKING AND DOMESTIC POLITICS

We saw earlier that the minutes of the ExComm meetings during the Cuban Missile Crisis produced no evidence that decisions were influenced by considerations of domestic politics. It is possible, of course, that because all involved were members or supporters of the Kennedy Administration, there was no need to articulate thoughts that might have been on several minds. During the 1990s, theorists have emphasized the requirement for a more careful integration of thinking about foreign-policy decision making and domestic politics. Robert Putnam portrayed political leaders as positioned between the two tables of (1) international negotiation, whether in crisis or noncrisis situations, and (2) the pressures of domestic political forces. The diplomatic course to be pursued has to be tailored both to what other states are likely to find acceptable and to what domestic constituencies can be persuaded to ratify.[148]

Such an approach represents a deviation from that of Kenneth N. Waltz and other structural realists who, as shown in Chapter 2, make the international system rather than the internal processes of the state itself the primary determinant of a state's international behavior. Andrew Moravcsik has contended that it is not sufficient to "give priority to international explanation and employ theories of domestic politics only as needed to explain anomalies."[149] Pure international theories, he held, are attractive in principle, but they "tend to degenerate under the collective weight of empirical anomalies and theoretical limitations" to the point where the single level of analysis (international) must give way to the integration of two levels (international and domestic).[150] Peter B. Evans has found (a) that the logic of the international system, as well as the autonomy of the executive, is more pronounced in cases involving national security, whereas constituency pressures become more salient in matters affecting the domestic economy and foreign trade; (b) that the relative autonomy of leaders decreases substantially the longer negotiations last; and (c) that hawkish leaders have less autonomy than dovish leaders because they impose greater potential costs on both domestic and foreign groups.[151] Finally, James G. Richter has argued that both U.S. and Soviet leaders who sought to ameliorate Cold War behavior "had to overcome not simply the entrenched image of an aggressive enemy existing in the other superpower, but also the roots of a similar Cold War mythology in their own domestic systems," which helped to perpetuate Cold War attitudes even after upheavals had begun to change the international system.[152]

CONCLUSIONS

The field of decision making is a broad one, and we do not pretend to be able to cover it all. The decision-making process is a function of many different factors relating to the behavior of individuals and of large organizational structures. The DM role is shaped by both the system and the individual's interpretation of it, and the influence of personality in comparison with social ideology will vary markedly from one system to another. Democratic and totalitarian states make foreign policy in very different ways. Most decision-making theories developed in the United States have, quite understandably, focused on the American political experience—on the role of public opinion, the state of executive–congressional relations, the nature of the bureaucratic competition in the annual battle of the budget in Washington, and so on. There is an inevitable tendency on the part of social scientists, unless they guard against it, to universalize from particulars, and to assume that at least certain aspects of a phenomenon studied in one cultural-political context can be *mutatis mutandis* given a more generalized application. Thus, there is a danger that when Americans think about such basic concepts as rationality in decision making, bureaucratic competition for scarce resources, or action–reaction processes either in prolonged arms races or in acute crisis, lessons drawn from an observation of the behavior of American decision makers can be inappropriately carried over to the behavior of decision makers in vastly different environments—Moscow, Beijing, Tokyo, New Delhi, or Baghdad.

We must admit that we do not know a great deal about foreign-policy decision making in non-Western capitals, particularly those far removed from any constitutional democratic experience. Even among the Western democratic states with which American political scientists are generally most familiar—Britain, France, Italy, and the Federal Republic of Germany—considerable differences exist in the organization of governments for the conduct of foreign affairs, as well as in the ways that elites typically conceive of their national interests. The difficulties of extrapolating from American experience to foreign decision-making processes become even more pronounced when we are dealing with governments and countries that are politically, ideologically, socioeconomically, and culturally very different from those of the West. During the 1970s and 1980s, significant strides were made in the comparative study of leadership, bureaucracy, value orientations of elites, and decision making in communist, socialist, and Third World countries.[153] The student should become acquainted with the comparative study of foreign-policy decision making in Western and non-Western societies.[154] The field of comparative foreign policies is distinct from that of international-relations theory, and specifically from theories of decision making in the international system, but the former has much to contribute to the latter by way of concrete data and perhaps of insights leading to useful new theoretical approaches.

NOTES

1. See Paul Wasserman and Fred S. Silander, *Decision-Making: An Annotated Bibliography* (Ithaca, NY: Graduate School of Business and Public Administration, Cornell University, 1958).
2. "Decision-Making as an Approach to the Study of International Politics," in Richard C. Snyder, H. W. Bruck, and Burton Sapin, eds., *Foreign Policy Decision-Making* (New York: Free Press, 1963), p. 65; see also pp. 85–86.
3. Robert Jervis, *Perception and Misperception in International Politics* (Princeton, NJ: Princeton University Press, 1976), pp. 66–76 and 343–355.
4. Joseph Frankel, *The Making of Foreign Policy: An Analysis of Decision-Making* (New York: Oxford University Press, 1963), p. 4.
5. Michael Brecher, *The Foreign Policy System of Israel: Setting, Images, Process* (New Haven, CT: Yale University Press, 1972), p. 4. For a thorough discussion of objective environment and decision makers' perception, see Hyam Gold, "Foreign Policy Decision-Making and the Environment: The Claims of Snyder, Brecher and the Sprouts," *International Studies Quarterly*, 22 (December 1978), 569–586.
6. Students of decision making have suggested several different ways of analyzing the phenomenon. Harold Lasswell, for example, presents seven functional stages: information, recommendation, prescription, invocation, application, appraisal, and termination. *The Decision Process: Seven Categories of Functional Analysis* (College Park, MD: University of Maryland Press, 1956). See also James A. Robinson and R. Roger

Majak, "The Theory of Decision-Making," in James C. Charlesworth, ed., *Contemporary Political Analysis* (New York: Free Press, 1967), pp. 178–181, including bibliographical references; John P. Lovell, *Foreign Policy in Perspective: Strategy, Adaptation, Decision-Making* (New York: Holt, Rinehart and Winston, 1970), especially pp. 205–261. Michael Brecher makes the elite image the decisive input of a foreign-policy system; op. cit., p. 11.

7. David Braybrooke and Charles E. Lindblom, *A Strategy of Decision* (New York: Free Press, 1963), p. 40.

8. Max Weber, *Economy and Society: An Outcome of Interpretative Analogy,* edited by Guenther Roth and Claus Wittich, Vol. 2. (Berkeley: University of California Press, 1978), p. 1393. For Weber's brilliant pioneering views on charismatic leadership and legal–rational bureaucracy, see chaps. X, XII, and XIII in Reinhard Bendix, *Max Weber: An Intellectual Portrait* (Garden City, NY: Doubleday, 1960; Anchor Books, 1962).

9. James A. Nathan and James K. Oliver, *Foreign Policy Making and the American Political System,* 2nd ed. (Boston: Little, Brown, 1987), pp. 10–11.

10. Morton H. Halperin, with the assistance of Priscilla Clapp and Arnold Kanter, *Bureaucratic Politics and Foreign Policy* (Washington DC: Brookings Institution, 1974). See also Morton H. Halperin and Arnold Kanter, "The Bureaucratic Perspective" in the book they edited, *Readings in Foreign Policy: A Bureaucratic Perspective* (Boston: Little, Brown, 1973). Other literature includes Robert J. Art, "Bureaucratic Politics and American Foreign Policy: A Critique," *Policy Sciences,* 4(4) (December 1973), 467–490; Steven D. Krasner, "Are Bureaucracies Important? (Or Allison Wonderland)," *Foreign Policy,* (7) (Summer 1972), 159–179; David C. Kozak, "The Bureaucratic Politics Approach: The Evolution of the Paradigm," in David C. Kozak and James M. Keagle, eds., *Bureaucratic Politics and National Security Theory and Practice* (Boulder, CO: Lynne Riemer, 1988), pp. 3–15; Jiri Valenta, "The Bureaucratic Politics Paradigm and the Soviet Invasion of Czechoslovakia," *Political Science Quarterly,* 94(1) (Spring 1979), 55–76; Jiri Valenta, *Soviet Intervention in Czechoslovakia, 1968: Anatomy of a Decision* (Baltimore, MD: Johns Hopkins University Press, 1979); Karen Davisha, "The Limits of the Bureaucratic Politics Model: Observations on the Soviet Case," *Studies in Comparative Communism,* 13(4) (Winter 1980) 300–326.

11. Francis Rourke, *Bureaucracy and Foreign Policy* (Baltimore, MD: Johns Hopkins University Press, 1972), pp. 49–50.

12. Ibid., pp. 62–65. See also chaps. 7 and 8 on advocacy of interest groups and competing elites in Brecher, *The Foreign Policy System of Israel,* op. cit.

13. Alexander L. George, "The Case for Multiple Advocacy in Making Foreign Policy," *American Political Science Review,* LXVI (September 1972), 751–785, quoted at 758.

14. Alexander L. George, *Presidential Decisionmaking in Foreign Policy: The Effective Use of Information and Advice* (Boulder, CO: Westview, 1980), pp. 25–27, 145–148.

15. Ibid., pp. 25–27; 145–148.

16. Edward Rhodes, "Do Bureaucratic Politics Matter?" *World Politics,* 47 (October 1994), 1–41, especially pp. 1 and 39–41.

17. Richard C. Snyder et al., *Foreign Policy Decision-Making,* op. cit., p. 144.

18. David Easton, *The Political System* (New York: Knopf, 1953), p. 129.

19. Paul Diesing attributes a distinctive rationality to economic, social, technical, legal, and political decisions; *Reason in Society: Five Types of Decisions and Their Social Conditions* (Urbana: University of Illinois Press, 1962). Others, too, including R. C. Wood and William L. C. Wheaton, have cautioned against extrapolating from private to public decision behavior. Cf. Robinson and Majak in Charlesworth, ed., op. cit., pp.

177–178. Anthony Downs, on the other hand, is thought to equate private with public decision making; in Charlesworth, ed., ibid., 178. However, even he differentiates sharply between individual and organizational decision making. See Downs, *Inside Bureaucracy,* A RAND Corporation Research Study (Boston: Little, Brown, 1967), pp. 178–179.

20. See, for example, Marshall Dimock, *A Philosophy of Administration* (New York: Harper & Row, 1958), p. 140; J. David Singer, "Inter-nation Influence: A Formal Model," *American Political Science Review,* LXII (June 1963), 424; Bruce M. Russett, "The Calculus of Deterrence," *Journal of Conflict Resolution,* VII (June 1963), 97–109.

21. Richard Snyder et al., op. cit., p. 176. Snyder emphasizes that the explanation of decision-making motivation implies a concept of multiple membership of the individual (a) in a culture and society, (b) in such social groupings as the profession and class, (c) in the total political institutional structure, and (d) in the decisional unit; ibid., p. 172.

22. Snyder had accepted earlier the notion of "maximization of expected utility." See his "Game Theory and the Analysis of Political Behavior," in *Research Frontiers and Government* (Washington, DC: Brookings Institution, 1955), pp. 73–74.

23. As we have noted in Chapter 9, most theorists of deterrence appeared to accept Max Weber's notion that modern governmental bureaucracies act according to rational procedures in pursuing state interests. Many agreed implicitly with Bruce Bueno de Mesquita's expected-utility model in arriving at how decision makers order their policy priorities. See section on Bueno de Mesquita's theory and Notes 175–185 in Chapter 8. Bruce Bueno de Mesquita and David Lalman added the role of domestic politics to their expected-utility models; the domestic factor, combined with misperception, may induce states mistakenly to shun war and to choose a negotiated compromise; *War and Reason: Domestic and International Imperatives* (New Haven, CT: Yale University Press, 1992), pp. 267–269.

24. J. David Singer, op. cit., 428–430.

25. Martin Patchen, "Decision Theory in the Study of National Action," *Journal of Conflict Resolution,* LVII (June 1963), 165–169.

26. Sidney Verba, "Assumptions of Rationality and Nonrationality in Models of the International System," in James N. Rosenau, ed., *International Politics and Foreign Policy,* rev. ed. (New York: Free Press, 1969), p. 231.

27. David Braybrooke and Charles Lindblom, op. cit., ch. 4.

28. See Herbert A. Simon, *Administrative Behavior* (New York: Macmillan, 1958); "A Behavioral Model of Rational Choice," *Quarterly Journal of Economics,* LXIX (February 1955), 99–118; and "A Behavioral Model of Rational Choice," in Simon, ed., *Models of Man: Social and Rational* (New York: Wiley, 1957), pp. 241–260. See also William D. Coplin, *Introduction to International Politics: A Theoretical Overview* (Chicago: Markham, 1971), pp. 32–37.

29. David Braybrooke and Charles Lindblom, op. cit., pp. 71–79 and chap. 5.

30. James Robinson and Roger Majak, op. cit., pp. 180–183.

31. Ibid., p. 182. The references are to Arthur F. Bentley, *The Process of Government* (Chicago: University of Chicago Press, 1908); David B. Truman, *The Governmental Process* (Chicago: University of Chicago Press, 1951); and William H. Riker, *The Theory of Political Coalitions* (New Haven, CT: Yale University Press, 1962).

32. Graham T. Allison, *Essence of Decision: Explaining the Cuban Missile Crisis* (Boston: Little, Brown, 1971), pp. 4–5, 10-11.

33. Ibid., pp. 13–18.

34. Ibid., pp. 29–30.

35. Ibid., p. 5.
36. Ibid., p. 67.
37. Ibid., p. 68. For more on this, see the section "The Cybernetic Theory of Decision" in the text.
38. Allison, ibid., pp. 71–77.
39. Ibid, pp. 144–145; see also Graham T. Allison and Morton H. Halperin, "Bureaucratic Politics: A Paradigm and Some Policy Implications," *World Politics*, XXIV (Spring Supplement 1972), 40–79.
40. Jonathan Bendor and Thomas H. Hammond, "Rethinking Allison's Models," *American Political Science Review*, 86 (June 1992), 301–322.
41. Ibid., 305.
42. Ibid., 319. "Whatever their ultimate worth, rational choice models were not given a fair test"; ibid.
43. Ibid; see the matrix on 303.
44. Ibid., 319. See also the article by Edward Rhodes cited in aforementioned Note 16.
45. David A. Welch, "The Organizational Process and Bureaucratic Politics Paradigms: Retrospect and Prospect," *International Security*, 17(2) (Fall, 1992), 112–146.
46. Ibid., 138.
47. Glenn H. Snyder and Paul Diesing, *Conflict Among Nations: Bargaining, Decision-Making and System Structure in International Crises* (Princeton, NJ: Princeton University Press, 1977).
48. Ibid., p. 355.
49. Ibid., pp. 355–56. The authors did not find that attitudes of leading decision makers are significantly determined by bureaucratic role. "Thus the most distinctive point of the Allison–Halperin bureaucratic politics theory does not survive our analysis" (note on p. 408).
50. Ibid., pp. 333–335.
51. Ibid., pp. 337–338.
52. Ibid., pp. 338–339.
53. Miriam Steiner, "The Elusive Essence of Decision," *International Studies Quarterly*, 21 (June 1977), 419.
54. Ibid.
55. John D. Steinbruner, *The Cybernetic Theory of Decision: New Dimensions of Political Analysis* (Princeton, NJ: Princeton University Press, 1974), chap. 1.
56. Ibid., pp. 48–67. Steinbruner acknowledges that some of his own criticisms of the analytic paradigm had been anticipated in Herbert Simon's satisficing model, but in his view, Simon had not gone far enough; ibid., p. 63. Simon's satisficing model is less intuitional then the cybernetic model.
57. Ibid., p. 68.
58. Ibid., p. 69.
59. Ibid., p. 72. The reference is to Richard M. Cyert and James G. March, *A Behavioral Theory of the Firm* (Englewood Cliffs, NJ: Prentice-Hall, 1963), chap. 6. It should be noted that Steinbruner incorporates into the cybernetic paradigm the work of Charles Lindblom (especially his incrementalism) and the organization process model of Graham Allison (see Allison, *Essence of Decision*, pp. 77 and 80). Steinbruner fully agrees with those who hold that organizational routines, once established, are very difficult to alter.
60. John Steinbruner, op. cit., p. 92. Cf. also Robert Jervis, *Perception and Misperception and International Politics*, chap. 4. (Princeton, NJ: Princeton University Press, 1976.)

61. Steinbruner, op. cit., chap. 4. According to Snyder and Diesing, Steinbruner's "theoretical thinker" is equivalent to their "irrational bargainer"; *Conflict Among Nations,* op. cit., p. 337.

62. Steinbruner devoted the major part of his work to applying his modified cybernetic–cognitive paradigm to a single complex policy decision issue—the effort to share control of nuclear weapons within the Atlantic Alliance in the early 1960s. The United States was caught in a value trade-off between its general political purposes in Europe and its antiproliferation policy. He concluded that the ability of the U.S. State Department to generate momentum for the deployment of a NATO Multilateral Force (MLF), to which the U.S. Secretary of Defense, most U.S. military leaders, and European policymakers in general were opposed, was a political anomaly that could best be understood in terms of the cognitive and cybernetic processes of bureaucratic decision makers rather than in terms of the analytic paradigm. In contrast, President Johnson's decision in December 1964 to reverse his diplomatic advisers and kill the MLF, wrote Steinbruner, "can readily be understood by analytic logic." Steinbruner, *The Cybernetic Theory of Decision,* op. cit., chaps. 6 to 9, and pp. 320–321.

63. Ibid., p. 70. See also chap. 10, especially p.329.

64. Zeev Maoz, *National Choices and International Processes* (Cambridge, England: Cambridge University Press, 1990), pp. 330–336.

65. Charles F. Hermann and Linda P. Brady, "Alternative Models of International Crisis Behavior," in Charles F. Hermann, ed., *International Crisis: Insights from Behavioral Research* (New York: Free Press, 1972), pp. 218, 304–320.

66. See, for example, Ole R. Holsti, "The 1914 Case," *American Political Science Review,* LIX (June 1965), 365–378; Ole R. Holsti, Robert C. North, and Richard A. Brody, "Perception and Action in the 1914 Crisis," in J. David Singer, ed., *Quantitative International Politics* (New York: Free Press, 1968); Glenn D. Paige, *The Korean Decision, June 24–30, 1950* (New York: Free Press, 1958); Erskine B. Childer, *The Road to Suez* (London: MacGibbon and Kee, 1962); Charles A. McClelland, "Access to Berlin: The Quantity and Variety of Events, 1948–1963," in Singer, ed., op. cit., pp. 159–186; and "Decisional Opportunity and Political Controversy: The Quemoy Case," *Journal of Conflict Resolution,* VI (September 1962), 201–213; Graham T. Allison, *Essence of Decision: Explaining the Cuban Missile Crisis* (Boston: Little, Brown, 1971); and Herbert S. Dinerstein, *The Making of a Missile Crisis* (Baltimore, MD.: Johns Hopkins Press, 1976); Michael Brecher with Benjamin Geist, *Decisions in Crisis: Israel 1967 and 1973* (Berkeley and Los Angeles: University of California Press, 1980); Alan Dowty, *Middle East Crisis: U.S. Decision-Making in 1958, 1970, and 1973* (Berkeley and Los Angeles: University of California Press, 1984); Richard G. Head, Frisco W. Short, and Robert C. McFarlane, *Crisis Resolution: Presidential Decision-Making in the Mayaguez and Korean Confrontations* (Boulder, CO: Westview Press, 1978); Thomas M. Cynkin, *Soviet and American Signaling in the Polish Crisis* (London: Macmillan, 1988).

67. See, for example, Oran R. Young, *The Intermediaries: Third Parties in International Crisis* (Princeton, NJ: Princeton University Press, 1967); Oran R. Young, *The Politics of Force: Bargaining During International Crises* (Princeton, NJ: Princeton University Press, 1968); Mark W. Zacker, *International Conflicts and Collective Security, 1946–77* (New York: Praeger, 1979).

68. Glenn D. Paige, op. cit., p. 10.

69. Glenn D. Paige, op. cit., pp. 276–279.

70. Ole R. Holsti et al., "Perception and Action in the 1914 Crisis," in Singer, ed., op. cit., pp. 123–158. Ole R. Holsti later discussed the limits of validity of relying on financial

data as indicators of international tensions and concluded that such data constitute only a partial and indirect check on the validity of content data from other sources, such as diplomatic documents; see the section, "Perceptions of Hostility and Financial Indices in a Crisis," in chap. 3 of *Crisis, Escalation, War* (Montreal: McGill-Queens University Press, 1972), pp. 51–70.

71. Holsti, "Perceptions of Hostility," ibid., p. 46. The phenomenon described here is similar to the hostility–friendliness continuum and the unstable reaction coefficients studied by Lewis F. Richardson in his research on the arms races of 1908–1914 and 1929–1939; see *Arms and Insecurity* (Pittsburgh, PA: Boxwood, 1960), and *Statistics of Deadly Quarrels* (Chicago: Quadrangle Books, 1960), discussed in Chapter 8.

72. Ole Holsti et al., "Perception and Action," in Singer, ed., op. cit., p. 152.

73. Ibid., p. 157.

74. L. L. Farrar, Jr., "The Limits of Choice: July 1914 Reconsidered," *Journal of Conflict Resolution,* 16 (March 1972), 1–23. Reprinted in Melvin Small and J. David Singer, eds., *International War: An Anthology,* 2nd ed. (Chicago: Dorsey Press, 1989), pp. 264–287.

75. Early accounts included Henry M. Pachter, *Collision Course: The Cuban Missile Crisis and Coexistence* (New York: Praeger, 1963); Arthur M. Schlesinger, Jr., *A Thousand Days* (New York: Fawcett, 1965), pp. 250–277; Theodore C. Sorensen, *Kennedy* (New York: Harper & Row, 1965), pp. 667–718; Elie Abel, *The Missile Crisis* (Philadelphia: J. B. Lippincott, 1966); Robert F. Kennedy, *Thirteen Days: A Memoir of the Cuban Missile Crisis* (New York: Norton, 1969); and Graham T. Allison, *Essence of Decision* (see Note 32).

76. Allison, op. cit., p. 245.

77. Ibid., pp. 40–56. Albert and Roberta Wohlstetter provided the military argument for the "rectifying the nuclear balance" hypothesis in *Controlling the Risks in Cuba,* Adelphi Papers No. 17 (London: Institute for Strategic Studies, April 1965).

78. Bruce J. Allyn, James G. Blight, and David A. Welch, "Essence of Revision: Moscow, Havana and the Cuban Missile Crisis," *International Security,* 14 (Winter 1989/1990), 136–172, especially 138. The authors cite extensive references to Soviet literature on the subject. Other significant later works in English include Marc Trachtenberg, ed., "White House Tapes and Minutes of the Cuban Missile Crisis," *International Security,* 10 (Summer 1985), 171–194; James G. Blight, Joseph S. Nye, Jr., and David A. Welch, "The Cuban Missile Crisis Revisited," *Foreign Affairs,* 66 (Fall 1987), 170–188; David A. Welch and James G. Blight, "An Introduction to the ExComm Transcripts," *International Security,* 12 (Winter 1987/1988), 5–29; McGeorge Bundy, transcriber and James M. Blight, ed., "October 27, 1962: Transcripts of the Meetings of the ExComm," ibid., 30–92; Raymond Garthoff, *Reflections on the Cuban Missile Crisis* (Washington, DC: Brookings Institution, 1989); James A. Nathan, ed., *The Cuban Missile Crisis Revisited* (New York: St. Martin's Press, 1992); James G. Blight and David A. Welch, *On the Brink: Americans and Soviets Re-examine the Cuban Missile Crisis* (New York: Noonday Press, Faarrar Straus and Giroux, 1990).

79. Allyn et al., "Essence of Revision," op. cit., 139.

80. Blight et al., "The Cuban Missile Crisis Revisited," op. cit., 176.

81. Allyn et al., "Essence of Revision," op. cit., 143–144.

82. Allison, op. cit., pp. 102–106.

83. Ibid., pp. 106–108.

84. Ibid., pp. 109–113.

85. Ibid., pp. 113–117.

86. Ibid., pp. 117–126.

87. David A. Welch and James G. Blight, "An Introduction to the ExComm Transcripts," op. cit., 25. Welch and Blight, "Introduction . . . ," op. cit., 25. The authors nevertheless cite Robert Kennedy's reference in *Thirteen Days* (op. cit., p. 67) to the President's admission that if he failed to act he would be impeached; "Introduction," op. cit., pp. 24–25. In the same place, they also cite Fen Osler Hampson's view that leaders, forced into difficult trade-offs between key values, may act out of concern for their political survival; "The Divided Decision-Maker: American Domestic Politics and the Cuban Crises," *International Security*, 9 (Winter 1984/1985), 142–149.

88. Arthur Schlesinger, Jr., *Robert Kennedy and His Times* (Boston: Houghton Mifflin, 1978), pp. 506–507.

89. Allison, op. cit., pp. 187–210.

90. Ibid., p. 210.

91. Ibid., p. 228.

92. See ibid., pp. 220–330, 248–249.

93. Welch and Blight, "Introduction . . . ," op. cit., 11, 15–18; Allyn, Blight, and Welch, "Essence of Revision," op. cit., 158–159. It seems that Robert Kennedy virtually assured Soviet Ambassador Anatoly Dobrynin that the Jupiter missiles would soon be removed from Turkey, but that sensitivity to the Allies prevented a formal pledge to that effect; ibid., 165.

94. At the symposium on Cuba held in Moscow in January 1989, Soviet participants sought to maximize the danger of the missile crisis by suggesting that 20 nuclear warheads were ready to be fitted into nose cones. Ray S. Cline asserted that U.S. intelligence knew that warheads were en route, but that massive photo reconnaissance found no evidence that they ever reached Cuba; "The Cuba Missile Crisis," *Foreign Affairs*, 68 (Fall 1989), 191–192.

95. Irving Janis, *Victims of Groupthink* (Boston: Houghton Mifflin, 1972), cited in Welch and Blight, op. cit., 23. On groupthink, see text infro, p. 491.

96. Mark Kramer, "Remembering the Cuban Missile Crisis: Should We Swallow Oral History?" *International Security*, 15 (Summer 1990), 212–216.

97. Ole R. Holsti, Richard A. Brody, and Robert C. North, "Measuring Effect and Action in the International Reaction Models: Empirical Materials from the 1962 Cuban Crisis," *Journal of Peace Research*, I (1964), 174. See also Eliot A. Cohen, "Why We Should Stop Studying the Cuban Missile Crisis," *National Interest*, 2 (1986), 3–13; Richard Ned Lebow, "The Cuban Missile Crisis: Reading the Lessons Correctly," *Political Science Quarterly*, 98 (1983), 431–458.

98. Holsti, Brody and North, Ibid.

99. Ibid., 158. See also Ole R. Holsti, "Time, Alternatives and Communications: The 1914 and Cuban Missile Crises," in Charles F. Hermann, ed., op. cit., pp. 58–80.

100. James A. Robinson, "An Appraisal of Concepts and Theories," in Charles F. Hermann, ed., op. cit., p. 27.

101. In addition to the works cited previously on the Cuban Missile Crisis, other early contributions to the subject include Ole R. Holsti, *Crisis, Escalation, War*, op. cit.; and the articles in the March 1977 issue of *International Studies Quarterly*. See also Thomas J. Price, "Constraints on Foreign Policy Decision-Making," *International Studies Quarterly*, 22 (September 1978), 357–376; Michael Brecher, "State Behavior in International Crisis," *Journal of Conflict Resolution*, 23 (September 1979), 446–480.

102. Michael P. Sullivan, *International Relations: Theories and Evidence* (Englewood Cliffs, NJ: Prentice-Hall, 1976), p. 82.

103. Charles A. McClelland, "Crisis and Threat in the International Setting: Some Relational Concepts," unpublished memo cited in Michael Brecher, "Toward a Theory of

International Crisis Behavior," *International Studies Quarterly*, 21 (March 1977), 39–40.

104. Charles F. Hermann, "International Crisis as a Situational Variable," in James N. Rosenau, ed., *International Politics and Foreign Policy: A Reader in Research and Theory* (New York: Free Press, 1961), p. 414.

105. Gilbert R. Winham, ed., *New Issues in International Crisis Management* (Boulder, CO, and London: Westview Press, 1988), p. 5.

106. Michael Brecher and Jonathan Wilkenfeld, "Crises in World Politics," *World Politics*, 35 (1982), 383. Glenn H. Snyder and Paul Diesing had also specified the "perception of a dangerously high probability of war" as a defining ingredient of crisis; *Conflict Among Nations: Bargaining, Decision-Making and System Structure in International Crises* (Princeton, NJ: Princeton University Press, 1977), p. 7. Richard Ned Lebow included in his criteria a perceived threat to concrete national interests, the country's bargaining reputation, and the ability of its leaders to remain in power; the perception by leaders that action taken may increase the possibility of war; and perceived time constraints for response; *Between Peace and War: The Nature of International Crisis* (Baltimore and London: Johns Hopkins Press, 1981), pp. 9–12.

107. Richard K. Betts, "Analysis, War and Decision: Why Intelligence Failures Are Inevitable," *World Politics*, 31 (October 1978) 61–89.

108. Snyder and Diesing, *Conflict Among Nations*, op. cit., p. 4.

109. Ibid., p. 455. Although crises are dangerous, they are seen to be more functional than dysfunctional.

110. Oran R. Young, *The Intermediaries: Third Parties in International Crises,* op. cit., p. 10.

111. Glenn H. Snyder, "Crisis Bargaining," in Charles F. Hermann, ed., op. cit., p. 217.

112. Alexander L. George and Richard Smoke, *Deterrence in American Foreign Policy: Theory and Practice* (NY: Columbia University Press, 1974), p. 697.

113. Glenn H. Snyder and Paul Diesing, *Conflict Among Nations*, op. cit.

114. Richard Ned Lebow, *Between Peace and War.* The discussion here is based on Lebow's own summary in the form of excerpts from his 1981 book. See his "Decision Making in Crises," in Ralph K. White, ed., *Psychology and the Prevention of Nuclear War: A Book of Readings* (New York: New York University Press, 1986), pp. 397–410.

115. Ibid., pp. 407–408.

116. Glenn H. Snyder, "Crisis Bargaining," in Charles F. Hermann, ed., op. cit., p. 217.

117. Ibid., pp. 419–445.

118. Ibid., pp. 450–453.

119. Richard Ned Lebow, *Between Peace and War: The Nature of International Crisis* (New York: Free Press, 1981), p. 275.

120. Michael Brecher, Jonathan Wilkenfeld, and Sheila Moser, *Crises in the Twentieth Century: Handbook of International Crises*, Vol. I (Oxford: Pergamon Press, 1988), p. 1.

121. Ibid., Vol. 2, pp. 171–201.

122. See, for example, Howard Gardner, *The Mind's New Science: A History of the Cognitive Revolution* (New York: Basic Books, 1985); Philip Tetlock and Ariel Levi, "Attribution Bias: On the Inconclusiveness of the Cognition–Motivation Debate," *Journal of Experimental Social Psychology*, 18 (1982), 68–88, Marilynn Brewer, "A Dual Process Model of Impression Formation," in Thomas Srull and Robert Wyer, eds., *Advances in Social Cognition*, Vol. 4 (Hillsdale, NJ: Lawrence Erlbaum Associates, 1990), pp. 1–36; Steven J. Sherman, Charles M. Judd, and Bernadette Park, "Social Cognition," *Annual Review of Psychology*, 48 (1989), 2281–2326; and Herbert Simon, "Human Nature in Politics: The Dialogue of Psychology with Political Science," *American Political Science Review*, 79(2) (1985), 293–304.

123. Richard K. Herrmann and Michael P. Fischerkeller, "Beyond the Enemy Image and Spiral Model: Cognitive–Strategic Research After the Cold War," *International Organization,* 49(3) (Summer 1995), 421.

124. Herrmann and Fischerkeller, ibid., pp. 426–427.

125. Ole R. Holsti, *Crisis, Escalation, War,* op. cit., p.10; see also Thomas C. Wiegele, "The Psychophysiology of Elite Stress in Five International Crises," *International Studies Quarterly,* 22 (December 1978), 467–512.

126. Martha L. Cottam, *Foreign Policy Decision-Making: The Influence of Cognition* (Boulder, CO: Westview Press, 1986). The author's sources are drawn more from social and cognitive psychology than from political science.

127. Robert Jervis, *Perception and Misperception in International Politics* (Princeton, NJ: Princeton University Press, 1976), p. 2; Cottam, op. cit., p. 1.

128. Cottam, op. cit., p. 22. The author explains her dissatisfaction with the "Operational Code" and "Cognitive Map" approaches; ibid., pp. 8–21.

129. Ibid., pp. 23–29, 33–56.

130. Ibid., pp. 61–108: The seven political categories are described, with some empirical evidence (from 51 U.S. policymakers out of 500 who received surveys).

131. Lebow, *Between Peace and War,* op. cit., p. 335.

132. Ibid., p. 223.

133. Ibid., p. 225.

134. Jonathan M. Roberts, *Decision-Making During International Crises* (New York: St. Martin's Press, 1988), chap. 9, "General Health of Decision-Makers During International Crises," pp. 181–226.

135. John T. Lanzetta, "Group Behavior Under Stress," *Human Relations,* VIII (1955); reprinted in J. David Singer, ed., *Human Behavior and International Politics: Contributions from the Social-Psychological Sciences* (Chicago: Rand McNally, 1965), 216–217. See Kurt Back, "Decisions Under Uncertainty," *American Behavioral Scientist,* IV (February 1961), 14–19.

136. Robert L. Hamblin, "Group Integration During a Crisis," *Human Relations,* XI (1958), in J. David Singer, ed., *Human Behavior and International Politics,* op. cit., 226–228. See Wilbert S. Ray, "Mild Stress and Problem Solving," *American Journal of Psychology,* LXXVIII (1965), 227–234.

137. Zeev Maoz, *National Choices and International Processes* (Cambridge, England: Cambridge University Press, 1990), pp. 318–321.

138. Jonathan M. Roberts, op. cit., chap. 9, "General Health of Decision-Makers During International Crises," pp. 218–219.

139. Dean G. Pruitt, "Definition of the Situation as a Determinant of International Action," in Herbert C. Kelman, ed., *International Behavior: A Social-Psychological Analysis* (New York: Holt, Rinehart and Winston, 1965), p. 395.

140. See ibid., p. 396, where Pruitt refers to the work of M. J. Driver and Charles E. Osgood.

141. Ole R. Holsti, *Crisis, Escalation, War,* op. cit., p. 13.

142. Ibid., pp. 14–15.

143. Peter Suedfeld and Philip Tetlock, "Integrative Complexity of Communications in International Crises," *Journal of Conflict Resolution,* XXI (March 1977), 169–184.

144. Thomas C. Wiegele, Gordon Hilton, Kent Layne Oots, and Susan S. Kiesell, *Leaders Under Stress: A Psychophysiological Analysis of International Crisis* (Durham, NC: Duke University Press, 1985).

145. Ibid., pp. 26–27.

146. Thomas C. Wiegele, "Is a Revolution Brewing in the Social Sciences?" in Thomas C. Wiegele, ed., *Biology and the Social Sciences: An Emerging Revolution* (Boulder, CO:

Westview Press, 1982), p. 6. See also Thomas C. Wiegele, *Biopolitics: Search for a More Human Political Science* (Boulder, CO: Westview Press, 1979); Thomas C. Wiegele, "Behavioral Medicine and Bureaucratic Processes: Research Foci and Issue Areas," in Elliott White and Joseph Losco, eds., *Biology and Bureaucracy: Public Administration and Public Policy from the Perspective of Genetic and Neurobiological Theory* (Lanham, MD: University Press of America, 1986), pp. 503–525.

147. Irving Janis, *Victims of Groupthink* (Boston: Houghton Mifflin, 1972), pp. 197–198.

148. Robert D. Putnam, "Diplomacy and Domestic Politics: The Logic of Two-Level Games," *International Organization,* 42 (Summer 1988), 427–460.

149. Andrew Moravcsik, "Introduction: Integrating International and Domestic Theories of International Bargaining," in Peter B. Evans, Harold K. Jacobson, and Robert D. Putnam, eds., *Double-Edged Diplomacy: International Bargaining and Domestic Politics* (Berkeley, CA: University of California Press, 1993), pp. 1–42, quoted at 6.

150. Ibid.

151. Peter B. Evans, "Building an Integrative Approach to International and Domestic Politics: Reflections and Projections," in Evans, Jacobson, and Putnam, eds., *Double-Edged Diplomacy,* pp. 397–430, especially pp. 399–405.

152. James G. Richter, "Perpetuating the Cold War: Domestic Sources of International Patterns of Behavior," *Political Science Quarterly,* 107 (Summer 1992), 271–301.

153. See R. Barry Farrell, ed., *Political Leadership in Eastern Europe and the Soviet Union* (Chicago: Aldine, 1970); Alvin Z. Rubinstein, Carl Beck, et al., *Comparative Communist Political Leadership* (New York: McKay, 1973); Vernon V. Aspaturian, "Moscow's Options in a Changing World," in Gary K. Bertsch and Thomas W. Ganschow, eds., *Comparative Communism* (San Francisco: Freeman, 1976), pp. 369–393.

154. See David Wilkinson, *Comparative Foreign Relations* (Encino, CA: Dickenson, 1969); James N. Rosenau, "Foreign Policy as Adaptive Behavior," *Comparative Politics,* II (April 1970), 365–387; Roy C. Macridis, ed., *Foreign Policy in World Politics*, 7th ed. (Englewood Cliffs, NJ: Prentice-Hall, 1974); James N. Rosenau et al., *World Politics* (New York: Free Press, 1975).

Chapter
12

Game Theory, Gaming, Simulation, and Bargaining

GAME THEORY AND
THE STUDY OF POLITICAL PHENOMENA

Game theory is based on an abstract form of reasoning, arising from a combination of mathematics and logic. The *theory* of games, as a branch of pure mathematics, sets forth mathematical postulates from which mathematical conclusions are derived. In the social sciences, game theory (utilizing mathematics) specifies what would happen in a situation in which actors—each with strategies, goals, and preferred outcomes—engage in interaction in the form of a game.[1] Nearly all game theorists agree that the theory with which they deal is addressed to what is rationally correct behavior in situations in which the participants are trying to win—to maximize gain or minimize loss—rather than to the way they actually may behave in such situations. For the sake of theoretical analysis, game theorists assume rational behavior, simply because they find this assumption more profitable for theory building than the obverse of it. If we were to assume that all human behavior is fundamentally absurd, neurotic, or psychotic, then there could be no theory, either of games or of any other social phenomena. Game theorists, then, subscribe to some such notion as the following: If people in a certain situation wish to win—that is, to accomplish an objective that the other party seeks to deny them—we can sort out the intellectual processes by which they calculate what kind of action is most likely to be advantageous to them, assuming that they believe their opponents also to be rational calculators like themselves, equally interested in second-guessing and trying to outwit the opponent.[2]

A few rudimentary concepts should be considered. Every game is characterized by the following elements: players who presumably are trying to win (optimize outcomes); payoffs that may mean various things to different players, depending on their value systems; a set of ground rules appropriate to the game; information conditions that determine the quantity, quality, and immediacy (i.e., immediately available or delayed) of the knowledge each player has of the environment and of the choices made by the other player(s); a strategy on the part of each of the players, designed to relate means to ends; the total environment in which the game is played, whether fully perceived by the players or not; and the interaction of competing moves, in which each successive choice by a player may prompt the other player(s) to modify subsequent choices.

Because it is based on rationality, the importance of game theory is said to lie in the extent to which it can be used to enhance an understanding of the rational-actor model in situations of conflict, as well as in conditions of cooperation. As we have noted elsewhere, in discussions of realist theory and decision making, for example, the rational actor forms an important basis for theorizing about political (and other forms of) behavior. How goal-seeking actors, be they collectivities or individuals, engage in purposeful action designed to achieve their posited objectives, provides a major focal point for the development of theory based on preferences, strategies, and payoffs that can be modeled accurately. According to writers such as Duncan Snidal, Steven J. Brams, and D. Marc Kilgour, game theory, based on the use of game models, holds important potential to contribute to a unified theory of international relations.[3] It is suggested that game theory can contribute to rigorous thought and analysis of critical security problems extending from deterrence to crisis management and arms control. The stronger the assumption of rationality, the more applicable game theory may be to the development of international-relations theory. Rationality encompasses how an actor views its short-term versus longer-range advantages and goals. To what extent, for example, is the actor prepared to sacrifice immediate gain for longer-term benefit? Moreover, rationality includes one actor's calculations of how other actors will behave. In determining how to act, rational actors take into account the anticipated response by other actors in determining their own behavior. Such dynamic interactive elements can be encompassed in the models set forth in game theory.

Game models are said to be applicable across a broad spectrum encompassing political, military, and economic issues that are often treated as fundamentally different from each other but nevertheless contain actors seeking goals reflected in strategies and anticipated payoffs or benefits. According to Snidal, the application of game theory to international relations gives rise to a large number of important empirical questions. They include the issue of who are the relevant actors, as well as what are the rules of the game, and the choices and payoffs available to each of the actors. Far from being merely a descriptive tool, game theory is said to provide a deductive basis for testing empirically its analytic assumptions about rational behavior. Game models, such as Prisoner's Dilemma, described here subsequently, can help illuminate important substantive issues of international politics, including how and why actors evolve their strategies, based on goals and anticipated benefits in negotiations, whether for arms control or for trade agreements. We turn now to a brief description of the basic models of game theory that, taken together, are said to have broad applicability, allowing diverse international issues to be "handled within a common game-theoretical framework which does not suppress that diversity but builds upon it to explore the implications of various contextual differences."[4]

Zero-Sum Games

The most commonly drawn preliminary distinction in game theory is that between a zero-sum game (ZSG) and a non-zero-sum game (NZSG), with variations of each. In a ZSG between A and B, what A wins, B loses. (NZSGs are those in which the sum of players' gains need not add up to zero. These are treated later.) Chess, checkers, two-person poker, or blackjack—all of these are ZSGs. Each game ends with one player having a score of plus one and the other minus one, and the value of one for the game depends on either the stakes or the size of the pot. Examples of real-life situations that contain aspects of ZSGs include an electoral race between two candidates for a congressional seat; most military tactical situations in which the military objective that one side seizes is thereby lost to the other, at least temporarily, such as an air duel or a battle over a hill; and the rivalry of two men for a woman's hand in marriage. It should be noted that a three-person race for an elective office is not really a ZSG unless we break it down into two different contests between the winner and each loser. We might also observe that in a tactical military situation, the ground gained by one side equals the ground lost by the other, but there might have been a considerable discrepancy in the cost to each side when measured in casualties. The same notion holds true for the election campaign and for courting: There is a single payoff, but the contending parties may spend widely varying sums in the effort to win. Writers on game theory distinguish the *outcome* of a game (win, lose, or draw) from the *payoff* (the value attached by a player to an outcome). The relationship between payoff and motivation is critically important, but it is difficult to establish.[5]

Two-Person Zero-Sum Games

In most of the literature on the subject, games are schematically represented in a normalized form, in which no details of the game are given, but in which the strategies for each player and the accompanying payoffs are depicted in a matrix. Moreover, the payoff values are often assigned in a purely arbitrary manner, merely to facilitate the illustration of a point. (The student therefore need not worry too much about how the payoff values were determined—at least not yet.) Moreover, the strategies may consist of fairly complex plans and yet be designated simply as Strategy 1, Strategy 2, or Strategy N for each player. Thus, in mathematical theory, both strategies and payoffs are treated abstractly. In the most helpful form of notation, each matrix contains the payoff that each player receives when he or she chooses one of the two strategies that converge at that point. The student may, however, come across a matrix that shows only the payoffs to one player. The following three simplified 2-by-2 matrices, borrowed or adapted from Shubik, are sufficient to illustrate our discussion of two-person ZSGs:

Matrix I   Strategy for Player 2

		A	B
Strategy for Player 1	A	+4, −4	−3, +3
	B	−3, +3	+4, −4

Matrix II   Strategy for Player 2

		A	B
Strategy for Player 1	A	−5, +5	−7, +7
	B	+8, −8	+1, −1

Matrix III   Strategy for Player 2

		A	B
Strategy for Player 1	A	−20, −20	+5, −5
	B	−5, +5	−2, −2

Matrix I refers to a game in which there is no saddle point. First, in each matrix, the sum of the payoffs is zero.[6] However, there is no point at which the strategies of the competing players logically converge. If both players opt for the A strategy, Player 1 wins 4, and the other player loses 4. If Player 1 plays the B strategy, and Player 2 chooses the A strategy, the former loses 3, and the latter gains 3. If readers analyze this payoff matrix for a minute, they will see that the best strategy for each player in a long series of runs is a random strategy, determined by the toss of a coin, for this will eventually produce a balancing-out of the wins and losses of 4s and 3s. In other words, the game schematized in Matrix I reduces to a game of chance, with which game theory does not deal.

Matrix II refers to a ZSG in which there is a saddle point, at which the minimum values in the rows (across) and the maximum values in the columns (up and down) converge at equality, or where the maximum values in the rows and the minimum values in the columns converge. The point of convergence is known as the *minimax value.* In a two-person ZSG, a rational strategy is based on the minimax principle: Each player should seek to maximize the minimum gain of which he or she can be assured, or to minimize the maximum loss that needs to be sustained. If both parties do this, their strategies may converge at a *saddle point,* and they will tend to balance wins or losses in the long run. If one does this and the other plays hunches, the former should win over a large number of plays.

Strategic theorists, military commanders, stock-market speculators, labor-management negotiators, employees seeking a raise or a promotion and diplomats bargaining over a bilateral treaty all have an intuitive understanding of this minimax principle, with its upper and lower boundaries. Put most simply: When you hold the right cards, press your advantage as far as possible; when luck turns against you, cut your losses. Strictly speaking, the utility of the minimax strategy can be validated only in an extended series of plays, not in a one-shot game. In certain types of simple games, it can be a rather dull, no-fun strategy, but it may be unavoidable under the circumstances of a prolonged context with a series of plays.

Let us suppose, again following Shubik, that Player 1 is a police force in a country torn by guerrilla insurgency and Player 2 is the guerrilla force. The police in this particular game can choose either to go into the jungle in pursuit of the insurgents (Strategy A) or to avoid the jungle and to protect key areas (Strategy B). The choice of open battle or attritional skirmishes is up to the guerrilla force. The police do better out of the jungle than in it, where they stand to lose in both battles and skirmishes (–5 and –7, respectively). The guerrillas' preferred strategy, whether in or out of the jungle, is to skirmish, for in this way they can maximize their gains (+8) or hold their losses to a minimum (–1). In the simplified game described, two rational players would tend to converge at the saddle point of +1, –1; that is, the police would probably choose key areas outside the jungle, whereas the guerrillas would skirmish and eschew open battle, thus holding their losses to –1 instead of –8.[7] This, of course, only describes the tactical encounter between guerrillas and police. For an insight into the strategic outcome of a guerrilla insurgency, something much more complex than a simple 2-by-2 matrix would be required. (In real life, the guerrillas might lose most tactical exchanges and yet win strategically because of psychopolitical factors.)

The minimax strategy is a cautious strategy. Five points are to be remembered in connection with the minimax strategy: (1) It applies only to ZSGs. (2) It is not jeopardized by information leakage. (3) It is useful and normative only against an opponent who is presumed to be playing a rational game. If the adversary is stupid, prone to make blunders, or usually motivated by emotional factors (which might incline the person to play his or her hunches), then the minimax strategy is not necessarily the optimum one to pursue. (4) The utility of the minimax strategy is validated in a series of plays, not in a one-shot game. (5) It is a rather unexciting, no-fun strategy, but it may be advisable. Shubik offers the following caveat:

> Apart from appreciating the two-person zero-sum game as the definition of a strictly competitive situation, the general political scientist will not gain too much insight from an intense study of this topic. . . . There is also a considerable amount of misinterpretation concerning the role in general game theory of the famous result concerning two-person zero-sum games known as the minimax or saddlepoint theorem. Zero-sum games are of extremely limited interest in the behavioral sciences in general.[8]

Non-Zero-Sum Games

The type of game referred to in Matrix III leads us partially out of two-person ZSGs toward the NZSG, in that it is not exclusively competitive, in the sense that what one gains, another must lose. The sum of gains and losses need not add up to zero. NZSGs may involve only two or a larger number of players. There is room in this type of game for elements of both conflict and cooperation; on some plays, both or some parties might win, and at the end of the game, both or some parties might be ahead by varying amounts. In an NZSG, there are often several different payoffs, some of which may be very good or very bad, some marginally good or bad. The payoffs depend on whether the players cooperate with each other, cut each other's throats, or mix their strategies of conflict and cooperation in varying combinations.

What is interesting about Matrix III is the fact that it refers to a game that might be a ZSG under some circumstances and an NZSG under others, depending on the outcome. Actually, this matrix depicts the possible payoffs in a game of Chicken, similar to that popularized many years ago in a Hollywood film, in which two youths drive toward each other in their fathers' automobiles at 80 miles an hours, each with his left set of wheels on the highway dividing line. If neither one swerves to the right, they will both be killed in the crash—an outcome that is arbitrarily assigned a numerical value of −20 for each. It could just as easily have been −200 or another figure, but in any event, this becomes a minus-sum game in which both players lose as heavily as possible. If one stays on the course and the other veers, one gains esteem, and the other loses in the eyes of the peer group. The latter is "chicken." This condition is indicated in the two matrices containing a +5 and −5. Thus if either driver swerves and the other holds longer to the course, the game turns out to be zero-sum. If both veer to the right simultaneously, each suffers dishonor in the eyes of the peer group, but because the reputation for being chicken is shared between them, so that no invidious comparisons can be drawn, each suffers only a −2.

We should hasten to point out that the payoff matrix as shown is partly a function of the distorted value system of the youthful peer group, as perceived by the two drivers. Actually, the peer group chiefly craves the excitement of the game and regrets the tragic outcome later. Certainly, the parents and fiancées of the two youths would assign a larger negative valuation to their deaths and a higher positive valuation to an outcome in which both have enough sense to veer off course before it is too late.[9] It ought to be made clear that the game of Chicken, played with human life at stake, is a game that is entered into only by irrational players, one or both of whom may become rational enough during the course of the game to save their lives. The analogy between the game of Chicken and the collision course of two nuclear superpowers in a crisis was drawn many times during the Cold War, but the latter is vastly more complex than the former. There is ample evidence to believe that the governmental decision-making structures of the two superpowers were of a higher order of rational caution than that of two adolescents in a game of Chicken. More is said about this later.

Two-person NZGSs can be played either cooperatively or noncooperatively. In a cooperative game, the players are permitted to communicate with each other directly and to exchange information in advance concerning their intended choices. In a noncooperative game, overt communication is not permitted, but the choice of each becomes obvious to the other after the play. There is, however, a slight ambiguity in this terminology. Even if a game is noncooperative, insofar as the rules prohibit overt or direct communication, it is possible for the players to cooperate tacitly through inferred communication, by which one player interprets the other's intentions from the kinds of choices made in a long series of plays.

The Prisoner's Dilemma Game

The best-known example of a two-person NZSG is "Prisoner's Dilemma." As we noted in Chapter 10, two individuals are taken into police custody and accused of a crime. Because they are interrogated separately, neither knows what the other will tell the district attorney. Each is aware that if both remain silent or deny all allegations, the worst they can expect is a sentence of 60 days in the county jail for vagrancy. If one turns state's evidence and the other remains silent, the former will receive a 1-year commuted sentence and the other will be sent to the state penitentiary for 10 years. If both confess, both will receive from 5 to 8 years in prison, with a parole possible at the end of 5. Their optimum strategy is a tacit agreement to remain silent, but in the absence of communication, neither can trust the other. Each makes the following assessment of the situation: If I remain silent, I will get either 60 days or 10 years, depending on whether my partner confesses. If I confess, I will receive a commuted sentence of either 1 or 5 to 8 years, depending on whether he confesses. In either case, I can assure myself of a lighter sentence by confessing. Because my partner is undoubtedly making the same sort of calculation, the chances are that my partner will confess, and hence I would be foolish to remain silent and count on the slim chance that my partner would do likewise. Thus, each, by choosing what seems to be the safer course, contributes to an outcome highly disadvantageous to both—a sentence of 5 years instead of 60 days.[10]

In political analysis, the Prisoner's Dilemma game can be illustrated by reference to the question of why and how states came into existence, identified by political philosophers, including notably Thomas Hobbes in the seventeenth century. As Arthur A. Stein suggests, the state of nature described in political theory by Hobbes and others is a condition, stated in game-theory terminology, in which individuals have a dominant strategy of defecting from common action in favor of pursuing their own competitive and conflictual acts.[11] The result is a situation that is recognized to be a dilemma for all actors. Although some individuals may wish to cooperate under these circumstances, they face the prospect that others will take advantage of them by accepting their cooperation move without reciprocating in kind, or becoming free riders. In other words, some actors can derive immediate benefit by cheating even if they agree in principle to cooperate with other actors. For this reason, Stein suggests, individuals join together to form a state that has the authority to coerce all of its members, in order to make sure that no individual can take advantage of another's cooperative behavior by defecting or getting a free ride. Stein goes on to suggest that international regimes, discussed in Chapter 10, are formed to help reconcile the competing interests of the individual actor with those of the collectivity. He contends that, like the formation of the state, international regimes in an anarchic society, are "created to deal with the collective suboptimality that can emerge from individual behavior."[12] How the dilemma of individual interest and common interest is resolved is central both to political theory generally and to game theory, and in particular, especially the Prisoner's Dilemma game.

According to the Prisoner's Dilemma game, the dilemma arises, we reiterate, simply because each of the players, taking only into account its own interest, receives a higher payoff from defecting rather than cooperating. What is best for each individual leads both to defect. If both defect, however, both are worse off than they would have been if both had cooperated. Robert Axelrod, whose work on cooperation theory we have discussed in Chapter 10, makes extensive use of the Prisoner's Dilemma game.[13] According to Axelrod, despite the individual disincentive to cooperate, contrasted with the mutual benefits from cooperation, players are drawn toward cooperative behavior by the prospect that they will meet each other again. Such a possibility leads them to make choices today that will influence their subsequent decisions.

Axelrod suggests that the contemplation of the future can help shape how the players view the present strategic situation. Nevertheless, the payoff expected from the next move counts less than the payoff anticipated from the immediate move. Axelrod terms the relative importance attached to a subsequent move, compared to the present move, the *discount parameter.* Stated in concrete terms, this means that it is preferable to cooperate today with someone who is likely to reciprocate in the future. The prospect for achieving ongoing mutual cooperation depends on the extent to which there is likely to be continuing interaction between the two players. According to Axelrod, a continuing opportunity for interaction between players constitutes a necessary but not sufficient condition in itself for the evolution of cooperation. If individuals develop a stake in their future interaction, Axelrod concludes, cooperation between larger entities can evolve from small groups of individuals who cooperate on the basis of reciprocity. Cooperation, after it has been established as a result of interactive reciprocity, can gain a momentum that helps protect it against less cooperative strategies. Axelrod suggests that Prisoner's Dilemma is applicable to the development of cooperative strategies to address a broad spectrum of situations from individual choice to the business setting to the international arena. The international arena includes arms races, nuclear proliferation, crisis bargaining, escalation, and de-escalation. He asserts that an understanding of the *process* by which cooperative emerges, based on the Prisoner's Dilemma, will contribute to the evolution of cooperation.

Games theorists have devised several variations of Prisoner's Dilemma, but at this juncture, two general points must be reiterated. First, there is an important difference between *game theory,* which is based on mathematical–logical analysis and which purports to show what kind of strategy a rational player *should* play (when he or she presumes the opponent to be rational), and *experimental gaming,* which is designed to furnish empirical evidence of how individuals *actually do behave* in game situations. Second, there is an important difference between one-shot games and games that are played over a series of runs by the same players, who, as a result of experience, acquire insight into the strategic thought processes of each other.

Games (both Prisoner's Dilemma and Chicken) have also been devised to determine whether sex differences influence the choice for cooperative or competitive behavior. The results have been somewhat inconclusive, whether subjects play against programmed opponents (who have been instructed as to their choice) or play against each other (in mixed-sex and same-sex pairs).[14] The results have been less ambiguous for Prisoner's Dilemma than for Chicken. Three PDG experimenters all found that males opposing males tend to be more cooperative than females opposing females.[15] Another concluded that females are more rational (i.e., capable of earning more money) in a one-shot game, whereas males earn more in a series, when optimal strategy requires a longer time horizon.[16] Conrath, after research on games of Chicken, finds the explanations of sex-role behavior in games thus far inadequate. If differences do exist, the why is important. "It is not likely that the biological aspect . . . is the determining factor, but rather the social and educational roles which distinguish the sexes."[17]

Prisoner's Dilemma has become a staple item in the literature of games, a full bibliography of which now runs into scores of articles, book chapters, and other studies. *The Journal of Conflict Resolution, The Journal of Social Psychology, The Journal of Personality and Social Psychology, The American Political Science Review, World Politics,* and other periodicals have consistently carried articles on the subject for many years. One authority on games has noted that "research in bargaining utilizing the Prisoner's Dilemma paradigm has become less concerned with questions of cooperation, competition, and the bargaining process, and more concerned with studying the Prisoner's Dilemma paradigm itself."[18] However, Schlenker and Bonoma defend the preoccupation with the paradigm as being "necessary to understand the limits and dimensions of the laboratory world before useful experiments can be conducted."[19]

N-Person Games

This brings us to *N*-person NZSGs, involving three or more players, all of whom are assumed to be independent decision-making units and to possess some method for evaluating the worth of outcomes.[20] As might be expected, much less is known about these than about two-person games, because the number of permutations or interacting strategies increases at an exponential rate with the number of players. Physicists have never found a mathematical solution to the "three-body problem." Hence it is not surprising that no single theory has yet been developed for *N*-person games. Probably the most fruitful avenue of inquiry to date has been in the area of coalition formation. (For an examination of literature on alliances and coalitions, see Chapter 10.) When several players are in a game, it becomes quite natural for two or more to form a coalition against the others, in which case the others are induced to do likewise in order to ensure their survival and maximize their gains. Sometimes the rules of the game may encourage the alignment of coalitions before starting to play; sometimes coalitions are formed, either tacitly or overtly, after the game is in progress. If two coalitions emerge, forcing all players to choose one or the other, the game in effect is reduced to a two-person ZSG.[21] It is conceivable, however, that at a particular stage of the game, there might be three coalitions, one of which would eventually find itself under pressure to coalesce with one of the other two. The crucial question, it would appear, is to work out to the satisfaction of all the allies "a rational division of the spoils."[22]

If coalitions are formed before the start of the game, all the partners should be considered equal and entitled to an equal share of the payoff. What is much more interesting, of course, is a situation in which the payoff is divided according to the contribution each partner makes to the victory of the coalition, and in which the contribution is in some sense a function of power and weakness. Sometimes there may be founding members of the coalitions, with others permitted to join later after bargaining for terms that reflect both the power of the coalition leaders and the more desperate straits of the applicants for entry. In addition to the division of the payoff and to the circumstances under which coalitions are formed, other questions worthy of game theorists' attention pertain to the motives that might drive a member of one coalition to defect to another and whether it is possible for a coalition to enforce against its own members any sanction that is stronger and more efficacious than the bond of mutual interest.[23] Questions such as these are quite germane to the study of alliance cohesiveness in crisis.

INTERNATIONAL RELATIONS AS A GAME

One is entitled to ask what all this has to do with international relations or, more narrowly, with international politics. First, it should be made clear that international relations—or the operation of the international system—cannot be fully comprehended merely within the analytical framework of a game. Nonetheless, the patterns and processes of international relations often manifest certain gamelike characteristics. Because game theory and gaming are closely related to decision making and bargaining, they are bound to have some relevance to the study of international relations—a field in which we commonly speak of making moves on the diplomatic chessboard, bluffing, upping the ante, using bargaining chips, and trying to second-guess or outwit the opponent. The application of analytical techniques derived from game theory can therefore aid in improving our understanding of the subject, provided that this approach is employed with the balanced intellectual perspective of those who regard it as one among several useful tools.

Virtually all international theorists who perceive some utility in game theory agree that international relations can be best conceptualized as an N-person NZSG, in which gains by some parties are not necessarily at the expense of other parties. The more advanced industrialized countries need not suffer a loss in their absolute or relative economic position as less developed economies advance. Indeed, economic expansion in less developed countries often leads to an intensification of trade, aid, and investment relations with wealthier countries. Several writers who pioneered in the effort to apply game theory to the social sciences (e.g., Oskar Morgenstern, Thomas C. Schelling, Martin Shubik, and J. C. Harsanyi) had economic training or conducted extensive research into problems of economic competition. Competition between economic firms can be either a ZSG or an NZSG. Economic analysts see the latter as the preferable, more rational alternative because both firms stand to gain, at least in the shorter run, if the mutual wounds of excessive competition can be avoided. Perhaps it is not too much to say that within the American economy, the desirable has gradually become, or is becoming, the actual: The rivalry among the largest corporations in a field is looked on as an NZSG. "Most social phenomena," writes Martin Shubik, ". . . are best represented by nonconstant sum games. In other words, the fates and fortunes of the parties involved may easily rise or fall together. There is no pure division into total opposition."[24]

International Relations as a Game of Conflict and Cooperation

Whether international politics can be as readily reduced as international economics to an NZSG will probably be for a long time a subject of debate between political scientists and economists. To be sure, there are some political scientists who do not distinguish sharply between politics on the one hand and economics or psychology on the other. However, the authors of this book are convinced that the political is not perfectly interchangeable with the economic or the psychological. As we pointed out in a previous chapter, there are important differences between political decisions and decisions made by business firms or by individuals.[25] William D. Coplin has also persuasively argued that there is a considerable difference between the bargaining process in domestic society and the process that goes on in the international setting.[26] Hence, we caution against efforts to make a hasty and uncritical transfer of the NZSG concept to international politics. In our view, international politics can be best understood within the game-theoretical framework as involving a complex and fluctuating mixture of tendencies toward zero-sumness and non-zero-sumness.

Joseph Frankel suggests that French relations with Germany, for example, "developed from a zero-sum game in the early post–World War II period, when the French wished—and hoped to be able—to keep the Germans down, into a variable-sum game within the [European] Communities in which cooperation changed the competitive character of the game and rapidly increased the payoff for both sides."[27] John W. Burton has proposed a method of resolving such conflicts as the one between Greeks and Turks over Cyprus by inducing the parties to view the situation as one not with a fixed-sum outcome that requires a compromise cutting of the cake, but with outcomes from which both sides can gain through functional cooperation that will produce a larger cake.[28] There may be a circularity in the reasoning that prescribes resolving a political conflict of passionate nationalism by transforming it into a process of mutually beneficial economic cooperation. Yet that is what was accomplished in the Franco-German rapprochement in the decades after World War II and that is what many hope to see achieved in relations between other countries. The Bosnian conflict, however, exemplifies the difficulties.

The shift from the ZSG to the NZSG perspective does not, of course, solve all problems of conflict in international relations or in other dimensions of life. Both Prisoner's Dilemma and Chicken games are mixed-motive NZSGs that human beings do not always play according to the strategies prescribed by rationality. In the former, the player is tempted to choose a noncooperative strategy by suspicion that the other player will not cooperate; in the latter, the players must make a last-moment choice between prestige and survival. Glenn H. Snyder has drawn the following contrast:

> The spirit or leading theme of the prisoner's dilemma is that of the frustration of the mutual desire to cooperate. The spirit of a chicken game is that of a contest in which each party is trying to prevail over the other. In both games, perceptions of the other party's intentions are crucial, and the actors face a problem of establishing the credibility of their stated intentions. But in the prisoner's dilemma, establishing credibility means instilling *trust,* whereas in chicken it involves creating *fear.*[29]

Neither game, when applied to international relations, is likely to lead to optimistic conclusions. Anatol Rapoport has applied the Prisoner's Dilemma model to the problem of international disarmament and found that, although ideally both parties might prefer to benefit economically from disarmament, neither one can be sure of the long-range intentions of the other, and thus both pursue the more prudent course of maintaining a costly balance of armaments.[30] Critical Cold War confrontations between the nuclear superpowers, such as the Cuban Missile Crisis, were often likened to the game of Chicken.[31] Schelling distinguishes between a game of Chicken, in which one has been deliberately challenged in a test of nerves, and a game into which two parties have been drawn by the course of events. He admits that in the real international world, it is hard to know which kind of crisis is being confronted.[32] In a dangerous international crisis requiring careful management, the rules of procedure are well defined.[33] Those who treated critical confrontations between superpowers as instances of Chicken usually did not want to press the analogy too far. In the Cuban Missile Crisis, Brams observes, "Neither side was eager to take any irreversible steps, such as the teenage driver in a game of Chicken might do by defiantly ripping off his steering wheel in full view of his adversary, thus foreclosing his alternative of swerving."[34]

R. Harrison Wagner has analyzed the balance of power within the framework of games theory, beginning with William Riker's contention that international systems are inherently unstable.

> Several scholars have tried to dispute Riker's conclusion in two major ways. One is to maintain that it rests on the false assumption that the international system has the properties of a zero-sum game. The other is to maintain that it rests on the false assumption that the international system has the properties of a game that is played only once. No one, however, has provided rigorous proof that either of these two changes in Riker's assumptions is necessary or sufficient to lead to a different conclusion.[35]

Wagner examined a simple model of an international system as an *N*-person noncooperative game, and he investigated the stability of systems with two, three, four, and five major actors.

> I found not only that constant-sum systems are stable, but also—contrary to most people's intuition—that stability is actually fostered by conflict of interest among states. I also found that . . . a nonconstant-sum system will have most of the properties of a constant-sum system. Thus, paradoxically, uncertainty about the future, by fostering conflict, promotes stability.
>
> Systems with any number of actors from two through five can be stable but, contrary to some unsupported assertions in the literature, there is a well-defined sense in

which the most stable system is one with three actors. Moreover, for any number of actors from two through five, there is at least one distribution of power that leads not only to system stability but also to peace. Some of these peaceful distributions are more stable than others. . . . These more stable distributions are characterized by inequality among states. If one wants to say that power is "balanced" when it is distributed in one of these ways, then one can say that there is no connection whatever between a balance of power and an equal distribution of power.[36]

The anarchical character of the international system invests that system with the essential trait of a multiperson NZSG—namely, the absence of a central authority capable of defining common goals and regulating the players' choices. Each player-state determines for itself the requirements of survival, vital self-interest, and policies conducive to the enhancement of its own well-being. Sometimes, the calculus of national interest demands a promise among player-states—whether two, several, many, or nearly all—to cooperate with a view toward advancing mutual benefits. This fact goes a long way to explain, although not fully, why there are such things as international customary laws, treaties, and conventions that prescribe certain types of decent reciprocal behavior and create legally obligating regimes in specific functional areas—communications, transport, maritime law, narcotics control, trade, arms limitation, environmental protection, and so on. State promises, however, cannot be considered absolutely binding in an anarchical system where there is no mechanism to enforce the rules. The observance of promises and rules is contingent on each player-state's continuing assessment of the degree to which other actors seem to be observing *their* promises.

There can be no doubt that it is highly desirable in the nuclear age to stress the elements of mutual interest and tacit cooperation in the avoidance of general war, in the hope that these will outweigh the elements of divergent interests and conflict. However, the understandable desire to attenuate the dangerous excesses of international ideological conflict has perhaps led some analysts to overlook the fundamental difference between the *ought* and the *is*. The conduct of international politics would probably be more restrained if the political leaders of all the major powers were convinced that international politics is an NZSG in the nuclear age. However, to assert that it always has been so, and always will be necessarily so, is to propound conclusions that a serious study of history does not substantiate.

It might be more accurate to say that international politics is usually an NZSG for most players, because most governments normally tend to observe rational limits in their decision-making processes. However, in every age, there may be some political–strategic adversaries who view their confrontation with each other as having certain characteristics analogous to those encountered in a two-person ZSG. Undoubtedly, much of the zero-sum quality that marks certain bilateral interstate relations in this century is a function of ideological attitudes, combined with the dialectics of communications systems and mass politics. In some cases, leaders may feel compelled to pay lip service to the ideological objective of the annihilation of the enemy, even if they have no serious intention of embarking on an Armageddon during their tenure of rule. Nonetheless, if individuals and groups in one country speak frequently as if the bilateral relationship is a ZSG, their counterparts in the second country will sooner or later do likewise. It will always be important to distinguish the way in which a bilateral conflict is viewed by the governmental policy-makers, by various politically conscious social groups, and by individuals. If an ideologically oriented group that perceives the conflict as a ZSG should seize control of the government, the conflict may indeed become a ZSG.

International Relations: Limitations of Game Theory

Those who would apply the game-theoretical framework to the analysis of international politics require a greater precision of language than they have sometimes employed in the past. It is not enough to say merely that we are dealing with an NZSG. We must carefully define the structure of the game we are discussing: the players, the rules, and the objectives of the game; the payoffs and the values the players attach to them; the whole context in which the game is played; and the interaction of the various strategies pursued. A specific game might appear to be a ZSG in the eyes of the country's leaders but not in the eyes of the whole people. Take, for example, World War II as it was waged between Germany and the Allied Powers. The strategic objective of unconditional surrender enunciated by Roosevelt and Churchill certainly made the war look like a ZSG to Hitler's Nazi regime because the latter could not possibly accept such terms and still survive politically, even though the German people could survive unconditional surrender and endure as a nation, albeit a divided one, until German unification at the end of the Cold War. In short, when two parties are striving toward mutually exclusive objectives and one succeeds and the other fails, this is a ZSG. If the contest ends in a complex compromise that leaves neither party entirely satisfied, but in which both parties are willing to settle for less than their original objectives rather than bear the cost of prolonging the struggle, then this is an NZSG. Thus the zero-sumness or non-zero-sumness of a subgame in international politics must be defined in terms of the various alternative outcomes and payoffs as these are perceived by the players.

The difference between a ZSG and an NZSG does not, contrary to popular opinion, depend on whether the game is conceptualized in such a way that one side must survive while the other perishes. Extreme Marxist ideologues might perceive their conflict with capitalism in this way, and so might extreme Arab nationalists describe the solution of the problem of Israeli-occupied Palestine. However, true zero-sumness pertains to the exclusive winning or losing of a payoff, not necessarily to the players' survival, except in a weird game of tic-tac-toe in which the loser forfeits his or her life, or in a game of Russian Roulette, which goes on until one player dies. Fortunately, most ZSGs are not so absurd, either in the parlor or in the international arena. Take, for example, the conflict between India and Pakistan over Kashmir. Control over this region is the payoff in a ZSG; as long as India retains control, Pakistan is deprived of it. However, the Pakistanis may continue to hope that someday the situation may be reversed, just as a person who has lost a chess game to the opponent may aspire to win the next round. This raises the interesting question as to when both parties in a specific international conflict recognize that the ZSG is over and is not to be replayed. This might require an uncommonly high degree of political rationality. The frequent replay of ZSGs between two states over the control of a disputed territory might eventually arouse political passions to such a point that the stakes are escalated far beyond the original objective of the game, to include the physical integrity of the players.

Kenneth A. Oye has probed the question as to what strategies states can adopt to foster cooperation. He begins by discussing how payoffs affect the prospects for cooperation. He found that the structure of payoffs in a given round of play—the benefits of mutual cooperation, relative to mutual defection, and the benefits of unilateral defection, compared with unreciprocated cooperation—is fundamental to analyzing international cooperation in both the security and economic fields. He illustrates his analysis with examples drawn from the games of Prisoner's Dilemma, Stag Hunt,[37] and Chicken. He remarks that "these games have attracted a disproportionate share of scholarly attention precisely because cooperation is desirable but not automatic."[38] He warns that conscious cooperation is not always required for parties to advance their mutual interests:

> Where harmony prevails, cooperation is unnecessary to the realization of mutual interests. Where deadlocks exist, . . . conflict is inevitable. . . . When you observe conflict, think Deadlock—the absence of conflict—before puzzling over why a mutual interest was not realized. When you observe cooperation, think Harmony—the absence of gains from defection—before puzzling over how states were able to transcend the temptations of defection.[39]

Payoff structures, then, are of critical significance. Oye agrees with Robert Jervis's finding[40] that the long-term likelihood of cooperation can be increased by willful modification of the payoff structure through unilateral, bilateral, and multilateral strategies. Examples include a government's decisions to procure weapons that are defensive rather than offensive, thereby reducing both the adversary's fear of being attacked and the gains that would accrue to itself by launching an attack; to deploy troops along the vulnerable border of an ally to make defection by either ally more costly and less likely; and to publicize agreements for a similar purpose. In situations resembling single-play Prisoner's Dilemma, Stag Hunt, and Chicken, states may be tempted to defect. States, however, must consider the long shadow of the future, in which they expect to continue dealing with each other. Every defection for the sake of immediate one-time gain decreases the prospects for cooperation; concern for repeated interactions in the future increases it.[41]

In the final analysis, it is difficult in the extreme—perhaps impossible—for either the human mind or the world's largest computer to grasp the game of international politics in its utter complexity. A three-person parlor game in which a very limited number of simple moves and countermoves can be made may be reducible to mathematical analysis. However, the triangular relationship of the United States, the former Soviet Union, and the People's Republic of China during the Cold War was comparable not to such a parlor game but to the three-body problem in Newtonian physics, which, as we noted previously, is still insoluble in a precise mathematical formula.[42] Moreover, it is impossible to conceive of a purely triangular relationship in which the interactions of those three powers are insulated from interactions with Western Europe, Eastern Europe, Japan, and other actors on the world scene. Nevertheless, although recognizing the limitations of game theory, we can still find it a useful means for suggesting hypotheses that may illuminate the study of strategic choices faced by foreign-policy decision makers.[43]

To the extent that it assumes that actors act rationally in pursuit of defined goals based on interests, game theory bears a similarity to realist theory. However, game theory does not hold that the key actors are necessarily states or that they inevitably strive to maximize power. Nevertheless, game theory can be used to test key propositions that form realist–neorealist theory and, as Robert Jervis suggests, to ascertain how states can cooperate under conditions of anarchy and when they have conflicting interests.[44] The realist conception of international politics, as discussed in Chapter 2, contains as defining characteristics anarchy, the security dilemma, and a combination of conflict and cooperation.

In the international system described in realist theory, two actors have a choice either to cooperate with each other or to reject cooperation (to defect), for example, in the Prisoner's Dilemma game. Several major questions arise in utilizing game theory to study the behavior of states under conditions of anarchy and the security dilemma. To what extent, for example, can the actor's preferences be inferred from its behavior, especially if states strive to conceal such goals? When and why do decision makers view cooperation, rather than conflict, to be desirable? How do various ideologies affect the utilities attached to various outcomes, based on the strategies adopted by the actors?

Because game theory focuses on the preferences of actors at a specific time, how can we account for changes in preferences as one group of decision makers replaces another group? The process by which preferences undergo transformation, according to realist theory, includes the position of the state in the international system. Great powers adopt strategies and establish goals based on interests substantially different from those of smaller powers. Preferences may also be shaped by the interactive process between states, as for example, the positive or negative interpretation placed by one state on the action of another state. If the United States acts unilaterally to abolish certain categories of weapons or trade restrictions, other states may see such action as evidence of generosity or of weakness. It may lead other actors either to reciprocate in kind or to decide that, because the United States has acted unilaterally, there is no need, or incentive, to take corresponding action. Thus, a cooperative strategy by one actor may produce either a cooperative or competitive response by the opposite party. The conditions under which one response or the other is forthcoming represent important questions for game theory and for international relations-theory.

The complexity of utilizing game theory to study cooperation and defection between actors in an anarchical international system is heightened by the fact, Jervis asserts, that some policies simultaneously exhibit elements both of cooperation and of defection. States may threaten to walk out of trade negotiations or of arms-control talks, or they may indicate that they will leave the European Union or NATO, if their demands are not met. The possibility of defection may then become the basis for negotiations leading to cooperation. By the same token, how do values and beliefs affect an actor's decision either to cooperate or to defect? How do shared values shape cooperative behavior between actors that may have political or economic differences? For example, our discussion of democratic peace theory in Chapter 8 placed emphasis on the development of normative standards that lead such states to reject war in favor of negotiation and adjudication as a basis for resolving disputes between them. Jervis concludes that game theory can help frame the analysis of international interaction, based on assumptions drawn from realist theory. Game-theory models can accommodate the realist theory emphasis on anarchy and conflict, while contributing to an understanding of motivations and behavior by actors based on premises other than, or extending beyond, variously defined self-interest or national interest.

Neoliberal institutionalist theory and structural-realist theory are both based on assumptions about conflict and cooperation to which game theory is said to be applicable. According to structural-realist theory, as we have noted in Chapter 2, emphasis is placed on prospects for conflict in an international structure in which states necessarily concern themselves with relative gains, often at the expense of other states (ZSG). In a self-help system, according to structural-realist theory, states are concerned not only about how well they themselves do (absolute gains) but also about how their gains compare with those of other states (relative gains). Gains for one state that are considered to be disproportionate or excessive are seen to threaten the security of other states and therefore to be destabilizing in an anarchic international system. In contrast, neoliberal institutionalist theory holds that cooperation is both feasible and likely to produce absolute gains for both sides (NZSG).

Using game theory, Robert Powell suggests that structural realism and neoliberal institutionalism can be examined in a model of the international system in which the feasibility of cooperation is shown to be related not to sharply contrasting assumptions about state preferences but instead to changes in the constraints that states face.[45] If the emphasis is shifted from preferences to constraints, Powell maintains, the possibility emerges for greater common ground between structural realism and neoliberal institutionalist theory. In the game model, states seek to maximize their economic welfare within constraints imposed by the anarchic international system. If the cost of using force to achieve state goals is perceived to be low, cooperation is said to be less likely, in keeping with structural-realist theory. If military force becomes too costly, a quest for cooperative solutions is enhanced. Thus, Powell shifts the structural realist and neoliberal institutionalist debate to a focus on the options considered to be available to states faced with a variety of constraints in an anarchic international system in which there is no common government capable of enforcing agreements. In Powell's game-theoretic model, the neorealist option to use force is represented, together with the possibility that, like the Prisoner's Dilemma, the neoliberal institutionalist theory leading to cooperation solutions is also present. The model is designed to help explain why the existence of anarchy does not necessarily imply a lack of cooperation. In other words, the constraints imposed on states by anarchy may impede cooperation or actually enhance the prospects for cooperative solutions.

The issue of relative gains as an obstacle to international cooperation is addressed in other game-theoretic work as well. Duncan Snidal makes use of game theory to refine the relative-gains assumption contained in realist theory.[46] Snidal sets forth a two-actor game matrix in which states, if they cooperate, each receive a payoff from mutual cooperation. If only one of the states cooperates, for example unilaterally reducing trade restrictions, the state that does not cooperate receives a free ride in the form of access to the other's markets. If neither state cooperates, neither receives any payoff. If the two states are symmetrical, each is equally situated either to benefit or to injure the other. Snidal describes a series of strategic situations confronting the states as players spanning a range of cooperation. Although joint cooperation may provide the best outcome for both, fear that the other will not cooperate, as in Prisoner's Dilemma, may lead risk-averse states to decide not to cooperate. One state may prefer to play a game of Chicken in order to exact maximum concessions from the other state. Alternatively, both may recognize that coordination is best for both, but they nevertheless may differ on what strategy to choose in order to achieve a desired equilibrium.

Based on this two-state game as well as on separate analysis among large numbers of actors, Snidal concludes that relative-gains considerations do not necessarily impede cooperation between two states in an anarchic setting. The assumption that states are exclusively relative-gains seekers and that therefore they are only, or even largely, engaged constantly in zero-sum, or conflictual–competitive, games is not accurate. Instead, there are mixtures of relative and absolute considerations, he finds, that affect cooperation within a Prisoner's Dilemma game framework. Furthermore, he suggests that cooperation prospects may be greater in a multipolar world than in a bipolar setting. Under conditions of multipolarity, relative gains spread over a larger number of states are less likely than in a bipolar system to have disproportionate effects resulting in the destabilizing growth of one state's capabilities, relative to those of other states. Whether, on this basis, post–Cold War trends toward greater multipolarity will facilitate international cooperation remains uncertain in Snidal's mind. Nevertheless, he concludes that because realist theorists are concerned that relative gains pursued by one state will be perceived to have adverse consequences for other states, thereby producing a security dilemma, realist theorists should prefer multipolarity over bipolarity. It is in tight bipolar systems, he concludes, that the relative-gains premise diminishes most the prospect for international cooperation. Although it is premature, based on game theory, to assert that multipolarity increases cooperation, there is game-theoretical evidence in support of the proposition that increasing the number of actors does not necessarily diminish the possibility of greater cooperation among such entities.

SCHELLING'S BARGAINING THEORY

Thomas C. Schelling, whose contributions to game theory have been widely regarded as seminal, is not primarily concerned with the mathematics of games. Like Morgenstern, he began as an economist and soon began to focus his attention on bargaining.[47] In Schelling's work, we find a combination of the social-psychological and the logical–strategic approaches to the subject of human conflict–conflict viewed not exclusively as the opposition of hostile forces, but rather as a more complex and delicate phenomenon in which antagonism and cooperation often subtly interact in the adversary relationship. His theory seeks to make use of game theory, organization and communication theory, and theory of evidence, choice, and collective decision. This strategic theory, according to Schelling, "takes conflict for granted, but also assumes common interest between the adversaries; it assumes a 'rational' value-maximizing mode of behavior; and it focuses on the fact that each participant's 'best' choice of action depends on what he expects the other to do, and that 'strategic behavior' is concerned with influencing another's choice by working on his expectation of how one's own behavior is related to his."[48]

Schelling, then, is mainly interested in such problems as conducting negotiations, maintaining credible deterrence, making threats and promises, bluffing, double-crossing, waging limited conflict, and formulating formal or tacit arms-control policies. His writing reflects a conviction that in most international strategic situations the notion of the ZSG is simply irrelevant. In his view, the two Cold War superpowers could not have rationally supposed themselves engaged in a zero-sum rivalry that would have been played out to the bitter end of a full-scale nuclear exchange. The resultant score of such a game would in all probability have been not zero but minus two. (If one asks "minus two what?" the answer is, at the very least, "minus two superpowers.") Schelling therefore devoted little attention to the rational analysis of this ultimate irrationality. Indeed, his "theory of interdependent decisions," as he prefers to call it, is addressed less to the *application* than to the *threat* of violence as a means of influencing another party's behavior. Going to war might be the height of folly under certain circumstances, but posing a controlled threat or risk of war might prove to be a strategically shrewd move.[49]

Although Schelling is very much interested in what constitutes rational behavior between parties in a conflict situation, he shies away from the notion that rationality can be neatly measured along a quantitative utility scale. This may be possible in respect to human action in the economic order, in which a precise monetary standard is available. However, he deems the concept of utility as applied to international political and strategic decision making much more ambiguous and fluid, and hence less relevant. Thus, instead of looking for the minimax solution to conflict situations, Schelling is more interested in what we might not inaptly call motivational dialectics. He goes so far as to suggest that even though rationality is a desirable commodity, it is not always and under all circumstances desirable to *appear* rational.

> It is not a universal advantage in situations of conflict to be inalienably and manifestly rational in decision and motivation. . . . It is not true, as illustrated in the example of extortion, that in the face of a threat it is invariably an advantage to be rational, particularly if the fact of being rational or irrational cannot be concealed. It is not invariably an advantage, in the face of a threat, to have a communication system in good order, to have complete information, or to be in full command of one's own actions or of one's own assets. . . . The very notion that it may be a strategic advantage to relinquish certain options deliberately, or even to give up all control over one's future actions and make his responses automatic, seems to be a hard one to swallow.[50]

Schelling focuses particularly on what is sometimes called the "limited adversary relationship," or what he himself refers to as "the theory of precarious partnership or . . . incomplete antagonism."[51] This implies a situation in which parties to a conflict, despite their strategic opposition to each other, perceive some minimum mutual interest, even if this amounts to no more than the avoidance of reciprocal annihilation. Even when, for one reason or another, parties cannot carry on direct or overt communication with each other, they can nevertheless tacitly coordinate their moves by fixing on certain salient points of common interest and converging expectation. He illustrates the possibility of tacit communication by citing several examples from nonhostile relationships in which two parties share an interest in finally arriving at the same meeting place.

If a husband and wife become separated in a department store, each might try to figure out where the other is most likely to go, with a view to rendezvous. In another situation, two parachutists drop into the same vicinity at some distance from each other. In order to be rescued, they must get together quickly, but they cannot communicate directly concerning their exact location. Each one knows, however, that the other carries a copy of the same map of the area, showing a central salient feature (such as a bridge) that furnishes a focal point for coordinated behavior. In a third example, a number of people in New Haven, Connecticut, were told that they were to meet someone in New York City on a specified date, but they received no instructions as to the exact place or time. Because they could not communicate with the other party, they had to make an intelligent guess. A majority of those queried chose the information booth in Grand Central Station at high noon on the date given.[52]

It might be objected in reference to this last illustration that people taking the train from New Haven to New York always pass through Grand Central Station. However, this need not vitiate the validity of Schelling's theory. Perhaps it only serves to demonstrate that choices based on mutual expectation of convergent decisions reflect not merely abstract logic but also concrete historical experience— an input that might help to render prediction more reliable. There is no guarantee, of course, that this method of tacit bargaining will work in any particular two-party situation. Schelling modestly claims no more than that a shrewd selection of those convergence points that seem likely, in the mind of each party, to be relatively unique and unambiguous is superior to a system of purely random guesses as to a focal point of agreement.

Bargaining parties are not motivated solely by a desire to agree. Divergent interests skew the quest for convergence. However, if agreement is finally reached, it means that forces for agreement proved stronger than forces for severance of negotiations. Moreover, although tacit coordination does not at first glance seem applicable to explicit bargaining in which formal communication is normal, nevertheless it is probably present even under explicit bargaining conditions. As examples, Schelling cites the tendency to split the difference in price haggling, and the recurring willingness to follow a conspicuous precedent embodied in an earlier compromise. Although the power to communicate alters a bargaining situation, it does not repeal the relevance of convergent expectations and the role of objective coordinating signals. Granted that in bargaining contests, one side often manifests either greater power or a stronger determination to press for a unilaterally favorable settlement, still Schelling notes that the outcome can often be predicted "on some basis of some 'obvious' focus for agreement, some strong suggestion contained in the situation itself, without much regard to the merits of the case."[53]

Schelling contends that the limitation of conflict is not only theoretically possible but also historically actual. Cases in point include the mutual abstention from using gas weaponry in World War II and the various restrictions imposed on the conduct of the Korean War, with respect to geographical boundaries, the political identification of parties involved, the kinds of weapons employed, and the types of military operations permitted. Thus, protagonists, even in wartime, have often bounded or limited the extent and scope of their operations, as in the Korean conflict when, for example, China itself was not attacked after its forces entered the war. If restraints were (and could be) imposed on military operations as a type of informal arms-control in wartime, Schelling asked, could such tacit agreements or understandings be utilized in peacetime arms-control settings? As a matter of national policy, nations did (and could) postpone the development or deployment of specific weapons systems as a signal and incentive to an opponent to take similar action. Such measures could be undertaken outside the cumbersome and often protracted negotiations leading to a treaty. Thus, tacit bargaining offered a highly flexible approach designed to assess the intentions of an enemy or to signal resolve or a willingness to accommodate. Tacit bargaining, in the form of unilateral or reciprocal restraint, it was recognized, could take place as part of, or outside of, a formal negotiating process leading to a treaty.

Schelling also suggests that it may be possible, prior to the outbreak of conflict, to make arrangements that increase the likelihood that limits could be observed once hostilities are under way. This involves keeping channels of communication open, clarifying in advance the authority and authenticity of messages calculated to reduce the pressures for uncontrollable escalation, and identifying parties who might plausibly act as intermediaries.[54]

Perhaps Schelling's principal contribution to this sector of international-relations theory is his emphasis on the necessity of avoiding extreme formulations. At one extreme of the spectrum, he sees the ZSG as the limiting case of pure conflict, not as a point of departure for realistic strategic analysis. At the opposite extreme, he places the pure-collaboration game in which there is no divergent interest because the players always win or lose together. Schelling is primarily interested in the situations that lie in between—that is, in those bargaining or mixed-motive games that contain elements of both conflict and mutual dependence, of divergence and convergence of interest, of secrecy and revelation—all in what he calls the "spiral of reciprocal expectations,"[55] which is usually a matter more of psychological than of mathematical calculus.

The major objective in bargaining, Schelling constantly reiterates, is for each party to make commitments, threats, and promises credible to the other party, so that the each party cannot conclude that the other party is bluffing. An adversary who thinks that you are leaving yourself an avenue of retreat will take seriously neither your commitment nor your threat. Hence, there may be a strategic advantage in making an overt commitment from which there can be no retreat and in communicating this clearly to the adversary. This can be achieved by staking your reputation on the adherence to the commitment or the execution of the threat, or by making it clear that if the other party commits an act you wish to deter, you will have no flexibility in respect to punishing the party, simply because you have already set up an automatic response that is irreversible. This makes the threat of punishment not merely probable but certain, and the adversary must take this into account before deciding to make a move.[56] It is the rich variety of subtle signaling problems associated with this type of political game that makes Schelling's *The Strategy of Conflict* one of the most interesting and readable works in international-relations theory.

LATER CONTRIBUTIONS TO BARGAINING THEORY

More recent work has built on Schelling's writings on tacit bargaining. According to George W. Downs and David M. Rocke, tacit bargaining occurs "whenever a state attempts to influence the policy choices of another state through behavior, rather than by relying on formal or informal diplomatic exchanges."[57] What differentiates tacit bargaining from negotiations is the fact that in tacit bargaining, communications are based on actions rather than on words. As Downs and Rocke point out, examples of tacit bargaining abound in the history of international statecraft. They encompass retaliatory actions such as the imposition of tariffs or quotas in response to a state that refuses to liberalize trade relationships. Tacit bargaining also includes, as in the Korean conflict, decisions to refrain from using certain kinds of weapons or to exempt one or more categories of targets from military action.

Tacit bargaining has the advantage of being iterative in nature. Small and incremental changes can be made, as deemed to be necessary or appropriate, either in the absence of a formal agreement, as already noted, or as part of a strategy designed to achieve a new agreement or to maintain an existing treaty. The means by which international agreements between adversaries are maintained after they are negotiated and ratified is of obvious importance and interest. Treaty preservation depends vitally on tacit bargaining, which itself is closely related to deterrence. Parties seeking to uphold an existing treaty have before them the need to deter a rival nation from violations. Although models of nuclear deterrence differ from models of deterrence applicable to treaty maintenance, tacit bargaining represents a potentially important dimension of the process of assuring treaty compliance. Whether a signatory chooses to violate a treaty depends on the relationship between compliance advantages and potential gains to be derived from measures such as circumvention or abrogation.

Basing their work on the extensive utilization of formal modeling, Downs and Rocke nevertheless set forth what they consider to be the strengths and limitations of an approach that relies on the use of such models. Their objective is to evaluate the potential contribution of differing tacit bargaining strategies, both to achieve arms control and to maintain agreements once concluded. They make use of a combination of modeling based extensively on Prisoner's Dilemma and on decision-oriented simulation models. Appropriately, given the complexity and large number of variables operative in decisions regarding national-security issues such as arms control, an attempt is made to reconcile the needs for rigor and for realism.

As Downs and Rocke acknowledge, there are pitfalls in the exclusive reliance on formal modeling as a basis for understanding the process by which tacit bargaining takes place and by which arms-control agreements are negotiated and maintained. Crucially important questions, such as the optimal mixture between sanctions and acceptance of treaty violations, as a basis for tacit bargaining, can only be answered by reference to an adversary's motives, not always known or easily knowable, and therefore not necessarily capable of being encompassed within the various boundaries of the axiomatic apparatus of the formal model. Precision in determining the respective priorities of state actors requires a form of measurement as a part of the formal modeling process. Even the most knowledgeable authorities would have difficulty estimating with maximum accuracy the priorities on which U.S. and Soviet bargaining strategies were based. Only to a limited extent can such problems be mitigated by the use of formal models sufficiently broad to take account of variations in important assumptions and decision variables.

In the final analysis, an assessment of the role of tacit bargaining in arms control depends vitally on assumptions about the motives leading to arms races. A state may embrace armaments as a necessary part of its quest for hegemony. Its commitment to achieving military superiority may dwarf any interest in tacit bargaining for the sake of arms control. In themselves, arms races may be stabilizing or destabilizing, just as their absence can be stabilizing or destabilizing. If World War I was said to be the logical outcome of an arms race, the Second World War has widely been held to have resulted from the absence of an arms race. The antistatus-quo power in possession of superior (however defined) military power represents a destabilizing element, just as a status-quo power with military forces greater than those of the revisionist state may contribute to stability. Therefore, as Downs and Rocke point out, "there is no way that a student of arms races can examine four or five historical cases and come away with the impression that the underlying pattern of motives was identical."[58] According to Downs and Rocke, any model that purports to encompass the key variables of an arms race must take account of such factors as perceived advantages from superiority; the cost of maintaining or changing a given level of weaponry; and the domestic considerations associated with weapons policy.

Attempting with considerable success to combine the rigor of formal modeling with the realism of historical experience and example, Downs and Rocke conclude that "under most circumstances, it is possible to assume that both of the nations that have achieved a tacit or formal arms agreement would prefer that the agreement survive than that it be replaced by an intense arms race."[59] Several other conclusions relate to the implications of imperfect information about an opponent's actions. It may prove difficult to maintain a treaty in the absence of a strategy that balances deterrence of violations (through tacit bargaining) with an understanding of the fact that imperfect information may give the appearance of a violation where none exists.[60] In fact, they continue, the inadequacy of information about an opponent's motivations, strategies, and goals holds profoundly important implications for the success or failure of tacit bargaining. For example, there may be a tendency to underestimate (or overestimate) the extent of an opponent's willingness to engage in cooperative behavior or to overestimate (or underestimate) the extent of an opponent's propensity to defect from, or discard, an existing arms-control agreement or to engage in a continuing weapons buildup. Such misperceptions, based on imperfect information, enhance the potential difficulties and dangers in tacit bargaining. Because the likelihood of less than adequate information is more the rule than the exception, the potential for failure in tacit bargaining is considerable. Precisely for this reason, tacit-bargaining initiatives are likely to be less than radical in nature and substance, especially when the costs of failure based on imperfect information in situations of hostility are greatest and thus under conditions in which it would be most useful for the policymaker to have tacit bargaining as an available option.

Realization of the true potential of tacit bargaining, according to Downs and Rocke, depends on answers to such questions as, How important is it that a unilateral action taken by one party in the bargaining process be generous in order to be politically important to the other side? How long should such a gesture be held out in the hope of reciprocity? When should a retaliatory action be initiated by a party in response to a violation? If tacit bargaining, like the broader negotiations process, takes place under conditions of imperfect information, the prospects for satisfactory answers to such questions are not promising. Although such questions define the authors' agenda, their ability to provide adequate answers is limited by the nature of the phenomena with which they (and the policymaker) are dealing.

With an emphasis on crisis decision making, as discussed in Chapter 11, Glenn H. Snyder and Paul Diesing have developed a series of formal bargaining models.[61] Their work cuts across decision-making theory as well as game theory and neorealist–structural-realist theory. Snyder and Diesing have attempted to develop a theory of international-crisis behavior based on a synthesis among several theories of international politics, basing their theoretical work on the rationale that crises "highlight in microcosm many of the essential features of international politics."[62] They assess the implications of the structure of the international system for crisis bargaining. In a multipolar crisis, for example, the relative bargaining power of the principal protagonists will depend on the intentions of their allies and especially how those intentions are perceived by the opponent. In multipolar systems, there is a potential for the principal parties to miscalculate the extent to which support will be forthcoming from allies as a result of uncertainties about the extent to which the ally's interests are shared by other alliance members. Snyder and Diesing note that, in multipolar crises, there is extensive bargaining uncertainty within alliances. Protagonists attempt to solidify support within their respective alliances and to weaken support within the opposing alliance for the antagonist.

In contrast, in bipolar systems, Snyder and Diesing found that the role of allies was of marginal importance if the crisis, as in the case of the Cuban Missile Crisis, was a direct superpower confrontation. Here, they set forth two other crisis categories in a bipolar system in which bargaining was of greater importance. They included, first, cases in which one of the superpowers initiated the crisis with a smaller state on the other side as the target (the Soviet Union blockading the access routes to West Berlin); and, second, crises outside Europe, as in the Middle East, in which both principal parties were states other than the superpowers, but in which the superpowers had an interest based on a client–state relationship (the Yom Kippur Crisis of 1973). Thus, in multipolar and bipolar systems, structural characteristics, as in structural-realist theory, shape the crisis bargaining process. For Snyder and Diesing, the *structure* means the distribution of military capabilities, while they use the term *alignment* to mean the beliefs held by actors about how such capabilities are aggregated in the system.

Depending on their levels of mutual dependence, or interdependence, also shaped by system structure, states engage in interactions that include bargaining, defined as a "communicative process in which the parties attempt to influence each other's decisions in a future substantive interaction." According to Snyder and Diesing, the outcome is a bargain, based usually on a "change in the parties' *intentions* and/or expectations regarding each other's behavior in future interactions, whether in a single transaction implementing the bargain, or a series of them, or in hypothetical future contingencies."[63] Moving beyond the international systemic level of analysis set forth in structural-realist theory, Snyder and Diesing suggest that international bargaining is shaped also by the national characteristics of the state actors, including for example the nature of their political systems and decision-making processes, values, images, and domestic participants in policy formulation.

Such conclusions are based on the utilization of game models, and principally one in which there was an ordinal ranking, by crisis participants, of their values for each of four general outcomes: winning, losing, compromising, or capitulating. With such a model, they examined a series of crises from the end of the nineteenth century until the 1970s. They encompassed the Balkan crises in the years preceding World War I, the outbreak of World War I, the Munich Crisis of 1938, the Suez Crisis of 1956, and the Yom Kippur Crisis of 1973, to mention only several of the 16 crises that were included in their analysis. In the crises studied, Snyder and Diesing examined bargaining processes that, as in the Prisoner's Dilemma game, produced compromise based on the replacement of conflictual behavior with cooperation. They also studied cases in which one side capitulated. Included also were cases in which one party played a game of Chicken but later compromised, as well as situations in which one party played according to Prisoner's Dilemma principles and the other engaged in a game of Chicken.

They concluded that the two crises that ended in more or less even compromises were Prisoner's Dilemma crises, in which the parties perceived that each was prepared to go to war or to engage in an escalation process leading possibly to war if the only alternative to war or escalation was to accept the opposite party's initial demand. In a bargaining process in which both parties possessed relatively equal power, both came to a reassessment of their original demands and goals, leading to concessions and compromise. The two crises that exhibited these characteristics were the pre–World War I Agidir Crisis of 1911 and the Berlin Crisis of 1961.

By the same token, Snyder and Diesing found, in cases of unequal compromise or capitulation by one side, a mutual recognition by the protagonists that there was an inequality in their respective resolve or commitment to originally stated goals. One party turned out to have interests that were greater than those of the other protagonist, or the dominant party appeared to be prepared, as a result of greater bargaining power, to pursue such interests to their logical conclusion. Among the crises that bore such characteristics was the Cuban Missile Crisis of 1962. Thus, Snyder and Diesing examined a variety of international crises within game models designed to assess strategies, goals, and payoffs based on the bargaining power of the participants, defined as "a function of the relative values the parties attach to the possible outcomes, especially the outcomes of losing, winning, and of bargaining breakdown and possible war."[64]

Bargaining provides a point of convergence between international relations and domestic politics that has formed a basis for analysis with the use of game theory. According to Robert D. Putnam, negotiators faced with domestic constituencies whose interests they must satisfy in an international agreement confront what is called "two-level games," or "domestic–international interactions."[65] As an example, Putnam quotes Robert Strauss, U.S. negotiator at the Tokyo Round trade negotiations: "During my tenure as Special Trade Representative, I spent as much time negotiating with domestic constituents (both industry and labor) and members of the U.S. Congress as I did negotiating with our foreign trading partners."[66] Putnam suggests that it is necessary analytically to consider the bargaining process within two stages. The first, termed Level I, consists of bargaining between the negotiators, leading to a tentative agreement. The second, designated Level II, comprises the discussions that take place within each group of constituents about whether, and on what terms, the agreement should be approved or ratified. Further, Putnam develops what he calls "win-sets," or the set of all possible Level I international agreements that would be acceptable to a majority of constituents voting yes or no. The configuration of such win-sets at the domestic Level II is of crucial importance for understanding the latitude available to international (Level I) negotiators. By definition, Putnam contends, any successful agreement must fall inside the Level II win-sets of each of the parties to the accord. Otherwise, an agreement reached between international negotiators may fail to achieve ratification.

In multi-issue negotiations, as in the case of trade, negotiators face the need to make concessions on one issue in order to gain benefits on others. How much to yield on imports of citrus fruit in order to gain a greater overseas market for other products will be shaped by the effects of one move or another on the domestic support required in order to ensure ratification of the resulting agreement. Putnam suggests the need to analyze the respective trade-offs and their implications for alternative win-sets, with the objective of maximizing the win-set needed for ratification. He suggests that Level I negotiators have a strong interest in maximizing the other side's win-set, to the extent of ensuring that its negotiations can achieve necessary ratification at the domestic level.

At the same time, Putnam recognizes that the ability of a negotiator to point to domestic difficulties standing in the way of ratification and limiting international negotiating flexibility may be turned to advantage. For example, an American negotiator can argue, with great plausibility, that the separation of powers contained in the U.S. Constitution, together with the important role accorded thereby to the U.S. Congress, imposes major constraints on what can be agreed at the international level by the executive branch of the U.S. government. Because two-level games as bargaining processes are said to be ubiquitous because of the intersection of domestic and international politics, it becomes essential to reflect such linkages in international-relations theory.

Here we have another example of the levels of analysis that we described in Chapter 1. Game theory, it is suggested, represents a useful basis for understanding how decision makers reconcile their domestic and international needs and constraints. This includes, within a game-theoretical context, the development of preferences, strategies, and payoffs within and between the international and domestic levels. If two-level games, as Putnam suggests, are a major feature of political relationships, diplomacy, and bargaining—from security policy to trade agreements—what is required is greater empirical research designed to extend knowledge about how such games are actually conducted in real life, drawing to the extent possible from game theory.

SIMULATION IN INTERNATIONAL RELATIONS

Simulation differs from game theory and gaming, although it is related to them. Whereas game theory seeks the optimum mathematically rational strategy for playing a game (purely as a game, with no reference to the real world), simulation theory deals with a "let's pretend" situation. A simulation experiment is a game that has been designed not merely for the sake of playing the game, but rather for the purpose of demonstrating a valid truth about actual social processes through the unfolding of an artificially constructed yet dynamic model. Thus, simulation techniques are essentially laboratory techniques or nonlaboratory contrivances that permit the study of replicated human behavior. Through the use of these techniques, researchers attempt to learn something significant about a complex phenomenon *out there*, which they cannot control, by creating *in here* a more simplified version of a specific phenomenon that they can control and that is in some way analogous or isomorphic to the phenomenon of interest. Social scientists have long complained that it is virtually impossible to obtain from the real world certain kinds of data needed to verify their hypotheses. The experimental method of simulation represents an effort to compensate for these data deficiencies.[67]

The Uses and Limitations of Simulation

Simulation is widely used in government as a means of sensitizing policymakers to hypothetical, but nevertheless plausible, contingencies. Simulation exercises are conducted within the civilian–military policy community. Often, the focus of simulation is a crisis scenario in which players confront the need to act quickly and decisively in order to cope with the situation set forth in the scenario. Simulation exercises have been conducted in which the players were the senior policymakers, including the U.S. President and Cabinet members, as well as the Chair of the Joint Chiefs of Staff and the other military leadership. Simulation exercises provide a unique opportunity to inform key decision makers about existing or emerging security threats and issues, to identify problems and opportunities for decision makers, and to expose future leaders to plausible international challenges. Simulation exercises have been widely and successfully used in the military, civilian government, academic, and even corporate communities for many years.

Simulation as a Teaching Device

Many proponents of simulation techniques are convinced that their greatest utility is in teaching. There are many types of simulation exercises. In one rather well-known version, Inter-Nation Simulation, which was developed as an educational device by Harold Guetzkow, participants role-play the key domestic- and foreign-policy decision makers of five or six fictitious states. (Fictitious rather than real states were used so that subjects could make their decisions in response to the interactive process of the game, uncomplicated by presuppositions and theories as to how the leaders of actual countries ought to act in various situations.)[68] Players learn about their roles and their country situations by reading background papers. They learn the game both by orienting themselves to its rules and even more by playing it. This, like the great majority of all political games, is characterized by the compression of real time; for example, a few hours of play might be made to represent a month or a year of historical time. National goals may be either given at the outset or defined by the participants as play proceeds. Periodically, each nation is assigned basic resources that can be allocated by the leaders' choices to internal or external purposes. Aside from national goals, action is guided by the presumed desire of the decision makers to remain in office. They can be replaced if either domestic consumer satisfaction or national security falls below a minimum standard that fluctuates somewhat arbitrarily, according to rules that permit differentiation of democratic and totalitarian regimes. The game permits both bilateral and multilateral communications—the former through restricted messages and the latter through a world newspaper.[69] Simulation experiments may involve the periodic feeding of game results to a computer for the purpose of speeding up the evaluation of decision consequences according to a preprogrammed formula, but computerization is not a necessary part of simulation.

Other exercises, such as SIMULEX, an annual crisis-management simulation held at the Fletcher School of Law and Diplomacy, Tufts University, provide an opportunity for students and invited participants from the official gaming agencies of the U.S. government to simulate a crisis-management exercise in which decision-making units of actual countries are represented. Although drastically reduced in scope and limited in time, the SIMULEX simulation exercise is designed to represent an operating model of reality. Despite the fact that the real-world context of international behavior is missing, there is still intense personal involvement in making decisions and taking other actions called for within a specified time limit. There is an opportunity to take part in, and observe, the processes of situation definition, information search, risk taking, group compromise, and policy formulation. Simultaneously, at the interteam level, there are present such phenomena as bargaining, negotiation, and communication of intent, of commitment, and of resolve. The exercise is not predictive; nor is its purpose to practice actual contingency planning for any particular nation. However, it is intended to provide a useful approach and methodology for generating new hypotheses, and for learning and testing the policy-planning process. SIMULEX, like comparable exercises, is designed to furnish a technique for generating insights and contributing to a greater understanding of the factors underlying national strategies, goals, and policies. A series of issues related to crisis escalation, de-escalation, bargaining, negotiations, the role of force, and intelligence policy are examined in the various game-move periods. Scenarios are written to be somewhat provocative in order to facilitate discussion of important issues that may have greater or lesser degrees of plausibility and probability in the real world. The scenario is designed to acquaint players with the key issues, dilemmas, constraints, challenges, and opportunities that could arise in an actual crisis, and the results are analyzed in light of lessons learned.

Advocates of simulation for teaching purposes argue that participation in such exercises enables a student to become actively involved in an interactive process that emulates selected basic features of international reality. Those educators who evaluate gaming most highly are likely to be those who believe that doing something is a superior learning experience to hearing something. They point out that games stimulate interest and motivation, essentially because games are fun; they provide an opportunity for students to test their theoretical knowledge gained from reading, lectures, and other sources; they introduce students to the concrete pressures that impinge on the policymakers, the dilemmas that policymakers face, and the constrictions that limited resources place upon policymakers; games enable students to experience decision making in a group context; and they furnish a glimpse into a model world that students can grasp more easily than they can the real international system.[70]

Simulation as a heuristic device, however, is not without its critics. It has been pointed out that a substantial proportion of students can be expected to be uninterested or skeptical; that gaming may arouse interest in the fun of the game without producing a serious attitude toward the study of international relations; that students seldom know enough about either the real political world or the roles they are supposed to play to act "even remotely as real-world politicians do in making their institutions and their political machinery work."[71]

Gaming and the Policy Sciences

In games designed to serve the policy sciences, an effort is usually made to achieve as much realism as possible. For instance, in some simulation exercises, used within and outside of government, scenarios are developed for situations such as international crises. The participants are students or even policymakers, who play the roles of decision makers in real states such as the United States, Japan, France, or India. Professional policymakers thereby derive greater profit by representing officials not of fictitious countries but of actual states engaged in the subtleties and complexities of the international interactive process that professionals understand best. Players might be instructed to play either *predicted strategies* (based on the way specific governments would be expected to behave, from historical experience) or *optimal strategies* (based on what the individual deems best under the circumstances, regardless of existing domestic and other constraints), or a combination of the two approaches.

Frequently the element of nature or fate is introduced into the game by allowing the control group to provide for such unexpected events as technological breakthroughs, the death of key leaders, and the outbreak of civil turbulence. Occasionally, the scenario will be used to project the opening of the game sufficiently far into the future to prevent the simulation from being overtaken by daily news developments. Participants have found that by participating in a gaming experiment of a critical international problem, they have acquired fresh insights into the complexities of situations, into the unexpected turns that events might take, and into the psychological–moral–intellectual pressures and uncertainties that accompany making foreign-policy decisions.[72] It is impossible, however, from the outcome of a crisis game to predict the actual outcome of a real-world political encounter, no matter how many times the game is played with similar results.

Gaming and Theory Building

The third principal use of political gaming is in the area of research and theory building. Here the primary objective is not to provide a worthwhile personal experience via the gaming process either to student or to policymakers, but rather to test social-science hypotheses. The utility of simulation as a tool for confirming or disconfirming theoretical propositions about the international system is a matter of considerable controversy within the field of international-relations theorists and among the simulators themselves. One might admit that from carefully observing the behavior of a group of experienced policymakers in a realistically simulated crisis (e.g., a future Persian Gulf or Korean Crisis), one might be able to make some interesting inferences concerning the political values, strategic preconceptions, psychological attitudes, and preferred methods of conflict management that would be likely to characterize those particular policymakers if a real crisis were soon to arise in a closely similar form. However, this specific simulation, after all, would be a highly particularized and concretized kind of prediction, more appropriate to diplomatic intelligence than to social science. The social scientist is much more interested in universally applicable generalizations than in those subtle nuances of unique historical situations that compose the special intellectual competence of the country or area expert. Policymakers wish to know as much as possible about this particular crisis or policy situation, so that they can favorably influence its outcome. Social scientists, on the other hand, are not primarily oriented to this situation. Their principal concern is with universal generalizations and probabilities. Of what use can simulation be to them in this more comprehensive quest?

The crucial question is this: What is the relation between a game and reality? What can we learn about the real political world from empirically observing the results of political gaming? A game, after all, is only an analogical model, which may or may not be partially parallel to the real world in respect to both elements and interactive processes, depending on the intelligence that has gone into the construction of the model, combined with the maturity and seriousness with which the game is played out. Eugene J. Meehan lays down the following useful guidelines:

> If a model is used as an aid to explanation, then the interaction of elements in the system is prime; if the model is used for prediction, the outcome of dynamic processes in model and empirical world must be similar. . . . Models are always partial and approximate, as are analogies. It follows that there will be properties of observed reality not duplicated in the model, at least potentially, and it is always possible that models have properties that are not duplicated in the empirical world. Furthermore, models and analogies may be useful in creating some expectations with regard to reality (supposing them to have congruence with reality) but may be quite useless and even misleading in other respects.[73]

THE GAME WORLD AND THE REAL WORLD

The first question to be asked is whether the game is isomorphic (congruent) with reality. Richard E. Dawson has implicitly recognized the need for traditional political knowledge in simulation experiments when he noted that before researchers can validly model a real political system, they have to know a great deal about the workings of that system.[74] It is not enough that a game be realistic in flavor: In its substantive details, a game might bear a superficial resemblance to a real-world political situation and yet be quite unlike reality in the playing—that is, in its basic dynamic processual features.

Richard C. Snyder asks whether participants can ever escape the realization that what they are involved in is only a game and not the real thing. He then cites evidence to the effect that people can become totally absorbed in the simulation exercise.[75] The fact remains, however, that total absorption in a game does not necessarily bridge the gap between simulation and reality. We are faced here with such problems as the compression of time and the concomitant pressure of hurried decisions from a sketchy information base; the selection of a small number of nations out of the whole complex international system; the cultural provincialism of nearly all gaming experiments to date—virtually all decision makers have been Americans; the fact that national decisions are made by a small number of decision makers, completely abstracted from an institutionalized context; and the realization that the reward–punishment matrix and indeed the whole sociopsychological environment of decision making in a game are quite different from those in real life.

For guidance in constructing models and evaluating the results of simulated international interaction, students of simulation have turned to the writings of scholars in other fields, both traditional and contemporary, who have theorized about international relations. Similarly, models of international simulation have provided for the observation of the behavior of actor participants in differing environments and in a multiplicity of relationships over time. Although simulation models have necessarily been more parsimonious than the literature of international relationships, students of simulation have attempted to compare simulation models with models explicit or implicit in international-relations literature to compare the *results* of simulation runs with empirically derived descriptions of inter-national behavior—for example, in crisis simulations.[76]

GAMING AND SIMULATION: THE DEVELOPMENT OF INTERNATIONAL RELATIONS

To summarize, it can be said that simulation experiments are widely regarded as potentially useful heuristic devices, provided that suitable facilities are available and the students are properly motivated to learn from them. Policy-oriented games played by experienced decision makers can also prove to be valuable tools for the improved understanding of specific foreign-policy problems, insofar as they may cast light on factors and suggest alternatives that might otherwise be over-looked. As for the use of simulation in research and theory building, some writers are more optimistic than others about the possibility of using political games to val-idate hypotheses about the real political world. Nonetheless, nearly all the author-ities in this area cautiously refrain from asserting that simulation techniques can produce any predictive capability. Most would probably agree that much more needs to be known before simulation can be accepted as a reliable tool for the ver-ification of theory.

Last but not least, game theory, as we have seen, cuts across international-rela-tions theory. It provides a basis for the development of more rigorous theory based on models in which actors with strategies, goals, and anticipated payoffs engage in an interactive process, based on rational behavior and including bargaining. In light of the enduring focal points of international-relations theory, including its emphasis on conflict and cooperation as well as war and peace, game-theory mod-els would appear to offer prospects for analyzing the process by which actors relate to each other over time, in a variety of situations of theoretical importance.

NOTES

1. For an extensive discussion of game theory, see Michael Nicholson, *Rationality and the Analysis of International Conflict,* Cambridge Studies in International Relations: Vol. 19 (Cambridge, England: Cambridge University Press, 1992), pp. 57–103; Steven J. Brams and D. Marc Kilgour, *Game Theory and National Security* (New York: Basil Blackwell, 1988); Robert Axelrod, *The Evolution of Cooperation* (New York: Basic Books, 1984); Steven J. Brams, *Biblical Games: A Strategic Analysis of Stories in the Old Testament* (Cambridge, MA: MIT Press, 1980); Steven J. Brams, *Superpower Games: Applying Game Theory to Superpower Conflict* (New Haven, CT: Yale Uni-versity Press, 1985); Martin Shubik, *Game Theory in the Social Sciences: Concepts and Solutions* (Cambridge, MA: MIT Press, 1982).

2. As Anatol Rapoport has asserted quite cogently, a theory is a collection of theorems, and a theorem "is a proposition which is a strict logical consequence of certain defini-tions and other propositions"; "Various Meanings of 'Theory,'" *American Political Sci-ence Review,* LII (December 1958), 973. He notes that Freudian *depth psychology* is "singularly poor in predictive capacity, either deterministic or statistical" (ibid., 982),

but Rapoport does not suggest that the reason for this perhaps resides in the basic irrationality of the subject matter. If one really assumes the irrationality of behavior, a person must at the same time accept its unpredictability, at least for the time being, until the behavior becomes rationally penetrable. In the social universe, observers can ascribe no greater rationality to their own theoretical explanation of a phenomenon than they are willing to attribute to the decision makers who collectively constitute the action-situation or process they are trying to describe and explain. Rapoport does concede, however, that the special merits of game theory derive from its assumption of "perfectly rational players" (ibid., 984). This may, of course, also constitute a major weakness if, in contrast to Freudian psychoanalytic theory, which emphasizes irrationality, game theory runs to the opposite extreme and places excessive stress on the mathematically rational factors that enter into human decisional behavior. The notion of second-guessing may be more psychological than logical–mathematical. Which strategic philosophy do good strategists adopt? Do they play the board, or do they play the opponent? Do they formulate their strategy on the basis of a mathematical computation of available moves, or do they formulate it much as psychological-warfare experts would try to size up their adversary? Rapoport, who is a mathematician–psychologist–game theorist at the University of Michigan, concedes that pure game theory is essentially mathematical and hence contains no uncertainties. "Although the drama of games of strategy is strongly linked with the psychological aspects of the conflict, game theory is not concerned with these aspects. Game theory, so to speak, plays the board. It is concerned only with the logical aspects of strategy. It prescribes the same line of play against a master as it does against a beginner." "The Use and Misuse of Game Theory," *Scientific American,* CCVII (December 1962), 110. For seminal work in game theory, see John von Neumann and Oskar Morgenstern, *Theory of Games and Economic Behavior,* 3rd ed. (Princeton, NJ: Princeton University Press, 1953).

3. Duncan Snidal, "The Game Theory of International Politics," *World Politics,* XXXVIII(1) (October 1985), 25–27; Steven J. Brams and D. Marc Kilgour, *Game Theory and International Security* (New York: Basil Blackwell, 1988), pp. vii–viii; 1–3. See also Stephen J. Majeski and Shane Fricks, "Conflict and Cooperation in International Relations," *Journal of Conflict Resolution,* 39 (4) (December 1995), 622–645.

4. Duncan Snidal, "The Game Theory of International Politics," *World Politics,* XXXVIII(1) (October 1985), 56. See also, in the same issue of *World Politics,* the following articles on various aspects of game theory and international-relations theory: Kenneth A. Oye, "Explaining Cooperation Under Anarchy: Hypotheses and Strategies," and "The Sterling–Dollar–Franc Triangle: Monetary Diplomacy 1929–1937"; Robert Jervis, "From Balance to Concert: A Study of International Security Cooperation"; Stephen Van Evera, "Why Cooperation Failed in 1914"; George W. Downs, David M. Rocke, and Randolph M. Siverson, "Arms Races and Cooperation"; John Conybeare, "Trade Wars: A Comparative Study of Anglo–Hanse, Franco–Italian, and Hawley–Smoot Conflicts"; Charles Lipson, "Bankers' Dilemmas: Private Cooperation in Rescheduling Sovereign Debts"; and Robert Axelrod and Robert O. Keohane, "Achieving Cooperation Under Anarchy: Strategies and Institutions." For examples of other applications of game theory to international relations, see Peter Bennett and Malcolm Dando, "Complex Hypergame Analysis: A Hypergame Perspective of the Fall of France," *Journal of Operational Research Society,* XXX(1) (January 1979), 23–32; Dina J. Zinnes, J. V. Gillespie, and G. S. Tahim, "A Formal Analysis of Some Issues in Balance of Power Theories," *International Studies Quarterly,* XXII (September 1978), 323–353; Curtis S. Signorino, "Simulating International Cooperation

under Uncertainty: The Effects of Symmetric and Asymmetric Noise," *Journal of Conflict Resolution,* 40(1) (March 1996), 152–205.

5. Martin Shubik, *Games for Society, Business and War: Towards a Theory of Gaming* (New York: Wiley, 1964), pp. 50 and 56. See also Michael Nicholson, *Rationality and the Analysis of International Conflict* (New York: Cambridge University Press, 1992), pp. 89–103.

6. Details of a simple game may help the student to envisage the game. Let us call it "Defenders and Attackers." The latter can strike at either of two towns. The Defenders can fully protect only one. If the Defenders select the right town and meet the Attackers, the Attackers will be destroyed. If Defenders select one town and Attackers select the other, the town is destroyed. Martin Shubik, "The Uses of Game Theory," in James C. Charlesworth, ed., *Contemporary Political Analysis* (New York: Free Press, 1967), p. 247.

7. Martin Shubik, "Game Theory and the Study of Social Behavior: An Introductory Exposition," in Martin Shubik, ed., *Game Theory and Related Approaches to Social Behavior* (New York, Wiley, 1964), 15–17.

8. Martin Shubik, "The Uses of Game Theory," in Charlesworth, ed., op. cit., p. 248. See also Shubik's *Games for Society, Business and War,* op. cit., pp. 93–97. "Social, political, and economic problems," Shubik notes, "almost always call for a non-zero-sum formulation"; ibid., pp. 97–98.

9. The mathematicization of utilities or value preferences is always a tenuous business. Even in respect to zero-sum games, Thomas C. Schelling notes that the value systems of two individuals are incommensurate. "If two feudal noblemen play a game of cards, one to lose his thumb if he loses and the other to lose his eyesight, the game is 'zero-sum' (as long as neither cares about the other's gain) and there may be no way of comparing what they risk losing. It is precisely *because* their value systems are incommensurable that, if their interests are strictly opposed, we can arbitrarily represent them by scales of value that make the scores of payoffs add up in every cell to zero." "What Is Game Theory?" in Charlesworth, ed., op. cit., p. 216. An approach that contrasts with that of Schelling is presented by Morton A. Kaplan in his discussion of the work of Duncan Luce and Howard Raiffa. In an analysis of some variant games, Kaplan agrees with Luce and Raiffa that in certain games, the outcome will be determined by the *psychologies* of the players; "A Note on Game Theory and Bargaining," in Morton A. Kaplan, ed., *New Approaches to International Relations* (New York: St. Martin's Press, 1968), pp. 507–509.

10. Many descriptions of Prisoner's Dilemma can be found. See A. W. Tucker and P. Wolfe, eds., *Contributions to the Theory of Games,* Vol. III, *Annals of Mathematic Studies,* No. 30 (Princeton, NJ: Princeton University Press, 1957); R. Duncan Luce and Howard Raiffa, *Games and Decisions* (New York: Wiley, 1957), p. 94ff; Anatol Rapoport and A. M. Chammah, *Prisoner's Dilemma: A Study of Conflict and Cooperation* (Ann Arbor: University of Michigan Press, 1965); Anatol Rapoport, *Two Person Game Theory* (Ann Arbor: University of Michigan Press, 1966); and Martin Shubik, "The Uses of Game Theory," in Charlesworth, ed., op. cit., pp. 264–268. The problem of trust and suspicion between players in mixed-motive games has been dealt with by Morton Deutsch, "Trust and Suspicion," *Journal of Conflict Resolution,* VII (September 1963), 570–579. Two psychologists at Kent State University conducted gaming experiments on a variation of Prisoner's Dilemma in which they separated *temptation* (i.e., the desire to obtain the largest payoff by being the only defector) from *mistrust* (i.e., the fear that the other would like to be the lone defector), and found that temptation is a more likely source of noncooperative behavior than is mistrust; V. Edwin Bixenstine and Hazel Blundell, "Control of Choices Exerted by Structural Factors in Two-Person, Non-Zero-Sum Games," *Journal of Conflict Resolution,* X (December 1966), especially 482.

11. Arthur A. Stein, "Coordination and Collaboration: Regimes in an Anarchic World," *International Organization*, 36(2) (Spring 1982), 299–324.

12. Ibid., 307.

13. Robert Axelrod, *The Evolution of Cooperation* (New York: Basic Books, 1984), pp. 3–27, 169–191.

14. Daniel R. Lutzker, "Sex Role, Cooperation and Competition in a Two-Person, Non-Zero-Sum Game," *Journal of Conflict Resolution*, V (December 1961), 366–368. See also Philip S. Gallo, Jr., and Charles G. McClintock, "Cooperative and Competitive Behavior in Mixed-Motive Games," *Journal of Conflict Resolution*, IX (March 1965), 68–78; and J. T. Tedeschi et al., "Start Effect and Response Bias in the Prisoner's Dilemma Game," *Psychonomic Science*, 11 (4) (1968).

15. David W. Conrath, "Sex Role and Cooperation in the Game of Chicken," *Journal of Conflict Resolution*, XVI (September 1972), 433–443. For additional subtle sex-related differences, see William B. Lacy, "Assumptions of Human Nature, and Initial Expectations and Behavior as Mediators of Sex Effects in Prisoner's Dilemma Research," *Journal of Conflict Resolution*, 22 (June 1978), 269–281.

16. Conrath, op. cit., 434.

17. Ibid., 442.

18. C. Nemeth, "A Critical Analysis of Research Utilizing the Prisoner's Dilemma Paradigm for the Study of Bargaining," in Leonard Berkowitz, ed., *Advances in Experimental Social Psychology*, Vol. 6 (New York: Academic Press, 1972), p. 204. See also Jeffrey Pincus and V. Edwin Pixenstine, "Cooperation in the Decomposed Prisoner's Dilemma Game: A Question of Revealing or Concealing Information," *Journal of Conflict Resolution*, XXI (September 1977), pp. 510–530. See also Alvin E. Roth, ed., *Game-Theoretic Models of Bargaining* (New York: Cambridge University Press, 1985).

19. Barry Schlenker and Thomas Bonoma, "Fun and Games: The Validity of Games for the Study of Conflict," *The Journal of Conflict Resolution*, 22 (March 1978), 14–15. The December 1975 issue of *The Journal of Conflict Resolution* carried seven articles on the subject.

20. Martin Shubik, *Games for Society, Business and War*, op. cit., p. 32.

21. Anatol Rapoport and C. Orwant, "Experimental Games: A Review," *Behavioral Science*, VII (January 1962), 1–37.

22. Abraham Kaplan, "Mathematics and Social Analysis," *Commentary*, VII (September 1952), 284. The mathematical and psychostrategic intricacies of the three-person game can be appreciated by reading William H. Riker, "Bargaining in a Three-Person Game," *American Political Science Review*, LXI (September 1967), 642–656.

23. For theoretical insights into the formation and dissolution of coalitions, see Chapter 10 and the following works: George F. Liska, *Nations in Alliance: The Limits of Interdependence* (Baltimore, MD: Johns Hopkins Press, 1962); William H. Riker, *The Theory of Political Coalitions* (New Haven, CT: Yale University Press, 1962); Julian R. Friedman, Christopher Bladen, and Steven Rosen, *Alliance in International Studies* (Boston: Allyn & Bacon, 1970); Swen Groennings, E. W. Kelley, and Michael Leiserson, eds., *The Study of Coalition Behavior: Theoretical Perspectives and Cases from Four Continents* (New York: Holt, Rinehart and Winston, 1970); and Martin Shubik, *Games for Society, Business and War*, op. cit., pp. 49–51, 149–151, 170, and 259–260.

24. Martin Shubik, *Games for Society, Business and War*, op. cit., p. ix.

25. See Chapter 11.

26. William D. Coplin, *Introduction to International Politics: A Theoretical Overview* (Chicago: Markham, 1971), pp. 258–269.

27. Joseph Frankel, *Contemporary International Theory and the Behavior of States* (New York: Oxford University Press, 1973), p. 96.

28. John W. Burton, "Resolution of Conflict," *International Studies Quarterly*, 16 (March 1972), 530.

29. Glenn H. Snyder, "Prisoner's Dilemma and Chicken Models in International Politics," *International Studies Quarterly*, 15 (March 1971), 84. For an analysis of the qualitative differences between Prisoner's Dilemma and public good conceptions of international trade (or, put differently, hostile and punitive tariff policies versus policies that benefit the larger international common good), see John A. C. Conybeare, "Public Good, Prisoner's Dilemma and the International Political Economy," *International Studies Quarterly*, 28 (March 1984), 5–22.

30. Anatol Rapoport, *Strategy and Conscience* (New York: Harper & Row, 1964), pp. 48–52.

31. See Steven J. Brams, *Game Theory and Politics* (New York: Free Press, 1975), pp. 39–47; Thomas C. Schelling, *Arms and Influence* (New Haven, CT: Yale University Press, 1966), pp. 120–123.

32. Schelling, ibid., p. 121.

33. Martin Shubik, *Games for Society, Business and War*, op. cit., p. 37.

34. Steven J. Brams, *Game Theory and Politics*, op. cit., p. 42.

35. R. Harrison Wagner, "The Theory of Games and the Balance of Power," *World Politics*, 38 (October 1986), 547.

36. Ibid., 574–575.

37. Jean-Jacques Rousseau devised the analogy of the Stag Hunt to demonstrate the difficulty of cooperation under international anarchy. If all members of a hunting team work together to trap the stag, all will eat well. However, if one or more chase a passing rabbit, all will eat less well, and some perhaps not at all. Rousseau, *The First and Second Discourses* (New York: St. Martin's, 1964), pp. 165–167.

38. Kenneth A. Oye, "Explaining Cooperation Under Anarchy: Hypotheses and Strategies," *World Politics*, XXXVIII (October 1985), 6.

39. Ibid., 7.

40. Robert Jervis, "Cooperation Under the Security Dilemma," *World Politics*, 30 (January 1978), 167–214.

41. Kenneth A. Oye, op. cit., pp. 9–13.

42. Pierre Maillard, "The Effect of China on Soviet–American Relations," in *Soviet–American Relations and World Order: The Two and the Many*, Adelphi Papers, No. 66 (London: Institute for Strategic Studies, 1970).

43. Steven J. Brams, *Game Theory and Politics* op. cit., p. 50.

44. Robert Jervis, "Realism, Game Theory, and Cooperation," *World Politics*, XL(3) (April 1988), 318–319.

45. Robert Powell, "Absolute and Relative Gains in International Relations Theory," *American Political Science Review*, 85(4) (December 1991), 1303–1320.

46. Duncan Snidal, "Relative Gains and the Pattern of International Cooperation," *American Political Science Review*, 85(3) (September 1991), 704–726.

47. Thomas C. Schelling, *National Income Behavior: An Introduction to Algebraic Analysis* (New York: McGraw-Hill, 1951), and "An Essay on Bargaining," American Economic Review, XLVI (June 1956), 281–306.

48. Thomas C. Schelling, *The Strategy of Conflict* (New York: Oxford University Press, 1963), p. 15.

49. Ibid., p. 15. Schelling notes that inmates of mental hospitals often seem to cultivate, deliberately or instinctively, value systems that make them less susceptible to disciplinary threats and more capable of exercising coercion themselves. A self-destructive

attitude expressed as a threat (I'll cut a vein in my arm if you don't let me) can put an irrational person in an advantageous position vis-à-vis a rational one. Ibid., p. 17.

50. Ibid., pp. 18–19.
51. Ibid., p. 15.
52. For these and analogous examples, see ibid., pp. 53–58.
53. Ibid., p. 68. See also pp. 71–74, where Schelling speaks of the mutually identifiable resting place, the search for which characterizes both tacit and explicit bargaining. If a person is to make a finite concession that is not to be interpreted as capitulation, the person needs an obvious place to stop; ibid., p. 71.
54. Ibid., pp. 77–80. For other discussions by Schelling of the problems of limiting conflict, see his "Reciprocal Measures for Arms Stabilization," in Donald G. Brennan, ed., *Arms Control, Disarmament and National Security* (New York: Braziller, 1961); see also Thomas C. Schelling and Morton H. Halperin, *Strategy and Arms Control* (New York: Twentieth Century Fund, 1961), especially chaps. 2 and 8.
55. Thomas C. Schelling, *The Strategy of Conflict,* op. cit., p. 87.
56. Ibid., pp. 22–46, 119–139. Hardly anything epitomizes strategic behavior in the mixed-motive game so much as the advantage of being able to adopt a mode of behavior that the other party will take for granted. Ibid., p. 160.
57. George W. Downs and David M. Rocke, *Tacit Bargaining, Arms Races, and Arms Control* (Ann Arbor: University of Michigan Press, 1990), p. 3.
58. George W. Downs and David M. Rocke, ibid., p. 195.
59. Ibid., p. 190.
60. Ibid., p. 191.
61. Glenn H. Snyder and Paul Diesing, *Conflict Among Nations: Bargaining, Decision-Making, and System Structure in International Crises* (Princeton, NJ: Princeton University Press, 1977). See especially pp. 33–183; 471–570.
62. Ibid., p. 471.
63. Iibd., p. 475.
64. Ibid., p. 525.
65. Robert D. Putnam, "Diplomacy and Domestic Politics: The Logic of Two-Level Games," *International Organization,* 42(3) (Summer 1988), 433.
66. Robert S. Strauss, "Foreword" in Joan E. Twiggs, *The Tokyo Round of Multilateral Trade Negotiations: A Case Study in Building Domestic Support for Diplomacy* (Washington, DC: Georgetown University Institute for the Study of Diplomacy, 1987), p. vii. Quoted in Robert D. Putnam, "Diplomacy and Domestic Politics: The Logic of Two-Level Games," *International Organization,* 42(2) (Summer 1988), 433.
67. Richard C. Snyder, "Some Perspectives on the Use of Experimental Techniques in the Study of International Relations," in Harold Guetzkow et al., *Simulation in International Relations: Developments for Research and Teaching* (Englewood Cliffs, NJ: Prentice-Hall, 1963), pp. 2–5.
68. The notion of relating game decisions to personality factors was given an interesting reverse application in a study designed to investigate the use of an actual historical situation to validate simulation. An effort was made (with somewhat inconclusive results) to select participants for the roles of such figures as Edward Grey, Raymond Poincaré, the Kaiser, and the Tsar by matching personality characteristics as much as possible. See Charles F. Hermann and Margaret G. Hermann, "An Attempt to Simulate the Outbreak of World War I," *American Political Science Review,* LXI (June 1967), especially 404–405.
69. Harold Guetzkow, "A Use of Simulation in the Study of Inter-Nation Relations," in Guetzkow et al., op. cit., pp. 24–38. This is a reprint of his article that appeared in

Behavioral Science, V (July 1959). For a description of student games that involved a specific international crisis, see Lincoln P. Bloomfield and Norman J. Padelford, "Three Experiments in Political Gaming," *American Political Science Review,* LIII (December 1959), 1107ff.

70. Chadwick F. Alger, "Use of the Inter-Nation Simulation in Undergraduate Teaching," in Guetzkow et al., op. cit., pp. 152–154.

71. Bernard C. Cohen, "Political Gaming in the Classroom," *Journal of Politics,* XXIV (May 1962), 374. Cohen is quite skeptical in regard to what it is that the students find interesting about the game, as well as their level of political knowledge, their serious desire to emulate real decision makers, and their willingness even to observe the basic rules of the game, compared with their determination to make sport of their personal acquaintances who are supposed to represent foreign countries. For evidence that simulation is not superior to the case study as a teaching device, see James A. Robinson et al., "Teaching with Inter-Nation Simulation and Case Studies," *American Political Science Review,* LX (March 1966), 53–65.

72. Herbert Goldhamer and Hans Speier, in Rosenau, ed., *International Politics: Foreign Policy—A Reader in Research and Theory* (New York: Free Press, 1961), pp. 499–502. Richard E. Barringer and Barton Whaley report that (a) the political–military game is a very intense and vivid experience, seemingly for even the most sophisticated individuals; (b) the insights gained depend largely on the knowledge and experience of the participant; and (c) the game suggests unanticipated policy alternatives. "The M.I.T. Political–Military Gaming Experience," *Orbis,* IX (Summer 1965), 444–448.

73. Eugene J. Meehan, *Contemporary Political Thought: A Critical Study* (Homewood, IL: Dorsey, 1967), pp. 31–32.

74. Richard E. Dawson, "Simulation in the Social Sciences," in Harold Guetzkow, ed., *Simulation in Social Sciences* (Englewood Cliffs, NJ: Prentice-Hall, 1962), p. 13ff.

75. Richard C. Snyder, "Some Perspectives on the Use of Experimental Techniques in the Study of International Relations," op. cit., pp. 12–14.

76. See, for example, William D. Coplin, "Inter-Nation Simulation and Contemporary Theories of International Relations," *American Political Science Review,* IX (September 1966), 562–578; Richard W. Chadwick, "An Empirical Test of Five Assumptions in an Inter-Nation Simulation About National Political Systems," *General Systems,* XII (1967), 177–192; Walter C. Clemens, Jr., "A Propositional Analysis of the International Relations Theory in Temper—A Computer Simulation of Cold War Conflict," in William D. Coplin, ed., *Simulation in the Study of Politics* (Chicago: Markham, 1968), pp. 59–101.

Chapter *13*

International Relations Theory: Into the Third Millennium

E. H. Carr has suggested that "when the human mind begins to exercise itself in some field an initial stage occurs in which the element of wish or purpose is overwhelmingly strong, and the inclination to analyze facts and means weak or nonexistent."[1] Whatever the validity of this statement in the development of other disciplines, it describes the growth of international relations, especially in its formative years between the two world wars of the twentieth century, although the theories that shaped twentieth-century international-relations theory can be traced from the ancient world, and many are discussed in previous chapters of this text.[2] The history of international-relations theory contains ample evidence of normative theory based on "wish or purpose," together with efforts to analyze "facts and means."

Since the early twentieth century, the study of international relations has passed through three major stages, which have been termed *utopian, realist,* and *behavioral.*[3] By the last two decades of the twentieth century, international-relations theory had entered a fourth, or postmodernist, postbehavioral, postpositivist, phase that was more difficult to define in summary fashion. Its principal characteristic has been diversity that included paradigmatic disagreement and debates even about the ability to produce a cumulative theory of international relations. At the same time, in its fourth phase, at the end of the twentieth century, international-relations theory was being shaped by numerous efforts focused on neorealist–structural-realist theory, neoliberal theory, debate about the agent–structure question within the levels-of-analysis context and the extent to which international-relations theory should be state-centric or transnational; in other words, theorists have asked who are the actors and what is their relative importance, and how do they relate to, or interact with, each other.

Among the most obvious features of its evolution, international-relations theory has had recurring and continuing debates about contending approaches to theoretical development. Instead of one dominant paradigm being replaced by another paradigm as the agreed basis for the development of theory, we have witnessed competing paradigms and theories. The debates of one era resurface in a later period. The earlier twentieth-century utopian–realist controversy returned in the form of the neoliberal–neorealist debate of the final decades of the century. Theories that have been cast aside by some scholars are refurbished, elaborated, and modified by others and brought back into fashion, the most notable example being realism in its more recent form of neorealist–structural-realist theory.

In this respect, international-relations theory has not developed in linear fashion. We see no clearly delineated paradigmatic change like the change that marked the discovery by Italian astronomer, mathematician, and physicist Galileo, noted in Chapter 1, based on telescopic observation in the early seventeenth century; that is, contrary to the convention of the day, Galileo found that the sun, not the earth, lies at the center of the solar system. Instead, the state of international-relations theory at the end of the twentieth century remains that of interparadigmatic debate.

The present phase of international-relations theory contains extended discussion of the meaning of the reality on which we base theory. Does reality, as in the physical sciences, exist outside our theories about the phenomena that we study? Alternatively, is reality, in the social sciences generally and in international relations in particular, formed by the human beings who compose the phenomena that we are observing and theorizing about at any given time? As we move into the next century, international-relations theory, in its diversity, will consist of contrasting paradigms, theories, methodologies, ongoing debates, and parallel efforts across a spectrum of work, such as that set forth in previous chapters.[4] Our challenge will be to find broadly acceptable criteria for evaluating the worth of alternative theoretical approaches. This may not prove easy in a world of growing diversity.

The present debate includes controversy about the units that compose the paradigm, which encompasses not only actors other than states but also the meaning and utility of the state itself as a delineating concept. The state remains an important unit of analysis, although the extent to which it is adequate as a basis for the development of international-relations theory has been questioned. Yale H. Ferguson and Richard W. Mansbach go so far as to assert that the definitions of the word *state* are so numerous that they obscure all meaning.[5] The state is said to represent a conception of normative order, an ethnocultural unit, a functional unit, a center of monopoly over legitimate violence, the embodiment of a ruling class, a decision-making process based on bureaucratic politics, an executive authority in the form of a leader such as a president or monarch or political system, and a sovereign unit among other such units.

As a result of such conceptual and semantic confusion, the state is said to have "little substance as an empirical concept and virtually no utility as an analytic concept; it obscures far more than it clarifies."[6] Accordingly, the state is a failed concept and, at the same time, we are in an era of failed states, the breakdown and breakup of existing states, and the emergence of new entities. The authority patterns on which political legitimacy is based sometimes transcend and supersede the state. Values are authoritatively allocated by a variety of institutions—political, religious, economic, cultural, social—other than governments, many of which are transnational, with little regard for formal state structures or boundaries. Thus, the ability of the state, however it is defined, to exercise full sovereignty in its domestic affairs without regard for external influences is doubtful and is likely to face increasing challenges in the years ahead. Therefore, a state-centric model does not adequately describe the contemporary global system.[7] Although there has been an extensive literature, the authors of which have sought to examine linkages between national and international systems and to study penetrated systems, the extent to which the domestic and the international are linked in a seamless web has yet to be fully determined.[8]

We have clearly moved beyond the classical paradigmatic assumption that international relationships—beyond the state's frontiers—are separable from domestic politics in some impermeable fashion. The question before us is whether what we call international-relations theory is simply part of a broader theoretical setting that somehow transcends the domestic–international separation. To what extent, as James N. Rosenau has suggested, have we entered an era of "cascading interdependence," with larger numbers of groups engaged in a quest for recognition, status, and independence contributing not only to the breakdown of existing units, but also to greater volumes of interactions accelerated by the impact of technology in global relationships? If there is no clear separation between international and domestic politics, how can there be a differentiation between international theory and other theories? If such distinctions are not readily evident, the basis for theory lies in an effort to cut across the boundaries of the various subfields, such as international relations and comparative politics, that comprise political science. Under such circumstances, if Rosenau is correct, the behavior of groups, whether they be termed states or other units, existing in alternative patterns of relationships with each other or with other entities, would (or should) become the object of theory building at a more general level than simply international-relations theory.

The quest for theory is complicated by the fact that we are in the midst of a transformation in structures, alongside an unprecedented acceleration in the volume of interactions among groups other than states, as well as among states themselves, and between states and nonstate actors. The accelerating and turbulent change that is shaping the world on the threshold of the third millennium encompasses a variety of actors in what Rosenau calls an era of "postinternational politics."[9] The turbulence to which Rosenau refers includes abnormalities comparable to those that, in climatic terms, exist during a hurricane or tornado, when uncertainty and unpredictability abound. If we have only limited ability to predict the path that a hurricane or tornado will follow, how can we develop predictive theories about political behavior? Events such as hurricanes and tornadoes, Rosenau points out, are comparable to revolutionary change in political relationships, a defining characteristic of the late twentieth-century world.

In the last decade of the twentieth century, as noted elsewhere in this text, the international system has contained as many as 185 members of the United Nations, contrasted with 51 at the time of its founding. Thus, in the second half of the century, there had emerged for the first time in history a global system. Of increasing importance are increasing numbers of nongovernmental organizations having links at the state and individual levels. The diversity of actors—state and other-than-state—together with vast asymmetries and disparities in their respective political, military, technological, and economic capabilities, represented important defining characteristics of the global system in an era of postinternational politics. Theoretical questions encompassed the nature of stability, based on theories of polarity, alignment patterns, integrative forces, conflict, fragmentation, and interdependence.

A new and largely unexplored set of dimensions has been added to international relations, thereby lengthening the list of issues to be reflected in emerging theory. Such dimensions include the rise of international organizations at the global and regional levels, the increasing importance of global financial markets and multinational corporations (MNCs), and instantaneous mass communications, as well as terrorist, revolutionary, and transnational religious fundamentalist movements. So rapid and pervasive is the pace of change that the gap between theory and the phenomena that are the basis of theoretical explanation is widening. How much of what we know about the past will help us to develop a theoretical basis for comprehending the future? To what extent has change reduced the utility of generalizations from the past in assessing emerging circumstances? To ask such questions is to inquire about the extent to which theory can transcend time and place, and to inquire about the adequacy of existing theory to explain the most momentous change of our time—how and why the Cold War ended as it did.[10]

We have noted that political behavior in an international context, it was once assumed, differs fundamentally from political behavior within the national unit. While domestic political structures were based on accepted authority patterns, including governments and laws, the international setting was anarchical. Therefore, studies of international political behavior could be separated from the analysis of political activity within the national unit. The distinction between domestic and international behavior stemmed principally from a model in which decision making was centralized in the former case and decentralized in the latter instance. Governments within states held a monopoly of the coercive capabilities of the units, in contrast to the decentralization of decision making and coercive capabilities in the international system.

Increasingly, as we have noted, emphasis has been placed on similarities rather than differences between the political process at the national and the international levels, although the centralization–decentralization distinctions still appear relevant in delineating international relations and studies of other political phenomena. Students of international relations have shown interest in political systems in which tribal loyalties often compete with modernizing forces and effective political power remains decentralized; such study has contributed to a reassessment of older notions about the uniqueness of international political processes, as contrasted to those at other levels. The breakdown and breakup of states in the post–Cold War era, the growing numbers of conflicts based on ethnic–sectarian cleavages, and the inability of states to assert control over their borders or territory provides further evidence of the need to transcend the traditional distinction between what is deemed to be international and what is said to be subnational.

Central to the present paradigmatic debate remains the perceived need to identify and categorize nonstate actors and to analyze their respective roles in the emerging international system. Richard W. Mansbach and John A. Vasquez call for the replacement of the state-centric paradigm by one that is based on issues, with politics being defined as the "authoritative allocation of values through the resolution of issues; i.e., through the acceptance and implementation of a proposal(s) to dispose of the stakes that compose the issue under contention."[11] The actors of international politics are said to encompass individuals operating on their own behalf, as well as large collectivities having common strategies and goals and working in collaborative fashion. Of direct interest is the process by which issues are defined, addressed, and resolved within and among the manifold entities—state and nonstate. In this respect, Mansbach and Vasquez cite and echo the call of John W. Burton for a new paradigm in which the study of international relations would be superseded by the study of world society. In Burton's perspective, the concept of world society can best be seen "if we were to map it, without reference to political boundaries, and indeed without reference to any physical boundaries."[12] Richard K. Ashley goes so far as to ask, in critique of the state-centric paradigm, how "are actions coordinated, energies concerted, resistance tamed, and boundaries of conduct imposed such that it becomes possible and sensible simply to represent a multiplicity of domestic societies, each understood as a coherent identity subordinate to the gaze of a single interpretative centre, the sovereign state?"[13] In this perspective, such a paradigm is clearly inadequate at a time of vast transnational interaction on the part of a variety of nonstate actors.

International-relations research, as has been noted throughout this book, has been guided by a variety of concepts, theories, models, and paradigms. One widely cited authority on the history of science, Thomas S. Kuhn, has suggested that in the natural sciences, periods of "scientific revolution" have alternated with eras of "normal science." One set of concepts has furnished the basis for cumulative knowledge only eventually to be discarded and superseded by yet another paradigm. Science advances in such a fashion that one dominant paradigm is replaced by another, with each in turn furnishing a new framework for intellectual inquiry, setting the research agenda, and providing the basis for the cumulative growth of scientific knowledge and theory. He defines scientific revolutions as "noncumulative developmental episodes in which an older paradigm is replaced in whole or in part by an incompatible new one."[14]

According to Arend Lijphart, the study of international relations has followed such a pattern of development.[15] The traditional paradigm, based on conceptions of state sovereignty and international anarchy, was challenged, as noted previously, even though a large body of theory about international relations had evolved, dating from antiquity and furnishing a "basis for a coherent tradition of research."[16] The scientific revolution embodied in the quantitative–behavioral phase was based on a large number of new approaches and methodologies. It was believed that Kuhn's characterization of paradigmatic change in the natural sciences was similarly applicable in the social sciences. In turn, the paradigm that eventually emerged in the study of international relations, it was assumed, would form the basis for broad theoretical advances based on the widespread application of agreed methodologies to important research questions. It is this assumption that has been questioned, and often rejected, by the advocates of postbehavioral, postpositivist, and postmodernist approaches to international-relations theory. In this interpretation, however valid the applicability of Kuhn's understanding of paradigmatic development for the physical sciences, it does not provide an adequate explanation of the evolution of international-relations theory. In retrospect, the behavioralist phase was focused more on research methods, or methodology, as a basis of theory, rather than on the development of a new paradigm or other theoretical basis for building theory.

As we have seen, the paradigmatic debate of the late twentieth century has had numerous dimensions. Since the 1970s, as K. J. Holsti and others have pointed out, the state-centric paradigm has faced challenges beyond those resulting from the emergence of nonstate actors in a global system. The state-centric paradigm has as its focal point a concern with "peace, war, and order," while one of its principal competitors, dependency theory (discussed in Chapter 6), is preoccupied with issues of "inequality, exploitation, and equality. The empirical connection between war and inequality remains problematic."[17] The present paradigmatic disagreement includes issues related to the high-priority problems to be addressed in the field, as well as "fundamentally different ideas about the appropriate units of analysis, the important processes, and the kind of context in which actions and processes take place."[18] According to Philippe Braillard, the study of international relations is fragmented to such an extent that it is "characterized by the absence of a paradigm and by the fact that there are several general explanatory models pitted against one another, several conceptions of its object," a situation that is said to be "characteristic of the whole field of investigation covered by the social sciences."[19]

As we have noted, other critics question whether the scientific progression set forth by Thomas Kuhn and widely accepted during the quantitative–behavioral phase even describes accurately the process of theory building in the social sciences, contrasted with natural science. In Kuhn's perspective, it has been suggested, the replacement of one paradigm by another occurs as a result of the inability of the then-existing dominant paradigm to account for important phenomena. However, the evolution of theory, following the rejection of an existing paradigm, depends in Kuhn's frame of reference on the ability of the community of scholars to reach agreement on a new paradigm as the basis for future inquiry. Conceivably, the present period of dissensus represents a necessary prelude to the emergence of an eventual paradigmatic consensus on which the research agenda of the early twenty-first century can be built. From the vantage point of the present, however, it may be equally plausible to suggest that the fragmentation of international-relations theory simply mirrors the heterogeneous global system of the late twentieth century, including the growth of a scholarly community that is politically, ideologically, intellectually, methodologically, and geographically more diverse and diffuse than in any previous era. If such is the case, the prospects for the formation of an agreed paradigm on which scholarly inquiry can be based may have receded. The problem of theory building is further complicated by the fact that existing theory is largely that of the Western world. If theory is the product of the social context in which it is developed, how would theories from other cultures and civilizations differ from Western theory? What, in turn, does this mean for paradigmatic consensus as a basis for theoretical advances?

The heterogeneity of the international system is reflected not only in the difficulty of developing consensual paradigm but also in the diverse approaches to the study of international relations represented by the theoretical diversity of the late twentieth century. If international relations constitutes an interdiscipline, its scope is global. The rise of new actors in many parts of the world will heighten the globalization of the study of international relations—its transformation from a literature that has been heavily influenced by the scholarship of Western Europe and the United States to a much broader global focus. As a result of such change, the prospect for any one comprehensive, agreed paradigm or unifying theory is likely to diminish rather than to be strengthened in the years ahead. For example, Hayward R. Alker, Jr., and Thomas J. Biersteker suggest the need to encompass such diversity by considering international relations as the "intersection and union of behavioral-scientific, dialectical Marxist and traditional approaches."[20] Partly because of the deeply political divisions of the world, "no single research approach has managed to gain worldwide acceptance in, or impose a globally shared intellectual interpretation on, this century of disorder."[21] Their proposal has been superseded by a lengthening list of approaches, at least some of which can be expected to generate their own paradigms and research programs, as well as criteria for evaluating the theoretical results.

MAJOR FOCAL POINTS OF CONTEMPORARY THEORY

In addition to various islands of theory, theory-building efforts of the past two generations have even included several macrotheories, or grand theories. For example, in political science, Gabriel Almond's and David Easton's formulations of the political system theorize at a macrolevel, and in international relations, realist theory and neorealist–structural-realist theory may be viewed as grand theories. Realist theory was based on an effort to isolate one variable—namely, power—in order to explain and predict a broad range of international behavior. In addition to its focus on power as a crucially important variable, realist theory attempted to explain behavior by reference to the international system (macrotheory) and at the level of the unit-actor, or agent. In other words, for realist theory, the source of behavior could be found both at the level of systemic structure and at the level of the unit, state, or agent.

In contrast, we have noted in Chapter 2, neorealist theory places principal emphasis on the international systemic structure within which political interaction takes place. The neorealist literature since the late 1970s has emphasized both the enduring importance of power and the impact of systemic structure—what Hedley Bull and Kenneth Waltz, among others, termed an anarchical system—on the latitude available to actors in shaping their policies and actions. In its broadest dimension, neorealist theory represents an attempt to derive from the realist tradition a theoretical approach for the late twentieth century and beyond, although, as we have seen, this theoretical approach has faced challenges from many quarters, including neoliberal contenders. As we have seen in the neorealist–neoliberal debate set forth in Chapter 2, neorealist and neoliberal theorists share common ground on, for example, the existence of anarchy at the international level, differing principally on its extent and significance. If anarchy is a delineating characteristic and enduring focal point for international-relations theorizing into the twenty-first century, our task is to answer questions related to its extent and meaning.

By the same token, the debate about the relationship between political behavior and structure that has preoccupied older and more recent theoretical discussions needs to be addressed more extensively. To what extent do structures at the international systemic and at the national (or other) levels shape the perceived options or behavioral characteristics of actors (the agent–structure problem noted in various chapters of this text)? In the same vein, the neorealist–neoliberal debate about institutions needs to be addressed in a way that contributes to a greater understanding of the ways and circumstances in which, for example, the United Nations or NATO simply reflect an existing systemic structure (neorealist) or actually change or otherwise shape the behavior of the units or agents (neoliberal). In short, what is the basis for an agreed synthesis that might contribute to a comprehensive theory of international relations? Such questions form a basis for an agenda for theory development into the twenty-first century.

Many of the theorizing efforts of the past generation and before, we have noted, represent islands of theory that theorists have hoped could be linked one day into a grand theory of international relations, although, as we have seen, consensus is lacking about the appropriate paradigm, or the methodologies, for a macrolevel or grand theory of international relations. Such agreement, if it eventually comes about, is likely to be the result of a conceptual breakthrough that points the way toward the theoretical integration of existing islands of theory and of setting agreed priorities for future research and data analysis. How such linking might take place, whether by enlarging existing islands or by creating new islands of theory, or by a major advance toward macrotheory within which middle-range theories could be linked, has been an object of debate among social scientists, especially during the quantitative–behavioral phase. The emphasis of the 1970s on the narrow theory-building efforts in the so-called islands of theory produced, in turn, a concern that the larger dimensions of theory at the macrolevel—the linking of the islands in a grand theory—would be neglected. Whatever the apprehension, it quickly was overshadowed in the final generation of the twentieth century by the even broader debate about the adequacy of existing paradigms of the global system that we have described. Such issues are likely to remain unresolved for at least some time to come.

Expectations of major theoretical breakthroughs characteristic of the quantitative behavioral era have proven premature, and the results of theory-building efforts based on social-science methodologies have been slim indeed. The behavioral revolution did not result in a cumulative theory of international relations that fulfilled earlier expectations. Perhaps for this reason, a broader and less ambitious conception of the nature of the growth of knowledge and theory emerged in the postbehavioral, postpositivist, postmodernist phase. This includes the suggestion that the reconceptualization of existing theories—the development of a variety of comparative methodologies and databases, and the constant quest for knowledge by research at more than one level of analysis—represents in itself a contribution to cumulative theory. As a proponent of this broader conception, Bruce Russett contends that a greater effort should be made to link and expand various islands of theory through detailed incremental research on specific problems. At the same time, however, it is doubtful, as Russett suggests, that a "narrow and exclusive application of the cumulative model would produce marginal returns comparable to those to be expected from maintaining, along with it, a more broad-based attack on international relations theory and substance."[22]

If the prospects for cumulative theory are limited by the lack of paradigmatic consensus, as well as the epistemological limitations of scientific method applied to social science, what criteria should be utilized to assess international-relations theory? What makes one theory better than any other theory? Is the quest for truth more a process than an end state? John A. Vasquez suggests the need to move beyond a postmodern relativism that limits the role of the theorist to the deconstruction and criticism of existing theories,[23] leading to the relativist assumption that any theory is as good (or as bad) as any other theory. Instead, more widely accepted criteria by which to determine truth are needed. The nature of scientific method, as we have discussed, is to furnish such criteria, although we acquire knowledge by other means, including intuition and reason. Without embracing the postmodernist idea of relativism, we may nevertheless accept the proposition that theory both arises from a social context and is formulated by dominant groups, or elites, of the time in which it is created. As we have already noted in this chapter, the basis for the development of international-relations theory in the years ahead lies in agreement or criteria by which to separate good from bad theory. We seek theory that helps to explain relationships among the phenomena that constitute international politics. Nevertheless, even if we acknowledge that theory arises from a particular social context, there must nevertheless be standards that transcend time and place, which are designed at least to approximate truth. To assert otherwise is to deny the essential basis for any theory and knowledge.

In its present phase, the theoretical and substantive interests of a large and diverse community set a complex agenda for the development of international-relations theory into the next millennium. Such work proceeds within a series of trends that, beyond the aforementioned paradigmatic debates includes the following:

1. Not only will theorists continue the effort to delineate the nature and scope of international relations, or postinternational relations, but also, they will attempt to establish international relations more firmly as an autonomous field of study, although the viability of such a claim to autonomy is weakened, if not destroyed, if the state based on legal sovereignty lacks substance as an empirical concept or utility as an analytic construct. Even though numerous problems of scope, definition, and conceptualization remain largely unresolved, such issues have been superseded by a renewed emphasis on substantive, in contrast to methodological, debates of the quantitative–behavioral phase.

2. The kinds of theorizing will be appropriate for building theories with greater explanatory capacity, with a realization that quantitative *and* qualitative analyses are indispensable to any such effort. Although the prospects for theory that is cumulative and therefore enduring may be uncertain, the increasing and complex issues of behavior between legally constituted units called "states," between such entities and nonstate actors, and among groups other than states, provides a rich agenda for theorizing and for

research that will only lengthen and broaden in the increasingly complex and heterogeneous world of the twenty-first century.

3. Theorists will try to develop more precise linkages among various levels of analysis (or actors) along the continuum from the microcosmic (the individual person) to the macrocosmic (the international system) and to resolve the agent–structure problem in international-relations theory by locating within and among the various levels of analysis the source of behavior being studied.[24] Such a research focus will enhance the prospects for linking levels of analysis and for bridging the ideals of theory represented by the neoliberal–institutionalist and neorealist–structural-realist traditions.

In summary, the paradigmatic, theoretical, methodological, and substantive diversity of international relations at the end of the twentieth century enhances the need to continue to draw on the numerous disciplines that have focused on problems of central interest to international relations, which remains an interdiscipline, drawing necessarily from a multiplicity of disciplines. Among others, these disciplines include anthropology, economics, history, political science, psychology (especially social psychology), law, public administration, and sociology.[25] As an interdisciplinary field addressing multidisciplinary issues, international relations will continue necessarily to incorporate, build on, and synthesize insights from most, if not all, of the social sciences and, where appropriate, from the natural and physical sciences into the twenty-first century.[26] The greater the complexity and quantity of issues that have an international or global dimension, the greater will be the need for a multidisciplinary focus (drawing on relevant academic disciplines) to produce interdisciplinary answers (based on the integration of approaches, findings, and insights from other disciplines).

EMERGING SUBSTANTIVE INTERESTS

Several specific substantive interests are likely to shape international-relations theory-building efforts into the third millennium. In light of the raison d'être of international relations from its early years, together with the large number of conflict-laden issues and the widespread availability of weapons of unprecedented lethality to a growing number of state and nonstate actors, the problems of war and peace will necessarily continue to attract principal attention both among scholars and policymakers, although such studies will form a part of a discipline, the global focus of which encompasses other issues and priorities, unprecedented in their number and diversity, with an obvious focus that transcends the state as the only and even the principal actor in increasing instances. Some of the subject areas likely to be the object of research for theory-building purposes are elaborated on briefly in the following section.[27]

The Long Peace, the Collapse of the Soviet Union, and the End of the Cold War

The two World Wars had a major impact on the development of international-relations theory. The theories of the two generations following World War II were shaped by the Cold War, just as the issues that formed the basis for theory in the two decades from 1919 to 1939 arose from the international context of the time. If utopian theory was an outgrowth of World War I, and realist theory was a product of the experience leading to and arising from World War II, what are the comparable post–Cold War theoretical constructs?[28] The collapse of the Soviet Union and the end of the Cold War present international-relations theory with questions at least as numerous and complex as those that framed these earlier focal points of inquiry. Will these momentous events have as profound an effect on international-relations theory into the next century as the earlier transformations had in their day?

The theoretical issues posed by the collapse of the Soviet Union and the end of the Cold War encompass, first, the question of why the Cold War ended without the Soviet Union having been militarily defeated in armed conflict, or why armed rivalry did not lead to a Third World War. What was responsible for the existence of a condition that, in retrospect, is called the "long peace"? Instead of resorting to massive military power as its political and economic system disintegrated, the Soviet leadership opted instead to surrender power, granting to the West concessions, in the form of German unification and withdrawal from Eastern Europe, that seemed impossible even to contemplate during the two generations before 1989, when the West confronted a seemingly strong, resolute, tenacious, and expansionist Soviet leadership. Closely related, what were the strengths and weaknesses of existing theories of international relations in predicting the end of the Cold War or in explaining why and how it ended as it did? What were the roles of Soviet leaders, and, if Mikhail Gorbachev and Boris Yeltsin had not been present, would the collapse of the Soviet Union have been postponed or averted? In other words, what is the place of individuals—the idiosyncratic variable—in great events, contrasted with the forces of history in situations such as the end of the Cold War? To what extent were Gorbachev and Yeltsin swept up in events beyond their control—events that they did not, and could not, foresee? In itself, the quest for answers to such questions provides an extensive, if not impossibly ambitious, agenda for international-relations theory in the years ahead.

Although much remains to be done, the effort to find answers to such questions has begun. It would be unusual if such a quest does not exert an increasing impact on the emerging international-relations theory agenda. What is remarkable, however, is the limited nature of the intellectual inquiry into the 1990s. Just as the end of the Cold War, however unexpected and unprecedented, was not marked by widespread popular celebration, it has yet to produce an upheaval in international-relations theory comparable to those that accompanied the two World Wars. As John Lewis Gaddis suggests, the immense significance of the end of the Cold War should have been sufficient to allow at least one major theory or another to have predicted or forecasted its coming.[29] That none of the theories did so should lead to questions about the adequacy of the theories and methods with which we have studied international politics. If the theories of the past two generations could not explain or predict the end of the Cold War, how helpful can they be in the transformed post–Cold War era? To the extent that our theories of international relations have had as an objective an understanding of forces shaping the future, they were surely deficient, even by their own standards, in anticipating the end of the Cold War.

What remains, therefore, is yet another extensive agenda for post–Cold War international-relations theory. This includes an effort to locate the sources of Soviet collapse within and among the various levels of analysis and to understand how and why fundamental change in international relationships takes place. The most obvious contending explanations encompass hypotheses about the relationship between nuclear bipolarity and the absence of superpower war.[30] Did the Cold War end without war between the United States and the Soviet Union because of the deterrence provided by nuclear weapons, which created unacceptable risks that overshadowed any conceivable gain? In what ways were alliances, especially NATO, stabilizing contributions to the long peace? Were negotiations leading to arms-control agreements, and arms-control treaties themselves, important contributing factors? Did the arms race, and especially the armaments strategies and policies of the United States and its allies, lead to stability and ultimately to the collapse of the Soviet Union without war? Why did the numerous East–West international crises not result in World War III?[31] Although there was no nuclear war between the two major possessors of such weapons, the Cold War political map contained scores of conventional wars and engaged the United States, in particular, in major regional conflicts in Korea and Vietnam. If nuclear weapons helped to sustain the long peace of the Cold War at the superpower level, or to channel U.S.–Soviet political competition away from the actual use of their huge military capabilities against each other, what are the lessons of this experience for post–Cold War stability in a world in which there are likely to be additional possessors of weapons of mass destruction? This question already gains attention in light of trends toward the increasing availability of weapons of mass destruction.

Existing theories of international relations provide contending explanations for change such as the one that accompanied the end of the Cold War and kept the peace, such as it was, during that era. The international system of superpower nuclear bipolarity, according to structural-realist theory, was primarily responsible for the relative stability that prevailed. A contrasting explanation is to be found at the unit/actor level, to the effect that the Soviet Union collapsed not so much because it could not match the United States militarily but instead because of the inevitable inability of the communist command economy and the Soviet political system, with its corrosive corruption, to compete with democratic and capitalist systems.[32] Western containment strategy, as originally set forth by George Kennan (to whose realist theory reference was made in Chapter 2), had as a central premise the need to deny the Soviet Union external victories in order to compel its concentration on domestic communist contradictions. Whether the Soviet Union would have imploded on itself in the absence of the political–military containment provided by the West and led by the United States is a question of great interest as the theoretical implications of the end of the Cold War are identified and assessed.

To ask such a question is to place in this context the structure–agent issue that we have discussed elsewhere in this text. Conceivably, the answer lies in an explanation that locates the sources of change leading to Soviet collapse at each of the levels of analysis. The demands made on the Soviet economy by massive military expenditures detracted from its already greatly limited ability to compete in postindustrial-age technologies with the far more innovative and dynamic capitalist economies of the West, and particularly with the United States. In other words, the international systemic structure of bipolarity imposed demands on the Soviet Union that it could not sustain in Cold War competition. Whatever the explanation, the need clearly exists to identify the sources of Soviet collapse and specifically to find answers to such questions as whether it was nuclear weapons that were primarily responsible for U.S.–Soviet stability and deterrence or whether the Soviet Union fell apart largely because of its own internal contradictions and weaknesses.

As an alternative explanation, it may be asserted that the source of change lies in the units or agents—whatever they may be—state or nonstate actors. As the actors change, so does the structure of the international system, which itself is defined by the numbers and types of actors and the interactive patterns among them. Thus, the growth of democracies with market economies produces units with characteristic normative standards and interactive patterns substantially differing from units with political systems that are totalitarian and economies that are state owned. In this case, a post–Cold War world of greater numbers of democratic states with market economies would be expected to be more peaceful if democracies do not go to war with other democracies. If, however, the explanation for international change is usually found in more than one of the levels of analysis, the issue is the relationship between alternative explanations for the collapse of the Soviet Union. What was the link between the events leading to the end of the Soviet Union (and its empire) and Western military power, technological superiority, democracy, religions, political freedom, market economies, the political ideology represented by individual rights grounded in natural law, and superior economic growth?

Closely related are questions associated with the emergence, since the collapse of the Soviet Union, of some 25 new states, some of them, of course, within the boundaries of the former Soviet Union itself. The fact that the state-centric map of the world has been so dramatically transformed by the end of the Cold War leads to numerous questions of major theoretical importance. What, for example, are the implications for international systemic structure resulting from the numbers and types of units that are created? Such units compose the new international systemic structure. How, why, and when do existing political units, or states, fall apart, or what are the essential conditions for political disintegration as the reverse side of integration? What are the precise effects of international systemic structure, including change, on existing and emergent units, and how do they, in turn, shape the interactive patterns that characterize international systemic structure? What will be the post–Cold War international systemic structure? To what extent, it should be asked, was the Cold War structure in fact bipolar, and what were its multipolar elements? If the structure contributed to strategic stability between the superpowers themselves, why were there so many armed conflicts in other parts of the system? There is already an emerging debate about the new systemic structure that will shape the early twenty-first century.[33] In the midst of such a transformation in the 1990s, with substantial numbers of theories purporting to address such questions, there is an ample basis for theoretical investigation and analysis, and thus for research agendas for the years ahead.

Conflict

There remains a relative dearth of knowledge concerning the relationship between international and intrasocietal aggression, and those studies, especially quantitative in nature, completed since the early 1970s, have failed to yield definitive insights. The causes of conflict are said to lie within and among each of the levels of analysis—the structure of the international system, the states and the domestic structures, nonstate actors, and the individuals who ultimately form the larger political entities. The questions that remain to be adequately answered are those that have long been of central importance. To what extent, for example, are the causes of conflict traceable to the structural, institutional, and other environing circumstances? In what sense, by contrast, is conflict a manifestation of political differences that, once resolved, lead to a diminution in tensions and the end of conflict? What is the relationship between systemic structure and conflict? Was a bipolar structure less stable before the advent of nuclear weapons and more stable as a result of nuclear weapons as the essential basis for deterrence? To what extent does the spread of democracy diminish the prospects for war, at least among states having democratic political systems as set forth in democratic peace theory discussed in Chapter 8? How rapidly will democracy spread in the next century, and with what consequences for global or regional stability?

Over the past generation, intrasocietal conflict has risen in many states, including, as noted elsewhere in this text, some of those most politically and industrially advanced. The emergence of large numbers of new entities and other groups into the political process, together with the increased availability and lethality of weaponry as a result of advances in technology, will undoubtedly accelerate and exacerbate conflict at differing levels of intensity. What are the implications of various modes and levels of socioeconomic development for the incidence of tensions, conflict, and violence, as well as for stability or instability, within and among the units that compose the international system? This question is of long-standing interest to those scholars who have studied conflict, and especially revolution, as noted in Chapter 8. Intrasocietal conflict is relevant to international-relations research not only because it gives rise to a large number of the nonstate actors in the late twentieth century—groups seeking revolutionary change and autonomy or independence based on ethnicity within existing states and, in some instances, the formation of new political entities—but also because it can lead to intervention by outside powers.

Finally, what part do the electronic media, global communications, and the information revolution play in molding attitudes with respect to issues of international cooperation and conflict within states and at the international level, and in establishing and accelerating international–domestic linkages? Such questions need to be addressed in the case of societies (such as the United States) having pluralistic political systems and high levels of technological development, with citizens who are linked by instantaneous communications, including global access to information by computer-based networks. These questions also need to be considered in societies that traditionally have been less open—states with authoritarian regimes, the power of which has included the ability to control access to outside information, ideas, and other influences.

Such questions have been the object of increasing interest in the late twenti-eth century, although analysis that includes the implications of global communica-tions for shaping public opinion or foreign policy remains in its infancy. We are in the unprecedented situation in which information once available only to official decision makers now reaches the entire society at the same time that it arrives in government offices. The time available for reaching important decisions is thus greatly reduced, with consequences that may shape behavior and thus our theories of international relations.

Integration and the Basis for Political Communities

The study of integration and how political communities are formed—of long-standing concern to students of international relations, especially since the work of David Mitrany in the period between the two world wars—continues to attract the attention of scholars. The Single European Act (SEA), the Treaty on European Union (TEU), and the debate about the deepening and widening of the European Union (EU) in the 1990s gave renewed impetus to the study of integration. An era of failed states, political fragmentation, and ungovernability coincides with a large number of integrative forces. In the generation after World War II, the creation of international organizations at the global and regional levels not only contributed to rising interest in the study of integration, but also provided an important source of data for scholarly investigation. Similarly, more recent trends of the post–Cold War era provide a new agenda for integration studies. Such questions, as we noted in Chapter 10, encompass why and how political entities cooperate with each other and the frameworks in the form of institutions, organizations, and regimes they develop for this purpose. The growing importance of the global corporation, in a global economy, together with the emergence of a multiplicity of nonstate actors, added yet other objects of study of international relations.[34] In turn, this coincided with the publication of numerous books and article-length studies based in partic-ular on neofunctionalist propositions and analyzing transnational relationships between and among nongovernmental entities in a world hypothesized to be increasingly interdependent, with a vast growth in the numbers of relationships across state boundaries between official and nongovernmental units.

The conceptualization of interdependence, and its relationship to concepts of integration and of power, attracted the interest of scholars in the 1970s; similarly, in the 1980s, attention came to be focused on the role of hegemonic states in shap-ing regimes at the international level, within which cooperative relationships are developed and sustained (see Chapters 3 and 10). Regime analysis has been a focal point of academic attention as a basis for studying and understanding the frame-works, norms, decisional procedures, and processes in such issue areas as diplo-macy, defense, economics, and law within which collaborative patterns evolve in response to international needs. The patterned relationships characterized as regimes are said to form the basis for more integrated structures and processes. In this sense, regime analysis focuses on the study of relationships that are the result of mutual need and interest in an international system, leading to higher levels of integration. It also furnishes a basis for analyzing and evaluating the behavior or performance of international organizations and their various institutional frameworks. As a result, it has been suggested, such study "has become more theoretical, more rigorous in a social science sense and has generated a better understanding of the general phenomenon of international cooperation."[35]

The end of the Cold War produced an extensive focus on the role to be played by the United Nations in the numerous conflicts that have been part of the global setting. This includes institutional development for conflict prevention, peacemaking, and peacekeeping, in accordance with Chapters 6 and 7 of the United Nations Charter. It encompasses situations of conflict, as in Bosnia, and examples of humanitarian activities, as in Somalia. This post–Cold War agenda is based also on the need to assess the role of alliances, notably NATO, and other regional security arrangements, in a transformed global structure.

Numerous questions of theoretical importance arise. They include the effects of global systemic structure on the latitude available to international organizations and the implications of changing global structures for the transnational tasks that such organizations are likely to be called on to address. Before 1989, the United Nations had been engaged in fewer than 25 peacekeeping operations. In the six-year period after the end of the Cold War, the United Nations was called on to undertake more than 25 such operations. NATO, which was never engaged in actual military operations during the Cold War, has undertaken numerous combat missions under international authorization in Bosnia in the 1990s. Questions about global systems structure, international organizations, the relationship between institutions and the regional security setting, structural constraints on the operations of global systems, and the ways in which global and regional organizations relate to each other and their members compose an extensive theoretical agenda for the years leading into the twenty-first century. To what extent do existing theories of integration provide a useful basis for further theoretical development? Functionalist–neofunctionalist theory emphasized the expansive logic of sector integration. More recent theory, related to the implementation of the SEA and the TEU, has built on and revised functionalist–neofunctionalist theory.

Existing theories of political integration owe a considerable intellectual debt to earlier studies of nationalism, as well as to cybernetics and systems theory. The study of the normative conditions for political community, especially characteristic of international relations in its first stage, gave way to specific case studies and comparative analyses of integration, at both the global and the regional levels, although scholars concerned with the development of empirically based theory have usually had a strong interest in the normative implications of integration. The earlier work, especially of Karl Deutsch, on transactions as indicators of integration led to further such efforts, especially in the 1970s. Such studies, discussed in Chapter 10, examined and in some cases refined relationships among transactions, such as exchanges of people and trade flows, communication patterns, and memberships and voting behavior in international organizations. To what extent, and under what conditions, are such types of transactions likely to transform the global system of the early twenty-first century? To what extent are such forces at work in the EU and elsewhere in the 1990s?

Integration theory has also included efforts to conceptualize more fully the linkages among institutional growth, intergovernmental cooperation, and elite and mass attitudes—that is, to consider integration as a phenomenon having institutional and attitudinal dimensions. At the same time, a need remains for greater definitional and conceptual clarity in the integration literature. This is a task to which students of international relations have turned in the past generation. The neofunctionalist refinement of propositions with respect to spillover, for example, is illustrative.

More recently, efforts to modify or revise existing integration theory by reference to the SEA and the evolution of the EU in the 1990s is indicative of such an interest. The achievement of greater agreement among writers about the nature of integration, its necessary components, and the stages and transformation rules by which it is achieved, if such progress is indeed possible, might contribute to major breakthroughs in knowledge about the building and disintegration of political communities. The need exists to develop a theory, or theories, of integration encompassing interaction between and among official elites (governmental decision makers), nonofficial elites (important nongovernmental groups and actors), and the mass level, as took place at the end of the 1980s when German unification was propelled forward by mass demonstrations that far outpaced governments.

To what extent has integration taken place, or at least been pressed forward decisively, by nongovernmental elites? At what level, and at what stage in an integrative process, is support at each of these levels indispensable to success? Moreover, a theory of integration adequate to the needs of the future should probably be based on conceptualization including a process model—how and when does the integrative process lead from a condition of separateness to a condition defined as political community, and what are the stages and relevant indicators that are present during the integrative process?

Subnational Forces

If a major thrust of scholarly literature and thought in international-relations theory has been to build political units beyond the nation-state, there is evidence of the need to place greater emphasis on centrifugal or fragmenting forces within the existing national units. Neither developed nations nor developing states have been immune from the rise of linguistic–ethnic nationalism. Even units such as the United Kingdom, France, and the United States, where the literature of political science, in its conventional wisdom, long ago dismissed forces making for separateness in favor of assumptions about the homogeneity of population and in the case of the United States, the melting pot, have faced disintegrative forces. Leaving aside the collapse of the Soviet Union and the disintegration of Yugoslavia, other states, including, for example, Canada, Cyprus, Belgium, Nigeria, India, Pakistan, Sri Lanka, and Zaire, have been beset with separatist movements that sometimes have resulted in communal strife and, in some cases, even secession and civil war, which have sometimes raised questions about the political future of these states. If the decade following World War II was characterized by a movement toward regional organization, as reflected in the literature of international relations, it was followed by a period of growing dissatisfaction by peoples in many parts of the world with the political units in which they live, and this dissatisfaction has yet to run its course. The rise to political consciousness of larger numbers of previously quiescent groups in the years ahead is likely to heighten the problems confronting political entities in many parts of the world. Indeed, as noted elsewhere in this chapter, one of the principal forces shaping the global system at the end of the late twentieth century is the quest of large numbers of groups in all parts of the world for greater status, power, and recognition.

Although the causes of this ferment are complex, those who have expressed dissatisfaction with the status quo aspire to such goals in order to (1) gain a greater voice in the decision-making process of existing units, (2) achieve in some cases greater decentralization of power, or (3) replace existing units with wholly new structures. The end of the twentieth century is an era of opposition to the bigness of units that reflect the impersonal forces of bureaucracy and technology—an era that has spawned literature on technology and society and, in particular, the effects of technology on political, social, and economic structures.[36] We face several conflicting forces, some of which, such as technology, give impetus to larger political units; others contribute to the perpetuation of existing political units; and still others enhance the prospects for the fragmentation of present units. The study of such forces is a task that will confront scholars of international relations and policymakers alike into the next century. In addition, both scholars and policymakers will consider how to devise political forms that reconcile the need for bigness with people's desire for local empowerment and freedom from centralized controls. At the very least, however, an understanding of the nature of integration and the conditions for cooperation and political community could yield insights into the process by which existing units are fragmented, as well as the necessary conditions for integration.

Comparative International Studies and Decision Making

The effort to examine linkages between the international system and domestic politics, as well as to understand the domestic and international determinants of foreign policy, reflects the growth of interest in comparative international studies. In the 1970s, increased emphasis was placed on the comparative study of foreign policy, although such interest was by no means new to international relations. The quest for theoretical frameworks for decision making and notably the conceptualization and research more than two generations ago of Richard C. Snyder[37] and his associates, as well as such efforts as those of Wolfram F. Hanrieder and James N. Rosenau,[38] are indicative of such interest. Events data analysis, together with the study of decision making, especially under crisis conditions, is illustrative of an interest in the comparative study of foreign policy, although the study of foreign policy on a comparative basis has not been of any notable proportions. The end of the Cold War, together with the emergence of additional states and the presumption that the world would contain larger numbers of democracies, brought to the forefront the question of the relationship between democracies and peaceful foreign policies. Examined in Chapter 8, the large number of hypotheses generated by such literature creates an extensive basis for research and theory building. To what extent, and under what conditions, do states with representative political institutions develop similar foreign policies and national-security approaches?

As in other areas, such as conflict and integration, numerous propositions about decision-making behavior (see Chapter 11) have been generated and tested, with uncertain results. In the Cold War era, the importance of international crises led to a focus on decision making under crisis conditions. The potential linkage between theory and policy in crisis decision-making studies contributed to a growing interest in crisis indicators that could be made available to official policymakers. A capability for the analysis of intelligence and other relevant data with the use of crisis indicators would have obvious implications both for crisis management and decision-making and for the development of more adequate theories of crisis management, escalation, de-escalation, communications, and other phenomena related to patterns of interaction within, between, and among decision-making units. With the end of the Cold War, the need remains for crisis indicators, especially in a world in which there are likely to be greater numbers of conflicts with crisis potential.

Theory and Security Studies

Closely related to crisis management is the need for conceptualization in the field of security studies that takes as full account as possible of the rapidly changing global setting, as well as the revolution in military technologies, in order to understand both the meaning of security and its requirements. The study of security as a central component of international-relations theory is itself interdisciplinary, for it encompasses the historical, economic, cultural, and psychological dimensions, together with the military, political, legal, and technological components.[39] The study of military strategy and the development of theories of security have concerned both the scholarly community and the military to an unprecedented level since World War II, although the causes of war, the role of military power, the legal norms for the use of force, and the conditions under which alliances are formed and dissolved have long been the focal point of much of international-relations theorizing.

Just as the advent of nuclear weapons and the onset of the Cold War framed security studies for much of the latter half of the twentieth century, the collapse of the Soviet Union and the emergence of new issues have had a major impact on the field, which can be expected to continue well into the new millennium. Stephen M. Walt traces what he calls the "renaissance of security studies" from the mid-1970s into the 1990s.[40] Among the topics that have sparked theoretical interest are the impact of offensive and defensive advantages on strategy; the effects of domestic politics on war (are democracies less warlike than nondemocracies?); the causes and consequences of arms races (under what conditions do arms races lead to war, and when and how do armaments contribute to peace?); the sources and implications of military innovation; the requirements for extended deterrence; the prospects for security cooperation; and the role of military forces in operations other than war, including peacekeeping. In a major project and publication that assessed the impact of the end of the Cold War on security studies, Richard Shultz, Roy Godson, and Ted Greenwood set forth an extensive agenda of topics that include the relationship between military capabilities and other forms of power; weapons of mass destruction, proliferation, and deterrence; arms control; conventional forces; the environment and security; regional security systems; low-intensity conflict; the defense decision-making process; and the role of ethics and values in national security.[41]

It was the development of nuclear weapons, together with the emergence of the United States as a global superpower in the aftermath of World War II, that to an unprecedented extent attracted scholars to the study of security. The result was seminal theoretical analyses, the purpose of which was to create a strategic framework within which nuclear weapons could be integrated into the other means of statecraft and national-security policy. This work produced an abundant literature on the nature of, and conditions for, the deterrence of war between the possessors of nuclear weapons. Its focus, as noted elsewhere in this text, was escalation, force survivability, nuclear retaliation, risk taking, and assured destruction as a basis for preventing the outbreak of atomic warfare. Yet, existing theories remain inadequate in several respects. First, the deterrence theory of the nuclear age was based, for the most part, on strategic-nuclear bipolarity. The post–Cold War security setting is characterized increasingly by larger numbers of states capable of acquiring nuclear weapons, as well as other types of weapons of mass destruction (WMD)—namely, biological and chemical capabilities. Stated in practical and specific terms, what are the conditions, including the force levels, necessary for deterrence in a world of several, or many, possessors of such capabilities? Alternatively, it has been hypothesized that nuclear multipolarity reduces the risks of nuclear confrontation by making it impossible for any single nuclear power to destroy the retaliatory capability of all or perhaps even several other nuclear powers. Among the questions that should be addressed is whether and to what extent, if at all, nuclear multipolarity will enhance the prospects for stable deterrence,[42] or whether and under what circumstances nuclear proliferation, ipso facto, is undesirable, as is generally assumed.

A second problem inherent in deterrence theory is ambiguity in the meaning of rationality—the assumption of a calculus between potential risk and potential gain. American strategic theory has contained such a calculus derived largely from a projection to adversaries of what for the United States would constitute unacceptable damage in a nuclear exchange. Are calculations made in America, or in any other state in fact, accurate in a post–Cold War world in which peoples have widely differing value systems, cultures, conceptions of national security, and international objectives? In a world of additional WMD possessors, about whose political and cultural values little may be known, to what extent will deterrence need to be customized? What might deter a Saddam Hussein might be different from what would be effective against another actor. Closely related are basic differences between states, as suggested in Chapter 9, in strategic-military doctrines and conceptions of the adequacy of force levels for attaining their respective objectives. Such issues enhance the need for a greater emphasis, in security studies, on the comparative study of military strategy and policy, as well as force levels and their composition, within the context of values and culture as the number of diverse possessors of such capabilities grows. Such comparative research might yield insights into such issues as the purposes of strategy and its relationship to force levels, political goals, and the nonmilitary dimensions of security; the decision-making process with respect to strategic-military capabilities and other elements of statecraft; the propensity of states to invoke various forms of military power to achieve political objectives; and the historical, doctrinal, and psychological factors that shape the propensities of diverse groups to resort to violence, or to threaten to do so on behalf of their respective interests.

Until the 1980s, the focal point of nuclear deterrence was offense dominance—the ability of a state to inflict unacceptable levels of devastation on its adversary as a basis for deterring the use of force by either side under conditions in which both would be destroyed. President Reagan's March 23, 1983, address, which posed the question of whether nuclear weapons could be made impotent and obsolete by the creation of the means of strategic defense, formed the basis not only for research on such technologies, but also for the development of a deterrence paradigm based on defense. To the extent that technologies for missile defense emerge in the years ahead, as in the decades of deterrence based on offense dominance, there is likely to be a burgeoning literature designed to build and analyze a paradigm based on the means to save rather than to avenge lives. The creation of defensively based theoretical deterrence constructs would in themselves represent an important contribution to strategic theory. In the 1990s, the discussion of missile defense was fueled by the threat of proliferation, leading to possessors of nuclear and other WMD capabilities in regions such as Southwest and Northeast Asia.

Among the other focal points of security studies that attracted interest in the 1980s, and that can be expected to endure is the ethical basis for conflict, spurred of course by the dilemmas of nuclear deterrence. Such inquiry built on the just-war tradition. Its purpose was to effect a reconciliation, if possible, between the requirements for deterrence and the ethics of Western societies under conditions of unprecedented weapons destructiveness. The result was an effort to make explicit the assumptions on which alternative schools of deterrence were based and to assess the means–ends relationships—or what could be termed the ethic of intention and the ethic of consequence inherent in the threat to use nuclear weapons, as contrasted to their actual use. The growth in lethality of nuclear weapons, as well as the other means of destruction, together with whatever potential emerges for defensively based deterrence in the years ahead, can be expected to give increased importance to the study of ethical issues associated with deterrence and security.

To a large extent, the academic study of security, as reflected in its literature, has been an American preoccupation. The danger inherent in such a condition, as Colin Gray has suggested, is that "the United States is only one culture, and for a field of inquiry as critical to the human future as strategic studies to be rooted in so narrow and unique a set of predispositions can only impoverish its capacity to accommodate the true diversity of strategic styles that exists worldwide."[43] Because the armed conflicts of the future encompass as direct participants a host of actors other than the United States or other Western nations, the need will be apparent for an understanding of diverse cultures, historical factors, differing value systems, and geostrategic relationships. In short, security studies can be separated from area and country studies only at grave peril because the strategic culture within which conflict unfolds represents a necessary point of departure for understanding the causes of war, the conditions for deterrence, the ways in which force will be used, and the basis for conflict resolution. The growth of interest in the study of low-intensity conflict and ethnic–sectarian conflict points up the need for such an understanding of the various states and regions as the setting for such wars.

In recent years, the focus of security studies, to a certain extent reflecting the multidimensional nature of conflict in a heterogeneous global international system, has broadened to take greater account of the pervasive impact of technology on strategy and to give increased place to the emergence of new types of conflict and actors. This includes interest in the domestic and psychological variables associated with deterrence; the examination of deterrence and war in nonnuclear situations; the greater utilization of history to assess its lessons for contemporary and future armed conflict; and the relationships among economic factors, military power, and conflict.

This focus also encompasses the study of the implications of rapid technological change for the conduct of warfare, or what has been identified as the revolution in military affairs. If we have entered an era of postinternational relations, as a result of phenomena associated with postindustrial societies, it becomes essential to understand the resulting ramifications for armed conflict. In U.S. military literature, there is increasing discussion of what is termed *information-age warfare.* Technologies of unprecedented sophistication confer unparalleled capacity to collect, analyze, and distribute information to render the battle space transparent and to deliver precision firepower to targets. What is termed the *digitized battlefield,* it is suggested, separates the conduct of future wars from the past as greatly as World War II blitzkrieg differed from the trench warfare of World War I. By the same token, the meaning of strategic warfare may be transformed by the ability of state and nonstate actors to disable banking transfers, stock exchanges, and vital communications systems, using the tools available to the computer hacker. In short, the agenda of security studies is increased by the impact of technologies that have an effect on strategy, deterrence, and military operations—on the theory and practice of postindustrial warfare. That impact needs to be discussed, and, in recent years, it has become the object of investigation within the field of security studies.

If traditional concepts of security had as their focus state-to-state conflict, the growing numbers of wars in which one or more actors were not states has been reflected in the literature of the field. Martin van Creveld has referred to a classical, trinitarian paradigm based on the state, its military capabilities, and its population.[44] To the extent that we have entered an era of political fragmentation that includes a growth in ungovernability at the state level, it follows that civil wars, coups d'etat, ethnic conflicts, and religious wars will form a growing part of security studies.[45]

Interstate war has been a defining characteristic of the international system based on the primacy of state actors. If postinternational politics gives prominence to nonstate actors, the emphasis of security studies will be changed as well. Although clearly a part of a postinternational politics paradigm, civil conflict antedates the international system. In this sense, patterns of warfare before the formation of the state system may provide insights into the types of armed conflict that will characterize the future.[46]

As Edward Kolodziej suggests, the security environment described in the seventeenth century by Thomas Hobbes was based on the destructive impulses unleashed by the English civil war, not the state system of Europe, which was only in the process of formation with the Treaty of Westphalia of 1648, with which the internal conflict in England coincided in time.[47] Of course, the state system itself has been the locus of numerous internal wars, including the American and French revolutions of the eighteenth century, as well as the revolutions that swept Russia and China in the twentieth century and other regions from Africa to Asia. Certain of these revolutions, as well as other political movements, spawned totalitarian regimes that inflicted brutal repression on their inhabitants. The millions who have died in the concentration camps and prisons of such societies bring a new dimension to the meaning of security, defined in its basic element as freedom from political oppression. In an era of post–Cold War ethnic cleansing in territories of the former Yugoslavia, we need not look far to find poignant examples of such problems of security. They include actions by successor states to eliminate undesired ethnic groups. They encompass violence against the Kurdish and Shiite populations of Iraq by Saddam Hussein. Violence by states and nonstate actors against weaker groups can be expected to increase in scope and intensity in an era of political fragmentation.

The emerging conflict map will be based on a changing security setting that has been described extensively, if not completely, by contributions to post–Cold War international-relations theory literature. In its security dimensions, according to Richard Shultz, Roy Godson, and George Quester, we confront what they term a *bifurcated environment* that contains a state-centric as well as a trans-state paradigm.[48] This includes state actors driven by radical forms of nationalism and fundamentalism, and possibly armed with WMD. Such states will often be prepared to support terrorism as an instrument of security policy. Thus, as in Southwest and Northeast Asia, the specter of major regional conflicts will continue to be present in the form of state-to-state warfare. The proliferation of WMD, as well as the wider availability of advanced conventional capabilities, will shape the emerging security landscape. At the same time, the trans-state paradigm, these authors suggest, will be based on a process of political fragmentation or fission, in which states disintegrate and lose both the authority and the power to govern. This paradigm highlights the development of larger numbers of substate and transnational actors, which include radical ethnic groups, secessionist movements, religious militants, criminal organizations, terrorists, and insurgents. Taken together, they will be major sources of instability, disruption, and armed conflict. Large geographical areas will become less governable, or even ungovernable, at least by existing states. As a result of the greater numbers and types of such state and trans-state actors, the conflict spectrum will broaden—and with it the definition and scope of security—and thus the agenda for the study of security and the development of theories about security.

As a result, there is a need for continued theory-building efforts focused on the enduring question of the causes of war; the deterrence paradigm with respect to offense and defense dominance; the impact of new technologies in deterrence, conflict, and war; the cultural dimensions of conflict; national-security decision making in crisis and noncrisis situations, especially in complex organizational contexts; the nexus, to the extent that it exists, between deterrence stability (offensively or defensively based) and arms control; the impact of domestic politics (especially in pluralistic societies) on national-security policy; concepts of security in their military, economic, and political dimensions under conditions of regional and global interdependence; the basis for conventional deterrence if nuclear-based deterrent relationships diminish; the causes, varieties, strategies, and effects of terrorism; and the implications of ungovernability in existing and fragmenting states for conflict. Thus, there is an abundant agenda for security studies, in both the building of theory and inevitably the generation of policy options having relevance in a conflict-laden world.

Power

Power has always been difficult to conceptualize in international relations, as we have noted especially in Chapter 2. The problems of measurement have grown as the components of power have increased. As a multifaceted phenomenon, the concept of power is inextricably linked to alternative structures of the international system, based, for example, on bipolarity and multipolarity. Polarity as a structural characteristic of the international system connotes not only the number and types of actors, but also the distribution of capabilities among them. Hence, a necessary prerequisite to understanding the implications of international systemic structure for the behavioral patterns of actors lies in the study of power itself. If we may foresee the growth in number of international actors—state and nonstate—into the twenty-first century, together with weapons of unprecedented destructiveness and new conflict issues, it follows that the study of power in its many dimensions—military, economic, psychological, and ideological—will continue to hold important interest.

Equally notable has been a lack of concern for the analysis of the techniques of statecraft—how power has been actually used to achieve specified objectives. Instead, as numerous commentators have pointed out, emphasis within international-relations literature, especially since World War II, has been placed on the study of the policy process—how policy is formulated, instead of the instruments by which policy is made and the actual outputs of the process. To the extent that studies of power have been comparative in scope, according to David Baldwin, their emphasis has been the comparison of actors rather than of techniques.[49] In Baldwin's perspective, the need exists to find answers to such questions as what types of influence are likely to succeed in achieving their stated objectives? What techniques, including violent and nonviolent means, together or in isolation from one another, can be expected to succeed or to fail? For example, under what conditions are economic embargoes likely to be more useful than military invasions? How and to what effect have the restrictions in foreign trade and the granting of foreign aid been used as techniques of statecraft?

Of fundamental importance in this context is a precise understanding of the relationship between the economic instruments and the other elements of power and influence that are available to and are actually employed in pursuit of security goals. Such a focus can be expected to grow in importance. It not only represents a logical extension of studies of power but also is integral to work that seeks more fully to link economic elements as necessary components of international politics.

Such an integral relationship is symbolized by the older term *political economy* and is embodied in contemporary writings, as noted elsewhere in this text, or, for example, in theories related to regime analysis and hegemony. Nevertheless, power can be expected to remain an important, but inadequately understood, variable, if only because of its multifaceted nature and as a result of the fact that power is relational.

Whether a given amount of power provides a means toward the achievement of goals depends, of course, on what are the objectives for which power is to be employed. However, power consists of physical instruments, such as military forces and the high-tech components of the information society. Such capabilities exist in a strategic context. How are they to be organized or maximized for some purpose? How this is done is the essence of strategy. Thus, power consists of physical means and strategy, further complicating its measurement as a variable of major importance in international-elations theory.

Comparative and Transnational Research

The late-twentieth-century tendency toward a more comparative focus in international-relations research has been reflected in a growth of interest in a broad range of subnational issues.[50] They include fundamentalist movements, ethnic conflict, the political values of elites, political fragmentation, ungovernability, violent conflict, environmental issues, and the nature of postindustrial, industrial, or industrializing societies. As in the past, we will be faced with both too much and too little data for development of theories about such phenomena and their relationship to each other. On the one hand, vast numbers of data are becoming available as a result of the technologies of the information age. Without leaving home or office, a researcher can gain access to libraries and other data sources around the world. Nevertheless, many of the most important kinds of data relevant, for example, to the study of foreign-policy decision making (including health records and psychological profiles of decision makers)[51] are not easily gathered, and, in fact, may never be available to the scholar. Much of decision-making analysis has emphasized international crises, which are, as Thomas C. Wiegele suggested, "stress-inducing" situations, the effect of which is to "put pressures upon the foreign policy decision-maker."[52] It follows that, as the author concluded, biological factors such as physical and mental health, fatigue, age, biological rhythms, and the use of various forms of medication should be included in studies of crisis decision making.[53] This in turn points up the need for research on the intersection between psychological variables and decision-making variables.

Information-age technologies now make it possible to make available greater volumes of data from governmental sources for the use of the scholarly community. The diffusion of computer technology to office, classroom, and home desktop and the acquisition of computer skills on a massive scale can be expected to influence both the study and the analysis of international relations in ways that are unprecedented. This includes the instantaneous transmission of data from storage systems, including bibliographic and literature surveys, quantitative materials, and other information. The cumulative effect is already to enhance greatly the human capacity for scholarly research and analysis. Clearly, we are entering an era in which the ability to utilize computers will be vastly enhanced to the extent that complex problems can be solved at increasing speed. The creation of global computer-based data sources contributes greatly to the conduct of research in international relations and other social sciences. Data sources are already as close to the researcher as the nearest computer, thus conferring unparalleled means for ascertaining rapidly the availability of, and for gaining immediate access to, relevant source materials, both in the form of bibliography and actual data. The diffusion of computerized data acquisition and processing capabilities, and the expansion of computer literacy, has already provided unprecedented means for the conduct of research.

POLICYMAKING AND INTERNATIONAL-RELATIONS THEORY

As Richard Smoke has suggested, policymakers have little interest, per se, in how often a particular combination of variables has been present in a historical context, unless, of course, that combination is present in a current situation of immediate interest.[54] Therefore, it is by no means accidental that the scholar interested in basic research and theory and the policymaker concerned with the immediate have often had interests seemingly irrelevant to each other. Much of international-relations research may seem not only unintelligible, but also irrelevant to the immediate concern of the policymaker, as perhaps indeed it is. Although it is difficult to assess with precision the impact of international-relations research on policymakers, nevertheless the policy community has made extensive use of academic writings. In particular, the development in international relations of a subfield in strategic affairs or national or international security studies, especially deterrence and defense, has furnished a body of literature on which policymakers have drawn not only insights, but also the theoretical framework and the explicit assumptions on which, for example, United States strategic-nuclear forces have been based. To an unprecedented extent, the development and study of strategy and, more broadly, military affairs, have passed from the professional military to the civilian policy analysts and theorists. As we noted in Chapter 12, gaming exercises designed to sensitize policymakers, including those at the highest level, to the opportunities and constraints confronting them, especially in hypothetical international crises, are widely utilized in the official policy community. Such models both draw on and contribute to the academic literature in the field of simulation.

The longer-range outcome of theory building and testing would be to produce a body of knowledge that would explain and perhaps even predict patterns of interaction among political variables. At the end of the twentieth century, such a goal remains unfulfilled for epistemological and methodological reasons discussed in this and various other chapters. Nevertheless, it would be useful at least to be able to specify with a higher degree of certainty than now exists, for example, the conditions essential to political integration within a national or international context, or to state with a greater degree of precision, within carefully specified parameters, the conditions that give rise to particular forms of conflict. If the study of international-relations theory were to reach this stage of development, we would have achieved an understanding of those international phenomena deemed most important to scholars, and we would have developed a body of theories of importance to the policymaker.

Among the ultimate benefits of our ability to develop and test theories about, for example, such phenomena as political integration or international conflict would be a series of if–then propositions relevant to the needs of both scholars and policymakers. For example, a greater knowledge of the essential conditions for integration or conflict would make possible an understanding of alternative outcomes of various policy choices because certain kinds of policy choices could be expected to produce certain kinds of outcomes. A new linkage between international-relations theory and policy formulation would have been forged, unless, of course, an understanding of the implications of alternative policy outcomes permitted policymakers to alter the basic variables on which the theory was based and thus to invalidate the theory itself. Herein may lie one of the fundamental differences between theory building in the physical and natural sciences and theory building in the social sciences—the capacity in the latter case for the objects of study—human beings—to effect changes in their behavior as a result of knowledge gained from a particular theory of behavior. In this respect, political and social phenomena, as we have noted elsewhere, differ fundamentally from elements in a test tube.

The literature of international relations—traditional and contemporary, qualitative and quantitative—contains assumptions and conclusions that may have relevance to the policymaker. Policy decisions are frequently dictated by the underlying assumptions of the policymaker, even though these assumptions may be only implicitly stated, or perhaps not even recognized as such. One objective of the study of international relations, we note parenthetically, should be to sensitize the student to the assumptions, or the propositions, contained in his or her theory of international relations, or in those of decision makers whose policy choices we must study as scholars or evaluate as citizens. Such an understanding is indispensable to one's own analysis of international relations, whether we are policymakers or observers of the political process. As Trevor Taylor has suggested, one of the functions of international relations is the development of explicitly stated assumptions and propositions on which to base research and policy, since all analyses of a problem of international relations or foreign policy rest on hypotheses of some kind.[55]

For this reason, the need exists to engage in a systematic examination of the assumptions that guide policymakers in the formulation of major policies. Policy statements can be analyzed to understand the assumptions that guide policy choices. An attempt should be made to match, compare, and contrast such assumptions, as well as policies, with assumptions and policies contained in theoretically oriented literature of international relations, both as a means of testing theories and as an aid to policymaking. Such an inventory and matching of major assumptions, theories, and findings about international phenomena from policy statements and from the literature of international relations would enhance the relevance of academic research to the needs of the policymaker. An exercise of this kind could provide insights into the theories, explicit or implicit, that guide policymakers, and it would contribute to a better understanding of those theories of international relations that have had the greatest impact on thought in the policy community.

THEORIZING ABOUT THE FUTURE

Although for centuries, efforts have been made to set forth conceptions of the future, the need for more systematic forecasts (the development of statements about the future to which is attached a higher or lower probability, as in a weather forecast based on, say, a 30 or 60 percent probability of rain or snow) has grown with the rapidity of change and the increasing complexity of issues and urgent problems facing policymakers. The result has been the emergence of the futurologist, who seeks to invent the future through technological forecasting.[56] If such means could clarify the choices available by reducing uncertainty about the future, it might become possible to calculate more accurately the lead time and the resources needed for alternative policy choices. Forecasts about future patterns of interaction among variables, especially resources, have existed at least since the writings of Thomas Malthus in the late eighteenth century. In the late twentieth century, there was renewed interest in forecasting, including the development of a series of neo-Malthusian projections into a future allegedly characterized by population pressure, resource scarcity, environmental degradation, and technological change. Whatever else can be said about the world of the early twenty-first century, it will contain burgeoning populations with likely heightened competition for resources and at the same time an unprecedented diffusion of economic and technological capabilities to new actors on a global scale.

The rapidity of change, together with the urgency of problems facing political systems—postindustrial, industrial, and less developed—together with the quest for as relevant a field of inquiry as possible is likely to give increasing impetus and importance to the development of futurology. Nonetheless, straight-line projections will be no more adequate in the future than they were in the past. The question of course is which, if any, of the trends that can be discerned in a present context will be operative in a future time frame. What new forces will intervene to shape the future? If projections based largely on extrapolating the future from the present are inadequate in themselves, can alternative hypothetical future international systems, or their subsystems, be developed? Such an exercise places a high premium on creative imagination about the future and on the generation of hypotheses about variables and about interaction among variables, all of which may have little or no place in today's scheme of things. Technologies that cannot presently be foreseen may transform the future, just as technologies that were not imaginable a century ago, or even 50 years ago, have profoundly altered the world leading into the twenty-first century. Such hypothetical models of international systems have their analogy in deductive theory, as discussed in Chapter 1. The projection of existing trends from the present to the future, in turn, is analogous to inductive theory, considered in the same chapter. Hence, understanding the forces shaping the emerging world lies in the creative intermingling of inductive and deductive approaches to futurology.

This is not to suggest that theories of international relations can ever achieve a level of predictability even about existing phenomena sufficient to make possible a high degree of specificity of alternative policy choices. To hold such expectations of international-relations theory, given the many variables that must be considered, would be to anticipate a level of performance that lies beyond even the theories in the physical sciences. As Morton Kaplan has suggested:

> Modern theoretical physical science has reared its present lofty edifice by setting itself problems that it has the tools or techniques to solve. When necessary, it has limited ruthlessly the scope of its inquiry. It has not attempted to predict the path a flipped chair will take, the paths of the individual particles of an exploded grenade, or the paths of the individual molecules of gas in a chamber. In the latter case, there are laws dealing with the behavior of gases under given conditions of temperature and pressure, but these deal with the aggregate behavior of gases and not the behaviors of individual particles. The physicist does not make predictions with respect to matter in general but only with respect to the aspects of matter that physics deals with; and these, by definition, are the physical aspects of matter.[57]

To complicate further the prospects for an explanatory and predictive theory of international relations, there has been increasing discussion of the implications of chaos theory for such theoretical development.[58] In the physical sciences, according to chaos theory, nearly identical entities, such as clouds, in similar environments can behave radically differently from each other. Chaos, or unpredictability, appears in systems that are in the process of transformation and subject to influences from within themselves and from their surrounding environmental circumstances. If systems, or certain categories of systems, are inherently chaotic, prediction will fail. Are there underlying causal laws leading to divergence among variables that produce the discontinuous behavior represented by chaos? To understand the nature of such laws forms the essence of an understanding of chaos theory. If relatively simple systems have discontinuities that are largely unpredictable, it follows that the prospects for chaos grow as the complexity of the system increases. If chaos characterizes behavior within the physical sciences, it is said to abound in the social sciences. To what extent are there categories of systems that display chaotic behavior or nonchaotic behavior in the physical sciences? Can we distinguish in the social sciences between chaotic and nonchaotic systems? To return to an earlier discussion in this chapter, was the end of the Cold War illustrative of chaos theory in the form of a situation characterized by large numbers of variables, the behavioral patterns of which were unpredictable even to the direct participants, as well as those who observed the unfolding events leading to the collapse of the Soviet Union and its empire? Thus, chaos theory casts a long shadow over the prospects for predictive social-science theory unless we can separate chaotic phenomena from nonchaotic phenomena.

Nevertheless, theories examined in preceding chapters, to varying degrees, have contained predictive statements that have enhanced, to a greater or lesser extent, our understanding of a period after they were formulated. For example, Mackinder's analysis of the impact of the technology of land mobility on power relationships in Eurasia, as noted in Chapter 4, is illustrative of a capacity to make use of certain variables in combination to examine the future with a considerable degree of accuracy. Such variables—implications of geography, resources, and technology for national capabilities—can be utilized in an analysis of the forces shaping the world of the future.

THE ROLE OF NORMATIVE THEORY

International relations has been marked by efforts to establish linkages between normative theory on the one hand and empirical–analytic theory on the other. As we have noted in this and other chapters, the question of a value-free study of politics is of long-standing interest to students of politics, although it is a matter of debate whether such an objective is either desirable or attainable. Given the nature of the objects with which international relations deals and the enormously important questions associated with war and peace, normative theory can be expected to remain central to this field. One of the leading proponents of quantitatively based scientific theory of the 1960s, Rudolph Rummel, writing in the mid-1970s, concluded that human behavior cannot be understood by reference to cause–effect processes comparable to those of physical objects. Because people are "teleologically guided by [their] future goals," Rummel maintained, "the future lies in [their] hands and not in some causative features of [their] environment such as distance, power, geography, poverty, deprivation, and underdevelopment."[59] Thus, Rummel raised fundamentally important questions for the conduct of scientific research about international behavior. Can the human being be studied scientifically, for example, as one would study the interaction of elements in a test tube? If people are guided in their political behavior by some objective, is there an inherent and logical contradiction in the idea of a value-free study of politics? Does the very selection of the object or topic to be studied represent a value choice on the part of the student or researcher?

By the end of the decade of the 1960s, as international-relations theory entered its postbehavioral phase, there was a growing belief that if social scientists and other scholars chose to emphasize empirical–analytic theory to the relative neglect of normative theory, they would have removed themselves from a problem area that historically had been of great concern. They would have opted to ignore the task of defining the meaning of good and evil, the designing of political structures, and the establishment of normative standards for humankind in a future fraught with growing problems and dangers of unprecedented dimensions. The urgent issues created by the impact of technology on institutions, the changes in the political environment resulting from ideology and technology, the proliferation of WMD, the breakup of existing political units, ethnic conflict, and problems resulting from ungovernability will continue to contribute to a greater interest in normative theory. Empirical–analytic theories in themselves cannot provide adequate answers to the question of the kinds of political institutions, practices, and values appropriate to the world of the future.

In almost dialectical reaction against the behavioral revolution, there was a new revolution of postbehavioralism that pointed toward the postmodernist critique of positivism that we have discussed elsewhere in this text. According to David Easton, this resurgence of interest was based on the following arguments: "(1) it is more important to be relevant to contemporary needs than to be methodologically sophisticated; (2) behavioral science conceals an ideology based upon empirical conservatism; (3) behavioral research, by its focus upon abstraction, loses touch with reality; (4) the political scientist has the obligation to make knowledge available for the general benefit of society."[60] The emphasis in this critique was on questions of values, goals, or preferences, and the development of policy choices for immediate problems and the generation of objectives and norms of behavior for future international systems. As Rosenau has suggested, in the early 1970s, there emerged in international-relations studies a "crisis of confidence," together with a loss of faith in the "slow, painstaking methods of science," as scholars sought to make themselves "relevant in ways that but a few years ago we would have found irresponsible and illusory."[61]

That crisis remained unresolved into the 1990s, in part because the international system was itself in the midst of change so profound and pervasive that theoretical efforts, it appeared, could not keep pace. Theory itself faced the prospect of diminishing relevance and correspondence to a world that was in the process of rapid transformation. Nevertheless, in keeping with a renewed emphasis on normative theory that accompanied the end of the Cold War and optimistic expectations of a new world order, Charles W. Kegley, Jr., suggested the need for a "neo-idealist conception of world politics" that would assure that "moral ideals can play a constructive role in the creation of a more stable world order."[62] Such a formulation would draw on a synthesis of "the moral idealism of the liberal creed with the sober conservatism of the realist approach." It would derive its validation from empirically verified theories.

By the end of the decade of the 1980s, the paradigmatic uncertainty discussed earlier in this chapter included the normative basis for theory. According to Ferguson and Mansbach, as we have noted, the history of theory from the ancient world to the present follows the value (normative) preferences of the age. The theoretical controversies at any time represent debates about normative commitments and political preferences. In this perspective, schools of thought based on realism and idealism, on neorealism and neoliberalism, form competing sets of norms more than they represent coherent theories of international relations. In the history of political thought, it is possible to delineate a series of central concepts—notably, anarchy and interdependence, community and conflict, war and peace—that form the basis for theory. Normative arguments and commitments lie at the core of discussions about which concepts, actors, variables, or levels of analysis should be studied. The objects chosen for investigation are derived from value-based interests and concerns. Research agendas based on issues such as conflict and cooperation change as human needs are altered; that is to say, international relations research and theory are contextually specific, just as the raison d'être for the emergence of international-relations in the early decades of the twentieth century lay in the quest for an understanding of the means necessary to eliminate war.

To assert, as Ferguson and Mansbach do, that theoretical preoccupations derive from the normative theories of the age "fully as much as do ideas in art and literature" is to suggest yet another limitation to the emergence of an agreed paradigm and, of course, to indicate the inherent inability completely to separate research from values. To be sure, the research preferences of those who work in the physical and biological sciences are shaped by the normative issues of the day, such as environmental pollution or finding a cure for dreaded diseases. However, what is said to distinguish the physical and biological sciences from international relations is the number of variables and their various combinations and permutations likely to be relevant in the case of international relations. Of even greater importance, moreover, is the fact that, unlike the physical and biological sciences, where we seek purposely to isolate the elements from their environment in, for example, a test tube, the study of international phenomena outside their social context or milieu is self-defeating and counterproductive. That such a separation has often been consciously attempted, especially in quantitative analyses devoid of historical or societal context, further diminishes the value of such research. To quote Ferguson and Mansbach again, "There is a more important set of complexity that becomes apparent in efforts to isolate and study specific variables; such reductionism isolates selected factors from their milieu when it is the milieu itself in which we are interested."[63] In sum, the environing circumstances constitute the normative context that gives meaning to the data that are analyzed. By the same token, in this perspective, from the milieu are derived the normative issues of the age and the theoretical interests that become the focus of intellectual inquiry in international relations.

Last but not least, in the field of international relations, there have always been groups of scholars whose principal interest was the development and analysis of public policy. In the second half of the twentieth century, this preoccupation has been evident in the literature of international relations. In its utopian and realist phases, moreover, international-relations study was strongly focused on policy. The efforts of quantitative–behavioral scholars to emphasize the methodological basis of inquiry have represented more a supplement to, rather than a replacement of, a concern for policy problems.[64] Indeed, considerable emphasis has been placed on the creation of more rigorous techniques for the analysis of public policy, especially in the form of systems analysis.[65] Here, the goal has been to devise criteria to aid in choosing and evaluating alternative policies or strategies, or mixes of policies or strategies, for the attainment of specified objectives. The effort has been to find optimal or at least preferable solutions among a series of alternatives, based on relative costs and benefits, by using such techniques as mathematical models, game theory, gaming (e.g., simulations), and the canvassing of expert opinion. Such cost–benefit studies represent a reaction against policy recommendations based on unstated assumptions, untested hypotheses, and uncertainty as to the implications of alternative choices and outcomes. The deficiencies of systems analysis in dealing with such factors as charisma and ideology, or the propensity of actors to adopt high-risk or low-risk strategies, and its inadequacies in explicating the value assumptions of analysis all serve to point up the need for additional work toward a policy science field, either within international relations or as a separate discipline, or "interdiscipline."[66]

Given the likely increase in pressing political problems, it is necessary to strike an acceptable balance, if possible, between empirical–analytic theory and normative theory, and between basic and applied research. Normative theory can continue to suggest alternative goals and preferences for political institutions and can also provide propositions for testing; empirical–analytic theory can furnish guidance as to the kinds of political behavior that are essential for attaining desired goals.

In summary, just as the study of international relations moved from the extreme preoccupation with the normative theory of the 1920s to the empirical–analytic theory of the 1960s, more recent generations of scholars have sought to develop theories of international relations in a rapidly changing world. Attempts have been made to find broadly based explanations and to develop a predictive capacity, but perhaps with a greater realization at the end of the twentieth century than in earlier decades of the difficulties inherent in achieving such a goal. There is a continuing pursuit of the normative and analytic objectives that have been sought by preceding generations of international relations theory, based on a recognition of the need for greater synthesis among those concerns that have been of principal importance in each of the stages through which the field has passed since the early years of this century, and noted in and derived from antecedents dating from the ancient world of Plato and Aristotle to our own day and age. Thus, the search for a theory, or theories, adequate to the needs of an ever-changing world continues as we move into the third millennium.

NOTES

1. E. H. Carr, *The Twenty Years' Crisis, 1919–1939* (New York: Harper & Row Torchbooks, 1964), p. 4. See also Richard Little, "The Evolution of International Relations as a Social Science," in R. C. Kent and G. P. Nielsson, eds., *The Study and Teaching of International Relations: A Perspective on Mid-career Education* (New York: Nichols Publishing Co., 1980), pp. 5–7.

2. See Kenneth W. Thompson, *Political Realism and the Crisis of World Politics* (Princeton, NJ: Princeton University Press, 1960); William T. R. Fox, *The American Study of International Relations* (Columbia: University of South Carolina Press, 1968), pp. 1–35; Torbjörn L. Knutsen, *A History of International Relations Theory* (Manchester, England, and New York: Manchester University Press, 1992), especially chaps. 1–7.

3. This is not to suggest that the concerns of students of international relations during each of these stages have been mutually exclusive. Examples of each can be found at every stage of the development of international relations.

4. For an examination of such trends in political science, see David Easton, "The New Revolution in Political Science," *American Political Science Review,* LXIII(4) (December 1969), 1051–1061. Because the study of international relations has been linked closely to political science, the methodological, conceptual, and substantive trends of political science have been expected to influence the development of international relations.

5. Yale H. Fersuson and Richard W. Mansbach, *The State, Conceptual Chaos, and the Future of International Relations Theory,* GSIS Monograph Series in World Affairs, the University of Denver (Boulder, CO, and London: Lynne Rienner Publishers, 1989), pp. 41–80.

6. Yale H. Ferguson and Richard W. Mansbach, ibid., p. 81.

7. See Andrew M. Scott, *The Functioning of the International System* (New York: Macmillan, 1967), pp. 2–6.

8. See, for example, James N. Rosenau, ed., *Linkage Politics: Essays on the Convergence of National and International Systems* (New York: Free Press, 1969); Rosenau, "Compatibility, Consensus, and an Emerging Political Science of Adaptation," *American Political Science Review,* LXI(3) (December 1967), 983–988; and Wolfram F. Hanrieder, "Compatibility and Consensus: A Proposal for the Conceptual Linkage of External and Internal Dimensions of Foreign Policy," *American Political Science Review,* LXI(3) (December 1967), 971–982.

9. James N. Rosenau, *Turbulence in World Politics: A Theory of Change and Continuity* (Princeton, NJ: Princeton University Press, 1990), p. 6.

10. For an extended discussion of this issue, see Robert Jervis, "The Future of World Politics: Will It Resemble the Past?" *International Security,* 16(3) (Winter 1991/1992), 39–73.

11. Richard W. Mansbach and John A. Vasquez, *In Search of Theory: A New Paradigm for Global Politics* (New York: Columbia University Press, 1981), pp. 68–69.

12. John W. Burton, *World Society* (Cambridge, England: Cambridge University Press, 1972), p. 42.

13. Richard K. Ashley, "Untying the Sovereign State: A Double Reading of the Anarchy Problematique," *Millennium: Journal of International Studies,* 17(2) (Summer 1988), 229.

14. Thomas S. Kuhn, *The Structure of Scientific Revolutions* (Chicago: University of Chicago Press, 1970), p. 92.

15. Arend Lijphart, "The Structure of the Theoretical Revolution in International Relations," *International Studies Quarterly,* 18(1) (March 1974), 41–73.

16. Ibid., 207.

17. K. J. Holsti, *The Dividing Discipline: Hegemony and Diversity in International Theory* (Boston: Allen & Unwin, 1987), p. 74.

18. Ibid., p. 11. See also M. Banks, "Inter-Paradigm Debate," in M. Light and A. J. R. Groun, eds., *International Relations: A Handbook of Current Theory* (London: Francis Pinter, 1985), pp. 7–26; See also Mark Hoffman, "Critical Theory and the Inter-Paradigm Debate," 231–249; Fred Halliday, "State and Society in International Relations: A Second Agenda," 215–230; Steve Smith, "Paradigm Dominance in International Relations: The Development of International Relations as Social Science," 189–206; Ekkehart Krippendorf, "The Dominance of American Approaches in International Relations," 207–214; all in *Millenium: Journal of International Studies,* 16(2), (Summer, 1987).

19. Philippe Braillard, "The Social Sciences and the Study of International Relations," *International Social Science Journal,* 36(4) (1984), 631.

20. Hayward R. Alker, Jr., and Thomas J. Biersteker, "The Dialectics of World Order: Notes for a Future Archeologist of International Savoir Faire," *International Studies Quarterly,* 28(1) (1984), 121.

21. Ibid., 122.

22. Bruce M. Russett, "Apologia pro Vita Sua," in James N. Rosenau, ed., *In Search of Global Patterns* (New York: Free Press, 1976), p. 36.

23. John A. Vasquez, "The Post-Positivist Debate: Reconstructing Scientific Enquiry and International Relations Theory After Enlightenment's Fall," in Ken Booth and Steve Smith, eds., *International Relations Theory Today* (University Park, PA: Pennsylvania State University Press, 1995), pp. 216–240.

24. See, for example, Barry Buzan, "The Level of Analysis Problems in International Relations Reconsidered," in Ken Booth and Steve Smith, eds., *International Relations Theory Today* (University Park: Pennsylvania State University Press, 1995), pp. 198–217; Alexander E. Wendt, "The Agent–Structure Problem in International Relations Theory," *International Organization*, 41(3) (Summer 1987), 335–370.

25. For a useful effort to delineate the boundaries of international relations, see E. Raymond Platig, *International Relations Research: Problems of Evaluation and Advancement* (Santa Barbara, CA: Clio Press, for the Carnegie Endowment for International Peace, 1967), especially pp. 26–44.

26. One contemporary student of international relations, Johan Galtung, has suggested, "One may say that the relationship between international relations and political science is the same as the relationship between sociology and psychology: It is the transition from the meticulous study of one unit at the time to the study of the interaction structure between the units that characterize the relations between these pairs of sciences." Johan Galtung, "Small Group Theory and the Theory of International Relations," in Morton A. Kaplan, ed., *New Approaches to International Relations* (New York: St. Martin's Press, 1968), p. 271.

27. See Walter Isard, in association with Tony E. Smith, Peter Isard, Tze Hsiung Tung, and Michael Dacey, *General Theory: Social, Political, Economic, and Regional* (Cambridge, MA: MIT Press, 1969).

28. For a discussion of this topic, see Fred Halliday, "The End of the Cold War and International Relations: Some Analytic and Theoretical Conclusions," in Ken Booth and Steve Smith, eds., *International Relations Theory Today* (University Park: Pennsylvania State University Press, 1995), pp. 38–61.

29. John Lewis Gaddis, "International Relations Theory and the End of the Cold War," *International Security*, 171(3) (Winter 1992/1993), 6. See also John Lewis Gaddis, *The Long Peace: Inquiries into the History of the Cold War* (New York: Oxford University Press, 1987), especially pp. 215–247. See also Janice Gross Stein, "Political Learning by Doing: Gorbachev as Uncommitted Thinker and Motivated Learner"; Thomas Risse-Kappen, "Ideas Do Not Float Freely: Transnational Coalitions, Domestic Structures, and the End of the Cold War"; Rey Koslowski and Friedrich V. Kratochwil, "Understanding Change in International Politics: The Soviet Empire's Demise and the International System," all in *International Organization*, 48(2) (Spring 1994), 155–249.

30. For contrasting explanations, see John Mueller, "The Essential Irrelevance of Nuclear Weapons: Stability in the Postwar World," *International Security*, 13(2) (Fall 1988), 55–79; Robert Jervis, "The Political Effects of Nuclear Weapons: A Comment," *International Security* 13 (2) (Fall 1988) 80–90; Kenneth M. Waltz, "Nuclear Myths and Political Realities," *American Political Science Review*, 84(3) (September 1990), 731–745; Richard Ned Lebow, "The Long Peace, the End of the Cold War, and the Failure of Realism," *International Organization*, 48(2) (Spring 1994), 249–279.

31. For an extended discussion of such questions and related issues, see Charles W. Kegley, ed., *The Long Postwar Peace: Contending Explanations and Projections* (New York: Harper Collins, 1991), especially pp. 1–25.

32. For a discussion of this topic, see Richard Little, "International Relations and the Triumph of Capitalism," in Ken Booth and Steve Smith, eds., *International Relations Theory Today* (University Park: Pennsylvania State University Press, 1995), pp. 63–89.

33. See, for example, Henry Kissinger, *Diplomacy* (New York: Simon and Schuster, 1994), pp. 804–835; Christopher Layne, "The Unipolar Illusion: Why New Powers Will Rise," *International Security,* 17(4) (Spring 1993), 5–51.

34. See, for example, Richard W. Mansbach, Yale H. Ferguson, and Donald E. Lampert, *The Web of World Politics: Nonstate Actors in the Global System* (Englewood Cliffs, NJ: Prentice-Hall, 1976).

35. Philip Alston and Raul Pangalangan, *Revitalizing the Study of International Organizations* (Report of a Conference on "Teaching About International Organizations from a Legal and Policy Perspective"), Medford, October 28–31, 1987 (Medford, MA: Fletcher School of Law and Diplomacy, Tufts University), 25.

36. See, for example, Zbigniew Brzezinski, *Between Two Ages: America's Role in a Technetronic Era* (New York: Viking, 1970); Victor Basiuk, *Technology, World Politics, and American Policy* (New York: Columbia University Press, 1977); Hans J. Morgenthau, *Science: Servant or Master?* (New York: American Library, 1972); Eugene B. Skolnikoff, *International Imperatives of Technology: Technological Development and the International Political System* (Berkeley, CA: University of California International Studies, 1972); Hilary Rose and Steven Rose, *Science and Society* (Baltimore, MD: Penguin, 1970); Ira Spiegel-Rosing and Derek de Solla Price, eds., *Science, Technology and Society* (Beverly Hills, CA: Sage, 1977).

37. See Richard C. Snyder, H. W. Bruck, and Burton Sapin, eds., *Foreign Policy Decision Making* (New York: Free Press, 1963).

38. See Wolfram Hanrieder, op. cit.; James N. Rosenau, "External Influences on the Internal Behavior of States," in R. Barry Farrell, ed., *Approaches to Comparative and International Politics* (Evanston, IL: Northwestern University Press, 1966), pp. 27–92; James N. Rosenau, "Comparative Foreign Policy—Fad, Fantasy, or Field," paper prepared for presentation at the Conference Seminar of the Committee on Comparative Politics, University of Michigan, 1967; Randolph C. Kent, "Foreign Policy Analysis: Search for Coherence in a Multifaceted Field," in R. C. Kent and G. P. Nielsson, eds., op. cit., pp. 90–110.

39. For recent analyses of international-security studies as a field, see, for example, Barry Buzan, *Peoples, States and Fear: The National Security Problem in International Relations* (Brighton, England: Wheatsheaf Books, 1983); Barry Buzan, *An Introduction to Strategic Studies, Military Technology, and International Relations* (New York: St. Martin's Press, 1987); Colin Gray, *Strategic Studies: A Critical Assessment* (Westport, CT: Greenwood Press, 1982); Robert Jervis, Joshua Lederberg, Robert North, Stephen Rosen, John Steinbruner, and Dina Zinnes, *The Field of National Security Studies: Report to the National Research Council* (Washington, DC: 1986); Richard Smoke, "National Security Affairs," in Fred I. Greenstein and Nelson W. Polsby, eds., *Handbook of Political Science*, Vol. 8, *International Politics* (Reading, MA: Addison-Wesley, 1975); Colin S. Gray, *Strategic Studies and Public Policy* (Lexington: University Press of Kentucky, 1982); Joseph S. Nye, Jr., and Sean M. Lynn-Jones, "International Security Studies: A Report of a Conference on the State of the Field," *International Security* (Spring 1988), 5–27; Richard H. Ullman, "Redefining Security," International Security, 8(1) (1983), 129–153; A. J. R. Groom, "Strategy: The Evolution of the Field," in R. C. Kent and G. P. Nielsson, eds., op. cit., pp. 47–59; Helga Haftendorn, "The State of the Field: A German View," *International Security*, 13(2) (1988); Helga Haftendorn, "The Security Puzzle: Theory-Building and Discipline-Building in International Theory," *International Studies Quarterly*, 35 (1991), 3–17; Stephen M. Walt, "The Renaissance of Security Studies," *International Studies Quarterly*, 35 (1991), 211–239; Edward J. Kolodziej, "Renaissance in Security Studies:

Caveat Lector!" *International Studies Quarterly,* 36 (1992), 421–438; David Dewitt, David Haglund, and John Kirton, eds., *Building a New Global Order: Emerging Trends in International Security* (New York: Oxford University Press, 1993).

40. Stephen M. Walt, "The Renaissance of Security Studies," *International Studies Quarterly,* 35 (1991), 211–239; David A. Baldwin, "Security Studies and the End of the Cold War," *World Politics,* 48(1) (October 1995), 117–141.

41. Richard Shultz, Jr., Roy Godson, and Ted Greenwood, eds., *Security Studies for the 1990s* (Washington: Brassey's [US], 1993). See especially the editors' introduction, pp. 1–13.

42. See Geoffrey Kemp, Robert L. Pfaltzgraff, Jr., and Uri Ra'anan, *The Superpowers in a Multinuclear World* (Lexington, MA: D. C. Heath, 1974). See also Robert L. Pfaltzgraff, Jr., "The Evolution of American Nuclear Thought," in B. Mitchell Simpson, III, ed., *War, Strategy and Maritime Power* (New Brunswick, NJ: Rutgers University Press, 1977), pp. 280–282.

43. Colin S. Gray, *Strategic Studies and Public Policy,* op. cit., 194.

44. Martin van Creveld, *The Transformation of War* (New York: Free Press, 1991), pp. 33–63.

45. See, for example, Edward A. Kolodziej, "Renaissance in Security Studies? Caveat Lector!" *International Studies Quarterly,* 36 (1992), 421–438.

46. Martin van Creveld, op. cit., pp. 57–62.

47. Edward A. Kolodziej, op. cit., p. 424.

48. Richard Shultz, Jr., Roy Godson, and George Quester, eds., *Security Studies for the Twenty-First Century* (Washington, DC: Brassey's, 1996).

49. For an extended survey of such literature, together with an important effort to define, categorize, and analyze economic policies as instruments of statecraft, see David A. Baldwin, *Economic Statecraft* (Princeton, NJ: Princeton University Press, 1985), especially chap 2. See also Roger Tooze, "The Unwritten Preface: International Political Economy and Epistemology," *Millennium: Journal of International Studies,* 17(2) (Summer 1988), 288–293.

50. See, for example, Robert T. Holt and John E. Turner, *The Methodology of Comparative Research* (New York: Free Press, 1970).

51. However, there are two volumes of potential use in a study of decision-making that take account of the medical histories of key participants. They include Hugh L'Etang, *The Pathology of Leadership* (London: William Heinemann Medical Books, 1969); L'Etang, *Lord Moran, Churchill: Taken from the Diaries of Lord Moran, The Struggle for Survival, 1940–1965* (Boston: Houghton Mifflin, 1966).

52. Thomas C. Wiegele, "Decision-Making in an International Crisis: Some Biological Factors," *International Studies Quarterly,* 17(2) (June 1973), 305. See also Thomas C. Wiegele, ed., *Biology and the Social Sciences* (Boulder, CO: Westview Press, 1982); Thomas C. Wiegele, *Biopolitics: Search for a More Human Political Science* (Boulder, CO: Westview Press, 1979); Thomas C. Wiegele, Gordon Hilton, Kent Layne Oots, and Susan V. Kisiel, *Leaders Under Stress: A Psychophysiological Analysis of International Crises* (Durham, NC: Duke University Press, 1985); Thomas C. Wiegele, "Models of Stress and Disturbances in Elite Political Behaviors: Psychological Variables and Political Decision-Making," in Robert S. Robins, ed., *Psychopathology and Political Leadership* (New Orleans: Tulane University, 1977), pp. 79–111; Kent Layne Oots and Thomas C. Wiegele, "Terrorist and Victim: Psychiatric and Physiological Approaches from a Social Science Perspective," *Terrorism: An International Journal,* 8(11) (1985), 1–32; James M. Schubert, Thomas C. Wiegele, and Samuel M. Hines, "Age and Political Behavior in Collective Decision-Making," *International Political Science Review,* 8(2) (1987), 131–146; Samuel Long, ed., *Political Behavior Annual,*

Vol. 1 (Boulder, CO: Westview Press, 1986); Thomas C. Wiegele, "Signal Leakage and the Remote Psychological Assessment of Foreign Policy Elites," in Lawrence S. Falkowski, ed., *Psychological Models in International Politics* (Boulder, CO: Westview Press, 1979); Thomas C. Wiegele, "The Psychophysiology of Elite Stress in Five International Crises: A Preliminary Test of a Voice Measurement Technique," *International Studies Quarterly,* 22(4) (December 1978), 467–511; Thomas C. Wiegele, "The Life Sciences and International Relations: A Bibliographic Essay," *International Studies Notes of the International Studies Association,* 11(2) (Winter 1984/1985), 1–7.

53. Thomas C. Wiegele, "Models of Stress and Disturbances in Elite Political Behaviors: Psychological Variables and Political Decision-Making," in *Psychological and Political Leadership* (New Orleans: Tulane University Studies in Political Science); see also, by the same author, "Physiologically Based Content Analysis: An Application in Political Communication," in Brent D. Rupin, ed., *Communication Yearbook 2* (New Brunswick, NJ: Transaction Books, 1978), pp. 423–436; "Health and Stress During International Crisis: Neglected Input Variables in the Foreign Policy Decision-Making Process," *Journal of Political Science,* III(2) (Spring 1976), 139–144.

54. Richard Smoke, "Theory for and About Policy," in James N. Rosenau, ed., *In Search of Global Patterns,* op. cit., p. 191.

55. Trevor Taylor, "Introduction: The Nature of International Relations," in Trevor Taylor, ed., *Approaches and Theory in International Relations* (New York: Longmans, 1978), p. 3.

56. There are three general types of technological forecasts: the exploratory, opportunity, and normative. The *exploratory forecast* suggests future technology that is likely if the current level of support continues. The *opportunity forecast* depicts probable effects of increased effort in one technological problem area or another. The *normative forecast* combines desired goals and technological possibilities, using the goals as a guide for the allocation of resources.

Numerous techniques have been used to obtain such forecasts. The most frequently used is still the trend correlation and its variations: trend correlation in several fields and growth analogy. A new technique for obtaining intuitive rather than statistical forecasts is the *Delphi method,* an elaborate polling device for obtaining an expert consensus without a conference or panel discussion. Systems analysis, such as program evaluation and research technique (PERT), originally developed by the U.S. Navy, has been especially helpful for opportunity forecasting, as well as research and development (R&D) administration. Finally, mathematical modeling and the feedback concept are intended to aid normative forecasting in correlating the goals of government and industry with technological capabilities.

The most comprehensive general treatment of technological forecasting is Eric Jantsch, *Technological Forecasting in Perspective* (Paris: OECD Publication, 1967). An explanation of forecasting techniques may be found in Robert V. Ayres, *Technological Forecasting and Long-Range Planning* (New York: McGraw-Hill, 1969). See also James R. Bright, *Technological Forecasting for Industry and Government: Methods and Applications* (Englewood Cliffs, NJ: Prentice-Hall, 1968). For the more literary and speculative side of the movement, see Bertrand de Jouvenel, *The Art of Conjecture,* trans. N. Lary (New York: Basic Books, 1967); Herman Kahn and A. J. Wiener, *The Year 2000: A Framework for Speculation* (New York: Macmillan, 1967); Dennis Gabor, *Inventing the Future* (New York: Knopf, 1964); Daniel Bell, ed., *Toward the Year 2000: Work in Progress* (Boston: Houghton Mifflin and the American Academy of Arts and Sciences, 1968); and Neville Brown, *The Future Global Challenge: A Predictive Study of World Security, 1977–1990* (New York: Crane, Russak, 1977).

57. Morton A. Kaplan, "Problems of Theory Building and Theory Confirmation in International Politics," in Klaus Knorr and Sidney Verba, eds., *The International System:
Theoretical Essays* (Princeton, NJ: Princeton University Press, 1961), p. 7.

58. See, for example, Hal Gregersen and Lee Sailer, "Chaos Theory and Its Implications
for Social Science Research," *Human Relations,* 46(7) (1993), 777–801; H. Mitchell
Waldrop, *Complexity: The Emerging Science at the Edge of Order and Chaos* (New
York: Simon & Schuster, 1992), especially pp. 9–13; 140–143; 318–323; 330–335; Lau-
rent Dobuzinskis, "Modernist and Postmodernist Metaphors of the Policy Process:
Control and Stability vs. Chaos and Reflexive Understanding," *Policy Sciences,* 25
(1992), 355–380; L. Douglas Kiel and Evel W. Elliott, eds., *Chaos Theory in the Social
Sciences: Foundations and Applications* (Ann Arbor: University of Michigan Press,
1995); Diana Richards, "A Chaotic Model of Power Concentration in the International System," *International Studies Quarterly,* 37 (1993), 55–72.

59. Rudolph J. Rummel, "The Roots of Faith," in James N. Rosenau, ed., *In Search of
Global Patterns,* op. cit., p. 30.

60. David Easton, "The New Revolution in Political Science," *American Political Science
Review,* LXIII(4) (December 1969), 1052. Similarly, Easton was among the first to
discern the behavioral revolution in political science. See David Easton, *The Political
System: An Inquiry into the State of Political Science* (New York: Knopf, 1954), espe-
cially 37–125; by the same author, *A Framework for Political Analysis* (Englewood
Cliffs, NJ: Prentice-Hall, 1965), pp. 6–9.

61. James N. Rosenau, "Assessment in International Studies: Ego Trip or Feedback?"
International Studies Quarterly, 18 (September 1974) 346.

62. Charles W. Kegley, Jr., "Neo-Idealism: A Practical Matter," *Ethics and International
Affairs,* 2 (1988), 195–196; and Charles W. Kegley, Jr., and Gregory A. Raymond,
"Normative Constraints on the Use of Force Short of War," *Journal of Peace Research,*
23(3) (1986), 213–227. For other recent normative analyses, see Mervyn Frost,
Toward a Normative Theory of International Relations (Cambridge, England: Cam-
bridge University Press, 1986); Hidemi Suganami, "A Normative Enquiry in Interna-
tional Relations: The Case of Pacta Sunt Servanda," *Review of International Studies,*
9(1) (1983), pp. 35–54; Robert Cordis, "Religion and International Responsibility," in
Kenneth W. Thompson, ed., *Moral Dimensions of American Foreign Policy* (New
Brunswick, NJ: Transaction Books, 1984), 33–52; Ray Maghroori and Bennett Ram-
berg, eds., *Globalism Versus Realism: International Relations Third Debate* (Boulder,
CO: Westview Press, 1982); Louis Ren, *Reason and Realpolitik* (Lexington, MA: Lex-
ington Books, 1984); J. E. Hare and Carney B. Joynt, *Ethics and International Affairs*
(New York: St. Martin's, 1982); John A. Vasquez, *The Power Politics: A Critique* (Lon-
don: Francis Pinter, 1983); Stanley Hoffmann, "The Political Ethics of International
Relations," Seventh Morgenthau Memorial Lecture on Ethics and Foreign Policy,
Carnegie Council on Ethics and International Affairs, New York, 1988; Kenneth Kip-
nis and Diana T. Meyers, eds., *Political Realism and International Morality: Ethics in
the Nuclear Age* (Boulder, CO, and London: Westview Press, 1987); Terry Nardin,
Law, Morality and the Relations of States (Princeton, NJ: Princeton University Press,
1983); Charles R. Beitz, Marshall Cohen, Thomas Scanlon, and A. John Simmons,
eds., *International Ethics* (Princeton, NJ: Princeton University Press, 1985); Chris
Brown, "The Modern Requirement? Reflections on Normative International Theory
in a Post-Western World," *Millennium: Journal of International Studies,* 17(2) (Summer 1988), 339–348; Bruce M. Russett, "Ethical Dilemmas of Nuclear Deterrence,"
International Security, 8(4) (Spring 1984), 36–54; Charles R. Beitz, *Political Theory
and International Relations* (Princeton, NJ: Princeton University Press, 1979); James

W. Child, *Nuclear War, The Moral Dimension* (New Brunswick, NJ: Transaction Books, 1986); Michael Novak, *Moral Clarity in the Nuclear Age* (New York: Thomas Nelson Publishers, 1983); Joseph S. Nye, Jr., ed., *Nuclear Ethics* (New York: Free Press, 1986); William V. O'Brien and John Langan, eds., *The Nuclear Dilemma and the Just War Tradition* (Lexington, MA: Lexington Books, 1986); Robert L. Pfaltzgraff, Jr., *National Security: Ethics, Strategy, and Politics, A Layman's Primer* (Washington, DC: Pergamon-Brassey's, 1986); and James E. Dougherty, *The Bishops and Nuclear Weapons* (Camden, CT: Archon, 1984).

63. Ferguson and Mansbach, op. cit., p. 216. For a discussion of continuity in the major premises and issues of international-relations theory, see N. J. Rengger, "Serpents and Doves in Classical International Theory," *Millennium: Journal of International Studies,* 17(2) (Summer 1988), 215–225.

64. For a collection of essays by scholars concerned with the relationship between social science and public policy in the post–World War II period, see Daniel Lerner and Harold D. Lasswell, eds., *The Policy Sciences* (Stanford, CA: Stanford University Press, 1951). For a more recent discussion, see Norman D. Palmer, ed., *A Design for International Relations Research: Scope, Theory, Methods, and Relevance.* Monograph 10, American Academy of Political and Social Science (October 1970), especially pp. 154–274.

65. Charles J. Hitch and Roland N. McKean, *The Economics of Defense in the Nuclear Age* (Cambridge, MA: Harvard University Press, 1963); Roland McKean, *Efficiency in Government Through Systems Analysis* (New York: Wiley, 1958); Raymond A. Bauer and Kenneth J. Gergen, eds., *The Study of Policy Formation* (New York: Free Press, 1968); Harold Lasswell, "Policy Sciences," in *International Encyclopedia of the Social Sciences* (New York: Macmillan and Free Press, 1968), pp. xii, 181–189.

66. See Yehezkel Dror, *Analytical Approaches and Applied Social Sciences* (Santa Monica, CA: RAND Corporation, 1969); monograph.

Subject Index

Name Index

Abbé de Saint-Pierre, 7–8
Abdolali, Nasrin, 342n
Abel, Elie, 236n, 475n
Abel, Theodore, 314n, 475
Abelson, Robert P., 471
Achen, Christopher, 380
Adams, M.L., 36n
Adie, W.A.C., 225n
Adler, Emanuel, 162–163
Adorno, T.W., 279–280
Ajami, Fouad, 5, 32–33
Alberts, Donald, 307n
Alderfer, E. Gordon, 191n
Alexander the Great, 226
Alford, Jonathan, 390n
Alger, Chadwick F., 531n
Alighieri, Dante, 7
Alker, Hayward R., Jr., 104, 547
Allison, Graham T., 16, 314n, 462,
     465–468, 471n, 472n, 475–477
Allport, Gordon W., 261n, 279, 280
Allyn, Bruce J., 475n
Almond, Gabriel A., 110–111, 112, 242n, 547
Alston, Philip, 555–556n
Altfeld, Michael F., 323n, 447–448
Ambrose, Saint, 188
Amery, Leopold, 170n
Andelman, David, 238n
Anderson, Ewan, 148
Andrew, Christopher, 375n
Andrews, William G., 303n
Andropov, Yuri, 225, 390, 396
Angell, Norman, 12, 61, 184, 193, 341, 399
Anthias, F., 36n
Antoninus of Florence, 188
Appleby, R. Scott, 310n
Apter, David E., 28n, 242n
Aquinas, Saint Thomas, 188
Archer, J.C., 147n
Archimedes, 301
Ardener, A., 36n
Ardrey, Robert, 268n
Arendt, Hannah, 218–219n, 303n
Aristotle, 22, 25, 62, 145, 185

Armstrong, Scott, 396n
Aron, Raymond, 18n, 31, 148, 226, 228n,
     229n, 273n, 377, 392
Ashby, W. Ross, 116–117
Ashley, Richard K., 36, 93n, 329, 545
Asmus, Ronald D., 236n
Aspaturian, Vernon V., 493n
Attlee, Clement, 216n
Augustine, Saint, 188, 225
Axelrod, Robert, 419, 504n, 510
Ayala, Balthazar, 189
Ayres, Robert V., 568n

Babai, Don, 426n
Bacevich, A.J., 309n
Back, Kurt, 489n
Bialer, Seweryn, 236n
Bainton, Roland H., 188n, 201n
Bakunin, Mikhail, 198
Baldwin, David A., 14n, 59, 62n, 63n, 66,
     68, 564
Baldwin, Robert, 250n
Ball, Desmond, 387
Bandura, Albert, 264, 268, 271n, 272–273,
     279n
Banks, Arthur S., 295n
Banks, Michael, 128, 546n
Barash, David P., 264n, 273n, 282n
Barber, Benjamin R., 32
Barghava, G.S., 329–330n
Barghoorn, Frederick C., 224n
Bark, Dennis, 308
Barlow, George, 264n
Barnett, Frank, 309
Barrera, Mario, 128n
Barringer, Richard E., 532n
Basham, A.L., 185n
Basiuk, Victor, 558n
Bate, John P., 189n
Baudrillard, J., 35n
Bauer, P.T., 233
Bauer, Raymond A., 572n
Beard, Charles A., 72n
Beck, Carl, 493n

Page numbers followed by n indicate location of notes in text to be found at the end of the chapter.